ISBN 978-1-330-53016-0
PIBN 10074471

1 MONTH OF
FREE
READING

at

www.ForgottenBooks.com

By purchasing this book you are eligible for one month membership to ForgottenBooks.com, giving you unlimited access to our entire collection of over 1,000,000 titles via our web site and mobile apps.

To claim your free month visit:

www.forgottenbooks.com/free74471

English
Français
Deutsche
Italiano
Español
Português

www.forgottenbooks.com

Mythology Photography **Fiction**
Fishing Christianity **Art** Cooking
Essays Buddhism Freemasonry
Medicine **Biology** Music **Ancient**
Egypt Evolution Carpentry Physics
Dance Geology **Mathematics** Fitness
Shakespeare **Folklore** Yoga Marketing
Confidence Immortality Biographies
Poetry **Psychology** Witchcraft
Electronics Chemistry History **Law**
Accounting **Philosophy** Anthropology
Alchemy Drama Quantum Mechanics
Atheism Sexual Health **Ancient History**
Entrepreneurship Languages Sport
Paleontology Needlework Islam
Metaphysics Investment Archaeology
Parenting Statistics Criminology
Motivational

61ST CONGRESS }
2d Session }
SENATE
{ DOCUMENT
{ No. 633

REPORTS OF THE IMMIGRATION COMMISSION

IMMIGRANTS IN INDUSTRIES

(IN TWENTY-FIVE PARTS)

PART 25: JAPANESE AND OTHER IMMIGRANT RACES IN THE PACIFIC COAST AND ROCKY MOUNTAIN STATES

(IN THREE VOLUMES: VOL. I)

JAPANESE AND EAST INDIANS

PRESENTED BY MR. DILLINGHAM

JUNE 15, 1910.—Referred to the Committee on Immigration and ordered to be printed, with illustrations

WASHINGTON
GOVERNMENT PRINTING OFFICE
1911

THE IMMIGRATION COMMISSION.

Senator WILLIAM P. DILLINGHAM, *Chairman.*
Senator HENRY CABOT LODGE.
Senator ASBURY C. LATIMER.[a]
Senator ANSELM J. McLAURIN.[b]
Senator LE ROY PERCY.[c]

Representative BENJAMIN F. HOWELL.
Representative WILLIAM S. BENNET.
Representative JOHN L. BURNETT.
Mr. CHARLES P. NEILL.
Mr. JEREMIAH W. JENKS.
Mr. WILLIAM R. WHEELER.

Secretaries:
MORTON E. CRANE.   W. W. HUSBAND.
C. S. ATKINSON.

Chief Statistican:
FRED C. CROXTON.

Extract from act of Congress of February 20. 1907, creating and defining the duties of the Immigration Commission.

That a commission is hereby created, consisting of three Senators. to be appointed by the President of the Senate, and three Members of the House of Representatives. to be appointed by the Speaker of the House of Representatives. and three persons to be appointed by the President of the United States. Said commission shall make full inquiry. examination, and investigation, by subcommittee or otherwise, into the subject of immigration. For the purpose of said inquiry, examination, and investigation said commission is authorized to send for persons and papers, make all necessary travel, either in the United States or any foreign country, and, through the chairman of the commission, or any member thereof. to administer oaths and to examine witnesses and papers respecting all matters pertaining to the subject, and to employ necessary clerical and other assistance. Said commission shall report to Congress the conclusions reached by it, and make such recommendations as in its judgment may seem proper. Such sums of money as may be necessary for the said inquiry, examination, and investigation are hereby appropriated and authorized to be paid out of the " immigrant fund " on the certificate of the chairman of said commission, including all expenses of the commissioners, and a reasonable compensation, to be fixed by the President of the United States, for those members of the commission who are not Members of Congress; * * *.

---

[a] Died February 20, 1908.
[b] Appointed to succeed Mr. Latimer, February 25, 1908. Died December 22, 1909.
[c] Appointed to succeed Mr. McLaurin, March 16, 1910.

II

LIST OF REPORTS OF THE IMMIGRATION COMMISSION.

Volumes 1 and 2. Abstracts of Reports of the Immigration Commission, with Conclusions and Recommendations and Views of the Minority. (These volumes include the Commission's complete reports on the following subjects: Immigration Conditions in Hawaii; Immigration and Insanity; Immigrants in Charity Hospitals; Alien Seamen and Stowaways; Contract Labor and Induced and Assisted Immigration; The Greek Padrone System in the United States; Peonage.) (S. Doc. No. 747, 61st Cong., 3d sess.)

Volume 3. Statistical Review of Immigration, 1819-1910—Distribution of Immigrants, 1850-1900. (S. Doc. No. 756, 61st Cong., 3d sess.)

Volume 4. Emigration Conditions in Europe. (S. Doc. No. 748, 61st Cong., 3d sess.)

Volume 5. Dictionary of Races or Peoples. (S. Doc. No. 662, 61st Cong., 3d sess.)

Volumes 6 and 7. Immigrants in Industries: Pt. 1, Bituminous Coal Mining. (S. Doc. No. 633, 61st Cong., 2d sess.)

Volumes 8 and 9. Immigrants in Industries: Pt. 2, Iron and Steel Manufacturing. (S. Doc. No. 633, 61st Cong., 2d sess.)

Volume 10. Immigrants in Industries: Pt. 3, Cotton Goods Manufacturing in the North Atlantic States—Pt. 4, Woolen and Worsted Goods Manufacturing. (S. Doc. No. 633, 61st Cong., 2d sess.)

Volume 11. Immigrants in Industries: Pt. 5, Silk Goods Manufacturing and Dyeing—Pt. 6, Clothing Manufacturing—Pt. 7, Collar, Cuff, and Shirt Manufacturing. (S. Doc. No. 633, 61st Cong., 2d sess.)

Volume 12. Immigrants in Industries: Pt. 8, Leather Manufacturing—Pt. 9, Boot and Shoe Manufacturing—Pt. 10, Glove Manufacturing. (S. Doc. No. 633, 61st Cong., 2d sess.)

Volume 13. Immigrants in Industries: Pt. 11, Slaughtering and Meat Packing. (S. Doc. No. 633, 61st Cong., 2d sess.)

Volume 14 Immigrants in Industries: Pt. 12, Glass Manufacturing—Pt. 13, Agricultural Implement and Vehicle Manufacturing. (S. Doc. No. 633, 61st Cong., 2d sess.)

Volume 15. Immigrants in Industries: Pt. 14, Cigar and Tobacco Manufacturing—Pt. 15, Furniture Manufacturing—Pt. 16, Sugar Refining. (S. Doc. No. 633, 61st Cong., 2d sess.)

Volume 16. Immigrants in Industries: Pt. 17, Copper Mining and Smelting—Pt. 18, Iron Ore Mining—Pt. 19, Anthracite Coal Mining—Pt. 20, Oil Refining. (S. Doc. No. 633, 61st Cong., 2d sess.)

Volume 17. Immigrants in Industries: Pt. 21, Diversified Industries, Vol. I. (S. Doc. No. 633, 61st Cong., 2d sess.)

Volume 18. Immigrants in Industries: Pt. 21, Diversified Industries, Vol. II—Pt. 22, The Floating Immigrant Labor Supply. (S. Doc. No. 633, 61st Cong., 2d sess.)

Volumes 19 and 20. Immigrants in Industries: Pt. 23, Summary Report on Immigrants in Manufacturing and Mining. (S. Doc. No. 633, 61st Cong., 2d sess.)

Volumes 21 and 22. Immigrants in Industries: Pt. 24, Recent Immigrants in Agriculture. (S. Doc. No. 633, 61st Cong., 2d sess.)

Volumes 23-25. Immigrants in Industries: Pt. 25, Japanese and Other Immigrant Races in the Pacific Coast and Rocky Mountain States. (S. Doc. No. 633, 61st Cong., 2d sess.)

Volumes 26 and 27. Immigrants in Cities. (S. Doc. No. 338, 61st Cong., 2d sess.)

Volume 28. Occupations of the First and Second Generations of Immigrants in the United States—Fecundity of Immigrant Women. (S. Doc. No. 282, 61st Cong., 2d sess.)

Volumes 29-33. The Children of Immigrants in Schools. (S. Doc. No. 749, 61st Cong., 3d sess.)

Volumes 34 and 35. Immigrants as Charity Seekers. (S. Doc. No. 665, 61st Cong., 3d sess.)

Volume 36. Immigration and Crime. (S. Doc. No. 750, 61st Cong., 3d sess.)

Volume 37. Steerage Conditions—Importation and Harboring of Women for Immoral Purposes—Immigrant Homes and Aid Societies—Immigrant Banks. (S. Doc. No. 753, 61st Cong., 3d sess.)

Volume 38. Changes in Bodily Form of Descendants of Immigrants. (S. Doc. No. 208, 61st Cong., 2d sess.)

Volume 39. Federal Immigration Legislation—Digest of Immigration Decisions—Steerage Legislation, 1819-1908—State Immigration and Alien Laws. (S. Doc. No. 758, 61st Cong., 3d sess.)

Volume 40. The Immigration Situation in Other Countries: Canada—Australia—New Zealand—Argentina—Brazil. (S. Doc. No. 761, 61st Cong., 3d sess.)

Volume 41. Statements and Recommendations Submitted by Societies and Organizations Interested in the Subject of Immigration. (S. Doc. No. 764, 61st Cong., 3d sess.)

Volume 42. Index of Reports of the Immigration Commission. (S. Doc. No. 785, 61st Cong., 3d sess.)

IMMIGRANTS IN INDUSTRIES.

JAPANESE AND OTHER IMMIGRANT RACES IN THE PACIFIC COAST AND ROCKY
MOUNTAIN STATES (IN THREE VOLUMES: VOL. I).

This report, which was prepared under the direction of the Commission by
H. A. Millis, superintendent of agents, forms part of the general report of the
Immigration Commission on immigrants in industries. Dr. Millis was assisted
in the preparation of certain parts of his report as follows: Immigrant labor
in the hop industry, Immigrant labor in California fruit and vegetable canneries, Immigrant labor in the manufacture of cement, Immigrant labor in the
salmon canneries of Alaska, Immigrant labor in the manufacture of cigars
and cigarettes in San Francisco, Immigrant labor in the powder factories of
California, Immigrant laborers employed by street railway companies operating in the cities of the Pacific Coast and Rocky Mountain States, Immigrants
employed in miscellaneous industries in California, and Immigrant labor in
the coal and coke industry of the Western States, by Samuel Bryan; Immigrant labor in the orchards about Suisun Valley, Immigrant labor and farming in the Imperial Valley, The wine-making industry of California, and The
celery industry of Orange County, Cal., by Evan J. Hughes; Immigrant labor
in the beet-sugar industry in the Western States and Immigrant labor in the
metalliferous mining, smelting, and refining industry in the Western States,
by W. M. Duffus; and Immigrants in Los Angeles, Cal., by Ralph D. Fleming.

v

CONTENTS.

PART I.—THE JAPANESE IMMIGRANTS IN THE UNITED STATES.

Page.

CHAPTER I.—Introductory 3
CHAPTER II.—Formation, geographical distribution, and composition of the
  Japanese population in the United States 5
CHAPTER III.—Japanese wage-earners in industries 33
  Japanese as railroad laborers 36
  Japanese employed in the lumber and timber industries of Oregon and
    Washington 46
  Japanese employed in the salmon-canning industry in Washington, Oregon,
    and Alaska 48
  Japanese employed in fruit and vegetable canneries of California 51
  Japanese employed in coal mines in the Western Division 52
  Japanese employed in the mining and smelting of metalliferous ores in the
    Western Division 56
  Japanese employed in other industries 57
  Summary 57
CHAPTER IV.—Japanese in agriculture 61
  Agricultural laborers 61
  California 62
  Oregon 68
  Washington 69
  Idaho 70
  Utah 71
  Colorado 72
  Yearly earnings 74
  Japanese farmers 75
CHAPTER V.—Japanese in city employments and business 91
  Japanese in domestic and personal service and related employments 91
  Japanese in business 99
    Laundries 118
    Restaurants serving American meals 121
    Barber shops 123
    Shoe repairing 126
    Tailoring, cleaning, and dyeing 128
    Provision and grocery stores 129
    Organization 131
    Summary 132
CHAPTER VI.—Other economic considerations 135
CHAPTER VII.—Social and political considerations 145
CHAPTER VIII—Pacific coast opinion of Japanese immigration and the desire
  for Asiatic laborers 167

Contents.

PART II.—THE JAPANESE IN CITY EMPLOYMENTS AND BUSINESS IN THE PRINCIPAL CITIES OF THE PACIFIC COAST AND ROCKY MOUNTAIN STATES.

Page.

CHAPTER I.—Introductory.. 181
CHAPTER II.—Japanese in city employments and business in San Francisco. 183
  Introduction.. 183
  Japanese employed by white persons.. 183
  Japanese in business... 187
    Laundries.. 189
    Cobbler shops... 197
    Restaurants serving American meals..................................... 200
    Boarding and lodging houses and labor agencies....................... 202
    Tailors, dressmakers, and suit cleaners.................................. 205
    Barber shops.. 207
    Bath houses... 207
    Men's furnishing stores.. 207
    Jewelry and watch repairing.. 207
    Art goods stores.. 208
    Provision and grocery stores.. 208
    Other stores... 208
    Photographers... 209
    Billiard and pool halls and shooting galleries........................... 209
    Other business.. 209
  Personal data relative to Japanese business men.......................... 209
  Personal data relative to Japanese wage-earners.......................... 213
  Sociological data.. 215
CHAPTER III.—Japanese in city employments and business in Los Angeles... 223
  Introduction.. 223
  Data relating to Japanese business... 226
    Barber shops.. 226
    Baths.. 227
    Laundries.. 227
    Pool rooms.. 229
    Restaurants.. 229
    Cobbler shops... 231
    Tailoring and cleaning establishments.................................... 231
    Provision and grocery stores.. 232
    Fish and poultry and meat markets....................................... 233
    Art or curio stores... 233
    Other stores... 234
    Cigar, confectionery, and ice-cream stands.............................. 234
    Boarding and lodging houses.. 235
    Employment agencies.. 236
    Petty manufacture.. 237
    Other business.. 237
    Japanese professional men... 238
  Summary and statement of the essential facts relating to Japanese business.. 238
  Personal data relative to Japanese business men.......................... 239
  Data relating to wage-earners... 243
  Sociological data.. 244
CHAPTER IV.—Japanese in city trades and employments in Sacramento.... 249
  Introduction.. 249
  Data relating to Japanese business... 251
    Barber shops.. 251
    Baths.. 252
    Laundries.. 252
    Restaurants.. 252
    Hotels and lodging houses... 253
    Tailor shops... 253
    Men's furnishing stores.. 254
    Grocery stores.. 254
    Other stores... 255
    Employment and real estate agencies.................................... 256
    Places of amusement... 256

CHAPTER IV.—Japanese in city trades and employments, etc.—Continued.
Data relating to Japanese business—Continued.   Page.
    Photograph galleries.. 256
    Other branches of business... 256
    Summary.. 257
    Labor employed... 258
    Organization... 259
    The Japanese and real estate values.................................. 260
  Personal data relating to Japanese engaged in business................. 261
  Personal data relating to employees of Japanese business men........... 264
  Sociological data... 265
CHAPTER V.—Japanese in city employments and business in Washington,
with special reference to Seattle.. 271
  Japanese in cities other than Seattle................................. 271
  The Japanese in Seattle—historical.................................... 273
  Japanese employed by white persons.................................... 274
  The Japanese district in Seattle...................................... 276
    Laundries.. 277
    Tailor shops... 281
    Barber shops... 282
    Restaurants serving American meals................................... 283
    Restaurants serving Japanese meals................................... 285
    Japanese stores.. 285
    Hotels and lodging houses.. 288
    Employment agencies.. 289
    Newspapers and periodicals... 290
    Other kinds of business.. 290
    Summary.. 291
  Japanese business men of Seattle...................................... 292
  Japanese wage-earners in Seattle...................................... 296
  Sociological data... 297
CHAPTER VI.—Japanese in city employments and business in Portland...... 303
CHAPTER VII.—Japanese in city employments and business in Denver 307
CHAPTER VIII.—Japanese in city trades and business in Salt Lake City and
Ogden.. 313
  Introduction.. 313
  Japanese in city trades and employments in Salt Lake City............. 314
  Japanese in business in Ogden... 316
CHAPTER IX.—Japanese in business in Idaho................................ 319

PART III.—THE EAST INDIANS ON THE PACIFIC COAST.

                                                                                     Page.
CHAPTER I.—Introductory... 323
CHAPTER II.—Settlement and progress of East Indians in Pacific Coast States.. 325
CHAPTER III.—Employment of East Indians in Coast States................. 331
  In lumber mills and rope factory...................................... 331
  In railroad work.. 332
  In agricultural work in California.................................... 333
  In other employments.. 336
  Summary... 336
CHAPTER IV.—Age and conjugal condition.................................. 339
CHAPTER V.—Standard of living... 341
  Agricultural workers.. 341
  Mill workers.. 342
  Tamale men.. 344
CHAPTER VI.—Sociological data... 347

General tables.. 351
List of text tables... 397
List of general tables.. 401

PART I.—THE JAPANESE IMMIGRANTS IN THE UNITED STATES.

PART I.—THE JAPANESE IMMIGRANTS IN THE UNITED STATES.

CHAPTER I.

INTRODUCTORY.

Special emphasis was placed upon Japanese immigration by the agents of the Commission attached to the western office maintained in San Francisco. Every industry in which the members of that race have extensively engaged has been investigated, and the results are set forth in the various reports in this volume. Among the industries investigated and in which the Japanese have been extensively employed are the growing of fruit, vegetables, sugar beets, and hops, the canning of salmon in Oregon, Washington, and Alaska, and the canning of vegetables in California, railroad work, and coal mining. An investigation was made also of Japanese engaged in city employments and in business in the more important cities of the West. Independent farming by the members of that race was investigated in all of the States in which it has become extensive. Special investigations were made of farming by Japanese in nine localities in California, in several localities in northern Colorado, in northern Utah, in Oregon, and in Washington. Moreover, agents attached to the eastern office investigated Japanese farming in the States of Texas and Florida. The detailed results of these special investigations have been set forth in reports dealing with each city and with each agricultural community. In the present report the more general results have been brought together with the personal data obtained for 13,307 Japanese for whom schedules were taken. Of the 13,307 Japanese 12,905 were foreign-born, 402 native-born. The representative character of the personal data is indicated by the following table, which shows by industry the number of foreign-born Japanese for whom information was obtained.

TABLE 1.—*Total number of foreign-born Japanese for whom information was secured, by sex and by industry.*

WAGE-EARNERS.

Industry.	Male.	Female.	Total.
Agriculture	6,064	112	6,176
Fish canneries	458		458
Fruit and vegetable canneries	201	36	237
Laundries	161		161
Lumber mills	333	11	344
Mining, coal	447		447
Smelting	65		65
Transportation:			
Steam railroads—			
Maintenance of way and construction	1,142	3	1,145
Shops, bridges, and buildings, water and signal service	631		631
Electric railways	102		102
Miscellaneous	1,277	61	1,338
Total	10,881	223	11,104

3

TABLE 1.—*Total number of foreign-born Japanese for whom information was secured, by sex and by industry*—Continued.

IN BUSINESS FOR SELF.

Industry.	Male.	Female.	Total.
Agriculture	857	280	1,137
Miscellaneous	459	205	664
Total	1,316	485	1,801
Grand total	12,197	708	12,905

It is the opinion of the agents of the Commission that in point of accuracy the data secured in the schedules taken for the Japanese are superior to those collected for most other races investigated in the Western Division of the country. In making the investigation the Commission has had the fullest cooperation of the Japanese consular officers stationed in the different Western States and of the Japanese press. In fact, everyone has given the Commission every assistance in its efforts to secure the information desired. The Commission is placed under special obligation to four Japanese students who at different times have served it as interpreters and translators. It must be added, however, that the investigation of Japanese immigration was made at an inopportune time. Direct emigration from Japan for the continental United States had been greatly restricted by the Japanese Government for approximately a year before the work of the Commission was begun. As a result of this fact it has been impossible to ascertain with a satisfactory degree of certainty the normal workings of an unrestricted immigration of that race. Because of the restrictions made, the differences between the wages of Japanese and of white men, which had obtained, had tended to disappear, while changes had been brought about in the position and work of the Japanese labor contractors, boarding houses, and emigration companies. It has not been possible to deal with a number of vital points with the same degree of certainty as would have been possible had the investigation been made when emigration from Japan was without great restriction.

CHAPTER II.

FORMATION, GEOGRAPHICAL DISTRIBUTION, AND COMPOSITION OF THE JAPANESE POPULATION IN THE UNITED STATES.

The number of Japanese in the continental United States has about quadrupled since the Census of 1900 was taken. At that time the number of Japanese reported, excluding Alaska, was 24,326. Estimates made by the agents of the Commission from all available sources—from the numbers engaged in various occupations, from the numbers reported as living in different places, from the censuses made in Oregon, Colorado, and parts of California by Japanese associations, and from the annuals published by Japanese newspapers printed in different cities—would give a total for the summer of 1909, including the native-born, of between 95,000 and 100,000.

Until after 1890 the number of Japanese immigrants to the United States was small. One Japanese is reported to have immigrated to this country in 1861, 7 in 1866, 67 in 1867, 14 in 1868, 96 in 1869, and 55 in 1870. The Census for 1870, however, reported only 55 persons of that race as residing in this country. The number reported in 1880 was 148, in 1890, 2,039. The number of Japanese ("immigrants" and "nonimmigrants") arriving at the ports of the United States and Canada have been separately reported in the annual reports of the Commissioner-General of Immigration since 1893. The figures presented in the following table have been compiled from that source and show the number of Japanese or of Japanese "immigrants" admitted to the continental United States, excluding Alaska, in so far as they have not come to the mainland from the Hawaiian Islands.

TABLE 2.—*Number of Japanese (exclusive of those coming from the Hawaiian Islands) admitted to the continental United States,a fiscal years 1893 to 1910.*

Year ending June 30—	Number.b	Year ending June 30—	Number.b
1893	1,380	1902	5,325
1894	1,931	1903	6,990
1895	1,150	1904	7,771
1896	1,110	1905	4,319
1897	1,526	1906	5,178
1898	2,230	1907	9,948
1899	3,395	1908	7,250
1900	12,626	1909	1,593
1901	4,908	1910	1,552

a Not including Alaska.

b These figures for the years 1893 to 1899 include "immigrants" and "other alien passengers" of the Japanese race, the two classes not being separately reported previous to 1900. Since 1900 "other alien passengers" have been excluded from the figures given. Since 1901 the number given has been obtained by deducting from the total number of immigrants the number giving their destination as Hawaii or Alaska. The number of "alien passengers" other than immigrants were 268, 311, 191, 195, 248, 794, 511, 612, 1,591, and 319 for the years 1900 to 1909, inclusive, respectively.

5

This direct immigration has been greatly augmented by an indirect immigration by way of Hawaii. A large number of Japanese who went there to work on the sugar plantations have later come to the mainland seeking higher wages or better opportunities for independent farming or business than were offered in the islands. Still others, when the Japanese Government discouraged emigration to the continental United States, emigrated to Hawaii as a stepping-stone to the Pacific coast. It has been reported that 20,641 Asiatics, of whom perhaps 300 were Koreans and less than 75 Chinese, departed from Hawaii for the mainland during the four years January 1, 1902, to December 31, 1905.[a] The figures, by shorter periods, are as follows:

TABLE 3.—*Departures of orientals from Hawaii to the mainland.*

Period.	Number.
Jan. 1, 1902, to Sept. 30, 1902	1,054
Oct. 1, 1902, to Sept. 30, 1903	2,119
Oct. 1, 1903, to June 30, 1904	3,665
July 1, 1904, to June 30, 1905	11,132
July 1, 1905, to Sept. 30, 1905	1,798
Oct. 1, 1905, to Dec. 31, 1905	873

The number of Japanese who came during the years 1906 and 1907 also was large. According to the Hawaiian Board of Immigration the number of Japanese departing from that Territory to the mainland during the year 1906 was 12,227.[b] The corresponding figure for 1907 was 5,438, of whom 5,149 were adult males, 198 adult females, and 91 children.[c] As a result of the President's order of March 14, 1907, issued in accordance with section 1 of the immigration act approved February 20, 1907, excluding from the continental United States " Japanese or Korean laborers, skilled or unskilled, who have received passports to go to Mexico, Canada, or Hawaii, and come therefrom," the corresponding number for the calendar year 1908 was only 69.[d] Thus the number of Japanese coming to the mainland from Hawaii during the seven years, 1902–1908, was more than 37,000, as against 46,779 who immigrated from Japan or other countries during the seven years, July 1, 1901, to June 30, 1908. A third element is found in those who crossed the Canadian or the Mexican border without permission of the officials connected with the Bureau of Immigration—a matter discussed later in this report.

The great majority of the Japanese immigrants have come to this country when young men, a smaller number when they had become older but had failed in business or found their prospects as farmers

[a] Third Report of the Commissioner of Labor on Hawaii, Bulletin of the Bureau of Labor, No. 66, September, 1906, pp. 378–379. These figures, with those to follow, cover fairly accurately Japanese immigrants regularly admitted to the continental United States since the last census was taken, save those who came from Honolulu during the six months July 1 to December 31, 1901.

[b] First Report of the Board of Immigration to the Governor of the Territory of Hawaii, 1908.

[c] Second Report of the Board of Immigration to the Governor of the Territory of Hawaii, 1909, p. 17.

[d] Ibid.

or laborers in Japan unattractive. The ages of 11,585 Japanese males from whom information was obtained at time of coming to the continental United States are shown in the following tables, the first giving the number, the second the percentage of the total number, falling within each specified age group:

TABLE 4.—*Age of foreign-born Japanese males at time of coming to the United States, by industry: Numbers.*

WAGE-EARNERS.

Industry.	Number reporting complete data.	Number within each specified age group.							
		Under 18.	18 and 19.	20 to 24.	25 to 29.	30 to 34.	35 to 39.	40 to 44.	45 or over.
Agriculture.................	5,985	703	718	1,700	1,297	807	491	191	78
Fish canneries..............	360	47	56	127	65	33	18	9	5
Fruit and vegetable canneries	198	22	32	67	38	15	17	6	1
Laundries..................	160	24	27	56	25	15	7	5	1
Lumber mills..............	230	17	19	70	57	38	18	4	7
Mining, coal..............	408	29	37	123	117	58	31	12	1
Smelting..................	65	3	5	23	13	8	10	1	2
Transportation:									
Steam railroads—									
Maintenance of way and construction ..	975	83	118	306	192	131	92	39	14
Shops, bridges, and buildings, water and signal service..	587	41	71	162	157	84	42	30	......
Electric railways........	88	7	8	29	26	8	5	4	1
Miscellaneous.............	1,268	130	169	470	271	121	73	25	9
Total..................	10,324	1,106	1,260	3,133	2,258	1,318	804	326	119

IN BUSINESS FOR SELF.

Agriculture.................	816	89	84	270	184	114	50	21	4
Miscellaneous...............	445	41	35	145	123	56	31	7	7
Total..................	1,261	130	119	415	307	170	81	28	11

TABLE 5.—*Age of foreign-born Japanese males at time of coming to the United States, by industry: Percentages.*

WAGE-EARNERS.

Industry.	Number reporting complete data.	Per cent within each specified age group.							
		Under 18.	18 and 19.	20 to 24.	25 to 29.	30 to 34.	35 to 39.	40 to 44.	45 or over.
Agriculture.................	5,985	11.7	12.0	28.4	21.7	13.5	8.2	3.2	1.3
Fish canneries..............	360	13.1	15.6	35.3	18.1	9.2	5.0	2.5	1.4
Fruit and vegetable canneries	198	11.1	16.2	33.8	19.2	7.6	8.6	3.0	.5
Laundries..................	160	15.0	16.9	35.0	15.6	9.4	4.4	3.1	.6
Lumber mills..............	230	7.4	8.3	30.4	24.8	16.5	7.8	1.7	3.0
Mining, coal..............	408	7.1	9.1	30.1	28.7	14.2	7.6	2.9	.2
Smelting..................	65	4.6	7.7	35.4	20.0	12.3	15.4	1.5	3.1
Transportation:									
Steam railroads—									
Maintenance of way and construction...	975	8.5	12.1	31.4	19.7	13.4	9.4	4.0	1.4
Shops, bridges, and buildings, water and signal service..	587	7.0	12.1	27.6	26.7	14.3	7.2	5.1	......
Electric railways........	88	8.0	9.1	33.0	29.5	9.1	5.7	4.5	1.1
Miscellaneous.............	1,268	10.3	13.3	37.1	21.4	9.5	5.8	2.0	.7
Total..................	10,324	10.7	12.2	30.3	21.9	12.8	7.8	3.2	1.2

TABLE 5.—*Age of foreign-born Japanese males at time of coming to the United States, by industry: Percentage*—Continued.

IN BUSINESS FOR SELF.

Industry.	Number reporting complete data.	Per cent within each specified age group.							
		Under 18.	18 and 19.	20 to 24.	25 to 29.	30 to 34.	35 to 39.	40 to 44.	45 or over.
Agriculture..................	816	10.9	10.3	33.1	22.5	14.0	6.1	2.6	0.5
Miscellaneous..............	445	9.2	7.9	32.6	27.6	12.6	7.0	1.6	1.6
Total..............	1,261	10.3	9.4	32.9	24.3	13.5	6.4	2.2	.9

Thus, of 10,324 wage-earners from whom data were collected, 2,366, or 22.9 per cent of the total, were under 20 years of age, and 5,499, or 53.2 per cent, were under 25 years of age when they immigrated (from Japan or elsewhere) to the continental United States. Only 1,249, or 12.2 per cent, were 35 years of age or over. Of 1,261 farmers and business men comprising the second main group shown in the tables, 249 were under 20 years of age, 664, or 52.6 per cent, were under 25, and only 120, or 9.5 per cent of the entire number, were 35 years of age or over when they came to this country. Were allowance made for the time spent by many of these in Hawaii, it would be seen that the great majority had left their native land when young men.

Perhaps three-fifths, or even more, of the Japanese immigrants to the United States have been of the agricultural class. The various city classes have been small in comparison. This is shown by the occupations of Japanese aliens arrived at the ports of the United States (including Hawaii) and Canada, as reported by the Commissioner-General of Immigration. The following table has been compiled from the reports of that official for the years 1901 to 1909, inclusive. The classes who have immigrated to the United States directly or indirectly do not differ sufficiently from those who have gone to Hawaii and remained there to prevent broad comparisons based upon the table from being of value.

TABLE 6.—*Occupations of Japanese aliens arrived at ports of United States and Canada, as reported by Commissioner-General of Immigration.*

Year.	Total number.	Professional.	Merchants, grocers, and bankers.	Farmers.	Farm laborers.	Skilled laborers.	Laborers.	Personal domestic service.	Other occupations.	Without occupation.[a]
1901..............	5,249	167	660	897	1,153	603	830	181	173	585
1902..............	14,455	222	1,211	5,212	451	1,047	1,558	173	193	4,388
1903..............	20,041	274	1,445	5,010	5,816	922	572	132	588	5,282
1904..............	14,382	373	1,189	121	6,775	641	1,474	317	248	3,244
1905..............	11,021	280	791	380	5,883	358	743	207	167	2,212
1906..............	14,243	256	649	522	8,435	329	835	195	567	2,446
1907..............	30,824	610	783	817	20,636	546	1,334	166	2,174	3,855
1908..............	16,418	378	687	378	6,766	457	1,144	284	1,742	4,582
1909..............	3,275	139	108	15	628	85	200	67	268	1,765
Total.........	129,908	2,699	7,523	13,352	56,543	4,988	8,690	1,722	6,129	28,359
Percentages.........	100.0	2.1	5.8	10.3	43.5	3.8	6.7	1.3	4.7	21.8

a This includes women and children.

Thus, according to these data, 10.3 per cent of the immigrants for the nine years had been farmers in Japan, while 43.5 per cent had been "farm laborers" most of whom were youths or young men working on their fathers' farms without wages, for farm laborers working regularly for wages have been relatively few. Moreover, 21.8 per cent, including women and children, had not been gainfully occupied. A large percentage of these were the wives and small children of farmers and farm laborers and should be added to the percentages given above in order to obtain an estimate of the relative number of the farming class emigrating from Japan. As opposed to the 53.8 per cent who had been gainfully employed in agricultural pursuits, 2.1 per cent were professional men (physicians, teachers, preachers, actors, etc.), 5.8 per cent were merchants, grocers, and bankers, 3.8 per cent skilled laborers in a great variety of trades, 6.7 per cent common laborers, 1.3 per cent had been occupied in the various branches of domestic and personal service, and 4.7 per cent in other occupations of which fishing was no doubt one of the more important. Thus, the majority of the Japanese immigrants have been drawn from the rural sections of the country. Yet many classes have found large representation among those who have come to the United States.

The primary motive to immigration of the Japanese as of most other races coming to this country has been economic. It is true that 2,825 of 8,466 passports issued in 1906 for the continental United States, and 2,843 of 38,559 issued for this country, including Hawaii, were for the purpose of study.[a] Yet, while the number of "students" has been large, a majority of those who have come as such have not pursued a regular course of study after their arrival in this country but have engaged in gainful pursuits, so that these figures exaggerate the numerical importance of the student class. That the economic motive should have appealed strongly to the Japanese is shown by the advantages which the members of that race have found offered by this country over those in the parts of Japan from which the emigration has largely taken place. Moreover, the activity of emigration companies in Japan and of the "contractors" in this country, and the part played by Hawaii have been such as to encourage immigration to the continental United States.

The Japanese population has a greater density than that of European countries, except Belgium, Holland, and England. Moreover, though less than one-fifth of the land of the Empire, exclusive of Formosa, is arable, Japan is primarily an agricultural country, as shown by the fact that in 1901 some 60 per cent of those gainfully occupied were engaged in agricultural pursuits. Most of the farms are exceedingly small and are cultivated most intensively. The majority of the farmers are tenants of at least a part of their holdings, and, with an increasing population, rents have been high.[b] Moreover, the improvements in agriculture, including the consolidation of scattered holdings into one tract, the improvement of irrigation and

[a] The Twenty-sixth Annual Statistical Report of the Japanese Empire, p. 67.
[b] According to returns made to the Government in 1888, there were in 38 prefectures about 1,470,000 farmers owning the land they tilled, about 2,000,000 farmers who owned a part and leased a part of their holdings, while 950,000 were tenants. The number of tenant farmers is increasing. (Japan in the Beginning of the 20th Century, 1904, p. 90.)

drainage, and the use of animals, machinery, and better tools in culti-vation, have rested heavily upon the small freeholders. In this con-nection it is noteworthy that a large percentage of the Japanese in the United States have come from a few districts, among which are Hiroshima (of first importance), Yamaguchi, Fukuoka, Okayama, and Hyogo. It is stated that 46,500 of the 84,576 passports issued by the Government between 1898 and 1903 to Japanese emigrating to countries other than China and Korea were issued to residents of these five districts. In all of these cases the majority of the farms are small. In Hyogo in 1888, 73 per cent of the holdings were of less than 8 tan, or 1.96 acres. The corresponding percentages for small holdings in Hiroshima, Okayama, Yamaguchi, and Fukuoka were 70, 66, 61, and 56, respectively.[a]

The wages of farm laborers, though they have risen rapidly, are small. According to the Twenty-fifth Annual Statistical Report of the Department of Agriculture and Commerce of Japan, the wages of those employed by the year, living with the employer and receiv-ing board and lodging and perhaps clothing twice a year, were $16 in 1900 and $23.01 in 1908—for the year. Those employed by the day in 1900 were paid 14.8 cents; in 1908, 19.3 cents, without board and lodging.

Work in the factories, mines, and various urban occupations has proved more attractive than farming or farm labor. In 1876, 77.8 per cent of those gainfully occupied were engaged in agricultural pur-suits. In 1886 66.12 per cent, in 1900 60 per cent, of the families were reported as being agricultural in their interests.[b] A large number of men have found employment in factories, where they con-stitute an increasing percentage of the increasing number employed, and in other nonagricultural pursuits. The wages in some of these occupations are shown in the following table, translated from the statistical report to which reference has just been made, the wages being reduced to American money:

TABLE 7.—*Wages of males in specified occupations in Japan.*

[Unless otherwise specified the amounts are wages per day without board and lodging.]

Year.	Farm laborers on yearly contract, with board and lodging.[c]	Farm laborers employed by the day.	Sericultural laborers.	Gardeners.	Fishermen.	Weavers.	Dyers.	Cotton whippers.	Tailors, Japanese dress.	Tailors, European dress.	Shoemakers.	Confectioners.	Carpenters.
1900....	$15.995	$0.148	$0.153	$0.254	$0.193	$0.163	$0.143	$0.183	$0.193	$0.294	$0.234	$0.148	$0.269
1901....	15.845	.158	.163	.284	.168	.143	.153	.178	.223	.309	.249	.153	.294
1902....	15.810	.158	.158	.284	.168	.163	.148	.188	.223	.299	.269	.168	.289
1903....	15.925	.153	.158	.274	.183	.168	.163	.198	.234	.284	.269	.178	.294
1904....	18.750	.163	.148	.264	.163	.173	.153	.193	.223	.294	.279	.163	.294
1905....	18.695	.158	.143	.274	.208	.168	.158	.203	.234	.319	.284	.168	.299
1906....	18.590	.168	.168	.294	.198	.208	.183	.218	.249	.339	.289	.163	.324
1907....	19.575	.178	.208	.309	.234	.208	.208	.249	.259	.369	.289	.178	.374
1908....	23.015	.193	.208	.344	.254	.218	.228	.244	.269	.382	.341	.193	.402

[a] Yosoburo Yoshida, " Sources and causes of Japanese emigration," Annals American Academy of Political and Social Science, vol. 34, pp. 159–162.

[b] Y. Ichihashi, " Movement of population in feudal and modern Japan," unpublished manuscript.

[c] Wages per year.

TABLE 7.—*Wages of males in specified occupations in Japan*—Continued.

Year.	Plasterers.	Stonecutters.	Bricklayers.	Paperhangers.	Cabinetmakers.	Coopers.	Harness makers.	Foundrymen.	Blacksmiths.	Potters.	Day laborers.	Male servants.[a]
1900....	$0.269	$0.304	$0.314	$0.249	$0.249	$0.213	$0.234	$0.234	$0.239	$0.188	$0.183	$1.345
1901....	.294	.334	.339	.269	.274	.228	.254	.249	.244	.213	.193	1.355
1902....	.294	.349	.364	.269	.269	.234	.274	.269	.259	.223	.193	1.399
1903....	.304	.339	.369	.279	.269	.234	.299	.264	.259	.208	.198	1.479
1904....	.299	.324	.354	.269	.259	.223	.289	.254	.274	.223	.198	1.504
1905....	.299	.329	.354	.279	.274	.228	.309	.264	.274	.228	.203	1.603
1906....	.324	.364	.407	.289	.294	.249	.314	.274	.284	.269	.208	1.643
1907....	.377	.432	.478	.329	.339	.269	.324	.309	.324	.274	.244	1.917
1908....	.417	.478	.528	.369	.354	.284	.339	.329	.339	.279	.264	2.012

[a] Wages per month with board and lodging.

The sums entered in this table are small as compared to the $1 to $2 per day Japanese have generally earned in this country. Direct comparisons of wages in the two countries are not worth the while, however, for prices and conditions of living differ greatly. Nor can these differences be measured and allowed for. It may be said, however, that most of the Japanese immigrating to the United States have come with the intention of working for a few or several years and then returning to their native land with such gains as had not been sent on before them, and that the average laborer has been able to save much more to send home or to invest in this country than he could earn in his native land. Indeed, his annual earnings in Japan at the rates of wages indicated above are a mere fraction of the amount of surplus over and above living expenses reported by Japanese laborers engaged in different occupations. These figures, together with the amount of money sent abroad, are shown in detail later in this report.[a] It should be added, however, that the wages earned by Japanese laborers are somewhat higher and their employment more regular than before restrictions were placed upon their emigration to this country, with the result that their savings are naturally somewhat larger than formerly. It has always been possible for a Japanese to meet the expense of immigrating to this country—some 65 to 69 yen since 1906 for passage and a smaller sum for incidentals [b]—and after a few years of work, if he did not remain longer in this country because of the gain to be realized, to return to Japan with sufficient means to establish himself as a small landowning farmer or in some higher economic position. When he has not returned to his native land it frequently has been because of opportunities found here to become an independent farmer or business man. It is this possibility of economic gain, witnessed when persons have returned to Japan, commented on by the Japanese press in some instances, and written about to friends by those residing in the United States, which has given rise to emigration from Japan directed toward the United States.

This movement, moreover, when unrestricted by the Japanese Government has been stimulated in various ways. As one of these is

[a] In Chapter VI.
[b] Since 1906 the fare for immigrants from Japanese ports to San Francisco has been from 65 to 69 yen and from San Francisco to Japan $51.

to be noted the publication and circulation among the Japanese of guides to different occupations and similar literature, most of which have exaggerated the advantages presented by the United States. Of far more importance, however, has been the influence of the emigration companies in Japan and the institutions in this country, which, with or without cooperation with the emigration companies, have paved the way and found ready employment for such as came. Little of the immigration to this country, except of the student class, has been independent of the emigration company; usually the first employment in this country has been under the Japanese contractor.

The Japanese Government has been paternal in its treatment of its subjects. The inhabitants are registered in the localities in which they live, and if one emigrates it is with the consent and under the protection of the Government. Those who emigrate are selected, passports are granted for limited periods, and security is required for the welfare of the emigrant while abroad, and in some cases for the care of his family while he is absent, and for his return to Japan when sick or disabled.

The regulations of this character, adopted by the Japanese Government after the prohibition of emigration from the country was discontinued, have been instrumental, if not in calling into existence, at any rate in providing opportunity for and strengthening the position of the emigration companies, of which there were 12—some of them with branches—in existence in 1899.[a] Most of the emigration has been through these companies, whether for contract labor in Mexico, Peru, or elsewhere, or for the United States, where the immigration of laborers under contract has been unlawful. In return for a fee, varying from 10 to 20 yen, these companies, when the individual secures his passport, arrange for his emigration and perhaps for the surety required by the Government. Moreover, these companies, in pursuit of profit, have advertised for contract laborers to go to Peru, Mexico, and elsewhere, and some years ago, according to a report made in 1899, " in a general way through circulars, pamphlets, and by means of traveling solicitors, for emigrants going to the United States." [b]

For several years before this was discouraged by the Japanese Government, emigration for the United States was thus encouraged; from first to last, through the efforts of the companies, emigration has been rid of its inconveniences and made easy for the individual.

In this country the Japanese employed as section hands on the railroads, as " cannery hands," as laborers in the sugar-beet fields, as laborers in large groups in other branches of agriculture—in fact, in most occupations outside of various city trades, have worked under " bosses " or contractors who serve as employment agents for one or a few employers. This has been the most characteristic thing in connection with Japanese labor and accounts in no small degree for the success which the Japanese have attained in this country. Except during the winter season, the demand for Japanese labor in the West has been such that these contractors could readily find employment within a short time for all the men they could bring under their control, and frequently the contractors have been unable to

---

[a] Rice: " Immigration of Japanese " (House Doc. No. 686, 56th Cong., 1st sess.).
[b] Ibid.

supply as many as were wanted for railroad work. The larger contractors have usually conducted boarding houses and supply stores, the one as a means of assembling laborers, the other as a means of providing those employed under their control with the larger part of the goods consumed. Moreover, the keepers of boarding houses who have not directly engaged in " contracting," if they had many patrons of the laboring class, have usually had close connections with those who were supplying labor for different industrial establishments. These relations are evidenced by the fees boarding houses, according to their association rules, are to charge contractors for supplying them with laborers—as $1.50 in Seattle and $3 in San Francisco for each railroad laborer. The other phases of this organization of labor will be discussed elsewhere. The point to be emphasized here is that this situation has at least guaranteed the immigrant the quickest and the most regular employment, and its existence has in and of itself stimulated the immigration of this race.

To what extent the contractors and boarding house keepers in the United States and the emigration companies in Japan cooperated when immigration to this country was without restriction is unknown. There is little direct evidence of any business connection between them. In one instance, however, a member of one of the large emigration companies has conducted a business in this country and has supplied Japanese laborers to several railways. Their first employment in any considerable number was arranged for just previous to a visit to Japan, which visit was followed by the immigration of 200 laborers who were set at work under his control as section hands. Whether they came under contract is unknown. Another man who was formerly connected with supplying railway labor in one of the Rocky Mountain States, returned to Japan, where he became interested in the emigration business.[a] Most of the contractors in this country, however, have come as wage laborers and later have risen to the position they now occupy. Yet it is noteworthy in this connection that in 1899, when an investigation of this matter was made by the Immigration Bureau, six of the emigration companies had agents in California.[b]

As already noted, upward of 37,000 Japanese came from the Hawaiian Islands to the mainland during the seven years, 1902 to 1908. In 1900, partly as a result of the importation of contract laborers, partly as the result of voluntary immigration of laborers to work on the sugar plantations, a large Japanese population of 61,111 (of a total of 154,001) had been built up in those islands. In 1900, as a result of the rapid influx of Japanese to the continent at that time, many being diverted to San Francisco from Honolulu because of the bubonic plague which had made its appearance, agitation began in California for the extension of the Chinese exclusion law to include the Japanese as well, an agitation which has become more persistent since 1905.[c] The Japanese Government has been responsive to the feeling exhibited in the United States, with the result that emigration for the mainland was more or less discouraged from 1900 until it was greatly restricted in 1907. For several years, how-

---

[a] See Rice, op. cit., p. 6.
[b] Rice, op. cit., p. 6, where names and addresses were given.
[c] For a discussion of the opposition to Japanese immigration, see Chapter VIII.

ever, there was a strong demand for Asiatic labor for the plantations in Hawaii, and the immigration of Chinese laborers being unlawful after annexation of these islands many Japanese went there. Once there they were no longer under the control of the Japanese Government and many of them used Honolulu as a stepping stone to the United States, where not only were wages higher and the work more agreeable than upon the plantations, but more numerous occupations were open to them, and the opportunities to rise to an independent position as tenant or land-owning farmers very much better. Moreover, with the strong demand for common labor prevailing in the West, the Japanese contractors on the coast, and especially those doing business in San Francisco and Seattle, induced many to come to the United States. Some of these contractors were for a time regularly represented by agents sent to Honolulu, recourse was made to advertising in the Japanese papers published there, cheap rates were secured, and in some instances assistance was given in other ways to those desiring to reach the mainland.[a]

Japanese residents of Honolulu attempted to profit by a similar migration and transported 2,777 laborers during ten months in 1907 to British Columbia, whence no doubt a large percentage entered the United States.

It was under such circumstances as these that the immigration directly from Japan and from the Hawaiian Islands took place. The figures given for the number of arrivals do not show the total number who have come to the continental United States, however, for some have entered this country irregularly across the Canadian and the Mexican borders. As in the case of other races, there is no

---

[a] The character of the inducements offered by these contractors to laborers to come to the mainland are well shown by excerpts from Japanese papers published at Honolulu, printed in the "Third Report of the Commissioner of Labor on Hawaii," pp. 22–23. The advertisements were for the spring of 1905. That business was continued for some time.

"Recruiting Laborers to America.

"For the S. P. R. R. Company, 800 men; for Alaska, 200 men. Advance $20 for passage to San Francisco. Applications for Alaska close 28th instant. Egi. Kyujiro, proprietor, Shiranui Hotel, San Francisco. Apply to the below-mentioned hotels in Honolulu" (followed by the names of 11 Japanese hotels).— (From Hawaiian-Japanese Chronicle of March 22, 1905.)

"Great Recruiting to America.

"Through an arrangement made with Yasuzawa, of San Francisco, we are able to recruit laborers to the mainland and offer them work. The laborers will be subjected to no delay upon arriving in San Francisco, but can get work immediately through Yasuzawa. Employment offered in picking strawberries and tomatoes, planting beets, mining, and domestic service. Now is the time to go! Wages $1.50 a day. Tokujiro Inaya–Niigata Kenjin—care of Nishimura Hotel. Apply to the Honolulu agency for further particulars, giving the name of your plantation."—(From Hawaiian-Japanese Chronicle of March 22, 1905.)

"The undersigned has appointed Harutada Yasumura agent for recruiting laborers for the mainland. Any laborer will be given work upon presentation of a letter of introduction from the above agent. We guarantee that the laborers receive work from only responsible parties. Tooyo Boyeki Kwaisha (Oriental Trading Company), Seattle. Honolulu agency at Hong Song Hotel."— (From Hawaiian-Japanese Chronicle of March 22, 1905.)

doubt that a fairly large number have come across the Canadian border. The problem presented there, however, has been solved by an agreement entered into in 1908 between the Canadian and Japanese Governments limiting the number of passports which the latter shall issue to emigrants to Canada in any one year to 400. The number of Japanese who have come into the United States across the Mexican border has been materially larger. In 1906 and 1907 Inspector Braun was detailed by the Bureau of Immigration to investigate the influx of immigrants of different races from or through Mexico. With reference to the Japanese he reported that within two years more than 10,000 had been imported into Mexico as contract laborers, being sent out by the various emigration companies, but that most of them had left their employment, and that the entire number in the Republic at the time (June, 1907) was only about 1,000. Inasmuch as they had not left the country through the ports, it was concluded that they had migrated to the United States, lawfully previous to the issue of the President's order of March 14, 1907, " surreptitiously ever since." [a] Since that time, however, the importation of contract laborers to Mexico has been discontinued, and the large influx of that race across the border has ceased. The investigation of Japanese employed in different places failed to discover more than a comparatively few who had entered the United States since the summer of 1907 other than those who had come directly from Japan.

"Special Notice.

" In the next three months we shall recruit 1,000 laborers of Niigata Province, Japan, for the mainland. Apply to the hotel below. Don't miss a good chance! The Industrial Corporation of Japanese of Niigata Province have sent a representative to Hawaii to encourage their countrymen to go to America. This representative, Mr. Seisku Kuroishi, assists applicants in every way. Yamaichi Hotel, February 1, 1905. (Pro. Fuse Totazo.)"—(From Hawaiian-Japanese Chronicle of March 22, 1905.)

"Arrangements have been made with the Japanese-American Industrial Corporation of San Francisco whereby anyone leaving Hawaii for the mainland through us can find work. Naigwai Benyeki Shosha."—(From Hawaiian-Japanese Chronicle of March 22, 1905.)

"New Steamship Line Opened.

" With the steamship *Centennial* we shall inaugurate a new line between San Francisco and Hawaii, and will take freight and passengers. For the convenience of Japanese we have appointed two agents, one at Honolulu and the other at Hilo. This is a large steamer of 3,000 tons, well built, and perfectly safe for carrying passengers, making monthly voyages and passage within a week. Passage is cheap. No deposit of $50 required. Cooks and waiters Japanese and Japanese food furnished. First sailing March 25. Applications received until day before sailing. S. N. S. S. Company agents, Honolulu, Yukinosuki Shibata; Hilo, Yasikichi Toda."—(From Hawaii Shinpo of February 27, 1905.)

"Special Steamer for America—Sailing Direct for Seattle.

" Steamship *Olympia*. Accommodates 500 passengers. Fare, including commissions, $28. Sails April 18, 1905. Applications for passage received up to April 10, 1905. All wishing to go to America apply to the undersigned or to the following hotels (list of 16 Japanese hotels in Honolulu). Seattle Occidental Steamship Company, office Han Sang Hotel, Honolulu."—(From Hawaii Shinpo of February 27, 1905.)

[a] See reports published in " Annual Report of the Commissioner-General of Immigration for the year ended June 30, 1907," pp. 73–75.

Largely because of the rapid influx of Japanese from Japan, Hawaii, and Mexico, the feeling on the Pacific Coast, and especially in San Francisco, against the members of that race became so intense that a crisis was reached late in 1906. The particular points at issue [a] were disposed of by an agreement whereby the Japanese Government was to discontinue the issuing of passports to certain classes of its subjects who desired to emigrate to the continental United States, and by an amendment to the United States immigration law, authorizing the President to issue an order preventing the incoming of laborers from other countries and our insular possessions, who did not have passports to this country properly granted by their home Government. On March 14, 1907, the President, exercising the authority vested in him by section 1 of the amended immigration law [b] approved February 20, 1907, issued an order refusing admission to "Japanese or Korean laborers, skilled or unskilled, who have received passports to go to Mexico, Canada, Hawaii, and come therefrom."

The understanding with Japan contemplates "that the Japanese Government shall issue pasports to the continental United States only to such of its subjects as are nonlaborers or are laborers who, in coming to the continent, seek to resume a formerly acquired domicile, to join a parent, wife, or children residing there, or to assume active control of an already possessed interest in a farming enterprise in this country;" so that the three classes of laborers entitled to receive passports have come to be designated "former residents," "parents, wives, or children of residents," and "settled agriculturists." [c] After the order of March 14, 1907, above referred to, was issued, the Japanese Government applied the same rule to the granting of passports to the Hawaiian Islands as to the continental territory.

With the immigration of Japanese thus restricted, the number who have been admitted at the ports has been much smaller than for several years, ending with the year 1906-7. The number who applied during the year 1908-9, with or without passports, the number who were admitted and the number rejected, by classes covered by the agreement with reference to the granting of passports, are shown in the table following.[d]

---

[a] See Chapters VII and VIII.

[b] A proviso attached to section 1 of that measure reads as follows: "That wherever the President shall feel satisfied that passports issued by any foreign government to its citizens to go to any other country than the United States or to any insular possession of the United States or to the Canal Zone are being used for the purpose of enabling the holders to come to the continental territory of the United States to the detriment of labor conditions therein, the President may refuse to permit such citizens of the country issuing such passports to enter the continental territory of the United States from such other country or from such insular possessions or from the Canal Zone."

[c] Annual Report of the Commissioner-General of Immigration for the fiscal year ended June 30, 1908, pp. 125-126.

[d] Similar data for the month of June, 1908, may be found in a table, pp. 92-93 of the Annual Report of the Commissioner-General of Immigration for the year ended June 30, 1908. Similar data were not presented for the earlier months because of the "indefinite and tentative nature" of the arrangement and the slow progress that could be made in carrying it into effect. "The system did not begin to work smoothly in all its details until the last month of the fiscal year" (p. 126).

TABLE 8.—*Japanese arrivals in continental United States, fiscal year 1909.*[1]

	Former residents — Nonlaborers	Former residents — Laborers	Former residents — Total	Parents, wives, and children of residents — Nonlaborers	Parents, wives, and children of residents — Laborers	Parents, wives, and children of residents — Total	Settled agriculturists — Nonlaborers	Settled agriculturists — Laborers	Settled agriculturists — Total	Not former residents, parents, wives, or children of residents, nor settled agriculturists—nonlaborers	Total entitled to passport	Not entitled to passport, not former residents, parents, wives, or children of residents, nor settled agriculturists—laborers	Total with passport — Nonlaborers	Total with passport — Laborers	Total with passport — Total	Without proper passport — Nonlaborers	Without proper passport — Laborers	Without proper passport — Total	With and without proper passport — Nonlaborers	With and without proper passport — Laborers	Grand total
	In possession of proper passport															*Without proper passport*			*With and without proper passport*		
	Entitled to passport under Japanese agreement																				
Total applications	464	304	768	686	256	942				493	2,203	204	1,643	764	2,407	114	123	237	1,757	887	2,644
Disposition: Admitted	459	295	754	675	233	908				483	2,145	158	1,617	686	2,303	102	27	129	1,719	713	2,432
Debarred	5	9	14	11	23	34				10	58	46	26	78	104	12	96	108	38	174	212
Sex: Male	427	295	722	128	106	234				432	1,388	184	987	585	1,572	98	107	205	1,085	692	1,777
Female	37	9	46	558	150	708				61	815	20	656	179	835	16	16	32	672	195	867

[a] Taken from Annual Report of the Commissioner-General of Immigration for the fiscal year 1909 (p. 100).

It will be noted first of all that of the 2,644 who applied for admission, 2,407 came with proper passports, while 237 did not. Of those with passports, 2,203 are recorded as being entitled to them under the Japanese agreement as interpreted by the Bureau of Immigration. 204 were not. Of the former of these two groups, 768 were former residents returning to this country, 14 were parents, 658 wives, and 270 children of residents, a total of 942; while 493 were not former residents, parents, wives, or children of residents, nor settled agriculturists, but nonlaborers. Of the 2,203 members of classes entitled to passports, 2,145 were admitted while 58 were debarred. Of the 204 laborers who came with passports to which they were not entitled under the agreement, 158 were admitted and 46 debarred. Of the 237 " without proper passports," 53 were nonlaborers and 54 laborers holding passports limited to Hawaii, Canada, or Mexico; 1 had a passport which was not genuine; 3 were nonlaborers and 13 were laborers who were not rightfully in possession of the passports they had; 44 were nonlaborers and 43 were laborers who claimed to have lost or left the passports held at the time of their departure from Japan; 10 were nonlaborers, and 8 were laborers who were not in possession of any kind of passport at time of leaving Japan; while the other 8 were found not to have proper passports or not to require them in order to be admitted.[a] Something more than one-half— 129—were admitted, while 108 were denied admission. Thus, of a total of 2,644 Japanese applying for admission, 2,432 were permitted to enter the country while 212 were debarred.

The occupations of the 2,432, who were admitted (or readmitted after being abroad) as reported, are shown in the following table:[b]

TABLE 9.—*Occupations of Japanese admitted to the continental United States, fiscal year 1909.*

Occupation.	Number admitted.	Occupation.	Number admitted.
Actors	10	Barbers	9
Clergy	14	Carpenters	12
Government officials	45	Tailors	5
Teachers	24	Other artisans	7
Other professional	65	Cooks	60
Clerks	56	Farm laborers	206
Farmers	69	Gardeners	6
Merchants	274	Laborers	245
Restaurant and hotel keepers	64	Servants	114
Students	255	Not stated	49
No occupation (including women and children)	690		
Not stated	153	Total laborers	713
		Grand total	2,432
Total nonlaborers	1,719		

Thus the number of new Japanese admitted (excluding the 768 who were former residents) in 1909 was 1,678. Of these, 409, or about 24.4 per cent, were laborers of the classes indicated in the table. From 1901 to 1907, inclusive, these classes constituted a large percentage of the entire number entering the Hawaiian Islands and the continental United States, but a considerably smaller percentage

[a] See Annual Report of Commissioner-General of Immigration, 1909, p. 101.
[b] Ibid., p. 99.

of those immigrating direct to continental territory. The remaining 1,269 admitted in 1909 belonged to the classes the granting of passports to whom is not limited by the understanding between the two countries. One object of the regulation being to avoid any " detriment to labor conditions," one question which arises is with reference to the number of those of the classes not covered by the agreement who become wage-earners upon their arrival in this country. Most of the farmers, clerks, students, merchants, and others of these classes have become common laborers in the United States. This has been true of many of those who came during the years 1908 and 1909 as well as of those who came in earlier years. Yet the number entering this country in 1908–9 and 1909–10 was small and not equal to the number who departed from the country.

The departures of aliens from the United States have been made a matter of record only since 1908. During the year 1908 the number of Japanese admitted (not including the small number coming from Hawaii) was 9,544; the number who departed, 4,796. As opposed to the 2,432 admitted in 1909, 5,004 departed. The corresponding figures for the year ended June 30, 1910, were 1,552 and 4,377. If allowance is made for the net increase in the number of women and foreign-born children, it would appear that the number of Japanese . men has already begun to diminish somewhat. That the number has not increased during the last two years is in accord with all the information obtained from different sources during the investigation conducted.

The number of Japanese debarred and deported from the United States is shown in the table on the next page. Previous to 1901 they relate to continental territory alone; since that date they relate to Hawaii as well.

TABLE 10.—Number of Japanese debarred or deported from the United States, 1893 to 1910, by cause.

Year ending June 30—	Idiots	Imbeciles	Feeble-minded	Epileptic	Insane	Tuberculosis, noncontagious	Tuberculosis, contagious.a (Loathsome diseases)	Trachoma.a (Loathsome diseases)	Other diseases	Professional beggars	Paupers or likely to become public charges	Likely to become public charges	Surgeon's certificate of defect, mental or physical, which may affect alien's ability to earn a living	Contract laborers	Accompanying aliens	Assisted aliens	Criminals and convicts	Polygamists	Anarchists	Prostitutes	Aliens bringing in prostitutes	Without passports	Total debarred	After landing (Number deported)	After 1 year (Number deported)	After 3 years (Number deported)	Grand total
1893																							56				56
1894						1			2																		
1895																							1				1
1896											1												4				4
1897																											
1898									1		14			5									91				91
1899									39		40			91									148		25		173
1900		2							30		135			261		72							442		96		538
1901									29		158			125		2	4						319		2		321
1902											69			49		2							150				150
1903									538		109			67		6				3			717		4		721
1904									196		158			73						3	2		433		6	36	475
1905					1				285		238			13				1		2	2	1	541		2	53	596
1906									266		84			18		1	1			3	1		370			11	381
1907									709		320			156						1	1		1,239			65	1,304
1908							2	312	13			73	19	16			1		51	1	3	267	711		3	386	1,100
1909					1			129				29	5	19			3			4	3	80	273			291	561
To March, 1910																							101	139			240

a Not segregated from other diseases until 1908.

It will be noted that some have been rejected almost every year on the ground that they were assisted immigrants or contract laborers. An approximately equal number have been rejected lest they might become public charges, while a still larger number have been turned back because they had some disease, most frequently trachoma. Since 1908 a comparatively large number who had gained admission to the country have been deported. During the two years 1908 and 1909, the great majority of the 680 who were deported were returned to Japan because they had not complied with the rules concerning passports or had entered the country without inspection. The number of the former was 506, of the latter, 148—a total of 654 of the 680. Of the others, 4 had trachoma at the time of admission, 1 was insane, 4 became public charges within one year after entry, of whom 1 was afflicted with a contagious disease, 1 became insane, 1 became a public charge because of physical condition prior to entry, and 1 was a dependent member of a family. Sixteen were prostitutes, 3 at the time of their admission, and 13 within three years thereafter, while 1 was deported for attempting to bring prostitutes into the country.

The Japanese population of the continental United States, Alaska excluded, was reported by the census of 1900 as 24,326. Of these, 23,341, or 96 per cent of the entire number, were males, 985, or 4 per cent, females. The estimates made of the total number in 1909, the number of adult males, adult females, and of children, by States of the western division, and other States, are shown in the following table, in so far as an acceptable basis for making such an estimate could be obtained:

TABLE 11.—*Japanese population (estimated) of the continental United States in 1909.*

State.	Adult males.	Adult females.	Children.	Total.
Arizona	a 623	a 11	a 3	637
California	a 47,301	a 5,210	a 3,399	b 55,901
Colorado	5,932	a 68	(c)	d 6,000
Idaho				950
Montana	1,774	26	(c)	1,800
Nevada	1,050	a 22	a 8	1,080
New Mexico	a 653	a 5	(c)	
Oregon	3,573	213	87	3,873
Utah	2,823	55 to 60	60 to 65	2,948
Washington				16,322
Wyoming	1,470	a 14	a 10	1,494
Other States	(c)	(c)	(c)	a 5,757

a From Japanese-American Yearbook.
b This figure is larger than the number of arrivals would indicate. The figures of the Japanese Association, however, check very well with the numbers found in different localities by agents of the Commission. In this connection it should be added that the personal schedules obtained from Japanese show a much greater migration from the Northwest to California than in the contrary direction. It should be added, moreover, that many Japanese have come into the State from foreign territory elsewhere than through the port of San Francisco, so that calculations based upon the records of the steamship companies are apt to prove misleading.
c Not reported.
d A rough estimate during the summer, when the largest number are drawn from other States. Japanese-American Yearbook gives 3,489 men and 68 women, or a total of 3,557.

As these figures indicate, not much less than 95 per cent of the Japanese in the continental United States are in the 11 States and Territories of the Western Division. Moreover, 55 per cent or more of the entire number are in the State of California, while some 16 or

17 per cent are in the State of Washington.   No other State has a number approaching that in either of these States where most of those immigrating have arrived—at Seattle or at San Francisco.   In California the Japanese constitute between 3 and 4 per cent of the total population; the Japanese adult males perhaps between 6.5 and 7 per cent of the total number of males 16 years of age or over.   The corresponding percentages for the other States and Territories are considerably smaller.

It will be noted that the number of women has increased more rapidly than the number of men.   It is probable that the number of adult females, of whom the great majority are married women, was in 1909 not far from 7,000.   The majority of these women have entered the United States during the last five years as the wives of farmers or business men or as single women to be married upon their arrival to men of these classes.   The increase in the number of women has accompanied the rise of the Japanese from the rank of wage-earners to a position of independence.

The majority of Japanese wives, however, have not joined the husbands in this country, because either their husbands expect to return to Japan shortly, or there are children to be schooled, or the husbands have not been able to acquire settled residences and make proper provision for their families.   The conjugal condition of the Japanese of the wage-earning class is shown in the tables following, the second giving the percentages corresponding to the figures entered in the first.

TABLE 12.—*Conjugal condition of foreign-born Japanese wage-earners, by sex, age groups, and industry: Numbers.*

MALE.

Industry	Number reporting complete data	16 to 19				20 to 29				30 to 44				45 or over				Total			
		Single	Married	Widowed	Total	Single	Married	Widowed	Total	Single	Married	Widowed	Total	Single	Married	Widowed	Total	Single	Married	Widowed	Total
Agriculture	6,055	345	1		346	2,377	293	4	2,674	1,127	1,535	63	2,725	29	265	16	310	3,878	2,094	83	6,055
Fish canneries	458	29			29	224	20	1	245	60	91	5	156	3	22	3	28	316	133	9	458
Fruit and vegetable canneries	199	15			15	97	9	2	108	24	41		65		8		11	136	58	5	199
Laundries	159	14			14	81	11		92	15	33		48	6	5		5	110	49		159
Lumber mills	332	9			9	96	26		122	75	109	1	185	1	10	1	16	186	145	1	332
Mining, coal	447	12			12	138	23	4	165	126	117	11	254	6	14	1	16	277	154	16	447
Smelting	62	1			1	21	3		24	8	26		34	1	3		3	30	32		62
Transportation: Steam railroads— Maintenance of way and construction	1,137	39			39	459	61	3	523	164	342	12	518	1	55	1	57	663	458	16	1,137
Shops, bridges, and buildings, water and signal service	631	16			16	230	62	2	294	87	201	5	293	4	23	1	28	337	286	8	631
Electric railways	102	3			3	41	8		49	14	31	1	46	1	2	1	4	59	41	2	102
Miscellaneous	1,276	47			47	602	51	5	658	267	240	14	521	17	30	3	50	933	321	22	1,276
Total	10,858	530	1		531	4,366	567	21	4,954	1,967	2,766	112	4,845	62	437	29	528	6,925	3,771	162	10,858

FEMALE.

Industry	Number reporting complete data	16 to 19				20 to 29				30 to 44				45 or over				Total			
		Single	Married	Widowed	Total	Single	Married	Widowed	Total	Single	Married	Widowed	Total	Single	Married	Widowed	Total	Single	Married	Widowed	Total
Agriculture	111	2	3		5	1	47	1	49		53		53		4		4	3	107	1	111
Fruit and vegetable canneries	34		2		2		13		13		18		18		1		1		34		34
Lumber mills	11						5		5		5		5		1		1		11		11
Transportation: Steam railroads, maintenance of way and construction	3						1		1		2		2						3		3
Miscellaneous	58	1	4		5	2	28	1	31		16	2	18		2	2	4	3	50	5	58
Total	217	3	9		12	3	94	2	99		94	2	96		8	2	10	6	205	6	217

TABLE 13.—*Conjugal condition of foreign-born Japanese wage-earners, by sex, age groups, and industry: Percentages.*

MALE.

Industry.	20 to 29 years of age.				30 to 44 years of age.				45 years of age or over.				20 years of age or over.			
	Number reporting complete data.	Single.	Married.	Widowed.	Number reporting complete data.	Single.	Married.	Widowed.	Number reporting complete data.	Single.	Married.	Widowed.	Number reporting complete data.	Single.	Married.	Widowed.
Agriculture	2,674	88.9	11.0	0.1	2,725	41.4	56.3	2.3	310	9.4	85.5	5.2	5,709	61.9	36.7	1.5
Fish canneries	245	91.4	8.2	.4	156	38.5	58.3	3.2	28	10.7	78.6	10.7	429	66.9	31.0	2.1
Fruit and vegetable canneries	108	89.8	8.3	1.9	65	36.9	63.1	.0	11	.0	72.7	27.3	184	65.8	31.5	2.7
Laundries	92	88.0	12.0	.0	48	31.3	68.8	.0	5	(a)	(a)	(a)	145	66.2	33.8	.0
Lumber mills	122	78.7	21.3	.0	185	40.5	58.9	.5	16	37.5	62.5	.0	323	54.8	44.9	.3
Mining, coal	165	83.6	13.9	2.4	254	49.6	46.1	4.3	16	6.3	87.5	6.3	435	60.9	35.4	3.7
Smelting	24	87.5	12.5	.0	34	23.5	76.5	.0	3	(a)	(a)	(a)	61	47.5	52.5	.0
Transportation: Steam railroads— Maintenance of way and construction	523	87.8	11.7	.6	518	31.7	66.0	2.3	57	1.8	96.5	1.8	1,098	56.8	41.7	1.5
Shops, bridges, and buildings, water and signal service	294	78.2	21.1	.7	293	29.7	68.6	1.7	28	14.3	82.1	3.6	615	52.2	46.5	1.3
Electric railways	49	83.7	16.3	.0	46	30.4	67.4	2.2	4	(a)	(a)	(a)	99	56.6	41.4	2.0
Miscellaneous	658	91.5	7.8	.8	521	51.2	46.1	2.7	50	34.0	60.0	6.0	1,229	72.1	26.1	1.8
Total	4,954	88.1	11.4	.4	4,845	40.6	57.1	2.3	528	11.7	82.8	5.5	10,327	61.9	36.5	1.6

FEMALE.

Industry.	20 to 29 years of age.				30 to 44 years of age.				45 years of age or over.				20 years of age or over.			
	Number reporting complete data.	Single.	Married.	Widowed.	Number reporting complete data.	Single.	Married.	Widowed.	Number reporting complete data.	Single.	Married.	Widowed.	Number reporting complete data.	Single.	Married.	Widowed.
Agriculture	49	2.0	95.9	2.0	53	.0	100.0	0.0	4	(a)	(a)	(a)	106	0.9	98.1	0.9
Fruit and vegetable canneries	13	.0	100.0	.0	18	.0	100.0	.0	1	(a)	(a)	(a)	32	.0	100.0	.0
Lumber mills	5	(a)	(a)	(a)	5	(a)	(a)	(a)	1	(a)	(a)	(a)	11	.0	100.0	.0
Transportation: Steam railroads— Maintenance of way and construction	1	(a)	(a)	(a)	2	(a)	(a)	(a)	.....	.....	.....	....	3	(a)	(a)	(a)
Miscellaneous	31	6.5	90.3	3.2	18	.0	88.9	11.1	4	(a)	(a)	(a)	53	3.8	86.8	9.4
Total	99	3.0	94.9	2.0	96	.0	97.9	2.1	10	.0	80.0	20.0	205	1.5	95.6	2.9

a Not computed, owing to small number involved.

The corresponding data for the Japanese farming and business classes are shown in the tables next submitted.

TABLE 14.—*Conjugal condition of foreign-born Japanese in business for self, by sex, age groups, and industry: Numbers.*

MALE.

Industry	Number reporting complete data	16 to 19 Single	Married	Widowed	Total	20 to 29 Single	Married	Widowed	Total	30 to 44 Single	Married	Widowed	Total	45 or over Single	Married	Widowed	Total	Total Single	Married	Widowed	Total
Agriculture	828	14	...	...	14	207	49	...	256	179	315	23	517	...	40	1	41	400	404	24	828
Miscellaneous	445	1	...	...	1	95	33	1	129	87	193	5	285	2	25	3	30	185	251	9	445
Total	1,273	15	...	...	15	302	82	1	385	266	508	28	802	2	65	4	71	585	655	33	1,273

FEMALE.

Industry	Number reporting complete data	16 to 19 Single	Married	Widowed	Total	20 to 29 Single	Married	Widowed	Total	30 to 44 Single	Married	Widowed	Total	45 or over Single	Married	Widowed	Total	Total Single	Married	Widowed	Total
Agriculture	270	7	6	...	13	1	131	...	132	...	117	...	117	...	8	...	8	8	262	...	270
Miscellaneous	194	4	6	...	10	1	102	1	104	...	77	1	78	...	2	...	2	5	187	2	194
Total	464	11	12	...	23	2	233	1	236	...	194	1	195	...	10	...	10	13	449	2	464

TABLE 15.—*Conjugal condition of foreign-born Japanese in business for self, by sex, age groups, and industry: Percentages.*

MALE.

Industry.	20 to 29 years of age.				30 to 44 years of age.				45 years of age or over.				20 years of age or over.			
	Number reporting complete data.	Per cent who are—			Number reporting complete data.	Per cent who are—			Number reporting complete data.	Per cent who are—			Number reporting complete data.	Per cent who are—		
		Single.	Married.	Widowed.		Single.	Married.	Widowed.		Single.	Married.	Widowed.		Single.	Married.	Widowed.
Agriculture	256	80.9	19.1	0.0	517	34.6	60.9	4.4	41	0.0	97.	2.4	814	47.4	49.6	2.9
Miscellaneous	129	73.6	25.6	.8	285	30.5	67.7	1.8	30	6.7	83.6	10.0	444	41.4	56.5	2.0
Total	385	78.4	21.3	.3	802	33.2	63.3	3.5	71	2.8	91.5	5.6	1,258	45.3	52.1	2.6

FEMALE.

Industry.	20 to 29 years of age.				30 to 44 years of age.				45 years of age or over.				20 years of age or over.			
Agriculture	132	0.8	99.2	0.0	117	0.0	100.0	0.0	8	(a)	(a)	(a)	257	0.4	99.6	0.0
Miscellaneous	104	1.0	98.1	1.0	78	.0	98.7	1.3	2	(a)	(a)	(a)	184	.5	98.4	1.1
Total	236	.8	98.7	.4	195	.0	99.5	.5	10	0.0	100.0	0.0	441	.5	99.1	.5

a Not computed, owing to small number involved.

Comparing the data for the wage-earning males and those for the farmers and business men, it will be noted that 47.5 per cent of the former as against 52.1 per cent of the latter were reported as married. Of more importance, however, is the location of the wives, which is shown for the various groups of men in the following tables:

TABLE 16.—*Location of wives of foreign-born Japanese, by industry.*

WAGE-EARNERS.

Industry.	Number reporting complete data.	Number reporting wife—	
		In United States.	Abroad.
Agriculture	2,092	236	1,856
Fish canneries	91	3	88
Fruit and vegetable canneries	58	25	33
Laundries	49	23	26
Lumber mills	96	34	62
Mining, coal	153	13	140
Smelting	32	1	31
Transportation:			
Steam railroads—			
Maintenance of way and construction	397	6	391
Shops, bridges, and buildings, water and signal service	267	17	250
Electric railways	41	1	40
Miscellaneous	321	87	234
Total	3,597	446	3,151

IN BUSINESS FOR SELF.

Industry.	Number reporting complete data.	In United States.	Abroad.
Agriculture	405	263	142
Miscellaneous	251	191	60
Total	656	454	202

TABLE 17.—*Per cent of foreign-born Japanese husbands who report wife in the United States and per cent who report wife abroad, by industry.*

WAGE-EARNERS.

Industry.	Number reporting complete data.	Per cent reporting wife—	
		In United States.	Abroad.
Agriculture	2,092	11.3	88.7
Fish canneries	91	3.3	96.7
Fruit and vegetable canneries	58	43.1	56.9
Laundries	49	46.9	53.1
Lumber mills	96	35.4	64.6
Mining, coal	153	8.5	91.5
Smelting	32	3.1	96.8
Transportation:			
Steam railroads—			
Maintenance of way and construction	397	1.5	98.5
Shops, bridges, and buildings, water and signal service	267	6.4	93.6
Electric railways	41	2.4	97.6
Miscellaneous	321	27.1	72.9
Total	3,597	12.4	87.6

IN BUSINESS FOR SELF.

Industry.	Number reporting complete data.	In United States.	Abroad.
Agriculture	405	64.9	35.1
Miscellaneous	251	76.1	23.9
Total	656	69.2	30.8

Thus of 3,597 married wage-earners reporting data, 12.4 per cent reported their wives (446) as being in this country, 87.6 per cent (3,151) as living abroad. In strong contrast 69.2 per cent of the farmers and business men who had a settled residence and had succeeded in establishing themselves in an independent position reported their wives as living in the United States, while 30.8 per cent reported theirs as living abroad.

Further details with regard to the conjugal condition and residence of wife were obtained from 2,117 Japanese immigrants. While the number is small, the details presented in the following tables indicate certain facts of importance in the upbuilding of the Japanese population in this country.

TABLE 18.—*Conjugal condition at time of coming to the United States of foreign-born Japanese males now 16 years of age or over, and subsequent changes in conjugal condition and location of wife, by occupation and industry: Numbers.*

Occupation and industry.	Total number of arrivals.	Single or widowed at time of coming to United States.			Married at time of coming to United States.			
		Number.	Married during visit abroad.	Married in United States.	Number.	Wife abroad.	Accompanied by wife.	Wife joining later.
Business men	a 445	298	41	63	145	49	55	41
City wage-earners	427	343	6	4	84	64	16	4
Farmers	b 785	507	c 31	72	b 278	137	85	56
Farm laborers	416	259	1	9	157	138	15	4
Coal miners	44	30	....	3	14	14	....	....

a Including 2 who have wives in California (no further data).
b Not including 9 married persons with wives in United States but not reporting whether married in United States or abroad.
c Including 1 person whose wife is abroad.

TABLE 19.—*Conjugal condition at time of coming to the United States of foreign-born Japanese males now 16 years of age or over, and subsequent changes in conjugal condition and location of wife, by occupation and industry: Percentages.*

Occupation and industry.	Single or widowed at time of coming to United States.			Married at time of coming to United States.			
	Number.	Married during visit abroad.	Married in United States.	Number.	Wife abroad.	Accompanied by wife.	Wife joining later.
Business men......................	298	13.8	21.1	145	33.8	37.9	28.3
City wage-earners..................	343	1.8	1.2	84	76.2	19.0	4.8
Farmers...........................	31	6.1	14.2	278	49.3	30.6	20.1
Farm laborers.....................	259	(a)	3.5	157	87.9	9.6	2.5
Coal miners	30	.0	10.0	14	100.0	.0	.0

a Less than 0.05 per cent.

These tables indicate the conjugal condition of these male immigrants at the time of their arrival in the continental United States and the subsequent changes which have taken place. They indicate (1) that only a small percentage of those who immigrated were accompanied by their wives; (2) that a large percentage of those who have been successful in establishing themselves as business men or as farmers have been joined by their wives more recently, while their less successful countrymen, who have continued to work as wage-earners, have not been; (3) that a large percentage of those who have been successful in establishing themselves as business men or as farmers have been married since their immigration, the larger number of them in the United States, while few of those who have continued to work as wage-earners have contracted marriage subsequent to their immigration. The contrast between the two groups noted is striking, both with regard to the percentage who have been married and the percentage of those who were married previous to their immigration and have subsequently been joined by their wives. This contrast is partly explained by the fact that the Japanese who have sent for their wives have usually sent $200, $300, or $400 to cover the expenses of the trip. The cost is too great except for those who have met with considerable success. More important, however, is the fact that the wage-earners are almost invariably set at work and housed in groups, and that their employment and residence are uncertain, so that provision can not easily be made for the maintenance of a wife. It is only by rising from the ranks of the wage-earner that a Japanese can make suitable provision for a family. The contrast is explained partly also by the fact that ordinarily the formation of a family means a protracted residence in this country, and that most of the wage-earners still expect to return to Japan after a time.

The length of time which elapsed before wives who did not accompany their husbands joined them in this country is shown in the table following.

TABLE 20.—*Time of arrival of wives of foreign-born Japanese males who were married before coming to the United States, by occupation and industry.*

Occupation and industry.	Number who were married before coming.	Number whose wives are still abroad.	Number accompanied by wife.	Number who have been joined by wife later.	Number who have been joined by wife after each specified number of years.			
					Under 1.	1 and under 2.	2 and under 5.	5 or over.
Business men	145	a 49	b 55	41		3	18	20
City wage-earners	84	64	c 16	d 4		1	3	
Farmers	278	137	85	56		5	17	34
Farm laborers	157	138	15	4		2		2

a Including 1 whose wife is now in Japan on visit.
b Including 2 whose wives are now in Japan on visit.
c Including 5; 4 have wives in United States but not scheduled, 1 has wife in Japan.
d One has wife now in San Francisco on her way to join him.

Practically all of the Japanese have immigrated to the United States expecting after a few years to return to their native land. Many of this race, however, as of others who have come under somewhat similar circumstances, have later decided to become permanent residents of this country. This is especially true of those who have succeeded in rising from the ranks of the laboring classes, as is indicated by the following table, as well as by the immigration of the wives:

TABLE 21.—*Intention of Japanese males 18 years of age or over to stay permanently in United States, by occupation and industry.*

Occupation and industry.	Number reporting complete data.	Number intending to stay permanently in United States.	Number not intending to stay permanently in United States.	Number who are in doubt.
Business men	442	167	108	167
City wage-earners	427	54	228	145
Farmers	327	130	87	110
Farm laborers	414	33	313	68
Coal miners (Wyoming)	41	7	27	7

Thus 167 of 442 men engaged in business for themselves, most of them small shopkeepers, and 130 of 327 farmers, most of them tenants, state that they expect to remain permanently in this country, while an approximately equal number are in doubt as to what they will eventually do, and a smaller number still expect, sooner or later, to return to their native land. That so many are in doubt is explained chiefly by the restrictions which have been placed upon the immigration of Japanese laborers, upon which most of the business and farming conducted by them depends for its success. These restrictions also account for the fact that so many expect to return to their native land. Without the limitations which have been placed upon further immigration, there can be no doubt that a large permanent Japanese population would be developed in the cities and upon the land. The laborers stand in contrast to the more successful of their countrymen in that a large majority still expect to return to Japan, while only a small minority expect to become permanent residents of this country. A rather large number, however, state that they are in doubt whether they will settle here or return to their native land. As they say, " it all depends "—the deciding factors being the degree of success they meet with in this country, the amount of opposition shown toward them, and the difficulty involved in readjusting themselves to changed conditions in Japan after residing abroad.

With the increase of the number of married women living in this country the number of Japanese children under 16 years of age has increased to 4,000 or more. The great majority of these have been born in this country and are under 6 years of age. Many of the Japanese wives in this country have been picture brides or have been married upon their arrival. Moreover, because of the separation of husband and wife for some years, which has usually accompanied the emigration of the married men, the number of children born to them has usually been small. Finally, many children born in Japan of mothers now in this country have been left in their native land with grandparents or other relatives to receive their schooling. As yet few of those so left have joined their parents. Because of these three facts the number of foreign-born children is very small. Of 3,399 under 16, reported by the secretaries of Japanese associations in different localities of California, 2,855 were reported to be native-born. The number of Japanese births in the State, as reported by the secretary of the state board of health, were 156 in 1905–6, 134 in 1906, 221 in 1907, 455 in 1908, and 682 in 1909; a total of 1,648 for the five years.

The following tables show the number and percentage of foreign-born Japanese from whom personal schedules were obtained, who had been in the continental United States each specified number of years, by sex and by industry:

TABLE 22.—*Number of foreign-born Japanese in the United States each specified number of years, by sex and industry.*

WAGE-EARNERS.

MALE.

[By years in the United States is meant years since first arrival in the United States. No deduction is made for time spent abroad.]

Industry.	Number reporting complete data.	Number in United States each specified number of years.								
		Under 1.	1.	2.	3.	4.	5 to 9.	10 to 14.	15 to 19.	20 or over.
Agriculture...............	6,053	53	313	757	1,378	987	1,986	495	72	12
Fish canneries............	458	5	33	86	88	36	164	41	3	2
Fruit and vegetable canneries......	201	13	24	36	39	25	45	15	4	......
Laundries................	161	3	24	32	31	17	44	7	3	......
Lumber mills..............	332	5	14	53	62	35	118	42	2	1
Mining, coal..............	447	......	2	26	109	62	203	39	6	......
Smelting.................	65	......	......	1	20	18	20	6	......	......
Transportation:										
Steam railroads—										
Maintenance of way and construction............	1,140	2	47	160	295	200	367	64	3	2
Shops, bridges, and buildings, water and signal service................	628	4	29	98	149	125	183	37	2	1
Electric railways..............	102	......	3	18	31	20	25	5	......	......
Miscellaneous................	1,277	10	80	201	202	149	455	128	35	17
Total...............	10,864	95	569	1,468	2,404	1,674	3,610	879	130	35

TABLE 22.—*Number of foreign-born Japanese in the United States each specified number of years, by sex and industry*—Continued.

WAGE EARNERS—Continued.

FEMALE.

Industry.	Number reporting complete data.	Number in United States each specified number of years.								
		Under 1.	1.	2.	3.	4.	5 to 9.	10 to 14.	15 to 19.	20 or over.
Agriculture....................	111	9	15	17	25	25	14	4	1	1
Frut and vegetable canneries......	36	10	1	6	15	2	......	1	1	......
Lumber mills..................	11	1	......	2	......	......	7	1	......	......
Transportation:										
Steam railroads—maintenance of way and construction......	3	......	1	......	1	1	......	......	......	......
Miscellaneous..................	61	4	4	17	11	6	16	1	1	1
Total..................	222	24	21	42	52	34	37	7	3	2

IN BUSINESS FOR SELF.

MALE.

Industry.	Number reporting complete data.	Under 1.	1.	2.	3.	4.	5 to 9.	10 to 14.	15 to 19.	20 or over.
Agriculture....................	853	8	14	57	95	94	373	156	53	3
Miscellaneous..................	459	2	4	23	30	42	206	108	34	10
Total..................	1,312	10	18	80	125	136	579	264	87	13

FEMALE.

Industry.	Number reporting complete data.	Under 1.	1.	2.	3.	4.	5 to 9.	10 to 14.	15 to 19.	20 or over.
Agriculture....................	280	19	30	49	61	45	72	3	1	......
Miscellaneous..................	205	7	32	29	30	31	65	8	3	......
Total..................	485	26	62	78	91	76	137	11	4	......

TABLE 23.—*Per cent of foreign-born Japanese in the United States each specified number of years, by sex and industry.*

WAGE-EARNERS.

MALE.

[By years in the United States is meant years sin e first arrival in the United States. No deduction is made for time spent abroad.]

Industry.	Number reporting complete data.	Per cent in the United States each specified number of years.								
		Under 1.	1.	2.	∴.	4.	5 to 9.	10 to 14.	15 to 19.	20 or over.
Agriculture....................	6,053	0.9	5.2	12.5	22.8	16.3	32.8	8.2	1.2	0.2
Fish canneries.................	458	1.1	7.2	18.8	19.2	7.9	35.8	9.0	.7	.4
Fruit and vegetable canneries......	201	6.5	11.9	17.9	19.4	12.4	22.4	7.5	2.0	.0
Laundries.....................	161	1.9	14.9	19.9	19.3	10.6	27.3	4.3	1.9	.0
Lumber mills..................	332	1.5	4.2	16.0	18.7	10.5	35.5	12.7	.6	.3
Mining, coal..................	447	.0	.4	5.8	24.4	13.9	45.4	8.7	1.3	.0
Smelting......................	65	.0	.0	1.5	30.8	27.7	30.8	9.2	.0	.0
Transportation:										
Steam railroads—										
Maintenance of way and construction............	1,140	.2	4.1	14.0	25.9	17.5	32.2	5.6	.3	.2
Shops, bridges, and buildings, water and signal service..................	628	.6	4.6	15.6	23.7	19.9	29.1	5.9	.3	.2
Electric railways..............	102	.0	2.9	17.6	30.4	19.6	24.5	4.9	.0	.0
Miscellaneous..................	1,277	.8	6.3	15.7	15.8	11.7	35.6	10.0	2.7	1.3
Total..................	10,864	.9	5.2	13.5	22.1	15.4	33.2	8.1	1.2	.3

TABLE 23.—*Per cent of foreign-born Japanese in the United States each specified number of years, by sex and industry*—Continued.

FEMALE.

Industry.	Number reporting complete data.	Per cent in the United States each specified number of years.								
		Under 1.	1.	2.	3.	4.	5 to 9.	10 to 14.	15 to 19.	20 or over.
Agriculture.........................	111	8.1	13.5	15.3	22.5	22.5	12.6	3.6	0.9	0.9
Fruit and vegetable canneries......	36	27.8	2.8	16.7	41.7	5.6	.0	2.8	2.8	.0
Lumber mills......................	11	(a)	(a)	(a)	(a)	(a)	(a)	(a)	(a)	(a)
Transportation:										
Steam railroads—maintenance of way and construction......	3	(a)	(a)	(a)	(a)	(a)	(a)	(a)	(a)	(a)
Miscellaneous....................	61	6.6	6.6	27.9	18.0	9.8	26.2	1.6	1.6	1.6
Total....................	222	10.8	9.5	18.9	23.4	15.3	16.7	3.2	1.4	.9

IN BUSINESS FOR SELF.

MALE.

Agriculture.........................	853	0.9	1.6	6.7	11.1	11.0	43.7	18.3	6.2	0.4
Miscellaneous......................	459	.4	.9	5.0	6.5	9.2	44.9	23.5	7.4	2.2
Total......................	1,312	.8	1.4	6.1	9.5	10.4	44.1	20.1	6.6	1.0

FEMALE.

Agriculture.........................	280	6.8	10.7	17.5	21.8	16.1	25.7	1.1	0.4	.0
Miscellaneous......................	205	3.4	15.6	14.1	14.6	15.1	31.7	3.9	1.5	.0
Total......................	485	5.4	12.8	16.1	18.8	15.7	28.2	2.3	.8	.0

a Not computed, owing to small number involved.

The first point to be noted is the comparatively small percentage who had arrived in the United States within two years of the time the data were collected, between August, 1908, and July, 1909. Six and one-tenth per cent of the male wage-earners and 2.2 per cent of the business men and farmers reported that they had first arrived in this country within two years. The second point of interest is the contrast presented by the males and the females of each group. Of the male wage-earners, 42.8 per cent had been in this country five years or over, while 80.3 per cent had been here three years or over, while the corresponding percentages for the females of the same group were 22.2 and 60.9. Of the business men and farmers, 71.8 per cent had been in the United States five years or over, while 91.8 per cent had resided here three years or over. The corresponding percentages for the females of the same group are 31.3 and 65.8. A contrast between the male wage-earners and business men and farmers is indicated by the percentages just noted. The percentage of the former group who had been in the United States less than five years was 57.1; less than ten years, 90.3; less than fifteen years, 98.4. The corresponding percentages for the members of the other group are 28.2, 72.3, and 92.4, respectively. The longer residence of the farmers and business men is a significant fact in connection with the economic position they occupy—a fact commented on later. Finally, the tables show that a comparatively small percentage of the number had been in this country as long as ten years, which is explained by the fact that the great majority of the immigrants have come to this country since 1899, and that until recently a large percentage have returned to their native land after a few years spent in working for wages.

Chapter III

JAPANESE WAGE-EARNERS IN INDUSTRIES.

The great majority of the Japanese in this country have been employed in railroad and general construction work, as agricultural laborers, cannery hands, lumber mill and logging camp laborers, in the various branches of domestic service, and in business establishments conducted by their countrymen. Smaller numbers have been employed in coal and ore mining, smelting, meat packing, and salt making. In the building trades they have done little save in making repairs and in doing cabinet work for their countrymen. They have found little place in manufacturing establishments in cities. In contrast to the Chinese, and partly because of the earlier agitation against the Chinese so employed, they have found little employment in shoe, clothing, and cigar factories.

Many Japanese laborers migrate from one locality and from one industry to another during the year. The following statement shows roughly, however, the occupational distribution of those in the West during the summer of 1909. Approximately 10,000 were employed by the steam railway companies, chiefly as maintenance of way and shop and roundhouse laborers. More than 2,200 were employed in 67 of the 1,400 or 1,500 lumber mills in Oregon and Washington. Some 3,600 were employed in salmon canneries in Alaska, Oregon, and Washington, while a few hundred were engaged in fishing along the coast of California. The number of Japanese employed in the mines of Wyoming, Utah, southern Colorado, and northern New Mexico was 2,000. Nearly 200 were employed in three smelters in Utah and Nevada and an approximately equal number in an iron and steel plant at Pueblo, Colo. Several hundred, all told, including those employed in constructing irrigation ditches in the arid districts of the Rocky Mountain States, were engaged in general construction work. Perhaps during the summer months the number engaged as farmers and farm laborers in agricultural pursuits in Washington was 3,000; in Oregon, 1,000; in Idaho, 800; in Utah, 1,025; in Colorado, possibly 3,000; in California, 30,000, with smaller numbers in the other States and Territories of the Western Division. Including the 30 or more farmers in Texas and Florida, the number of Japanese farming on their own account was probably in excess of 6,000; the number of farms or smaller holdings cultivated by them, 4,000; the acreage controlled by them, in excess of 210,000. The numbers employed by street railway companies (in Los Angeles), in two salt refineries near San Francisco, and otherwise outside of towns and cities, were comparatively small, though amounting to several hundred all told. As opposed to these, the number engaged in city trades and business—in the West—may be estimated at from 22,000 to 26,000. The majority of those found in the central and eastern States are engaged in business or are connected with business establishments.

This occupational distribution of the Japanese is the resultant of opposing influences. On the one hand, the Japanese are ambitious

33

ind in many respects capable, so that, speaking of them as a whole, they have tended to rise rapidly from the ranks of laborers to the economic position they occupied in their native land. Upon the other hand, the race prejudice against them, a prejudice in part due to that earlier exhibited against the Chinese, has prevented their employment in many branches of industry and, in those in which they have been employed, has cooperated with the lack of command of English and of technical knowledge to retard their occupational progress. Moreover, the fact that they are Asiatics caused them to fall heir to much of the work formerly done by the Chinese and to some extent to limit them to the fields of activity to which the Chinese had been restricted. These limitations upon their occupational advance have placed a premium upon engaging in petty business and farming on their own account.

The great majority of the Japanese immigrants to the Western States have found their first employment as railroad laborers, agricultural laborers, or in domestic and personal service, using the term in its broader sense. The first two branches of employment have been well organized under the Japanese " contractors " and " bosses; " the last has been found largely through the employment offices or house-cleaning firms. That the majority were thus employed upon their first arrival in this country is indicated by the following table, which shows the first gainful occupation of 1,808, from whom complete data were obtained with reference to the various ways in which they had been employed since their immigration.

TABLE 24.—*First occupation of Japanese in the United States, by present occupation and industry.*

Present occupation and industry.	Total number reporting.	Number who engaged in—								
		Business for self.	Farming.	Farm labor.	Railroad labor.	Sawmill labor.	Domestic service.	Other city wage-earners.	Other occupations.	Occupations unknown.
Business man..........................	439	70	5	88	49	6	143	66	6	6
City wage-earners......................	424	3	....	99	38	3	158	94	15	14
Japanese farmers.......................	490	10	18	259	103	4	54	11	31	......
Coal miners (Wyoming).................	41	......	....	8	20	2	4	3	4	......
Farm laborers..........................	414	......	....	276	97	2	19	8	11	1

Thus, of 439 men now engaged in business for themselves, 17.1 per cent were at first so occupied or were farmers. As opposed to these, 32.6 per cent were engaged in domestic or personal service, 20 per cent as farm hands, 15 per cent in various city occupations, and 11.2 per cent as railroad laborers. The occupational distribution of the 424 who are now city wage-earners was very similar. The great majority of the farmers and farm laborers, on the other hand, were first employed as farm hands. Of 490 farmers, only 18 began as such and 10 as business men, while 259, or 52.9 per cent of the entire number, found their first employment as farm hands, 103, or 21 per cent, as railroad laborers, and 54, or 11 per cent, as domestic servants. Two-thirds of the 414 farm laborers secured such as their first employment, while 23.4 per cent were first employed as railway laborers, and 4.6 per cent as domestic servants.

In this connection the following tables relating to their present and their last regular occupation before immigrating to the continental United States are of interest.

TABLE 25.—*Occupation of foreign-born Japanese males before coming to the United States, by present industry.*

WAGE-EARNERS.

/ Present industry.	Number reporting complete data.	Number who were—				
		At home.	In farming or farm labor.	Common laborers.	In business for self or wage-earners in city.	In other occupations.
Agriculture	5,983	733	4,360	36	658	196
Fish canneries	450	137	239	2	59	13
Fruit and vegetable canneries	198	50	121	1	23	3
Laundries	160	56	61		33	10
Lumber mills	300	21	192	2	58	27
Mining, coal	405	25	327	7	32	14
Smelting	65	4	44		15	2
Transportation:						
Steam railroads—						
Maintenance of way and construction	1,087	85	817	65	97	23
Shops, bridges, and buildings, water and signal service	587	43	361	58	90	35
Electric railways	88	9	63	2	7	7
Miscellaneous	1,265	392	442	59	302	70
Total	10,588	1,555	7,027	232	1,374	400

IN BUSINESS FOR SELF.

Agriculture	511	51	332		118	10
Miscellaneous	439	78	126		227	8
Total	950	129	458		345	18

TABLE 26.—*Per cent of foreign-born Japanese males in each specified occupation before coming to the United States, by present industry.*

WAGE-EARNERS.

Present industry.	Number reporting complete data.	Per cent who were—				
		At home.	In farming or farm labor.	Common laborers.	In business for self or wage-earners in city.	In other occupations.
Agriculture	5,983	12.3	72.9	0.6	11.0	3.3
Fish canneries	450	30.4	53.1	.4	13.1	2.9
Fruit and vegetable canneries	198	25.3	61.1	.5	11.6	1.5
Laundries	160	35.0	38.1	.0	20.6	6.3
Lumber mills	300	7.0	64.0	.7	19.3	9.0
Mining, coal	405	6.2	80.7	1.7	7.9	3.5
Smelting	65	6.2	67.7	.0	23.1	3.1
Transportation:						
Steam railroads—						
Maintenance of way and construction	1,087	7.8	75.2	6.0	8.9	2.1
Shops, bridges, and buildings, water and signal service	587	7.3	61.5	9.9	15.3	6.0
Electric railways	88	10.2	71.6	2.3	8.0	8.0
Miscellaneous	1,265	31.0	34.9	4.7	23.9	5.5
Total	10,588	14.7	66.4	2.2	13.0	3.8

TABLE 26.—*Per cent of foreign-born Japanese males in each specified occupation before coming to the United States, by present industry*—Continued.

IN BUSINESS FOR SELF.

Present Industry.	Number reporting complete data.	Per cent who were—				
		At home.	In farming or farm labor.	Common laborers.	In business for self or wage-earners in city.	In other occupations.
Agriculture	511	10.0	65.0	0.0	23.1	2.0
Miscellaneous	439	17.8	28.7	.0	51.7	1.8
Total	950	13.6	48.2	.0	36.3	1.9

These tables show three things of interest: (1) That the student class and the younger immigrants who had not been gainfully occupied at home are largely represented in the city trades and in trades drawing upon the city population; (2) that the rural employments have by far the largest percentages of those who were farmers or farm laborers abroad; and, (3) conversely, that most of the city employments have the largest percentage of those who were similarly occupied previous to their immigration. The city employments are those of the business men, of the miscellaneous wage-earners, and the laundry workmen, while those which draw chiefly upon the city population are the fish, fruit, and vegetable canneries. These show the largest percentage of those who had not been employed in their native land. The other industries are nonurban employments, and among their employees were from 61.5 to 80.7 per cent who had been engaged in agricultural pursuits previous to their immigration. The percentage of this same class employed in the other occupations varies from 28.7 of the business men to 61.1 of the laborers in the fruit and vegetable canneries. The contrast in the distribution of those who at home had been engaged in business and in city occupations is not so clearly marked, yet the representation of these classes in the groups of business men, laundry workers, and miscellaneous city wage-earners is much above the average for all occupations.

The more important of the data relating to the employment of and business conducted by Japanese in this country are best presented in three parts, the first relating to wage-earners in industry, the second to agricultural laborers and farmers, the third to employees in urban occupations and business. The employment of Japanese in industry constitutes the body of this chapter. The other data are presented in Chapters III and IV. Further data bearing upon these matters may be found in the special reports to which reference is made in connection with the several topics discussed.

JAPANESE AS RAILROAD LABORERS.[a]

In spite of a well-defined tendency on the part of the Japanese to leave their employment as section hands in order to engage in agricultural labor and farming, or to engage in business in the towns

---

[a] Further information bearing on most of the points touched upon in this section will be found in a report on "Immigrant laborers employed by the steam railways of the Rocky Mountain and Pacific Coast States."

and cities, or to take employment with their countrymen who are so engaged, perhaps one-eighth of those gainfully occupied at the close, of the year 1909 were on the pay rolls of the steam railway companies operating in the States comprising the Western Division, and chiefly in Washington, Oregon, Montana, Idaho, Nevada, Utah, Wyoming, and Colorado. Few are employed in the States farther east and comparatively few in California. Between 6,000 and 7,000 [a] were employed as section hands and members of extra gangs during the late spring and summer months of 1909. During the other seasons of the year, when many return from their work in the beet fields and other agricultural labor of a seasonal nature, the number is materially larger. On the average they constitute between one-seventh and one-sixth of the laborers in the maintenance-of-way departments in the western division. Smaller numbers are employed in railway shops and still smaller numbers in the departments of bridges and buildings. All told, at the close of the year 1909 the Japanese employed in the three departments of railway work perhaps aggregated some 10,000.

As against this, it is estimated that as many as 13,000 [b] were similarly employed in 1906, when the number reached its highest point. In order to indicate the importance of railroad work as a source of employment for Japanese immigrants to·the Western States, those engaged in railway construction work as members of general construction gangs must be added to the numbers given.

The Japanese were first employed as section hands near the close of the year 1889 or early in the year 1890, when they replaced some Chinese at work on a road with a terminus at Portland, Oreg. Their employment on other roads with terminals at that place soon followed. The railroads with western terminals at Tacoma or Seattle began to employ Japanese as section hands in 1896 and 1898. On the railroads in the Southwest their employment dates from the close of the nineties, while on the railroads centering in San Francisco and Oakland and extending north to the Oregon line, east to Ogden, and south to Los Angeles, their employment began somewhat earlier. With these beginnings, when the Japanese in the country were comparatively few, the number employed increased with the expanding immigration from Japan and Hawaii until 1906.

Three causes contributed to this increase in the number of Japanese engaged in railroad work. In the first place, they were made available through contractors at a time when industries were expanding and it was impossible to retain as section men (at the wages which had obtained) the Americans, Irish, and north Europeans, who had constituted the majority of such laborers previous to 1895, and when the number of Chinese available had become small as a result of the operation of the exclusion laws and the tendency of that race to seek agricultural employment or to withdraw to the cities. In the second place, they were willing to work for a lower wage than the

---

[a] Estimate based upon records of the Japanese contractors for railroad labor and of most of the railroad companies.

[b] Estimate contained in the Japanese-American Yearbook. Judging from the records of the larger contractors who are still in business, it was perhaps not far wrong. A large number, especially in California, have ceased to be contractors for railway labor since limitations were placed upon the immigration of Japanese laborers.

Italians, Greeks, and Slavs, who were being steadily employed in large numbers. In the third place, except where Mexicans have been available, they have generally been regarded as satisfactory laborers. The same set of circumstances explains their employment in railway shops and in bridges and building departments during the last ten years, and after they had established their position in the maintenance of way work. Of the circumstances mentioned, the organization of the Japanese through contractors serving as employment agents must be emphasized above all others. Greeks, Italians, and Slavs must be "recruited" from the East and usually through general employment agencies. Standing orders with Japanese contractors at the western ports have given greater assurance of the necessary labor supply, and, moreover, such an arrangement was more convenient for the railway companies. The only race as easily and as conveniently secured has been the Mexican through the supply companies organized within the last ten years to provide certain railroads, with which they made contracts, with laborers of that race. The details supporting the above statements and supplying the more complete information which the importance of this branch of employment requires are best presented by summarizing briefly the history of the employment of Japanese as section hands and as members of "extra gangs" on a few of the more important steam railways of the West.

The first Japanese employed as section hands were secured near the end of 1889 or early in 1890 from a Portland contractor who was or had been a member of a large emigration company in Japan. From that time, when possibly 100 were substituted for as many Chinese, they increased in number on the road which first gave them employment until 1906, and, with the Italians, Greeks, and various Austrian races, gradually took the places of the Irish and natives, who were permitted to leave for more remunerative work elsewhere. In 1896 600 Japanese were employed at $1 per day. In 1905 the average number employed was 1,052; in 1906, 1,221; in 1907, 1,049; in 1908, 782. Before 1902 their wages had been increased to $1.50, and they were then increased to $1.60, the rate which has since obtained, except for a short time beginning in 1908, when the wage was fixed at $1.40 per day. The Japanese, at first paid considerably less than the members of any race save the Chinese, are now paid the same as the Italians and Greeks, who, with the Japanese, have constituted for several years the majority of the employees in the maintenance of way department. With few exceptions, the roadmasters have preferred the Japanese to the Italians, Greeks, and Austrians, so that it has been the policy of this company to employ as many Japanese as the Portland contractor could supply. From 1905 to 1907 they constituted about two-fifths of the maintenance of way laborers employed.

Two railroads operating farther north began to employ Japanese as section hands in 1896 and 1898, respectively. The laborers have been obtained through a supply company with its main office in Seattle, but with branch offices at the various division points in Washington and Montana. The average number of men supplied by this Japanese corporation for the eleven years 1898 to 1908, inclusive, were 200, 600, 2,145, 1,199, 1,082, 1,069, 1,515, 1,372, 1,824, 2,295, and 1,936, respectively. When first employed, the Japanese were paid 10 or 12 cents per hour, according to the division of the road to which they were assigned. For some years previous to 1907 the corresponding rates of wages per hour had been 13 and 15 cents. At that time they were reduced somewhat because of the financial depression, but were soon increased to 12 and 14 cents, or $1.20 and $1.40 for a ten-hour day—the wages which prevailed at the time of the investigation in 1909. At these wages the Japanese have always been lower paid than any race save the few remaining Chinese. Their wages have usually been 25 cents per day less than those paid the Italians, for example. Most of the Greek, Scandinavian, and Austrian section hands are paid $1.50 per day, but whatever the wage in the different localities investigated, it was found to be somewhat higher than that paid the Japanese similarly employed.

On another road operating in the Northwest the Japanese were first employed as section hands in 1897 or somewhat earlier, these laborers being secured from a contractor to whom reference has already been made and who for years has supplied Japanese laborers to several railroad companies. The number employed in 1900 was reported as 313, or about one-fifth of the entire number of section hands. By 1905 the number had increased to an average of 793, but since then it has diminished to an average of 685 in 1906, 626 in 1907, 550 in 1908, and 430 in 1909. The wages paid in 1897 were $1.05 per day; in 1900, $1.10; for some years previous to 1907, $1.50; in 1907–8, $1.20; at the time of the investigation, $1.35. These wages have been less than those paid to white laborers, most of whom since 1900 have been south and east Europeans. The Japanese have generally been preferred to the other races for this kind of work at the wages which have been paid. In this case it may be added—for it is very exceptional—preference for Japanese over Chinese was expressed by a prominent official of the company who had had much personal experience with the members of both races employed as railroad laborers.

The history of the employment of Japanese in the maintenance of way departments of two railways operating in the Southwest differs from that in all of the cases to which reference has thus far been made. In one case previous to the employment of Japanese, native whites, Indians, Chinese, and natives of Mexican descent had comprised the larger number of the section hands and laborers in "extra gangs," all but the first mentioned being employed for the greater part in the desert country of Arizona and California. The Chinese, for reasons already noted, decreased in number and the Indians worked irregularly, while with the development of new industries there was a tendency among the white men to find other work. Under these circumstances Japanese were employed through a contractor of that race and in 1900 constituted slightly more than one-half of the total number employed on the western sections of the road, the members of this race being assigned to those divisions where the conditions of work and living were least desirable. The Japanese were paid $1.10 per day, the Mexicans (including the native-born of that race), the Indians, and most of the white men $1.25. Though the Japanese were at this time the lowest paid laborers, they were less strong and less satisfactory than some of the other races. Moreover, they were not suited to the warm climate and were unsatisfactory in other ways, and particularly, when compared with the Mexicans, in the matter of discipline.

Under these circumstances a contract was entered into with a supply company then organized for that purpose to provide Mexican laborers for maintenance of way. The men were drawn from El Paso and were paid $1 per day—the wage they have since been paid—except for a short time in 1906–7 and since the autumn of 1909, when it was $1.25. Since 1902, few persons other than Mexicans have been employed as common laborers by this company, except for a time in 1905 when Japanese were again tried. The Mexicans, though inferior to native white men and north Europeans, are regarded as more satisfactory than the Japanese, and when the present contractor has proposed to employ Japanese, the officials of the company have not given their consent. The Mexicans are preferred at the same wage. Though given to drink and irregular at work after pay days, they are stronger and more obedient than the Japanese, and unlike the latter, are not given to making organized demands for higher wages or better conditions. The increase of wages granted to them on two occasions has been due to the employment of Mexicans elsewhere at higher wages, this making it necessary for the company in question to increase its wage in order to obtain a sufficient number of men. With variations in detail the history of the competition between these two races has been about the same on the other railroads operated in southern Nevada, southern California, Arizona, and New Mexico. The Mexicans have been cheaper laborers than the Japanese. Moreover, though they do not accomplish as much work and are not so satisfactory in other respects as white men of the type formerly employed rather extensively, they are preferred to the Japanese at the same wage. At present few of the latter race are employed in maintenance of way work in that entire section of the country save by one railway company which has not the same advantage as the others in reaching the supply of Mexican labor at El Paso.

Formerly Japanese were employed in large numbers on all of the railways in that part of California lying north of the Tehachapi as well as in the part lying to the south. They were invariably paid lower wages than any other race save the few remaining Chinese and the Mexicans working as far north as Fresno. Because of the opportunities to engage in agricultural work, however, their wages rose considerably even while the number arriving at San Francisco was greatest. Within the last few years the one company controlling most of the railways of northern California has transferred its remaining Japanese section hands to Nevada, where the conditions are such as to render it difficult to secure men of other races, and their places have been filled chiefly by Italians, Greeks, and Slavs at higher wages than had been paid to the Asiatics.

In Nevada and Utah the Central Pacific, the Western Pacific, and the Salt Lake and San Pedro, employ many Japanese. On one of these roads which has a history covering a rather long period, Chinese were at one time employed in large numbers, but it would appear that with the decrease in the number of that race, more natives and Irish were employed. During the nineties all of the races mentioned gradually disappeared and their places were filled by the incoming Italians and Japanese. the former at $1.50, the latter at $1.10 per day.

From 1895, when they were first employed, until 1901 the Japanese were the most numerous of the races employed as laborers. They were then displaced by Greeks at a higher wage, but were later reemployed at a lower wage than that paid to the displaced race. In 1906 they numbered 1,000; in 1908, 900; at the beginning of 1909, 700. They are now paid $1.40 per day, while the Italians, the other important racial element in maintenance of way work, are in some cases paid $1.50. On the other two roads referred to, the Japanese are paid the same wages as all white men, $1.45 per day, and in one case more than the Mexicans employed on the southern end of the route. They are also paid the same wage as Greeks, Italians, and Slavs, and all white men employed on another road with its western terminus in Utah. The Japanese are employed in Utah and Wyoming, while the majority of the members of the other races are employed farther east. The Japanese were first employed in 1900. In 1904, 600 of this race were employed; in 1905, 1,000; in 1906, 1,400; in 1907, 1,200; in 1908, 900. In 1900 they were paid $1.20. Since then, because of the tendency of the Japanese to engage in the more remunerative occupations of coal mining and sugar-beet growing, their wages have been increased until they receive the same as most of the others, viz, $1.45 per day of ten hours. At the higher wage more have been wanted than the contractor, through whom they are supplied, can furnish.

These instances are sufficient to present the variations in the history of the employment of Japanese in the maintenance of way in the West and to indicate the more-important conclusions to be drawn. These conclusions are: First, that with the exception of the Chinese and the Mexicans, until recently, the Japanese have been the most lowly paid laborers employed, and that in the majority of cases in 1909 they were paid less per day than Italians, Greeks, and Slavs. Secondly, that with their acceptance as desirable laborers and the expanding opportunities presented in agriculture, mining, and other occupations (as well as with clever bargaining on the part of the contractors), their wages rose materially, and that the difference between their wages and those paid to white men of various races tended to diminish, even while the number immigrating to this country and finding employment on the railways was greatest. Thirdly, that the Japanese have been displaced by other races at higher wages in a few cases, and more extensively by Mexicans at lower wages. Finally, that the opinions of the Japanese, as section hands, vary considerably. Where they and the Mexicans have been employed the latter are preferred almost without exception. Of several men who had had experience with both Chinese and Japanese, all but one preferred the former because more tractable, more painstaking in their work, and more satisfactory generally in spite of the fact that they are less intelligent, less adaptable, and less progressive—all qualities receiving little emphasis in work of this kind. With few exceptions the Japanese are preferred to the Greeks, who are almost invariably ranked as the least desirable section hands, because they are not industrious and are intractable and difficult to control. As between Japanese and Italians, opinion is fairly evenly divided. The same may be said of them and the Slavs. Though the Japanese are usually ranked below the Chinese and Mexicans, they compare favorably with the south and east Europeans, who constitute a still larger percentage of the common laborers in maintenance of way work.

Reference has been made to the tendency on the part of the Japanese to leave their employment as common laborers in the maintenance of way department in search of more remunerative or more agreeable work elsewhere. The annual earnings of 73 Japanese employed as section hands on three railroads were secured from personal schedules taken. Their average earnings were $435. The minimum was $150 for a few months work; the maximum, $900, secured in large part from contract work in beet fields. Of the other 71, 2 earned between $200 and $250; 13 between $300 and $400; 42 between $400 and $500; 12 between $500 and $600; 1, $640; and 1, $720. In several instances the men had done other work as well as that in which they were engaged at the time of the investigation, so that the earnings given can not be accepted as showing the possibilities offered by maintenance of way work.

The Japanese, like other laborers employed as section hands, are usually provided with lodging in box cars " set " on the sidetrack. The men live in a cooperative group, purchasing much, if not most, of their supplies from the contractor under whose control they work. The limitations imposed upon them by these conditions are not the least important in explaining the strong tendency exhibited by the Japanese to secure other employment. Their desire for better equipped and clean " bunk cars " was cited by one roadmaster as an important source of trouble with the Japanese. The Greeks and Italians were satisfied with less.

In addition to the above facts, this branch of employment has offered little opportunity for progress. Some Japanese serve as subforemen, and a few, on one railway, as foremen. However, like the Mexicans and most of the other races not known as " white," they usually work under foremen of other races, and chiefly the natives and north Europeans, who occupied an important place as railway laborers fifteen or twenty years ago and who have more experience, better technical knowledge, better command of English, and the confidence of the roadmaster.

Comparatively little construction work was in progress at the time of the investigation. The Japanese have been employed in many instances, but not so generally as in maintenance of way, for they are deficient in weight and muscular strength. They were or had been employed on three railways under construction during the time covered by the investigation made by the Commission. In one instance they were employed in comparatively large numbers and with satisfactory results. In another case they were employed only to level and straighten track and were found to be superior for that work to the other races employed, chiefly Greek and East Indian. In the third case they were found to be less desirable than white men of many races, but chiefly foreign born, and orders had been issued that no more should be employed. In a general way what was said in some detail concerning the wages paid to Japanese and others employed as section hands applies to railroad construction work as well.

The same circumstances which explain the gradual substitution of Japanese, Italians, Greeks, Slavs, and Mexicans for the native and north European white men and Chinese in the maintenance of way departments, explain also a partial substitution of the one group for the other in the unskilled work of the railroad shops and round-houses maintained at terminals and division points—the substitution becoming apparent about ten years ago. In one case, however, the change was largely incidental to a strike covering a considerable period of time. The Japanese and other races conspicuously employed as section hands, being readily available, have been substituted for other races as they have risen in the scale of occupations with expanding industry or as they have been attracted elsewhere for more attractive or better paid work than found in the lower occupations of the railroad shops. Agents of the Commission investigated 25 shops. Japanese were employed in 12 of these, in fact in practically all of those belonging to railway systems employing them as section hands. They were first employed to do the most unskilled labor, as in the yards, or the most disagreeable work, such as engine wiping. Though most of the work done by them now is unskilled, they have risen somewhat in the scale of occupations and in several instances were found to occupy positions which are stepping stones to skilled work. Of 470 Japanese employed in the shops investigated, 240 were common laborers, 71 engine wipers, 14 boiler washers, 80 car cleaners, 9 car repairers, 33 boilermakers' helpers, 22 machinists' helpers, and 1 a blacksmith's helper. They were employed as common laborers in 12 shops, as engine wipers in 8, as boiler washers in 6, as car cleaners in 4, as car repairers in 2, as boilermakers' helpers in 3, as machinists' helpers in 3, and as blacksmiths' helpers in 1. They are found in a wider range of occupations than the Greeks, Slavs, and the Chinese, but in a less wide range than the Mexicans and the Italians.

Though more Mexicans than Japanese are engaged in semiskilled work, this is explained by the fact that most of the former are employed in shops located in places where it is difficult to secure men of other races. Indeed, the foremen of shops in the Southwest usually rank the Japanese ahead of the Mexicans for shopwork, but regard both as distinctly inferior to the native white laborers. The Japanese are more industrious, more alert, more progressive, and more temperate than the Mexicans, who, when of the peon class, are generally deficient in these qualities. They are invariably preferred for such work as engine wiping, though the Chinese are regarded as still better than the Japanese. For other than this and the most unskilled labor, however, the Japanese are regarded as better than the Chinese because they learn the details of the work more quickly. Both are preferred to south and east European races also for engine wiping and similar work. Moreover, in only one of several shops where both Greeks and Japanese were employed were the former, though generally paid higher wages, preferred to the latter. The Japanese are more industrious, more ambitious, and more tractable. In several instances the Japanese were preferred to the Italians also, but these instances were less numerous than those where the contrary was true.

While the Japanese have generally been employed to replace the Chinese, who have become fewer, or white men no longer available for unskilled work at the rate of wages which obtained, the replacement has not always taken place at the rate of wages which had been paid to white men. As would be expected, there seems from the first to have been a close relation between the wages paid to them as section hands and as laborers, engine wipers, and car cleaners in the shops. Though paid somewhat more than for track work, frequently 15 cents per day more, their wages have usually been less than those paid the men they have replaced. " In one shop the Japanese, when introduced, were paid 16 cents, while those whom they replaced had been paid 18 cents per hour. In another place they were set at work at 12½ cents per hour where the various white races which had been employed had received 18 cents per hour. In a third place they were given work as car cleaners at $1.25 per day where white men had been paid $1.50. In a fourth instance Japanese at $1.25 replaced white men who had been paid $1.60 as engine wipers. In still another shop they began work as engine wipers at 15 cents whereas the white men they replaced had received 20 cents per hour. The substitution elsewhere in these occupations seems to have been made on much the same terms.

" Beginning at a lower rate of pay the Japanese, when not serving as helpers, are still very generally paid less than the members of other races doing the same kinds of work. In one city there are three railway shops. In one of these Japanese are employed as laborers at $1.25 per day; in the second, Greeks and Italians at $1.80 per day; in the third, Austrians and Italians at $1.80 per day. One railway pays Japanese laborers in one of its shops $1.60 per day, all white laborers $1.90. Usually, however, the differences are less great. The highest rate paid Japanese laborers is $1.75 per day; the lowest, $1.25, and the rates most frequently paid are $1.35, $1.40, and $1.60. As engine wipers they receive from $1.25 to $1.60 in the several shops investigated. As car cleaners they earn from $1.25 to $1.60 per day. As boiler washers they earn from about $1.60 to $1.80 per day; white men when employed somewhat more." [a]

The Japanese are, however, usually paid more than the Mexicans as unskilled laborers in the shops. In one city, for example, the Mexicans employed as common laborers in one shop are paid $1 per day, the Japanese similarly employed in another $1.20. Other instances of the same kind might be cited, though the two races are not often employed in the same localities, thus limiting possible comparisons to a few cases.

Finally, passing over the employment of Japanese as janitors and cleaners of station buildings on a few of the railroads included in the investigation made by the Commission, the members of this race were found to be employed in the department of bridges and buildings of one. These men were employed at pumping stations, tunnels, and in similar places, and as cooks, however, and not as regular members of " crews " engaged in construction work. That they have not been more extensively employed is no doubt partly explained by the fact that provision must be made for boarding and lodging the workmen while not at work in large towns, and that the Japanese prefer to work and live in their own groups and are not welcomed by the other races as members of general groups. In some instances the inconvenience involved in making separate provision for them has caused the rail-

---

[a] Quoted from " Immigrant Laborers Employed by the Steam Railways of the Rocky Mountain and Pacific Coast States."

ways not to employ Japanese, Mexicans, or negroes at all as laborers in the department of bridges and buildings.

Numerous references have been made to the way in which Japanese are secured for railroad work. Those employed in maintenance of way are always obtained through a Japanese " contractor " and those employed in the shops or elsewhere are usually obtained in the same way. One corporation in Seattle supplies two railroads, one in Portland four, one in Salt Lake City two. In other cases, with one exception, there is a separate contractor for each road. Late in the spring of 1909, 8 of these men or firms were supplying some 5,600 laborers as section hands and still others for the shops.

These Japanese agents collect their men in various ways. Some apply directly to them for work, most have been obtained through boarding houses, while others are " recruited " through advertising and the more usual methods used with other races in Seattle, Portland, San Francisco, and Los Angeles. The most important of these methods has been the second, where the laborers have been collected through large boarding houses.

Each of the large boarding houses in the coast cities has or has had affiliations with large Japanese contractors, or has been conducted by a contractor as a means of collecting laborers. The hotel keepers' organizations in San Francisco and Seattle establish the fee which the contractor shall pay the boarding-house keeper for each man obtained through him—at $3 in the one city, at $1.50 in the other.

"Agents for Japanese labor invariably collect from each person employed as a railroad laborer an " office fee " or " interpreter's fee " of $1 per month and a second payment of so much per day or a given percentage of their earnings. Two of the largest of the contractors, and several of the smaller ones collect, in addition to the interpreter's fee, 5 cents for each day worked. One of these formerly collected 10 cents per day without an interpreter's fee, but in 1904 changed to the present rule in order to compete more successfully for laborers. Another agency collects an interpreter's fee of $1 per month and 5 cents for each day worked during the month up to 20, thus limiting the total deduction on account of the agency to $2 per month. Two agencies collect only 2 cents per day for each day worked, in addition to the interpreter's fee of $1 per month.

" It may be pointed out in passing that this arrangement is very much more satisfactory to the laborers than where each " job " is paid for in a lump sum commission. It, at any rate, protects the men from the graft sometimes practiced by foremen and agencies cooperating in collecting, hiring, and discharging laborers." [a]

As a second source of profit the contractors usually supply their men with most of the goods they consume, or else act through auxiliary organizations which do. Scarcely ever is the supply business absent. It is well worth the while, for the Japanese, for the most part, consume Japanese wares, and as the laborers are far removed from towns, these can usually be had only from the contractor who finds employment for them. It is estimated that 30 per cent of the food used is American in its origin and 70 per cent Japanese. Most

---

[a] Quoted from " Immigrant Laborers Employed by the Steam Railways of the Rocky Mountain and Pacific Coast States."

of this Japanese food and a small part of the clothing and miscellaneous goods purchased are supplied by the contractor.

If property accumulation is a good criterion, the commissions and profits from supplies sold have given the larger contractors a handsome profit. However, the contractor himself, or his interpreters through whom he usually acts, looks after all difficulties and disputes arising between laborers and foremen or other representatives of the company in regard to work, wages, bunk cars, and other matters. He does much more than find employment for laborers and supply them with goods at a profit.

As a general rule, the Japanese employed in railroad work are paid directly by the company, deductions to cover commissions and supply bills due being made, which sums are paid directly to the agency. However, the several railway companies supplied with laborers by two of the largest of the Japanese agents pay these agents for the men supplied, they, in turn, paying the laborers after deducting commissions and sums due for supplies purchased.

JAPANESE EMPLOYED IN THE LUMBER AND TIMBER INDUSTRIES OF OREGON AND WASHINGTON.[a]

In 1909 more than 2,200 Japanese were employed in the lumber industry in Oregon and Washington, while in 1905 the total number of employees of all races in the industry was 35,307.[b] The first Japanese employed in the lumber mills were deserting sailors, whose employment in the industry is reported to date from about thirty years ago. Their numbers were small, however, and they did not constitute an important factor in the labor supply until after the year 1900, when they numbered less than 350 and were employed in only a few mills. Within the last decade, however, there has been a large immigration of Japanese to the Northwest and especially to Seattle. For example, between the years 1901 and 1908 no less than 20,011 entered the ports of Seattle and Portland. When the unusually prosperous times preceding the financial stringency of 1907 gave rise to a scarcity of labor, this Japanese immigration was drawn u n along with a much larger number of recent immigrants from Europe and a smaller number of East Indians, for lumber mill work. It is estimated that in 1907, 2,685 members of this race were working in the lumber mills of Washington alone. In 1909 they were employed in 67 mills and logging camps in Washington, and numbered 2,240, while some 200 Japanese were employed in the lumber and shingle mills of Oregon.

The Japanese have never been employed in the majority of the mills of the Northwest, though the mills in which they have been employed have been among the largest. In fact, because of race prejudice exhibited by white employees, they have been discriminated against to the point of being refused employment in most of the mills.

In one instance 50 Japanese sent out from Portland were not allowed to leave the train by the inhabitants of the mill town. In another community they were used to replace Italians at lower wages,

---

[a] See "Immigrants in the Lumber and Shingle Industries of Oregon and Washington."

[b] Census Bulletin 77, 1905, "Lumber and Timber Products."

but so strong was the sentiment against them that they found it difficult to live in the locality. Partly as a result of this prejudice against them the Japanese, with few exceptions, have been able to enter the least remunerative occupations only. In fact, of 231 employed in mills investigated and from whom personal information was obtained, 89 per cent were common laborers, usually laborers in the lumber yards, oilers, or teamsters—the most unskilled and least remunerative work offered by the industry.

Where the Japanese have been employed they have, without exception, been paid lower wages than men of other races engaged in the same occupations. In the one mill investigated where they were employed in skilled and semiskilled positions also, their wages were considerably lower than those paid to white men employed in similar positions in other mills. While the Japanese were employed as trimmers, edgermen, planing-mill feeders, lumber graders, lath-mill men, and carpenters at wages varying from $1.65 to $2 per day, at other mills the white men engaged in these occupations were paid from $2.75 to $3.50 per day. Of 205 Japanese common laborers 76 earned $1.25 per day, 84, $1.50, and 45, $1.75. Nineteen others were employed at difficult or semiskilled work and earned from $2 to $2.25 per day. The wages paid to other men, including the small number of East Indians, engaged in common labor are higher than those paid to the Japanese similarly employed. While " white men " are paid $1.75, $2, and $2.25 as common laborers, Japanese are paid $1.50, $1.60, and $1.75, and rarely $2, and in one mill employing a large number they receive only $1.25 per day.

Corresponding differences have from the first existed between the wages paid to Japanese and white laborers employed in this industry. The average earnings of 48 Japanese employed in lumber mills in northwestern Washington was $515.75 for an approximate average of 11.2 months in employment during the twelve months immediately preceding the investigation in the spring of 1909.

As already indicated, the employment of the Japanese in comparatively large numbers in lumber mills has been coincident with a period of rapid industrial expansion. They not only worked for less than other men, they were also more easily secured, for they are obtained here, as in most other industries, through a contractor or bookman, and are generally reported by employers to be more steady and less inclined to leave their employment for other work than are the members of other races.

On the whole, the mill managers who have employed Japanese are of the opinion that they are more satisfactory at the rate of wages they are paid than the white men available for work as common laborers at the wages they command in the industry. While the Japanese have never been employed in the majority of the mills and have been discharged from some others, this has been due chiefly to the race feeling exhibited against them and seemingly closely connected with the facts that they are of a different race and tongue and have always worked for lower wages than were paid to white men.

Organized opposition by the Shingle Weavers' Union and the presence of conditions which for efficiency require a kind of apprenticeship explain why the ᴗJapanese have been employed in only a few shingle mills, and in so far as could be ascertained had been discharged from these. In a few instances the Japanese have established shingle mills of their own. However, the developments in this direction have been slight, because a relatively large capital is required for investment in plant and timber, and because the Japanese have been unable to secure insurance on such mills since one owned by them in Washington was destroyed by fire. In so far as could be ascertained only one mill is now owned by Japanese, and this was recently started in Oregon by a corporation doing business in Portland.

JAPANESE EMPLOYED IN THE SALMON-CANNING INDUSTRY IN WASHINGTON, OREGON, AND ALASKA.[a]

Japanese laborers were first introduced in the salmon canneries on the Columbia River in 1901, and soon thereafter in the establishments located on Puget Sound and in Alaska. Few were employed, however, previous to 1904, but since then their number has increased greatly. A rough estimate of the number of Japanese engaged in canning salmon in 1909 is about 3,600 of an approximate total of 10,000, largely Chinese, but including some white men in the Puget Sound and Columbia River canneries and a rather large number of Indians and a few Filipinos in the Alaskan establishments. Of the 3,600 Japanese, 2,132 were employed in Alaska and about 1,500 in the Puget Sound and Columbia River canneries.

Of the 18 canneries located on the Columbia River, 16 were investigated by an agent of the Commission. These employed from 253 to 367 Japanese during the season, the number varying with the "catch" of salmon. In 19 of 23 establishments on Puget Sound 953 Japanese were found to be employed, as against 1,024 Chinese. The Japanese are employed almost exclusively in the more unskilled and disagreeable parts of the work. They clean and cut fish, operate butchering and soldering machines, truck and pile cans, and act as helpers in the "bathrooms." It is only in exceptional cases, when Chinese are not obtainable, that the Japanese are used for skilled work. In fact, the Chinese are said to have used their superior position to prevent the Japanese from learning the processes requiring skill. The Chinese have taught other races the art of canning fish, but because of race antipathy they seek to retard the advance of the Japanese in the industry in so far as they are able.

The few unskilled Chinese employed in the canneries are paid more than the Japanese. For example, where they are employed in the same establishment, in northwestern Washington, the Chinese earn $5 per month more than do the Japanese. Where, as is usually the case, the earnings are paid by the season, rather than by the month, the difference is notable between those received by the Chinese and the Japanese. In the Columbia River canneries the latter race receive from $130 to $140 for the season's work, while the minimum amount paid to the Chinese engaged in similar work was $150. The packers operating on Puget Sound employ Japanese for a short season, ordinarily of about two months' duration, for which they pay from $60 to $75. On the other hand, the Chinese, most of whom are skilled workmen, average about $500 each for the season. However, their

---

[a] See "Salmon Canneries of the Columbia River and Puget Sound" and "Immigrant Labor in the Salmon Canneries of Alaska."

period of work is several months longer, including the labeling and packing of the cans after the actual canning is completed. Although still engaged in the most lowly paid occupations in the industry, the Japanese are earning more than when first employed in 1901. They were then paid only at the rate of $1.10 per day. At present most of the members of this race earn $35 or $40 per month, with board and lodging, a substantial increase over the former $1.10 per day. The normal day's work is eleven hours.

During the large part of the year in which the canneries are not in operation the Japanese find their way into various occupations. The most common of these are railroad construction and maintenance of way, agriculture, and wood chopping. A considerable number, however, are of the student and city classes, and are employed for the greater part of the year in the urban centers as domestics or in the various city trades. Thus the earnings of the cannery hands in these localities are drawn from diverse sources. Data were secured from 90 Japanese employees from various establishments in Washington and Oregon with regard to their yearly earnings from work of various kinds. They are as follows:

Number of persons earning—								
Less than $200.	From $200 to $250.	From $250 to $300.	From $300 to $400.	From $400 to $500.	From $500 to $600.	From $600 to $700.	From $700 to $800.	Average amount per year.
1	2	5	55	22	2	1	2	$378.27

The smallest earnings were $196, while the largest were $760. The average of the yearly earnings for the group of 90 was $378.27.

Practically all of the Japanese work under the "boss" system. In the great majority of establishments the Chinese have contracts for canning the fish, and they employ Japanese through "subbosses." Where the packers do not let the work out to Chinese contractors, they, too, secure their Japanese laborers from "bosses." Formerly these "bosses" were paid from $2 to $3 per man supplied, but this system had been superseded by one under which the employer pays nothing to the "bosses" direct, but the latter derive their income from fees for securing employment deducted from the wages of the men, and from profits on merchandise and board furnished them. However, where they are employed by Chinese contractors, the latter as a rule furnish them with board. Where the "bosses" deal directly with the white employers, they are allowed $7.50 or $8 for each man per month for boarding the men under them, in addition to the regular wages. Ordinarily a "boss" makes about $15 per man during the canning season. Wages are paid at the close of the season, but advances of supplies and cash up to the amount of $50 are made by the "bosses" to the men.

The situation in the Alaska salmon canneries is different from that in Oregon and Washington in a number of respects. Practically all of the Japanese are employed by Chinese contractors through "bosses" of their own race. The distant location of the field, the long journey involved, and the impossibility of changing from place to place during the season serve to give the "bosses" unusual powers over the men. The latter are of a roving type, and rated as of a low order by their fellow-Japanese of the cities. They are sent out in sailing vessels from San Francisco, Astoria, Portland, and Seattle, late in the spring, and return early in the autumn. Their work is the most unskilled and disagreeable offered by the industry—similar to their employment in the canneries of Washington and Oregon. The Chinese in nearly all cases do the skilled work.

Wages are paid entirely by the season, which, including the time spent on the voyage, amounts to above five months. During the heaviest "run" the men work from sixteen to twenty hours per day. Season wages vary from $160 to $225. The majority, however, earn less than $200. These wages are in addition to board and lodging. The book earnings, however, do not furnish a true index of the actual earnings of the men, for under the "boss" system, as it has generally operated in the past, a large part of their earnings have been taken from them by exploitation. Indeed, the individual is considered fortunate who returns to the home port with as much as $30 to his credit.

The exploitation carried on by Japanese "bosses" controlling Alaskan cannery laborers is worthy of especial comment. They secure the men through subagents (usually connected with Japanese boarding houses in the cities), who receive for this service a commission of $5 per man, which is deducted from the wages of the men engaged. An advance is usually made by the packers to the "boss" in the spring of the year on the basis of the labor to be furnished. With the money so obtained the cost of securing the laborers is paid, they are advanced enough money to equip themselves for the trip, and a stock of goods is secured for boarding the men. In addition to these expenditures an extensive stock of eatables is bought, which is destined to be sold at high prices to the men en route. This is made possible by the fact that the food regularly furnished is poor and frequently insufficient in quantity, costing the "boss" about $3 per month per man. The men buy these extra eatables and gamble at tables conducted by subbosses, on credit, their expenditures and losses being deducted from their total earnings for the season. The income of the "boss" is thus obtained from two sources—the sale of goods to the men at monopoly price and the profits realized from gambling. This income is comparatively large for the ability represented; frequently, if not generally, amounting to from $2,000 to $5,000 for the year. It is entirely the result of the exploitation of the wages of Japanese laborers, since as much or more than the total sum paid by the packers to the "bosses" is spent in wages and regular board for the men.

The Japanese keep very much to themselves in the camps, usually lodging and eating together. They are given to gambling among themselves and often to excessive drinking.

Though the Japanese are industrious the canners prefer the Chinese, on the ground that they are more careful and conscientious workmen and more satisfactory in contractual relations. The preference is so decided that it is not unusual for the companies to stipulate in their contracts with the Chinese "bosses," who enter into contract to do the cannery work, that the number of Japanese employed shall not exceed the number of Chinese. The Filipinos, who have been employed in the Alaska canneries in small numbers, are also preferred to the Japanese.

Though the Japanese have been employed as fishermen in British Columbia, they have not been employed in this capacity by the packers in Alaska, Oregon, and Washington. On the coast of California, however, a few hundred have been engaged in fishing on their own account. The largest groups of these are about Monterey, where they numbered about 150 in 1909. The more important markets of the State, however, are controlled almost entirely by the Italians and chiefly by those from the southern Provinces.

JAPANESE EMPLOYED IN FRUIT AND VEGETABLE CANNERIES OF CALIFORNIA.[a]

Japanese were first employed in fruit and vegetable canneries about twenty years ago, but they have never occupied an important place in the industry. Together with Portuguese, Italians, Greeks, and other recent immigrants, they have gradually filled the places vacated by the north European immigrants and Chinese, who have found more remunerative employment elsewhere. Few of the Japanese were employed in canneries before 1900, and since that time their increase has not been rapid. Among the employees of 19 canneries investigated were 237 Japanese. The 201 males constituted 16.3 per cent of the total number of that sex, and the 36 females 2.2 per cent of the total number of that sex, employed in the establishments investigated. Of a total of 2,890 employed, 756 were native females, 357 native males. Among the 1,777 foreign-born were 860 Greeks and Italians, 172 Portuguese, 132 Chinese, and 58 Mexicans. The Japanese have been employed chiefly by canneries operated by Chinese, who began to employ Japanese when the supply of Chinese laborers became too small. The Japanese are given employment, however, in a number of establishments operated by white men, but a number of white employers discriminate against them to the extent of not employing them at all. Where employed in canneries they are under the control of " bosses " who arrange for their work and through whom their wages are paid.

While in some cases they earn less than do white persons in similar occupations, discrimination in wages is not general. The differences are due largely to the occupations at which they work. Of the 201 male Japanese employees from whom data were secured, more than one-half were cutting and canning fruit, work which is paid on a piece basis and which is almost monopolized by women. The Japanese work at the same piece rates as do other employees. The 34 Japanese women who reported their earnings were all canners or cutters. Of the remaining 75 males, 44 were common floor laborers, 24 were employed in the cooking and soldering rooms, 4 were used in warehouse work, and 3 were foremen or clerks.

Of the males, 72.2 per cent earned less than $2 per day, while of the total foreign-born only 64.2 per cent earned less than $2 per day. Of the Italians and Greeks only 58.1 per cent earned less than $2

---

[a] See " Immigrant Labor in California Fruit and Vegetable Canneries."

per day, as did 57.1 per cent of the Portuguese. Moreover, only 12 Japanese earned more than $2.50 per day, while 186, or 44.3 per cent, of the Greeks and Italians earned more than $2.50. The apparent difference between the wages of Japanese and Italians and Greeks is accounted for chiefly on the basis of occupation. Many of the Italians are used as subforemen and in the more responsible positions at higher wages than pieceworkers and common laborers command. The Japanese women earn less than others of the more recently arrived races. None of them earned as much as $2 per day, whereas 29 of the Portuguese and 57 of the Italian and Greek women earned $2 or over per day. No discrimination in the piece rates paid was noted, however.

Information was obtained concerning six vegetable canneries near the lower Sacramento River, which conserved asparagus almost exclusively. Here the Chinese have always done most of the work of canning since the inception of the industry ten years ago. They were formerly used for the warehouse labor also, but because of their increasing scarcity have recently been replaced at this work by white men and Japanese. Japanese were employed in one establishment, but discharged as being unsatisfactory. The foreman of this cannery stated that Chinese were cheaper at $1.50 per day than Japanese at $1.25. In another cannery, however, 20 Japanese who were employed in the warehouse and paid at the rate of 15 cents per hour with lodging, were proving satisfactory to their employers. They were also used recently as common laborers (cleaning rusty cans) by another firm, but were not employed at the time of the investigation. In the other asparagus canneries no Japanese were employed in the early summer of 1909.

JAPANESE EMPLOYED IN COAL MINES IN THE WESTERN DIVISION.[a]

Something less than 2,000 Japanese are employed in the coal mines of southern Colorado, New Mexico, Wyoming, and Utah. The great majority of the 27,000 to 30,000 persons employed in the coal-mining industry of these States are immigrants from south and east European countries and Mexico. The Japanese were first employed in Wyoming in considerable numbers about 1900, when during a period of labor scarcity the operators of Wyoming secured " gangs " of laborers through a Japanese employment agency on the Pacific coast. Other Japanese entered the mines from the railroad section " gangs " in the locality because of the larger earnings which might be made. In southern Colorado, New Mexico, and Utah, on the other hand, few Japanese were employed in the mines previous to 1903. In that year they were used as strike breakers. Those who entered the mines of southern Colorado at this time have left the work, a few at a time, for agricultural pursuits, until at the present time they constitute a relatively unimportant part of the labor supply. In New Mexico a somewhat greater number have remained in the mines, while in Utah their numbers have increased materially in recent years. That no Japanese are employed in the coal mines of northern Colorado is due to the complete unionization of the district and the opposition of the

---

[a] See " Immigrant Labor in the Coal and Coke Industry in the Western States."

union to all oriental labor. In Washington, while the field is less completely organized, the hostile sentiment displayed in the community has been strong enough to preclude the employment of Japanese as miners.

Of 65 Japanese employed in southern Colorado and reporting their earnings 4.6 per cent earned $3.50 and under $4 per day, while 69.2 per cent earned $3 and under $3.50, and 15.4 per cent $2.50 and under $3. The remaining 10.7 per cent earned $1.50 and under $2.50. No discrimination in wages was noted in this district between the Japanese and other races.

Members of this race are segregated as much as possible at their work. Furthermore, they live in separate camps, and all of their business is managed by "bosses." Their camps are often outside of the town limits. Other races employed are extremely hostile to the Japanese, classing them in this regard with negroes. Wherever they are employed, however, the superintendents regard them as satisfactory miners.

The situation in New Mexico is essentially the same as that in southern Colorado. A somewhat larger proportion of Japanese are employed. For example, 90, or 7.9 per cent, of the total number of employees on the pay rolls of the mines investigated in the northern part of the State were Japanese. Of these, 88 were miners or loaders, 1 a common laborer, and 1 a foreman. Their earnings, however, were somewhat larger than in Colorado. During the month covered by the pay rolls secured the percentage earning each specified amount was as follows:

Number of Japanese.	Under $10.	$10 and under $20.	$20 and under $30.	$30 and under $40.	$40 and under $50.	$50 and under $60.	$60 and under $70.	$70 and under $80.	$80 and under $100.	$100 and under $120.	$120 or over.	Average earnings per day.
88	2.3	3.4	1.1	4.5	5.7	11.3	17.1	13.6	25.0	12.5	3.4	$3.60

Their average daily earnings were $3.60, while the average for all miners and loaders was $3.26. Furthermore, the Japanese earned on the average a greater amount per day than did the more recently arrived European immigrants and the Mexicans, except the Italians, whose average daily earnings were 3 cents higher than those of the Asiatics. The average daily earnings of the races most conspicuous in mining and loading were as follows:

Italian _____ $3.63 | Bulgarian _____ $2.97
Japanese _____ 3.60 | Greek _____ 2.96
Montenegrin _____ 3.09 | Mexican _____ 2.87

The number of Japanese employed in the coal mines of Utah has increased steadily since their introduction in 1903–4 with other races to fill the places of the "trouble makers" connected with the coal strike. The number employed in 1905 was 46; in 1908, 114; in 1909, 126. Laborers of this race are supplied to the operators by a Japanese contracting agency in Salt Lake City. As in the other sections, they are controlled by " bosses," who conduct their business and direct their work.

The position of the Japanese coal-mine employees in Wyoming is substantially different from that in the other States where they are engaged in this industry. A much larger proportion of the labor supply is drawn from this race. It is estimated that 512 Japanese in a grand total of 6,915 are at work in the coal mines of the State. Data were secured from 337 of these. As noted above, they were first employed about 1900 during a time of labor scarcity. Since that time they have been continuously employed, but within the last two years their numbers have fallen off considerably. In one community, for example, where 200 were employed in 1907 only 135 were reported in 1909.

As in other districts, the Japanese in Wyoming are chiefly miners and loaders. However, 16 of the 274 who reported their specific occupation were common laborers, 5 were mechanics, and 2 foremen. Previous to 1907 Japanese were paid $2.10 per day in the mines—which was somewhat less than the earnings of European miners. In 1907 the United Mine Workers of America extended its organization to Wyoming. The presence of a large number of Japanese and a few Chinese miners made organization difficult. It is stated that the operators expected to be able to use these orientals at lower rates than those fixed upon in the union agreement. However, a delegation of Japanese was sent to the convention of the union, which was held in Denver, to present their side of the case, with the result that a special dispensation was granted, and the Chinese and Japanese who were on the ground were allowed to become members of the union on an equal footing with other races. The Japanese now earn wages equal to those of other races—$3.10 per day for company men and the uniform piece rates for mining and loading. In this State the Japanese earn higher wages than in any of the other Western States where they are employed in coal mines. The difference is due to their participation in the results of union organization. The percentages of the 335 reporting wage data, who earned each specified amount, are as follows:

Total number.	Percentage earning each specified rate per day.						
	$1.50 and under $1.75.	$1 75 and under $2.	$2 and under $2.50.	$2.50 and under $3.	$3 and under $3.50.	$3.50 and under $4.	$4 or over.
335	0.3	1.5	4.5	30.2	38.5	1.8	23.3

Data were obtained from 39 of these men relating to their annual earnings, in part from other work, however, in those cases where they had been otherwise employed at any time during the twelve months preceding the investigation. A few had made large earnings in the sugar-beet fields. The earnings of 3 were reported as being $400 and under $500; of 2, $500 and under $600; of 2, $600 and under $700; of 5, $700 and under $800; of 23, $800 and under $1,000; of 4, $1,000 and under $1,250. The average for the 39 was $820.

The earnings of the 39 are shown, by the number of months worked, in the following table:

TABLE 27.—*Yearly earnings ᵃ (approximate) of Japanese coal miners 18 years of age or over.*

Months worked.	Number working for wages and reporting amount.	Average earnings.	Number earning—							
			Under $400.	$400 and under $500.	$500 and under $600.	$600 and under $700.	$700 and under $800.	$800 and under $1,000.	$1,000 and under $1,250.	$1,250 or over.
6...............	1	$450.00	....	1	....	....	....	....	....	....
7...............	1	500.00	....	....	1	....	....	....	....	....
9...............	8	650.00	....	2	1	2	1	2	....	....
10..............	14	859.29	....	....	....	....	1	13	....	....
11..............	9	886.67	....	....	....	....	2	6	1	....
12..............	6	970.00	....	....	....	....	1	2	3	....
Total........	39	820.00	....	3	2	2	5	23	4	....

ᵃ Without board.

Though they are members of the union, the individual Japanese are not masters of their own affairs. They are in most cases controlled by a Japanese contracting agency in Salt Lake City. All of their affairs are managed by this agency, in return for which numerous deductions are made from the earnings of the men, on behalf of the agency, by the operators. These deductions include items for board, "bunks," baths, transportation, coupons exchangeable for merchandise, and commissions. So extensive are these charges that often the employee receives no cash payment, all of his wages being taken in the form of deductions. Data with regard to this matter were secured from one mine where 118 Japanese were employed. Their total earnings for a period of two weeks were $2,828.15, or an average of $23.97 per man. Of this amount $1,933.75, or an average of $16.39 per man, was deducted by the company on behalf of the Japanese agency. In other words, only $894.30, or an average of $7.58 per man, was paid in cash. Indeed, 60 men received less than $5 in cash, while 37 earned nothing over and above the claims of the agency. In this case the men are boarded at a rate of $19 per month and furnished lodging in bunk houses for 50 cents per month. This charge is materially higher than the cost of living at the other mines investigated.

The Wyoming coal fields are extremely cosmopolitan and few race antipathies are apparent. The Japanese are treated in the same manner as other immigrants. They prefer to associate with natives rather than with other foreigners, however. They are loyal members of the union, and exhibit considerable pride in their connection with the organization. At work they are under Japanese foremen, but are usually employed at tasks with other races. In their living quarters, however, they are segregated from other races, living in bunk houses, often beyond the boundaries of the mining towns. Employers were unanimous in characterizing the Japanese as regular and attentive workmen giving satisfactory service.

JAPANESE EMPLOYED IN THE MINING AND SMELTING OF METALLIFEROUS
ORES IN THE WESTERN DIVISION.[a]

Japanese have never played an important part in the mining and
smelting of metalliferous ores in the Western States. In most places
they are not considered eligible to employment, while in the few localities where they have been used their numbers have always been
small. In the investigation of metal mining in the Rocky Mountain States they were found in the iron mines of one locality alone.
In the investigation of smelting in the several States they were
found employed in only three smelters, two of these located near
Salt Lake City and one in Nevada. The Japanese employed in the
smelters near Salt Lake City were secured through a contracting
agency which received as its commission 5 per cent of the wages of
the men. They were first employed in 1908 to replace Greeks who
were on strike for higher wages. They were confined to "general
labor," for they had had no previous experience in the industry, and
at the time of the investigation they were still paid less than the
Greeks for the same kind of work.

All of the 63 Japanese from whom wage data were secured were
paid a flat rate of $1.60 per day, while Greeks received from $1.60 to
$2.50—the majority earning $1.75 per day. These two races were the
only ones whose wages fell below $2 per day in the locality. The
Japanese worked eight hours per day, while most of the Greeks
worked nine, but those Greeks who worked only eight hours were
paid more than the Japanese—$1.80 to $2.50. Bunkhouses were
furnished the Japanese by the companies at $1 per month per man.
These are built apart from the quarters of the other employees. Besides this segregation in living quarters the men are set at work in
"gangs" to themselves. In the two establishments in Utah where
they were employed, Japanese were preferred to other races used as
general laborers and were characterized as industrious, attentive,
tractable, sober, and progressive.

The only other place in which they were employed at the time of
the investigation, in so far as could be learned, was in a newly established smelter, where 35 found work as common laborers.

Although no Japanese were employed in Colorado smelters when
investigated by agents of the Commission, it was found that they had
formerly been employed at two establishments. At one smelter they
were introduced as an experiment in 1907, but proved unsatisfactory
for the work and were subsequently discharged. At another smelter
in Colorado about 100 Japanese were employed when the plant was
first established in 1903, and were retained until 1907. They did not
work in the smelter proper, but were engaged as common laborers in
constructing the railroads and other auxiliaries. When this work
was completed, in 1907, they were discharged, and many of them
found work in the near-by sugar-beet fields. In this instance they
were regarded as lacking in industry and too weak physically for the
heavy construction work.

---

[a] See "Metalliferous Mining, Smelting, and Refining in the Western States."

JAPANESE EMPLOYED IN OTHER INDUSTRIES.

As has already been indicated, few Japanese have been employed in other industries. They have been employed by electric railway companies operating in and near Los Angeles, by the Colorado Fuel and Iron Company as laborers in its iron and steel plant at Pueblo, in two packing houses at Omaha, Nebr.,[a] in three or more salt refineries about the bay of San Francisco, and in a few quarries. In none of these instances, however, have the conditions of their employment been dissimilar to those indicated in connection with the other industries. They have been paid comparatively low wages in almost all of these instances. An additional reason assigned for their employment in salt refineries is that it has been difficult to retain good white laborers because of the bad conditions under which the work must be done. In one instance, however, the Japanese were discharged on the ground that they were unsatisfactory laborers, and their places were filled by white laborers at a higher wage.

SUMMARY.

Any general statement concerning the employment of Japanese is apt to prove misleading because the circumstances have differed from industry to industry and from one establishment to another. The following general statements may be made, however, as a result of the investigation of the several industries in which the members of this race are employed:

(1) In a number of instances the first employment of the members of this race has been to break strikes. This is true of coal mining in southern Colorado and Utah, where they were first employed in 1903–4, of meat packing in Omaha, of smelting in Utah, where they replaced Greeks striking for higher wages in 1907, and of the shops of one railway company. In the great majority of instances, however, they have been introduced to replace Chinese or when employers were experiencing difficulty in finding an adequate number of steady white men to work as common laborers and as helpers at the rate of wages which had obtained. Seldom have other classes been discharged in large numbers to make room for the Japanese; on the contrary, Japanese have usually been employed to fill places vacated by others because of the more remunerative or agreeable employment to be found elsewhere.

(2) A premium has been placed upon the substitution of Japanese rather than of other immigrant races by the fact that they were made easily available by the Japanese contractors, and that because of the position of the contractors their employment involved the least inconvenience to the employers. These contractors have had a

---

[a] The employment of Japanese in packing houses in Omaha dates from 1904, when they were introduced as strike breakers. Some 200 were then brought from the West, but most of these have drifted away, and those who have come more recently have not been quite sufficiently numerous to maintain the number at that point. They are paid the same wage—17½ to 20 cents per hour—as other employees engaged in the same kind of work. They are entirely satisfactory for the lighter kinds of work, and especially that ordinarily done by women.

supply of labor available; other cheap laborers must be " recruited " largely through employment agents in the cities of the Middle West, which involves competition with the industries more conveniently reached from these supply centers. This organization of the Japanese laborers must be emphasized above all other things in explaining the demand for them.

(3) Moreover, the Japanese have usually worked for a lower wage than the members of any other race save the Chinese and the Mexican. In the salmon canneries the Chinese have been paid higher wages than the Japanese engaged in the same occupations. In the lumber industry all races, including the East Indian, have been paid higher wages than the Japanese doing the same kind of work. As section hands and laborers in railway shops they have been paid as much as or more than the Chinese, and more than the Mexicans, but as a rule less than the white men of many races. In coal mining they have been employed chiefly as miners and loaders and have worked at the common piece rate, but in Wyoming, where they have been employed as " company men," they were paid less per day than the European immigrants employed in large numbers, until their acceptance as members of the United Mine Workers in 1907 gave them the benefit of the standard rate established by bargaining between the union and the operators. As construction laborers they have usually, though not invariably, been paid less than the other races employed except the East Indian and the Mexican. Competition between the races engaged in unskilled work appears generally to have hinged upon the rate of wages paid rather than the efficiency of the races employed.

(4) It must be added, however, that the difference between the wages paid to Japanese and those paid to the members of the various white races engaged in the same occupations tended to diminish, and in some instances disappeared, while the number of immigrants arriving in the country was largest. This is accounted for partly by the skillful bargaining of the few large contractors who have supplied the great majority of the laborers for work in canneries, on the railroads, in the lumber mills, and for other industrial enterprises, partly by the fact that there was an increasing demand for their labor in other industries, which, one after the other, had been opened to them.

(5) Though regarded as less desirable than the Chinese and the Mexicans, roadmasters and section foremen usually prefer Japanese to the Italians, Greeks, and Slavs as section hands. In the railway shops they are usually given higher rank than the Mexicans and Greeks, and sometimes the Italians as well. They are versatile, adaptable, and ambitious, and are regarded as good laborers and helpers. In salmon canning, on the other hand, they are universally regarded as much less desirable than the Chinese, and are inferior to the Filipinos who have recently engaged in the industry in Alaska. In the lumber and other industries there is greater difference of opinion. On the whole, however, the Japanese have been regarded as satisfactory laborers at the wage paid. In salt refineries and in some other places where the labor conditions are hard, they find favor because they are willing to accept such conditions.

(6) In spite of these considerations, however, in most branches of industry the Japanese have found it difficult to make much advance. In the lumber industry, for example, the great majority of employers have never employed them at all. In some instances this is explained by the race antipathy of the employer, more frequently by that of the white employees or that of the community in general. The same situation is found in most industries in which the Japanese have been employed in so far as large groups of men are brought together at one place and the work is of such a character that the members of different races must work in close association. While exceptions are found in a few other industries, it is mainly in the salmon canneries and in railway work that a hostile public opinion has had little effect upon the employment of Japanese.

(7) Chiefly because of the attitude of other laborers and the fact that many of the Japanese do not understand English and must be set at work in groups with an interpreter, the Japanese have always been engaged chiefly in unskilled work. In the lumber industry a few have advanced to semiskilled positions, but they have not made the progress the members of the same race have in British Columbia, where skilled white men have been more scarce.

In fact, in Washington and Oregon few Japanese have been employed except in the "yards." Nor have they found a place in catching fish for the canneries as they did in British Columbia, while in the canneries they are, as a rule, employed to do the unskilled work during the busiest season, while the Chinese are employed more regularly and fill the positions requiring skill. They likewise occupy the lowest positions in the fruit and vegetable canneries and are engaged chiefly in preparing fruit and vegetables for canning. In the coal mines, with the exception of Wyoming, they are employed as miners and loaders—occupations in which the great majority of the new immigrants are employed, because the work is less regular and more disagreeable than in the other occupations. Likewise, in the three smelters where they are employed they share the commonest labor with Greeks and other recent immigrants from south and east European countries. Perhaps the Japanese have made greater progress in railway shops than in any other nonagricultural employment. Though most of those employed in shops are unskilled laborers, they have risen somewhat in the scale of occupations, and in several instances are found occupying positions which, with their versatility and capacity, might serve them as stepping stones to skilled work.

These, in brief, are the more general facts relating to the employment of Japanese in these nonagricultural industries. The Japanese, who found their first employment in the canneries and as section hands and general-construction laborers, have shown a strong tendency to leave such employment for agricultural work or to find employment in the cities. The explanation of the movement is found partly in the higher earnings which might be realized, partly in the better conditions of living which might be found, partly in a very evident tendency exhibited by the Japanese to rise to the occupational and economic position they had enjoyed in their native land. In this way the large number who have engaged in agricultural pursuits or in city trades upon their arrival have been added to by those who were leaving their employment in other industries. As a result of this movement the number of Japanese engaged in railroad and general construction work and in coal mining in all of the States save Utah has been decreasing, especially since restrictions were placed upon the immigration of laborers from Japan and Hawaii. Their places have been filled by an increasing number of European immigrants, as a rule at higher wages. Business having been in a more or less depressed condition throughout the West since the end of 1907, the partial substitution involved has not caused much difficulty. Moreover, it may be said that none of these industries, save the salmon canning, has been materially assisted by or has become dependent upon Japanese labor. In the salmon canneries more Chinese or more laborers of some other race than Japanese are desired. With the beet-sugar industry in several States and certain other agricultural industries in California it is different, for the farmers in many localities have for years relied upon Asiatic labor until a situation has developed in which the substitution of other races will involve inconvenience and will require radical changes in order to make the necessary readjustment.

CHAPTER IV

JAPANESE IN AGRICULTURE.

AGRICULTURAL LABORERS.[a]

The farms of the Western States furnish employment during the summer months to more than 40 per cent of their Japanese population. The number so employed in California during the summer months of 1909 was probably 30,000, in Washington 3,000, Colorado 3,000, Oregon 1,000, Idaho between 800 and 1,000, Utah 1,025, and Montana 700 or 800. Comparatively few are employed in the other States of the western division, in Texas, and in Florida. Of these, perhaps 6,000 are farmers (chiefly tenants), the others farm laborers.

The work performed by Japanese farm hands is practically all connected with the more intensive crops, such as sugar beets, grapes, deciduous and citrus fruits, berries, vegetables, and hops, which require much hand labor during certain seasons. They also engage in clearing land in some localities. Japanese are rarely employed on ranches devoted to general farming. The most important branch of agriculture as regards Japanese laborers is the raising of sugar beets, in which between 10,000 and 11,000 out of a total of 25,500 persons in the industry as a whole are employed during the busiest season. The great majority of the Japanese farm laborers in Idaho, Montana, Colorado, and Utah are working in the beet fields of those States during the busy season, and a part of those in Washington, Oregon, and California are also similarly employed. In Washington and Oregon, however, the great majority of the Japanese farm laborers are employed in berry patches and truck gardens and very few find employment in fruit orchards. In California the Japanese are extensively employed in nearly all districts, raising vegetables, berries, citrus and deciduous fruits, nuts, etc. The range of their work, as well as their number, in California is much greater than in the other States.

---

[a] The investigation of immigrant agricultural labor embraced studies of the beet-sugar industry of all of the Western States, the hop industry in Oregon and California, and intensive farming in several localities in California. The reports submitted relating to these give much more detail concerning Japanese agricultural labor than is here presented. The reports are as follows: "Immigrant labor in the beet-sugar industry in the Western States;" "Immigrant labor in the hop industry of California and Oregon;" "Immigrant labor in the agricultural and allied industries of California;" "Immigrant farming on the reclaimed lands of the Sacramento and San Joaquin rivers;" "Immigrants in Fresno County, Cal.;" "Immigrant labor in the deciduous-fruit industry of the Vaca Valley;" "Immigrant labor in the garden-seed and deciduous-fruit industries of Santa Clara County;" "Immigrant labor in the orchards about Suisun;" "Immigrant labor in the citrus-fruit industry;" "Immigrant labor in the fruit industries of the Newcastle district;" "The celery industry of Orange County;" and "Immigrant labor in the Imperial Valley."

The history and conditions of employment of Japanese differ from one State to another. For that reason the facts are best presented for several of these States separately.

CALIFORNIA.

The Japanese were first employed in agricultural work in California about 1887. The entry and the subsequent extensive employment of Japanese in the farming districts of this State was made easy, because of the previous employment of Chinese. In many parts of the State the Chinese had predominated for years, so that the restrictions on their immigration paved the way to the extensive employment of the Japanese, who soon adapted themselves so as to fit into the Chinese system of labor and living conditions. Among other things they adopted the Chinese "boss" system. At first the Japanese worked in small unorganized groups, but as their numbers increased and they were more extensively employed, they soon became organized into "gangs" under leaders or bosses. Though individuals move rather freely from one group to another, this form of organization has been important in explaining the advance made by the Japanese in agriculture as in other industries.

One of the first of the agricultural districts in which the Japanese found employment was the Vaca Valley, where four came in the winter of 1887–8. In 1890 4 Japanese went to Fresno, and the following year 30 found work there in the vineyards. In 1891 they first sought employment in the Newcastle fruit district. In 1892 13 Japanese were employed as hop pickers in the Pajaro Valley. They appeared also in the Lower Sacramento and San Joaquin River country, and in the Marysville and Suisun districts in the early nineties. In the early nineties the members of this race gained a foothold in the beet fields of the State. After once securing work, the number of Japanese in a district increased rapidly, and they found employment on more and more ranches, especially while the immigration was at its height—from 1899 to 1906. They were later in entering agricultural work in southern California than in the northern part of the State. This was due largely to the fact that the districts of the south had been more recently developed, and that few Chinese, whom the Japanese followed in agricultural work in the north, had been employed there. Japanese were just beginning to find employment in the citrus fruit industry in 1900, and their employment in most localities of importance in citrus fruit growing dates from 1903 or 1904. Large numbers of the first Japanese brought to the southern part of the State were employed on the railroads, from which most of them were discharged in favor of Mexicans about 1902. The discharged men drifted into farm work, in certain parts of which they predominated or constituted a large percentage in most districts in 1909.

In some localities the Japanese laborers have merely made good the decrease in the number of Chinese due to natural causes, and supplied a part or all of the laborers needed for the expanding industries. In other localities there has been a net displacement of Chinese and white men engaged in certain agricultural occupations. The chief competition with the Japanese in the handwork involved in sugar-beet growing are Mexicans, Chinese, Koreans, and Hindus.

In fact, white men have never been employed to any great extent in this work. In other cases, as in the citrus fruit industry and in the deciduous fruit industry in most of the localities in which this industry centers, the competition is principally between white persons and Japanese.

In most localities the Japanese at first offered to work for less pay than any other race. Underbidding of white men was all but if not quite universal, of Chinese, previous to 1900, very general. Underbidding of the Chinese and white men was the method commonly used by Japanese for some years to gain a foothold in the various districts. In one community where the Chinese were paid $5 per week, the Japanese first worked for 35 or 40 cents per day in the early nineties. In another locality the price for work done by Japanese by contract was first estimated on a basis of 45 cents per day as against $1 for Chinese, and in the later nineties at day work Japanese were paid 75 to 90 cents per day where Chinese were paid $1. In a third district they were paid 70 cents per day and for two or three years their wages varied from 60 to 90 cents as against $1.25 per day for Chinese and $1 per day, including board, for white men. Before the close of the nineties, however, the wages paid Japanese had begun to rise and the increase in their wages continued even when the influx of the members of this race was greatest. The continued rise in the wages of Japanese farm laborers during the years since 1900, when the number of immigrants of this race was largest, is explained by the employment of these laborers in more and more of the rapidly expanding agricultural districts and also the greater opportunity and employment offered them at better wages in other industries and in the Pacific coast cities. They were also well organized under " bosses," which greatly aided them in securing work at the higher wages. The Chinese were decreasing in number and the better class of white men did not care to engage in the seasonal farm work when regular work could be found at good wages elsewhere. With prosperous times and an inadequate labor supply under prevailing conditions, with new opportunities opened for them, and especially with restrictions upon their further immigration, the wages of Japanese have increased more than 50 per cent within fifteen years and, especially since great restrictions were placed upon the further increase of their numbers, they have ceased to greatly underbid other laborers. Their organization has, in fact, been used in some instances to effect an increase in the prices paid for contract work.

That California should give employment to more Japanese farm laborers than the other States of the West is due mainly to the greater specialization of large districts in intensive agriculture and because they were convenient substitutes for the disappearing Chinese in those industries which had been built up with comparatively few white hand laborers. These intensive crops require large numbers of handworkers at certain stages in their production and it has been most difficult to secure these temporary laborers. The migratory Japanese have assumed such great importance in the agricultural districts of the State by supplying the greater part of this urgent demand for seasonal workers. They have been well adapted to the disagreeable handwork and have generally been secured at lower wages than white men. They have been convenient for ranchers to secure through " bosses," for they are well organized into " gangs," as has been described elsewhere in this report, while white men are not organized and so are more difficult to secure, and with Japanese available few white ranchers have made any effort to find white men for such work. Like the Chinese, they have put up with poor living quarters and have boarded themselves, which has been a convenience and a saving to the ranchers. The prominence of Japanese in farm work has been confined mainly to temporary handwork, but in recent years they have become more firmly established in regular hand-work also, principally on farms leased by their countrymen, but to a certain extent on farms conducted by white men as well.

The Japanese have been employed in practically all of the inten-sive branches of agriculture in California. In the beet industry they number 4,500 of between 6,000 and 7,000 handworkers employed during the thinning season. They predominate and control the handwork in the beet fields of all except three districts in the State— two in southern California, where they are outnumbered by the Mexicans, and one northern district, where they do not care to work and Hindus were the most numerous race employed in 1909. In the grape picking of the various parts of California they are also the most numerous race, some 7,000 or 8,000 being employed during the busiest season of a few weeks in the fall. They do practically all of the work in the berry patches of the State. In the various districts specializing in certain vegetables and on truck farms near the cities they do much of the work. Much of the seasonal work in most of the deciduous-fruit districts is also controlled by Japanese laborers.

Of the 4,000 extra laborers brought in to work in the orchards of the Vaca Valley during the summer of 1908, one-half were Japanese. About 2,000 of the 2,500 or 3,000 persons employed in the Newcastle fruit district at the busiest season in 1909 were Japanese. About 1,000 members of this race remain in the Pajaro Valley all year, while for the intensive work during the summer and autumn some 700 or 800 Japanese and about the same number of Dalmatians come into the district from other places. In the citrus-fruit industry of Tulare County a little less than one-half of the pickers are Japanese, while some 5,000 Japanese pickers in southern California constitute more than one-half of the total number of citrus-fruit pickers in that part of the State during the busy spring months. Some 200 Japanese are employed regularly in the handwork on celery ranches in Orange County, while at the height of the transplanting season the number is increased to 600. These instances are sufficient to show the im-portance of this race in various industries and districts.

The majority of the Japanese farm laborers in California are seasonal workers, employed only during busy seasons in the produc-tion of crops involving much hand labor. The Japanese found their first employment in these various farming districts as transient tem-porary laborers, and the majority of them are still thus employed, but in the years since their first coming a considerable number of them have become permanently located in these communities and work as regular farm hands for both white farmers and their own countrymen.

It is generally true that the Japanese are now paid somewhat less than white men when working on a day-wage basis. The day wages of Japanese in farm work in California are shown in the following table:

TABLE 28.—*Day wages of Japanese in farm work in California.*

	Number reporting.	Average wage.	Number earning—																		
			$0.88	$1.	$1.25	$1.30	$1.35	$1.40	$1.50	$1.55	$1.60	$1.65	$1.70	$1.75	$1.80	$1.85	$1.90	$1.95	$2.	$2.15	$2.25
Regular employees:																					
With board	93	$1.396	8	3		27	2		36	2	8		6				1				
Without board	863	1.623			25		24	4	243	123	77	39	71	193	7	12	17	3	23	1	1
Temporary employees:																					
With board	40	1.421				7	3	13	17												
Without board	2,654	1.615				11	143	918	104	193	225	268	688	56	23	10		13			2
Total Japanese	3,650																				

This table is, however, of limited value, for the differences between districts, industries, seasons of the year, etc., tend to become equalized in such a compilation. The differences in wages and hours as between different districts, different races of employees, and between different farms in the same district are of great importance and will be found in the separate reports on various California communities investigated.

The above table includes only those laborers who are paid on a time basis. Nearly two-thirds of the Japanese from whom data were obtained were temporary workers not boarded; but as most of the seasonal workers were paid on a piece basis, they are not included in the table. It will be seen that very few Japanese farm hands are boarded, and these few are employed either by Japanese or Chinese, for white employers never board Asiatic field hands. Of the 863 regular employees not boarded, 86.4 per cent received between $1.50 and $1.75, and of the 2,654 temporary men not boarded, 90.3 per cent received from $1.50 to $1.75, inclusive. There are more Japanese receiving $1.50 per day than any other specific wage—243, or 28.2 per cent, of the regular men received this amount without board; and 918, or 34.6 per cent, of the temporary employees received the same. A comparison between the average of the wages of the Japanese on a time basis and the averages of other races is shown in the following table, which gives the average wage in each case for the persons reported from all parts of the State:

TABLE 29.—*Comparison between the average wages of the Japanese on a time basis and the averages of other races.*

Race.	Regular with board.		Regular without board.		Temporary with board.		Temporary without board.	
	Number.	Average.	Number.	Average.	Number.	Average.	Number.	Average.
Miscellaneous, White	411	$1.311	199	$1.889	53	$1.286	286	$1.855
Italian	101	1.108	22	1.667	181	1.121		
Mexican			85	1.422			82	1.721
Chinese	108	1.406	26	1.559	35	1.454	99	1.743
Japanese	93	1.396	863	1.623	40	1.421	2,654	1.615
Hindus			66	1.534			253	1.441

It will be seen that the averages for both Japanese and Chinese regularly employed and receiving board, $1.396 and $1.406, respectively, are higher than those for "miscellaneous white" men, $1.311, and Italians $1.108. This fact is accounted for by the higher cost of board for the white races than for the Asiatics. For Japanese, board by their countrymen is reckoned at from 20 to 30 cents, while for white men board is valued at from 50 to 75 cents per day. This is made plain by comparing the averages for the regular employees without board. "Miscellaneous white" men were paid $1.889 per day without board, as against $1.623 paid to Japanese—a difference of more than 25 cents in favor of the white races. The average daily wage of the temporary employees is not very different from the regular wages, and they show the Japanese receiving more than white men where board is included and less than white men where board is not included. The wages of the Chinese do not differ much from those of the Japanese, except for temporary laborers without board, where they averaged about 13 cents more than Japanese, although it must be borne in mind that the number of Japanese is many times larger. Of the regular employees without board, the Mexicans averaged the least, $1.422, with Hindus next lowest at $1.534. As temporary employees, the Hindus were paid the least, $1.441, while Mexicans received about 10 cents more than Japanese.

Wages vary considerably between different districts of the State, and these averages only show the general conditions for the State as a whole. In most districts of the State there is a discrimination of about 25 cents per day in favor of white men as against Japanese and other Asiatics engaged in the same work, although in a few localities for seasonal work the day wages are the same for both classes of laborers. The wages reported were in most cases those at the height of the busy season when the demand for laborers was greatest and the wages highest. During the slack months of the year in most districts the wages of the Japanese are usually about $1.25 per day.

The larger part of the seasonal farm laborers of California are working on a piece basis, and their earnings have not been tabulated above, for they vary greatly with the number of hours worked per day, condition of the crop, amount of skill, and the degree of application of the worker. Working on a piece basis, the Japanese who predominate in such seasonal work, make from 10 to 100 per cent larger average earnings per day than at day rates. The average daily earnings of the Japanese in picking raisin grapes were in 1908 in excess of $4, and there were many members of the race who earned as much as $6 per day. Americans, working shorter hours and less extensively, averaged about $3 per day; German-Russians, $2.50; and the Mexicans, Hindus, and Indians, about $2. During most of the longer season of wine-grape picking Japanese averaged about $1.91 per day, while other races earned somewhat less. In the handwork of the beet fields the Japanese have the highest average earnings of any race, for they do more work. More than one-half of the Japanese reporting data in 1909 earned $1.75, but less than $2, while 37.4 per cent earned $2 or more as against 8.5 per cent who earned less than $1.75. In the hop industry, also, the Japanese make the largest earnings, because they are quick and are willing to work intensively for longer hours than white persons. Of 239 Japanese males reporting in 1909, 91 earned $3, but less than $4, while 18 succeeded in earning $4 or more per day. Only 47, or one-fifth of the Japanese, earned less than $2 per day. Of the natives and north Europeans, about one-half earned $2, but less than $3 per day, one-third earned between $1.50 and $2, and the remainder earned from $1 to $1.50.

It should be stated, however, that these data were secured at the beginning of the season, before many of the white persons had had much experience in picking hops. These important industries show the larger earnings of the Japanese in the seasonal work where paid on a piece basis. That they earn more than white persons is explained by the fact that they work longer hours and with closer application to their work, for piece rates are now usually the same for all races.

In the early years of their employment in the different localities the Japanese were regarded by the farmers with great favor. They were younger, neater, and more active than the Chinese who were employed. They were more accommodating and accomplished more work in a day and for lower wages than the latter, who, as a consequence of the restrictions on further immigration, were growing old and were unable to meet the labor demands of the expanding farming districts. For some work such as grape picking, beet thinning, and the raising of vegetables and berries, the Japanese have been regarded as physically well adapted to the "stoopwork," as they are short of stature and endure the extreme heat found in a few localities better than most other races. For some of the fruit picking they are considered less well suited because of their short reach. For several years the Japanese were favorably received and praised for their industry, quickness, adaptability, and eagerness to learn American ways.

Within the last few years, however, since the Japanese have come to predominate in the handwork connected with the production of most of the intensive crops, there has been much opposition to them on the part of ranchers. Complaints are heard that they are less accommodating and do less work in a day; they have become very independent and hard to deal with; by strikes and threats of strike and boycott they have raised wages; and they can not always be depended upon to perform their contracts. At day wages the Japanese now very often, like other laborers, shirk work and are slow, while on a piece basis they work extremely fast, but require constant supervision, as they are careless and wasteful in their eagerness to make large earnings. In spite of this widespread dissatisfaction with the Japanese, they are hired because they are so numerous and easily secured through their "bosses." The consensus of opinion in the older districts of the State is that the Chinese were far more satisfactory farm laborers and are much preferred to the Japanese. In a few districts where the employment of Japanese has been more recent and in industries, such as citrous-fruit growing, where few growers have had experience with Chinese, the opinion of the Japanese is more favorable. In some of the districts specializing in the production of intensive crops, and in the production of beets and grapes in particular, the ranchers very generally regard Asiatic labor as essential to the success of these crops, and while they regard the

Chinese as the best laborers, consider the Japanese as better suited to the work and the conditions under which it is performed than are white men. White employers nearly always prefer white men as teamsters and usually state that they would prefer reliable white men for all work, but the Japanese are better workers than the irregular white men usually available for handwork.

OREGON.

Comparatively few Japanese farmers and farm hands were to be found in Oregon before 1900, and the number in the State in 1909 was only about 1,000 during the busy summer season. Previous to 1900 most of the Japanese coming to Portland were employed by the railroads through "bosses," who had contracts with the transportation companies for all of the men they could furnish. Since 1900, however, more Japanese have sought agricultural work, some working on farms regularly throughout the year, while others leave other industries to engage in the harvest work only. The Japanese in Oregon have been employed by white employers in the agricultural districts merely to supplement the inadequate number of white laborers and have not been employed as the main supply for any kind of work as in California. This is largely due to the more recent development with white labor of the intensive farming districts of Oregon.

In 1909 the Japanese farm laborers were found in the following districts: About 400 were in the vicinity of the city of Portland working on truck and berry farms, about 300 were in the berry patches and fruit orchards near Hood River, at The Dalles some 30 men were employed by Japanese farmers, and between 150 and 200 about Salem were employed in truck gardens and in the hopyards during the vine training and hop-picking seasons. In the beet fields at La Grande some 125 Japanese did 95 per cent of the handwork during the busy season of 1908, but the industry has waned and has been practically abandoned. In the State as a whole the Japanese do not occupy a very large place in farm work. They are usually engaged in raising berries and vegetables. Handwork of this character and the cutting of wood and clearing of land are the principal occupations in which Japanese are engaged in agricultural districts. White persons do nearly all of the work in the orchards of the State.

The larger percentage of the Japanese in Oregon work for farmers of their own race. Because of this fact and the small extent to which they are employed, the organization of the agricultural laborers of this race under contractors has not been noticeable.

During the early nineties the few Japanese farm laborers were paid only 40 to 50 cents per day, and for clearing land in winter only 30 or 40 cents per day, without board. Even as late as 1898, when they were paid $1 and $1.10 as section hands on the railroads, 75 cents per day was considered good wages for Japanese farm hands. Only a few received as much as $1 for summer work before 1902. Since that time the wages of Japanese farm laborers have varied with and corresponded closely to the wages of the section hands of that race.

These changes for the years 1905 to 1909 were, approximately, as follows:

Year.	Wages per month (with board and lodging).	Wages per day (without board).
1905	$25	$1.25
1906	30	1.35
1907	$40 to 45	a 1.75
1908	30	b 1.35
1909	35 to 40	c 1.50

a Wages of section hands at the maximum.   b Wages of section hands reduced.
c Wages of section hands increased.

The wages of Japanese have never been as high as those paid to white men. At first there was about 50 cents per day discrimination against the Japanese, but that difference has become less until it is now about 25 cents.

In communities where Japanese have come in numbers there has been a growing prejudice against them on the part of white men, but it has not been as pronounced in Oregon as in California.

WASHINGTON.

The earliest Japanese immigrants to Washington were of the sailor class and found employment in the lumber mills and in the cities. The number of immigrants was small, however, until 1897 or 1898, when large numbers began to arrive from Japan to engage in railroad work under Japanese contractors. It is stated that a few were employed on farms near Tacoma and Seattle as early as 1888 or 1889, and that the first lease of land was made in that locality as early as 1892. But few engaged in agricultural work until after a great number were employed upon the railroads. During the last ten years many have left their employment as section hands to find work as agricultural laborers or to lease land, and there has been a smaller movement of the same kind on the part of Japanese employed in other occupations. In 1909 some 3,000, and possibly a few hundred more, were engaged in agricultural work in the State. The great majority of these were in western Washington about Tacoma and Seattle, where the maximum number of Japanese on farms conducted by the members of that race was estimated in 1909 at 2,484, while the minimum during the year was estimated at 834.

The majority of the Japanese farm laborers in this district work on berry, truck, and dairy farms, conducted by the members of that race. In eastern Washington more than 200 are found for a few weeks each year in the beet fields near Waverly engaged in the hand-work, which is done almost exclusively by them. This sugar-beet industry is in a sparsely-settled district where it is difficult to get help. For the first year or two of beet growing, which was begun in 1899, "transient whites" were employed, but they were too irregular to be satisfactory. The sugar company turned for relief to a

Japanese contractor in Portland, Oreg., who agreed to furnish men. At present local contractors provide all of the Japanese required. As gardeners and nursery laborers near North Yakima about 75 Japanese are employed and about Wenatchee some 20 or 30 are engaged in farm work. The regular and the seasonal work in the numerous orchards of these two districts are performed almost entirely by white farmers and laborers. Near White Salmon on the Columbia River some 40 Japanese were, in 1909, engaged in clearing land. In Washington also very few Chinese have engaged in agriculture and these have been truck gardeners near cities. The fruit and berry farms of the State have been developed recently and the Chinese-exclusion law limited the immigration of that race before a demand for many laborers arose in these districts devoted to intensive crops. This fact and the consequent development of these districts with white labor accounts for the small part taken by the Japanese in the farm work of Washington as compared to California.

The wages of Japanese farm laborers have changed materially since they first appeared. From 1890 to 1895 Japanese were paid from 75 to 90 cents per day without board, while white men received from $15 to $18 per month with board. From 1895 to 1900 Japanese averaged $1 per day without board and white men $20 to $25 per month with board. In 1900 Japanese were paid $1.10 and by 1906 $1.25 per day. In 1909, $1.35 per day without board was the usual wage for regular work throughout the year, while $1.50 was the standard wage for seasonal work. During berry picking and potato harvesting, when the demand for men is greatest, $1.75 per day was frequently paid. The white farmers pay for most of the seasonal work on a piece basis, and some of the Japanese farmers do likewise. On such a basis the laborers make larger earnings per day. Japanese gardeners on a monthly basis were paid from $25 to $35 per month with board and lodging, and dairy hands were paid $40 or $45 per month with board. White laborers employed regularly by white farmers were usually paid $35 or $40 per month with board and white milkers were paid $45 and $50. The Japanese have always shown a tendency to underbid white laborers, but to a less extent now than formerly, and since restrictions have been placed upon further immigration their wages have more nearly approached those of white men.

There has been some opposition to the Japanese in Washington, but as a rule they have been favorably received in agricultural districts.

IDAHO.

The Japanese farm laborers in Idaho are and have always been chiefly engaged in the seasonal handwork connected with the raising of sugar beets in four districts—Nampa, Idaho Falls, Blackfoot, and Sugar City. The beet-sugar industry in Idaho dates from 1903, when the factory at Idaho Falls was opened.

The Japanese do the greater part of the handwork in the beet fields of the State, while white persons do most of the work with teams. The German-Russians who were brought by the sugar company into one district to give competition to the Japanese and to place them " on their good behavior," are an important element in that locality. In another district about one-half of the work is done by white persons, principally natives, and among them many school children who find the employment in thinning suitable.

The Japanese beet workers have generally been secured through the " bosses " of organized gangs. In one important district, however, the " boss " system has been modified, so that the growers contract directly with the men employed. The Japanese are brought in by a large Japanese contracting company which is paid by the sugar company $1 per acre for each acre worked by the Japanese laborers plus 35 cents per acre to defray part of the cost of transporting laborers to the community. The sugar company also pays the salary of the resident agent of the Japanese contractors. The Japanese laborers are distributed among the growers who contract with them directly and they are paid the full contract price by the growers, without any " boss's " commission deducted. They are paid on a piece basis for the various processes, so that their earnings vary with the amount of work accomplished. The German-Russians are usually paid a flat rate of $20 per acre for doing the handwork in the beet fields. The Japanese contracts are now usually on a basis of $20 per acre for beets running 12 tons to the acre, with a reduction of 50 cents for each ton under 12 and an addition of 60 cents per ton for each ton over 12.

This graduated scale has been found advisable in the case of the Japanese to secure the best work, for by putting a premium upon good work, their tendency, when paid on a straight rate per acre, to overthin in the spring in order to have less beets to harvest in the fall, is overcome. During the slack months many of these Japanese remain in these localities and engage in other branches of agricultural work.

The Japanese have been generally preferred by Idaho beet growers to German-Russians and to such transient white men of other races as are occasionally employed. The German-Russians are considered more acceptable by some growers, however, for they settle permanently with their families in the community.

UTAH.

In Utah also the employment of Japanese in agricultural work is mainly confined to the handwork in the beet fields. There are probably a little more than 1,000 employed in the whole State. In the oldest beet-growing district in the State, where the industry dates from 1889, the handwork has always been done by the white farmers, their families, and the regular farm hands. In the other three districts of the State the Japanese do much of the work, white farmers and their families doing the remainder. In one of these districts the Japanese do nearly all of the thinning and hoeing, but almost no harvesting, in another district they do three-fourths of all the handwork, while in a third they do only one-half of it.

The first Japanese farm laborers in Utah were brought directly from California by a beet-sugar company in 1903, and set at work in a district where beet growing was introduced in that year. The locality was thinly settled and the sugar company and the employment agency contracting to supply laborers were unable to secure enough white men from surrounding towns, so 40 Japanese were imported from the beet districts of California, and later in the season 60 more were secured from other places. Much loss resulted from the inability to secure laborers. The following year several Japanese contractors appeared, but still white men were employed to do much of the work. The third year enough Japanese to do practically all of the handwork came to the district. In another place the establishment in 1904 of a second sugar factory in a more thinly settled part of a district led to the bringing in of Japanses in 1905. In the third community, where previously the work had all been done by white persons, the Japanese employed in railroad work began to bid for the handwork in the beet fields in 1906.

The first Japanese were brought to Utah through labor " bosses," and they were employed mainly under " bosses " for three or four years. An interesting feature of the labor situation has been a partially successful attempt in two districts to eliminate Japanese " bosses." As a substitute the sugar companies employ salaried agents, in one case a Japanese and in the other an American who speaks the Japanese language, to secure Japanese laborers and distribute them among the growers as needed. The purpose of this movement was to eliminate the evils of subcontracting under which the laborers who actually did the work would often receive only three-fourths of the contract price, which resulted in poor work. Under the present system the workers receive the full contract price paid by the growers.

As a rule the opinions of beet growers in Utah are favorable to the Japanese laborers. The principal complaint against them has been the evil of subcontracting under the " boss " system, which has been largely removed by eliminating the Japanese " boss " himself. About Ogden, and to a very slight extent elsewhere, Japanese find a place as laborers in growing asparagus and garden truck, but, with the exception of 25 employed by a company growing asparagus and operating a cannery, they are almost all employed by their countrymen who have purchased or leased land and are farming on their own account. They find very little employment in harvesting the crops of the orchards which have been rapidly developed in different localities and now cover a large acreage.

COLORADO.

Colorado is another State in which the employment of Japanese agricultural laborers is connected mainly with beet growing. The Japanese numbered 2,627 out of a total of more than 15,000 persons engaged in the handwork of the sugar-beet industry of the State in 1909. Of other races so employed there were 6,560 German-Russians, 2,632 Mexicans, and over 3,000 " miscellaneous white persons," besides a few Indians, Koreans, and Greeks. The importance of the Japanese, however, is greater than their numbers indicate, as they do more work per individual than the laborers of any other race. The " miscellaneous white persons " are largely farmers who plant beets on only a part of their lands, and the women and children of the families do much of the work in the fields. The German-Russian men are less efficient than Japanese, doing only about two-thirds as much work per man, and a large part of the German-Russian laborers are women and children, who accomplish still less work. The

Japanese excel the Mexicans also in the amount of work accomplished by each man during the season. In Colorado, where "miscellaneous white persons," German-Russians, and Mexicans predominate, and Japanese constitute only one-sixth of the total number, the average hand worker in the beet fields cares for a little more than 8 acres per season, while in California, where Japanese constitute two-thirds of the total number, the average hand laborer attends to nearly 11 acres.

The Japanese began coming into northern Colorado as early as 1903, when 200 of them were secured in one district to increase the supply of laborers and to afford competition against the German-Russians. During the same year about 100 appeared in other northern Colorado communities. For a time trouble with irresponsible " bosses " caused some decrease in the number of Japanese, but by 1909 the number of Japanese in northern Colorado had increased to 2,100, as against 5,800 German-Russians and 1,000 Mexicans. In southern Colorado the " miscellaneous white persons," German-Russians and Mexicans, did all of the handwork until 1904, when the Japanese were first employed. In 1909 the latter race in southern Colorado numbered 442 in a total of 3,918 handworkers, the Mexicans with 1,630 being the most numerous. In western Colorado only 25 Japanese were found among the 550 handworkers in that part of the State in 1909. Their small number is explained by a strong local race prejudice against them.

The organization of Japanese laborers under " bosses " similar to the " gang " system in California prevails in Colorado. The Mexicans and German-Russians also work in groups, but the group in the case of the latter is the family. The beet districts of Colorado are so situated that formerly they had a very small local labor supply. The German-Russians were brought in from Nebraska for the season by the sugar companies and the Mexicans and Japanese were secured from distant places. At first the companies paid the transportation of the laborers, but now those coming from other districts must pay their own railroad fare. Many German-Russians and Japanese have purchased or leased lands and are permanently located in these districts throughout the year.

The contract prices for the handwork in the beet fields of Colorado are higher than those paid in California, which is accounted for largely by the greater difficulty of securing laborers. As a rule, a flat rate of $20 per acre is paid for the thinning, hoeing, and topping. For this reason the rates of earnings for Japanese laborers are somewhat higher than in California. Out of 370 representative Japanese beet workers in northern Colorado, 200 averaged between $3 and $3.50 per day during the thinning season of 1909. The earnings of handworkers in the beet fields of Colorado are sufficiently above those of common laborers in other industries to attract them from other localities and from neighboring States for the season. The Japanese come principally from the coal mines and smelters of Wyoming and Colorado, and from maintenance of way work on the railroads.

Opinion concerning the Japanese in Colorado varies all the way from extreme race antagonism to extreme favor. In northern Colorado where most of them are found the attitude of white persons toward them is favorable, and on the whole they stand higher in the esteem of the beet growers than they do in California. Except in western Colorado, what opposition exists to the Japanese is apparently due primarily to the previous mismanagement of "bosses." Several attempts to introduce Japanese into the orchards of the western part of the State have been abandoned because of the opposition of white laborers.

These are the States in which Japanese occupy an important place as agricultural laborers. In Montana they are employed in smaller numbers in the beet fields about Billings. The 135 or 140 Japanese farm laborers in Texas do a small part of the work on the rice farms, in the truck gardens, and about the nurseries conducted by their countrymen.

YEARLY EARNINGS.

The approximate earnings during the preceding year of 375 Japanese farm laborers, from whom such information was secured in some of these States, are shown in the two following tables.

TABLE 30.—*Approximate earnings during the past year of Japanese farm laborers 18 years of age or over.*

WITH BOARD.

States.	Number working for wages and reporting amount.	Average earnings.	Under $100.	$100 and under $150.	$150 and under $200.	$200 and under $250.	$250 and under $300.	$300 and under $400.	$400 and under $500.	$500 and under $600.	$600 and under $700.	$700 and under $800.	$800 and under $1,000.	$1,000 and under $1,250.	$1,250 and under $1,500.	$1,500 and under $2,000.	$2,000 or over.
California	25	$327.72	1	1	1	2	1	11	8								
Colorado and Utah	2	390.00						1	1								
Washington and Oregon	44	405.32					1	20	19	3	1						

WITHOUT BOARD.

States.	Number working for wages and reporting amount.	Average earnings.	Under $100.	$100 and under $150.	$150 and under $200.	$200 and under $250.	$250 and under $300.	$300 and under $400.	$400 and under $500.	$500 and under $600.	$600 and under $700.	$700 and under $800.	$800 and under $1,000.	$1,000 and under $1,250.	$1,250 and under $1,500.	$1,500 and under $2,000.	$2,000 or over.
California	260	$379.03	1		1	19	18	96	102	19	3		1				
Colorado and Utah	22	386.64		1	1	1		9	7	1	2						
Washington and Oregon	22	439.86		1				3	14	3	1						

TABLE 31.—*Approximate earnings during the past year of Japanese farm laborers.*

WITH BOARD.

Months worked.	California. Number working and reporting data.	California. Average earnings.	Colorado and Utah. Number working and reporting data.	Colorado and Utah. Average earnings.	Washington and Oregon. Number working and reporting data.	Washington and Oregon. Average earnings.
1	1	$40.00				
6	1	130.00				
7	1	180.00				
8	1	240.00				
10	3	320.00	1	$360.00	1	$250.00
11	1	420.00			1	403.00
12	17	366.65	1	420.00	42	409.07
Total	25	327.72	2	390.00	44	405.32

TABLE 31.—*Approximate earnings during the past year of Japanese farm laborers*—Continued.

WITHOUT BOARD.

Months worked.	California.		Colorado and Utah.		Washington and Oregon.	
	Number working and reporting data.	Average earnings.	Number working and reporting data.	Average earnings.	Number working and reporting data.	Average earnings.
2..	....	....	2	$133.50	....	....
3..	1	$90.00	....	....	....	....
4..	....	....	....	....	1	$145.00
5..	2	219.00	....	....	....	....
6..	7	208.14	2	375.50	....	....
7..	6	248.33	2	370.00	....	....
8..	16	311.38	2	291.25	....	....
9..	25	326.80	5	429.13	1	380.00
10..	29	317.38	2	462.50	....	....
11..	45	391.36	1	450.00	2	412.00
12..	129	427.18	6	440.63	18	462.67
Total......................................	260	379.03	22	386.64	22	439.86

It is apparent from the first table that the Japanese in Washington and Oregon earned the most ($405.32 with board and $439.86 without board as an average) during the year, while those in Colorado and Utah ($390 with board and $386.64 without board) earned more than the men in California ($327.72 with board and $379.03 without board). The second table shows the number of months worked during the year and the average earnings for those working each specified number of months. Of the Japanese receiving board in addition to wages 17 of the 25 in California and 42 of the 44 reporting in Washington and Oregon worked for twelve months, and of those not boarded, 129 of the 260 in California, 6 of the 22 in Colorado and Utah, and 18 of the 22 in Washington and Oregon worked twelve months. The larger percentage working twelve months in Washington and Oregon partly accounts for the larger average earnings for the year in those States.

JAPANESE FARMERS.

The investigation of the Japanese included an extensive investigation of the independent farming carried on by them in several States.

This was always investigated in connection with the investigation of agricultural labor, and in 13 different localities included the collection of " family " and " agricultural " schedules from representative farmers of that race. Schedules were obtained for practically all of the 25 farms in Texas, and for 490 of the approximate 4,000 in the States of the Western Division. The schedules from the latter group of States were collected from various localities in northern Colorado and Utah, various localities in Oregon and Washington, and from eight localities or districts in California. The results of the special investigation have been presented in a number of special reports.[a] The following statement is merely a summary of some of the details there presented. At most points this section is the same as one section of a general report on "Immigrant farmers of the Western States." Its presentation here is due to the desire to make this report comprehensive of the entire situation in so far as the Japanese are concerned.

It is probable that more than 6,000 Japanese, including all partners, are farming on their own account in the continental territory of the United States. The number of farms or subdivisions of farms controlled by them in 1909 was perhaps in excess of 4,000, with a total acreage of more than 210,000. The following table is submitted as indicating roughly the acreage owned, the acreage leased, the total acreage owned or leased, and the number of holdings or farms the tenure of which was by Japanese, in the States of California, Colorado, Idaho, Oregon, Texas, Utah, and Washington. The number of holdings in the other Western States and in one colony in Florida is small and the total acreage only a few thousand.

TABLE 32.—*Land farmed by Japanese in 1909, by form of tenure and estimated number of holdings.*

	Acres owned.	Acres leased for cash.	Acres leased for share of crop.	Total acres leased.	Total acres owned or leased.	Number of holdings or farms.
California	a 16,449.5	a 80,232	a 57,001.5	a 137,233.5	a 153,683	b 3,000 or 3,200
Colorado	120	c 14,750	5,000	19,750	19,870	200 or over
Idaho		d 4,870	d 2,202	d 7,072	d 7,072	
Oregon	c 2,048			e 1,157	e 3,205	e 91
Texas	12,642			2,546	15,188	25
Utah	157.6			f 5,724.5	f 5,882.1	105 to 115
Washington				g 7,000	g 7,000	g 325

a According to the Japanese-American Yearbook.
b A rough estimate based upon the average size of holdings in the several localities investigated.
c Estimated in part upon data contained in Japanese-American Yearbook; in part upon data collected by field agents.
d Data collected by field agents. Does not include land leased for the production of sugar beets about Preston and Whitney.
e Not including several tracts of land leased, exact number and acreage not ascertained.
f Not including three or more farms, acreage not ascertained.
g Including an estimate of 16 farms with 654 acres in localities from which exact data were not secured.

These figures should not be regarded as complete or as possessing a great degree of accuracy. Those for California are taken from the Japanese-American Yearbook and are compiled chiefly from the records of the secretaries of local Japanese associations. The form of tenure, number of acres, and use made of each holding are published in detail in this annual. The agents of the Commission were able to check these figures in several localities and found them to be fairly satisfactory, except that in some instances not all holdings

a "Japanese and German-Russian farmers of northern Colorado;" "Japanese farmers of northern Utah;" "Immigrant labor in the deciduous fruit industry of the Vaca Valley;" "Immigrants in the fruit industries of the Newcastle district." Part II.—"Immigrant farming of the reclaimed lands of the Sacramento and San Joaquin rivers, California," Ch. I–III; "Immigrants in Fresno County, Cal.," Ch. IV; "The Japanese farmers of Los Angeles County, Cal.;" "Japanese tenant and landowning farmers of the Florin district, California;" "Japanese in the Pajaro Valley;" "Japanese truck gardeners about Sacramento, Cal.;" "Japanese and Italian farmers in Oregon;" "Immigrant farmers about Seattle and Tacoma, Wash.;" and "The Japanese in Texas."

were reported.   The figures presented, therefore, should be regarded as somewhat smaller than the proper figures would be.   The figures submitted for Colorado are based in part upon the local reports of the Commission's agents, which covered 13,686 acres.   The others are estimates based upon the Japanese-American Yearbook.   Those for Idaho were secured from the different localities in which Japanese are farming, but are incomplete in that they do not include the holdings of some tenant farmers growing sugar beets about Preston and Whitney, in the southern part of the State near the Utah boundary.   Nor are the Oregon figures complete, for they do not include several tracts of leased land in localities not visited by an agent of the Commission.   The figures for Utah were collected by agents of the Commission, but do not include three, or possibly more than three, farms, the acreage of which could not be ascertained.   The figures for Texas were returned by an agent who visited practically all of the 25 farms in the course of his investigation in that State. Finally, the figures for Washington are estimates, based in large part, however, upon a census made by an agent of the Commission.   This agent found 309 farms or holdings, with a total acreage of 6,344, in the vicinity of Seattle and Tacoma.   Several farms were found or reported in other parts of the State, bringing the total number of holdings to approximately 325, with 7,000 acres as a probable total.

In many cases the holdings of the Japanese are only subdivisions or parts of farms.   The leases may cover only the fields which are devoted to the production of sugar beets, vegetables, or berries, or the orchards.   Hence the figures relating to "holdings" should not be interpreted as equivalent to as many "farms" as the term is ordinarily used.

The next table, which is designed to show the kind of farming in which the Japanese are engaged, is still less accurate.   The figures do, however, indicate in a general way the place occupied by the farmers of this race.   Those for California and Colorado are taken from the Japanese-American Yearbook, to which reference has been made; the others are based upon reports made by agents of the Commission.

TABLE 33.—*Kinds of farming in which the Japanese are engaged.*

	Acres devoted to specified crops in 1909 in each specified State.					
	California.	Colorado.	Idaho.	Texas.	Utah.	Washington.
General crops (cereals and forage).........	12,528	3,653	1,310	....	(a)	(b)
Poultry, live stock, dairying..............	1,187½	300	....	....	....	1,084
Deciduous fruit and grapes...............	53,679½	....	....	....	....	....
Citrus fruit.............................	237	....	....	76	....	....
Berries.................................	5,535	....	....	....	....	769
Sugar beets.............................	8,042	10,839	4,922	....	5,190	....
Vegetables.............................	56,243½	2,899	840	276	425	3,449
Rice farms..............................	....	....	....	13,961	....	....
Mixed intensive crops....................	9,960½	....	....	....	875	1,044
Other land.............................	4,348	....	....	....	267	....
Total......................	c 151,767	c 17,691	7,072	15,188	5,882	c 6,346

a Reported under "Other land."
b Reported under "Mixed intensive crops."
c Acreage accounted for does not include total acreage for the State.

In Colorado, Utah, and Idaho the Japanese are chiefly growers of sugar beets. These they rotate to some extent with other crops, while in recent years they have engaged extensively in growing potatoes and, less extensively, other vegetables. In Colorado in 1909 the Japanese numbered 158 in a total of 5,298 farmers growing sugar beets under contract with the beet-sugar companies. In Utah they leased something less than one-fifth of the acreage devoted to beet growing. In Idaho in 1909 they leased 4,922 acres for growing sugar beets, which was almost one-fourth of the acreage devoted to the production of that crop. In several localities in these States the Japanese are the chief truck gardeners. In no case do they have effective control of the beets grown in these States, and the localities in which they produce most of the vegetables, though increasing in number, are still few. In Washington and Oregon the farmers of this race are primarily growers of potatoes, vegetables, and berries, though a few have orchards or poultry yards or dairies. They practically control the acreage devoted to berry growing about Tacoma, Seattle, and Portland and are competing with the growers of other races, but chiefly the Italian, in the vegetable markets of these places. Thirteen of the Texas farms are devoted primarily to growing rice, two are citrus fruit orchards, two are large nurseries, while the remaining eight are truck gardens.

The Japanese farmers of California also are engaged chiefly in intensive farming, which requires much hand labor. Seventy-four were reported among a total of 834 farmers contracting to deliver beets to sugar factories in 6 different localities of the State. They grow by far the larger part of the strawberries, the more important centers of production being Los Angeles County, Florin, Watsonville, and Alviso and Agnews, near San Jose. They grow the larger part of the truck for the markets of Sacramento and Los Angeles, sharing the former chiefly with Chinese and Italians and the latter with Chinese and white men of various races. They grow a large part of the celery in southern California, where all of it was formerly grown by white farmers employing Chinese and Japanese laborers. They also grow much of the deciduous fruit, potatoes, asparagus, beans, and other vegetables. In some of the localities devoted chiefly to growing deciduous fruit, as about Vacaville, Winters, and in the "Newcastle district," the farmers of this race control by lease or purchase the majority of the orchards. In the Santa Clara Valley—another important center of the industry—on the other hand, they control as tenants only a few of the orchards. In several reclamation districts on the Sacramento River, where the land is devoted largely to growing fruit and vegetables, the Japanese in 1909 leased 17,597 of a total of 64,056 acres. Most of the remaining acreage is leased by Chinese, Italians, and Portuguese. On a few islands on the lower San Joaquin they leased 8,592, or 21.4 per cent, of the 40,082. Here the Italians and Chinese are tenants of much of the land, while Americans lease extensively for the production of barley, which is used in the rotation of crops. Japanese are also conspicuous as tenants of vineyards and hopyards in a few communities, as on the American River above Sacramento, and as nurserymen in various parts of the State. Few have engaged in general agriculture.

The Japanese are engaged almost exclusively in producing for the market. They grow sugar beets, fruit, berries, potatoes, or vegetables and little else. Most of those who are not producing fruit do not have orchards. Few of those who are producing fruit have gardens. Their specialization is extreme, as compared to that of other races, and as a rule their leases are for the production of only one or a few crops. Few of them keep cows, unless they are conducting dairies; or pigs, unless they are engaged primarily in raising live stock; or poultry, unless they are conducting poultry yards.

It is difficult to make a general statement concerning the size of farms controlled by Japanese tenants and owners. The great majority of the tracts devoted to the growing of berries and garden truck are small, from 1 to 10 acres, but much larger tracts devoted to these purposes are frequently found. In the growing of potatoes, asparagus, beans, and similar crops, many of the holdings are as large as 50 or 100 acres, but many small holdings are also found. The orchards leased are of various sizes, from a few to 100 acres or even more. The leases of land for the growing of sugar beets frequently cover 100 acres or more, but tracts of 40 or 50 acres or even much less are found.

Perhaps a better index of the scale of production by Japanese farmers is found in the values of crops produced for sale on 444 farms during the year preceding the investigation. In 2 cases the value of the crops sold was less than $50; in 2 others, $50 but less than $100; in 7, $100 but less than $250; in 24, $250 but less than $500; in 49, $500 but less than $1,000; in 47, $1,000 but less than $1,500; in 50, $1,500 but less than $2,000; in 59, $2,000 but less than $3,000; in 79, $3,000 but less than $5,000; in 84, $5,000 but less than $10,000; in 29, $10,000 but less than $25,000; in 12, $25,000 or over. In connection with the comparatively large number where the value of crops sold was small, it should be stated that a large percentage of the holdings had not been fully developed. Of course, it can not be assumed that the proportions here indicated hold true of the Japanese farmers as a whole. The figures do indicate roughly, however, that there are many small and also many large producers among them. The figures presented are for farms in the States of the Western Division and do not include any in the State of Texas where the rice farming is conducted on a large scale.

The Japanese have rapidly risen to the position they now occupy as farmers. In 1900 only 39 Japanese farmers were reported by the census, their holdings aggregating 4,698 acres. The acreage of small subdivisions of farms under lease, and not included in these figures, was very small. Indeed, most of the acreage controlled by them has been acquired since 1904. In California they were reported in the Japanese-American Yearbook as then owning 2,442 acres, leasing 35,258½ acres for cash and 19,572½ acres for a share of the crops. The corresponding figures for 1909 were 16,449½, 80,232, and 59,001½. Most of the land controlled in Oregon and Washington has been acquired within the last five or six years, and in Colorado, Utah, and Idaho within the last three or four.

Their progress has been marked also by a change in the form of tenure, a general advance being evident in most communities from " contract " work to share tenantry, with little capital provided by the tenant, to share tenantry where the tenant furnishes most of the capital and gains some independence as a farmer, to cash tenantry, where he usually provides much of the capital required and is fairly free from control by the landlord. The number of purchases has been small as compared to the number of leases, but has been increasing in recent years as the farmers have accumulated more capital and as the number who have decided to remain permanently in the United States has increased. Moreover, it has been found that a large percentage of those who are tenant farmers are looking forward to the purchase of land. This progress is all the more noteworthy because, with the exception of the large rice growers in Texas and a very few capitalists who have purchased land in the Pacific Coast States, these farmers have practically all risen from the ranks of common laborers. It has been seen that of 490 for whom personal data were secured, 10 upon their arrival in this country engaged in business for themselves and 18 became farmers, while 259 found employment as farm laborers, 103 as railroad laborers, 4 as laborers in sawmills, 54 as domestic servants, and 42 in other occupations.[a]

Among the Japanese farmers every form of land tenure is found, from the nearest approach to a labor contract to independent proprietorship. About Watsonville, Cal., for example, there are many contracts for the handwork involved in growing potatoes, according to which the laborer is paid so much per sack harvested. In the berry fields of the same locality there have been numerous contracts covering a period of years, under which the work done by the laborers is paid at so much per crate harvested. The acreage covered by contracts of this kind has not been included in that reported above as leased by Japanese. Much of the leasing by them in the past and no small part of the leasing by them at present, however, differs but little from such contracts as these. The landowner provides all necessary equipment, except, perhaps, crates needed for shipping, does the work with teams or hires it done, possibly pays the wages of a part or all of the employees, manages the business in all of its details, sells the products and collects the selling price, and shares this with the tenant after all bills have been paid. Much of the leasing of orchards about Vacaville and elsewhere in California and a considerable part of the leasing of land for the growing of sugar beets and of vegetables on an extensive scale takes this form and differs little in most respects from a contract for the hand labor for the season, except that the tenant's remuneration depends upon the amount of the crop produced and its price in the market. In still other cases the landowner furnishes all permanent equipment but very little of the other capital required, and the tenant does all of the work or hires it done, many of the details of management, but few of the details of marketing the product passing into his hands, and the crop is shared between the contracting parties. Much of the leasing of orchards in the Newcastle district, of land for growing sugar beets in several localities, and of some strawberry patches about Watsonville takes this form. In still other cases the share tenant provides some, possibly most, of the equipment. Not very different from this is much of the leasing with cash rent. In some instances the landowner provides all or almost all of the equipment required, while in others he provides little or none, and the tenant pays so much per acre or a variable sum per acre, according to yield, as rent. As a rule, however, the change from share to cash rental signifies that the tenant provides more of the capital required, becomes responsible for all of the labor which must be performed, and is fairly independent in the management of the business, except, perhaps, the marketing of the product. A large part of the land devoted to the growing of sugar beets, many of the orchards, most of the berry fields, and much, if not most, of the land devoted to the production of "green vegetables" takes this form. As stated, the Japanese tenants in many localities have progressed from labor under contract to share tenantry, to cash tenantry, as they have gained experience, commanded the confidence of landowners, and accumulated the necessary capital.

In connection with these details relating to tenure, it is noteworthy that of 490 Japanese farming as individuals or as senior partners, covered by the investigation, 165, or 33.7 per cent of the entire number, owned no horses, and 99 owned neither horses nor implements. Of the 325 who owned horses, 95 had 1; 116, 2 or 3; 55, 4 to 6; and 57 from 7 to 25, and in some cases even more. The value of the live stock and implements owned by 48 was less than $50; by 17, $50 but less than $100; by 88, $100 but less than $250; by 83, $250 but less than $500; by 75, $500 but less than $1,000; by 24, $1,000 but less than $1,500; by 33, $1,500 but less than $2,500; by 19, $2,500 but less than $5,000; and by 4, $5,000 but less than $10,000, the total number reporting being 391.

Several factors have cooperated to make possible the progress of the Japanese as tenant farmers, which has been indicated. Not the least important in many localities has been the dominant position occupied by the laborers of this race. In many instances leasing has been resorted to as a method of securing a nucleus of a desired labor supply and of transferring to the tenants the solution of the problem of obtaining the other laborers needed. The beet-sugar companies in Colorado, Utah, and Idaho have encouraged the leasing of land by Japanese as well as by German-Russians, brought to the community to do the seasonal work in the beet fields, in order to keep them in the community, and to make it easier year after year to secure the desired number of men.

In many localities in California the same motive has caused many orchardists and others to lease their holdings to Japanese as the predominant element in the labor supply just as they did less extensively to the less ambitious Chinese at an earlier time. By leasing to one or several Japanese, the nucleus of the necessary labor supply is obtained and the tenant or tenants serve as "bosses" to obtain the other laborers needed during the busiest seasons. In many cases leases have been transferred from Chinese to Japanese as the number of Chinese laborers decreased, and the Japanese became the predominant element in the labor supply. Moreover, as a large number of farms have been leased to the Japanese in one locality and the members of that race have done more of the work on these holdings, it has become increasingly difficult for other farmers to obtain desirable laborers of that race, so that a still greater premium is placed upon leasing the land. Thus the system tends to spread and become general, the farms falling under the control of the race which predominates in the labor supply, especially if the race is ambitious and capable as the Japanese is.

At the same time the Japanese have been very anxious to lease land and have generally been the highest bidders among those wishing to become tenant farmers. Their strong desire to lease land is explained by several facts. In the first place, the members of this race do not like to work for wages, are ambitious, and desire to establish themselves as business men or as independent producers, as most of them were in their native land. This ambition to rise from the ranks of the wage-earners has been one of the characteristics most strongly exhibited by the Japanese and must be emphasized in explaining their progress either in business or in independent farming. Moreover, as has been indicated, decided limitations have been placed upon the occupational advance of the Japanese. Unless employed by their countrymen few have been able to rise to occupations above that of common unskilled labor. This situation has cooperated, with the general ambition of the Japanese, to place a great premium upon independent farming or business. Moreover, by leasing land the farm laborer secures a settled residence, more regular employment, and, if he has a family, an opportunity to reunite it in this country under normal conditions. The differences shown by the Japanese farmers and the farm laborers as groups, as regards the percentage who are married and the percentage who have their wives with them in this country, are not explained entirely by the difference in their age distribution or in their incomes. The differences in both cases are closely connected with the fact that most of the laborers can not secure tolerable conditions under which to live with their families, while the farmer and his family can lead a normal family life.

Furthermore, the Japanese are venturesome. They are not deterred by risk to the same extent that the members of other races are, and are greatly attracted by the unusual profits realized by a few of their countrymen. In some instances it has been found that not only are they highly speculative in their economic activities, but that they are inclined to reckon expenses and losses at too low a figure. All of these things have combined to cause the farm laborer to desire to become a farmer on his own account, and pride and the limited field of employment have frequently kept him from returning to the wage-earning class when the profits realized from farming have been small.

But whatever the explanation of the strong desire evinced by the Japanese to become independent farmers, it is true that the desire is so strong that they have been willing, as a rule, to pay comparatively high rents. In a few localities, as about Vacaville, Cal., they have even resorted to coercion in the form of threat to withhold the necessary labor supply, in order to secure the tenure of orchards or farms they desired. Such instances, however, have been limited to a few localities. The offer of comparatively high rents, though not universal, is fairly general. About Los Angeles the Japanese tenants have offered higher rents than had previously been paid by the Chinese for the same kind of land to be used for similar purposes.

On the Sacramento and San Joaquin rivers the Japanese have in some instances displaced Chinese by paying higher share or cash rents. In another instance they displaced the Italian tenants. About Vacaville and Newcastle—in fact, in almost every locality in California, it was found that the farmers of this race had been willing to pay higher rents than had previously obtained. This is true also about Portland, Oreg., Tacoma and Seattle, Wash., and in the beet fields of Colorado. The rivalry among the Japanese for land in Colorado was so great that an agricultural association, which they had organized about Lupton, fixed a maximum rental which should not be exceeded in the leasing of land for the production of sugar beets. As a fairly general phenomenon, the Japanese, for reasons already stated, have been willing to pay higher rents than the members of other races, and because of that fact much land has been leased to them, for it was more profitable to the owner to do so than to farm it himself, and, other things being equal, the Japanese have been preferred in the selection of tenants.

Not only have they been willing to pay comparatively high share or cash rents; in some instances their advance has been due to a willingness to make improvements upon lands, which the farmers of other races not so prominent in the labor supply were not willing to do. Thus about Tacoma much of the leasing of land by Japanese has been incidental to removing the brush and stumps from " logged-off " land, drainage of the land, and reducing it to cultivation. The land has been leased for a period of one or a few years, reclaimed, and brought under cultivation. The Japanese show a greater willingness than others to do such work as a part of their contracts. The same thing is found to be true in the leasing of the newly reclaimed land of the Sacramento and San Joaquin River Valleys, and has been met with in various other localities in the course of the investigation.

Another reason for the preference for Japanese in many cases has been that they are more easily provided with living quarters than white men are. In many cases the Japanese lease only the orchards, or the " beet land," or the " berry land;" or the " vegetable land " on a farm, and live in the laborers' quarters, while the farmer with his family continues to occupy the farmhouse and to cultivate the rest of the land. Moreover, where the entire farm is leased to Japanese, the owner and his family usually continue to live there and the tenant is housed in a cheap cottage or in the " bunk house." The buildings erected for Japanese tenants are usually much less expensive than those required for a white farmer and his family. In some instances, as about Los Angeles and Tacoma, they have built their own shelters of materials provided by the landowner or by themselves. Thus the Japanese have had the advantages incidental to the fact that in many instances they have been the predominant element in the labor supply, that they have generally been willing to pay higher rents and to take land on conditions not acceptable to white tenants, and have been the most easily provided for when settled upon the land.

Another fact of importance in this connection is that many of the Japanese farmers have required little or no capital to begin with. As already indicated, many, in fact most of them to begin with, have leased land for a share of the crop, the landlord supplying all or practically all of the equipment. This is especially true in all localities where much seasonal labor is required and the Japanese are the predominant element in the labor supply. In these localities not only have the farmers provided most of the necessary equipment, but have also frequently provided the money necessary to pay current expenses, so that the tenant required no capital at all. Moreover, in the production of sugar beets the beet-sugar companies have ordinarily advanced a part of the necessary capital.[a] At Newcastle and Vacaville, and in other localities devoted to the growing of fruit and vegetables, the commission merchants usually make advances of supplies for shipping the product, and of cash, taking a lien upon the crop in order to secure the loan. In several instances the competition between the shippers for business has led to the making of advances long before the crop matures, and in large amounts. About Newcastle it was found that some of the shippers had leased land and then subleased it to Japanese tenants in order to control the business of shipping the product. With assistance in these forms (extended to other growers also) the Japanese laborers with little or no capital have been able to begin tenant farming. And even where the system of making advances has not been extensively adopted the tenants who pay cash rent usually do not need much capital of their own, for it is customary to pay the rent in installments, and credit is extended by the Japanese and other provision merchants. In some instances, as about Florin, Cal., leasing has been encouraged by arranging for the larger rentals to be paid during the later years covered by the lease.

Finally, the Japanese in many localities have usually formed partnerships when leasing land. In some cases this is virtually required by the landlords, in order that there may be a larger nucleus for the needed labor supply and that the tenants may be more closely held to the terms of their contract because of the greater amount of labor they invest in growing the crops. It is significant that 194 of 462 tenant farms investigated were leased by partners. There were two partners in 116 of the 194 cases, three in 36, four in 22, five in 12, six in 2, seven in 3, nine in 1, and ten in 2. The formation of partnerships enables the Japanese to engage in farming with less individual capital, and has made it possible for them, like the Italians among whom this form of organization prevails in leasing land, to quickly establish themselves as farmers.

Most of the land owned by Japanese is in California, Texas, and Oregon. In the other States the number of farms which have been purchased is few and the acreage is small. That no land has been purchased by them in Washington and Idaho is explained by the fact that in those States aliens may not acquire title to it by purchase.[b] Most of the land purchased in Texas is in a few large tracts and is owned by corporations or by wealthy individuals who have come to this country to invest their capital in speculative enterprises. Some have immigrated with $10,000 or more; one of the farms owned by them embraces 3,500 acres, another 2,224, a third 1,734. At Liv-

---

[a] See "Japanese and German-Russian Farmers of Northern Colorado" and "Japanese Farmers of Northern Utah."

[b] Constitution of Washington, Article II, section 33, and Idaho, Revised Code, section 2609. In both States these provisions were adopted before there was any question as to the desirability of Japanese immigrants.

ingstone, Cal., a large tract of land has been purchased by a Japanese corporation and is being disposed of to Japanese farmers in small holdings on the installment plan.[a] Moreover, in a few instances, as in Oregon, large tracts have been purchased by Japanese who have accumulated wealth by selling supplies or by contracting for labor.

With such exceptions as these, the purchases have been made in comparatively small tracts by men who have risen from the ranks of labor, and have successfully engaged in farming as tenants. They have been assisted in making their purchases by the extension of liberal credit. Some of these farms are valuable, however. Of 44 investigated, embracing 1,849 acres, four were worth $500 but less than $1,000, four, $1,000 but less than $1,500, eight, $1,500 but less than $2,500, fourteen, $2,500 but less than $5,000, five, $5,000 but less than $10,000, seven, $10,000 but less than $25,000, and two more than $25,000. In all of these cases the owners had come to this country with little or no capital. High prices have been paid for land in some instances, but the number of purchases has been so small and scattered over so many communities that they have had no effect upon the market value of land.

In a large number of localities the Japanese farmers are organized into farmers' associations. Such institutions are found in various localities about Tacoma and Seattle, about Ogden, about Lupton, Colo., and along the Sacramento River, about Agnews, Moneta, and in various other localities in California. In some instance these act as agents in finding ranches for Japanese who wish to become tenants; in a few cases they limit the competition for land by fixing a maximum rental, as about Lupton, Colo.; in a very few cases they assist in marketing the product and in obtaining supplies, as some of those

---

[a] Somewhat similar to the venture at Livingstone is that in Dade County, Fla., where the Yamato colony was organized in 1904. This colony is incorporated under the statutes of the State of Florida. The president of the corporation and the head of the colony is one J. Sakai, a Japanese land agent of the Florida East Coast Railway. The corporation owns or has an option on a few sections of land, a part of which is being farmed in the name of the colony until such time as it can be sold to Japanese. When the colony was first established it had 23 members, all of whom were adult men. Sakai has gone to Japan at different times to secure more members, but of those who have come some 60 have deserted, leaving 37 in the colony in the spring of 1908. Of these 37, 34 were men, 2 women, and 1 an infant. Almost all of the members of the colony came directly from their native land, but it is said that 3 or 4 have joined the colony after having lived in the Western States. Practically all of those who have come have been drawn from the larger cities of Japan. Some of them were novelty makers, other silk weavers, and still others students and bankers. Being used to city life and city trades, the majority have found the hard agricultural work in the warm and humid climate disagreeable, hence the desertions mentioned above.

The majority of those residing in the colony work for wages for the corporations; a minority have purchased land or leased land for a share of the crop. About 80 acres have been set in pineapples. While these are developing the colonists raise tomatoes, peppers, and other vegetables of various kinds.

The land is sold on the installment plan, for from $6 to $25 per acre in its "wild" condition. After it is cleared and reduced to cultivation it is worth as much as $300 per acre. Most of the land has been cleared by negro laborers.

Some of the Japanese find employment in a packinghouse at Del Rey, not far away, while others were employed during the season of 1908 in a canning factory near by.

about Tacoma, Seattle, and Ogden; in several instances they interest themselves where disputes arise between landlord and tenant; while in several instances they have had more or less to do with the dissemination of scientific knowledge of horticulture and agriculture among the Japanese farmers.   One publication issued by the organization in the Stockton district is particularly interesting in this last connection.   These organizations are of interest, chiefly, however, as evidence of the capacity of the Japanese to cooperate and secure the advantages of organized effort in meeting the problems confronting them.

Independent farming by Japanese has had several effects upon the communities in which it is carried on.   It is evident from what has been stated that the competition of Japanese tenants has caused the rental value of land to increase.   It is evident, also, that tenants of other races, to some extent, have been displaced by them.   Another effect more difficult to measure has been that of the presence of farmers of this race upon the influx of white families to the community.   There can be no doubt that the extensive leasing by them about Newcastle and in a few other localities has caused prospective settlers to locate elsewhere, and the white population of some neighborhoods has actually diminished.   In other words, there has been a partial substitution of Asiatic for white families.   But it should be noted in this connection that in some communities much of the land leased was reclaimed and reduced to cultivation by Japanese, or was first devoted to intensive farming by them.   In such cases they have added to the wealth of the community and their farming has not necessarily affected the white population adversely.   Another effect of leasing by Japanese, as by Chinese and other races similarly circumstanced, has been to encourage the holding of large tracts of land by corporations or as " estates," and to remove the premium which would otherwise be placed upon their subdivision and sale to white farmers.   This is very evident upon the Sacramento and San Joaquin Rivers, where in some instances several hundred or several thousand acres are owned in one or a few tracts, and the managers prefer to retain them as investments and to lease them to Italians or Asiatics at comparatively high rentals, rather than subdivide them and dispose of them to permanent settlers.   While some of these holdings are in communities which have not been developed to the point where white families would care to live, this is by no means true of all.   Leasing in the form which there obtains places a premium upon landlordism which will stand in the way of the normal settlement and development of these communities.

One characteristic of Japanese farming is that with their short-time interests the farmers frequently specialize greatly in the production of the crop which has proved to be more than usually profitable.   As a result of the rapid increase in the number of these farmers in certain localities and this specialization, overproduction has resulted and profitable prices could not be maintained.   This is especially true of the strawberry industry, which has been expanded rapidly by the Japanese because of handsome profits realized a few years ago, until the prices have become very unremunerative.   Nearly all of the few white farmers and many of the Japanese have now withdrawn from this branch of production.   A similar instance of overproduction is found in asparagus growing on the Sacramento River, where many of the Japanese tenants have been involved in great loss during the last two years. The prices of some vegetables about Tacoma and Seattle also appear to have been adversely affected by the larger acreage devoted to their production with the increasing number of Japanese farmers. It appears that other farmers withdraw from the production of such crops before the Japanese, because they are not satisfied with as small profits.

But the instances where the prices realized for crops have been adversely affected as a result of Japanese competition are comparatively few. As a matter of fact, where their acreage has been added to that productively used in the community it has generally been devoted to growing crops not extensively grown by white farmers. Moreover, most of the markets are not local and narrowly limited. The effect of Japanese farming upon the rental value of land is much more general than any effect upon the prices of produce.

Another effect of the leasing of orchards and other ranches under cultivation to Japanese has been to cause a further displacement of laborers of other races. Except for some of the work with teams and the cutting of fruit preparatory to drying nearly all of the laborers employed by these farmers in the West are of their own race.[a] While numerous instances are found in which white men and women and Hindus are temporarily employed by them, these are after all comparatively few. Like the Italian, Portuguese, and Chinese farmers, they usually employ the members of their own race in so far as they can secure them. The only essential difference between the races in this regard is found in the fact that the Japanese laborers have been available in larger numbers than the others. In so far as comparisons of wages have been possible, it has been found that the Japanese farmers frequently pay their countrymen somewhat more than they are paid by other farmers for work of the same kind. It must be noted in this connection, however, that the workday is somewhat longer, and that, in some instances, they have been able to secure the best laborers in the available supply.

Moreover, until a few years ago, they had the advantage, as compared to farmers who employed higher priced laborers, possessed by all farmers who employed the Japanese at the lower wages which then prevailed. Yet the Japanese farmer's workday is not so long as that of the Italian, and he has always paid his laborers as high or higher wages. It is clear that Japanese farming has given rise to a further displacement of laborers of other races. While it is not clear that their outlay for labor is now less than that of their white competitors, and while it is clear that it is certainly not less than that of the Italians, the situation was somewhat different a few years ago when Japanese labor was cheaper.

In several localities in California where the Chinese have been employed or have leased land there is much dissatisfaction with the Japanese tenants. There is no doubt that they are less careful workmen than the Chinese, and that their farming is frequently inferior. It is generally agreed that the Chinese who have had long experience, and this counts for much, are better pruners of trees and vines and

---

[a] On the rice farms in Texas this is not true.

prepare the product better for shipment. There has also been much complaint of broken contracts in the case of the Japanese. The complaint is not without reason, for the Japanese do not regard a contract as inviolable, while the Chinese do. In some communities a few Japanese farmers have not fulfilled their contracts, just as a few " contractors " have run away with the wages due their laborers. In some localities the preference for Chinese, partly racial, however, has been so great that farms have been leased to them for a lower rental than Japanese have offered.

This is not infrequently true in the leasing of orchards. The preference for Chinese tenants has become just as marked as for Chinese laborers in most of the California communities. It is noteworthy, however, that in communities where Chinese have not been employed and do not serve as a standard for comparisons no complaint was made of the character of the farming of the Japanese, and little complaint was heard of failure to fulfill their contracts. On the contrary, in such communities they are generally regarded as good tenant farmers and as " fairly reliable " in their contractual relations.

Some of the Japanese farmers have realized large profits and have accumulated wealth rapidly, while many have met with loss. In some cases they have fallen back into the ranks of the wage-earning class. Some of those who have not been successful have been too inexperienced in the kind of farming undertaken. A more common cause of failure, however, has been found in the fact, already commented on, that they produce almost entirely for the market and specialize greatly, and in some cases have depressed the prices of produce until they would not cover the expenses incidental to the harvest. This is notably true of strawberry growing for the Los Angeles market and of asparagus growing on the lower Sacramento River, cases to which reference has previously been made. A comparatively large number of the tenant farmers in these localities have become bankrupt, and some of them have been led to break their contracts with the landowners from whom they leased. Moreover, the wages paid to laborers of their race have recently advanced rapidly and it has become difficult to secure laborers in sufficient numbers. This change in the labor market has been a further source of difficulty to the Japanese farmers. It is proving so serious that in some localities they insist upon leases for one or a few years, where a few years ago they desired to secure leases for a period of several years.

Of 647 Japanese farmers, including partners, from whom information was obtained, 432 reported that they had made a surplus over living expenses during the preceding year. Of the other 215, 114 were involved in a deficit while 101 reported that they had neither surplus nor deficit. The average amount of surplus realized was $579.88; of deficit, $561.02. Some of the gains were very large. Those of 31 of the 432 were less than $100; of 92, $100 but less than $250; of 146, $250 but less than $500; of 114, $500 but less than $1,000; of 35, $1,000 but less than $2,500; of 14, $2,500 or over. Some of the deficits also were large. Those of 5 of the 114 were less than $100; of 27, $100 but less than $250; of 37, $250 but less than $500;

of 23, $500 but less than $1,000; of 20, $1,000 but less than $2,500; of 2, $2,500 or over. These figures must not be taken too literally, however, for the amount of surplus and deficit, especially in farming, is difficult to estimate. Moreover, and more important, no allowance is made for investments in developing strawberry patches and asparagus and other crops which require two seasons before the plants begin to yield a remunerative harvest. The failure of the figures to make allowance for such cases greatly exaggerates the number who sustained deficits and increases the amount of deficits reported.

The estimated value of property owned by 488 Japanese engaged in farming as individuals or as senior partners was ascertained by the agents of the Commission. Many of them are in debt for land or supplies purchased or for advances made, so that the value of their property over and above indebtedness is frequently very much less than the gross value of the property in their possession. Of the 488, 86 had nothing over and above the indebtedness outstanding against them; 16 had less than $50; 10 had $50 but less than $100; 45, $100 but less than $250; 77, $250 but less than $500; 92, $500 but less than $1,000; 48, $1,000 but less than $1,500; 43, $1,500 but less than $2,500; 41, $2,500 but less than $5,000; 17, $5,000 but less than $10,000; 10, $10,000 but less than $25,000; and 3, $25,000 or over. In considering these figures, it must be held in mind, however, that they do not include the value of growing crops and of such improvements made upon leased land as do not become the property of the tenant upon the expiration of the lease. The fact that allowance is not made for these causes the number who are represented as having little or no property to be unduly large, for most of the data were collected during the harvest season when large investments had been made but before the returns for the crop had been received. Moreover, many of the Japanese invest heavily in improvements in the land, hoping to secure a profit from them before the expiration of the lease. The value of such improvements can not be estimated, however, and is not included in the values given.

In most localities the Japanese are the most recent race to engage in farming on their own account, so that there is a striking contrast between them and the other farmers in the West—in wealth as well as in the form of tenure and permanency of their relations in the community. While many of the Japanese farmers have accumulated considerable property and have become fairly independent in the conduct of their holdings, the largest number have little property and many of them have a form of tenure which limits their freedom in production. Moreover, because of the circumstances under which they have engaged in farming an unusually large number of the Japanese have failed. Yet it must be held in mind that most of them have begun to farm much more recently than the farmers of other races. The wealth accumulated by a small minority in a few years has induced many to undertake farming on their own account.

CHAPTER V

JAPANESE IN CITY EMPLOYMENTS AND BUSINESS.

JAPANESE IN DOMESTIC AND PERSONAL SERVICE AND RELATED EMPLOYMENTS.

As opposed to those employed in the various industries discussed in the preceding chapters, perhaps between 12,000 and 15,000 Japanese are employed in the 11 States and Territories comprising the Western Division, as domestic servants in private families, and as "help" in restaurants, hotels, barrooms, clubs, offices, and stores conducted by members of the white races,[a] while some 10,000 or 11,000

---

[a] It is estimated that between 8,000 and 10,000 are employed in these capacities in the cities and towns and on the farms of California, but any estimate for the State as a whole or for any city must necessarily be largely a matter of guesswork. The nature of these employments is such that even those most familiar with them differ widely in the estimates made. Only a census would reveal the approximate number. The estimates here made are based upon the estimates of Japanese employment agents, those of union officials in the trades embraced under personal service, and those of the secretaries of Japanese associations. The corresponding number for Washington is perhaps between 2,800 and 3,000; for Oregon, 600; for Colorado, 300; for Utah, 250; for Nevada, 175; for Arizona, 150; for Montana, 120; for Idaho, from 40 to 70, according to the season of the year; for Wyoming, 50.

Agents of the Commission made a general investigation of Japanese employed in domestic service and related occupations in Seattle, Tacoma, Portland, San Francisco, Los Angeles, Denver, and Salt Lake. The character of the employments is such that only the more general facts can be ascertained without the expenditure of much more time than the details warrant and than that at the command of the Commission's agents. Japanese business was investigated in a comparatively large number of places named below. General information was collected with reference to the situation, and schedules were collected for 368 business establishments conducted by them in Seattle, San Francisco, Los Angeles, Sacramento, Fresno, and Watsonville, for 439 business men of these cities, and for 427 wage-earners and salaried men. "Individual slips" were also collected from several hundred men employed in the establishments investigated or elsewhere, or living in boarding and lodging houses or in groups of house cleaners. The general results of the investigation are set forth in this chapter, the emphasis being placed upon those cities in which the largest number of Japanese residents are found, and in which they have been engaged in domestic and other work and in business for the greatest length of time. The details are set forth at greater length in a number of special reports as follows: "The Japanese in city employments and business in Washington, with special reference to Seattle;" "The Japanese in city employments and business in Portland, Oreg.;" "The Japanese in city employments and business in San Francisco;" "The Japanese in city employments and business in Sacramento;" "The Japanese in city employments and business in Los Angeles;" "Japanese in city employments and business in Salt Lake City and Ogden, Utah;" "Japanese in city employments and business in Denver, Colo.;" "The Japanese in business in Idaho;" "Immigrants in Fresno County, Cal.;" "The Japanese of Pajaro Valley, Cal.;" and "Immigrant laborers and farmers in the Vaca Valley, Cal." The first eight of these are grouped so as to form a series, while the last three are reports dealing primarily with immigrant agricultural labor and immigrant farming (in which the Japanese in the town trades and employments are incidentally discussed), and are therefore to be found in Volume II of this report, relating to agriculture.

91

more are engaged in business for themselves or are employed by those who are thus occupied, or are professional men and craftsmen working on their own account. Few are found in city employments other than those indicated.

The number engaged in this group of occupations varies greatly from one season to another, for during the spring and summer months many leave most of the cities and towns, in which they spend the winter, for work in fish and vegetable canneries and in the beet fields, orchards, and gardens. With the close of the " busy " season in these places many return to the cities to find employment as house cleaners, domestic, and general help, or to live upon their savings until the spring months return. The figures given would perhaps be too conservative as an estimate of the number of Japanese engaged in these occupations during the winter months.

Most of the Japanese employed in this group of occupations are found in a few cities which have large populations of that race, and are with one exception ports at which many immigrants of this race have arrived. The number so employed in Seattle is perhaps about 2,400, in Tacoma 150, in Portland 470, in San Francisco possibly 4,000, in Los Angeles possibly 2,000. Upon their arrival most have found work through Japanese " contractors " and employment agents. The Japanese contractors have directed the majority into railway or agricultural work, while a large percentage of the others have engaged in domestic service in its broader meaning. The student class and farmers' sons and those who had not been gainfully occupied in their native land have furnished a large percentage of those engaging in domestic service. The same is true of the business men. The work is less arduous than in the country, the conditions of living are materially better, and the opportunity to learn English and certain American methods are present. It is a significant fact that of 490 men now engaged in farming 54 found their first employment in domestic service. The corresponding figure for 317 employed at present as agricultural laborers was 13. Only 11 of the former and 7 of the latter engaged in other city occupations. Of 433 men now engaged in business on their own account, on the other hand, 138 found their first employment as house servants, 5 as members of house-cleaning groups, and 66 in other city employments, but chiefly as restaurant "help." The corresponding figures for 410 wage-earners in various city occupations were 148, 10, and 101. The large number found in Los Angeles is explained partly by the favorable climatic conditions which prevail there, but largely by the fact that many migrated to that city as a result of the fire in San Francisco in 1906. These cities, with Oakland, have the largest numbers of Japanese engaged in this group of occupations. Sacramento has perhaps 300, Denver 230, Salt Lake City 150, and other cities comparatively small numbers. In the aggregate, however, the number found in the smaller cities and towns of Washington and California, and upon farms in the latter State, is large.

For convenience this general group may be divided into four minor groups, viz, those engaged as cooks and other servants in private families; house-cleaners, and other " day workers;" those employed in restaurants, hotels, barrooms, and clubs; and those employed as general help in offices and stores conducted by white men.

It is very difficult to obtain accurate data with reference to the number of Japanese and other house servants, the wages they are now and have in the past been paid for the same kind of work, and what the effect of Japanese competition has been. Briefly the results obtained in San Francisco and Seattle and set forth at greater length in the special reports dealing with the Japanese in city trades and employments in those places are these: In San Francisco it is probable that some 700 or 800 Japanese were employed as house servants in 1898, and that the number had increased to more than 3,600 in 1904. More recently, however, with the restrictions upon immigration, their tendency to leave domestic service for other work or to engage in business, and the higher wages they command so that there is no longer the same pecuniary advantage that was formerly found in employing them, their number has diminished and is possibly at present not far from 2,000 in a total of several times as many. Perhaps from 300 to 500 of these are " school boys " who work short hours and in return receive board and lodging and from $8 to $16 per month, the sum depending upon the number of hours of work over that (three or four per day) regarded as an equivalent for board and lodging. A part of the day or the evening is spent in attending classes or in private study. Those regularly employed as domestics in 1909 were paid from $25 per month for those with little experience as house servants to $60 per month for the most experienced cooks. The average wage per month of 70, from whom personal data were secured, was $36.86. Though the number from which this average is derived is small, it probably reflects the situation very well. The wages now paid are materially higher than those formerly prevailing. According to the records of Japanese employment agents the prevailing rate for plain cooks in 1900 was $20 to $30 per month. By 1903 the rate had advanced $5 per month, and ·by 1907 another advance of $5 had taken place.

The field of domestic service in private families is shared chiefly by Japanese and Chinese men,[a] and white women, of whom many are foreign born. Since the Japanese have immigrated to San Francisco in large numbers the Chinese have materially diminished in number as a result of the exclusion acts. The Japanese have much more than made good the decrease in the number of Chinese employed, but with the growth of population and the larger number of families keeping servants, it appears unlikely that the increasing number of Japanese servants at any time caused an actual decrease in the number of white domestics in employment. Though the Japanese, at any rate until recently, have been regarded as the cheapest servants for cooking, waiting on table, and cleaning (the kinds of work they have done),[b] there has generally been a scarcity of white

[a] Contrary to the custom in Honolulu, very few Japanese women take employment as domestic servants in the Western States.

[b] It is impossible to compare the wages of Chinese, Japanese, and white women, for the occupations of these persons when employed as domestics differ. For years the Chinese men have done practically no work except cooking and some cleaning incidental to that; the Japanese have been occupied in the same way, except that they do somewhat more of the work about the house. A large percentage of the white females, on the other hand, are " women of all work."

servants at the wages offered, though these wages have been increasing.[a]

In Seattle the Japanese domestics number about 1,200. The number of Japanese now employed is about the same as the number (1,217) of female servants and waitresses in Seattle reported by the census in 1900. With the phenomenal growth in population, the number of domestics has increased several fold, and doubtless the number of females so employed has increased during this time, in spite of the fact that the wages of Japanese were formerly lower than they now are. No doubt, however, the influx of Japanese has caused the wages of other domestics to rise less rapidly than they would otherwise have done, for the Japanese have added greatly to the number available for such work. But here, as throughout the Western States, and especially in the Pacific Coast States, there has been a scarcity of servants at the comparatively high wages which they command—wages which compare most favorably with those of women engaged in other occupations in the same cities and much higher than the wages which prevail in eastern localities. It should be added, moreover, that the presence of Asiatics in domestic service has not had the effect of causing it to be regarded as essentially Asiatic work, and to be shunned by others, as has been the case with certain occupations in some agricultural communities of California.

Closely related to the branch of domestic service just discussed is the work done by Japanese " day workers." These men usually live in groups, averaging 5 or 6 in San Francisco, but in some instances containing sevral times as many, and go to private houses to do house cleaning, window cleaning, cooking, waiting on table, and gardening " on call." Frequently they live with cobblers, and at the cobbler shops, or other offices maintained, receive orders for work to be done.

The Japanese alone have made an organized effort to meet the desires of those in need of temporary and irregular service, and in California for years a large number have been thus occupied. The largest number are found in San Francisco, where in 1909 the number of groups reported by the Japanese-American Yearbook was 148. The number of persons in the groups was reported at 984, so that if allowance is made for individuals not connected with the groups reported, the number in the winter season, when it is largest, would be somewhat in excess of 1,000. The number of groups in Los Angeles is reported for 1909 as 18, a few of which are comparatively large. In almost every California town in which the Japanese have settled one or more of these house-cleaning groups is to be found. In other States, however, few exist, the largest number being in Denver, where there are 4 groups with an aggregate membership of about 130.

The position these " day workers " occupy is best shown by the investigation made of them in San Francisco. In addition to obtaining general information covering them, 14 groups, comprising 53 men, were investigated and personal schedules taken for each member.

[a] See Report on Japanese in City Trades and Employments and Business in San Francisco for such statistical data as are available in the reports of the (California) State Bureau of Labor Statistics.

The wage for cleaning was 30 or 35 cents per hour (depending largely upon whether calls from the given place were numerous or infrequent), or $2.50 per day; for waiting on table, 35 or 50 cents (with white coat), or $1 (with dress coat); for gardening, 50 cents per hour; for window cleaning, 5 cents per window. As would be expected, the work is irregular, so that the earnings of the 53 house cleaners varied between $20 per month as a minimum and $70 as a maximum. The average of the earnings of the 53 was $42.74 per month and $512.83 per year. The earnings of 4 were less than $30 per month; of 15, $30, but less than $40; of 12, $40, but less than $50; of 15, $50; of 6, $60, but less than $70; of 1, $70 per month. Their earnings per day were higher than formerly, when the number of newly arrived Japanese was larger than during the last two years. According to the testimony of Japanese employment agents, the rate per day for ordinary cleaning was $1.50 in 1900. By 1903 it had risen to $1.75, by 1907 to $2 per day.[a]

A large number of Japanese were found to be employed in restaurants, hotel kitchens, barrooms, and similar places in Seattle, San Francisco, and Los Angeles. Smaller numbers were so employed in Portland, Sacramento, Salt Lake City, and other localities. In Seattle some 400 (not including 300 employed on boats on Puget Sound) were, in 1909, employed in restaurants and hotels, and some 200 more in barrooms and clubs. In San Francisco and Los Ageles the number employed in these places is much larger. In Portland, on the other hand, if the few employed as porters in stores conducted by white persons are included, the corresponding number is about 120, in Salt Lake, possibly 35. Any estimate, however, is at best a rough one, for accurate data as regards the number of Japanese and of others employed in these places can be obtained only by making a census of a very large percentage of them—which the Commission did not undertake to do. Any considerable number of Japanese gainfully employed in these places conducted by white men, however, are to be found only in the cities of the Pacific Coast States, where the settled Japanese population is large, and where comparatively large numbers have resided for more than eight or ten years.

In San Francisco a few hundred Japanese are employed as cooks' helpers, dishwashers, and general "kitchen help" in restaurants and hotels conducted by white men, as against, perhaps, 1,000 white persons employed in these capacities. They are generally paid $30, $35, or $40 per month, with board. These wages are less than the union scale—about one-third of the white men engaged in these occupations in 1909 were members of the Cooks' Helpers' Union—for a six-day week of twelve hours per day. The union scale in effect provides for a wage of $12 per week for cooks' helpers and pantrymen, and $10 per week for "vegetable men," dishwashers, porters, and "miscellaneous help," with 25 cents per hour for overtime, with board, in restaurants, and for $45 and $35 per month for the two classes, respectively, with "found," in hotels. The nonunion whites, many of whom are very young or very old men, have no trade, and shift from place to place, are paid smaller wages. For 947 men supplied during 1907 and 1908 by San Francisco employment agencies for positions as "kitchen help," the median wage reported was $30 per month.[b]

---

[a] Quoted from Report on the Japanese in City Employments and Business in San Francisco.

[b] As reported in the Thirteenth Biennial Report of the Bureau of Labor Statistics of the State of California, p. 150. Approximately 45 per cent of the number reported were employed outside of San Francisco, but chiefly in the cities on the other side of San Francisco Bay, where about the same scale of wages prevails.

The Japanese now earn higher wages than those reported for the nonunion white men, but they are men in the prime of life and frequently, if not usually, work for seven days per week. Moreover, the wages of Japanese have increased in these occupations, as they have in domestic service. White men have been displaced to a certain extent because the Japanese have been—

willing to do various kinds of work regarded by the union man as no part of his occupation, and to work seven days per week, as the union men do not. Moreover, they have worked for less than the union scale of wages, while they are more capable and more regular in their habits than many of the nonunion white men, who receive about the same or less wages.[a]

In so far as known, Japanese have not been employed as cooks or as waiters in restaurants or hotels in San Francisco. They have, however, been employed in these capacities to some extent in saloons, but here Chinese cooks have been far more numerous and the Japanese have commonly been employed to serve the free lunches, to do cleaning, and to act as porters. They have never been employed in any considerable number in saloons frequented extensively by workingmen, however, and as a result of a movement initiated in the spring of 1909 by the Asiatic Exclusion League to restrict their employment, by the end of the year they were employed in fewer public houses than formerly. Before the "campaign" was made against them they were found in a large percentage of the saloons of the city, which in 1907 numbered 2,375.[b]

It would appear that the situation in Seattle and Los Angeles is not materially different from that in San Francisco. As kitchen and barroom help, the Japanese in Seattle have displaced white persons, though this displacement is by no means complete. Their wages are usually $10, less frequently $11, $12, or $13, per week of seven days, with board, but not lodging, included. The secretary of the Cooks and Waiters' Union of Seattle asserts that—

there is no longer any regular scale of wages for white employees engaged in this line of work, but from the few data collected the wages of this class are about the same as, or a little higher than, those paid to Japanese. The change of races employed is explained by the fact that reliable white persons have found it easy to secure more remunerative and more agreeable employment, while the Japanese, being more regular in their work, more willing to work long hours, and more easily secured when needed, have been preferred by the employers to the less desirable class of white persons available.[c]

The Japanese have not been employed as cooks and waiters, for this trade is well organized, requires skill and experience, and for waiters a good knowledge of the English language. In barrooms they number about 200 and earn $10, $12, or $14 per week for work like that described in San Francisco.

The most important difference between Seattle and San Francisco is found in the absence in the former city of any well-organized opposition to the employment of Japanese. This has enabled the members of that race to secure and retain employment as bell boys in the

---

[a] Quoted from Report on the Japanese in City Employments and Business in San Francisco.

[b] Number based upon number of license taxes paid as reported in Census Bulletin 105.

[c] Quoted from special report on Japanese in City Employments and Business in Washington, with Special Reference to Seattle.

hotels, an occupation they have not been admitted to in San Francisco. Perhaps the Japanese working in this capacity in Seattle are almost as numerous as the other classes taken collectively. Such employment is of recent date, though in at least one instance an experiment was made with them in this capacity several years ago. In a few instances negroes, but in most instances white youths, have been displaced.

The displacement appears to have been due to difficulties met with in securing a reliable class of young men for such work rather than to a desire to economize in the matter of wages. The Japanese are paid from $15 to $25 per month, and from " tips " they frequently receive as much as $30 more.[a]

The Japanese, though not numerously employed in establishments conducted by white men in Portland, are conspicuously employed as bell boys in the hotels. In this capacity they are now employed to the exclusion of other races in most of the high-priced hotels of the city. They earn about $30 per month and board. Japanese were similarly employed in a number of hotels in southern California, but within the last two or three years, largely because of the sentiment prevailing against them, especially in other employments than as common laborers, they have been discharged from several hotels, so that their employment in this capacity is now exceptional.

As janitors of office buildings, cleaners, porters in stores, and as elevator boys, some Japanese are employed in all of the larger cities of the Pacific Coast States. With few exceptions, however, their numbers are small, though the work is of such a character that the collection of accurate data would involve the taking of a census. In Seattle they are more numerously employed as porters and " general help " in stores than in any other city. In fact, they are very generally found in the larger stores in the better shopping district, and it is estimated that at least 300 are so employed. Their wages are $10, $12, or $14 per week, the rates which are paid to Japanese porters employed in other establishments. In most of these stores they were first given employment within the last few years, when with the phenomenal growth of the city it has been difficult to secure responsible men to serve in such capacities at the wages which have been paid. It has been difficult to get and to keep good white employees. In San Francisco and other California cities the number of Japanese similarly employed in white stores appears to be smaller, judging from the comparatively small numbers so employed living in boarding and lodging houses. Yet one or a few are employed as porters in a considerable percentage of the drug stores, and in some of the grocery, clothing, and millinery stores. In some instances they are employed merely as " general help," in others as attendants to replace goods which have been displayed to prospective purchasers.

These are the more important occupations in which the Japanese have been employed in the western cities. Excluding the employment in industrial establishments discussed in the preceding chapter, in so far as it happens to be located in cities and towns, the Japanese have not been employed to any considerable extent by white persons in any other occupation or trade. A few Japanese carpenters are found following their trade in practically all of the cities in which

[a] Quoted from special report on Japanese in City Employments and Business in Washington, with Special Reference to Seattle.

there is any considerable number of that race, but they are employed largely in making alterations in buildings occupied and in installing fixtures in establishments conducted by their countrymen. In this the situation differs materially from that which obtains in Honolulu, where the Japanese engage regularly in practically all of the building trades and enter into contracts for the construction of some substantial structures. The fact that, from the data collected, there are many carpenters and other builders in the continental United States who are not following their trades is explained partly by the extreme differences in the character of building practiced here and in their native land, but more by the same general group of facts which explain why the Japanese have not engaged to any great extent in city occupations other than domestic service and those closely related to it and in establishments conducted by their countrymen. A few details with reference to Japanese in industry in San Francisco, where the instances of such employment have been more numerous than elsewhere, will make the situation clear.

The Japanese have not made the headway the Chinese made in industry in San Francisco at an earlier time, partly because they have had less time in which to make progress, but largely because of other factors in the situation.

The members of the latter race at one time predominated in the shoe factories, in the manufacture of clothing, and in cigar making. The opposition to them was so strong, however, that most of them were discharged from the factories engaged in these branches of production.[a] Moreover, this widespread opposition to the Chinese prevented occupations in other establishments conducted by white proprietors from being opened to them. No doubt this experience accounts largely for the fact that the Japanese have never been conspicuously employed in any branch of manufacture in San Francisco. At the same time a large influx of Italians and the immigration of smaller numbers of Russians, Mexicans, Spaniards, and Porto Ricans, along with other races, has provided an abundance of cheap labor for manufactures requiring little skill and which are not attractive to higher classes of workmen. At the time of the immigration of Chinese in large numbers these classes of " cheap labor " found little place in the population of San Francisco.

An attempt to employ Japanese in the manufacture of shoes soon resulted in failure.[b] Because of the strong opposition to them, they have been employed only to a slight extent in the manufacture of cigars and cigarettes. Even the small number employed has decreased in recent years, with the result that the agents of the Commission found them employed (as cigarette makers) in only one of the cigar factories investigated.[c] In the large overall and shirt factories they have not been employed. The employment of a few at $2 per day in minor positions in the stove industry a few years ago was discontinued because of the organized opposition of the

---

[a] See reports on "Immigrants in the cigar and cigarette industry of San Francisco" and "Immigrant labor in the manufacture of clothing in San Francisco."

[b] See discussion of the shoe-repairing industry, p. 126.

[c] See report on "Immigrant labor in the cigar and cigarette industry of San Francisco."

molders, and, it is said, because they were not regarded by the employers as satisfactory workmen. In tea packing, partly because of their efficiency in such work, they are employed in two establishments, but in comparatively small numbers. In one of these they are found engaged in several occupations at wages varying from $40 to $65 per month, and corresponding to those paid to white women and men engaged in the same or similar work. With unimportant exceptions such as these, the Japanese have not been employed in industrial enterprises conducted by white persons in San Francisco.

In business the Japanese have made more progress than in the various wage occupations in cities.

JAPANESE IN BUSINESS.

It is probable that between 10,000 and 11,000 Japanese in the 11 Commonwealths comprising the Western Division of the continental United States are engaged in business on their own accounts or are employed for wages by their countrymen who are thus occupied.[a] The great majority of these Japanese establishments are located in a comparatively few large general supply centers—San Francisco, Oakland, Los Angeles, Sacramento, San Jose, Portland, Seattle, Tacoma, Spokane, Ogden, Salt Lake City, and Denver—but a few Japanese business establishments are found in almost every town of importance near which the members of this race are employed. Agents of the Commission investigated the business conducted by Japanese in Seattle, Tacoma, Spokane, Bellingham, North Yakima, and Wenatche, in the State of Washington; Portland, in Oregon; San Francisco, Los Angeles, Sacramento, Fresno, Watsonville, and Vacaville, in California; Ogden and Salt Lake City, in Utah; Denver, in Colorado; and several towns in Idaho and Montana.

General information was collected in all of these places, while details were obtained and set down in schedules for representative establishments, proprietors, and employees in those having the largest number of Japanese engaged in business.[b] The results of these investigations are set forth in a number of local studies.[c] In this section of the report only the more general and significant phases of the situation are presented.

Many of the Japanese business establishments are of such a character that they are difficult to classify. In some branches of business their numbers change rapidly, old establishments disappearing and new ones appearing. The number of establishments devoted to each kind of business, as classified by the agents of the Commission in each town or city investigated, at the time the investigation was made (during November and December, 1908, and the first half of the year 1909), together with the total for each town or city and

---

[a] According to the Japanese-American Yearbook, the number of persons in these groups in California in 1909 was 7,078. Investigation by agents of the Commission, in all places in which any considerable number of Japanese are found, give the following corresponding figures for the States specified: Washington, 2,025; Oregon, 450; Utah, 300; Colorado, 200; Montana, 100; Idaho, 80; Wyoming, 50; Nevada, 50. The numbers for New Mexico and Arizona are very small.

[b] Seattle, San Francisco, Los Angeles, Sacramento, Fresno, and Watsonville.

[c] See note, p. 91.

the total of the numbers for the several places, is shown in the following summary table:

TABLE 34.—*Number of Japanese establishments engaged in each specified kind of business in selected localities in 1909.*

Kind of business.	Seattle.	Tacoma.	Spokane.	Bellingham.	North Yakima.	Portland.	San Francisco.	Los Angeles.	Sacramento.	Fresno.	Watsonville.	Vacaville.	Salt Lake City.	Ogden.	Denver.	Eleven Idaho towns and cities.	Total.
(a) STORES AND SHOPS.																	
Art and curio	12	5	2			4	42	15	1				3		1	1	86
Book and drug stores	4						14	8	4	2					1		33
Fruit and vegetable		3					8	20									31
Furnishing							13		9								22
Importing and exporting							5										5
Meat and fish	5					1	5	3	3	4					1		22
Provision and supply	26		5	2		8	22	27	12	4	3	4	4	2	2	3	124
Sake (liquor)	2						7	5									14
Watch and jewelry	7					1	8	5	4	6					1		32
(b) PERSONAL SERVICE.																	
Barber shops	46	9	5	2		10	18	44	26	12	2	1	3	4	4	1	187
Bath houses	26	5				13	13	26	7	4	4		2	2	3		105
Hotels, boarding and lodging houses	72	8	7		1	12	51	90	37	12	10	4	9	10	10	4	337
Laundries	37	6	4	3	1	2	19	7	6	5	1	1	1	1	3		97
Restaurants (American meals)	36	5	11	1	3	14	17	25	8	5	5	1	5	1		12	149
Restaurants (Japanese meals)	51	7	4		1	11	33	58	28	15	1	1	3	8	10	1	232
Tailoring, dyeing, and dressmaking	45	3	2	3		2	52	16	6				3	1	2	1	136
(c) AMUSEMENTS.																	
Moving-picture shows							1	1	2								4
Pool and billiard parlors and shooting galleries	25	4	2		1	4	28	33	15	10	4	3	3	6	3	3	144
(d) OTHER.																	
Bamboo shops							7	1					1		1		10
Banks	3						1	2	1	2		1		1	1		12
Confectioners	5					1	4		4			4			4		22
Contractors						2	12						7	4	7		32
Employment agents	17	1				2	12	7	4						1		44
Embroidery							3										3
Expressmen	10	3				2	5	10	6			3		2	2		43
Florists							4										4
Job printing shops	7						5	2	2								16
Magazines and newspapers	12					1	6	7	1			1					28
Photograph galleries	5	1					8	6	3			1	1	1			26
Rice mills							2										2
Shoe stores and cobbler shops	5					1	76	17	3	2	1						105
Tofu makers						1	2	3	3						1		10
Miscellaneous	20	3	3			5	43	35	15	22	6				8		160
Total	478	63	45	11	7	97	545	473	209	107	37	23	46	43	67	26	2,277

In the larger cities there were doubtless some business establishments conducted concerning which information was not obtained by the agents. These omissions are more than offset, however, by the duplications contained in the table presented. In the larger cities the agents found it necessary to rely upon the records kept by the secretaries of Japanese associations, trade societies, and newspapers publishing yearbooks, checking the data thus secured by information gained at establishments actually visited and for which schedules were taken. The records thus made use of contain much duplication, due to the fact that frequently two or more businesses, separately reported, are conducted as one and that much of this duplication has not been eliminated from the figures presented in the table. Labor contractors, in addition to the employment agency, almost invariably conduct hotels or boarding houses as a further source of profit and as a means of assembling laborers, and frequently conduct provision and supply stores as well. Many of the restaurants serving Japanese meals are carried on in connection with hotels and boarding houses. Billiard and pool halls and cigar stores are frequently connected with barber shops. Bath houses are usually connected with barber shops, small laundries, or boarding houses. The selling of books and drugs is usually combined in one business or affiliated with other branches of business enumerated in the table. The job printing is more frequently than not carried on in connection with the publication of a newspaper or magazine. Hence the table presented is of more value to show the variety of business and relative importance of the several branches engaged in by the Japanese than the actual number of establishments conducted by them. The table does indicate, however, that the number of establishments conducted by the Japanese is large—probably about 2,100 in the cities and towns covered by it.

The foregoing table covers all but a few of the establishments in Washington, Oregon, Idaho, Utah, and Colorado. The total number in Nevada is about 22 (including 7 restaurants serving American meals, 2 serving Japanese meals, 2 laundries, 1 barber shop, and 4 stores); in Wyoming, 21 (including 5 restaurants serving American meals, 1 serving Japanese meals, 1 barber shop, 2 laundries, 2 photographers, and 5 stores and shops). The statement next presented for California is translated from the "Japanese-American Yearbook, 1910." The number of establishments and amount of capital and number of employees are as of November 1, 1909, the other figures for the year July 1, 1908, to June 30, 1909. The figures for the number of establishments are not complete.

Business.	Number of establishments.	Capital invested.[a]	Volume of transactions. 1908-9.	Number of employees.[b]	Wages paid.	Rent per annum.
Art and curio stores.........................	84	$420,470	$917,250	209	$96,360	$105,100
Provision stores.............................	179	1,422,340	2,483,730	323	161,200	89,689
Bookstores.................................	25	32,250	234,350	32	15,060	12,080
Fancy goods stores.........................	21	26,300	165,930	36	17,180	10,410
Watch repair and jewelry stores............	32	32,800	89,430	11	6,890	9,514
Sake dealers...............................	13	107,600	330,380	20	5,940	6,070
Importers..................................	5	85,500	396,500	11	5,940	4,620
Drug stores................................	15	18,750	72,760	12	5,840	5,880
Bamboo shops..............................	9	6,800	41,300	14	7,430	4,780
Fruit and vegetable stalls..................	73	25,830	279,106	33	12,970	14,947
Florists....................................	9	11,450	55,100	16	8,160	6,220
Confectionery (Japanese cake)..............	23	17,550	85,150	27	14,475	8,090
Fish dealers...............................	27	27,960	199,220	25	12,710	8,390
Farm products, dealers in..................	8	32,300	581,000	17	7,440	4,844
Dealers in miscellaneous goods.............	30	16,600	62,900	13	5,560	7,730
Florists (owners of greenhouses)............	89	855,000	625,000	209	96,800	5,000
Laundries..................................	98	293,050	996,320	927	444,080	61,144
Hotels and boarding houses.................	295	344,850	886,490	231	94,489	149,098
Lodging houses.............................	68	34,180	85,540	15	5,950	23,470

a Value of real estate used for business purposes included, if owned.
b Includes second and third partners, and members of family working without wages, as well as those who are hired for wages. Hence adding 2,937 for the hired partners or managers, the total number gainfully occupied in these establishments was estimated at 7,038.

Business.	Number of establishments.	Capital invested.	Volume of transactions, 1908–9.	Number of employees.	Wages paid.	Rent per annum.
American restaurants......................	105	97,230	957,890	326	142,995	56,830
Tailor shops..............................	57	64,550	360,060	104	65,230	26,460
Cleaning and dye shops...................	49	22,850	146,110	82	34,000	18,470
Japanese restaurants (sake)..............	173	148,480	1,080,850	389	144,755	73,725
Japanese meal houses.....................	63	30,365	134,220	52	19,875	17,065
Barber shops.............................	178	73,701	256,149	88	41,785	38,705
Bathhouses...............................	131	118,790	202,122	39	15,415	38,891
Billiard and pool parlors................	221	136,160	390,380	82	34,380	68,644
Shooting galleries.......................	14	8,050	41,010	11	6,010	11,520
Photograph galleries.....................	26	26,900	64,890	22	8,254	12,704
Job printing offices.....................	11	20,250	40,780	30	16,100	3,130
Expressmen...............................	42	31,310	76,840	19	16,620	7,242
Shoe store and repair shops..............	208	99,060	426,060	139	51,680	47,190
Employment offices.......................	53	5,983	69,990	....	....	3,530
Miscellaneous............................	381	60,810	187,655	253	29,965	28,572
Total....................	2,937	4,816,573	13,020,462	4,101	1,655,886	1,109,476

The agents of the Commission found as a result of their investigation of Japanese business in the cities and towns mentioned in the above table:

(1) That most of the Japanese business establishments have been started in recent years; that the number in the large cities serving as supply centers has rapidly increased; and that a few establishments have been started in many smaller places as well.

(2) That with comparatively few exceptions the Japanese business establishments are small, employing comparatively little capital, being conducted with the assistance of comparatively few employees and having a comparatively small volume of annual transactions.

(3) That in the larger cities where there are many Japanese there are many branches of business and professions represented, so that because of clannishness, convenience in point of location and language, and the character of the goods carried in stock, as well as because of a feeling of opposition toward the Asiatics, with the result that they are not welcomed at white establishments engaged in personal service, the majority of the wants of the Japanese are met by their countrymen engaged in business and the professions.

(4) That while many of the Japanese establishments have been called into existence primarily to meet the needs of the members of that race, others have been started, chiefly in recent years, for "American trade," and are patronized largely or almost exclusively by white persons.

(5) That rather frequently, in competing with white establishments, the Japanese have underbid through a lower scale of prices.

(6) But that because of organized opposition in some instances, and of the small number of Japanese establishments as compared to those conducted by other races, the trades which have been seriously affected by Japanese competition in most cities have been few.

(7) That in some instances the changes in the character of the population resulting from the settlement of Japanese, who trade chiefly at shops conducted by their countrymen, have seriously affected the business of shopkeepers and others located in or near Japanese colonies.

(8) That few white persons are employed in Japanese establishments.

(9) That usually, where there is competition between white and Japanese business men, the former maintain a shorter workday and a higher scale of wages than the latter. While the above statements represent general conclusions from the facts ascertained, the details differ materially in certain respects in the several localities.

Three facts go far toward explaining the rapid increase in business conducted by the Japanese during the last eight or ten years: First the great influx of Japanese to the Western States; second, their well-defined tendency to rise from the ranks of wage laborers; and third the tendency more recently exhibited by them in some branches of business to seek American patronage and trade.

The number of Japanese business establishments in Seattle in 1900 was about 50, in 1905 about 216, in 1909, 478. The number in Tacoma in 1905 was 23, in 1909, 63. The number in Portland in 1900 was about 28, in 1909, 97. In 1904 there were some 160 establishments in Los Angeles, in 1909 the corresponding figure was 495. The establishments in San Francisco numbered about 336 in 1904, perhaps 500 in 1909.[a] In all of these cases the Japanese population had increased between the dates indicated, but not in proportion to the increase in the number of business establishments. In Utah and Colorado, and most of the other Rock Mountain States, the comparatively small number of establishments is the result of a rapid growth during recent years, since the Japanese who first found employment there as laborers not more than ten years ago have become a more settled part of the population.

This rapid increase in the number of business establishments is closely connected with the classes from which the Japanese immigrants have been drawn and the opportunities which have been opened to them as wage-earners in this country. It is a significant fact that of 394 business men who had migrated directly from Japan to this country and whose occupations previous to their emigration from their native land were ascertained, no fewer than 132, or approximately one-third of the entire number, had been engaged in business on their own accounts, 20 had been employed in stores, 54 had been city wage-earners, while 78, practically all from the non-wage-earning city classes coming to this country as students, had not been gainfully employed previous to their immigration. Opposed to these persons of the city classes there were 104, 14 of whom had been independent farmers, the other 90, farmers' sons, working on the father's farm before coming to the United States. These data drawn from 6 cities show (1) that a large majority of these men engaged in business in this country came from the cities of Japan, and (2) that a still larger number at home had not belonged to the wage-earning classes. In this country, however, most of them began as wage-earners. Indeed, less than one-sixth of 439 (45 of whom came to the continental United States from Hawaii or from Canada) whose first occupations were ascertained engaged in business on their own accounts as their first gainful occupation in this country. As opposed to the 70 who engaged in business, 143 found their first employment in

---

[a] Exclusive of the offices of house-cleaning groups.

domestic service, 88 as farm hands, 5 as independent farmers, 49 as railroad laborers, 6 as laborers in lumber mills, 3 in canneries, and some 69 in various city employments other than those already mentioned, but chiefly as " restaurant help " and in other unskilled work. These are the chief branches of employment which, as has been explained, have been opened to Japanese wage-earners.

Few opportunities have been afforded to the members of this race to rise from the ranks of the lowest to those of the higher-paid laborers in railroad work, lumber mills, canneries, smelters, and other noncity industries in which they have been employed. Moreover, the conditions of living which have very generally prevailed have been unsatisfactory from the point of view of the single man, and such that normal family life was impossible. Because of these facts a heavy premium has been placed upon acquiring land for independent farming and upon migration to the cities. It was found that few of those who immigrated from the cities of Japan remained long at work outside of the cities, while many of those coming from the nonwage-earning agricultural classes soon sought work in the cities when they had become railroad or farm laborers upon their arrival. In the cities, however, similar limitations upon the employment of Japanese have prevailed. Few opportunities for employment by white persons other than as domestics and in related trades have been open to them, with the result that a premium has been placed upon engaging in business on their own account, which has been rendered easy by the small amount of capital required in most businesses engaged in and the frequent formation of partnerships. The last occupation regularly engaged in previous to their migration to the continental United States and their first gainful employment in this country are shown for the Japanese business men investigated in Seattle, San Francisco, Los Angeles, Sacramento, Fresno, and Watsonville, in the following table:

TABLE 35.—*First occupation in the United States of foreign-born Japanese, by occupation abroad.*

IN BUSINESS FOR SELF.

Occupation abroad.	Number.	Number who were—															
		In business for self.	Farmers.	Farm hands.	Railroad laborers.	Sawmill laborers.	Cannery hands.	Laborers in industrial establishments.	Store help.	Restaurant help.	House cleaners.	In domestic service.	Tailors and dyers.	Barbers.	Wage-earners in city.	In other occupations.	Occupation unknown.
In business for self	a/145	42	....	23	18	1	....	1	7	5	....	32	....	....	11	1	4
Farmer	b f 18	1	....	9	3	2	....	....	....	3	1	2	....	....	....	....	....
At home	78	5	1	3	6	....	1	....	5	3	....	51	....	....	2	....	1
Farming for father	a 102	3	4	35	15	2	1	....	....	4	4	26	....	....	7	1	....
Farm hand	c 6	2	....	1	1	1	....	....	....	....	....	....	....	....	....	1	....
Store help	d 22	6	....	2	1	....	....	....	4	2	....	7	....	....	....	....	....
Laborer in industrial establishments	e 7	4	....	2	....	....	....	....	1	....	....	....	....	....	....	....	....
Wage-earner in city	b f 53	7	....	9	4	....	....	....	2	4	....	20	2	2	2	....	1
In other occupations	d 8	....	....	4	1	....	1	....	....	....	....	....	....	....	2	....	....
Occupation unknown	....	....	....	....	....	....	....	....	....	....	....	....	....	....	....	....	....
Total	439	70	5	88	49	6	3	1	19	18	5	138	2	2	24	3	6

a Including 12 who came via Hawaii.
b Including 4 who came via Hawaii.
c Including 6 who came via Hawaii.
d Including 2 who came via Hawaii.
e Including 1 who came via Hawaii.
f Including 1 who came from Canada.

TABLE 35.—*First occcupation in the United States of foreign-born Japanese, by occupation abroad*—Continued.

WAGE-EARNERS.

Occupation abroad.	Number.	In business for self.	Farmers.	Farm hands.	Railroad laborers.	Sawmill laborers.	Cannery hands.	Laborers in industrial establishments.	Store help.	Restaurant help.	House cleaners.	In domestic service.	Tailors and dyers.	Barbers.	Wage-earners in city.	In other occupations.	Occupation unknown.
							Number who were—										
In business for self	a 53	2	....	13	5	....	....	1	4	3	1	15	2	....	4	....	3
Farmer	a e 16	..	....	6	5	....	....	....	1	....	3	....	1	....	....	....	
At home	a 134	1	....	12	6	2	2	3	14	9	1	72	2	....	9	....	1
Farming for father	b f 128	....	....	43	19	1	2	1	4	9	7	32	....	....	4	2	4
Farm hand	c 2	....	....	....	....	....	....	1	....	....	....	1	....	....	....	....	
Store help	a 33	....	....	6	1	....	....	....	8	4	....	9	....	....	2	1	2
Laborer in industrial establishments	7	..,	....	3	1	....	....	....	....	1	1	....	....	....	1	....	
Wage-earner in city	d 41	....	....	13	1	....	....	1	....	....	....	12	5	....	5	....	4
In other occupations	c 9	....	....	3	....	....	....	....	....	....	1	....	4	....	1	....	
Occupation unknown	1	....	....	....	....	1	....	....	....	....	....	....	....	....	....	....	
Total	424	3	....	99	38	3	5	7	30	28	10	148	9	1	26	3	14

a Including 2 who came via Hawaii.
b Including 17 who came via Hawaii.
c Including 1 who came via Hawaii.
d Including 4 who came via Hawaii.
e Including 1 who came from Canada.
f Including 1 who came from Mexico.

In addition to the above-mentioned facts there has been a tendency for men who had acquired a trade at home to seek an opportunity to engage in it here; in fact most of them immigrated with the hope of soon being able to do so. A detailed investigation reveals the fact that in all of the cities included in the investigation the majority, and in some instances practically all, of those conducting tailor shops, barber shops, carpenter shops, and watch-repairing shops had been tailors, barbers, carpenters, or watchmakers in their native land. This same correspondence between business engaged in in this country and abroad is also generally shown in the business of conducting curio stores, drug stores, and shoe-repairing shops, though in a comparatively large number of instances the business engaged in here is entirely unrelated to the occupation in which they had gained experience abroad. In most other branches of business it is surprising to find how few have undertaken branches of business for which their previous experience would fit them. Nevertheless, the effort of craftsmen and of others so to establish themselves that they may profit by their skill and experience acquired previous to their immigration assists in explaining the rapid growth of numbers in a few branches of trade.

While the conditions of work, the occupations open to them, and their wages where employed by others have generally been such as to place a premium upon entering upon business or farming on their own accounts, much emphasis must be placed upon the fact that the Japanese like to be free from the wage relation. That they take great pride in being independent of that relation is a very important fact in explaining the spread of Japanese business and independent farming in this country. Moreover, the opportunities presented in many branches of business have been attractive, and the profits realized by a large percentage of those engaged in them much larger than the earnings of the wage-earning classes. The profits realized by 410 proprietors of or partners in Japanese establishments located in Seattle, San Francisco, Los Angeles, Sacramento, Fresno, and Watsonville, during the twelve months preceding the collection of the data, are shown in the following table. The figures given are for net income derived from the main business conducted only. A rather large percentage of those from whom information was secured had other incomes from subsidiary business carried on, from investments, or from labor performed other than in connection with the business conducted by them:

TABLE 36.—*Number of persons having each specified income during the past year, and average income, by branch of business engaged in.*

Business engaged in.	Number reporting complete data.	Number having each specified amount of income.									Total income.	Average income.
		Under $300.	$300 and under $400.	$400 and under $500.	$500 and under $750.	$750 and under $1,000.	$1,000 and under $1,500.	$1,500 and under $2,000.	$2,000 and under $2,500.	$2,500 or over.		
Restaurant proprietor	54	1		5	19	10	6	6	1	5	$69,430	$1,285.74
Lodging house	46	....	1	1	16	12	9	3	1	3	55,980	1,216.96
Storekeeper	109	....	3	1	29	27	21	8	7	13	173,790	1,594.40
Barber shop	34	1	1	1	20	10	1	....	....		23,844	701.29
Tailor	21	....	....	....	5	4	8	4	....	....	23,970	1,141.43
Shoemaker	26	....	1	3	9	10	1	1	1		21,500	826.92
Real estate and labor agencies	16	....	....	1	2	3	6	1	2	1	20,120	1,257.50
Laundry	33	....	....	6	13	3	4	5	....	2	36,495	1,105.91
Pool room	12	....	1	1	4	3	3	....	....		9,880	823.33
Miscellaneous	59	2	2	....	26	12	9	4	3	1	54,740	927.80
Total	410	4	10	19	143	94	68	32	15	25	489,749	1,194.51

Of course the success of those who have undertaken business for themselves is not measured by the profits realized by those who have remained in business. In estimating the degree of success attained, those who have failed and returned to the ranks of the wage-earners must also be taken into consideration. What proportion of the Japanese engaging in business have failed is not ascertainable. Japanese business establishments have frequently changed hands, but in the data obtained from wage-earners in city trades, the number who had at any time engaged in business in this country upon their own account was found to be very small. It should be stated also that for reasons set forth in detail below, the figures here given for business are not entirely representative of the incomes of Japanese business men as a class in other cities and towns as well as the six from which these data were collected, and exaggerate somewhat the differences between the incomes of the business men as a class and those of wage-earners.

Moreover, the profits shown in the table presented are in part to be regarded as interest upon the capital invested in the business conducted, and the percentage of the total which should be so regarded varies from trade to trade and from one establishment to another in a given trade, because of the differences which are found to obtain. The data relating to the capital employed in, and the profit realized from, business establishments in the cities mentioned above are shown in a table presented below. A comparison of profit and capital and number of persons working without wages, in each establishment, shows that upon the whole, when interest upon invested capital is allowed for, the profits are usually much in excess of the earnings of the wage-earners from whom data were secured in the same cities, in spite of the fact that the restrictions placed upon the further immigration of laborers had already adversely affected the business and profits of a rather large percentage of them. Moreover, with few exceptions, most of the capital employed represents gains from the business carried on, so that the incomes shown in the table presented above show roughly the opportunities offered to the Japanese engaged in the several branches of business mentioned. This is particularly true of the proprietors of restaurants, barber shops, tailor, cleaning and dye shops, cobbler shops, and pool rooms, for few of these employ as much as $1,000 of capital in their business. The results of the investigations made by the agents of the Commission would tend to show that with the exception of a few instances where the Japanese have met with organized opposition, as in the restaurant and laundry trades in San Francisco, or where, as in Los Angeles, the grocers have extended credit too freely to their countrymen who were unsuccessful in farming, the Japanese business men have generally made good profits.

Of 54 proprietors of restaurants covered by the above table, it will be noted that while the incomes realized varied greatly, 19 realized profits for the year of $500 but less than $750; 10, of $750 but less than $1,000; and 6, of $1,000 but less than $1,500—a total of 35. As opposed to these, 12 earned $1,500 or over, and 5 employing considerable capital, from $2,600 to $9,600, while 7 earned less than $500. The average for the 54 was $1,285.74. The 34 proprietors of barber shops with 4 exceptions earned $500 but less than $1,000; 20 of them, $500 but less than $750; 10, $750 but less than $1,000—the average being $701.29. Five proprietors of tailor and dye shops netted for the year $500 but less than $750; 4, $750 but less than $1,000; 8, $1,000 but less than $1,500; and 4, $1,500 but less than $2,000—the average for the 21 being $1,141.43. Of the 26 shoemakers, 4 earned less than $500; 9, $500 but less than $750; 10, $750 but less than $1,000; and 3 between $1,000 and $2,500—the average for the entire number being $826.92. Of 12 proprietors of pool rooms and billiard parlors, 2 earned less than $500 net; 4, $500 but less than $750; 3, $750 but less than $1,000; and an equal number $1,000 but less than $1,500. The average for the 12 was $823.33. The incomes of the proprietors of other business establishments require no comment. These incomes have proved attractive to the more ambitious of the laboring class, and many Japanese working for wages, in answering the query contained in the schedule used as to why they had come to the locality in which they resided, stated that they did so with the expectation of engaging in business for themselves. As they have accumulated a small capital many of the Japanese have sought an opportunity to rise from the ranks of the wage-earning class and have engaged in business, and a not inconsiderable percentage of the city wage-earners from whom information was obtained have expected to do likewise.

Though 70 of 439 business men reporting data engaged in business for themselves, as their first gainful occupation after arriving in this country, only 20 of 435 reporting the amount of money brought to this country, had upon their arrival as much as $500; and the total amount reported by 8 who brought more than $1,000, was only $30,400. Indeed, only 59 brought as much as $200; while 21 brought $150 but less than $200; 53, $100 but less than $150; 131, $50 but less than $100; and 171 less than $50. By forming partnerships and to some extent by means of loans, it would appear that the majority of those who came as wage-earners soon engaged in business. Complete information was obtained in Sacramento and Los Angeles for 143 of these men, with reference to their employments from their arrival until the time of the investigation. Thirty-one engaged in business at once, while 112 first worked for wages. Of these 112, however, 24 engaged in business within one year of their arrival, 39 within two years, 25 within three years, 15 within four years, and the remaining 19 after from four to eleven years. Thus it would appear that the majority soon established themselves in business and when the amount of property possessed by them was comparatively small. In some instances this was done by forming partnerships or entering those already organized or by borrowing money.

The aggregate value of property now controlled by 438 men in business, as reported by them, was $1,597,900, or an average of $3,648.17. Against this, however, were the debts of 178, aggregating $266,649. The net value of property owned, therefore, was $1,318,916, or an average of $3,011.22 each. The net value of the property owned by 437 of the 438, and by 427 wage-earners, most of whom were employed in the establishments conducted by these business men, is shown in the following table.

TABLE 37.—*Net value of all property now owned by Japanese 18 years of age or over.*

IN BUSINESS FOR SELF.

Years since first arrival in United States.	Number reporting complete data.	None.a	Under $50.	$50 and under $100.	$100 and under $250.	$250 and under $500.	$500 and under $1,000.	$1,000 and under $1,500.	$1,500 and under $2,500.	$2,500 and under $5,000.	$5,000 and under $10,000.	$10,000 and under $25,000.	$25,000 or over.
Under 1 year													
1 year	3				2					1			
2 years	22	b 1			5	3	6	5	1	1			
3 years	26			1	2	1	13	1	5	3			
4 years	38				1	6	15	6	6	3	1		
5 to 9 years	200	c 1			6	18	43	45	40	30	11	5	1
10 to 14 years	105	b 1			2	6	28	20	21	18	6	2	1
15 to 19 years	33	b 1				1	7	3	9	2	5	3	2
20 years or over	10						2	1		1	2	1	3
Total	437	4	....	1	18	35	114	81	82	59	25	11	7

a Including 3 in debt (2 for $7.50 each and 1 for $250).
b Gross value of property minus indebtedness is nothing or less than nothing.
c Having gross value of property $2,000 and encumbrances $4,000.

TABLE 37.—*Net value of all property now owned by Japanese 18 years of age or over*—Continued.

WAGE-EARNERS.

Years since first arrival in United States.	Number reporting complete data.	Number having each specified amount of property.											
		None.	Under $50.	$50 and under $100.	$100 and under $250.	$250 and under $500.	$500 and under $1,000.	$1,000 and under $1,500.	$1,500 and under $2,500.	$2,500 and under $5,000.	$5,000 and under $10,000.	$10,000 and under $25,000.	$25,000 or over.
Under 1 year	2	1	....	....	....	1	....	....	....	....	....	....	....
1 year	29	2	....	7	13	6	1	....	....	....	....	....	....
2 years	74	7	2	11	28	16	9	....	1	....	....	....	....
3 years	64	a 5	3	6	21	17	9	3	....	....	....	....	....
4 years	38	5	....	....	13	8	8	2	2	....	....	....	....
5 to 9 years	151	b 29	....	11	41	33	20	12	3	2	....	....	....
10 to 14 years	46	7	2	....	14	6	10	2	3	2	....	....	....
15 to 19 years	17	5	....	....	2	2	4	1	1	1	....	1	....
20 years or over	6	....	....	....	3	1	2	....	....	....	....	....	....
Total	427	61	7	35	135	90	63	20	10	5	....	1	....

a Including 1 having no gross value of property and encumbrances $200.
b Including 1 having deficit of $40.

Forty-three, or 9.8 per cent, of the 437 business men had property with a net value (over and above all incumbrances) of $5,000 or more; 59, or 13.3 per cent, $2,500, but less than $5,000; 82, or 18.8 per cent, $1,500, but less than $2,500; 81, or 18.5 per cent, $1,000, but less than $1,500; while 172, or 39.4 per cent, had property the net value of which was less than $1,000. Thus the majority of these men have comparatively little wealth, and hence little capital to invest in business. Moreover, for reasons pointed out below, a larger percentage of these than of Japanese business men as a class have a considerable amount of property. The men from whom data were obtained can not be regarded as entirely typical of the class to which they belong.

The above table shows also, when taken in connection with the amount of money brought, the progress in accumulating property these men have been able to make. It is a fairly good index to the degree of success they have realized. The contrast between the amount of property owned by business men and the wage-earning class is explained partly by the larger incomes the former have earned and partly by the fact that they have sent less of their earnings abroad. The last-mentioned matter is discussed later in this report.

The amount of capital employed in Japanese establishments investigated is shown by branches of business engaged in in the following table. In each case where two or more branches of business are conducted in the same establishment the establishment is entered under the branch of business of most importance in the given case, and the full amount of capital, as reported, is imputed to it.

TABLE 38.—*Capital employed in Japanese establishments investigated, by branch of business.*

Branch of business.	Number of establishments reporting capital.	Total amount of capital employed.	Average amount of capital employed per establishment.	Number of establishments reporting capital as—					
				Less than $500.	$0 but under $1,000.	$1,00 but under $, 500.	$2,500 but under $, 000.	$5,00 but under $, 000.	$10,00 but under $25,000.	$25,000 and over.
Boarding and lodging houses............	44	$100,200	$2,277.27	5	9	14	10	6	0	0
Barber shops......................	28	24,799	885.68	11	9	6	2	0	0	0
Tailor shops......................	21	22,800	1,085.71	5	8	6	1	1	0	0
Art and curio stores...............	9	222,900	24,766.66	0	0	0	2	2	2	3
Books, drugs, and stationery stores......	9	25,760	2,862.22	0	2	2	4	1	0	0
Jewelers and watchmakers' shops	9	31,000	3,444.44	0	0	5	1	3	0	0
Meat and fish markets.................	9	11,100	1,233.33	3	1	3	2	0	0	0
Cake, confectionery, and tobacco stores..	16	17,450	1,090.65	0	10	4	2	0	0	0
Shoe-repairing shops...................	11	3,800	345.45	9	2	0	0	0	0	0
Billiard and pool halls.................	13	23,150	1,776.92	0	3	8	1	1	0	0
Baths...........................	4	8,600	2,150.00	1	0	1	2	0	0	0
Laundries.........................	24	98,880	4,120.00	1	6	8	6	0	2	a 1
Restaurants.......................	40	71,620	17,905.00	3	6	18	11	2	0	0
Provision and general merchandise stores...................	32	446,650	13,957.81	0	2	12	9	3	1	
Miscellaneous establishments...........	44	370,780	8,426.82	11	11	8	7	3	1	5

a Includes value of the real estate occupied by the laundry.

The average amount of capital employed and the relative number of the larger establishments for the cities and towns of the West, taken as a whole, are somewhat exaggerated by the figures here given in practically all cases and very much so in a few. Most of the exaggeration is due to the fact that the establishments investigated were located in the several cities mentioned, and that these are among the cities in which the Japanese have made the greatest progress in business enterprise, and that in the larger cities the amount of capital employed and the proportion of the larger establishments are both materially larger than in the smaller cities and towns. Moreover, in attempting to secure data bearing upon competition between the Japanese and the other races and for the business of contractors, in some instances the agents selected for investigation more than a fair proportion of the larger establishments in the cities investigated. The number of large boarding and lodging houses and provision and general merchandise stores conducted by labor contractors investigated constituted a far larger proportion of the entire number of these than the number of the smaller ones for which data were obtained. Five of the largest curio stores, conducted by corporations, were investigated, so that the figures for that branch of business are misleading. The other data are more nearly representative of conditions in the five cities to which they relate.

For the reasons pointed out, however, the data published in the Japanese-American Yearbook and presented above, though they doubtless contain inaccuracies and are in some cases based upon rough estimates, afford a better index to the size of Japanese establishments and the amount of capital employed. Using approximate figures, the average amount of capital these reported for 361 boarding and lodging houses (including a large number of so-called "camps" in agricultural districts) is $1,044; for 178 barber shops, $414; for 106 tailor and cleaning and dye shops, $825; for 84 art and curio stores (including many general shops), $5,006; for 40 book and drug stores, $1,225; for 32 watch-repairing shops and jewelry stores, $1,025; for 27 fish dealers (including peddlers), $1,036; for 23 confectionery stores, $763; for 208 shoe-repair shops, including a few shoe stores, $476; for 221 billiard and pool parlors, $616; for 98 laundries, $2,996; for 105 restaurants serving American meals, $926; for 173 restaurants serving Japanese meals and drinks, $861; for 63 restaurants serving Japanese meals only, $482; for 179 provision stores, $7,923. The average amount of capital for the 2,937 establishments reported for the State was approximately $1,640.

Data relating to the volume of transactions for 282 of the establishments included in the above table are presented in the following table. The figures for each establishment were for the twelve months immediately preceding the collection of the data. The transactions reported are subject to the same limitations as the figures in the preceding table.

TABLE 39.—*Volume of transactions during the past year, by branch of business.*

Branch of business.	Number of establishments reporting transactions.	Aggregate of annual transactions.	Average amount of transactions per establishment.	Less than $1,000.	$1,000 and under $2,500.	$2,500 and under $5,000.	$5,000 and under $10,000.	$10,000 and under $25,000.	$25,000 and under $50,000.	$50,000 and under $75,000.	$75,000 and under $100,000.	$100,000 and over.
Boarding and lodging houses...	a 24	$83,680	$3,486.66	0	9	8	7	0	0	0	0	0
Barber shops.......................	b 25	65,680	2,627.20	2	14	5	3	1	0	0	0	0
Tailor shops......................	c 20	126,560	6,328.00	2	5	3	6	4	0	0	0	0
Art and curio stores............	9	390,000	43,333.33	0	0	1	2	2	1	1	0	2
Book, drug, and stationery stores..........................	9	66,300	7,366.66	0	1	2	3	3	0	0	0	0
Jewelers' and watchmakers' shops.........................	d 8	59,700	7,462.50	0	1	3	2	2	0	0	0	0
Meat and fish markets........	9	145,300	16,144.44	0	1	0	2	4	1	1	0	0
Cake, confectionery, and tobacco stores......................	16	42,900	2,681.25	0	9	6	1	0	0	0	0	0
Shoe-repairing shops..........	9	12,900	1,433.33	1	8	0	0	0	0	0	0	0
Billiard and pool rooms........	e 12	30,452	2,537.66	1	6	4	1	0	0	0	0	0
Baths...........................	4	10,110	2,527.50	1	1	2	0	0	0	0	0	0
Laundries......................	f 23	221,740	9,640.87	0	8	2	6	4	3	0	0	0
Restaurants....................	40	475,700	11,892.50	0	4	6	9	17	4	0	0	0
Provision and general merchandise stores..................	32	1,131,100	35,315.62	0	2	3	8	11	1	2	2	3
Miscellaneous establishments...	g 42	1,525,805	36,328.69	2	17	9	7	4	1	0	0	2

a Does not include 20 boarding and lodging houses investigated in San Francisco having a total capital of $49,800 and total profits of $38,450.

b Does not include 3 barber shops, 2 investigated in San Francisco and 1 in Seattle, having a total capital of $1,350 and total profits of $2,400.

c Does not include 1 tailor shop investigated in San Francisco having a total capital of $1,000 and total profits of $1,200.

d Does not include 1 jeweler's shop investigated in San Francisco having a total capital of $1,300 and total profits of $900.

e Does not include 1 billiard and pool room investigated in San Francisco having a total capital of $900 and total profits of $720.

f Does not include 1 laundry investigated in San Francisco having a total capital of $3,200 and tota profits of $1,500.

g Does not include 2 establishments, 1 in San Francisco, with a capital of $30,000 and profits reported $1,440; 1 in Sacramento with a capital of $4,900, transactions of $1,650—in business only 3 months.

The profits realized from the business transacted during the period of twelve months were secured from most of the establishments investigated. The figures are necessarily in some cases approximations of the true amounts. On the whole, however, they are regarded as fairly accurate.

TABLE 40.—*Amount of profits realized during the past year, by branch of business.*

Branch of business.	Number of establishments reporting profit.	Total of profits realized.	Average amount of profit realized per establishment.	Number of establishments reporting amount of profit realized as—								
				Less than $300.	$300 and under $400.	$400 and under $500.	$500 and under $750.	$750 and under $1,000.	$1,000 and under $1,500.	$1,500 and under $2,000.	$2,000 and under $2,500.	$2,500 and over.
Boarding and lodging houses...	44	$66,551	$1,512.52	0	1	1	12	10	8	7	2	3
Barber shops	28	20,440	730 00	0	1	1	16	9	1	0	0	0
Tailor shops and dye shops....	21	23,370	1,112.86	0	1	1	2	7	8	1	0	1
Art and curio stores	a 5	6,390	1,278.00	1	0	0	1	1	1	0	0	1
Book, drug, and stationery stores	9	11,760	1,306.66	0	0	0	3	3	2	0	0	1
Jewelers' and watchmakers' shops	9	14,340	1,593.33	0	0	0	1	4	1	1	0	2
Meat and fish markets	9	13,720	1,523.33	0	0	0	3	0	2	1	2	1
Cake, confectionery, and tobacco stores	16	13,150	821.88	1	3	0	6	2	2	1	1	0
Shoe-repairing shops	9	6,360	706.66	0	1	1	3	4	0	0	0	0
Billiard and pool rooms	13	10,908	839.08	1	1	1	2	4	4	0	0	0
Bathhouses	4	3,600	900.00	0	0	0	2	1	1	0	0	0
Laundries	b 19	30,235	1,591.32	0	0	0	5	2	5	3	0	4
Restaurants	c 38	50,406	1,326.47	1	1	2	10	6	7	6	2	3
Provision and general merchandise stores	d 31	69,300	2,235.48	0	0	1	7	8	5	1	3	6
Miscellaneous establishments...	e 43	66,840	1,554.42	1	1	0	8	7	13	8	2	3

a Does not include 4 art and curio stores investigated in Los Angeles, having a total capital of $170,000 and total annual transactions of $182,000.

b Does not include 5 laundries investigated in Los Angeles, having a total capital of $6,000, and total annual transactions of $25,400.

c Does not include 2 restaurants investigated in San Francisco, having a total capital of $1,700, and total annual transactions of $10,000.

d Does not include 1 grocery store investigated in Los Angeles, having a total capital of $7,500 and total annual transactions of $140,000.

e Does not include 1 gents' furnishing store investigated in Sacramento, having a total capital of $4,900 and transactions of $1,650 for the 3 months that it has been in business.

While the Japanese first engaged in the restaurant trade, serving American meals at low prices, chiefly to white workingmen, in Seattle, Portland, Los Angeles, Denver, and in a large number of the smaller towns, especially in the Rocky Mountain States, the majority of the establishments opened by them until recently in the large centers of population in the West have been primarily to provide Japanese laborers with Japanese goods or to provide them with such personal service as they required. In recent years, however, there has been a tendency to open establishments more with reference to "American" patronage which may be secured, as is shown by the expansion of the laundry, barber, tailor and dyeing, and restaurant trades in a comparatively large number of localities. Yet this tendency is not so evident from a comparison of the number of establishments patronized by Japanese almost or quite exclusively, on the one hand, and the number of those with a large majority of white patrons on the other; for the number of small shops catering to the wants of the Japanese has very rapidly increased. Until recently the number of Japanese in the Western States and in the larger cities has been rapidly increasing.

Inasmuch as the members of the Japanese wage-earning class have not as a rule been accepted as guests at hotels, boarding and lodging houses conducted by white men, or been served in white barber shops or many of the white restaurants, the demand for such establishments, as well as billiard parlors, bathhouses, and the like, conducted by Japanese, has grown rapidly. With the increasing number of Japanese, the majority of whom have purchased most of their foods, drinks, and work clothes from their countrymen, the number of general supply houses and stores has increased. The number of small establishments of this kind has increased the more rapidly as more of the laborers have severed their relations with large labor contractors, who usually sell to the men under their control such supplies as they need. Banks, real estate offices, newspapers, printing plants, and several other branches of business enterprise, have come into existence or increased in number as a larger percentage of the Japanese have ceased to be migratory laborers and as other branches of business have been developed. In spite of the increase in the number and size of the establishments having much " white " patronage, the majority of the Japanese establishments are now engaged in business chiefly with the members of the Japanese race.

The minority are competing for white patronage. The situation as regards the extent to which the Japanese establishments are patronized by the white races, and the more general effects, as found in the more important of the localities investigated by the agents of the Commission, may be briefly presented. Following this, the details relating to the terms upon which Japanese and others have competed will be set forth in summary form.

Of the business conducted by Japanese in Seattle, the great Japanese supply center of the Northwest, much is conducted primarily to meet the wants of their own people, most of whom have immigrated within the last ten years, many of whom do not speak English, and who are usually discriminated against in white barber shops, restaurants, lodging houses, and places of amusement. The 3 banks, the 17 employment and real estate agencies, the bookstores, and the 51 restaurants serving Japanese meals are patronized exclusively by Japanese. The same is true, with few exceptions, of the general supply stores, the few drug stores, the 2 liquor stores, the 7 job printing establishments, the 5 photograph galleries, the 25 billiard parlors and pool rooms, the 72 boarding and lodging houses, and the 10 expressmen. The patronage by whites is in all of these branches of business comparatively small. Some of the grocers, and most of the 45 tailors and dyers, the 12 curio dealers, the 7 watchmakers, the 5 shoe repairers, the 5 fish markets, the 36 restaurants serving American meals, the 46 barber shops, and the 37 laundries (the smaller hand laundries excepted), on the other hand, have among their patrons a very large percentage of white people.

The competition of the Japanese in several of these lines has been sufficient to give their white competitors serious concern. This is true particularly of the laundries, tailors and dyers, barbers, restaurants serving American meals, and some of the grocery stores, branches of business in which the Japanese, as a rule, have charged or now charge somewhat lower prices than their competitors and are in sufficient number to take as their share more than a small percentage of the business of the community or of the district in which their shops are located.

Portland, Oreg., for ten years following the introduction of direct steamship connection with Japan, in 1887, was the most important supply center in the Northwest; but more recently this position has been lost to Seattle. In 1909 there were some 97 business establishments conducted by Japanese in Portland. Practically all of the establishments, the business of one contractor being an important exception, are small, and most of the business conducted is incidental to supplying the needs of the Japanese. In fact, the 10 barber shops, the 14 restaurants serving American meals, and the 4 art and curio stores alone have more than a small percentage of white patrons. Though the prices charged are the same as at the other small barber shops, about 50 per cent of the patrons of the Japanese shops are white persons, chiefly laborers. The restaurants serving American meals have only a very small percentage of Japanese patrons. Inasmuch as the curio stores have been conducted by Asiatics chiefly, the competition of the Japanese engaged in business has been limited practically to the barber and restaurant trades.

San Francisco has been the port of arrival of the majority of the Japanese immigrating to the United States, and has also been a more important center of Japanese business than any other American city. Its establishments have been more numerous than those of any other place, and a larger percentage of the business has been conducted on a large scale. It is here, too, that the Japanese have met with the strongest resistance offered to their advances and that race lines are most clearly drawn against the laboring class. The more than 50 hotels and lodging houses, the 18 barber shops, the 13 bathhouses, the 28 pool rooms and shooting galleries, and a great many small shops conducted by Japanese are patronized almost, if not quite, exclusively by the members of that race. Among the small shops and other establishments to which reference is made are 8 book stores, 3 drug stores, 7 confectioners' shops, 1 meat and 4 fish markets, a few fruit stands, a sake store, and 1 sake brewery, the 4 dealers in bamboo goods, and 3 tofu (bean curd) manufacturers. On the other hand, 2 of 8 photographers have some white patrons, some of the 22 supply stores and groceries find as many as 20 or 25 per cent of their patrons among the white people, the watch repairers and jewelers from 10 to 15, the 18 tailors from 10 to 35, the 34 cleaning and dye shops from 30 to 100. The small gentlemen's furnishing stores also have a small percentage of white patrons. In none of these cases, however, has the gaining of white trade had any particular significance. The more complete provision for meeting the wants of the Japanese has (in some lines) had more. The 42 art and curio stores are patronized largely by white persons, but these compete chiefly with similar stores conducted by the Chinese. The three branches of business in which the percentage of white patrons has been large, in which the Japanese establishments have been relatively numerous, and where the prices charged have been comparatively low, are the laundries, restaurants serving American meals, and the shoe-repair shops, to which further reference will be made presently.

In Sacramento the Japanese have established 2 laundries, 2 restaurants serving American meals, 10 barber shops, and 1 gentlemen's furnishing store outside of the well-defined Japanese quarter, embracing some five or six city blocks, primarily to secure white patronage. The vast majority of their places of business, however, are located within the Japanese quarter. The 37 boarding and lodging houses, the 7 bathhouses, the 4 small hand laundries, the 28 restaurants serving Japanese meals, the 4 employment and real estate agencies located in the Japanese quarter are patronized exclusively by Japanese. The percentage of white patrons of the 1 dry goods store, the 2 drug stores, the 4 jewelry and watch-repair shops, the 1 curio store, the 3 fish markets, and 4 confectionery shops is comparatively small. Nor do the 6 small tailor and dye shops and the 8 gentlemen's furnishing stores located in the Japanese quarter have a large percentage of white patrons. On the other hand, from 15 to 40 per cent of the patronage of the 12 groceries, 2 of which are very large, from a very small percentage to 30 per cent of that of the 16 barber shops, and the larger part of the patronage of the 6 restaurants serving American meals, here located, are from white persons.

Thus the number of establishments having a large percentage of white patrons is comparatively small, and the establishments, with the exception of two grocery stores, are small shops. Of much more importance than the competition for white patronage, however, is the transference of Japanese trade from white shops formerly patronized by them to shops established by their countrymen in recent years, and the change in the population of the district constituting the present Japanese quarter. With the establishment of tailor shops and gentlemen's furnishing stores some of the white shopkeepers located in or within a few blocks of the large Japanese settlement have, within the last few years, lost a part of the business they formerly transacted with the Japanese. As the Japanese have come to the district in which they are at present located, the other races have gradually moved away, partly because of the fact that the rental value of property has increased as the Japanese have offered higher rents, partly because of the dislike most white people evince toward living in or near the Japanese colony. With this change in the character of the population, the white proprietors of the small groceries and other stores, the restaurant keepers, barbers, and others dependent for the greater part upon the patronage of those who live in the immediate vicinity, have suffered loss of business, for the Japanese, for reasons already mentioned, usually patronize shops conducted by their countrymen.

In Los Angeles the 90 boarding and lodging houses, the 58 restaurants serving Japanese meals, the 2 banks, besides the printing establishments and some petty manufacture of Japanese goods, are the principal Japanese places of business patronized exclusively or almost exclusively by the members of that race. The other branches of business are patronized to some extent, and most of them largely, by non-Asiatics. From 60 to 90 per cent of the patrons of the 7 laundries, something less than one-half of the patrons of the 26 baths, a little more than one-half of the patrons of the 44 barber shops, a considerable number of the patrons of most of the 33 pool halls and billiard parlors, the vast majority of the patrons of the

21 restaurants serving American meals, the majority of the patrons of the 17 cobbler shops, from 20 to 50 per cent of the patrons of the 16 tailor and dye shops, about 18.5 per cent of the patrons of the groceries and provision stores investigated, a considerable percentage of those of the 3 fish markets, about one-half of the patrons of the 5 watch-repairing shops, a small percentage of the patrons of the 8 drug and book stores, about 30 per cent of those of the 1 liquor store,[a] and a considerable percentage of the patrons of several of the numerous cigar and fruit stands were members of other races than the Japanese, as were practically all of the patrons of the 15 art and curio stores constituting one of the most important branches of Japanese business.

With the exception of the art stores and some of the laundries, practically all of the Japanese establishments are located in or very near the two districts in which the Japanese have colonized, and most of their patrons are residents of these same districts. Among them are some Mexicans, a small percentage of negroes, and a large percentage of foreign-born whites of the laboring class. Though a majority of the Japanese establishments are patronized by other races, and some of them almost exclusively so, the competition of these, because of the comparatively small amount of business done by them, has not been of any special importance except in the case of the cobbler shops, restaurants, pool rooms, barber shops, and laundries.

The California cities to which reference has thus far been made are the larger supply centers. Watsonville may be taken as the representative of the smaller cities and towns which serve as supply centers for the farmers and agricultural laborers of the community, with the qualification that the situation which obtains there is the result of a longer period of growth, and that Japanese count for much more than in most of the agricultural centers.

In this town of 5,000 inhabitants the number of Japanese business establishments is 37. The number of boarding houses patronized by Japanese only is 10; of restaurants serving Japanese meals, 1; of billiard and pool rooms and bath houses not frequented by white persons, 4 each. On the other hand, the 2 barber shops, the cobbler shop, the bicycle shop, and the 3 supply stores have a small percentage of patronage by white people, while persons of that race constitute the majority of the patrons of the small hand laundry and of the 5 small restaurants serving American meals. These are all small establishments save one store conducted by a Japanese corporation, and with the exception of the restaurants are of no special importance in so far as their patronage by white persons is concerned. Of more importance, however, is the more complete provision year after year for meeting the needs of the Japanese. Most of their wants are now supplied by their countrymen in business. However, one large store, conducted by a corporation of white men, being in better position to meet the needs of the numerous Japanese farmers and to extend credit to them, does more business with the Japanese than the large Japanese supply house to which reference was made above.

Because of their more recent settlement in the cities and towns of the Rocky Mountain States, the Japanese have not engaged so exten-

---

[a] The others entered in the table are little more than sale agencies.

sively in business there as in the cities of the Pacific Coast States, and most of the establishments conducted by them are devoted chiefly to supplying the laborers of that race at work in the rural communities. The number of Japanese business establishments in Salt Lake City in 1909 was 46; in Ogden, 43; in Denver, 67. These are the three important Japanese supply centers of the "Mountain States." In Salt Lake City the supply and grocery stores and the boarding and lodging houses, the most important branches of business engaged in by the Japanese, are patronized almost exclusively by their own countrymen. On the other hand, the 5 small restaurants serving American meals, the barber shops and baths, employing 8 men, the 3 curio shops, the 3 small tailor and dye shops, and the largest of 3 billiard and pool rooms are patronized largely or principally by white persons. These Japanese establishments are relatively very few, however, and the prices charged are, as a rule, the same as those charged at numerous shops of the same general character conducted by the members of other races. In Ogden most of the Japanese establishments of any particular importance are directly connected with Japanese labor. The establishments having any considerable percentage of their patrons among the white races are the 1 small laundry, with 5 employees; the 1 restaurant serving American meals; and the 4 barber shops, with a total of 8 chairs, and the pool rooms connected with them.

The growth of Japanese business in Denver has been chiefly since 1903 and has been incidental to the employment of many laborers in the growing of sugar beets. Most of the establishments are located in the ill-defined Japanese quarter, and the 10 boarding and lodging houses, the 10 restaurants serving Japanese meals, a bank, a fish market, 2 confectionery shops, and a drug store are patronized almost, if not quite, exclusively by Japanese. Two dairies, the 4 supply stores, the 4 barber shops, and a few other establishments are patronized to some extent by white persons, and in some instances by negroes, but except in the case of the first mentioned the Japanese patrons constitute a majority. The Japanese establishments are relatively few and unimportant. Indeed, the only instance in which Japanese competition has been of any importance in Denver was in the restaurant trade a few years before the influx of any large number of laborers of that race, and that was successfully opposed by the white restaurant keepers and their unionized employees.

In the other Rocky Mountain States the Japanese establishments are few, and these few are largely lodging houses and restaurants for Asiatic laborers and American restaurants and small laundries depending upon American patronage. The only thing noteworthy is the absence of any feeling against them—save in Butte, Mont., where they were not permitted to engage in business at all—and the freedom with which all classes of white persons patronize the small restaurants.

Of much more importance than the extent to which white people have patronized Japanese establishments in different places is the basis upon which such competition as has arisen has taken place. This phase of the matter is best brought out by an account of the laundry, restaurant, shoe repairing, tailoring and dyeing, barber, and provision trades, in which alone, it is evident from what has been said, has there been any great amount of competition between Japanese establishments and those conducted by the members of the various white races.

LAUNDRIES.

All told the Japanese conduct perhaps as many as 160 laundries in the cities and towns of the Western States. Most of these are in the cities of Washington and California. Of the cities investigated by the agents of the Commission, the largest numbers were found in Seattle with 37, San Francisco with 19, Los Angeles with 7, and Sacramento and Tacoma with 6 each. The approximate number of persons employed for wages in the Japanese laundries was 275 or 300 in Seattle, 75 in Tacoma, 350 in San Francisco, 30 in Sacramento, and some 75 or 80 in Los Angeles.

Thus the total number of laborers employed in the 75 laundries of these 5 cities is 800 or 850. The average number for each laundry is thus approximately 11; but this would be increased somewhat were proprietors, frequently two or more partners, included in the total given. The small average indicated is due to the fact that the majority of these laundries are small hand laundries, employing little capital and few men, and doing a small business. Twenty-one of the 37 in Seattle are small establishments connected with Japanese barber shops and bathhouses. Of the 16 independent establishments, 12 employ about 8 persons each; 1, 15; 2 about 30 each; and the largest about 40 men. In Los Angeles only 2 employed as many as 20 men, in Sacramento the largest number employed was 9, in San Francisco, 37. It is significant that 24 laundries for which detailed information was secured, in Seattle, San Francisco, Los Angeles, Sacramento, and Fresno, employed 213, but that 2 of these were operated without hired assistance, 3 with 1 employee each, 4 with from 2 to 5, 6 with from 6 to 9, 4 with from 10 to 19, and 3 with 25, 32, and 37, respectively.

The amount of capital employed was less than $1,000 in 7 of the 24 cases, $1,000 but less than $2,000 in 6, $2,000 in 2, $3,000 in 5, and $3,200, $10,000, $15,000, and $40,000 (including the value of the real estate occupied) in the remaining 4. The gross receipts from the business conducted during the year preceding the investigation were less than $2,000 in 4 cases, $2,000 but less than $3,000 in 4, $3,000 but less than $5,000 in 2, $5,000 but less than $10,000 in 6, $10,000 but less than $20,000 in 4, and $26,400, $35,000, and $42,000, respectively, in the remaining 3 of the 23 reporting data relating to their gross earnings for the year. The total gross earnings for the 23 were $220,740, an average of approximately $9,887.

In all of the five cities to which specific reference has been made, there are numerous white steam laundries, and in some cases, as in San Francisco, numerous French hand laundries, in which several times as many persons are employed as in the Japanese laundries. In San Francisco alone the employees of the white steam laundries number 3,000, while those of the Chinese and French laundries increase this number to 5,000 or more. Yet in Seattle, San Francisco, Los Angeles, Fresno, and in various smaller places serious complaint has been made of Japanese competition in the laundry trade, while in San Francisco and Los Angeles organized effort had been made to limit this competition.

The agents of the Commission found that the majority of the Japanese laundries, and especially the larger ones, had been established during the last few years; that the larger laundries draw most of their business from white persons; that the prices charged for work done have frequently been less than those charged by white laundrymen of various races and by French laundrymen in San Francisco; that Japanese are employed almost exclusively in laundries conducted by their countrymen; and that while they work longer hours per day, their wages are smaller than those paid to persons employed in white steam laundries and to those employed in French laundries in San Francisco. In Seattle the number of Japanese laundries had increased from 1 in 1900 to 20 in 1905, and to 37 in 1909. The number in San Francisco was 8 in 1904 and 19 in 1909. In Los Angeles the corresponding figures were 2 and 7 (with 4 branches); in Tacoma, 3 and 6. Moreover, nearly all of the larger laundries had been established during the last few years. The rapid increase of numbers, though not large as yet, and the introduction of improved methods has caused the sharing of the laundry business with them to be felt by the proprietors of white steam laundries in several cities. Unlike the numerous Chinese hand laundries throughout the West, devoted largely to doing washing " by the bag," the larger Japanese laundries, a few of which are equipped with steam, follow American methods. While in Sacramento, Denver, and Salt Lake the prices charged by Japanese were found not to differ materially from those charged by their competitors, in most places there had been a certain amount of underbidding by the Japanese in order to increase the volume of their business. This is especially true in Seattle and San Francisco, and in some of the small cities and towns where the number of laundries is small. Details bearing upon this point are presented in the special studies to which reference has been made.

The 218 wage-earners employed in the Japanese laundries of San Francisco, Sacramento, Los Angeles, Seattle, and Fresno were, with the exception of 9 white persons, Japanese. In Ogden and Denver, where there are fewer Japanese laborers available for such work, and where there is not so much opposition to the Oriental races as there is in the cities of the Pacific Coast States, more white persons are employed in the few small laundries which have been established. In Seattle, San Francisco, and Los Angeles the agents investigated the wages and hours of work in white as well as in Japanese laundries. The hours are rather irregular and vary greatly, but in general it may be said that in Seattle those of the Japanese laundries are regularly from 66 to 69 per week, as against 55 to 60 in white steam laundries. The corresponding figures for Los Angeles were $8\frac{1}{2}$ per day for the larger steam laundries and 10 per day for the small hand laundries and those conducted by Japanese—all with much overtime each week. In San Francisco the hours per week in Japanese laundries varied from 60 to 72, in 6 French laundries, from 50 to 63, while in unionized white steam laundries they were 49 per week.

Practically all of the Japanese laborers receive board and lodging in addition to wages. This, together with different periods for the payment of wages, makes it difficult to compare the wages of different classes of laundry employees. In San Francisco, however, the average wage of 89 Japanese male employees, with board and lodging, was $28.90 per month; of 32 men and 20 women employed in French laundries, with board and lodging, $37.69 and $33.18, respectively; of 52 men and 65 women employed in other French laundries, without board and lodging, $58.56 and $40.53, respectively; of 140 men and 204 women employed in white steam laundries, these also without board or lodging, $69.74 and $44.33, respectively. It is evident that if allowance is made for the value of board (it costs the Japanese employer from $8 to $10 per month), the wages of the Japanese were lower for a longer work day than those paid to the employees of the competing French and white steam laundries. Similar differences, though less great, were found to prevail in the wages paid to these classes of laundry workers in Seattle and Los Angeles, and in other places where the details as to wages were ascertained. In Los Angeles, which is perhaps more nearly typical than San Francisco of the cities as a whole, the wages of 30 Japanese employed in the 4 laundries investigated and who received board and lodging in addition to the wages paid, varied from $13 to $45 per month. The median wage, with board and lodging, was $25, the average $27.30 per month. Two other Japanese were paid $40 and $45 per month, respectively, without board or lodging, while two German-Russian women, employed for extra work, were paid $1.50 per day. The 5 white steam laundries investigated employed 179 women and 75 men, of whom 165 were native-born whites, 9 American negroes, 14 English, 10 French, 19 German, 8 Irish, 6 Italian, 8 Scandinavian, 3 Scotch, 3 Welsh, 3 Austrian, 1 Canadian, and 4 Mexican. The wages paid to men and women as a group varied from $1 to $2; the median wage, without board or lodging, for the two sexes, was $1.50 per day or about $39 per month, full time. If allowance is made for the cost of boarding and lodging the Japanese laborers (in the buildings used for laundry purposes), it is seen that the wages paid by the white laundries are somewhat higher, though the workday is shorter.

The increase in the number of Japanese laundries, the increase in their size, the improvements in their methods and equipment, and the expansion of their business, though its volume is in no large city more than a small percentage of the whole, together with the comparatively low rates of wages which prevail in the Japanese laundries, have caused the white laundrymen to fear their competition and in some places to organize in order to limit it. In Los Angeles, where the Japanese laundrymen, whose establishments were equipped to do hand work only economically, have taken household linen to the steam laundries to be laundered at " flatwork rates," this fear has taken the form of a resolution adopted in May, 1909, by the Laundrymen's Association to the effect that the members of the organization shall not accept work brought to them by their Asiatic competitors. Moreover, a " gentlemen's agreement " is said to exist between the laundrymen and the laundry machinery supply houses to the effect that the latter shall not furnish equipment to the Japanese, all of whom are now conducting hand laundries. In northern California local "Anti-Jap laundry leagues " are found in several localities, and the formation of a similar organization has been under consideration in Seattle.

The first of these leagues was organized in San Francisco in March, 1908, by the Laundry Drivers' Union, the Laundry Workers' Union, and the proprietors of the white steam laundries. Since then similar organizations have been effected in Alameda County, San Mateo County, San Rafael, Vallejo, Stockton, and Fresno. In Vallejo and Stockton, however, the leagues were short-lived. The methods pursued by these leagues are designed (1) to diminish the white patronage of Japanese laundries, and (2) to render it difficult for them to secure supplies and improve their equipment. Though the methods employed by the several organizations differ somewhat, those adopted in San Francisco have been copied by other leagues more recently organized in so far as they were applicable, and may therefore be regarded as fairly typical. Lists of patrons of Japanese laundries are prepared, and appeals are made in person, by card, or by letter to these patrons to discontinue sending laundry to Japanese establishments. Billboard advertising, making appeals along the same lines, has also been resorted to. At the same time, the league has been active in preventing the granting of the necessary permits to Japanese to operate steam laundries, and by appeals or threat of boycott the cooperation of some of the laundry-supply houses has been gained, with the result that difficulty has been experienced by some of the Japanese proprietors in securing needed supplies.[a]

Largely because of the opposition with which they had met, the proprietors of the Japanese laundries in San Francisco in March, 1909, effected a protective organization known as the Association of Japanese Laundries of America. Its objects are to protect and to "promote the development and prosperity of the business of its members." In order to do this an "emergency fund" is being formed from the dues of $2 per month paid by each member until his contributions shall amount to $100. The constitution of the association provides also for the extension of financial aid to members, and the lending of laborers in cases where extra help is needed, and for the regulation of the hours of labor and pay for overtime work.

RESTAURANTS SERVING AMERICAN MEALS.

As already stated, in a number of localities the Japanese, as the first branch of business engaged in, have conducted restaurants serving American meals. This was the case in Seattle, Portland, Los Angeles, and Denver, and in a much longer list of places, where restaurants were opened some years before these places became important as supply centers and when the resident Japanese population was small. While this is true, the greater number and especially the larger of these restaurants have been established in recent years, as the members of this race have accumulated some capital and have sought profitable employment for it.

The advance in some of the large cities has not been rapid because of the strong opposition encountered. The number in Seattle has increased from 10 in 1900 and 21 in 1905 to 36 in 1909; in Tacoma from 4 in 1905 to 5 in 1909; in Los Angeles from 21 in 1904 to 25 in 1909. In Portland the number in 1891 was 4; in 1900 and also in 1909, 14. In San Francisco there were 8 in 1904, and more than 30 in

---

[a] A full account of the methods employed by the Anti-Jap Laundry League will be found in the special report on the "Japanese in city trades and employments in San Francisco." Details will be found in the published proceedings of its Pacific coast conventions held in December, 1908, and May, 1909.

1906, but because of strong opposition the number in 1909 had decreased to 17. In the smaller towns the progress has been much more rapid, for the opposition has not been great, and, unlike that in the larger cities, has been unorganized. In many of the smaller places the conducting of restaurants serving American meals is the most important branch of Japanese business enterprise. Moreover, in many of these places the small number of these restaurants constitutes a much larger percentage of the total than the larger numbers in the cities constitute of the larger number found there.

Most of the Japanese restaurants are small and sell meals for 10, 15, or 20 cents " and up." The approximate number of persons employed in the 36 restaurants in Seattle is 200; in the 5 in Tacoma, 40; in the 14 in Portland, 94; in the 25 in Los Angeles, 125; in the 17 in San Francisco, 125. Most of them are patronized to some extent by Japanese who prefer American meals, but the great majority of the patrons in all cities are white persons, and principally of the laboring and low-salaried classes. Their competition is with the " quick-lunch " houses and the third and fourth class restaurants. The more extensive investigations of the restaurant trade were made by the agents of the Commission in Seattle, Sacramento, and Los Angeles. The details relating to the restaurants investigated may be found in the special reports dealing with the Japanese in city trades and employments in those cities.

In Seattle the Japanese restaurants serve 10 or 15 cent meals and are located, some in the older shopping district, some near industrial establishments, and some in the Japanese quarter. Previous to 1907 the price of meals was uniformly 10 cents. At that time, however, a union was formed, and the price was increased to 15 cents which now prevails except in a few establishments the proprietors of which did not become members of the organization. But, whatever the price charged, the agent of the Commission, as a result of his investigation, is of the opinion that the restaurants serve better meals at the price than the majority of their competitors, " white restaurants," also serving 10 and 15 cent meals. The former were found to have an advantage in the wages paid employees. In the 9 Japanese restaurants investigated it was found that first cooks were paid from $35 to $70 per month, with board and, as a rule, with lodging, the greater number being paid $35, $40, or $45 per month; second cooks were paid from $32 to $42 per month; and third cooks from $30 to $40. In 6 white restaurants conducted in the same localities, two of them by Slovenians and one by Greeks, cooks were paid, with board and usually with lodging, $16, $17, and $18 per week, and 2 head cooks $100 and $150 per month, respectively. The Japanese male waiters employed were paid from $25 to $40, the prevailing rate being $30 per month, or $1 per day. A few white waitresses were also employed in these Japanese establishments at the current rates—$8, $8.50, and $9 per week, with board. In the white restaurants, 8 waiters were paid $10; 3, $12; 2, $14; and 2, $15 per week. The waitresses were paid at the same rates as in the Japanese restaurants. The " general " and " kitchen " help in the Japanese restaurants were paid as follows: 5, $25; 1, $28; 1, $29; and 3, $30 per month. In the white restaurants men were paid $8, $9, $10, or $11, and women $8 per week.

The wages of the Japanese men employed by their countrymen are thus shown to be smaller than those of the white men employed in the competing restaurants. Within the districts in which the Japanese restaurants are located their competition has been seriously felt, and a few white restaurants have been closed because of the smallness of profit. The same is true, however, of some Japanese establishments which were not well managed, for in this trade the expense account depends far more upon economy and intelligence in management than upon the cost of labor.

In Los Angeles the same general situation obtains, except that some of the white proprietors of cheap restaurants investigated employed Japanese as "kitchen help." About the same differences as in Seattle are found in the wages paid. An added source of disadvantage encountered by the white restaurant keepers in one of the districts in which the Japanese have settled is that there has been a gradual change in recent years in the racial composition of the community. In Sacramento also it was found that higher wages were paid to the employees of 4 restaurants conducted by Americans, Germans, Danes, and Slovenians than in the Japanese establishments near by and which sold meals of the same general character at about the same price—10 and 15 cents " and up."

In almost all, if not in all, of the larger cities of the Pacific Coast States, and in Denver, the Japanese restaurants have met with opposition from organized labor. This has taken the form of union rules, sometimes vigorously enforced by fines in cases of violation, and of more general boycotts in Denver, San Francisco, and Seattle. As a result of the cooperation of the restaurant keepers and the cooks and waiters in Denver several years ago, the several Japanese restaurant keepers found it impossible to secure supplies and were forced to suspend business. They have not since engaged in this trade. In San Francisco the rioting directed against the Japanese restaurants as a result of a boycott conducted by the Cooks and Waiters' Union in 1906 resulted in considerable damage to property, and has been primarily responsible for the decline of the Japanese restaurant trade, which for some time, and especially after the fire earlier in the year mentioned, had been expanding rapidly.

BARBER SHOPS.

Another branch of Japanese business which has expanded rapidly and which has secured the patronage of a comparatively large number of white persons, most of them residents of the poorer districts of the cities in which the Japanese quarters are generally found, is that of conducting barber shops. This increase in the number of shops has been more rapid in such cities as Seattle, Tacoma, Portland, Sacramento, Los Angeles, Fresno, and Ogden, where they have not met with strong and persistent opposition, than where there has been strong opposition to the Japanese, as in San Francisco and Denver. The number of shops in Seattle increased from 1 in 1894, to 12 in 1900, to 18 in 1905, to 46 in 1909; in Tacoma from 2 in 1905, to 9 in 1909; in Portland from 2 in 1900, to 10 in 1909; in Los Angeles from 18 in 1904, to 44 in 1909; in Fresno from 6 in 1900, to 10 in 1904, to 12 in 1909; in Sacramento from a few in 1900 to 26 in 1909. In

Ogden there are 4 shops, but elsewhere in the Rocky Mountain States they are few and of little consequence. In San Francisco, where there has been much friction between the Japanese and the white races, the Japanese shops are seldom patronized by white persons, and the number of Japanese shops has increased and diminished with the increase and decrease in the size of the Japanese population. The number of shops in 1894 was 2; in 1899, 6; in 1904, 21; in 1909, 18. In most of the other cities mentioned, however, the number of Japanese shops has increased more rapidly than the population of that race, and they not only are sufficient to meet the needs of the Japanese patrons, but find a large percentage of their patrons among the other races, and especially among the members of the laboring classes who live in or near the districts occupied in part by the Japanese. The increase in the amount of this white patronage has made possible a part of the progress shown in this trade.

The great majority of the Japanese barber shops are of the same type as those characteristic of the districts in which they are located. With few exceptions, the most important of which is a shop in Los Angeles in which 12 white barbers are employed, they have only 1, 2, or 3 chairs, the proprietor usually working alone, or with the assistance of his wife or that of 1 employee. A total of 143 men were employed in the 46 shops in Seattle, 20 in the 9 in Tacoma, 31 in the 10 in Portland, about 50 in the 26 in Sacramento, 33 in the 18 in San Francisco, about 100 in the 44 in Los Angeles, 14 in the 12 in Fresno, and 8 in the 4 in Ogden. It is evident from the number of persons thus engaged in these cities that the trade has assumed greater proportions in Seattle, Los Angeles, and Sacramento than elsewhere. The agents of the Commission investigated the trade in these three cities, taking schedules for competing white shops as well as for the Japanese.

In Seattle the competition of the Japanese barbers, because of the rapid increase in number and the low prices charged, has been keenly felt—more so, perhaps, than in any other trade. The barbers of this race are competing with a large number of small shops of the same general character and a smaller number of larger shops, the former conducted by the members of various white races, the latter chiefly by Americans and located in the older business district adjoining the Japanese quarter of the city. Of 10 Japanese shops investigated, 2 reported that 30 per cent of their patrons were white persons; 2, 50 per cent; 2, 60 per cent; 1, 80 per cent: and 3, 90 per cent. White persons constitute perhaps two-thirds of the patrons of the Japanese shops, taken as a whole.

Since 1902 the prices charged by the Japanese barbers have been determined by a union which they then organized. Previous to 1907 the price for hair cutting was 15 cents; for shaving, 10 cents; but upon reorganization of the union at that time the former price was raised to 25 cents. Moreover, in some shops white customers are charged 15 cents for shaving. With the increase in the number of these Japanese shops the union scale in white shops has been lowered from 35 cents to 25 cents. Moreover, some of the "downtown" shops have reduced the price for shaving from 15 cents to 10 cents, in order, it is said, to meet the Japanese competition. Some of the white barbers on First Avenue South have changed locations because of the severe competition. In the several white shops investigated, all located near Japanese shops, the barbers were paid a percentage of their gross earnings, with a minimum wage guaranteed. Nineteen of the barbers employed in these shops reported their average earnings as about $16, while 24 reported their average earnings as about $18 per week. The Japanese barbers working for wages are paid less. Those employed in the 10 shops investigated received either $45 or $50 per month without, and from $15 to $30 per month with, board and lodging, the cost of which may be reckoned at from $10 to $12 per month.

In Los Angeles the Japanese shops are freely patronized by other races as well as by Japanese, the proportions of the latter varying for the 8 shops investigated from 1 to 90 per cent and averaging between 48 and 49 per cent. Some of the patrons are negroes and Mexicans, and practically all reside near the Japanese shops, which, with the exception of two, are located in the two districts of the city in which the Japanese have settled in large numbers. The prices charged by the Japanese barbers are uniformly 15 cents for hair cutting and 10 cents for shaving, which, with few exceptions, have been the rates charged at other shops located in the same districts. In a few shops conducted by other races, however, the prices charged have been even less. The union prices in the larger shops in other parts of the city are 25 cents for hair cutting and 15 cents for shaving, while the prices in still other shops are 20 and 10 cents. The patronage of Japanese shops is almost entirely local in character, however, and the effects of any competition equally restricted. The Japanese barbers in the majority cf the shops are paid $30, $35, $40, or $45 per month with board and lodging, but those in other shops, following the general rule in this trade, are paid 60 per cent of their gross earnings without board and lodging. In 5 white shops located near some of these Japanese establishments 10 barbers earned on the average $61 per month on the same percentage basis, while 1 was paid $10 per week. Thus the white and Japanese proprietors compete on about equal terms as regards wages and prices. Yet the former complain of the loss of business, and some have closed their shops. The explanation of the loss of business is evidently due to the increase in the number of shops and the change which has taken place in the character of the population of the two districts in which the Japanese have settled.

Formerly in Sacramento all of the Japanese shops were located in the " Japanese quarter," but in recent years several have been located in another district of the city. The white patrons of the 16 shops located in the first-mentioned district vary from practically none to 50 per cent, while those of the 10 located in the latter district vary from 50 to 80 per cent of the total. Partly because of the increase in the number of Japanese shops, and partly because of the lower prices which they have until recently charged, the barbers of other races complain of the competition. The prices charged at the Japanese shops have been determined by the union which has been maintained in the trade and previous to July, 1909, were 20 cents for hair cutting and 10 cents for shaving. In July, 1909, however, the former price was raised to 25 cents, so that now the Japanese prices are the same as those which have prevailed in the white shops of these districts of the city. In other shops not far away, however, the price for shaving is 15 cents. The chief complaint on the part of other barbers, however, is the increase in the number of Japanese shops, which has resulted in the sharing of the trade among a greater number. It was found, however, that a large percentage of the shops conducted by other races had also been established during the few years in which the Japanese shops have increased in number most rapidly.

In Stockton and Fresno, where the Japanese have opened a number of shops and have secured a considerable patronage by white persons, the situation differs from the preceding in that for some time there has been an agreement between the proprietors of white union shops and the Japanese Barbers' Union as to the prices which shall be charged. The difference in details between the two cities are not material. In Fresno the white patrons, chiefly laborers, of the 4 small Japanese shops investigated, constituted from 10 to 80 per cent of the total number. Most of this patronage has been secured in recent years, and especially shortly previous to 1907, when the prices charged were much lower than those maintained by union white barbers. Until that time the price for hair cutting maintained by the Japanese union had been 15 cents, for shaving 10 cents, while the union white shops maintained the scale of 35 and 15 cents respectively. This difference in prices, with the increasing number of Japanese shops, caused a loss of patronage of some of the competing barbers. To prevent this an agreement was entered into in 1907 providing that the Japanese shops should adopt the union (white) scale for their white patrons. At the same time 25 cents and 15 cents were fixed upon as the prices to be charged Japanese patrons. Some months later, however, the price for hair cutting at Japanese shops was reduced to 25 cents for all patrons in order to meet the competition of some nonunion white shops which had been opened and in which this price obtained.

SHOE REPAIRING.

Shoe repairing is another trade in which the Japanese have made rapid progress in recent years in California. The first establishment was opened in San Francisco in 1890, but many if not most of the 189 shops which in March, 1909, were on the list of the Japanese Shoemakers' Union have been started in the last six years. The number in Los Angeles in 1904 was 2; in 1909, 17; in San Francisco in 1904, 60; in March, 1909, 72. The great majority of the shops are located in the cities about San Francisco Bay, but one or more are found in most of the towns of the northern part of the State in which any Japanese have settled. In the cities and towns of other States the number of shops is very small and of no particular significance.

The Japanese cobbler shops are small and the older handwork methods are followed in making repairs. Practically all, if not all, of the master journeymen, journeymen, and apprentices employed in the Japanese shops in California are members of the Shoemakers' Union to which reference has been made, and in 1909 numbered 298.

In Seattle, Sacramento, San Francisco, Los Angeles, and in all other localities in which the shoe-repairing trade was investigated the Japanese prices were found to be lower than those which ordinarily prevail in the competing shops conducted by white craftsmen, most of them also foreign-born, in the same localities. This underbidding, together with changes in population, has given rise to much complaint of Japanese competition in such places as San Francisco and Los Angeles, where the number of Japanese shops in certain districts has become comparatively large.

In Los Angeles, where most of the cobbler shops established by Japanese are located in the older of the two districts in which the members of that race have settled, and in which as a result of the incoming of Japanese the composition of the population has changed, the proprietors of small cobbler shops located near by have lost much of their business. They have been adversely affected also by the competition of better equipped shops in other parts of the city. A large percentage of the patrons of the Japanese shops are white people, living or working in the vicinity of the shops. The chief inducement they have to patronize these shops is the lower prices which are charged for repairs. The price for half-soling men's shoes, hand sewed, is $1 or $1.25 at white, 90 cents at Japanese shops. Corresponding differences were found to obtain in the prices charged for other kinds of repair work.

In San Francisco, where the Japanese shops number more than 70 in a total of perhaps 1,000, the cobblers of other races located in some districts complain of underbidding by Japanese and of the increase of the number of cobblers, among whom the smaller amount of repair work since the fire of 1906 has been shared. The agents of the Commission found that the Japanese shops located in the city blocks in which many members of that race reside had white and Japanese patrons in about equal numbers, but that white persons constituted from 85 to 95 per cent of the patrons of the shops located elsewhere.

Though the price charged for half-soling shoes is $1.25, as against 90 cents in Los Angeles, the practically uniform prices of the Japanese cobblers were found generally to be lower than the varying prices of the white cobblers, most of whom are foreign-born, with almost every prominent European race represented among them. The net incomes of 17 Japanese cobblers investigated varied from $40 to $80, and averaged $61.76 per month. The net earnings of an equal number of white cobblers whose shops were in the same localities varied between $400 as a minimum and $1,200 as a maximum, and averaged slightly less than $800 ($799.06) per year.

Most of these Japanese shoemakers were engaged in the same craft before immigrating to this country. The craft was well organized in Japan, and in this country a corresponding organization was effected in 1893, when the number of shoemakers of that race in California was about 20. This organization not only fixes a scale of prices to be charged, usually minimum prices, but controls the location of shops and protects and furthers the interests of its members in various ways. In opening shops no two (Japanese shops) may be located within 1,000 feet of each other. A member of the union opening a shop in a locality where no Japanese shop is in existence may be assisted by a loan of money from the organization not to exceed $50 in all. The union also maintains a supply house in San Francisco and several thousand dollars of the "business fund," accumulated from dues paid, are invested in the stock of goods carried. Most of these goods are purchased from two firms in the East and are sold to the members of the organization at an advance of 10 per cent on the cost. Finally, this organization controls apprenticeship to the trade, and maintains a system of fraternal benefits along the lines commonly followed by craft organizations. The advantages in competition derived from the organization are apparent.[a]

TAILORING, CLEANING, AND DYEING.

In the cities and towns in which Japanese business was investigated by the agents of the Commission, there were 136 tailor shops, cleaning and dye shops, and dressmaking establishments. The great majority of these have been started in recent years. In San Francisco the number of such establishments was 5 in 1899, 15 in 1904, and 52 in 1909; in Los Angeles, 2 in 1904, and 16 (2 of which were dressmaking establishments) in 1909; in Seattle, 4 in 1900, 12 in 1905, and 45 in 1909. In the smaller cities and towns, such shops as have been established have been opened in recent years. Practically all of these shops are small and the majority are devoted to cleaning, dyeing, and pressing clothes as their main business. Of the 45 shops in Seattle only 5 have more than 5 employees each. In San Francisco 54 proprietors and 101 wage-earners—a total of 155—were employed in the 52 shops, while the corresponding number for the 16 shops in Los Angeles was about 40.

These small shops are located in the districts settled in part by Japanese and compete with many shops of a similar character conducted by the members of other races. In Seattle white persons constituted from 10 to 90 per cent of the patrons of 7 shops investigated. The corresponding figures for 4 shops in Los Angeles were 20 to 50 per cent, for 7 in San Francisco 10 to 100 per cent. The percentage of white patrons of a shop depends largely upon its location, for the business is almost entirely local in character, and upon the relative importance of tailoring as opposed to dyeing, cleaning, and pressing. Few white persons have suits made by Japanese tailors, while a large percentage of the Japanese do in San Francisco, Seattle, and Los Angeles, and a smaller percentage in Sacramento. The competition of Japanese tailors has not been seriously felt except in those cases, as in Sacramento, where as their shops have been established a part of the Japanese patronage which had been given to a limited number of white tailors has been transferred to them. In Seattle, San Francisco, and Los Angeles, however, these shops have secured a large percentage of the cleaning and pressing of suits for white persons residing near by. In Los Angeles this is usually done at the prices which have prevailed in the same localities—50 cents per suit for pressing and 75 cents for cleaning and pressing. In San Francisco the same prices with correspondingly low prices for other work, prevail in the

---

[a] A fuller account of the Kako Domei Kwai, or Japanese Shoemakers' Union, and of the circumstances under which the first cobblers immigrated to California and opened shops, will be found in "The Japanese in city employments and business in San Francisco, Cal."

Japanese shops. Here the prices are lower than those generally charged at shops conducted by other races, if the poorest shops are excepted.

The prices now charged were established as minima by the Japanese Suit Cleaning Union, which was organized in February, 1909, and which has as members the majority of the proprietors of cleaning, pressing, and dye shops. The competition of the Japanese cleaners and dyers has been more far-reaching in its effects in Seattle than elsewhere, if some small places, such as Bellingham, Wash., are excepted. In Seattle the agent of the Commission found that "high-class" and even "second-class" tailors were not affected by Japanese competition, but that the third-rate shops, and especially those which do cleaning and pressing as their chief business, were quite seriously affected. The Japanese tailors make suits for less money than white men and their workmanship is often as good. The charge for pressing suits has been reduced from $1 to 50 cents, and for pressing trousers from 25 cents to 15 cents, on account of low Japanese prices. Even at these rates the white establishments have lost much of their business to Japanese.

A few white tailors are employed in the larger Japanese shops in Seattle and one is employed in the largest shop in Los Angeles. These men are cutters or other skilled workmen. The other employees are Japanese. The wages paid in the shops investigated in Seattle, San Francisco, and Los Angeles varied from $20 to $65 per month with board and lodging; from $40 to $55 with lodging only; and from $35 to $80 per month with neither board nor lodging. The average monthly wage of 26, with board and lodging, was $39.23; of 8, with lodging only, $47.50; of 8, with neither board nor lodging, $51.88. Still other Japanese were employed at piece rates as are most of the workmen in American shops.

PROVISION AND GROCERY STORES.

The number of provision and grocery stores in the cities and towns in which Japanese business was investigated in 1909 numbered 124. Some of these are large establishments engaged chiefly in providing Japanese laborers employed in railroad and other work in country places with canned goods and other staple supplies, chiefly of Japanese origin. At the other extreme are many small establishments carrying Japanese and American goods in stock in varying proportions and patronized by varying percentages of white persons and Japanese. The stores of the large cities are located in the districts in which the Japanese are settled in largest numbers, and with the more specialized stores which have developed meet most of the wants of the Japanese save for clothing of a superior type. In Seattle, Sacramento, Los Angeles, San Francisco, and elsewhere, it was found that the Japanese traded chiefly at stores conducted by their countrymen, though some of them have shown a tendency to seek better service or better bargains elsewhere.

The number of Japanese provision and grocery stores has increased rapidly in all of the cities in which the Japanese population is large. In Seattle they numbered 16 in 1905 and 26 in 1909; in San Francisco, 10 in 1904 and 22 and 1909; in Los Angeles, 6 in 1904 and 27 in 1909. In Sacramento there are now 12, most of which have been established in the last five or six years. This increase is due partly to the increase of the Japanese populations of these cities during this time, partly to the fact that a smaller percentage of the laborers are now controlled by contractors and provided with supplies by them, and partly by an increasing amount of patronage by other races.

In Seattle an agent of the Commission investigated 9 of the 26 grocery stores. Making allowance for differences in the volume of business transacted, a little less than three-fifths of their patrons were white persons, while some $51,800 of the total $96,800 of sales were of goods of Asiatic origin, most of which, together with some goods of non-Asiatic origin, were sold to Japanese. It is evident that the larger part of the business is done with Japanese. These stores are located in a district in which there are a large number of small shops and a small number of larger grocery stores. A large percentage of the small shops are conducted by Greeks, Italians, and Servians, and these places are patronized chiefly by persons of the same race as the proprietor. The competition of the Japanese has been chiefly with the stores conducted by other races than those just mentioned. While their rents are a larger percentage of their receipts, the wages paid to their employees were found to be lower than those paid in the few large white stores investigated by the agent. The wages of the 11 employees of 7 Japanese stores (the other 2 investigated were conducted without hired assistance) averaged $29.55 per month, with board and lodging, while the wages of the white men employed in other stores were very much larger.

The competition which exists in Seattle is purely local. In Sacramento, on the other hand, 2 of the 12 grocery stores employ large amounts of capital, and though located in the Japanese quarter, sell and deliver goods to families living in all parts of the city. From 30 to 70 per cent of the customers of 5 stores investigated were white persons, but their purchases were reported as being from 15 to 40 per cent of the total, and Japanese goods from 50 to 70 per cent of those sold. The facts that most of the goods were of Japanese origin and that most of the sales were to Japanese, while the majority of the customers were white persons, is due to the large amount of business done with Japanese agricultural "bosses" and Japanese farmers who purchase supplies in large quantities for their employees. While some of the Japanese grocers are selling goods to families living in various parts of the city, their competition affects the small grocers in and near the Japanese quarter far more than others.

The Japanese sell at somewhat lower prices than other grocers in Sacramento. Not only do they sell at lower prices, they also pay lower wages than the white proprietors of 5 groceries located in the same part of the city. The wages of 11 Japanese clerks and drivers varied between $25 and $40 and averaged $31.59 per month, with board and lodging. The wages of 9 white male and 2 female employees in white stores varied between $40 as a minimum and $90 as a maximum, and averaged $63.82 per month, without board and lodging. The most serious disadvantage under which the white storekeepers have labored, however, is that most of their trade is local, and that with the influx of the Japanese, many of their white patrons have moved to other parts of the city.

An agent of the Commission investigated 9 of the 27 Japanese grocery and provision stores in Los Angeles. Their annual sales aggregated $423,400. More than one-half, 51.5 per cent, of the goods sold were of non-Japanese origin, much of it being rice grown in Texas, and about 81.5 per cent of the sales were made to Japanese, a large percentage of them farmers in Los Angeles County and " bosses " of agricultural labor in the southern part of the State, who purchase provisions in large quantities for the men who work under their control. Such competition as has developed in this branch of trade has been scarcely felt by white grocers. At any rate, no especial complaint of Japanese competition was made by these men. Twenty-three Japanese men, 1 Japanese woman, and 1 white woman were employed in the 9 stores investigated. Omitting two managers, the wages of the 21 men varied between $30 and $50, and averaged $38.24 per month, with board and lodging. In San Francisco the competition between Japanese and other races is even less than in Los Angeles. The white patronage of Japanese provision stores investigated varied from 5 to 25 per cent of the total. About 50 per cent of the goods sold were reported to be of Asiatic origin.

ORGANIZATION.

Another detail of interest in connection with Japanese business is the extent to which they are organized into associations to limit competition among themselves or to protect themselves from injury by others and to further their own interests. Reference has been made to the Shoemakers' Union, in which practically, if not quite, all of the Japanese shoemakers of California have membership. The barbers are organized in almost every city in which more than a few shops have been established, to provide for relief of those in distress and to control apprenticeship, hours for opening and closing, and the prices which shall be charged. Among the places in which such unions exist are Seattle, Portland, Sacramento, Fresno, and Stockton. Organizations are even more generally found in the restaurant trades, among restaurants serving Japanese meals and drinks, as well as among those serving American meals. Prices are controlled, as well as other matters of mutual interest to the trade.

The boarding-house keepers are commonly very well organized, especially those who are also labor contractors. The proprietors of laundries are usually organized where more than a few exist, as in Seattle and San Francisco, to standardize wages and hours, and in some instances, as in San Francisco, to provide for their mutual defense. Other interesting instances of organization are found among the carpenters, the expressmen, and watchmakers in Sacramento, among the suit cleaners in San Francisco, among the tailors of San Francisco and Oakland, and among the house cleaners in San Francisco. The more important details relating to these organizations are set forth in the special reports dealing with the Japanese in the cities mentioned. They are of interest here: (1) As an expression of a tendency exhibited still more extensively in their native land, to organize the crafts and branches of business; (2) as an evidence in a large number of instances of the ruinous competition among themselves, said to exist at the time of organization because of new men constantly entering the trade and reducing profits; and (3) as a factor affecting the competitive ability of the Japanese engaged in the businesses in which these organizations exist.

SUMMARY.

A general summary of the persons employed for wages in the Japanese establishments for which schedules were taken in Seattle, San Francisco, Sacramento, Los Angeles, and Fresno, shows that of the 679 only 19 were white persons, and of the 660 Japanese all but 10 were males. The earnings of the 10 Japanese women were as follows: $15, but less than $20 per month in 6 cases; $20, but less than $25 in 1 case; and $25, but less than $30 in the remaining 3 cases, with board and lodging in all cases. Twenty-three of the Japanese males were paid at piece rates or on a commission basis. The earnings per month of the remaining 627 are shown in the following tables, those receiving board and lodging, those receiving board only, those receiving lodging only, and those receiving neither board nor lodging, in addition to their money earnings, being distinguished:

TABLE 41.—*Number of male Japanese employees with each specified amount of earnings per month, with board and lodging, by branch of business.*

Branch of business.	Under $20.	$20 and under $25.	$25 and under $30.	$30 and under $35.	$35 and under $40.	$40 and under $45.	$45 and under $50.	$50 and under $60.	$60 and under $70.	$70 or over.	Total.
Hotels			6	7	2	2		1			18
Barber shops		1			1	1					3
Tailor shops	1	6	1	3	4	3	1	2	3		24
Art and curio stores		1		1	3	1	6	5	7		3	26
Book, drug, and stationery stores	1		1	1							3
Jewelers' and watchmakers' shops		1		1	3						5
Meat and fish markets				6	3	3					12
Cake, confectionery, and tobacco stores	1			3							4
Shoe repairing shops	3	1		1							5
Billiard and pool rooms				1	1	1					3
Bathhouses				1							1
Laundries	19	15	24	50	30	5	4	12			159
Restaurants	5	3	15	33	33	16	6	5		2	118
Provisions and general merchandise stores		3	18	8	13	8	5	4		1	60
Miscellaneous establishments				7	6	11		2		1	27

TABLE 42.—*Number of male Japanese employees with each specified amount of earnings per month, with board, by branch of business.*

Branch of business.	Under $20.	$20 and under $25.	$25 and under $30.	$30 and under $35.	$35 and under $40.	$40 and under $45.	$45 and under $50.	$50 and under $60.	$60 and under $70.	Total.
Barber shops				1	1		1			3
Art and curio stores					1					1
Jewelers' and watchmakers' shops									2	2
Meat and fish markets				1	1	1				3
Cake, confectionery, and tobacco stores			1		1					2
Billiard and pool rooms			2							2
Bath houses						1				1
Restaurants	1	2	33	8	2	2	1		4	53
Provision and general merchandise stores			1							1
Miscellaneous establishments			1	3	2					6

TABLE 43.—*Number of male Japanese employees with each specified amount of earnings per month, with lodging, by branch of business.*

Branch of business.	Under $20.	$20 and under $25.	$25 and under $30.	$30 and under $35.	$35 and under $40.	$40 and under $45.	$45 and under $50.	$50 and under $60.	$60 and under $70.	Total.
Tailor shops						1	2	3		6
Book, drug, and stationery stores						1				1
Meat and fish markets									1	1
Miscellaneous establishments			1						1	2

TABLE 44.—*Number of male Japanese employees with each specified amount of earnings per month, without board or lodging, by branch of business.*

Branch of business.	Under $20.	$20 and under $25.	$25 and under $30.	$30 and under $35.	$35 and under $40.	$40 and under $45.	$45 and under $50.	$50 and under $60.	$60 and under $70.	$70 and under $80.	$80 and under $90.	$100 or over.	Total.
Barber shops	2			1			1	7	2				13
Tailor shops							1	2	2		1		6
Art and curio stores		1	1		1	3		2	2			1	11
Meat and fish markets					4								4
Cake, confectionery, and tobacco stores			1										1
Laundries						1	1						2
Provision and general merchandise stores	2							2			1		7
Miscellaneous establishments				2	3	2	2	6	4	1		1	21

In view of the remarks made concerning wages in the preceding pages of this report, the details presented in this summary table require no comment, save with regard to the general prevalence of the "living in" system among the Japanese. The 10 Japanese women and, including those working at piece rates or on a commission basis, 468 of the 617 Japanese men, received board and lodging; 74, chiefly in the restaurant trade, received board, but not lodging; 10 received lodging, but not board; while 65 received neither board nor lodging, in addition to their money wages.

The table on the next page shows the earnings of 425 Japanese wage-earners in Seattle, San Francisco, Sacramento, Los Angeles, Fresno, and Watsonville for the twelve months ending with the time the schedule in the given case was secured.

TABLE 45.—*Yearly earnings (approximate) of male Japanese 18 years of age or over, by months worked.*

WITH BOARD.

Months worked.	Number working for wages and reporting amount.	Average yearly earnings.	Under $100.	$100 and under $150.	$150 and under $200.	$200 and under $250.	$250 and under $300.	$300 and under $400.	$400 and under $500.	$500 and under $600.	$600 and under $700.	$700 and under $800.	$800 and under $1,000.	$1,000 and under $1,250.	$1,250 and under $1,500.	$1,500 and under $2,000.	$2,000 or over.
12	204	$447.06	2	3	2	10	2	67	69	10	22	7	8	1		1	
11	8	311.63		1		2	1	2	2								
10	8	326.25				1	2	4	1								
9	7	405.00				1	1	2	1	1	1						
8	3	240.00			1	1		1									
7																	
6	5	224.40		1	1	1	1	1									
5	2	187.50			1	1											
4	3	200.00		1		1	1										
3																	
2																	
1																	
Total	240	424.81	2	6	5	18	8	77	73	11	23	7	8	1		1	

WITHOUT BOARD.

Months worked.	Number working for wages and reporting amount.	Average yearly earnings.	Under $100.	$100 and under $150.	$150 and under $200.	$200 and under $250.	$250 and under $300.	$300 and under $400.	$400 and under $500.	$500 and under $600.	$600 and under $700.	$700 and under $800.	$800 and under $1,000.	$1,000 and under $1,250.	$1,250 and under $1,500.	$1,500 and under $2,000.	$2,000 or over.
12	156	$582.63			1	2		16	41	22	35	24	11	1		3	
11	5	448.20						3	1		1						
10	4	578.75					1		2					1			
9	9	311.89				1	3	4	1								
8	5	670.00				1		1	2								1
7																	
6	4	291.00			1		1	2									
5	1	208.00				1											
4																	
3																	
2	1	60.00	1														
1																	
Total	185	556.95	1		2	5	5	26	47	22	36	24	11	2		3	1

The larger number of these men were employed in the business establishments investigated in the 6 cities just mentioned, but a smaller number were employed as domestics, as porters, and in other city occupations. The data being for a miscellaneous group, the table may be used properly to show only the large percentage of the Japanese who had been in fairly regular employment during the year, the wide range in the earnings of those employed full time, and the comparatively few whose earnings were as large as those of craftsmen and small shopkeepers from their labor and small capital, as shown in Table 36.

CHAPTER VI

OTHER ECONOMIC CONSIDERATIONS.

Certain of the economic phases of Japanese immigration remain to be considered. Among these are the standard of living of the Japanese, the articles entering into their consumption, the relation between their expenditures and incomes, the amount of money sent abroad, the savings retained in this country, the forms in which such savings are invested, and the amount of property they have accumulated.

The following table presents the data relative to the outlay per month per individual for food and drink ordinarily consumed, in so far as they can be combined and presented in tabular form:

TABLE 46.—*Cost of food and drink per month per person of Japanese 2 years of age or over, by occupation and industry.*

Occupation and industry.	Number reporting complete data.	Number spending each specified amount per month.							
		Under $6.	$6 and under $7.	$7 and under $8.	$8 and under $9.	$9 and under $10.	$10 and under $12.	$12 and under $14.	$14 or over.
Business men and city wage-earners...................	860	28	49	83	110	36	192	166	a 196
Farmers and farm laborers...	855	54	92	211	73	62	189	96	78
Coal miners (Wyoming).....	44	0	0	0	0	0	0	13	31

a Including 35 persons spending: 3, $23.33; 13, $25; 2, $27.50; 11, $30; 1, $35; 1, $40; 1, $45; 2, $50; 1, $60.

In considering the outlay for food and drink, it is necessary to divide the Japanese into groups. The above table presents data relating to 860 individuals who were engaged in business or were employed by those who were so engaged, or were members of the families of such persons. Inasmuch as the "living-in" system generally obtains in Japanese establishments, the two classes are found in the groups and must be considered together. The data for business men and city wage-earners were obtained from Seattle, San Francisco, Los Angeles, Sacramento, Watsonville, and Fresno. Those engaged in conducting restaurants and other enterprises such that the outlays would not be normal were eliminated from the tabulation. While few of the data have been taken from accounts kept, the estimates are indicative of the wide differences which prevail and the extremes which are found among the Japanese as among other races. Of 860 the cost per individual per month, as reported, was less than $6 for 28, $6 but less than $7 for 49, $7 but less than $8 for 83, $8 but less than $9 for 110, $9 but less than $10 for 36, $10 but less than $12 for 192, $12 but less than $14 for 166, and $14 or over for 196. The number of those whose outlay was $12 or over per month was larger among those investigated than the number of those whose outlay was less than $10. As will be noted, the expenditures of some were very much in excess of $14 per month, but most of these boarded at restaurants, and the outlay was for more than the articles constituting their food and drink, which alone are covered by the figures where the group had a table of its own. The average of reported expenditures per month in San Francisco was $11.08; in Sacramento, $8.32.

There are many Japanese in cities who do not live with their employers, but live in boarding houses. The cost of board and lodging at these establishments is a good index to the standard of living. In one boarding house in Los Angeles, practically all of the boarders at which were regularly employed in the city, the charge for board was $9 per month, and for lodging $3.50 to $7 per month. At another the charge for board was $10 per month; for lodging from $3 to $10. These are typical of the boarding houses patronized by the "rank and file" of Japanese. There are, however, many Japanese whose board and lodging is much more expensive. The members of shoemaking and house-cleaning groups in San Francisco may also be used for the purpose of illustration. Twelve groups of house cleaners living with shoemakers and paying for their board and lodging reported the cost at from $12 to $15 per month. It should be added that they usually take turns in preparing the meals.

The data for farmers and farm laborers presented in the table were secured from farmers and relate to them, the members of their families, and such of their employees as were provided with board in addition to wages. The figures are not entirely comparable with the others given, for a large percentage of the farmers produced a part of the food they consumed. A small percentage, it has been seen, keep cows, pigs, and poultry. Though their specialization in commercial farming is extreme, the majority of them have some vegetables and fruit, or both, which are available for home consumption. Hence the figures in the table, representing merely the outlay for goods purchased, do not measure the entire consumption. The cost of the whole would have been materially larger. Of the 855 reported, the cost for each of 54 was less than $6 per month; of 92, $6 but less than $7; of 211, $7 but less than $8; of 73, $8 but less than $9; of 62, $9 but less than $10; of 189, $10 but less than $12; of 96, $12 but less than $14; of 78, $14 or over.

Of much more importance is the cost of food and drink consumed by groups of farm laborers, who embrace a far larger number than the groups of farmers, their families, and employees provided with board. The food is usually prepared for these groups by the members, who work in turn, or by a cook provided by the employer or paid so much per day for each member of the group. The outlay reported by groups of farm laborers in California varied from 23 to 30 cents per day. In other cases, however, they are boarded by the " boss " under whose supervision they work, and the charge here varied from as little as 20 cents per day in a few to more than 30 cents in other cases. But however the board may be provided, the cost is far more frequently either 25 or 26 cents per day than any other amount. While at work the cost of the laborer's board is usually between $7 and $8 per month.

The cost of food consumed by Japanese section hands may be reckoned at from $8 to $8.50 per month, or, roughly, $2 per week. The figures reported by the men, those reported by the supply companies, and the deductions from earnings on account of purchases, as shown by pay rolls, all combined to cause this to be accepted as a fairly accurate estimate. Data were obtained from 41 coal miners at Rock Springs, Wyo. About three-fourths of them reported their outlay for food and drink at $12 but less than $14 per month, the remainder spending $14 or a slightly higher amount. Data were also secured for 146 Japanese employed in the packing houses of South Omaha. The group was so large that accurate accounts were kept of all outlays and the figures submitted were taken by an agent from those accounts. The cost of board and lodging per month for each of the 146 was $12.

Data relating to the cost of food and drink were not collected and tabulated for other races, save in exceptional instances. It may be said, however, that the outlay of the Japanese for food and drink does not differ materially from that of other races similarly circumstanced with reference to work and earnings and living largely as members of groups of single men. The outlay of Japanese section hands is somewhat larger than that of the Mexicans, for the rice and canned fish constituting a large part of the diet of the former are more expensive than the beans so largely consumed by the latter. The cost of living of the Japanese at boarding houses in Los Angeles and elsewhere does not differ particularly from that at boarding houses patronized by Slovenians and other recent immigrants. The expenditures of the Japanese do not differ particularly from those of the more recent and poorer Germans or of the Russians in Los Angeles. It is true, however, that while the board of white farm laborers is reckoned at 50 or 75 cents per day in California, and while these laborers frequently pay $14, $15, or $16 per month for the board they receive on ranches, the cost of the food consumed by the Japanese farm laborers, as stated above, is usually 25 or 26 cents per day. The important fact is, however, that the cost of food and other necessaries is covered by the smaller part of the earnings of those immigrants who are working and living as groups of single men and are not charged with the support of a family in this country.

The articles of food entering into the consumption of the Japanese vary greatly according to circumstances, those consumed by railroad laborers and others similarly circumstanced being chiefly of articles of Japanese origin, unless Texas rice is purchased as it is, except in the Northwestern States—while those consumed by those who make individual purchases include more items of food of non-Japanese origin. With the exception of that of a small percentage who patronize "American restaurants," however, their diet differs greatly from that of natives and the European immigrants. Tea, soft drinks, rice, canned fish, and sauce are among the more important articles purchased. Vegetables and fruit are important in the consumption of the agricultural classes. They do not use much milk or butter and the majority do not consume much fresh meat, though in some instances the consumption of meat is large. In short, the majority of the Japanese consume chiefly the food articles to which they were accustomed in their native land, where animal husbandry has only recently made much advance. A tendency is evident among them, however, to use more of the articles entering largely into the consumption of the other races. This substitution is being hastened by the fact that rice is not cheap food, especially since the price has increased so rapidly in recent years.

Lodging has not been an important item in the budget of the Japanese. The agricultural laborers, miners, cannery hands, railroad laborers, lumber-mill employees, in fact practically all employed outside of cities, are provided with lodging in addition to wages, such lodging as is provided, as a rule, not being regarded as a commercial consideration. Only here and there is any charge made for lodging provided, and in these very exceptional cases it is usually 50 cents or $1 per month. Similarly in the cities the Japanese employed in business establishments and shops conducted by their countrymen and in domestic service are generally provided with lodging, while the business and shopkeeping class more frequently than not live in the building sheltering the business conducted. Thus few Japanese, save those living as boarding or lodging groups and in the boarding and lodging houses of the cities, have a separate item for lodging in their budgets. The expense at the boarding houses has already been indicated. These Japanese laborers are much better housed than the Chinese, who are very gregarious, and their expenditures vary from $3.50 per month up to three times as much, as against the $2, or approximately that amount, paid by the Chinese laborers at the lodging houses conducted for them.

The expenditures of the Japanese for clothing and for incidentals vary greatly. No data have been tabulated with reference to these, but it is a notorious fact that such expenditures are larger among the Japanese than among any race the great majority of whose members are not charged with the immediate necessity of supporting a family and are employed as unskilled laborers. American dress has been adopted before these immigrants arrive in the continental United States and they almost without exception dress well. Most of them also spend money liberally on amusements and other incidentals. Though on the whole a thrifty race they spend more liberally than the Chinese, the Italians, the Portuguese, and the German-Russians, taking the members of each of these races as a whole.

The earnings and personal expenditures of the Japanese have been such that in the great majority of cases there has been a surplus at the close of the year. The annual earnings of 39 coal miners, 73 section hands, 48 lumber-mill laborers, 90 fish-cannery hands, 375 farm laborers, 425 city wage-earners, and 410 shopkeepers and business men in 6 cities of California and Washington have been noted in the preceding chapters.

The data relating to the surplus realized or deficit sustained by most of these classes and by farmers, are presented in the following table:

TABLE 47.—*Average surplus or deficit income for past year of Japanese males, by occupation and industry.*

Occupation and industry.	Total number reporting data.	Number reporting surplus.	Average surplus reported.	Number reporting deficit.	Average deficit reported.	Number reporting neither surplus nor deficit.	Average surplus, based upon total number reporting data.
Business men.....................	395	344	$699.99	14	$733.86	37	$583.60
City wage-earners...............	394	339	239.11	9	214.91	46	200.82
Farmers........................	647	432	579.88	114	561.02	101	288.34
Farm laborers..................	406	366	230.92	11	330.00	29	199.22
Coal miners (Wyoming)........	41	32	297.66	1	1,000.00	8	207.93

No great difficulty is involved in estimating the surplus left from wages earned after personal expenses and those of dependents in this country have been met. A few of the laborers included in the tabulation worked only a part of the year, while others had lost money in some business venture, hence the number as shown by the table whose earnings did not cover their expenditures. Allowance made for these cases, the average surplus reported is believed to indicate fairly well the net gains of these laborers. In the case of the business men, and especially the farmers, it is more difficult to estimate gains because of the nature of a part of the income and of the investments made in the business in the course of the year. The figures for shopkeepers and business men perhaps show with a fair degree of accuracy their net gains and deficits. This is not true of those for farmers, however, for the investments in the gardens, fields, and orchards have not been taken into consideration, with the result that the number incurring deficit and the amount of the deficits incurred are exaggerated, while the average surplus reported is diminished. These remarks apply equally to the following table, which shows surplus and deficit by occupation and industry and by groups:

TABLE 48.—*Surplus or deficit for past year reported by Japanese, by classified amount and by occupation and industry.*

Amount.	Number of business men reporting.		Number of city wage earners reporting.		Number of farmers reporting.		Number of farm laborers reporting.		Coal miners (Wyoming) reporting.	
	Surplus.	Deficit.	Surplus.	Deficit.	Surplus.	Deficit.	Surplus.	Deficit.	Surplus.	Deficit.
Under $100........................	4	1	38	2	31	5	28	1	1	0
$100 and under $250..............	61	4	148	3	92	27	166	4	17	0
$250 and under $500..............	129	4	130	4	146	37	163	3	8	0
$500 and under $1,000...........	95	3	20	0	114	23	8	3	5	0
$1,000 and under $2,500.........	42	0	3	0	35	20	1	0	1	1
$2,500 or over..................	13	2	0	0	14	2	0	0	0	0
Total......................	344	14	339	9	432	114	366	11	32	1

Thus the great majority realized a comfortable surplus during the year, while some made much money. Comparing the figures here given, it is evident that after allowance is made for the higher wages earned in this country during the last two or three years the average Japanese laborer has had as a disposable surplus, all of which might be sent to Japan, a much larger sum than his earnings as a laborer in Japan would have amounted to.[a]

The extent to which Japanese have sent money abroad has varied greatly as between classes and according to circumstances. The number of Japanese sending money abroad during the twelve months immediately preceding the investigation, and the total amount and the average amount sent, are shown for 2,075, by occupation and industry, in the following table:

TABLE 49.—*Money sent abroad by Japanese males during past year, by occupa-tion and industry.*

Occupation and industry.	Number reporting complete data.	Number not sending money.	Number sending money.	Total amount sent.	Average amount sent.
Business men	437	263	174	$48,751	$280.18
City wage-earners	426	226	200	32,505	162.53
Farmers	760	515	245	38,090	155.47
Farm laborers	411	160	251	39,805	158.59
Coal miners (Wyoming)	41	19	22	4,465	202.95

Among the more important factors controlling the sending of money abroad have been the extent of gains, whether or not there were dependent parents, wife, and children in Japan, the facilities for the safekeeping of money here, and the opportunities for profitable investment in this country. It is noteworthy that the majority of the three groups of wage-earners taken together sent money abroad during the year, while the majority of the business men and farmers did not. Though on the whole the gains of the business men and farmers are larger than those of the laborers, a larger percentage of them are married men with wives in this country. Moreover, engaging as they do in business or in farming on their own account, they can make profitable use of their savings. The wage-earners more frequently have dependents to support at home, have less opportunity for profitable investment of their savings here, and generally expect to return to Japan sooner or later. They usually send a large part, and frequently send all, of their surplus earnings to Japan for the support of dependents, for safekeeping, or for investment in some form or other.

Of 411 farm laborers from whom data were obtained, approximately 370 realized a surplus during the twelve months immediately preceding the investigation. Of these, 240 retained in this country a total of $45,450, some of which was invested in land, but most of which was placed in the bank or loaned to friends. As opposed to these, 251 sent various sums abroad, aggregating $39,805. In a few cases this was for the purchase of land. Thirty-two of the 41 coal

[a] See Table 7, pp. 10 and 11.

miners had a surplus. Of these 32, 22 sent money abroad during the year, while 23 retained savings in this country. The amount sent abroad was $4,465; the amount retained in this country was $5,060. Of the 426 city wage-earners, 200 sent money abroad, the aggregate amount sent by them being $32,505. As opposed to this amount, $45,557 was retained in this country.

It is a noteworthy fact that in all of these groups of laborers the savings retained in this country exceeded the money sent abroad during the preceding twelve months. This is far more strikingly true of the men who were engaged in business and of the farmers. Of 437 business men, 174 sent money abroad during the year, the total amount sent being $48,751, or an average of $280.18 each. As against this amount, the members comprising this group retained in this country a total of $195,130, or aproximately four times as much. The greater part of the savings retained in this country were used for extending the business engaged in, but no small part was invested in land. Of 760 farmers, 245 sent money abroad during the year, the sums sent aggregating $38,090, or an average of $155.47 each. The amount retained in this country and used to pay debts earlier incurred or invested in land or equipment of various kinds was several fold larger. Thus, taking seven groups of farmers for illustration, the amount of money sent abroad was $18,580; the amount retained in this country, $91,907.

There is one difference between the Japanese and other races with which we are more familiar with reference to the disposition of their gains not explained by the differences in the circumstances under which they reside in this country. The Japanese family differs from the European and the American in that the relation between parents and offspring is much closer in the case of the Japanese. Filial duty demands that the offspring assist the parents to an extent not found among the white races, so that unmarried men are usually charged with at least the partial support of their parents, and married men are not uncommonly charged with the necessity of contributing to the support of their parents as well as to the support of the members of their immediate families. But, more important, the disposition of gains is largely controlled by the circumstances under which immigrants reside in this country. In the percentage of wives and other dependents living in this country, in the percentage who expect to remain here for a long time or permanently, and in the opportunities for profitable investment open to them the Japanese differ from such races as the East Indian on the one hand and the German, Scandinavian, and Armenian on the other. The East Indian immigrants have no settled interest in this country; the immigrants of the other races referred to are practically all permanent settlers and their condition and interests are modified by that fact.

Thus, of 79 East Indians in Oregon and Washington, 31 sent $4,320 abroad during the year preceding the investigation. The total amount of the gains of the entire group retained in this country was approximately $1,130. Without permanent interests in this country and with need at home, they usually send their surplus earnings as soon as possible and frequently do not make adequate provision for themselves if work is not available. The amount of money sent abroad by European immigrants, on the other hand, is usually small, except by those who belong to the migratory and unsettled class of laborers. The Italian farmers, for example, send little money abroad, though the number who send nominal sums as gifts is comparatively large. In fact, the only group of immigrant white farmers investigated who sent much money abroad were the German-Russians about Fresno, and their remittances were chiefly to assist others to come to the United States. A larger percentage of the Japanese than of the European immigrants in the West send money abroad and they no doubt send a larger percentage of their net gains. Considered as a race group they live and work under different conditions. Moreover, the Japanese are charged with duties which increase the number to whose support they must contribute.

As a result of retaining the larger part of their savings in this country, the Japanese have accumulated much property. The net value of the property owned by the members of the various classes from whom data were obtained is shown in the following table:

TABLE 50.—*Net value of all property owned by Japanese 18 years of age or over, by occupation and industry.*

Occupation and industry.	Number reporting complete data.	Number owning property valued at each specified amount.											
		None.a	Under $50.	$50 and under $100.	$100 and under $250.	$250 and under $500.	$500 and under $1,000.	$1,000 and under $1,500.	$1,500 and under $2,500.	$2,500 and under $5,000.	$5,000 and under $10,000.	$10,000 and under $25,000.	$25,000 or over.
Business men	437	4	....	1	18	35	114	81	82	59	25	11	7
City wage-earners	427	61	7	35	135	90	63	20	10	5	....	1	....
Farmers b	488	86	16	10	45	77	92	48	43	41	17	10	3
Farm laborers	348	96	8	28	95	68	35	10	2	6	....	....	....
Coal miners (Wyoming)	41	18	....	....	8	9	2	1	3	....	....	....	....

a Gross value minus indebtedness is nothing or less than nothing.
b Does not include the value of furniture and growing crops, or the value of such investments by tenant farmers in or upon the land as do not become their property upon the expiration of their leases.

While a large percentage of the laborers have nothing (aside from their personal effects), or less than nothing, over and above such debts as they owe, a few have several hundred or a few thousand dollars' worth of property. Some of the city wage-earners look forward to the profitable employment of this in business, while a rather large percentage of the farm laborers have planned to become farmers on their own account. In fact, a few of them have already invested in land. The business men and farmers as classes, of course, have much more wealth than the laborers. Most of them have risen to their present positions because they are the most successful of the laborers, they have maintained their positions because not unsuccessful in business, and they have sent less of their earnings abroad than have the members of the laboring classes. The wealth of the farmers, as has been explained,a is greater than indicated by the table, for most of them are tenants and have only a tenant's equity in much of the

a See Chapter IV, p. 75.

investment made in the land, which for that reason is not included in the estimated values. Moreover, in many localities at the time of the investigation much had been invested in maturing crops which had not been marketed, and as the value of growing crops was not taken into consideration, the estimates are still further reduced below their true level.

Most of the property of the farmers is in live stock, tools, and other equipment, for, as has been indicated, a relatively small number own the lands they till. Similarly most of the property owned by the shopkeepers and business men is in stocks of goods and equipment. Very few of them own the real estate which they occupy for business or residence purposes. Comparatively few are yet firmly established in the communities in which they live and conduct business. Moreover, most of them have had to meet but recently the problem of securing sufficient capital for business purposes and have not been in position to invest in real estate.

The amount of money brought to the continental United States stands in sharp contrast to the net value of the property now owned in this country by the Japanese immigrants from whom personal data were obtained. The data with reference to the sums brought by 2,001 are presented in the following table:

TABLE 51.—*Money brought by Japanese males upon coming to the United States, by occupation and industry.*

Occupation and industry.	Number reporting complete data.	Number bringing each specified amount.									
		None.	Under $25.	$25 and under $50.	$50 and under $100.	$100 and under $150.	$150 and under $200.	$200 and under $300.	$300 and under $400.	$400 and under $500.	$500 and under $1,000.	$1,000 or over.
Business men	435	4	7	160	131	53	21	22	14	3	7	a 13
City wage-earners	426	3	5	189	170	33	8	9	5	2	2	.....
Farmers	689	13	29	269	202	86	29	31	12	7	7	4
Farm laborers	410	18	59	131	151	28	13	6	1	2	1	.....
Coal miners (Wyoming)	41	.....	3	8	18	9	1	2	.....	.....	.....	.....

a Five brought $1,000; 2, $1,200; 2, $1,500; 2, $2,500; and 2, $10,000 each.

A few farmers and business men arrived with sufficient capital to establish themselves in business or in farming at once, but the great majority came with little money, expecting to become wage-earners. The great majority of each of the classes shown in the table had upon their arrival less than $100, while not as many as 10 per cent in any class, save of business men where the percentage was 13.6, had as much as $200. In the amount of money brought, however, they present no strong contrast to most other races who have immigrated in large numbers to the United States. That they occupy an intermediate position is shown by the data relating to money in possession by immigrants, as reported each year by the Commissioner-General of Immigration. Taking the data for the year 1906–7 (the last year of normal immigration of Japanese), the average amount reported for the 30,444 Japanese was $31.33. The English immigrants had

$67.22 on the average; the Scandinavian, $64.62; the German, $55.31; the Bohemian and Moravian, $41.32; the East Indian, $39.30; the North Italian, $28.99; the Greek, $23.43; the Finnish, $21.48; the Portuguese, $20.23; the Russian, $16.88; the South Italian, $16.50; the Slovak, $16.22; the Croatian and Slovenian, $14.67; and the Polish, $13.61.

The data presented in Chapters III, IV, V, and VI summarize the results of the investigation in so far as they relate directly to the economic phases of Japanese immigration. It remains to present data obtained bearing more directly upon the social and political phases of the problem.

CHAPTER VII.

SOCIAL AND POLITICAL CONSIDERATIONS.

The capacity of the Japanese for assimilation, the progress they have made toward assimilation, and the place they occupy in the community are indicated by their literacy, the effort made to acquire and their knowledge of the English language, the character of their reading, their position in political life, their relations with other races, their religious ideals, and related matters.

The number and percentage of the Japanese from whom personal data were obtained who can speak English is shown by sex, by economic groups, and by industry, and by years in the United States, in the following tables:

TABLE 52.—*Ability to speak English of foreign-born Japanese, by sex, years in the United States, and industry.*

WAGE-EARNERS.

MALE.

[By years in the United States is meant years since first arrival in the United States.]

Industry.	Number reporting complete data.	Number who speak English.	Years in United States.					
			Under 5.		5 to 9.		10 or over.	
			Number.	Number who speak English.	Number.	Number who speak English.	Number.	Number who speak English.
Agriculture	6,041	3,973	3,479	2,047	1,984	1,438	578	488
Fish canneries	458	368	248	197	164	132	46	39
Fruit and vegetable canneries	201	112	137	70	45	30	19	12
Laundries	161	141	107	91	44	41	10	9
Lumber mills	333	164	170	66	118	65	45	33
Mining, coal	447	225	199	89	203	110	45	26
Smelting	63	18	38	7	20	8	5	3
Transportation: Steam railroads— Maintenance of way and construction	1,135	558	701	313	366	203	68	42
Shops, bridges, and buildings, water and signal service	628	294	405	150	183	114	40	30
Electric railways	102	60	72	36	25	19	5	5
Miscellaneous	1,277	1,101	642	538	455	390	180	173
Total	10,846	7,014	6,198	3,604	3,607	2,550	1,041	800

FEMALE.

Industry.	Number reporting complete data.	Number who speak English.	Under 5.		5 to 9.		10 or over.	
Agriculture	111	29	91	25	14	2	6	2
Fruit and vegetable canneries	36	4	34	3			2	1
Lumber mills	11	4	3	1	7	3	1	
Transportation: Steam railroads— Maintenance of way and construction	3		3					
Miscellaneous	61	31	42	19	16	10	3	2
Total	222	68	173	48	37	15	12	5

TABLE 52.—*Ability to speak English of foreign-born Japanese, by sex, years in the United States, and industry*—Continued.

IN BUSINESS FOR SELF.

MALE.

Industry.	Number reporting complete data.	Number who speak English.	Years in United States.					
			Under 5.		5 to 9.		10 or over.	
			Number.	Number who speak English.	Number.	Number who speak English.	Number.	Number who speak English.
Agriculture	847	791	263	226	373	358	211	207
Miscellaneous	458	446	100	95	206	200	152	151
Total	1,305	1,237	363	321	579	558	363	358

FEMALE.

Industry.	Number reporting complete data.	Number who speak English.	Under 5.		5 to 9.		10 or over.	
Agriculture	278	94	202	51	72	42	4	1
Miscellaneous	205	112	129	60	65	44	11	8
Total	483	206	331	111	137	86	15	9

TABLE 53.—*Per cent of foreign-born Japanese who speak English, by sex, years in the United States, and industry.*

WAGE-EARNERS.

MALE.

[By years in the United States is meant years since first arrival in the United States.]

Industry.	Number reporting complete data.	Per cent who speak English, by years in United States.			
		Under 5.	5 to 9.	10 or over.	Total.
Agriculture	6,041	58.8	72.5	84.4	65.8
Fish canneries	458	79.4	80.5	84.8	80.3
Fruit and vegetable canneries	201	51.1	66.7	63.2	55.7
Laundries	161	85.0	93.2	90.0	87.6
Lumber mills	333	38.8	55.1	73.3	49.2
Mining, coal	447	44.7	54.2	57.8	50.3
Smelting	63	18.4	40.0	60.0	28.6
Transportation:					
Steam railroads—					
Maintenance of way and construction	1,135	44.7	55.5	61.8	49.2
Shops, bridges, and buildings, water and signal service	628	37.0	62.3	75.0	46.8
Electric railways	102	50.0	76.0	100.0	58.8
Miscellaneous	1,277	83.8	85.7	96.1	86.2
Total	10,846	58.1	70.7	82.6	64.7

FEMALE.

Industry.	Number reporting complete data.	Under 5.	5 to 9.	10 or over.	Total.
Agriculture	111	27.5	14.3	33.3	26.1
Fruit and vegetable canneries	36	8.8		(a)	11.1
Lumber mills	11	(a)	(a)	(a)	(a)
Transportation:					
Steam railroads—					
Maintenance of way and construction	3	(a)	(a)	(a)	(a)
Miscellaneous	61	45.2	62.5	(a)	50.8
Total	222	27.7	40.5	41.7	30.6

*Not computed, owing to small number involved.

TABLE 53.—*Per cent of foreign-born Japanese who speak English, by sex, years in the United States, and industry*—Continued.

IN BUSINESS FOR SELF.

MALE.

Industry.	Number reporting complete data.	Per cent who speak English, by years in United States.			
		Under 5.	5 to 9.	10 or over.	Total.
Agriculture..........................	847	85.9	96.0	98.1	93.4
Miscellaneous........................	458	95.0	97.1	99.3	97.4
Total..........................	1,305	88.4	96.4	98.6	94.8

FEMALE.

Industry.	Number reporting complete data.	Under 5.	5 to 9.	10 or over.	Total.
Agriculture..........................	278	25.2	58.3	(a)	33.8
Miscellaneous........................	205	46.5	67.7	72.7	54.6
Total..........................	483	33.5	62.8	60.0	42.7

a Not computed, owing to small number involved.

These tables bring to light certain contrasts between the different groups. The more important of these are: (1) The contrasts which are found between those who have been in the United States less than five years and those who have resided here a longer time; (2) those which are found between the sexes, the males invariably showing a larger percentage than the females of the same households, who speak English; (3) those which are found between the more successful who have become business men and farmers and those who are wage-earners; (4) those which are found between the farmers and the members of their households and the business men and the members of their households; and (5) those which are found between the wage-earners in laundries, fish canneries, and miscellaneous occupations, representing city classes on the one hand and the wage-earners in the other industries on the other.

The contrasts pointed out are explained partly by the different classes represented in the different groups, partly by the possibility of association with the members of other races, and partly by the possibility of attendance at school. The " student class," which has been largely represented among the Japanese immigrants to the continental United States, is found chiefly in the city trades, in business, and in the canneries, which draw largely upon the city populations for seasonal labor during the summer months. The men so engaged, except in the fish canneries, also have more contact with white persons, and a large percentage of them have attended night schools for the study of English. The farm laborers, lumber-mill hands, coal miners, smelter employees, and railroad laborers on the other hand usually work in " gangs " under an interpreter, live apart from others, and have little opportunity to attend classes. These facts, together with the further fact that with the exception of farm laborers, the " student class " finds small representation among them, account for the difference shown between them and the other groups.

These same facts account for the slight differences found between the business men and the farmers. A knowledge of English is almost necessary to rise to either class and to maintain that position; hence the differences between them and the wage-earners. The marked differences found between the females and the males of the same industrial and length-of-residence groups are explained partly by the fact that with a lower standard of education for the latter few of them belong to the student class, but more by the fact that they do not take employment as servants and do not come into much contact with white persons, and, not finding it urgent to know English in order to be successful, do not so frequently attend classes for the study of English. The differences are of interest chiefly, however, in indicating the conditions upon which progress in learning to speak English depends. A more important question relates to the progress made. This is in a way shown by the percentages who speak English among those who have resided here for different lengths of time. But progress is a relative matter, and must be shown by comparing the Japanese with other immigrants whose mother tongue is some other language than English. Inasmuch as the conditions imposed by work and residence are important—a fact indicated by the contrasts between different groups of Japanese— comparisons between the Japanese and others should be limited to those engaged in the same industries.

The relative advance of the Japanese and Chinese is best shown by reference to the data gathered from agricultural laborers, while the mining of coal and the construction and maintenance of way departments of the electric and steam railroads offer the best field for comparison of the Japanese with the south and east Europeans and the Mexicans. In making comparisons between Japanese and others, however, it should be held in mind that a large number of the former have not immigrated directly from Japan, but first went to the Hawaiian Islands or to Canada. Those who first migrated to the Hawaiian Islands usually remained there from one to five years before coming to the continental United States, while those who came from Canada have frequently resided there for a few years. In both instances they have had some contact with English-speaking people, and this should have weight in drawing conclusions from a comparison of the Japanese with other races with regard to their progress in acquiring a knowledge of the English language. Another condition which would tend to make the apparent progress of the Japanese more rapid than that of other races is that many of the Japanese laborers have had high-school training before immigrating. Such an education includes instruction in English grammar, and thus provides the foundation for a rapid acquisition of our language after their arrival here. The members of no other race with which comparisons are made have had a similar advantage in their native land.

The contrast between the Japanese and the Chinese employed in agricultural pursuits is striking. Although 94.9 per cent of the Chinese from whom data were obtained have been in the United States 10 years or over, and the great majority 20 years or over, a smaller percentage of them than of the Japanese speak English, although 90.4 per cent of the latter have been here less than 10 years and 56.5 per cent less than 5 years. Indeed, of the Japanese who have resided in the United States less than 5 years, 58.8 per cent speak English, as opposed to 66.9 per cent of the Chinese who have been here 10 years or over. This wide difference between the two races is not due to differences in their environments, for the conditions under which Chinese farm laborers live and work are substantially the same as those which surround the Japanese, but it is the result chiefly of the different attitude of the two races toward American customs and our language. The Chinese are self-satisfied and indifferent in this regard, whereas the Japanese are eager to learn the English language or anything pertaining to western civilization. The same contrast between these races with regard to progress in learning to speak English is found in the other industries where Japanese and Chinese are employed in similar branches of work.

The race most distinctly opposed to the Japanese in the unskilled labor involved in conducting steam and electric railways is the Mexican, and members of this race are decidedly less progressive than the Japanese as regards the learning of English. Of those employed on street railways for example, 58.8 per cent of the 102 Japanese speak English, as against only 17.4 per cent of the 539 Mexicans, and this in spite of the fact that 70.6 per cent of the former as against 57.9 per cent of the latter have been in this country less than five years. Indeed, only 41.9 per cent of the 81 Mexicans whose period of residence is ten years or over speak English, while 50 per cent of the 72 Japanese who have been here less than five years have acquired our tongue.

A comparison of the Japanese employed in the mining of coal with the other races most commonly used in similar occupations in that industry shows that their progress in learning to speak English has been relatively rapid. Of the 199 Japanese who have been in the United States less than five years, 44.7 per cent speak English, as opposed to 38.8 per cent of the 129 Poles, 38.7 per cent of the 562 North Italians, 36.7 per cent of the 229 Slovenians, 31.8 per cent of the 44 Slovaks, and 28.7 per cent of the 216 South Italians. However, 48.7 per cent of the 152 Croatians, 51.8 per cent of the 170 Montenegrins, and 62.3 per cent of the 61 Finns in this residence group speak English. It should be noted, moreover, that with the exception of the South Italians the Europeans whose period of residence was more than five years, show more progress in this regard than the Japanese, indicating either that the percentage for Japanese who have been here a relatively short time is greatly affected by residence in Hawaii or Canada or that they continue longer than the Europeans under conditions which retard assimilation.

By way of summary, it may be said that when compared with other races employed in similar kinds of labor in the same industry, the Japanese show relatively rapid progress in acquiring a speaking knowledge of English. Their advance has been much more rapid than that of the Chinese and the Mexicans, who show little interest in "American" institutions. During their first five years of residence a greater proportion have learned to speak English than of most of the south and east European races. However, among those who have been in this country for a longer period of time, a larger proportion of the south and east Europeans than of the Japanese speak English. The progress of the Japanese is due to their great eagerness to learn, which has overcome more obstacles than have been encountered by most of the other races, obstacles of race prejudice, of segregation, and of wide differences in language.

The literacy of the Japanese immigrants upon their arrival in this country is shown fairly accurately by their ability to read and write their native language. Few immigrants, except those who came as children, have learned to read and write their native language since their arrival here. That the great majority of the Japanese immigrants are literate is shown by the following tables. The first gives the number, the second the percentage of the wage-earning group who read and write their native language, by sex and by industry.

TABLE 54.—*Number of foreign-born Japanese wage-earners who read their native language and number who read and write their native language, by sex and industry.*

MALE.

Industry.	Number reporting complete data.	Number who—	
		Read native language.	Read and write native language.
Agriculture	5,563	5,429	5,425
Fish canneries	368	368	368
Fruit and vegetable canneries	201	197	196
Laundries	161	161	161
Lumber mills	231	227	226
Mining, coal	403	388	387
Smelting	63	63	63
Transportation:			
Steam railroads—			
Maintenance of way and construction	1,000	982	981
Shops, bridges, and buildings, water and signal service	628	619	618
Electric railways	102	94	94
Miscellaneous	849	840	840
Total	9,569	9,368	9,359

FEMALE.

Industry.	Number reporting complete data.	Read native language.	Read and write native language.
Agriculture	81	60	59
Fruit and vegetable canneries	36	19	19
Miscellaneous	34	31	31
Total	151	110	109

TABLE 55.—*Per cent of foreign-born Japanese wage-earners who read their native language and per cent who read and write their native language, by sex and industry.*

MALE.

Industry.	Number reporting complete data.	Per cent who—	
		Read native language.	Read and write native language.
Agriculture	5,563	97.6	97.5
Fish canneries	368	100.0	100.0
Fruit and vegetable canneries	201	98.0	97.5
Laundries	161	100.0	100.0
Lumber mills	231	98.3	97.8
Mining, coal	403	96.3	96.0
Smelting	63	100.0	100.0
Transportation:			
Steam railroads—			
Maintenance of way and construction	1,000	98.2	98.1
Shops, bridges, and buildings, water and signal service	628	98.6	98.4
Electric railways	102	92.2	92.2
Miscellaneous	849	98.9	98.9
Total	9,569	97.9	97.8

FEMALE.

Industry.	Number reporting complete data.	Read native language.	Read and write native language.
Agriculture	81	74.1	72.8
Fruit and vegetable canneries	36	52.8	52.8
Miscellaneous	34	91.2	91.2
Total	151	72.8	72.2

Of the 9,569 male wage-earners from whom data were secured, 97.8 per cent read and write Japanese. The standard among the females is less good, for only 72.2 per cent of a total of 151 are literate. Little difference appears between the Japanese employed in the various industries investigated, but those showing the largest percentage who do not read and write Japanese are the farm laborers, the fruit and vegetable cannery hands, and the smelter hands, among whom the largest percentages of rural immigrants are found. It is likewise true that the largest percentage of illiteracy in Japanese among the females from whom data were secured appears among the groups of cannery hands and the agricultural laborers, as opposed to the "miscellaneous" group of city wage-earners.

A comparison of Chinese and Japanese agricultural laborers shows that 97.5 per cent of the latter, as opposed to 84.5 per cent of the former, read and write their native language.

The contrast between Japanese and Mexicans is very marked. Of the members of these races engaged in street-railway labor, 92.2 per cent of the 102 Japanese, as against 45.5 per cent of the 539 Mexicans, read and write their native language. Moreover the Japanese rank higher in this regard than most of the south and east European races. A comparison of the data secured from those engaged in mining coal shows that while 96 per cent of the 403 Japanese in this industry read and write their native language, only 66.3 per cent of the 474 South Italians, 78.5 per cent of the 214 Slovaks, 82 per cent of the 245 Poles, 83.9 per cent of the 193 Montenegrins, 85 per cent of the 419 Croatians, 88.5 per cent of the 479 Slovenians, 90.9 per cent of the 66 Greeks, and 91 per cent of the 1,175 North Italians, read and write their native language. However, 98.2 per cent of the 225 Finns read and write Finnish.

It is evident from the preceding discussion that the standard of literacy shown by the Japanese, as indicated by their ability to read and write their native language, is far higher than that shown by the Chinese, the Mexicans, and most of the south and east European races, if comparison is limited to those who are employed in the same industries and at the same kinds of work.

It should be noted, however, that the great majority of the Japanese have migrated as single adults, whereas a larger proportion of the European immigrants have come to this country in family groups, among them a number of children of school age who have received their elementary education in American schools, and hence are illiterate in their native language. In spite of this fact the differences shown between the Japanese and Europeans are wide enough to indicate that the standard of literacy in Japan is better than in most of the south and east European countries. The higher educational ideals of Japanese are further reflected in the relatively rapid progress which they have shown in learning to read and write English.

As noted above, with regard to their ability to speak English, many Japanese immigrants have attended high schools in Japan, where they have been given a foundation in English grammar. Furthermore, others have had the advantage of a slight association with English-speaking people in the Hawaiian Islands or in Canada before their arrival in the United States. But a further aid in mastering the English language is found in the schools which are conducted

in this country. Practically all of the few Japanese children of
school age in the West attend the American public schools, where
they are found in all classes from the primary grades through the
entire elementary and secondary system. It is estimated that in 17
California cities there were in February, 1909, 573 Japanese children
enrolled.[a]

The greater part of these were attending schools in the cities about
San Francisco Bay, Sacramento, and Los Angeles. Japanese children
also attend American schools in the cities of other States where their
parents are employed. Such schools, however, are not available for
adults, who are dependent upon schools (night schools or day schools)
conducted by various agencies, and on their own enterprise for any
education in the English language which they may acquire.

Numerous schools are maintained for the benefit of adult Japanese
immigrants. No less than 33, the primary aim of which is to in-
struct adult Japanese in the English language, were reported by
agents of the Commission in Los Angeles, San Francisco, Oakland,
and Sacramento, Cal., and Seattle and Tacoma, Wash. Of these,
several were designed primarily for the " student class," and embraced all subjects preparatory for high school, and in one or two
cases for college work. The great majority, however, were conducted
by the various religious missions and by private parties with the
primary aim of imparting a knowledge of English to Japanese
laborers.

In San Francisco and Oakland there are 15 such schools. Four
are conducted by private parties and amount to little more than
private tutoring institutions preparatory to high school or college.
The other 11, however, have regularly conducted classes and a large
number of pupils. Five are maintained by various Japanese missions. They offer work corresponding to that given in the public
schools from the primary to the high-school grades, mathematics
excepted, in both afternoon and evening classes. Japanese men and
American women are employed as teachers. The majority of the
pupils are between the ages of 20 and 23, and a majority have been
in this country less than 2 years. Some of the 6 private schools are
conducted in much the same manner, offering both elementary and
advanced courses of instruction. The majority of the pupils are
from 19 to 23 years of age, and are recent immigrants. Most of
the adults attending such schools are gainfully employed, largely in
domestic service. There is also a school the object of which is to
teach Japanese children born in this country the use of their mother
tongue and something of the history and institutions of Japan, and
to assist children, born in Japan and recently arrived in this country,
in learning English in order that they may be less handicapped in
the classes of the public schools. This school is therefore merely
supplementary to the public schools.

In Los Angeles there are 7 schools for adult Japanese, and in
addition some Japanese youths are tutored by Americans. The 7
schools are connected with religious missions and have from 20 to 50
pupils each. They offer about the same kind of instruction as the
similar institutions in San Francisco. In connection with the Budd-

[a] See San Francisco Call, Feb. 17, 1909, for partial census made by the
governor.

hist mission a school with an enrollment of from 20 to 30 pupils is conducted for Japanese children as supplementary to the public schools, giving instruction in the language and the history of Japan. A similar Buddhist school is conducted in Sacramento. In that city there are 4 schools designed to teach adult Japanese the English language. Six schools of the same nature were reported in Seattle, Wash. In fact, in all cities of the West with more than a few hundred Japanese there are schools the primary object of which is to teach adult Japanese the English language. The number of these institutions and the many Japanese who attended them at an earlier time when many immigrants were arriving are the best evidence of the ambition and eagerness of the members of this race to learn western civilization. No adult immigrants in the West, unless it is the Hebrews, show as great desire to learn the English language. Though the attendance of the Japanese at night classes is, of course, somewhat irregular, it is far less so than of Greeks and others at the classes conducted for them at Pueblo, Colo., and in a few other places where educational facilities have been organized for the benefit of non-English-speaking immigrants.

Because of the influence of the schools, the greater association with English-speaking people, which is an inevitable part of city life, and the larger representation of the student class among them, the Japanese who are employed in the cities are more advanced with regard to ability to read and write as well as to speak English than are those employed in the more isolated places, such as section hands on the railroads or laborers in the smelters. Much the same contrasts are noticeable in this regard as were noted in the speaking of English. The following tables show the number and percentage of the Japanese employed in the various industries who read and write English. Table 56 gives the number and Table 57 the percentage who read and write English, by sex and industry.

TABLE 56.—*Number of foreign-born Japanese who read English and number who read and write English, by sex and industry.*

WAGE-EARNERS.

MALE.

Industry.	Number reporting complete data.	Number who—	
		Read English.	Read and write English.
Agriculture	6,041	1,307	1,194
Fish canneries	368	206	194
Fruit and vegetable canneries	201	69	68
Laundries	161	95	95
Lumber mills	231	84	82
Mining, coal	447	215	211
Smelting	63	7	7
Transportation:			
Steam railroads—			
Maintenance of way and construction	1,000	428	422
Shops, bridges, and buildings, water and signal service	628	212	190
Electric railways	102	52	51
Miscellaneous	1,276	754	693
Total	10,518	3,429	3,207

TABLE 56.—*Number of foreign-born Japanese who read English and number who read and write English, by sex and industry*—Continued.

WAGE-EARNERS—Continued.

FEMALE.

Industry.	Number reporting complete data.	Number who—	
		Read English.	Read and write English.
Agriculture...	111	3	3
Fruit and vegetable canneries..................................	36	2	2
Miscellaneous...	60	14	13
Total..	207	19	18

IN BUSINESS FOR SELF.

MALE.

Agriculture...	841	315	308
Miscellaneous...	450	320	320
Total..	1,291	635	628

FEMALE.

Agriculture...	277	21	20
Miscellaneous...	198	44	43
Total..	475	65	63

TABLE 57.—*Per cent of foreign-born Japanese who read English and per cent who read and write English, by sex and industry.*

WAGE-EARNERS.

Industry.	Number reporting complete data.		Per cent who read English.		Per cent who read and write English.	
	Male.	Female.	Male.	Female.	Male.	Female.
Agriculture.................................	6,041	111	21.6	2.7	19.8	2.7
Fish canneries..............................	368	....	56.0	....	52.7	....
Fruit and vegetable canneries.............	201	36	34.3	5.6	33.8	5.6
Laundries...................................	161	....	59.0	....	59.0	....
Lumber mills...............................	231	....	36.4	....	35.5	....
Mining, coal...............................	447	....	48.1	....	47.2	....
Smelting....................................	63	....	11.1	....	11.1	....
Transportation:						
Steam railroads—						
Maintenance of way and construction...	1,000	....	42.8	....	42.2	....
Shops, bridges, and buildings, water and signal service........	628	....	33.8	....	30.3	....
Electric railways.........................	102	....	51.0	....	50.0	....
Miscellaneous..............................	1,276	60	59.1	23.3	54.3	21.7
Total.................................	10,518	207	32.6	9.2	30.5	8.7

IN BUSINESS FOR SELF.

Agriculture.................................	841	277	37.5	7.6	36.6	7.2
Miscellaneous..............................	450	198	71.1	22.2	71.1	21.7
Total.................................	1,291	475	49.2	13.7	48.6	13.3

The wage-earners employed in " miscellaneous " industries (largely city trades), in laundries, in fish canneries, and as construction and maintenance of way laborers on the electric railways, reported the largest percentages who could read and write English. With the exception of the fish cannery hands, all of these are employed near the Japanese centers of population. The fish cannery hands on the Columbia River and Puget Sound are largely of the urban class, who work in the various branches of domestic jobs in the cities during the greater part of the year, but engage in cannery work during the summer months. Moreover, a larger percentage of the Japanese business men of the cities than of the independent Japanese farmers could read and write English.

Of course a much smaller number of the Japanese can read and write than can speak English. While 64.7 per cent of the male wage-earners and 94.8 per cent of the business men and farmers speak English, only 30.5 per cent of the former and 48.6 per cent of the latter both read and write English. Among the females the difference is equally great. While 30.6 per cent of the females of the wage-earning groups and 42.7 per cent of those of the business and farming groups speak English, only 8.7 per cent of the former and 13.3 per cent of the latter are able to read and write English. This difference is due to the fact that the spoken language can be acquired through association, whereas a knowledge of the written language presupposes definite educational activity.

A comparison of the Japanese and Chinese males engaged in agriculture shows that 19.8 per cent of the former as opposed to only 1.6 per cent of the latter read and write English. An even wider difference is to be noted between the Japanese and the Mexicans employed at common labor on the street railways of southern California. While 50 per cent of the 102 Japanese read and write English, only 5.9 per cent of the 539 Mexicans have acquired these arts. Comparing the data gathered from immigrants employed in the mining of coal, a larger percentage of the Japanese read and write English than of most of the races from south and east Europe. Indeed, while 47.2 per cent of the 447 Japanese employed in this industry read and write English, only 34.2 per cent of the 225 Finns, 22.3 per cent of the 479 Slovenians, 20.7 per cent of the 214 Slovaks, 19.3 per cent of the 419 Croatians, 18.8 per cent of the 245 Poles, 17.6 per cent of the 193 Montenegrins, 14 per cent of the 1,175 North Italians, and 9.9 per cent of the 485 South Italians have acquired these arts. These comparisons, however, as noted above, should be somewhat modified because of the fact that many of the Japanese have resided in the Hawaiian Islands and Canada prior to their immigration to the continental United States, and, further, that some of them have studied English in Japanese schools. With due allowance for these factors in their progress, the proportion of Japanese who read and write English is unusually high as compared to most of the immigrant races employed in similar kinds of work.

As a general summary of the literacy of the Japanese employed in the western division, the following tables are submitted. The first shows the number and the second the percentage who read and who read and write some language, by sex and industry.

TABLE 58.—*Number of foreign-born Japanese who read and number who read and write, by sex and industry.*

WAGE-EARNERS.

MALE.

Industry.	Number reporting complete data.	Number who—	
		Read.	Read and write.
Agriculture...	6,041	5,910	5,903
Fish canneries..	458	457	457
Fruit and vegetable canneries.......................	201	197	197
Laundries...	161	161	161
Lumber mills..	332	327	326
Mining, coal..	447	429	4,128
Smelting..	63	63	63
Transportation:			
Steam railroads—			
Maintenance of way and construction..............	1,135	1,102	1,091
Shops, bridges, and buildings, water and signal service......	628	623	622
Electric railways.....................................	102	94	94
Miscellaneous...	1,277	1,267	1,267
Total..	10,844	10,630	10,609

FEMALE.

Agriculture...	111	88	87
Fruit and vegetable canneries.........................	36	19	19
Lumber mills...	11	10	10
Transportation:			
Steam railroads—			
Maintenance of way and construction..............	3	2	2
Miscellaneous...	60	55	55
Total..	221	174	173

IN BUSINESS FOR SELF.

MALE.

Agriculture...	838	816	815
Miscellaneous...	450	444	444
Total..	1,288	1,260	1,259

FEMALE.

Agriculture...	277	246	243
Miscellaneous...	198	182	182
Total..	475	428	425

TABLE 59.—*Per cent of foreign-born Japanese who read and per cent who read and write, by sex and industry.*

WAGE-EARNERS.

Industry.	Number reporting complete data.		Per cent who read.		Per cent who read and write.	
	Male.	Female.	Male.	Female.	Male.	Female.
Agriculture...........................	6,041	111	97.8	79.3	97.7	78.4
Fish canneries......................	458	....	99.8	....	99.8	......
Fruit and vegetable canneries..............	201	36	98.0	52.8	98.0	52.8
Laundries............................	161	....	100.0	....	100.0	......
Lumber mills........................	332	11	98.5	(a)	98.2	(a)
Mining, coal.........................	447	....	96.0	....	95.7	......
Smelting............................	63	....	100.0	....	100.0	......
Transportation:						
Steam railroads—						
Maintenance of way and construction...	1,135	3	97.1	(a)	96.1	(a)
Shops, bridges, and buildings, water and signal service........	628	....	99.2	....	99.0	......
Electric railways......................	102	....	92.2	....	92.2	......
Miscellaneous........................	1,277	60	99.2	91.7	99.2	91.7
Total...................	10,844	221	98.0	78.7	97.8	78.3

IN BUSINESS FOR SELF.

Agriculture...........................	838	277	97.4	88.8	97.3	87.7
Miscellaneous........................	450	198	98.7	91.9	98.7	91.9
Total...................	1,288	475	97.8	90.1	97.7	89.5

a Not computed, owing to small number involved.

With regard to general literacy no difference appears between the male wage-earners and those engaged in business for themselves. However, a sharp difference is to be noted between the females of the two groups. Of the females of the wage-earning groups only 78.3 per cent as opposed to 89.5 per cent of those of the business group are literate. As between industries the contrasts are much the same as those pointed out with regard to the ability to read and write Japanese. Of those of the business group the urban group are somewhat more literate than the agriculturists. Of the male wage-earners all except those employed on street railways, in construction and maintenance of way gangs on the steam railways, in the mining of coal, and as agricultural laborers reported a greater percentage of literacy than the average (97.8 per cent). The most illiterate groups are the laborers on electric railways, of whom 92.2 per cent as opposed to 95.7 per cent of the coal-mine employees, 96.1 per cent of the maintenance of way and construction laborers of the steam railroads, and 97.7 per cent of the agricultural laborers could read and write some language.

The difference between the Mexicans and Japanese with regard to general literacy is great. Of the former only 46.2 per cent of the 539 employed on street railways read and write, while 92.2 per cent of the 102 male Japanese similarly employed are literate. Of the agricultural laborers 97.7 per cent of the 6,041 male Japanese are literate as opposed to 84.8 per cent of the Chinese from whom data were obtained. Of the south and east European races employed at the coal mines only the Finns, of whom all are literate, reported a higher rate of literacy than the Japanese. Indeed, while 95.7 per cent of the 447 Japanese read and write, only 68.4 per cent of the 461 South Italians, 82.4 per cent of the 245 Poles, 82.7 per cent of the 214 Slovaks, 83.9 per cent of the 193 Montenegrins, 89.6 per cent of the 479 Slovenians, 90.9 per cent of the 66 Greeks, and 92.3 per cent of the 1,175 North Italians are literate. A comparison of the various races employed in the department of maintenance of way of the steam railways shows that more of the Japanese are literate than of the other races most numerously employed. Of 1,135 Japanese 96.1 per cent are literate as opposed to 82.2 per cent of the 714 North Italians, 81.9 per cent of the 1,127 Greeks, 66.4 per cent of the 456 South Italians, and 41.9 per cent of the 2,508 Mexicans employed at the same kind of work who can read and write some language.

Reviewing the whole field of literacy, the following facts are clearly disclosed. More progress in learning English has been made by Japanese employed in or near the centers of Japanese population than by others of the same race who work under other conditions. This is partially due to environment and partially to the fact that many Japanese employed in the cities are of the student class. Compared to the other races employed in similar kinds of work in similar industries, the Japanese appear to have progressed more rapidly than most of the other races, especially the Chinese and Mexicans. This seeming superiority must be discounted somewhat because of two facts: First, that many of the Japanese have had a high-school training in Japan, which usually includes a rudimentary knowledge of English grammar, and hence is a great aid in learning to use English; and second, that many Japanese have come into the continental United States by way of the Hawaiian Islands and Canada, where they have had some contact with English-speaking people. None of the other races have had these advantages before immigration. The differences between the Japanese and some of the other races with regard to the learning of English are so great, however, as to justify the statement that the Japanese have acquired the use of the English language more quickly and more eagerly than the Chinese, the Mexicans, and some of the European races.

The progress of those Japanese who have been in this country for a longer period of time has, on the other hand, been somewhat less rapid than that of the south and east Europeans, due largely to the fact that the extent to which the latter associate with the natives increases with their period of residence here, whereas there is little change in the course of time of the clannish conditions under which Japanese immigrants live and work. That a high standard of literacy on the part of the males obtains in Japan is evidenced by the fact that a much larger percentage can read and write their native language than that reported by most of the south and east European races employed in similar work. That the educational opportunities of females in Japan are not so good is likewise shown by the relatively low literacy of the female Japanese from whom data were secured.

The newspapers and periodicals taken by immigrants are of interest, because according to their character they assist or retard the process of assimilation. They also indicate the extent to which the immigrants have been assimilated and their standard of living. The data relating to newspapers taken by Japanese households are shown in the following table:

TABLE 60.—*Newspapers taken by Japanese households.*

Households.	Number of households.	Number taking—			
		No newspaper.	Only newspapers printed in Japanese.	Only newspapers printed in English.	Newspapers; some printed in Japanese, some in English.
City households...............	332	8	193	4	127
Farm households.............	490	136	322	0	32

Thus only 8 of 332 city households, as against 136 of 490 farm households, were without any newspaper or periodical publication. It is noteworthy that only 4 of the entire number subscribing for one or more publications were without any printed in the Japanese language. Of the 332 city households, however, 131 subscribed for one or more publications in English, but the corresponding number among the farm households was only 32. Some of the Japanese newspapers taken are published in Japan, but the majority are published in a few western cities. There are 4 Japanese daily newspapers published in San Francisco, 3 in Los Angeles, 1 in Sacramento, 2 in Seattle, and a few elsewhere. A few weekly and monthly publications are also found in these cities. These publications present Japanese and American news from the Japanese point of view.

The American publications subscribed for are largely local daily newspapers of the community in or near which the subscribers live. However, a number of households (in most cases those of the urban Japanese) subscribe for weekly or monthly magazines printed in English. Among these are the Literary Digest, the Independent, the Outlook, the Review of Reviews, the Pacific Monthly, and Collier's Weekly. Relatively few, however, are regular subscribers for such magazines. Without entering upon detailed comparisons, it is found that the number of Japanese subscribing for no newspaper is much smaller than that of the Italians and Portuguese. Moreover, the number of publications taken is very much larger. In all of these respects the Japanese compare favorably with the households of north European immigrants. It is true, however, that a far larger percentage of the publications subscribed for are printed in their native language in the case of the Japanese than in the case of the city and farm households of most of the other races investigated. This fact is of importance, for it shows at once the interests and an important source of information of the majority of the Japanese immigrants.

With regard to their political status in the United States, the Japanese, because of their race, occupy a position essentially different from that of the European immigrants. Under the provisions of the laws of the United States they can not become citizens by process of naturalization.[a] During the investigation a comparatively large number of the farmers and business classes expressed a desire to become naturalized and expressed regret at the discrimination against persons who do not belong to some white race. How many would become naturalized and how strong their allegiance to the United States would then be can not be said, for in no country have a sufficient number found it possible to become citizens to serve as a basis for drawing conclusions with reference to such matters. All that can be said is, that the Japanese are greatly interested in political matters, are intelligent, quick to absorb new ideas, and progressive, but have been accustomed to a somewhat different form of government and have exhibited a strength of feeling for and loyalty to their country and its Government and the Mikado, seldom, if ever, found among other people.

Their distinct racial characteristics, combined with the race prejudice of the "white" population, have made the conditions under which the Japanese live and work different from those of the non-Asiatics where employed. In industry they are for the most part kept in "gangs" of their own race under "bosses," who not only direct their labor but manage all their business affairs. It is usual for the Japanese quarters or "bunkhouses" to be located away from the homes of other races, as, for example, at the mines at Rock Springs, Wyo., where the railroad track separates the houses of others from those of the orientals. Moreover, in most cases they are limited in their work to the least pleasant and least remunerative tasks in the productive process. Thus the wage-earning Japanese are largely segregated from others and have little association with Americans or immigrants of other races, either in their living quarters or at their work. Moreover, the independent farmers, in the great majority of cases, have little intercourse with other races in matters other than of business, and even this relation is greatly limited by the fact that they usually employ laborers of their own race and make most of their purchases at Japanese stores. The same segregation, in a more modi-

---

[a] The following are four of the leading cases holding Japanese ineligible for naturalization:

In re Saito (62 Fed., 126, June, 1899). The court held that Japanese, like the Chinese, belong to the Mongolian race, and so are not entitled to naturalization, not being included within the term "white persons" in Rev. Stat., sec. 2169.

In re Buntaro Kumagai (163 Fed., 922, Dist. Ct. Washington, A. D. Sept., 1908). Held that Rev. Stat., par. 2166, authorizing the naturalization of aliens honorably discharged from the military service of the United States does not extend the right to a person of the Japanese race, although having an honorable discharge from the Army of the United States.

In re Knight (171 Fed., 299, D. C., E. D., New York, July, 1909). The petitioner whose father was an Englishman and his mother half Chinese and half Japanese, was born on a British schooner in the Yellow Sea. He enlisted in the United States Navy off the coast of China in 1882 and served honorably since his enlistment until his application for citizenship. It was held that the petitioner was not a free "white person" and was therefore not entitled to naturalization under Rev. Stat., sec. 2169.

In re Takiyi Yamashita (30 Wash., 234, 70 Pac. Rep., 482, Oct., 1902). Application of petitioner, a native of Japan, for admission as an attorney and counsellor at law was denied, as he was not entitled to naturalization, not being "a free white person." The judgment of naturalization given in the superior court was held void.

fied form, exists in the cities in which members of this race have settled in large numbers. Though not as distinct in their boundaries as the " Chinatowns," the Japanese quarters usually come to be rather sharply defined.

As the Japanese element becomes more numerous in a locality, the white residents, who object to their presence more than to the presence of any white immigrants, gradually move out of the district. The Japanese frequently use buildings for both business and residence purposes and are willing to pay higher rent. Thus in many cases as natives have given place to Japanese the rentals have increased, and this has hastened the departure of the white families. Property which Japanese desire to occupy commands a higher rent, but property surrounding the Japanese communities which is not sought by the Japanese falls in value, because it is less desired by other races on account of its proximity to the Japanese " quarter." [a] Many of the city Japanese, however, are employed in domestic and personal service and in other occupations where they are thrown into more direct contact with other races than are those employed in agriculture and industry. Such employment usually carries with it an inferior rank, with its limitations.

The segregation of the Japanese in their living quarters, and in many cases at their work, as well as their failure to obtain employment in a number of industries and localities, have resulted from an attitude of opposition to this race taken by the " white " races, which is more than a negative refusal of association, but an opposition which has taken organized form in some communities and in others has resulted in open violence. Reference has been made in the previous chapters of this report to the organized opposition to Japanese laundries in Los Angeles, San Francisco, and in a number of smaller communities in the State of California,[b] to the concerted action of union labor against and the several boycotts of Japanese restaurants in the leading cities of the West,[c] and to the opposition to the employment of Japanese laborers in the lumber industry in Washington and Oregon.[d] Moreover, the hostile attitude of employees toward all oriental races has prevented the employment of Japanese in the coal mines of northern Colorado and Washington, in most of the shingle mills in Washington and Oregon, in the majority of the fruit and vegetable canneries in California, and in a number of the city trades in which Chinese were used in the early days. In Butte, Mont., the Japanese are not permitted to live in the city, although the Chinese are.

Sporadic outbreaks of violence against the Japanese have occurred from time to time. In one case a group of 50 Japanese, sent out by an agency in Portland to a lumber mill, were not allowed to leave the train by the inhabitants of the mill town. More recently (in August, 1910) a group of Japanese were forcibly driven out of a lumber community in Washington by the " white " employees. Violence was

---

[a] See especially the report on " Japanese in city employments and business in Sacramento, Cal."

[b] See " Japanese in city trades and employments in San Francisco." Also Chapter V, p. 118, of this report.

[c] See Chapter V, p. 121.

[d] See Chapter III, p. 46.

used in the boycott of the Japanese restaurants in San Francisco in 1906, and resulted in considerable destruction of property. The proceedings of the Japanese and Korean Exclusion League of Denver, Colo., in 1908 (organized by labor leaders) were such as to make the Japanese population there fear violence. A counter protective organization was formed by the Japanese, paid detectives of which followed closely the movements of the exclusion league. Literature favorable to Japanese immigration was distributed by the Japanese with the hope of allaying the opposition. Moreover, instructions as to conduct were issued to all Japanese in the neighborhood, in order that no offense should be given by them in matters of morality, cleanliness, aggressiveness, etc. Provision was also made for a place of security in the event of riot, and the men were urged to wear whistles for protection rather than offensive weapons. In San Francisco, also, the Japanese have organized to protect their mutual interests and property.

Aggressive opposition on the part of the " white " population to the association of Japanese with other races has also been manifested with regard to the presence of the latter race in the public schools. As a result of a popular demand, voiced by the Japanese and Korean Exclusion League of San Francisco, the board of éducation of that city decided on October 11, 1906, to segregate Japanese and Chinese pupils in a school building designated as the Oriental School, " not only for the purpose of relieving the congestion at present prevailing in our schools, but also for the higher end that our children should not be placed in any position where their youthful impressions may be affected by association with people of the Mongolian race." The Oriental School was located in the burned district and was inconvenient for most of the Japanese pupils, who, with one exception, failed to appear there for instruction when debarred from the schools they had been attending, it being held by the members of that race that the action was taken in violation of their existing treaty rights, guaranteed by the Federal Government. The school board later rescinded its action and the Japanese pupils returned to the schools which they had formerly attended.[a] Yet in most localities Japanese pupils and the pupils of other races associate with little or no friction.

The race antipathy evidenced by the instances cited above has done much to cause and to perpetuate the clannishness of the Japanese immigrants. The feeling is also very general that marriage between Japanese and white persons should be discouraged. In fact, the strong popular sentiment in this connection has developed into a definite legal prohibition of such unions in the State of California,[b] and has been strong enough in the other Western States to prevent any widespread intermarriage between the Japanese and other races.

---

[a] See " The Japanese in city employments, and business in San Francisco, Cal."

[b] In 1880 section 69 of the California Civil Code was amended so as to prohibit the issuing of licenses for the marriage of white persons with negroes, mulattoes, or Mongolians. In 1905 section 60 of the Civil Code was amended so as to make the marriage of white persons with Mongolians, as well as with negroes and mulattoes, illegal and void. Japanese are regarded as Mongolians. In fact, the amendment of the law in 1905 was meant to relate specifically to marriages between them and white persons.

A few Japanese men have married American women in the West, but the number is too small to be of importance in this connection. In an investigation of the Japanese population of Denver conducted by the Japanese Association of Colorado, and completed July 15, 1909, 6 Japanese were reported as married to white women. In the other Western States, save California, such marriages have been occasionally contracted, but they are few in number. They are of interest chiefly in connection with the strong protests which are called forth and given expression through the press.

Furthermore, in their church affiliations, the Japanese have little opportunity to associate with other immigrant races and with the native-born Americans. A large number of them do not attend any religious services or belong to any religious organization. Moreover, the majority of those who take an interest in religious work adhere to the Buddhist faith. In 1906 there were 12 Japanese Buddhist temples in the Western Division, 9 located in California, 2 in Washington, and 1 in Oregon. These 12 temples had at that time a membership of 3,165 persons, of whom 2,387 were males and 778 females. Nineteen schools were conducted in connection with these temples, having a teaching staff of 48 persons and enrolling 913 pupils.[a] These Buddhist temples include no natives or Europeans in their membership.

In every community where any considerable number of Japanese have settled Christian missions have been instituted for their benefit. The membership of the Christian missions, while large and increasing year by year, is smaller than that of the Buddhist organizations. These missions are for Japanese alone, a recognition of a difference between them and other races and a condition which lessens their value as an assimilative force. All are Protestant missions, some five denominations (Episcopal, Methodist, Presbyterian, Congregational, and Baptist) being represented among them.

In Los Angeles there are five Japanese missions and a like number in San Francisco. The combined attendance of the Christian missions conducted for Japanese in the two cities is roughly 1,000 persons. Japanese Christian missions were reported in practically all of the urban centers having a considerable number of Japanese residents. In several of the rural settlements of the Japanese, however, no such institutions have been established. In some such cases a few Japanese who have accepted the Christian faith have united with local churches on an equal footing with the white members, but such instances are comparatively rare. On the whole, the religious ideas and the worship of the Japanese immigrants are not of such a character as to subject them to influences making for their assimilation. Their association is almost exclusively with members of their own race and their native language is ordinarily used in their public worship.

In no cases were Japanese from whom data were secured members of fraternal orders to which Americans belong. They are racially ineligible for membership in practically all of the American orders. The only organizations other than religious in which they as well as

---

[a] See Bureau of the Census, Special Report on Religious Bodies, 1906, Part II, p. 178.

white persons are members are of a business nature, as, for example, the " Fife Vegetable Growers' Association," in the State of Washington, the " Sacramento Grocers' Union," and the " Chamber of Commerce " of Sacramento.

Among themselves the Japanese are well organized. Most important are the " Japanese Associations," which exist in every urban center in which Japanese have settled in any considerable number. The local associations are branches of more general organizations, as, for example, the " Japanese Association of Colorado," the " Japanese Association of Oregon," and the " Japanese Association of Washington." These areas often correspond to the consular districts, and the associations are used to some extent by the Japanese consular service as administrative organs, as, for example, in the issuing of certificates of various kinds.

These associations have as their members the better-known Japanese of the communities in which they are organized. Most of the farmers and business men and some of the laborers have membership in them. Their objects, as stated in their constitutions, are general and vague. The Japanese Association in San Francisco sets forth its aims as: (1) To elevate the character of Japanese immigrants; (2) to promote association between Japanese and Americans; (3) to promote commerce, agriculture, and other industries; and (4) to further Japanese interests. They, in fact, interest themselves in whatever concerns the welfare of the Japanese. For example, the San Francisco organization came into existence for the purpose of protecting the " rights " of the Japanese immigrants, who felt that unduly harsh treatment was accorded them when San Francisco was threatened with the bubonic plague in 1900. Later, in protecting the Japanese from violence, " plain-clothes men " were employed upon the streets. So were they in Denver also during the anti-Japanese movement of a few years ago. The Japanese Association of Fresno was instrumental in closing the oriental gambling dens and houses of prostitution located in that city. They do whatever comes to hand, and in many localities have been of great value in promoting morality and orderly living as well as in preserving harmony between conflicting interests.

A large number of Japanese immigrants are members of prefectural societies, organizations of immigrants from the same prefectures in Japan. These societies are of a general and benevolent and social nature. Some provision is made for caring for members in case of sickness or misfortune. They also serve in some degree as a center of the social life of the Japanese. In San Francisco 27 prefectures in Japan are represented by as many prefectural societies, 24 in Seattle, 12 in Los Angeles, 8 in Sacramento, and smaller numbers in other communities.

In addition to these more widespread and general organizations, the Japanese have united in several localities for various purposes. The organizations among farmers, shopkeepers, and business men have been noted earlier in this report. Here and there mutual aid societies are conducted which collect dues, usually $1 per month, and in turn provide for the members who are sick or in financial distress. The Japanese Benevolent Society of San Francisco was organized in 1901, with the object of making more complete provision for the care of sick, injured, or unfortunate Japanese. It is of the nature of a charity organization society, organizing the relief-giving agencies of the race rather than dispensing material aid. However, in the period 1901–1908 some $7,000 was expended in caring for the unfortunate and in transporting persons back to Japan. A hospital is conducted in San Francisco by the organization. Japanese hospitals are found in Vacaville, Ogden, and in many of the places in which a few hundred or more Japanese have settled. Though they are without any great fraternal organizations, such as those found among the Portuguese, the Danish, and several other of the European races, the Japanese in a more or less organized way care for those who are in need of assistance. Seldom have the Japanese become public charges or been charity patients at public hospitals. Perhaps no race of equal numbers in this country has imposed upon the public charitable institutions as little burden as the Japanese.

With regard to criminal acts, the record of the Japanese immigrants is very good. With the exception of the cases of excessive gambling and of the operation of houses of prostitution in one or two localities few charges of misdemeanor or of criminality have been brought against them. For example, in San Francisco from 1900 to 1907 less than 100 Japanese were reported among the commitments, a remarkably small number if the size of the Japanese population of that city and the number of Greeks, Italians, and others committed are considered. Gambling is rather prevalent among the Japanese, both among those who live in isolated groups, as for example the employees of the salmon canneries or agricultural laborers and the residents of Japanese quarters in the cities. The gambling places are frequently conducted by Chinese or by other persons. A notable example of this exists in Fresno, Cal., where a number of Chinese dives were conducted until the fall of 1908. In the early summer of that year an agitation against them was initiated by the better element among the Japanese, who enlisted the native clergy and the press in their fight, with the result that the gambling houses were finally closed for several months, beginning in August, 1908. A few Chinese gambling houses, however, were opened in May, 1909, and were still in operation at the time of the investigation. Gambling is an evil which is often to be found in the Japanese just as it is found in other " camps " where any large number of laborers live and work together. In connection with the whole matter of law and order it should be noted, however, that the general attitude of the white people is that it is not important what the Asiatics do among themselves so long as violation of law or disorder does not endanger or inconvenience the members of other races.

This spirit is clearly shown by the circumstances surrounding the agitation and temporary suppression of the Japanese houses of prostitution in Fresno in 1908. The better element among the Japanese initiated the movement against these as well as against the Chinese gambling houses, which were largely patronized by the Japanese. In securing the desired reforms, however, they were consistently opposed by the chief of police and a considerable part of the native population, and not until the moral sense of the better native element was aroused by the appeals of the clergy and the progressive newspapers was action taken. The action was, however, temporary, and, although all the

Japanese societies protested against the reopening of the vicious resorts, several have been allowed to continue their business and were in operation in 1909. Here, in Vacaville, and in some other localities the attitude of the citizens toward law and order seems to have been lowered somewhat by the failure to enforce a single standard of observance.

The Japanese as a race are temperate. Though there is much drinking at restaurants and in " camps," instances are rare in which drunkenness has interfered with their efficiency in any branch of employment. However, some complaint has been made of the excesses of those who work in the Alaskan salmon canneries. These are of the most unsettled and reckless class of Japanese immigrants, and are inclined to excesses of different kinds. Where Japanese have been employed with other races in the same field of work, as for example as section hands on the railroads and as laborers in the cement works and smelters, they are regarded as far more temperate than the Mexicans or the races of south and east Europe.

Thus the Japanese have a comparatively small percentage of illitcrates among them, are intelligent and eager to learn of American institutions, make fairly rapid progress in learning to speak English, and unusually good progress in learning to read and write it. They have not proved to be burdensome to the community because of pauperism or crime. Yet the Japanese, like the Chinese, are regarded as differing so greatly from the white races that they have lived in but as no integral part of the community. A strong public opinion has segregated them, if not in their work, in the other details of their living, and practically forbids, when not expressed in law, marriage between them and persons of the white race.

PACIFIC COAST OPINION OF JAPANESE IMMIGRATION AND THE DESIRE FOR ASIATIC LABORERS.

For several years there has been strong opposition to the immigration of Japanese laborers to the continental United States, and not a little evidence of a desire not to accord to them and other Asiatics residing in this country all of the privileges and rights accorded to immigrants of the white races. Much which bears upon this phase of the matter has been noted in the preceding chapters of this report. It remains to mention still other matters necessary to give a more complete view of the situation.

It is a significant fact that the first strong note of opposition to the immigration of Japanese laborers came from a mass meeting called in 1900 to consider the reenactment of the Chinese-exclusion law, soon to expire.

It is true that the incoming of these laborers and the place they occupied in the industries of the State had been investigated by the California state labor commissioner shortly before,[a] and that an agent of the Federal Government had made an investigation in Japan of the circumstances under which the laborers emigrated from that country to the continental United States.[b] It was in 1900, when an unusually large number arrived, however, that the first organized demand was made for the exclusion of the Japanese. At the mass meeting called in San Francisco, May 7 of that year, not only was a resolution adopted urging Congress to reenact the Chinese-exclusion law, but it was further resolved to urge the adoption of an act of Congress or such other measures as might be necessary for the total exclusion of all classes of Japanese other than members of the diplomatic staff. "Such a law," it was added, "has become a necessity not only on the grounds set forth in the policy of Chinese exclusion but because of additional reasons resting in the fact that the assumed virtue of the Japanese—i. e., their partial adoption of American customs—makes them the more dangerous as competitors."[c] The following January Gov. Henry T. Gage, in his first biennial message to the legislature of the State of California, called attention to the facts that the Chinese-exclusion act of 1892 would expire in May of the next year, and the convention between the United States and China might be terminated in 1904, while the recent acquisition of territory by annexation and war made it particularly necessary that acts of Congress should be passed and the convention revised so as to cover beyond question every part of the territory of the United

---

[a] See Ninth Biennial Report of the Bureau of Labor Statistics of the State of California for the years 1899–1900.
[b] See Chapter II.
[c] Report of mass meeting in San Francisco, Cal., May 8, 1900.

States. While urging that action should be taken looking to this end, Governor Gage took occasion to add:

> The peril from Chinese labor finds a similar danger in the unrestricted importation of Japanese laborers. The cheapness of that labor is likewise a menace to American labor, and a new treaty with Japan for such restriction, as well as the passage of laws by Congress, is desired for the protection of Americans.
>
> I therefore most earnestly appeal to your honorable bodies for the passage as a matter of urgency of appropriate resolutions instructing our Senators and requesting our Representatives in Congress for the immediate institution of all proper measures leading to the revision of the existing treaties with China and Japan, and the passage of all necessary laws and resolutions for the protection of American labor against the immigration of oriental laborers.

As a result of this appeal a joint resolution was adopted by the legislature and a memorial addressed to Congress, praying for the restriction of Japanese immigration. The legislature of Nevada the same year adopted similar resolutions.

Though the American Federation of Labor, at its annual convention held in San Francisco in November, 1904, resolved, in response to a local demand, that the terms of the Chinese exclusion act should be extended so as to exclude Japanese and Korean as well as Chinese laborers, there was little discussion of Japanese immigration until in the spring of 1905. In spite of the fact that the Japanese Government for several years had discouraged the emigration of laborers intending to come to the continental United States the number immigrating directly to this country had increased in 1903 and 1904, while during the latter year, as a result of the inducements made by the Japanese contractors of the Pacific coast cities, a still larger number were migrating to the mainland from Hawaii.[a] From these combined sources many Japanese laborers were arriving in the United States in 1904 and 1905. It was under these circumstances that the San Francisco Chronicle, on February 23, 1905, began the publication of a series of articles upon the Japanese question, calling attention to the number of Japanese already in the country, discussing the supposed evils connected with their immigration, and emphasizing the dangers of future immigration of that kind. The Japanese question at once commanded the attention of the state legislature of California and has had a prominent place in the discussions of that body at every session since that time. On the 1st of March following the state senate adopted a resolution, which was concurred in the following day by the assembly, demanding that action be taken without delay, by treaty or otherwise, to limit the further immigration of Japanese laborers.[b] The same year similar resolutions were again adopted by the legislature of Nevada.

At this time the Union Labor party was in control of municipal affairs in San Francisco. On May 6, 1905, the board of education passed a resolution declaring its determination to effect the establishment of separate schools for Chinese and Japanese pupils. No action followed this resolution, however, for more than a year. The great fire following the earthquake of April, 1906, destroyed many of the school buildings of the city, and among them the one attended by the majority of the Japanese pupils. The difficulty of providing

---

[a] See Chapter II, p. 5 et seq.
[b] Senate joint resolution, No. 10, California Statutes, 1905, p. 1060.

for pupils of any race after the disaster brought the Japanese school question again into prominence, while the more conspicuous position the Japanese had made for themselves in the business of the city, and especially in the restaurant trade, immediately after the fire had added to the feeling against them as a race. In October, 1906, the board of education passed a " separate school order," which required the transfer of most of the Japanese pupils to the " Oriental School," located in the center of the city, far removed from the homes of most of the pupils to be transferred. The objections to this by the Japanese and the complaints from the Government at Tokio, immediately centered the attention of the whole country upon San Francisco, and the question of separate schools for Asiatics suddenly became an international one. At the same time, October, 1906, the Cooks and Waiters' Union conducted a boycott against the numerous Japanese restaurants which had been opened in various parts of the city. This boycott was accompanied by much damage to the buildings occupied for this purpose and by much violence to Japanese of all classes.[a] This was followed by an investigation by the Federal Government, a conference between the local officials and the President, the withdrawal of the separate-school order by the board of education, and an agreement between the governments of Japan and the United States in which the former agreed to discontinue the issuing of passports to laborers planning to come directly to the continental United States. The President, acting in accordance with an amendment to the immigration law approved February 20, 1907, issued an order refusing admission to "Japanese or Korean laborers, skilled or unskilled, who have received passports to go to Mexico, Canada or Hawaii and come therefrom." [b]

The opposition to Japanese immigration had assumed a definitely organized form in May, 1905, when the Asiatic Exclusion League [c] was organized in San Francisco. Later branches of the same body were organized in Seattle, Portland, Denver, Stockton, and other places, and a general international organization [d] was formed holding yearly conventions. The general organization states its principles and purposes in the preamble to its constitution as follows:

Two or more unassimilable races can not exist peaceably in the same territory. This action between such races results in the extermination of that one which, by reason of its characteristics, physical and mental, is least adapted to the conditions of life originating in the given territory.

The conditions of life are, in the last analysis, determined by the conditions of labor; consequently the question of adaptability as between two unassimilable races must be resolved in favor of that race the characteristics of which most nearly conform to the conditions of labor.

The labor of to-day in North America is a machine, as distinguished from a manual process. That race, therefore, which by its nature is best suited to complement the machine as the essential factor of production is in that respect the superior race, and therefore best adapted to the conditions of American industrial life.

---

[a] See " Japanese in city employments and business in San Francisco."

[b] For the restrictions placed by the Japanese Government upon the emigration of laborers, the amendment of the immigration law, and the order issued by the President, see Chapter II.

[c] The league was at first known as the Japanese and Korean Exclusion League, but the official title was later changed to that given above.

[d] With a membership drawn from British Columbia and several of the Western States.

The Caucasian and Asiatic races are unassimilable. Contact between these races must result, under the conditions of industrial life obtaining in North America, in injury to the former, proportioned to the extent to which such contact prevails. The preservation of the Caucasian race upon American soil, and particularly upon the west shore thereof, necessitates the adoption of all possible measures to prevent or minimize the immigration of Asiatics to America.

With these principles and purposes in view we have formed the Asiatic Exclusion League of North America, to the end that the soil of North America be preserved to the American people of the present and all future generations, that they may attain the highest possible moral and national standards, and that they may maintain a society in keeping with the highest ideals of freedom and self-government.

Of the several local organizations that in San Francisco alone has been active in its agitation against the Japanese for more than a very short time. Indeed, the other branches have usually been inactive, and in most places the organization has been little more than a name. The San Francisco league, however, has been well organized and very active. Nor did its agitation cease with the restriction of immigration in 1907, for it has maintained that the agreement was neither a logical nor an effective method of regulation. At the meeting of the general organization in Seattle in February, 1908, it was resolved in a memorial addressed to Congress that—

The first annual convention of the Asiatic Exclusion League of North America does hereby most respectfully protest against the administrative and executive officers of the United States entering into any agreement which will permit the ruler of any foreign country to make stipulations as to what class of persons and in what numbers shall leave said foreign country for the purpose of immigrating to the United States, and your memorialists further declare that the incoming of immigrants into the United States is a matter for domestic legislation and regulation, and is a prerogative of Congress and of Congress alone.

The composition of the Exclusion League is that of a number of affiliated bodies, the greater number of them labor organizations. In February, 1908, the membership in California was reported to be 110,000. In May, 1909, according to the official proceedings for that month, the organization in California consisted of 238 affiliated bodies, characterized as follows:

Labor	202
Fraternal	18
Civic	12
Benevolent	3
Political	2
Military	1
Total	238

This did not include the membership of leagues in the States of Oregon, Washington, Idaho, Colorado, and Nebraska.

While not limiting its membership in any way, the league has always been dominated by organized labor, and the position taken by it has always had the support of organized labor in general. The strength of feeling against the Japanese among union laborers has been shown by frequent boycotts of Japanese goods and services by fines imposed on members patronizing Japanese and by the fact that membership in labor unions has been closed to the Asiatics. The only exception to this is found in Wyoming, where Japanese miners have been admitted to membership in the United Mine Workers of America, though working agreements have been entered into by white and Japanese organizations representing the same trade, as by the Japanese and white barbers' unions in Stockton and Fresno.

The Exclusion League, however, has declared officially and emphatically that it is not in its province to take the lead in or advise any boycott either of Asiatics or their goods, and that such matters shall be left to the labor organizations. It has frequently emphasized the fact that its opposition to Asiatics was not alone on industrial but on racial and political grounds as well, and has consistently directed its efforts to arousing a sentiment in favor of the extension of the present exclusion law to the Japanese. It has sought anti-Japanese pledges from candidates for office, but has not affiliated with any political party. By its agitation no doubt the league has done much to increase the opposition to Japanese, especially in California.

It has already been mentioned that the anti-Japanese movement in San Francisco in 1900, followed by the message of Governor Gage on the subject and the renewal of the agitation in 1905, both resulted in resolutions being adopted by the California legislatures, then in session, calling the attention of Congress to the need of measures restricting Japanese immigration to this country. With the increase in the number of immigrants in the country until 1907, and the more serious and widespread agitation against them throughout the State at the session of 1907, some more definite measures in regard to the Japanese question were presented to the legislature. These proposed bills and resolutions provided for ascertaining and expressing the will of the people of the State upon the subject of Asiatic immigration, condemned the proposition of the President to extend the elective franchise to alien-born Asiatics, urged upon Congress the necessity of excluding objectionable Asiatics, fixed the age at which children might be admitted to the primary schools, and protested against the making or ratification of any treaty with Japan unless it should contain a proviso that nothing in the treaty should affect or impair any law of any State relating to the subject of education, marriage, suffrage, eligibility to hold office, or the exercise of the police powers of the State. As a result of the efforts of the President and governor all of the measures proposed failed to pass either one or both houses.

The session of 1909 was still more prolific of anti-Japanese bills. No fewer than 17 different bills relative to Japanese were introduced, but the interest centered largely in an " alien land bill " and a " school segregation " measure. The former bill was intended to prevent the acquisition of land by the Japanese, but the objections of the President led to its amendment so as to include all aliens, and in that form it failed to pass. The bill for segregating Japanese children in the public schools, however, passed the assembly by a vote of 48 to 26. The prompt intervention of President Roosevelt through the governor brought about a reconsideration of the bill and its defeat by a vote of 41 to 37. The only anti-Japanese measures passed at that session were one—

to provide for the gathering, compiling, printing, and distribution of statistics and information regarding the Japanese of the State, and making an appropriation therefor—

and a resolution in favor of exclusion. The report of the state labor commissioner, who has had charge of the investigation for which provision was made, has not yet been printed. The resolution adopted, quoted because it is the most recent expression of the legislature, is as follows:

Whereas the progress, happiness, and prosperity of the people of a nation depend upon a homogeneous population;

Whereas the influx of the overpopulated nations of Asia, of people who are unsuited for American citizenship or for assimilation with the Caucasian race, has resulted and will result in lowering the American standard of life and the dignity and wage-earning capacity of American labor;

Whereas the exclusion of Chinese laborers under the existing exclusion laws of the United States has tended to preserve the economic and social welfare of the people;

Whereas we view with alarm any proposed repeal of such exclusion laws and the substituting therefor of general laws;

Whereas the interest of California can best be safeguarded by the retention of said exclusion laws and by extending their terms and provisions to other Asiatic people;

Whereas the people of the Eastern States and the United States generally have an erroneous impression as to the real sentiment of the people of the Pacific coast relative to the Asiatic question;

Whereas we think it right and proper that the people of this country should be advised as to our true position on that question: Therefore be it

Resolved by the senate and assembly jointly, That we respectfully urge the Congress of the United States to maintain intact the present Chinese exclusion laws, and instead of taking any action looking to the repeal of said exclusion laws, to extend the terms and provisions thereof so as to apply to and include all Asiatics.

Resolved, That our Senators be instructed and Representatives in Congress requested to use all honorable means to carry out the foregoing recommendation and requests.

Resolved, That the governor of California be, and he is hereby, directed to transmit a certified copy of these resolutions to the President and Speaker, respectively, of the Senate and House of Representatives of the United States and to each of our Senators and Representatives in Congress.

During the session of 1909 of the Nevada legislature strong anti-Japanese resolutions, commending the Japanese land bill and the school segregation bill then pending in the California legislature, were adopted by the house but were defeated in the senate as a result of influence brought to bear from Washington through the United States Senators from Nevada. In the Oregon legislature also a resolution was introduced calling upon Congress to maintain the Chinese-exclusion act and requesting that the present laws be broadened so as to include all Asiatics. This was also defeated through the efforts of one of the United States Senators. In Montana a school-segregation measure was introduced and also a joint memorial calling for the enforcement of the present Chinese-exclusion laws and urging their extension so as to include all Asiatics. The school-segregation measure was referred to the committee on military affairs and was reported unfavorably.

In how far this abortive legislation represents the general sentiment of the people of the Western and Pacific Coast States can only be judged by the attitude toward the Japanese question of political parties, newspapers, chambers of commerce, and other organizations, and personal opinions as gathered by agents of the Commission. Without doubt there has been much difference of opinion as to the advisability of the proposed measures directed against Japanese already in the country, but it is equally certain that with reference to the further immigration of laborers the prevailing opinion is in favor of effective restriction.

Only now and then, and chiefly as a result of the movement in California, has the immigration of Japanese been regarded as a problem of commanding importance in the Western States other than California. This is explained largely by the difference in numbers, the greatest objection accompanying the largest numbers, but partly also by the greater advance the Japanese have made in California than elsewhere. No doubt the successful agitation against Chinese, which was limited very largely to California, has also been a factor in developing the feeling against the Japanese. That the sentiment of the great majority of the people in this one State is definitely opposed to any immigration of Japanese laborers is evidenced by the fact that the platforms of the three leading political parties of the State in 1910 all contained " exclusion planks." The exclusion plank in the Republican platform was as follows:

16. We declare our faith in the unswerving opposition of the people of California to the further admission of oriental laborers, and we urge upon Congress and the President the adoption of all necessary measures to guard against this evil.

The planks in the Democratic platform were:

7. The exclusion of all Asiatic labor.
20. The adoption of the Sanford bill, preventing Asiatics who are not eligible to citizenship from owning land in California.

The Socialist party's platform contained the following plank:

We favor all legislative measures tending to prevent the immigration of strike breakers and contract laborers and the mass immigration and importation of Mongolian or East Indian labor, caused or stimulated by the employing classes for the purpose of weakening the organization of American labor and of lowering the standard of life of the American workers.

Not only did the parties place themselves on record in favor of exclusion, but almost all of the leading candidates for office pledged themselves to work for the exclusion of all Asiatic laborers and many of them discussed the matter extensively during the campaign.

The general trend of editorial comment in Pacific coast newspapers within the last few years has been in favor of Japanese exclusion, either by agreement as at present or by an extension of the Chinese-exclusion law. Although it would be impossible to state exactly how general this attitude is, the newspaper clippings sent in from all parts of the West by agents of the Commission would indicate that there is a strong and increasing prejudice against the further admission of Asiatics. The few editors who have favored Japanese immigration have usually justified their position by the plea that certain agricultural industries were dependent upon Asiatics, or that exclusion would injure the trade between the United States and the Orient. There can be no doubt that those newspapers which are published in the localities where the Japanese have become established as an important element in the labor supply, and then have become farmers and business men, very generally declare emphatically against them, and that those papers reflect the general attitude of the community on the question.

Another important indication of popular sentiment in regard to the Japanese is found in the expression of boards of trade through their officers, as shown in correspondence with the Commission or in personal interviews with its agents. The opinion of the great majority of these men, representing the more important agricultural centers in California and a few in Washington and Oregon, was strongly opposed to further immigration of Japanese laborers. The objections to the Japanese were partly because of their personal characteristics, but more generally on the broader ground of the welfare of the community or of public policy. These boards of trade have been organized to advertise the resources of their particular localities, to induce the migration and settlement of families, to secure the reclamation and subdivision of lands and better exploitation of resources, and in other ways to promote the material welfare of the community. One almost universal objection made to the Japanese by the representatives of these organizations was that their presence, and especially the lease and ownership of land by them, prevented the migration of desirable white families to the district. The representatives of several of these boards of trade, even while opposed to the immigration of Japanese, stated that their communities would gladly make use of more Chinese if they were available. The reasons advanced for the favorable opinion of the Chinese as against the Japanese were their superiority as workmen, their faithfulness to the employer, a less general desire to acquire possession of land or to engage in business, and the absence of a desire on their part to associate with others on equal terms.

A few years ago several chambers of commerce in the larger cities of the Pacific Coast States adopted resolutions of a more or less pro-Japanese character. Most of these were adopted at the time of the difficulties growing out of the " separate school order " and the boycott of restaurants in San Francisco, and though the opinions of members of these organizations given expression in the general resolutions adopted differed, it would appear that these resolutions were usually adopted in order to allay the increasing hostility in Japan, which would result in a loss of trade. In most cases it appears, upon investigation, that these resolutions were not intended as an expression of opinion as to the desirability of the immigration of Japanese laborers, but as to the treatment which should be accorded to the Japanese in this country and as to the undesirability of any action which would result in friction between the two races. The very general feeling at present is to " leave well enough alone."

The prevailing sentiment in communities where Japanese are found in large numbers is in favor of exclusion of the laborers of this race, and in general the present policy of restriction by international agreement is considered satisfactory so long as it proves effective. Yet there are three classes who advocate a change in the present policy of restriction in this form. One class advocate the enactment of a positive Japanese exclusion law such as exists against the Chinese. Among the reasons assigned by them for desiring the enactment of such a law are that the present agreement with Japan in regard to a question of domestic policy creates an undesirable precedent and leaves the question in such form that it may be reopened at any time by the repudiation of the agreement. Though this view is taken by some who are not connected with that organization, it finds expression chiefly through the Asiatic Exclusion League. A second class is found at the other extreme in those who object to any discrimination between races and who favor the immigration of Chinese and Japanese on the same terms as other races and under a general immigration law, with little regard to the immediate effect of such a policy upon the community. The larger number of this small class—in the West—approach the matter from a religious or an ethical point of view.

There is a third class composed of some fruit growers and shippers and men engaged in other industries, who advocate a change in the present policy, so as to permit the immigration of both Chinese and Japanese, but the persons of this class usually state that the number of immigrants should be strictly limited. These men generally hold that Asiatics are essential, or at least desirable, for the development of their industries. In the growing of sugar beets, grapes, and certain other intensive crops, especially in California, and in the canning of salmon in Oregon, Washington, and Alaska, the Chinese, and more recently the Japanese, have been regarded as indispensable to the continuance of the industries. A noticeable feature of the attitude of those who desire Japanese and Chinese for work in their particular industries, however, is that their proposals for the admission of such classes are only of a temporary nature. They generally do not regard these races as desirable otherwise than in limited numbers, and as laborers in those employments which have been uninviting to white men under prevailing conditions and for which the organization, habits, and physical characteristics of the orientals make them peculiarly acceptable to the employer. It is noteworthy also that the greater part of those who believe Asiatic labor of some kind to be necessary to the continued development of the fruit, vegetable, or other intensive crops prefer Chinese to Japanese, as the former are more skillful and painstaking and strictly honest as to contracts, while much complaint and dissatisfaction is expressed with regard to the Japanese. Moreover, preference is frequently expressed for the Chinese because they are less ambitious than the Japanese and fewer of them rise to higher economic positions than that of the laborer. The attitude of this class is clearly expressed as follows in a report made by its committee on immigration to the Los Angeles Chamber of Commerce, February 16, 1910:

The other class of immigrants desired is concerned with handling our citrous industry, marketing our fruits and vegetables, and in general caring for the many agricultural products for which southern California is noted. For this work we need the Chinese and Japanese, and especially the former. To all practical intents a discussion of the immigration problem in southern California is synonymous with a discussion of the Chinese question. Your committee feels that the time is fast approaching when southern California is to be called upon to face an imminent need of Chinese laborers. While your committee is entirely in sympathy with the general spirit and idea of the exclusion laws, it feels that certain modifications should be enacted so as to preserve the original intent and yet satisfy needs which are at present a serious problem to some of our most important employers of labor. Our orchardists, our fruit-packing interests, our vegetable gardens, our great bean fields, our walnut groves, our vineyards, the raisin industry—these agricultural interests, together with the omnipresent domestic problem, are clamoring loudly at the present time. It is a fact a dearth of labor in such industries is approaching. These conditions demand your attention to this important phase of our economic problem.

In voicing what we believe to be a sane view of the matter, the Chinaman in this present instance is not a competitor of our American workman. He is a necessity. We feel the solution of our immigration needs, now felt seriously in some quarters, to be found in the modification of the present law providing for the admission of a restricted number of Chinese workers.

It should be added that this report was merely filed and was never acted upon by the chamber of commerce, so that it can not be said to represent the views of that body, but it does set forth the position taken by the class of employers to which reference has been made.

Thus the desire for a change in the present policy of exclusion of Japanese laborers by agreement and the further immigration of that class is closely connected with the assumption that there is a need for Asiatics specifically to perform certain kinds of labor, and the desire is for both Chinese and Japanese, or for the former in preference to the latter. It is evident from the details presented above that the laborers of both races have done much to develop certain industries, and notably fish canning and intensive agriculture, and that their labor in other instances, as in domestic service, has been a great convenience. It is evident also that the Chinese, and especially the Japanese, are conspicuously employed in the industries just mentioned. The investigation made by the Commission has not shown, however, that the dependence upon Asiatic labor is so great, that with the supply already available for work where the employment of other races would involve too great difficulty, a readjustment and the substitution of laborers of other races as the Asiatics diminish in number can not be made. General facts of importance in connection with the possibilities of such a readjustment and substitution of white laborers and the specific need for Asiatic labor have been discussed at length elsewhere.[a] They may be stated here in summary form:

Employers have naturally, as a rule, sought the cheapest and most convenient supply of labor. In this way the Asiatics have been employed extensively, and sometimes almost to the exclusion of others, in certain industries. These industries and the conditions under which they have been carried on, have been shaped in such instances by the Asiatics employed. Industries have been developed in advance of a settled labor supply and specialization has been carried to the extreme, so that a large migration of laborers has been required to meet the seasonal demands in the different localities, and the living conditions, especially for seasonal laborers, have been so shaped that they are bad from the point of view of the white laborer. The Asiatics fit well into this scheme of things; in fact, as stated, the situation has been given shape by them, and the substitution of other races involves difficulty. It should be noted, however, that with the exception of salmon canning in certain localities, there is no work engaged in by Asiatics in the West which is not engaged in by white laborers also to some extent and in which white men do not engage in other parts of the country under not dissimilar climatic conditions. With better provision for board and lodging there can be no doubt that the number of white men available for such work would be materially increased.

The problem of seasonal labor can be met in part in several ways. The white labor supply of the larger cities has not been fully utilized because of the abundant, organized and convenient supply of Asiatic labor at hand. That much more white labor can be made available for fruit picking and similar work is shown by the fact that by ad-

---

[a] See "Immigrant labor in California agricultural industries."

vertising, the large hop growers secure white laborers in very large numbers from the cities. One difficulty in the case of the orchardists and other small growers has been that they could not well secure this labor when they and it were both without organization and they could not guarantee enough work to make it attractive. In southern California, however, in several instances, the packing houses and the citrus-fruit associations have " crews " of white pickers who are sent to the ranches where needed for harvest work. In some other industries, as in the deciduous fruit industry, where the fruit is shipped "green," a similar organization is possible, or the matter might be taken care of by the shippers. In fact, some shippers now pack the fruit consigned to them. It would be possible to extend this system and maintain " gangs " of pickers and packers and send them to the places where needed. Mexicans, German-Russians, and other white races can be used more extensively in the hand work in the beet fields until such time as the lands are subdivided and the growing of beets takes its place in diversified farming—a condition which obtains at Lehi, Utah, where the families of American, English, and other farmers, with the assistance of regular farm laborers, do the work in the fields.

A greater diversity of crops and of industries in the community can be developed, so as more nearly to equalize the demand for labor and to provide fairly regular employment for laborers where it is not now to be found. With a diminishing number of Asiatic laborers there will be a tendency to subdivide the large vineyards and vegetable farms which have been conducted here and there as " estates " or by corporations. This would induce a settlement of families upon small farms, the members of the families would do most of the work, and this would go far toward solving the problem of labor, for smaller holdings would naturally be accompanied by a greater diversity of crops. A development of this kind, and a decreasing number of Asiatics, will increase the influx of families from the East and Middle West, which there can be no doubt has been retarded by the presence of the Asiatics. Finally, a larger influx of laborers and families, especially of the Italians and Portuguese, should follow the completion of the Panama Canal.

It is not evident that there is any need for Asiatic laborers as against laborers of other races, which can not be met indefinitely by those now in the country. There is need, however, for a much larger population, who will settle in the western country, exploit its resources more fully, and develop the communities along normal lines. The presence of Asiatics has in some localities prevented the influx of other races. It should be added, moreover, that the problem of labor does not stand alone. Without restrictions out of harmony with the policy to extend equal privileges to all within the country and without restrictions of such a character that they would give rise to difficult political and administrative problems the tenantry and ownership of land, the personnel of the business class, and the local institutions are determined largely by the race or races which become dominant in the labor supply.

PART II.—THE JAPANESE IN CITY EMPLOYMENTS AND BUSINESS IN THE PRINCIPAL CITIES OF THE PACIFIC COAST AND ROCKY MOUNTAIN STATES.

PART II.—THE JAPANESE IN CITY EMPLOYMENTS AND BUSINESS IN THE PRINCIPAL CITIES OF THE PACIFIC COAST AND ROCKY MOUNTAIN STATES.

CHAPTER I.

INTRODUCTORY.

The agents of the Commission made an investigation of the occupations, business, and social life of the Japanese in several cities in the Pacific Coast and Rocky Mountain States. The investigation in San Francisco was made between November, 1908, and May, 1909; in the other localities between March, 1909, and the 1st of July of the same year. In Seattle, San Francisco, Sacramento, Los Angeles, Fresno, and Watsonville, the general investigation was supplemented by the taking of schedules. Family schedules were taken for wage-earners and business men and their families. Business schedules also were taken for Japanese and some of the competing establishments conducted by white men, and individual schedules were obtained from their employees wherever possible, as in the industrial investigations. From the family schedules data were obtained for 887 foreign-born male Japanese, 232 foreign-born female Japanese, and 66 males and 80 females native-born of Japanese foreign-born father, residing in the 6 cities mentioned above. Business schedules were obtained for 92 Japanese establishments in Los Angeles, 91 in San Francisco, 86 in Seattle, 55 in Sacramento, 21 in Fresno, and 19 in Watsonville, while in the first 4 of the cities mentioned a smaller number of schedules were taken for white business establishments in trades where Japanese competition was asserted to work injury to white competitors.

This business schedule among other things contained inquiries concerning the kind of business conducted in the given establishment, the date at which it was started, the approximate amount of capital employed in it, the amount of the capital borrowed (including the cost of goods in stock but unpaid for), the approximate value of annual transactions, the annual rental value of the property occupied, the occupations, races, sex, and wages of employees, and the number of hours worked per day and per week, the percentage of patronage by white and by oriental races, and, if in mercantile trade, the proportions of oriental and other goods dealt in. In the case of the Japanese this schedule was employed as a supplement to the family schedule taken, which contained inquiries relating to family income, property, and other matters, affording possibilities of checking some of the entries in the business schedule.

The data obtained in this way are presented in a number of special reports, while the more significant facts are incorporated in Chapter V of the " General report on Japanese immigrants in the United

States." The special reports are as follows: "Japanese in city employments and business in the State of Washington, with special reference to Seattle; " "Japanese in city employments and business in San Francisco, Cal.; " "Japanese in city employments and business in Los Angeles, Cal.; " "Japanese in city employments and business in Sacramento, Cal.; " "Japanese in city employments and business in Portland, Oreg.; " "Japanese in city employments and business in Salt Lake City and Ogden, Utah; " "Japanese in city employments and business in Denver, Colo.; " and "Japanese in business in Idaho." In addition to these, sections of the reports on "Immigrants of Fresno County, Cal.," "The Japanese of the Pajaro Valley," and "Immigrant labor in the deciduous fruit industry of the Vaca Valley," deal with the members of the Japanese race in business in Fresno, Watsonville, and Vacaville, respectively.

In the reports on San Francisco, Los Angeles, Sacramento, and Seattle, which follow in the order named, the statistical tables based upon the schedules collected are not inserted in the text, but reference is made by number to these tables, which are published at the end of the special report to which they relate. The statistical data must not be regarded as having any degree of finality, but as illustrative and indicative. Some of the returns made are taken from books kept, while most are estimates, and therefore in some instances no doubt vary considerably from the true amounts in spite of an almost universal effort made by the persons questioned to furnish the agents with accurate data. Where a return has appeared questionable it has been eliminated. As a whole it is believed that the data are above the average in point of accuracy in matters in which much—such as the profits of a small business, the percentage of patronage by a given race, and the cost of food and drink consumed—must necessarily be more or less uncertain and difficult to reckon. Moreover, the numbers involved are comparatively small and the tables can not be accorded the same weight as tables based upon larger numbers collected with equal care. Finally, in some branches of business more than a fair proportion of the larger establishments were included in the investigation, the effect being to increase the average amount of capital invested, the amount of business done, the rent paid, and the profit realized by the business men of each city represented in the investigation in connection with which statistical tables are used.

JAPANESE IN CITY EMPLOYMENTS AND BUSINESS IN SAN FRANCISCO.

[For General Tables, see pp. 353–361.]

INTRODUCTION.

The majority of the Japanese immigrating to the continental United States have arrived at the port of San Francisco, from which city more Japanese laborers have been sent out by contractors to work in various employments than from any other place. Because of its position in this respect, San Francisco has always had the largest Japanese population, the largest amount of business conducted by the members of that race, and the largest number of them employed as wage-earners of all the cities of the West.

According to the census, the number of Japanese in San Francisco was 45 in 1880, 590 in 1890, and 1,781 in 1900. With the great influx of immigrants during subsequent years, the number reported for 1900 has increased several fold. In 1904 it is estimated to have been 10,132, in 1907, 11,380.[a] More recently, with the further immigration of laborers discontinued, a tendency on the part of those in the ports of arrival to migrate to other places, the strong agitation against them in San Francisco, and a gradually diminishing number in the United States, the number of Japanese in San Francisco has decreased. In November, 1909, the population was estimated at 8,746, of whom 6,938 were adult males, 1,187 adult females, and 621 children under 16 years of age. The number varies greatly during the year because of the exodus of some 1,500 in the spring and summer for agricultural and cannery work. A partial census conducted by the Japanese Association in the spring of 1910 was used as a basis for an estimate of 8,000 or somewhat less.

JAPANESE EMPLOYED BY WHITE PERSONS.

The Japanese, as well as the Chinese, have long been conspicuously employed as domestic servants in San Francisco. In 1898 it is probable that 700 or 800 were so employed. In 1904 it is estimated that the number had increased to more than 3,600, but recently the number has diminished with the smaller number of Japanese in San Francisco, because of a desire on their part to obtain other work and the higher wages which housekeepers have found it necessary to pay them. In 1909 it was estimated that about 2,000 were employed as domestics. A large percentage of these are "schoolboys," who work short hours, and in return receive board and lodging and from $8 to $16 per month, the money wage depending upon the number of hours of work over that regarded as an equivalent for board and lodging.

---

[a] Estimates contained in the Japanese-American Yearbooks for 1905 and 1908.

The Japanese who worked regularly as servants in 1909 earned from $25 per month for those of little skill to $60 per month for experienced cooks. It was difficult to secure personal information from persons thus employed, but data were secured for 70 "domestics." Of this number 4 earned $25; 17, $30; 16, $35; 20, $40; 9, $45; 3, $50; and 1, $55 per month. These wages are materially higher than those paid in earlier years. The wages paid previous to 1900. can not be ascertained with any degree of exactness, but the scales in effect for 1900 and subsequent years, as shown by the records of a Japanese employment agent, are presented in the following tabular statement:

Year.	Wages "plain cook."a	Wages waiter and house worker.a	Wages "school boy."b
1900	$20 to $30	$15 to $25	$1.50
1903	25 to 35	20 to 30	1.75
1907	30 to 40	25 to 35	2.00

a Per month.					b Per week.

The field of domestic service in private families is shared chiefly by Japanese and Chinese men and white women of various races, among whom many are foreign-born. It is impossible to estimate with any degree of accuracy the total number thus employed at present or at any time in the past, for such domestics are not reported separately by the census.a During the last fifteen years the number of Chinese has diminished somewhat as a result of the exclusion acts. It appears that the number of Japanese entering upon domestic service has not been sufficient to do more than offset the decreasing number of Chinese servants and to provide for the larger number of servants employed in consequence of the growth of population. Though the Japanese until recently have been regarded as the cheapest servants for such kinds of work as they have done, there has been also a scarcity of white servants at the wages offered, though these wages have been increasing.b

Japanese are also employed to do cleaning and related work about private houses and gardens. These " day workers," as they are called, usually live in groups of from 2 to 8, the average number being 5 or 6. Frequently they live with cobblers and at the cobbler shops or other offices receive orders for work to be done.

The " day workers " do house cleaning, cooking, waiting on table, and gardening " on call." The Japanese alone have made an organ-

a The census for 1900 reports 6,995 male servants and waiters and 6,837 female servants and waitresses. Of the 19,741 females thus employed in the State of California, 7,838 were foreign-born whites, among whom the Irish with 4,493, the Germans with 2,697, and the Scandinavians with 1,718, were the important elements.

b The statistical data presented in the reports of the Bureau of Labor Statistics are not entirely comparable. It would appear, however, that the median wage for 56 female cooks who received positions through employment agencies during April, 1908. was $35; for 209 seeking employment in the same way in 1895-96, about $25, while the median wages for general houseworkers at the two dates were $25 and $20, respectively. Were the computation of averages possible, they would indicate a greater increase in wages paid to these two classes of domestics.

ized effort to meet the desires of those in need of temporary and irregular service, and a large number have been thus occupied for several years. At the close of the year 1909 the number of groups reported by the Japanese-American Yearbook was 148, the number of persons included in them 984. This number is materially larger than during the summer months, when many men are attracted to the country for agricultural and related work. A few who are not members of the groups mentioned are similarly employed, so that the maximum number of "day workers" may be reckoned at about 1,000. Fourteen of the groups, comprising 53 men, were investigated. The wages for cleaning were 30 or 35 cents per hour, or $2.50 per day; for waiting on table, 35 to 50 cents (with white coat), or $1 (with dress coat); for gardening, 50 cents per hour; for window cleaning, 5 cents per window. As would be expected, the work is irregular, so that the earnings of the 53 house cleaners varied between $20 per month as a minimum and $70 as a maximum.

The average of the earnings of the 53 was $42.74 per month and $512.83 per year. The earnings of 4 were less than $30 per month; of 15, $30 but less than $40; of 12, $40 but less than $50; of 15, $50; of 6, $60 but less than $70; of 1, $70 per month. Their earnings per day are higher than formerly, when the number of newly arrived Japanese was larger. According to the testimony of Japanese employment agents the rate per day- for ordinary cleaning was $1.50 in 1900. By 1903 it had risen to $1.75, by 1907 to $2 per day.

A few hundred Japanese—how many can not be ascertained without making a census of the many restaurants and hotels of the city—are employed as cooks' helpers, dishwashers, and "general kitchen help" in the restaurants and hotels conducted by white proprietors.

It is estimated that the total number of white persons so employed is about 1,000. Of these about one-third are members of the Cooks Helpers' Union and are paid $12 per week as cooks' helpers and pantrymen and $10 per week as "vegetable men," dishwashers, porters, and "miscellaneous help." The union scale provides for a 6-day week and a day of 12 hours, with board in addition to wages for the days employed and 25 cents per hour for overtime work. In hotels the wages for the two classes mentioned are, respectively, $45 and $35 per month and found. The nonunion white men employed in these capacities are paid smaller wages. Many of these men are either very young or very old, have no trade, shift from place to place, and are willing to accept work at comparatively low wages. The earnings of most, it would appear, are between $5 and $10 per week, with board. Of 947 men supplied during 1907 and 1908 by San Francisco employment agencies for positions as kitchen help, 37 were to be paid less than $15 per month; 63, $20; 165, $25; 237, $30; 178, $35; 107, $40; 46, $45; 111, $50; and 3, $60 per month.[a] The median wage was $30 per month. The Japanese simi-

---

[a] Thirteenth Biennial Report of the Bureau of Labor Statistics of the State of California, p. 150. The above figures do not include the wages of 66 paid by the day—from $1 to $2.75. Of the total of 1,013, 447 were employed elsewhere than in San Francisco, but chiefly in the transbay cities, where the same level of wages obtains.

larly employed usually earn $30, $35, or $40 per month, but they frequently work 7 days per week. It should be added, also, that they are all in the prime of life and that their wages are higher now than formerly, the increase corresponding to that of the Japanese engaged in domestic work in private families.

The Japanese employed as " cooks' helpers " and " kitchen help " have displaced some white men. It is in fact asserted by officials of the Cooks' Helpers' Union that there has always been a large number of white men available for such work, but the Japanese have been preferred because willing to do various kinds of work regarded by the white union man as no part of his occupation and to work seven days per week, as the union man does not. Moreover, they have worked for less than the union scale of wages, while they are more capable and more regular in their habits than many of the white men who receive about the same wages.

Japanese have seldom been employed as cooks or waiters in " white " hotels and restaurants in San Francisco. They have, however, been employed in these capacities in saloons, but the number of Japanese cooks employed has been small, this work frequently, if not generally, falling to the Chinese. The Japanese employed in saloons usually serve the lunches—that is, stand behind the counter or bring food to the counter where patrons wait upon themselves—or else work as " scrub boys " and porters. In a number of the smaller saloons a Chinese cook prepares the lunch, serves it, and acts as porter or " scrub boy," while in other cases the several duties are performed by a Japanese.

How many Japanese were employed in 1909 in the saloons of San Francisco, which numbered 2,375 in 1907, it is impossible to estimate with any degree of accuracy, but they have aggregated several hundred. Most of the barrooms not frequented by workingmen in 1909 employed one or more, but the majority of the saloons conducted are on the streets occupied largely by workingmen, and because of the strong opposition to the Asiatics shown here few Japanese are employed in such establishments. Indeed, it would appear that with the organized opposition to the Japanese and the agitation against them, fewer are employed in public houses than formerly.[a] The wages earned vary between $12 and $18 per week of 7 days of 12 hours or more per day.

These are the more important instances in which Japanese have been employed by white persons in San Francisco. Several hundred who spend the winter in San Francisco each year—1,119 in 1909—are employed by fish packers and taken to Alaska, a large number are employed on seagoing vessels, and at times a considerable number have been employed by the steam railway companies in San Francisco. In the various employments within the city, however, the Japanese have not made the headway made by the Chinese at an earlier time.

---

[a] On March 26, 1909, the secretary of the Asiatic Exclusion League reported to the Labor Council that between 1,500 and 1,800 Japanese were employed in saloons, serving free lunches, and requested cooperation in reducing the number of Japanese employed. As a result of the attitude of the trade unions and their friends, the number of Japanese employed at the close of 1909 was very much smaller than at the beginning of the year.

As janitors, cleaners, porters in stores, and as laborers in similar capacities, all bordering upon or falling within the field of domestic service, more Japanese are employed. The janitors, however, are very few. The number employed in drug stores, grocery stores, and clothing and millinery stores, chiefly as porters or " help " can not be estimated with any degree of accuracy. In May, 1909, a list of 174 merchants said to employ Japanese in these capacities was submitted to the Asiatic Exclusion League, but upon investigation it was reported that a number of these merchants had never employed members of that race.[a] The number employed in any establishment is limited to one or a very few, and the total number so employed has never been sufficiently large to affect the terms upon which the members of other races are employed in the same capacities in other establishments. The Japanese employed in drug stores were in 1909 paid $50 or $55; in one large department store $45, in another $50 per month.

JAPANESE IN BUSINESS.

A large percentage of the Japanese in San Francisco are engaged in business for themselves or are employed by their countrymen. In the spring of 1909 there was a total of about 5C0 business establishments conducted by Japanese.[b] The number of Japanese connected with these as proprietors or as wage-earners was perhaps between 1,800 and 2,000.

The number of Japanese places of business reported for 1909 and the corresponding figures for December, 1904, as reported in the Japanese-American Yearbook (which since 1904 has presented a fairly accurate census of such establishments in San Francisco), are shown in the table following. No summary statement of the number of establishments of each kind is now available for any earlier date. Such data as the agents have been able to gather, bearing upon the beginning and progress of each branch of business, are presented in the later sections of this report.

---

[a] Proceedings of the Asiatic Exclusion League, May, 1909, p. 13, and June 1909, p. 3.

[b] The number reported in the census made by the California state bureau of labor was 497; the number reported by the Japanese-American Yearbook for November 1, 1908, exclusive of " day-workers " offices, was 545, but this involved some duplication, which when allowed for, left some 482. Not all were reported, however. The majority of these places of business are located in the " up-town district," in which most of the " white " shops and offices were located after the fire of 1906 and in or near " Chinatown." The former district lies between Van Ness avenue and Fillmore street and Geary and Post streets, while the latter centers in Grant avenue and Dupont street. Within these districts the Japanese places of business are rather widely scattered. The laundries, shoeshops, curio stores, and some other establishments patronized chiefly by white persons, are scattered throughout the city. Though 81 establishments are found on Geary street, 51 on Post, 33 on Sutter, 26 on Grant avenue, 26 on Laguna street, 23 on Buchanan, and 20 on Bush street, 101 streets are represented in the Japanese directory of business places. Because of this fact and the disappearance of old and the appearance of new establishments, no accurate census of Japanese establishments can be conveniently made and none was attempted by the agents of the Commission. Efforts were made, however, to check data presented in the Japanese Yearbook which have been used to some extent in this report, and while not always accurate in detail, they were found to indicate the more important facts with a fair degree of accuracy.

TABLE 1.—*Business conducted by Japanese in San Francisco, as reported by the Japanese-American Yearbook.*

Kind of business.	Number of establish-ments, 1904	Number of establish-ments, 1909.	Number of persons occupied, 1909.
(a) STORES AND SHOPS.			
Book	3	a 8	25
Curio and art	42	42	166
Drug	2	6	11
Fruit and vegetable	6	a 8	21
Furnishing	10	13	47
Importing and exporting	(b)	a 5	16
Meat and fish	1	5	12
Provision	15	22	112
Sake	(b)	c 7	19
Watch and jewelry	4	8	12
(b) PERSONAL SERVICE.			
Barber shops	21	18	33
Bath	a 10	a 13	28
Hotels and boarding houses	d 60	33	119
Laundries	8	19	347
Lodging houses	(d)	18	30
Restaurants, American meals	8	17	124
Restaurants, Japanese meals	} 27 {	12	41
Restaurants, sake		21	102
Tailors and dressmakers	} 15 {	18	67
Cleaners and dyers		34	89
(c) AMUSEMENTS.			
Pool halls	} a 16 {	a 22	34
Shooting galleries		a 6	15
(d) OTHER.			
Bamboo shops	(b)	7	15
Bank	3	1	15
Confectioners	5	4	22
Contractors	2	e 12	28
Employment agents	7	12	18
Embroidery		3	12
Expressmen	7	5	22
Florists	2	4	9
Job printing shops	3	f 5	19
Magazines	3	3	4
Newspapers	2	3	73
Photograph galleries	3	8	22
Rice mills		2	6
Shoe repair shops	60	76	146
Tofu makers	1	2	4
Miscellaneous	20	43	131
Total	366	545	2,019
Duplications		g 63	
Grand total		482	h 1,800–2,000

a Usually conducted in connection with other business.
b Not separately reported.
c Some are included in provision stores.
d Hotels, boarding and lodging houses reported together in 1904.
e With one exception, conducted in connection with hotels and boarding houses.
f Some are newspaper offices.
g About.
h Proprietors and wage-earners.

The agents of the Commission made a general investigation of all of the important branches of business engaged in by the Japanese save the importing and exporting of merchandise. Detailed information was obtained for 91 of the establishments, while personal information was secured from the proprietors of these and from a large percentage of their employees. The details relating to the business conducted are employed in this section of the report, while the personal data are used in subsequent sections and presented in tabular form in the appendix. The 91 establishments from which details relating to capital employed, amount of business transacted, number of employees, wages and rent paid, races of patrons and related matters were obtained included the following: Twenty-two boarding houses and hotels, 17 shoe-repairing shops and 1 shoe store, 7 tailoring and repairing shops, 7 grocery stores, 6 laundries, 4 watchmakers, 4 restaurants serving American meals, and 23 others representing branches of business of less importance or interest.

The details presented below show the following facts:

1. That most of the Japanese business is conducted on a small scale.

2. That Japanese are employed in these establishments almost exclusively.

3. That the Japanese have encountered so much opposition in a few branches of business that their progress has been slow, while in some cases they have found it impossible to maintain the position they formerly held.

4. That except in the restaurants serving American meals, shoe repairing, and the laundry trade, the competition with white business men has thus far been of little importance.

5. That most of the business establishments conducted by Japanese are patronized exclusively or principally by the members of that race.

6. That most of the wants of that race are provided for by Japanese establishments and professional men.

Inasmuch as the business of the Japanese laundries, shoeshops, and restaurants serving American meals has been of the most importance from the viewpoint of competition with others engaged in the same branches of business, the details relating to these may be presented at length, after which the other branches of Japanese business may be discussed more briefly.[a]

LAUNDRIES.

The first Japanese laundry was started in San Francisco in 1890. By 1904 the number had increased to 8, and by 1908, because of the handsome profits realized, to 18. Six of these were investigated by an agent of the Commission, and they are representative of the larger number.

---

[a] From the viewpoint of the number of persons employed, the capital invested, and the amount of business done, the most important branches of Japanese enterprise are the art stores, provision stores, restaurants, hotels and boarding houses, and shoeshops. The following figures are taken from the Japanese-American Yearbook for 1910 (p. 160). The figures seem to be based upon a thorough investigation undertaken two years before but not completed:

Branch of business.	Amount of capital.	Annual value of business transacted.
Art stores	$246,500	$558,300
Provision stores	559,400	932,940
Laundry	93,500	326,600
American restaurant	19,450	245,400
Hotel	59,300	267,400
Japanese restaurant	29,150	198,750
Shoeshop and repairing	39,250	169,890

The Japanese proprietors have not been able to secure the permits necessary in San Francisco to operate steam laundries. Hence, all have remained " hand laundries." With the exception of one equipped to operate with steam the amount of capital invested in the 6 investigated varied from $1,000 to $3,200, the number of employees from 6 to 37, the amount of gross receipts from $9,000 to more than $15,000, the amount of profit realized from $1,200 to $6,000 per year.

At an earlier time, because of the inexperience of Japanese men in laundry work, almost all of the Japanese laundries employed white persons for those occupations requiring any great degree of skill. As the orientals gained skill, however, they gradually filled the positions, until now they alone are employed in Japanese laundries. Of the 89 employed in the 6 laundries investigated, 82 were adult males, 7 adult females. They all received board and lodging in addition to wages. The wages per month for males varied from $15 to $50, for females from $15 to $21 per month. The median wage for those of the male sex was $30, the average $28.90 per month. The details of earnings are shown in the table given below.

These wages are for days varying in length. Though the Association of Japanese Laundries in America, organized in March, 1909, had fixed upon eleven and one-half hours per day and sixty-nine hours per week as normal and provided for overtime payment, the hours normally worked were found to be ten per day and sixty per week in one establishment, eleven per day and sixty-six per week in three, eleven and one-half per day and sixty-nine per week in one, and twelve per day and seventy-two per week in the sixth. There is considerable overtime during the summer months. For this and for work on holidays and Sundays employees who receive less than $20 per month are paid at the rate of 10 cents per hour; those who receive $20 but less than $30, at the rate of 15 cents per hour; and those who receive $30 or more per month at the rate of 20 cents per hour.

As stated above, all of these employees receive board and lodging in addition to wages. The agent of the Commission found the food provided at the laundries investigated to be satisfactory, both from the point of view of quality and quantity. The cost per employee averaged $8.50 per month at the laundries investigated, and with regard to lodgings, which are in the structures housing the business, each married couple was provided with a separate room, while two or three single men were ordinarily assigned to one room. In one instance, however, all of the men (there were no female employees) were sheltered in one large room serving as a bunkhouse.

The bedding was good and the linen was kept clean. Occasionally, however, the lodgings were deficient in one or more respects. In one case the two rooms were not well cared for, and the ventilation and lighting were poor. In another instance the rooms were crowded and not well cared for. In a third case 10 men were given lodging in three small rooms, which were in disorder, poorly lighted, and poorly ventilated. The lodgings in the ramaining three cases were on the whole satisfactory, though in one of these eight single men lived in one large room arranged as a bunkhouse.

As against the 18 hand laundries, some of which are large, operated by Japanese, there are in San Francisco some 102 small hand laundries operated by Chinese, perhaps as many French laundries, some of them large establishments, and 18 large white steam laundries. Included in the investigation were 6 French laundries, employing 169 persons, and 4 white steam laundries, employing 344 persons.

Though the amount of unremunerated overtime in the French laundries can not be accurately estimated, the hours of work per day and per week were found to be shorter and the wages higher than in the Japanese laundries. In two of the six French laundries the usual hours were nine per day and fifty per week; in two others, nine per day and fifty-four per week; in a fifth, ten per day and sixty per week; in the sixth, ten and one-half per day and sixty-three per week. Omitting drivers who receive commissions in addition to or in lieu of wages, 32 men employed received from $15 to $60 and averaged $37.69 per month, while 20 women received from $12 to $52 and averaged $33.18 per month, with board and lodging. Fifty-two men and 65 women did not receive board and lodging in addition to wages. The wages of the former varied from $26 to $97.50 and averaged $58.56, while those of the latter varied from $24 to $65 and averaged $40.53. The lodgings provided (by four of the establishments) were found to be simply but adequately furnished, and each of the rooms were occupied by 2 or 3 persons. In some cases living and reading rooms were maintained for the use of the employees. In none of the four cases where the "living-in" system obtained were conditions found to be unsatisfactory. Of the 169 employees 17 were native and 152 foreign-born. Of the latter, 77 were French, 31 Italians, 11 Portuguese, and 33 members of various other races, chiefly north European.

The steam-laundry trade in San Francisco is thoroughly unionized. The Laundry Workers' Union has about 1,500 members, while the Laundry Drivers' Union has a membership about one-sixth as large. According to the agreement between the Laundry Workers' Union and the laundry proprietors, the standard work week was forty-nine hours at the time of the investigation, but at the end of the year 1909 was to be reduced to forty-eight hours. The agreement fixes the rate of wages for each occupation and stipulates that all overtime, amounting to a few hours per week, shall be paid for at the rate of "time and a half." Working under this agreement, the wages of 140 males, 18 years of age or over, employed in 4 laundries investigated, were found to vary from $20 per month, paid to 2 apprentices, to $92 per month, paid to "head markers and distributers." Of the 140, 36.4 per cent earned less than $50 per month, 14.3 per cent $50 but less than $70, and 49.3 per cent $70 or over. The average wage for the males was $69.74 per month. The wages of 204 females, 18 years of age or over, varied from $20 per month for a beginner to more than $70 per month for 11 skilled persons. Of the 204, 79.9 per cent earned less than $50 per month, 14.7 per cent $56 but less than $70, and 5.4 per cent $70 or over. The average monthly wage of the female employees was $44.33, while the average monthly wage for both males and females was $53.94. It may be added that of the 344 employees (other than drivers) of the 4 steam laundries investigated, 162 were native-born, while 182 were foreign-born. Of the latter, 85 were French, 33 North or South Italian, and 8 Portuguese. Most of the remaining 56 were immigrants from north European countries other than France.

The details relating to the earnings of the several groups of laundry employees are shown in the following table:

TABLE 2.—*Number of employees working in steam laundries earning each specified amount per month, by sex.*

AMERICAN LAUNDRIES (WITHOUT BOARD).

Sex.	Number reporting complete data.	$12 and under $15.	$15 and under $20.	$20 and under $25.	$25 and under $30.	$30 and under $35.	$35 and under $40.	$40 and under $45.	$45 and under $50.	$50 and under $60.	$60 and under $70.	$70 or over.
Male	140	......	2	2	1*	17	9	14	6	7	13	69
Female	204	......	......	1	5	45	36	37	39	24	6	11
Total	344	......	2	3	6	62	45	51	45	31	19	80

FRENCH LAUNDRIES (WITHOUT BOARD).

Sex.	Number	$12–$15	$15–$20	$20–$25	$25–$30	$30–$35	$35–$40	$40–$45	$45–$50	$50–$60	$60–$70	$70 or over
Male	52	......	......	......	1	6	5	4	4	6	9	17
Female	65	......	......	1	1	3	37	6	5	11	1	......
Total	117	......	......	1	2	9	42	10	9	17	10	17

FRENCH LAUNDRIES (WITH BOARD).

Sex.	Number	$12–$15	$15–$20	$20–$25	$25–$30	$30–$35	$35–$40	$40–$45	$45–$50	$50–$60	$60–$70	$70 or over
Male	32	......	2	2	1	5	6	8	1	4	3	......
Female	20	1	1	......	3	5	5	2	......	3	......	......
Total	52	1	3	2	4	10	11	10	1	7	3	......

JAPANESE LAUNDRIES (WITH BOARD).

Sex.	Number	$12–$15	$15–$20	$20–$25	$25–$30	$30–$35	$35–$40	$40–$45	$45–$50	$50–$60	$60–$70	$70 or over
Male	82	......	17	10	8	14	9	12	1	11	......	......
Female	7	......	6	1	......	......	......	......	......	......	......	......
Total	89	......	23	11	8	14	9	12	1	11	......	......

Thus it is seen that if the cost of board and lodging of the Japanese employed in Japanese laundries is reckoned at between $8 and $10 per month, which is the approximate cost, their wages are materially less than those of the employees of French and white steam laundries, while their hours are longer. This of course can not be interpreted as indicating that the labor cost of the work done is necessarily less in the Japanese laundries than in the other establishments, for there are differences in the efficiency of the oriental and white employees and differences in the equipment of laundries, which are important factors to be taken into consideration in this connection.

The six Japanese laundries investigated estimated their annual receipts at $83,200. Something less than 80 per cent of this sum— $65,510—represented the value of the business done with white patrons, the remainder that done with Japanese. The establishment of these laundries in recent years has not affected the Chinese shops. In fact, the Chinese do little work which would be done by other laundrymen, and do it generally " by the bag " rather than at piece rates. The French laundries do a general business, but a large part of it is in laundering articles requiring handwork, such as shirt-waists, lace curtains, etc. The steam laundries do the kind of business done elsewhere by establishments of that type. Though there has been much competition, especially between the French and the steam laundries, there has been, in a way, a division of the business between Chinese, French, and the other laundries along the lines of the kinds of work to be done.

The Japanese doing handwork have competed with the French and the white steam laundries, but more with the former than with the latter. Their prices have been somewhat lower than those of the French laundrymen and these in turn, on certain articles, lower than those of the steam laundrymen. How much lower the Japanese prices have been it is impossible to estimate. At the time of the investigation the Association of Japanese Laundries, organized in 1909, had provided for a uniform list of prices to be charged. In most cases these are the same as those in the printed lists of other laundries, while in a few they are lower. Moreover, the association authorizes the members to accept family washings at reduced rates. It is conceded by all that in the past, and to a certain extent at present, the Japanese laundries charge somewhat less than their competitors. By locating in residence districts, where their shops are convenient for patrons, and by collecting laundry from all parts of the city and doing the work at lower rates than others the Japanese laundries have gained their present position. Though their establishments are not so numerous as those of the French and not so large or so well equipped as those of the " American " proprietors, their competition has come to be felt. Fear has been expressed that if their establishments were equipped with modern machinery while maintaining their lower wage scale and working longer hours their competition would become a serious matter.

Partly because of the facts noted and partly because of a general feeling of opposition among the working classes toward the Japanese, there has always been more or less agitation in San Francisco against the Japanese laundries. This has been directed chiefly by the trade unions, until recently the only type of organization which could well conduct an agitation against a business of this kind. In March, 1908, however, steps were taken to organize the "Anti-Jap Laundry League," an organization which has (August, 1909) locals in Fresno, San Mateo County, San Rafael, and Oakland (Alameda County), as well as in San Francisco. This organization was effected by the members of the Laundry Drivers' Union, to which reference has already been made. The drivers are usually paid a commission on the laundry they collect, or rather, have their routes and collect laundry which they deliver to their respective laundries, paying them for doing the laundering. Because of this arrangement the Japanese competition has directly affected the members of this union as well as the proprietors of the steam laundries. Through the activity of the Drivers' Union, the proprietors of steam laundries, the laundry workers, and the drivers, all working under agreements between their respective organizations, were brought together in the Anti-Jap Laundry League. The funds for conducting the campaign have been obtained from the proprietors, who contribute 10 cents per month for each employee on their respective pay rolls and from contributions of $100 per month from each of the two unions to which reference has been made. Since the organization of the league the proprietors of the French laundries have been added to its membership.[a] They pay 10 cents per month for each employee, but continue to conduct nonunion shops, and some of them pay less than the union scale of wages.

The campaign of the league against the Japanese laundries has been conducted along two general lines—one directed toward reducing the number of their patrons, the other toward preventing them from obtaining supplies and becoming equipped as steam laundries.[b] To accomplish the former object, to reduce the number of patrons, agents have followed Japanese collectors and reported the names of patrons, who have then been corresponded with and personally visited and an appeal made to them to patronize laundries conducted by and employing the white race.

The following are forms of letters used in the league's appeals to patrons of Japanese laundries (from report of convention held December, 1908, pp. 5–8) :

(Form I.)

In behalf of the white boys and girls engaged in the laundry business of this city we most urgently request your personal and earnest consideration to the following : The laundry industry, which has given to a considerable portion of our citizens a fair and substantial means of earning a livelihood, is being gradually monopolized by Asiatic competition. According to reliable statistics the increase in the number of Japanese laundries during the past two years has been over 100 per cent.

The continuation of this appalling rate means practically the elimination of our race from this field of industry. To prevent such a consummation we make a personal appeal to you (patron of a Japanese laundry) as a fellow-citizen of this community, asking you to make it possible, through your patronage, to give our boys and girls a fair chance of earning a white man's living in a white man's country.

In this connection we point out the significant fact that the Japanese by no means contribute toward your subsistence and therefore have no claim upon your sympathy or support. On the other hand, the white race, off whom you make your living exclusively, is entitled to your first consideration and patronage.

Place yourself in a similar position to ours. If the Japs should invade your field of industry to the extent of forcing you to the wall (which is a possibility), would you not be entitled to and justified in demanding the moral support of your fellow men and women to assist you in resisting the Mongolian invasion that threatened your separation from the bread and butter necessity of life?

Under these circumstances are we asking too much of you to desist from patronizing Japanese laundries?

Hoping to hear from you, we remain,

Respectfully,   ANTI-JAP LAUNDRY LEAGUE.

(Form II.)

We desire to call your attention to a subject to which perhaps you have given but little, if any, thoughtful consideration, and yet it is one that to a great extent menaces your individual prosperity.

Perhaps you do not realize that at present you are rendering aid and financial support to those who are more than likely later on to encroach upon your

---

[a] Through a branch organization known as the " French Anti-Jap Laundry League."

[b] For history of and methods employed by the Anti-Jap Laundry League in San Francisco and elsewhere, see reports of its "Pacific Coast Conventions," December, 1908, and May, 1909.

present means of earning a living. We refer to the fact that if our various sources of information be correct a Jap calls for and receives your laundry each week.

We cheerfully concede your right to patronize whom you choose. We are simply appealing to your sense of right and justice to others of your own race.

At present, along the limited avenues of employment open to women, a great many white girls depend upon the laundries as their means of support. To you comes the question direct—a question that is in your power to answer:

For a few cents a week difference in your laundry bill can you afford to help make life harder for our working girls by favoring the Jap, who has no interests in common with your own? By patronizing a Jap you help reduce the white girl's standard of living and you are also advertising the Jap, for a Japanese laundry wagon at your door means that others seeing your example may be inclined to follow it.

Again we appeal to you to look at the matter from this point of view, feeling fully confident that when it comes to a question of white or Jap you can but decide in favor of your own race, on whom you also depend for your means of happiness and prosperity.

Will you not help us maintain a white man's standard in a white man's country? Believing you will, we remain,

Respectfully,   ANTI-JAP LAUNDRY LEAGUE.

(Form III.)

Have you ever given any consideration to the thought that as a patron of a Japanese laundry you are in a great measure helping to undermine your own prosperity—that you are helping to deprive women and girls of your race of a chance to earn a respectable living, that you are encouraging and financially aiding a Jap, who has no interests in common with your own, that prosperity for a Jap spells ruin for white engaged in a similar line of avocation, and that success of Japs in one line of business simply encourages them to branch out along other lines, and that ere long the battle for a living as against oriental competition will have reached you direct?

While we concede your right to patronize whom you choose, we appeal to your sense of fair play by asking you whether for a few cents saved on your laundry bill you can afford by your actions to declare in favor of a Jap and against women and girls of your own race, many of whom are entirely dependent upon their own resources for a living.

The people of our city are becoming aroused to the danger menacing our industrial conditions from this Japanese invasion. Business men are responding to our appeals. Unions are passing laws fining their members, and from many sources we receive the names and addresses of patrons of Jap laundries.

You must surely realize that one can not compete with a Jap and maintain a white man's standard of living.

Are we asking too much of you, then, in urging you to unite with us in our endeavor to stay the onward march of the Japanese upon so many of the industrial lines?

Will you not cease giving your work to a Jap laundry and thus show by your actions that you indorse our plea and assist us in our effort to maintain a white man's standard in a white man's country?

Believing you will, and inviting you to attend our meetings, held at the above address each Thursday evening, we remain,

Respectfully,

ANTI-JAP LAUNDRY LEAGUE.

In cases where a Jap patron has been reported the second time, the following letter is sent:

A short time ago we made an earnest appeal to you on behalf of others of your own race who were gradually being deprived of an opportunity to earn a respectable living by being driven from an occupation that for years has been theirs, and why? Simply because an oriental accustomed to oriental standards of living, an oriental against whom no white girl or woman could compete and live according to a white man's standard, an oriental whose interests are by no means in accord with your own, is able to do your laundry work cheaper. And for this reason you have seemingly—if our reports be correct—

decided that you care not for the suffering of others, providing it nets you a little less outlay.

Oh, foolish policy! Surely you do not realize the ultimate results of its continuance. Will you wait until you find yourself like we, who are appealing to you face to face in a struggle with a Jap, who has learned to do well the task that is at present the means whereby your household is provided with the comforts and necessities of life? Do you think you can for long prosper financially while others are being forced down to a lower standard of living?

What does the Jap do with the dollars you give him? Does he spend them so as to increase the demand for whites as store clerks and business men? Not so, but just to the contrary, for he takes your coin and with it helps make some other Jap prosperous, sends some of it across the ocean to help some other Jap to America, where he may, because he works cheaper, deprive some family of its means of support.

Let this truth influence you, to the extent that you give financial aid and encouragement to a Jap in any line of business by just so much you are surely undermining your own prosperity. Do you doubt this? Go and investigate the many lines of business the Japs are engaged in in our city, and we know you will agree with us that it is necessary that we who prize American ideals and standards of living should be united in an endeavor to preserve the same as against the dangers menacing us from the oriental invasion bearing down upon us.

Trusting we may count upon your support along hese lines, we remain,

Respectfully,

ANTI-JAP LAUNDRY LEAGUE.

Billboard advertising, making an appeal along the same lines, has also been resorted to, while the cooperation of organized bodies, and especially trade unions, has been sought.[a] At the same time the league has been active in preventing the granting of necessary permits to Japanese to operate steam laundries, and by appeals or by threat of boycott the cooperation of some of the supply men has been gained, with the result that difficulty has been experienced by some of

---

[a] The following is a copy of a poster shown on the streets of San Francisco, Berkeley, Alameda, and Oakland; size about 4 by 7 feet:

The Jap Laundry Patrons.
Danger!
Yellow competition,
Fostered by the white man's money,
Is the ammunition that will
Orientalize our city and State.

ANTI-JAP LAUNDRY LEAGUE,
483 Guerrero Street.

The following is a copy of poster displayed in nearly every laundry; size about 12 by 15 inches:

Are our boys and girls wrong
In expecting you who make your living
Exclusively off the white race
To stop patronizing Jap laundries,
And thereby assist your fellow men and women
In maintaining the white man's standard in a white man's country?

ANTI-JAP LAUNDRY LEAGUE.

Another, more recently displayed, reads:

Foolish woman!
Spending your man's
Earnings on Japs.
Be fair, patronize
Your Own.
We support you.

ANTI-JAP LAUNDRY LEAGUE.

the Japanese proprietors in securing supplies needed.[a]   The business of the Japanese laundries in San Francisco has been injured somewhat by this hostile movement, but was found to be profitable.   The net earnings reported by six of them for the 12 months preceding the investigation by the agent of the Commission varied from $1,200 to $6,000 and averaged $2,646.67 per year.

Though their business was still profitable, the proprietors of Japanese laundries in March, 1909, effected a protective organization, known as the Association of Japanese Laundries of America.   Its object is to " promote the development and prosperity of the business of its members."   The extension of financial aid and the lending of laborers in case of need is provided for.   To collect an emergency fund each member is required to pay $2 per month until his contributions aggregate the sum of $100.   In addition to these provisions the association fixes upon a scale of hours and rate of pay for overtime—the former of which had not been placed in operation at the time of the investigation.

COBBLER SHOPS.

In March, 1909, there were 72 Japanese cobbler shops in San Francisco.[b]   Seventeen of these were investigated.

The first Japanese shop of this kind was opened in San Francisco in 1890.   The year before a member of the Japanese Shoemakers' Union came to this country, as a representative of that organization, to report with reference to the success of the Chinese employed in this city in the manufacture of shoes.   This representative and two other members of the union, who had immigrated in the meantime, opened a shop of their own in 1890.

The attention of a prominent manufacturer was then drawn to their work, with the result that one of the men was sent to Japan to bring others to this country, with the assurance that upon their arrival they would be given employment at good wages.   Thirteen were induced to come, and the entire number (16) were set at work in a room located on Market street.   The shoes manufactured in this shop bore the trade-mark borne by those manufactured in the large factory conducted elsewhere by the propieter and in which union men were employed.   When the manufacture by Japanese finally became known to the union employees of the same manufacturer, difficulties ensued which led to most of the Japanese seeking employment elsewhere, and finally to the shop being closed.   Some of these Japanese then opened a shop of their own for making and repairing shoes.   This was also in 1890.   A few months later a second shop was opened in San Francisco and another in Alameda.   These were well patronized by white persons, with the result that the number rapidly increased.   In 1909, as already stated, there were 72 Japanese shops in San Francisco and at least 119 in other cities and towns of Cali-

---

[a] In order to obtain necessary supplies, a Japanese laundryman in a small city arranged with a supply house in San Francisco to deliver the goods purchased by him through a grocer, whose business was conducted in the same block. Because of threatened boycott the dealer would not do business with the Japanese laundryman openly.

[b] From membership list of Shoemakers' Union.

fornia, all members of Nihojin Koko Domei Kwai, or the Japanese Shoemakers' Union, with which the history and progress of these craftsmen have been closely identified.

This Japanese Shoemakers' Union was organized in 1893, and from the first, when it had 20, until now, when (March, 1909) it has 298 members, has had practically every master journeyman, journeyman, and apprentice engaged in the shoemaking trade on its lists.[a]

The objects of the Koko Domei Kwai are "to promote a friendly association among the Japanese shoemakers, to provide means for their mutual assistance, and to limit and to control competition among themselves." All persons who are connected with the trade are eligible to membership. In furthering its objects it has accumulated a "business fund" amounting to $10,000 or more. This has been derived from payments of 50 cents per month by each master journeyman, until his contributions aggregated $50, and from the surplus from regular dues, which are 50 cents per month for master journeymen and 35 cents per month for ordinary journeymen and apprentice members.

The shoemakers' union maintains a supply house in San Francisco, and several thousand dollars of the "business fund" are invested in the stock of goods carried. Most of these goods are purchased from two firms in the East and are sold to the members of the organization at an advance of 10 per cent on the cost. The sales aggregate about $3,200 per month, or some $38,000 or $40,000 per year. In this connection it is interesting to note that the company, as it is called, sells also to white shoemakers, the amount of such sales being about $150 per month. The part of the "business fund" not invested in the supply business is retained in the bank to serve as an "emergency fund."

As already indicated, practically if not quite all of the Japanese engaged in the trade belong to this organization, which regulates the establishment and conduct of shops and stands ready to assist those in need of capital to conduct their business and those who meet with misfortune or are in distress. A journeyman member of the union must pass a test examination if he wishes to establish a shop within six months after gaining membership. An apprentice, after having served one year with a master journeyman, may establish and maintain an independent shop, but previous to doing so must have passed an examination. In opening shops, however, no two shall be located within 1,190 feet of each other. A member of the union opening a shop in a locality where no Japanese shop is in existence may be assisted by the organization by a loan of money not to exceed $50 in all. Provision is made for the repayment of such loans in monthly installments. Moreover, any member who, because of infirmity, is unable to meet his necessary expenses (including outlays for medicines, etc.) is to be given financial assistance by the union. In case of death the funeral expenses are paid from the funds of the organization.

---

[a] The agents of the Commission during their investigation found only one Japanese shoemaker in California who was not a member of this organization, and so much pressure was being brought to bear upon him that he soon joined the organization.

The union has established minimum and, in some cases, actual prices to be charged for repair work. The prices fixed in the by-laws of the organization and published in its report for 1906 and the prices actually charged at the time of the investigation by the Japanese cobblers in San Francisco are shown in the following tabular statement:

	Fixed in by-laws.	Actual prices.
Men's shoes, sole and heel (hand sewed)..	$1.00 and up.	$1.25
Women's shoes, sole and heel (hand sewed)..	.80 and up.	1.00
Men's shoes, sole and heel (nails)..	.60 and up.	1.00
Women's shoes, sole and heel (nails)..	.45 and up.	.70
Men's shoes, heels..	.30 and up.	.25—.30
Women's shoes, heels..	.20 and up.	.20
Patches..	.10 each.	.10
Rubber heels..	....	.45—.50
Slippers (hand sewed)..	....	1.00

Violation of the rules of the organization and failure to abide by its regulations are to be penalized by the payment of a sum of not less than $10 nor more than $50.

As already stated, there were 72 Japanese shops in San Francisco in March, 1909. Seventeen of these were investigated. The amount of capital employed varied from $100 as a minimum to $400 as a maximum. Only 4 of the 17 had an employee, and in each of these cases the 1 employee was an apprentice.

These men worked from 66 to 72 hours per week for their respective masters for which they received board and lodging and " pocket money," amounting to from $8 to $15 per month.

Some of the shops are located on Bush, California, Geary, and Sutter streets, where many Japanese live, while others are located in various other parts of the city, where most or all of the residents are white persons. The shops located on the streets first mentioned were found to have Japanese and white patrons in approximately equal numbers, while those located elsewhere drew from 85 to 95 per cent of their patrons from the members of the various white races.

The gross receipts from the business done, as reported, varied from $1,200 to $1,500 per year. The net earnings of the 17 master journeymen varied from $40 to $80, and averaged $61.76 per month. In detail their net earnings per month, as reported, were as follows:

Amount per month.	Number.	Amount per month.	Number.	Amount per month.	Number.
$40.....................	2	$65.....................	2	$80.....................	3
50.....................	4	70.....................	3		
55.....................	1	75.....................	1	Total..........	17
60.....................	1				

The Japanese cobblers compete with a much larger number of white shoemakers.[a] The majority of these are of foreign birth— German, French, Hebrew, and Italian craftsmen being conspicuous

---

[a] There are several hundred, perhaps 1,000, cobbler shops in San Francisco. The partial list presented in the San Francisco Directory for 1908 embraces 257.

among them.   Seventeen of these cobblers, including 5 Hebrews, 2 Germans, 3 French, 3 Italians, 1 American, 1 Swede, and 1 Spaniard, were included in the investigation made by the Commission.   The earnings for the preceding year varied between $400 as a minimum and $1,200 as a maximum.   One earned $400, four $600, one $624, one $700, one $780, three $800, two $900, one $1,000, one $1,080, and two $1,200.   These present somewhat greater variations than the earnings of the Japanese but average somewhat more.

Almost without exception the cobblers investigated complained of loss of business and smaller earnings than they had formerly made, in some cases less than one-half.   The business of several had been injured by the fire of 1906, which had caused their patrons who had lived near by to settle elsewhere, of others by the industrial depression at the time the investigation was made, of others by the incoming of too many cobblers to share the trade of a given district of the city.   In some blocks Japanese cobblers had opened shops and reduced the amount of work to be done by those who had previously located there.   Moreover, the Japanese prices were usually lower than those charged by other cobblers, and the loss of patronage by a few was ascribed to this underbidding which the agent found to exist.   The agent of the Commission found that the lower prices charged by the Japanese cobblers than by most of their competitors, together with the large number of Japanese shops recently opened in some blocks, had caused the business and earnings of competing white cobblers to perceptibly diminish.

RESTAURANTS SERVING AMERICAN MEALS.

The number of Japanese restaurants serving American meals was small previous to 1906.   As late as 1904 there were only eight.   Following the fire of 1906, however, numerous restaurants were opened by Japanese in the district of the city devastated by the fire, bringing the total number to more than 30.   These were all " cheap " eating houses charging from " 15 cents up " for meals.   For a while they prospered, because of the large number of laborers who came to engage in removing débris and rebuilding the city.   They were soon strongly opposed by organized labor, however, and during the labor troubles which developed at this time became an object of attack by rioters and several of the proprietors suffered serious loss because of destruction of property or loss of their patrons, or both.[a]   Since

[a]At this time there was a strong agitation against the Japanese.   This was directed largely by the Japanese and Korean Exclusion League and the various labor unions, many of which had laws forbidding their members to patronize Japanese or Chinese places of business.   At a meeting of the Exclusion League, held June 25, 1906, complaints were made that many white wage-earners, including some union men, were patronizing Japanese restaurants, and the league requested the labor organizations to enforce the penalties imposed by their rules for violations of the prohibition mentioned.   Among the unions at the meetings of which the members were urged or directed to refrain from patronizing the Japanese restaurants was that of the cooks and waiters.   A boycott was kept in force by this organization from October 3 to 24, 1906, and the destruction of property of the proprietors of restaurants by rioters followed peaceable appeals to patrons by the representatives of the organization.   The appeal took the form of a label bearing the words " White men and women, patronize your own race."   For details see Senate Document No. 147, Fifty-ninth Congress, second session.

then the Japanese restaurants serving American meals, being opposed by organized labor, have not prospered as they did earlier, and the number of establishments had decreased to 17 by the end of the year 1908. These are located in the poorer residence districts of the city, among the smaller shops and restaurants conducted by white persons of various races. Five of the 10 were investigated by an agent of the Commission.

Two of the five restaurants investigated were conducted by two partners and one by three, while the other two were conducted as individual enterprises. The size of these establishments is indicated by the fact that two were conducted by the proprietors with one employee in each case, another with two employees, a fourth with three, and only one with as many as eight. The annual gross receipts varied between $4,000 as a minimum and $20,000 as a maximum, the monthly rent between $25 and $200. The annual profits realized varied between $600 and $2,600.

The patrons of two of the restaurants are largely Japanese; of the others principally, if not exclusively, white people of various races. The competition of these small restaurants affected many cheap restaurants near which the Japanese establishments were opened.

There were 20 persons, all of whom were Japanese, employed in the 5 restaurants investigated. Two cooks were paid $50, a third $35 per month; 3 " cooks' helpers," $35 per month; 8 waiters, $35; 2 waiters and 1 waitress, $30; and 1 waiter employed " part time" (ten hours per day), $15 per month; and 2 dishwashers $30 and $25 each, respectively, all with board and lodging. Of those employed full time, 12 worked twelve hours per day and eighty-four hours per week; 7, thirteen hours per day and ninety-one hours per week. The union (white) scale of wages for cooks' helpers, it will be recalled, is $12 per week ($51 per month) ; for dishwashers, $10 per week ($42.50 per month) with board but not lodging. The majority of the persons so engaged, however, are not members of the unions and, as a rule, work for less than the union scale, for $5 to $10 per week, which is not materially higher than the wages paid to the Japanese, who, however, work longer hours.

The Japanese employees are all provided with lodging in rooms in the rear of the restaurants. In all but one of the establishments investigated the agent of the Commission inspected the lodgings and found them to be adequate and satisfactory, save in one instance, where the room occupied was poorly furnished and inadequately lighted and ventilated. The lodging provided is worth $4 or more per month.

Because of clannishness and language difficulties, as well as on account of the strong sentiment against them on the part of other races in the community, almost all of the Japanese patronize Japanese restaurants and usually those serving Japanese meals, which have always been more numerous than those serving American meals. In 1904 they numbered 27; in 1908, 38. Some of these are conducted in connection with hotels, while others are independent establishments. Many of the Japanese in San Francisco being unemployed, and a considerable number of those in employment not receiving board in addition to wages, these restaurants are largely patronized. Some of them sell alcoholic as well as soft drinks; in fact, 21 of 38 reported in November, 1909, were said to do so.

BOARDING AND LODGING HOUSES AND LABOR AGENCIES.

Because of the character of Japanese immigration and the place occupied by San Francisco as a port of arrival and departure and as a labor market, the keeping of boarding and lodging houses with their affiliations has always been the most important branch of business enterprise engaged in by the Japanese of that city. This business began with the immigration of the laboring class and has expanded and contracted with the increase or decrease in the size of the Japanese population. At the time of the investigation there were some 35 hotels and boarding houses and possibly as many rooming houses. A large number of the former and practically all of the latter are conducted by private families who take a few boarders and lodgers or rent spare rooms. Most of the patrons of places of this kind are Japanese regularly employed in San Francisco and not provided with board and lodging.

On the other hand there are some large hotels and boarding houses the majority of the patrons of which are laborers out of work, newly arrived immigrants, and Japanese departing for their native land or elsewhere. These larger boarding houses are generally connected with other kinds of business, such as conducting barber shops, baths, pool rooms, and supplying laborers for various kinds of work. The investigation by the agents of the Commission embraced 22 of the 35 boarding houses and 3 of the larger lodging houses.

The number of rooms in the 22 boarding houses investigated varied from 8 to more than 100. Nine of the 22 had more than 20 rooms each, and 7 of these 9 were of sufficient importance to have membership in the "Japanese Hotel Keepers' Association," about which something will be said presently.

The majority of the boarding and lodging houses are located in two districts of the city in which the Japanese have tended to congregate. Many are located in the "uptown" section on Geary, Sutter, and neighboring streets, and on the intersecting streets beyond Van Ness avenue. Several large houses, however, are located in South Park place, near the wharves. Still others, but fewer in number, are located in the business district, especially near the well-defined Chinatown, in which all but a comparatively few of the Chinese have congregated.

Except in the first-mentioned district the houses occupied by the Japanese have been erected since the fire of 1906 and were constructed for the purpose for which they are used. Most of the rooms are extremely small, but not more than two persons are provided with lodging in the same room. The houses in the "uptown" district, on the other hand, were built to serve as private residences. Most of them have become old and weatherbeaten and are no longer desirable as residences for private families who can afford to pay the comparatively high rents these houses command. Here the rooms are larger than in the newer houses in the other district spoken of, and in the majority of cases at least one or two rooms are equipped to accommodate from four to eight persons each. In some cases thin partitions, sometimes extending only part way to the ceiling, have been made to subdivide large rooms into smaller ones. Though the investigation was made in the winter of 1908–9, when the greatest number of Japanese were without employment and the number of persons in the lodging houses the largest, there were very few cases of overcrowding. In this connection, however, it should be added that the number of Japanese had already begun to diminish and that the business of the boarding houses was not so large as it had been in previous years.

Very few of the boarding houses are heated and few of them are provided with bathing facilities. With regard to bathing facilities, it should be said, however, that there are 13 bath houses in San Francisco conducted by Japanese primarily for their own race, and that several of these are operated in connection with boarding houses, the boarders and lodgers being served on the same terms as other patrons.

The character of the furnishings and care of the rooms in the boarding and lodging houses investigated varied greatly. The worst conditions found in any of the 25 houses investigated are described briefly as follows: The house is very old and is in a dilapidated condition. No care is taken of the rooms and hallways. The toilets and the bathroom are dirty and ill smelling. The floors are covered with matting and cheap dirty carpet. Of the 10 rooms for lodgers, 4 have been partitioned by thin boards, the partitions extending only halfway to the ceiling. A few establishments were found to be of the same general type as the following: The house is very old and dirty throughout. In one room there are four double beds; the furnishings are scanty and of the cheapest kind. The floors are bare and dirty. The patrons are all transient sailors, who pay 50 cents per day for board and lodging. The majority of the boarding houses differ only in detail from the following: The house is an old frame building, but the interior is kept clean. Two large rooms have been made into four by partitions of thin boards. Each room is furnished with an iron bed, a couple of chairs, and a desk. A few are provided with bureaus also. The floors are covered with cheap carpets and fancy mattings. There are two sinks for washing. The toilets are clean. The whole house is well lighted and the ventilation is good. Most of the patrons are transients, who pay 60 cents per day. The few persons who live there regularly pay $12 per month for board and various sums for their lodgings. A few of the boarding houses are somewhat better than the last one described.

As has been indicated incidentally in the cases cited, the prices charged for board and lodging vary. In a few instances the cost is as low as 50 cents per day for transients; in more numerous instances it is 60 cents, while in the majority of the large boarding houses it is 70 cents per day. Most of the large boarding houses have membership in the Japanese Hotel Keepers' Association, which provides in its rules, among other things, that " patrons shall not be charged less than 25 cents per night for lodging and not less than 15 cents per meal." The rates per month for regular lodgers and boarders are, of course, less.

With the exception of the " sailor boarding-house " keepers, the proprietors of the large boarding houses are organized into the Japanese Hotel Keepers' Association. The organization of this association dates back ten years or more, but it was reorganized and given its present form in 1905. Its primary object has been to limit or to eliminate the strong competition which existed between the large boarding-house keepers whose patrons were transients and laborers who were available for employment. The only written agreement or regulation in existence, roughly translated, reads as follows:

We, the members of the Japanese Hotel Keepers' Association, will maintain in good faith the following agreement:

1. Patrons shall not be charged less than 25 cents per night for lodging and not less than 15 cents per meal.

2. Storage: Trunks, 25 cents each per month; baskets and valises, 10 cents each per month.

3. Commissions to be charged as labor agencies: $5 on each Alaskan laborer, $3 on each railroad laborer, $1 on each ranch laborer.

The matter of commissions as labor agencies brings up the most important part of the business of most of the large boarding-house keepers. Hotel keeping and contracting for labor are closely related. Indeed, each of the 12 "contractors" now in business in San Francisco is a boarding-house keeper. In many cases the largest income is from the commissions charged as noted above (and deducted from the wages of the laborers); in these cases the keeping of the boarding house is more or less incidental to assembling a "gang" of laborers. One proprietor of a house of more than 30 rooms reported that his net income from the boarding and lodging business was $1,000; from commissions from laborers supplied, $2,500. Another proprietor of a house of about the same size reported a net income of $600 from boarding and lodging, $1,600 from his other business, but chiefly from commissions paid by laborers for whom work was found. The proprietor of another establishment reported a total annual income of $1,700, $500 of which was derived from his commissions. Finally, the proprietor of a comparatively small establishment reported an income of $600 from boarding and lodging and $400 from his services as a "labor agent." The importance of the business of the labor agency is thus shown.

With the exception of the proprietors of the "sailor boarding houses," the proprietors of the larger establishments have established connections with construction companies, railway companies, Japanese bosses supplying ranch laborers, and fish cannery companies. If the boarding-house keeper, who is a member of the Japanese Hotel Keepers' Association, receives an order for a given number of men and does not have them immediately at his command, he draws upon those at the command of other members of the Hotel Keepers' Association. In other words, the boarding-house keepers pool their men and cooperate in filling positions which come to them as labor agents. From this pooling arrangement the members of the association derive a gain not second to that resulting from the maintenance of uniform rates and prices.

The business of the Japanese "contractors" is much less extensive and less profitable than formerly, however. Prior to 1907, when many Japanese were arriving in San Francisco from Japan and the Hawaiian Islands, their business was very extensive. Employment was found by the contractors for most of the new arrivals. In 1906 the several contractors supplying laborers for railroad work kept from 216 to 1,500 men each employed—several thousand all told. In 1909 the number of railroad laborers supplied from San Francisco varied between 200 and 800. The number of fish cannery hands and agricultural laborers employed through and controlled by these contractors is also smaller than before immigration was restricted.   As a result of the restrictions which have been imposed, several firms have discontinued the contracting business.

As already stated, the proprietors of the " sailor boarding houses " do not serve as regular labor agents and do not charge any commission for any service they may render in securing employment for their patrons.   While this is true, employers frequently apply in person at these houses for laborers of the kind to be found there.

Because of alliances with employers of different kinds of labor, the classes of laborers found in the large boarding houses differ.   Practically all the laborers found at some are sailors, at others Alaskan cannery hands, at others railroad laborers or ranch hands.   Moreover, in many cases most of the patrons of the boarding houses were found to have come from the same provinces as the proprietors and labor agents.

Besides the " contractors " still in business, there are several employment agents.   These are engaged chiefly in supplying Japanese domestics and in connection with their labor agencies frequently conduct billiard parlors and fruit and cigar stands.

TAILORS, DRESSMAKERS, AND SUIT CLEANERS.

Tailoring, dressmaking, and suit cleaning, as carried on by the Japanese, are so closely related that it is impossible to discuss them separately.   In 1899 there were 5 shops where tailoring, dressmaking, and suit cleaning were carried on.   In 1904 the number of shops had increased to 15, by the close of 1909 to 52.   Most of the shops, however, are conducted on a very small scale, having from 1 to 3 employees at work.   A very few have as many as 5 persons employed, but a much larger number are conducted by 1 man or a man and wife or by 2 or 3 partners, without the assistance of any persons employed for wages.   Of 7 typical shops, 2 were conducted by the proprietor without assistance, 3 by the proprietors and 1 employee each, 1 by 2 partners and 2 employees, and 1 by the employer and 5 employees.   Some shops are devoted to suit cleaning, pressing, and repair work (" renovatories "), and have no more than $150 to $400 invested in them, while the larger shops in which tailoring as well as the cleaning and other work just mentioned is carried on represent an investment of $2,000 or more.   The rent per month paid in 7 cases varied from $10 as a minimum to $65 as a maximum, but in only 1 of the 7 cases did it exceed $25.   From these data it may be inferred that the tailoring business as conducted by the Japanese is a case of petty trade.   Three shops doing some tailoring reported that their gross business amounted to $10,000 in two cases and to $5,000 in the other case per year.   The shops doing repairing, cleaning, dyeing, and pressing only reported gross earnings varying from $360 to $1,500 per year.

The Japanese shops are scattered throughout a large section of the older residence and the small shop portion of the city in which or near which the larger number of the Japanese have settled.   The character of the patrons differs according to the location of the shops and also according to the amount of tailoring done.   The larger number of the patrons who have pressing and related work done at these shops are white persons, while the majority of those who have suits made to order are Japanese. In fact, in so far as tailoring and dressmaking are concerned, white patronage is so small as to be of little consequence. It is a significant fact that the proprietors of four small shops devoted to cleaning, pressing, and related work only reported that 100 per cent, 90 per cent, 40 per cent, and 30 per cent, respectively, of their patrons were white persons, while the proprietors of three shops, in which tailoring was done also, reported that 10, 30, and 35 per cent, respectively, of their patrons were members of the various white races.

That a large percentage of those having cleaning and pressing done at the Japanese shops are white persons is explained partly by convenience of location and partly by the low prices which are charged. The Japanese Suit Cleaning Union, which in February, 1909, had 23 members, has placed in effect the following scale of minimum prices, which the shops are required to adhere to:

Men's suits pressed	$0.50 up.
Women's suits pressed	.75 up.
Men's suits cleaned and pressed	.75 up.
Women's suits cleaned and pressed	1.00 up.
Men's and women's suits steam cleaned	1.50 up.
Men's and women's suits dyed	2.00 up.
Coats dyed	1.00 up.

Though this is a scale of minimum prices, the sums given are those usually charged. These are lower than the rates which have obtained in other than the poorest shops in San Francisco, with the result that the competition of the Japanese shops has been felt by others doing a similar business in the same localities.

In tailoring, on the other hand, there has been little competition. Yet it is true that the Japanese have much of their clothing made in establishments conducted by their countrymen and the number of shops has increased directly with the number of Japanese residing in San Francisco.

The profits reported by the proprietors of the small shops devoted to cleaning and pressing were $300, $720, $900, $1,200; by the other shops engaged in tailoring also, $1,440, $1,800, and $3,000, respectively, per year. The wages of tailors varied from $25 to $60 per month with board and from $40 to $80 per month without board. Of 20 men employed in Japanese shops 2 were paid $25; 2, $30; 2, $35; 1, $40; 3, $50; and 4, $60 per month with board; 3, $45, and 1, $55 per month with lodging only; and 1, $40, and 1, $80 per month with neither board nor lodging.

Reference has been made to the regulation of prices by the Japanese Suit Cleaning Union. It controls the location of shops as well, its rules providing that no two Japanese shops shall be located within 1,000 feet of each other. The union also provides for assistance to its members. Organization was not effected until the early spring of 1909. The tailors also are organized. The Tailors and Dressmakers' Union, including Japanese persons of this class in Oakland as well as in San Francisco, was organized several years ago and was incorporated under the laws of California in 1905. This organization provides that no two shops shall be located within 600 feet of each other on the same street or within 300 feet of each other on different streets. It also controls the matter of apprenticeship, forbids the employment of persons who are not members of the union, and provides for persons who are sick, have met with accident, or are in distress.

BARBER SHOPS.

The number and prosperity of the Japanese barber shops in San Francisco has always been dependent upon the number of Japanese in the city, for the members of that race have generally not been admitted to white shops, while the Japanese shops have had few white patrons. The first Japanese shop was opened more than twenty years ago. In 1894 there were 2; in 1899, 6; in 1904, 21; at the close of the year 1908, 18. Previous to 1907 the number of Japanese in San Francisco was increasing and the number of small shops kept pace with the growth of population. Since 1907, however, the population has been decreasing and a number of the barber shops have been closed.

The Japanese shops are small, the number of chairs, as a rule, not exceeding two, and the amount of capital invested varying from $150 to $400. The earnings of three proprietors from their establishments were $600, $720, and $960; from the commissions of 10 to 20 per cent on laundry collected, $120, $480, and $100, respectively, for the year preceding the investigation. The few barbers employed are usually paid either $35 or $40 per month, in addition to which they receive board and lodging.

BATH HOUSES.

The record of Japanese bath houses is in most respects similar to that of their barber shops. In 1894 there were 2; in 1899, 8; in 1904, 10; in 1908, 13. About one-half of these are located in or near the Chinese quarter and are largely patronized by Chinese, who have no public bath houses of their own. The others are located in the Japanese residence section and are patronized by the members of that race. Frequently they are conducted in connection with boarding and lodging houses, some of which are not provided with bathing facilities.[a]

MEN'S FURNISHING STORES.

The first establishment of this kind conducted by a Japanese was opened in 1900. By 1904 there were 8, at the close of 1908, 13 or more. More than one-half of these are very small shops, the capital invested varying from $500 to $1,500. They carry a variety of cheap goods, and their patrons are almost exclusively Japanese. The larger shops have several thousand dollars, in one case as much as $11,000, invested in Japanese and American goods carried in stock. Like the smaller shops, they find most of their patrons among the Japanese.

JEWELRY AND WATCH REPAIRING.

The first of the jewelry and watch repairing shops opened by a Japanese dates from the year 1900 or somewhat earlier. In 1904 they numbered 4; at the close of the year 1908, 7. Of these, 4 were investigated. With one exception the amount of capital employed, the

---

[a] Nine of the 13 are connected either with hotels and boarding houses or barber shops or with both.

volume of annual transactions, and the amount of profit were small. All but 1 were conducted without hired assistance, and in this case only 1 person was employed for wages, a watchmaker, at $30 per month, with board and lodging. The amount of capital employed in the 4 shops was $1,000, $1,300, $2,300, and $7,500, respectively. The profits realized for the year were $900, $900, $1,680, and $3,000, respectively, for the 4 shops in the order mentioned above. In one case the patronage of white persons was reckoned at 15, in the other cases at 10 per cent of the total. The significant facts relating to this branch of business are that most of the shops are small and engaged in repair work chiefly; that their patronage by white persons is so small as to be unimportant, but that they are sufficiently numerous to supply the greater number of the Japanese with such watches, clocks, and jewelry as there is demand for among them.

ART GOODS STORES.

The most important branch of business engaged in by Japanese in San Francisco, from the point of view of white patrons, is the conduct of art stores. In 1898 some 20 of these were devoted to selling brass ware, toys, china, etc. By 1904 the number had increased to 40; by the close of 1909 to 42. The majority of these carry stocks of goods valued at several thousand dollars, and practically all of the patrons are white persons. The articles sold have never been carried in stock to any great extent by white dealers. In San Francisco there are, however, many Chinese stores of the same type, and the patronage is shared by these two Asiatic races.

PROVISION AND GROCERY STORES.

The number of Japanese provision and grocery stores has rapidly increased in recent years. In 1904, 10 were reported; in 1909 there were 22. Most of these are comparatively small stores, employ a few thousand dollars of capital, deal largely in Japanese goods, and are patronized chiefly by Japanese. A few of these stores, however, are large supply houses and have much capital invested in their business, most of which is with Japanese outside of San Francisco. The percentage of American goods sold is about 50; the percentage of white patrons varies from 5 to 25.

OTHER STORES.

There are many other small stores, most of them patronized almost exclusively by Japanese. Among these are 8 book stores, selling books, stationery, and notions; 3 drug stores,[a] selling Japanese drugs and notions; 7 confectioners' shops, selling the confections manufactured by them, fruit, etc.; 4 fish dealers and 1 butcher, selling fish and meat to persons of their own race almost exclusively; a few fruit stands, and a sake (liquor) store.[b] In no case do these have any particular significance save that through them the Japanese are enabled to satisfy their wants while dealing with persons of their own race.

[a] Some other establishments also sell drugs.
[b] Several provision stores also sell sake.

Closely related to some of these branches of petty business are the businesses carried on by 4 manufacturers and retailers of bamboo goods, by the 3 tofu (bean curd) manufacturers, by the 2 small rice mills cleaning imported rice, and the small sake brewery. The Japanese have not engaged in any branch of manufacture of any importance.

PHOTOGRAPHERS.

There was 1 Japanese photographer in San Francisco in 1895, 3 in 1899, 5 in 1904, and 8 at the close of the year 1908. Formerly the Japanese studios were patronized rather extensively by members of the white race, but, with the development of a strong sentiment against the Japanese, much of this patronage has been lost. Two of the 8, however, still have a large number of white patrons.

BILLIARD AND POOL HALLS AND SHOOTING GALLERIES.

The chief places of amusement conducted by Japanese are the billiard and pool halls and shooting galleries, which numbered 16 in 1904 and more than 20 in 1909. Most of these are small places with two or three tables. Cigars and soft drinks are frequently carried in stock. Some of the places are patronized by Japanese only; the number of white patrons of the others is very small.

OTHER BUSINESS.

Besides the 3 newspaper offices engaged chiefly in the publication of daily papers, there are a few job printing houses engaged principally in printing in the Japanese language. There are also 5 Japanese real estate agents, engaged chiefly in acting as intermediaries in leasing property to be occupied by Japanese. Few of the members of this race have purchased the property they occupy. There is also a branch of the Yokohama Specie Bank, which alone survives the 4 banking institutions in existence in 1908. The other banks failed and were closed by the state bank commissioner. There are also 5 parties engaged in the transfer business. In 1907 one of these was organized as a corporation with a capital stock of $30,000, and combining the business of several persons formerly doing business independently. Most of the business done is in hauling goods under contract with the proprietors of Japanese establishments.

There are also about 10 carpenters, who are employed almost exclusively by their countrymen in altering and repairing buildings occupied by them. Of physicians there were 8 in 1904 and 5 in 1908; of dentists, 5 in 1904 and 3 in 1909.

PERSONAL DATA RELATIVE TO JAPANESE BUSINESS MEN.

Personal data were secured from 113 business men engaged in conducting the establishments investigated. Roughly speaking, two-fifths of them had been in the United States ten years or over, another two-fifths five years but less than ten, while the remaining one-fifth had immigrated within the last five years. In more detail, of 122 (including 9 male members of the families of these business men), 8 had been in the United States twenty years or over; 4, fifteen years but less than twenty; 34, ten years but less than fifteen; 48, five years but less than ten, while the remaining 28 had immigrated within the last five years. Fourteen of them had migrated to the continental United States from Hawaii, while another came from Canada. Of the 98 who had immigrated directly from Japan, 27 had been engaged in business on their own account, 7 had been employed in stores, 18 had been employed for wages in various city occupations, 23 had been with their fathers on the farm, while 22 had had no occupation previous to their immigration to this country. None of the 98 had been farming on his own account in his native land. From these details it is seen that more than one-fourth of these men had been in business, one-fourth had been wage carners in cities, another one-fourth had been farmers' sons, while the remainder had been at home without occupation.

It is evident from these details also that the great majority had come from the urban classes of Japan. Some of the immigrants came to the United States when young men to find their first work or to pursue their studies; some came when older because of failure to succeed in business at home; while others, more successful, transferred their business to this country to avail themselves of the opportunities offered. Of 116, 16 years of age or over at the time of the investigation, 21 had been under 20 years of age at the time of their immigration, 36 between 20 and 25, 34 between 25 and 30, 14 between 30 and 35, 7 between 35 and 40, and 4, 40 years of age or over. Inasmuch as representatives of the few large business firms were not included in the investigations, the amount of money brought to this country was found to be very small. In fact, of 112 reporting data with reference to this matter, 44 had less than $50 and 32 others less than $100 upon first landing in the continental United States. Of the remaining 36 (roughly one-third of the entire number), 16 had $100 but less than $150; 7, $150 but less than $200; 5, $200 but less than $300; 3, $300 and $400; and 5, from $500 to $1,200 each. (General Table 1.) It is apparent that most of them came without capital and were under the necessity of becoming members of the wage-earning class. Indeed, 87 of the 113 were first gainfully occupied in this country as wage-earners, 1 as a farmer and 25 as business men, usually in partnership with others and engaged in small enterprises requiring very little capital. The majority of those who first worked for wages found employment in San Francisco or other cities. Only 14 became farm hands and 1 a railroad laborer; 50 first engaged in domestic service, 4 worked in stores and an equal number in restaurants, and the remaining 14 in other city occupations. (General Table 2.)

Though the great majority of the immigrants investigated had become wage-earners upon their arrival in this country, most of them soon advanced from the wage-earning class, to which only a small minority had belonged in Japan, and established themselves in business. The great number of Japanese arriving at the port of San Francisco, and depending largely upon their countrymen for supplying most of their wants, made it possible for the members of that race to engage in business in increasing numbers, while because of the petty nature of most of the establishments and the rather common practice of forming partnerships, little capital was required of one who wished to establish himself as a business man. A further inducement was found in the fact that in San Francisco as elsewhere very few remunerative occupations have been open to the Japanese. As a rule the Japanese has had farming on his own account or the establishment of a small business enterprise as the only avenue of escape from the lower forms and least well-paid kinds of unskilled labor.

In this connection it is interesting to note that with the exception of the jewelers and watch repairers, barbers, and tailors, most of whom had been similarly occupied in Japan, few of those investigated were engaged in the same line of business here that they had engaged in abroad. Most of the business conducted is of such a character that experience is not highly essential to success.

As has been stated, most of the Japanese have come to the United States "to make money." How well they have succeeded is indicated by the value of the property they now own. The gross value of property possessed by the 113 men from whom personal data were secured was $352,520, or an average of $3,119.65 each. Of these 113, however, 47 were in debt, the total amount of such indebtedness being $63,830. The net amount of property owned was, therefore, $290,690, an average of $2,594.44 per man. (General Table 6.) One had a net indebtedness of $2,000 outstanding against him, while the remaining 112 had property over and above any indebtedness, varying from $100 to $45,000. Four reported $100, but less than $250; 9, $250, but less than $500; 33, $500, but less than $1,000; 27, $1,000, but less than $1,500; 16, $1,500, but less than $2,500; 14, $2,500, but less than $5,000; 4, $5,000, but less than $10,000; 2, $10,000, but less than $25,000; and 3, $27,000, $30,000, and $45,000, respectively. Thus 23, or one-fifth of the entire number, have property worth $2,500 or over. Fourteen of these 23 had been in the United States 10 years or more, the other 9 from 5 to 9 years. As opposed to the 14, 32 who have been here for 10 years or more have property worth less than $2,500, and 15 of them have property worth less than $1,000. As opposed to the 9 who have been in this country from 5 to 9 years and have property worth $2,500 or over, there are 35 who have less than $2,500, while 16 (including 1 who is insolvent) have less than $1,000. (General Table 3.)

The data relating to property are, however, a better index to the kind of business conducted by the Japanese than of the degree of pecuniary success with which they have met, for these property-owning business men remain of the larger number who have engaged in business on their own account and some of whom are now found in the ranks of the wage-earners, while, on the other hand, the property now owned represents the money not sent abroad but saved and invested in this country. A better index is found in the amount of profit realized during the year preceding the investigation. The net incomes of 110 from the main business or businesses conducted by them are shown in General Table 20. The net incomes derived varied from $300 to $9,600. Of the 110, a hotel keeper and a tailor had incomes of $300 and $360, respectively; 10 had incomes of $400, but less than $500; 32, $500, but less than $750; 27, $750, but less than $1,000; 14, $1,000, but less than $1,500; 12, $1,500, but less than $2,000; 6, $2,000, but less than $2,500; while 7 had realized incomes of $2,500 or over. The incomes of 22 lodging-house and hotel keepers varied from $300 to $7,000 and averaged $1,491.36. The incomes of 25 storekeepers from the stores conducted by them varied from $500 to $3,000 and averaged $1,404.80. Eighteen shoemakers had incomes averaging $814.44. Six proprietors of small laundries had incomes of less than $500, while the proprietor of a large one had a net income of $6,000 from his business. These data and others presented in General Table 20 show that the incomes vary between wide extremes, but that all but 12 of the 110 had incomes from the main business conducted by them of $500 or over, which is more than the average amount received by the wage-earning classes of Japanese from such occupations as are open to them, and that 66, or three-fifths of the entire number, realized net incomes of $750 or over.

The net incomes discussed above are those from the principal business or group of businesses conducted. No fewer than 29 of the 110 from whom data were obtained, however, had incomes from interests in other business establishments, investments, labor, lodgers, etc. The total amount of such subsidiary income was $42,172. If this were included, the average annual income, reported above as $1,259.64, is found to exceed $1,643, and the number having each a specified amount of income is shown in the following table:

Amount of income (all sources).	Number.	Amount of income (all sources).	Number.
Under $300.........................	....	$1,000 and under $1,500.................	15
$300 and under $400.....................	1	$1,500 and under $2,000.................	15
$400 and under $500.....................	9	$2,000 and under $2,500.................	10
$500 and under $750.....................	22	$2,500 or over	11
$750 and under $1,000...................	27		

a Ten men reported their total net incomes from all sources to be as follows: $2,600, $3,000, $3,000, $3,500, $4,200, $6,000, $7,200, $7,600, $9,600, and $20,000. The total income of the remaining one in this group was not ascertained.

Of 112 from whom data were obtained, 4 reported a deficit, 6 neither surplus nor deficit, and 102 a surplus, after all living and incidental expenses had been paid out of the net income for the year. The surplus reported varied from $100 as a minimum to $9,750 as a maximum, and averaged $726.86. The amounts reported by 12 were $100 but less than $250; by 40, $250 but less than $500; by 30, $500 but less than $1,000; by 17, $1,000 but less than $2,500; by 3, more than $2,500. (General Tables 4 and 5.) From these data it is evident that the Japanese business men as a class are fairly prosperous and that a few have large incomes and large balances over and above their personal expenses.

By far the larger part of the surplus amounts realized were retained in this country. Of 112 reporting data with regard to the matter, 51 had sent money abroad during the year, the total amount sent by them being $12,300, or an average of $241.18 each. Most of this ($8,950) was for the support or use of relatives and the education of children, the remainder for investment or safe-keeping. As opposed to the money sent abroad by 51 men, 98 reported that they disposed of $62,290 retained by them in this country as follows: Invested in business, $30,125; deposited in banks, $19,645; loaned to friends, $1,600; used to pay debts earlier incurred, $7,200; employed for other purposes, $3,720.

PERSONAL DATA RELATIVE TO JAPANESE WAGE-EARNERS.

Corresponding data were obtained from 231 members of the wage-earning classes. Some of these were employed in Japanese establishments, others in the homes and places of business of white persons. Though the total number of persons from whom complete data were obtained is comparatively small, the data are sufficient to indicate certain facts concerning the wage-earning classes of Japanese in the city.

The first significant fact is that 108 of the 231 wage-earners had been in the United States less than five years, 82 from five to nine years, while only 26 had been here ten to fourteen years, 9 from fifteen to nineteen years, and 6, twenty years or longer. The contrast between the members of this class and those of the business class is shown by the fact that 46.8 per cent of the former as against 23 per cent of the latter had immigrated to the United States within the last five years, while only 17.7 per cent of the former as against 37.7 per cent of the latter had been in the United States ten years or longer.

Twenty-two of the 231 wage-earners had come to the continental United States from the Hawaiian Islands, where most of them had been engaged in agricultural work, while one came from Mexico. The remaining 208, or 9 of every 10, had immigrated direct from Japan. Like the business men, most of them had belonged to the urban classes in their native land. Of the 208 immigrating direct from their native land, 57 had been on farms with their fathers, while one had been a farm hand. On the other hand, 35, or roughly one-sixth of the entire number, had been engaged in businesses on their own account, 14 had been employed in stores, and 23 in industrial establishments and in other city occupations. Finally, 68, almost all of whom had been reared in cities, had had no occupation before leaving their native land, while the occupation of one was not ascertained. (General Table 2.) That so many should not have been gainfully employed or should have been with their fathers on the farm before emigrating from Japan is indicative of the fact that the majority of those from whom data were obtained had come to the United States when young men. Indeed, 26.4 per cent of the 231 were under 20, 59.7 per cent under 25, and only 20 per cent 30 years of age or over at the time of their first arrival in the continental United States. Moreover, a comparatively large number of those who were 30 years of age or over had left Japan when young men and spent some years in Hawaii before coming to "the mainland." (General Table 9.)

Like the business men, these wage-earners had little money upon their arrival in this country. Indeed, the percentage of them who had only nominal sums was larger and the percentage who had more than $200 was smaller than among the business men from whom data were obtained. Of 230 reporting the amount of money in their possession upon landing, 127, or 55.2 per cent, had less than $50; 66, or 28.7 per cent, $50 but less than $100; while only 16, or 7 per cent, had $150 or more. Though one-sixth of the number immigrating direct from their native land had been engaged in business, the largest amount of capital brought to this country by any member of the group of 230 was less than $500. (General Table 1.)

A comparatively large percentage of those investigated had come to the United States upon the completion of their schooling in Japan and expected to pursue their studies in this country. Yet the motive of the great majority in immigrating to the United States was purely economic. Nearly all of those who had attended school in this country had combined labor with their school attendance. This is reflected by the fact that of 229 reporting their first gainful employment in this country 92 were domestic servants, many of them "schoolboys" working short hours and receiving small wages in addition to board and lodging. The next largest number, 58—or, roughly, one-fourth of the 229—were first employed as farm laborers. Of the remaining 79, 12 became railroad laborers, 10 house cleaners working by the day, 7 restaurant "help," 9 store "help," 5 cannery hands, and 28 wage-earners in various city occupations. Only 2 engaged in business for themselves and very few of the others had engaged in business at any time and again become members of the wage-earning classes. From these facts it is evident that the great majority of these men had come from the urban classes of Japan and that about two-thirds of them found their first employment in the cities and in San Francisco. (General Table 2.)

The earnings of 230 during the twelve months preceding the investigation were ascertained. Of the 230, 194 had been in continuous employment for the 12 months. As against these, 6 had been employed for eleven months, 3 for ten, 13 for nine, 2 for eight, 7 for six, 2 for five, and 3 for four months of the twelve. The earnings of 106 who received board and lodging in addition to their wages varied from $8 per month and $96 per year to $85 per month and $1,020 per year. The average for the year was $415.82; for those continuously in employment, $444.54. The median, however, was only $360. The yearly earnings of 124 who did not receive board in addition to wages varied from $180 to $2,000. The average for the group was $553.75, and for the 111 who had employment throughout the year, $566.76. The median was $540. (General Table 21.)

Two hundred and twenty-nine reported as to surplus or deficit after their expenses in this country had been paid. Of this number 8 reported a deficit ranging between $58 and $440, while 23 reported that they had spent all they had earned, but had not incurred any debts. The remaining 198, or 86.5 per cent of the number, had realized a surplus during the year.

The aggregate of the balances reported by 198 was $47,434, or an average of $239.52. The sums reported by 24 were less than $100, by 83 $100 but less than $250, by 76 $250 but less than $500, by 14 $500 but less than $1,000, by 1 $1,050. (General Tables 4 and 5.) It is evident that the incomes of the wage-earners from their labor are much smaller than those of the business men derived as a result of their labor and investments from their business, and that their balances over their personal expenditures average only about one-third as much.

Of 229 wage-earners who reported with reference to the disposition of their pecuniary gains for the year, 121 had sent money abroad, the total amount sent being $18,445, or an average of $152.44 for each. Few of them sent more than $200, and all but a negligible percentage was reported to be for the support of parents or of wives and children in Japan. As against the total of $18,445, reported by 121 as sent abroad during the year, 176 reported a total of $29,429 retained in this country. Of this total $4,680 was loaned to others, $24,749 deposited in banks or kept in hand. In the number sending money abroad, and especially in the percentage of their gains sent and the disposition of the part retained in this country, the wage-earners present a contrast to the business men. That the business men retained five times as much of their gains in this country as they sent abroad, while the wage-earners retained roughly 1½ times as much, and that the business men invested about one-half of the amount retained here, while the investments of the wage-earning class were found to be practically negligible are to be explained by the facts that the business men have much the larger incomes, comparatively fewer wives and children residing abroad to be supported, and have much better opportunities for profitable investment.

Few of the wage-earning classes have property worth as much as $1,000. Of 231 reporting with regard to their wealth, 1 was in debt $200 and 36 had no property other than their personal effects. The remaining 194 had property with an aggregate value of $66,444, an average of $342.49. (General Table 6.) The value of the property owned by 28 of these 194 was estimated at less than $100, by 91 at $100 but less than $250, by 38 at $250 but less than $500, by 23 at $500 but less than $1,000, by 6 at $1,000 but less than $1,500, by 5 at $1,500 but less than $2,500, by 3 at $2,500, $3,500, and $4,000, respectively. (General Table 3.)

SOCIOLOGICAL DATA.

As already stated, the Japanese population of San Francisco was in 1909 estimated at 8,746. In this investigation personal data were secured from 113 business men, 231 wage-earners, and the members of their families living with them, the total number of persons being 443. The 443 embraced 338 males 20 years of age or over; 9 male youths 16 years of age, but under 20; 55 females 20 years of age or over; and 41 children under 16.[a] All of these, save 33 of the children, were foreign-born. (General Tables 7 and 10.)

The majority of the Japanese women have come to the United States in recent years to join their husbands, or to be married upon their arrival. Moreover, most of them are wives of men engaged in business. Only 2 of the 57 (including 2 foreign-born female children) had been in this country 10 years, and 31 had immigrated within the last 5. (General Table 11.) Of 116 males of the business class, 16 years of age or over, 66 are married, and all but 17 of them have their wives with them in this country. Thirty-seven were married previous to their immigration to this country, and 13 of these were accompanied by their wives, while 11 have been joined by them more recently. Twenty-nine of the number investigated have been married subsequent to their first immigration, 19 of them to women coming to this country and 10 while on visits abroad.

Of 231 male wage-earners 16 years of age or over, only 46 are married, and only 9 of these have their wives in this country. Only 3 of

---

[a]As against these 41, most of whom had been born in the United States, there were some 63 other offspring of the married couples investigated who had remained in Japan with the mother or other relatives.

the 46 have married subsequent to their immigration, and 8 of the 9 wives in the United States came with their husbands when they first immigrated, nearly all of them from the Hawaiian Islands. That so comparatively few of the wage-earning class are married, and that so few of those who are married have their wives with them, is explained chiefly by the circumstances under which the wage-earners must live. The members of the business class, on the other hand, having a settled residence and being better established, have contracted marriages more freely, and almost three-fourths of them now have their wives with them in this country. (General Tables 8 and 9.)

The immigration of married women in recent years is indicative of a settled residence in the United States. Many of the Japanese, however, do not expect to remain in this country for an indefinite time. Of the 113 business men 38 signified their intention to remain permanently in this country; 18, including several whose wives were here, to return to Japan; while 57 were in doubt as to what they would eventually do. Of 231 wage-earners, on the other hand, only 34 stated that they expected to remain here permanently, 105 that they expected to return to their native land, 92 that they were in doubt as to what they would eventually do. Of course these answers can be taken only as indicative of the state of mind of the men at the time they were questioned, but they show that a large percentage of the business men, practically all of whom had come as temporary residents, had decided to remain permanently, while one-half of the entire number were in doubt as to what they would do, largely because of the opposition shown to the members of their race and the uncertainties of the future, because of the restrictions upon further immigration of the laboring classes. The number of wage-earners expecting to remain permanently is smaller, yet, in spite of the fact that few have families in this country and that they do not have business interests of importance, one-seventh state that they intend to remain in this country permanently.

Something has been said earlier in this report concerning the character of the lodgings and the cost of meals at the Japanese hotels and boarding houses, and the board and lodgings of the laundry and restaurant employees. The day workers, a large element among the Japanese, usually live in cooperative groups organized among themselves or with shoe repairers. Taking the latter as typical of these groups, it was found that in most instances the day workers contributed a certain amount per month toward the cost of food and drink and for their lodgings, and that the several members of the group, including the cobbler with whom they lived, cooked in turn. Where a wife was present, however, the domestic work was done by her. The cost per month of their board and lodging reported by 12 of these groups was as follows:

Number paying sum specified.	Cost per month per man.	Number paying sum specified.	Cost per month per man.
6	$12.50	4	$13.00
3	15.00	4	11.00
4	12.00	3	13.00
3	13.00	4	12.00
6	14.00	5	13.00
6	12.00	9	12.00

The cobblers and the day workers living with them—when there are any doing so—invariably live in rooms connected with the shops. In some instances the rooms are too few and are crowded, and a large percentage of them are neglected and in disorder.[a]

Living in the building sheltering the business conducted is the general rule among the Japanese business classes, except those who have the largest stores. Indeed, there were only some 9 exceptions among the 91 investigated. The employees are usually provided with board and lodging on the premises. Though several cases of overcrowding were found (elsewhere than among laundrymen and "day workers" and cobblers), conditions were not materially different from those which obtain among small shopkeepers generally.

Agents of the Commission collected data relating to the cost of food and drink of families and groups investigated. Excluding those conducting restaurants or other business where the cost is not normal or can not be estimated with a fair degree of accuracy, data were obtained for 347 persons, constituting 140 groups or single individuals. Seven persons, constituting 3 groups, reported the cost as less than $6 per month; 18, constituting 4 groups, as $6 but less than $7; 35, constituting 12 groups, as $7 but less than $8; 65, constituting 23 groups, as $8 but less than $9; 14, constituting 5 groups, as $9 but less than $10; 59, constituting 24 groups, as $10 but less than $12; 93, constituting 41 groups, as $12 but less than $14; and 56, constituting 28 groups, as $14 or over per month. The average cost per person per month was $11.08. Naturally the cost was higher for the single persons eating at restaurants. Eliminating all single persons and retaining only groups of 2 or more, the average for each of the 297 persons was $10.76 per month.

Of 405 foreign-born 10 years of age or over, all but 6 females were literate (General Table 15). All but 6 of 122 foreign-born males 6 years of age or over of the Japanese business class could speak English, and 75, or 53.6 per cent, of the 118 who were 10 years of age or over could read and write the language as well. Of 231 males of the wage-earning class, 200 could speak, 123 could read, and 121 could both read and write English. This fairly general command of English was acquired by some in the schools in this country

---

[a] Taking 14 of these groups, the number of persons and the number of rooms occupied (besides the cobbler shop) were as follows:

Number of men.	Number of women.	Number of children under 15 years.	Number of rooms occupied.
3	0	0	2
3	2	0	4
3	1	1	3
8	0	0	1
5	1	1	3
4	0	0	3
7	0	0	5
6	1	0	5
5	0	0	3
5	0	0	3
4	0	0	3
9	0	0	4
3	0	0	2
2	0	0	1

and by contact with English-speaking persons. The females, few of whom had studied English abroad, few or none of whom had immigrated as students, and who as a class have immigrated more recently than the males and have had little contact with members of the white races, show less proficiency in the use of the English language. Of 57, 6 years of age or over, 32 speak English (General Tables 12 and 13). Of 56, 10 years of age or over, 10 read and 8 both read and write the language.

Many of the Japanese have been trained in the use of English in schools maintained for that purpose in San Francisco. There are, all told, 15 schools for Japanese immigrants. Four of these conducted by American women, however, are not schools in the proper sense of the term, but places where individuals, chiefly well-to-do men and prospective college students, are tutored. The remaining institutions, on the other hand, have regularly organized classes and are conducted primarily for the instruction of adults in the use of English or for teaching the reading and writing of their mother tongue and the history and geography of Japan to Japanese children attending American public schools. Five of these are conducted by as many Japanese missions; the others by private parties, who, however, usually have the gratuitous services and contributions of others and, in some instances, subsidies from Japanese organizations.

The schools conducted by the five missions are very much alike, so that the following details relating to one would apply, with few changes, to the other four. This particular mission has conducted a school for twenty years in which courses are offered corresponding to the work given in the public schools from primary to the high school grades, mathematics excepted. The principal is assisted by four American women and an equal number of Japanese men. The tuition fee is $1 per month. The number of pupils is about 100. Of 54 attending the afternoon classes, all but 1—a youth of 14—were between 20 and 23 years of age. Fifty of the number were males and 4 females. Most of them had been in the United States only one or two years, and 42 of the 54 were "schoolboys," i. e., domestic servants working a part of the day in return for board and lodging and very small wages. Of the remaining 12, 1 was a reporter, 1 a clerk, 1 an office boy, 1 a nurse, 1 a teacher of Japanese, while the other 7 were not gainfully occupied. Thirty-one males in the night classes belonged to a somewhat different class as regards occupations, but they were practically all young men and the majority had been in the United States only one or two years. Three were "schoolboys," 14 regular domestics, 2 watchmakers, 2 tailors, 2 laundry hands, 2 house cleaners, 1 a tea packer, 1 a bookkeeper, while 2 were at the time without occupation.

The most successful of the schools on a private and nonmission basis and conducted primarily for adults may be described as follows: Both elementary and more advanced courses are offered, most of the instruction being in the use of English. The tuition is $2 or $3 per month, according to the courses taken. Most of the pupils are between 19 and 23 years of age and have been in the United States only one or two years. Data were obtained from 71 of some 80 in the classes. All but 2 of these were gainfully employed—50 as "houseworkers," 6 as cooks, 3 as waiters, 5 as clerks in Japanese stores, 3 as laundry hands, 1 as a tailor, and 1 as an apprentice to a photographer. Thus of the 71, 59 were engaged in some branch of domestic service.

Besides these schools for teaching adult Japanese, most of whom are gainfully employed, there is one [a] school designed primarily to teach children of primary and grammar school age to read and write their native language and to acquaint them with their native literature and history. However, three years ago the scope of the school was enlarged so as to interest children born in Japan and recently arrived in this country in the use of English so as to prepare them for the public schools. The tuition fee is $2 per month. The Japanese Association contributes regularly to the support of the school, as do a rather large number of Japanese men interested in educational work.

These educational institutions among the Japanese are, of course, entirely supplementary to the public schools of the city, which are open to pupils of all races.[b] The number of Japanese children, youths, and young men attending the public schools in the spring of 1909 was 128.

Closely connected with the use of the English language is the matter of newspapers and periodicals subscribed for. These are indicative of the standard of living and culture and show the interests and source of much of the information of the Japanese. Of 77 households reporting all had at least 1 newspaper and 58 had from 2 to 10 each. All of the households had one or more (some as many as 7) papers and periodicals printed in the Japanese language, some of them published in San Francisco and other American cities, others published in Japan. In addition to these, 25, or, roughly, one-third of the households, had from 1 to 5 newspapers and periodicals printed in English and published in San Francisco and other cities. Among the subscriptions to periodicals by those investigated were 3 to the Pacific Monthly, 9 to the Literary Digest, 1 to the Independent,

---

[a] There were two of these schools, but one conducted by the Buddhist mission has been discontinued.

[b] For a time during the fall term of 1906 the Japanese were refused admission to any of the public schools save the Oriental Public School, established for Chinese, Japanese, and Korean pupils. The board of education of San Francisco resolved, May 6, 1905, "that the board of education is determined in its efforts to effect the establishment of separate schools for Chinese and Japanese pupils, not only for the purpose of relieving the congestion at present prevailing in our schools, but also for the higher aim that our children should not be placed in any position where their youthful impressions may be affected by associations with people of the Mongolian race." On the 11th of October, 1906, after agitation conducted by the Japanese and Korean Exclusion League for separate schools, this board further resolved "that in accordance with article 10, section 1662, of the school law of California, principals are hereby directed to send all Chinese, Japanese, or Korean children to the Oriental Public School, situated on the south side of Clay street, between Powell and Mason streets, on and after Monday, October 15, 1906." The Oriental School was located in the burnt district of the city, and many of the 93 Japanese attending school at the time of the adoption of the above resolution lived many blocks from it. The Japanese, with one exception, failed to go to the Oriental School, and the resolution was claimed to be in conflict with the treaty rights guaranteed by the Federal Government. Later the resolution was rescinded by the board of education and Japanese children admitted to such schools as they were qualified to attend. See Senate Report No. 147, Fifty-ninth Congress, second session.

4 to Colliers' Weekly, 1 to the Outlook, and 1 to the North American Review.

The Japanese missions have already been mentioned in connection with educational institutions. Of these missions there are now five— the Methodist, Presbyterian, Congregational, Episcopal, and Buddhist—besides the Japanese Gospel Society. The last-mentioned institution was organized by Christian students as early as 1887. Independence of all denominations and its liberal Christian teaching and great emphasis upon educational work are as true of it now as at the time of its organization more than twenty years ago. The Methodist Mission, with a history covering twenty years, was the next to be organized, and was followed by the organization of the Presbyterian, Congregational, and Episcopal missions. The combined membership of these missions is some 700 or 800. The membership of the Methodist Mission is 306; of the Presbyterian, 325; of the Episcopal, 50. The Buddhist Mission was organized as recently as 1899. There are now 10 such missions scattered throughout California with a membership, exclusive of the wives and children of married men, of 2,350. Some 400 of these members reside in San Francisco. These Buddhist missions do not differ from the Christian missions save in religious teachings. That the Buddhist organization has made more rapid advance in securing members is explained largely by the fact that most of the Japanese were Buddhists at home.

Reference has been made to the various organizations among the Japanese engaged in business and to the several missions with Japanese members only. Besides these there are several organizations, the most important of which are the Japanese Association, prefectural clubs or societies, and the Japanese Benevolent Society.

The Japanese Association was organized in 1900, at the time of the threatened outbreak of bubonic plague, when the Japanese and Chinese, being Asiatic races, were dealt with in a different manner from other races. The organization was effected to protect the "rights" of the Japanese. When the crisis due to the fear of bubonic plague ended, the Japanese organization was continued in existence because of the strong anti-Japanese movement which had sprung up in San Francisco. Upon the renewal of this agitation in 1905 the association was reorganized and extended its activity to the entire State of California. Local associations were soon organized in no fewer than 33 different places. The general nature of the association is indicated by these details relating to its organization and reorganization. Its objects as set forth in its constitution are: (1) To elevate the character of the Japanese immigrants; (2) to promote association between Japanese and Americans; (3) to promote commerce, agriculture, and other industries; and (4) to further Japanese interests. The indefiniteness of this shows the general and elastic character of the association. It interests itself in whatever concerns the Japanese. In addition to this, the association has recently received recognition from the Japanese consulate, and has become an administrative organ of the consulate in issuing certificates of various kinds and in related matters. Its members number about 400.

The prefectural societies are very numerous. Of 344 men from whom personal data were obtained 99 had membership in these or-

ganizations, the societies of 27 different prefectures being represented among them. The societies indicate the strength of the local
ties among the Japanese. They serve as centers of social life and
give assistance to those who are in need.

The Japanese Benevolent Society was organized in 1901. Its
object was to make more complete provision for the care of the sick,
injured, and unfortunate than had been made by the several missions, the Japanese Association, the prefectural societies, and trade
associations. During the eight years 1901 to 1908, its expenditures
for the sick and for sending persons back to Japan amounted to
$7,000. This does not indicate the importance of its work, however,
for in its methods it is more a charity organization than relief society.
One of the more important branches of its work lies in securing reduced rates from the steamship companies for those who are sick
or in need in order that they may return to Japan. As a result of
the efforts of this society and of the other institutions to which reference has been made, no Japanese become public charges in San
Francisco.

CHAPTER III.

JAPANESE IN CITY EMPLOYMENTS AND BUSINESS IN LOS ANGELES.

[For General Tables, see pp. 361-372.]

INTRODUCTION.

A few Japanese came to Los Angeles about 1885. These men had served as cooks on a sailing vessel, and, leaving the ship at San Diego, drifted north to Los Angeles, where they opened a restaurant. With this as a beginning, the Japanese population of the city increased slowly until about ten years ago. There has been no direct steamship connection with Japan, and it was only a little more than ten years ago that Japanese were employed in large numbers by the railroad companies with terminals at Los Anegeles, first as section hands and then as laborers in the shops. The members of the race did not become conspicuous as farmers and agricultural laborers in the southern part of the State until some six or seven years ago. With the influx of laborers to engage in such occupations as those mentioned, however, the number of Japanese who have settled in Los Angeles and the number and variety of business establishments conducted by them have rapidly increased. According to the best-informed Japanese, the number of persons of their race in Los Angeles in 1897 was about 500.[a] According to the Japanese-American Yearbook for 1905, the number in December, 1904, was 3,358. Of these, 3,178 were adults males, 144 were married women, while 36 were children. In 1906 the number greatly increased as a result of the San Francisco fire, which caused many to leave San Francisco and settle in other places, principally in Los Angeles.

The number of Japanese in the city at the close of that year has been estimated as in excess of 6,000. During 1907 and 1908, however, the number decreased. Some returned to Japan and others found business unprofitable and sought employment elsewhere. The total number residing in the city in December, 1908, was estimated by the secretary of the Japanese Association of Los Angeles at 4,457. Of these, 3,925 were adult males, 427 adult females, and 105 children under 16 years of age. It would appear that the number of adult males had increased somewhat between 1904 and 1908, and that the number of women and children had increased almost threefold. These figures are for the settled population. There have been as many as 20,000 Japanese in southern California, and during those seasons when many are unemployed they have come to Los Angeles in large numbers, the lodging houses being crowded with transient

[a] According to the Census for 1900 (Population, pt. 1, p. 798), however, the number of foreign-born Japanese in Los Angeles was only 152. There is good reason to believe that the actual number was in excess of that reported.

laborers. According to the Japanese-American Yearbook for 1905, 2,025 of the 3,358 reported for the preceding December were laborers, 250 were students, 681 were engaged in business or employed for wages by business men, and 140 were tenant farmers in the suburbs. According to the same authority, in December, 1908, 1,661 of the total 4,457 were engaged in business or employed for wages in establishments conducted by their countrymen. In all probability between 2,000 and 2,500 were gainfully occupied in other ways. Some of these are employed in track work on the street railways, others as car cleaners, and still others as laborers in the yards and shops of the steam railways. A much larger number, however, are employed in stores, clubs, saloons, restaurants, and other places conducted by white persons and as domestics in private families. A small number are employed as janitors or cleaners about office buildings, at wages varying from $9 per week to $60 per month. As porters in saloons and in a few hotels they earn from $35 to $50 per month. A small number are employed as elevator boys at from $35 to $60 per month. By far the largest number are employed, however, as " kitchen help " in restaurants and hotels, as domestics in private families, or as " house cleaners," working by the hour or day. As dishwashers and " general help " in restaurants they are paid from $8 per week to $40 per month with board. Domestics earn from $30 to $50 per month with board and lodging. Most of the cooks are paid $40, the less skilled servants $30 or $35 per month. There are more than 20 establishments which send men to private houses to do cleaning and similar work. They are paid from 27.5 to 35 cents per hour and earn about $40 per month.

As already stated, the first Japanese to locate in Los Angeles started a restaurant. This was a low-priced place, patronized chiefly by white working men. A little later another Japanese located here and manufactured bamboo furniture, for which he found ready sale. By 1892 there were 14 restaurants serving 10, 15, and 25 cent meals, all patronized chiefly by white workingmen. In 1897 there were 15 restaurants, 7 bamboo-furniture stores, and a few other establishments conducted by Japanese. Since then, until recently, the number of branches of business enterprise and the number of establishments conducted by Japanese have rapidly increased. Most of the business engaged in has been designed to serve the needs of the increasing number of Japanese employed in Los Angeles and in other parts of southern California, but some of it, like the first establishments opened, has been designed to serve the needs of other races in this rapidly growing city. The number of establishments in which each specified kind of business was conducted in 1904 and in 1909 are shown in the following table. The figures for the year 1904 are taken from the Japanese-American Yearbook for 1905, while most of those for 1909 were reported by the agents of the Commission as a result of an investigation made by them during the months of June and July, 1909. The enumeration by these agents was not complete, so that in several instances use has been made of the figures reported in the Japanese-American Yearbook for the month of December preceding. In many branches of business the number of small establishments changes rapidly, so that the data presented in the table can not be accepted as being more than an approximation of the true number, and are intended merely to indicate in a general way the extent to which the members of this race have engaged in the different branches of business enterprise.

TABLE 3.—*Business conducted by Japanese in Los Angeles, Cal., December, 1904, and June, 1909.*[a]

Kind of business.	Number in June, 1909.[b]	Number in December, 1904.[c]
(a) STORES AND SHOPS.		
Book stores	5	5
Curio	15	7
Drug	3	....
Fish markets	3	1
Fruit and cigar stands	20	....
Liquor stores	*5	....
Provision and grocery stores	27	6
Shoe store	1	....
Watch and jewelry	5	2
(b) PERSONAL SERVICE.		
Barber shops	44	18
Bath houses	d*26	8
Boarding and lodging	90	18
Restaurants (American meals)	25	21
Restaurants (Japanese meals)	*58	12
Tailor shops	14	2
Dressmaking establishments	2	....
Laundries	7	2
(c) AMUSEMENTS.		
Pool rooms	d*33	13
Moving-picture show	1	....
(d) OTHER.		
Bamboo furniture manufacturers	*1	5
Tofu manufacturers	3	....
Cobbler shops	16	2
Expressmen	10	....
Banks	2	....
Employment offices	7	12
Photograph galleries	6	....
Newspapers	2	
Periodicals	5	5
Job printing offices	2	
Miscellaneous (about)	35	21
Approximate total	e 473	160

a Does not include physicians, midwives, dentists, interpreters, and other professional men and women.
b As ascertained by agents of Commission. Those marked (*) taken from Japanese-American Yearbook, and are for December, 1908.
c According to Japanese-American Yearbook for 1905.
d In most cases conducted in connection with other business.
e Number of establishments somewhat smaller because of fact noted in (d).

Most of the Japanese places of business are located in two colonies. The older colony finds its center in East First street from Alameda to Main, but many shops are located on Alameda and San Pedro, while a small number of Japanese are located on the short streets running from Main to Alameda and lying north of First street. In this section of the city, laborers and petty business men of many races are found, but the Japanese alone have colonized there. The Chinese, the Mexican, and the Italian colonies are found in other parts of the city not far away. As the number of Japanese has increased, the older white element has tended to move elsewhere, so that most of the residents of the district at the present time are foreign-born. In recent years, however, the Japanese have opened shops in another part of the city several blocks away. At present a large number of their establishments are located on South Sixth and Seventh and Hill, Olive, and Hope streets. That is a distinctly better part of the city than the other district in which the Japanese have colonized. Yet it is a mixture of small shops, small residences, and large old residences which the original occupants have tended to vacate, making possible the gradual formation of another foreign quarter. In these two districts practically all of the business of the Japanese, save the curio shops or "bazaars" (these are located in the shopping district), are located. Moreover, all but a comparatively few of the Japanese who provide their own lodgings live in the one "quarter" or the other, usually in boarding and lodging houses or in the structures in which business is conducted.

Agents of the Commission collected data relating to 92 of the business enterprises conducted by Japanese, the men who conducted them and the members of their households and some of their employees, together with general data relating to the competition between Japanese and other races in some lines of business. The detailed investigation covered the following Japanese establishments: Two book stores, 6 curio stores, 3 drug stores, 5 fish and poultry markets, 9 fruit, confectionery, and cigar "stands," 9 provision and grocery stores, 2 watch and jewelry stores, 2 men's furnishing stores, 8 barber shops, 6 boarding and lodging houses, 9 restaurants, 4 tailor shops, 7 laundries (including separate shops), 6 pool rooms, 3 cobbler shops, 2 photograph galleries, 2 employment agencies, and 7 other establishments of various kinds. Data were also obtained for the purpose of comparison from 23 establishments conducted by members of other races in the same districts. The data relating to the date of establishment, capital employed, the amount of capital borrowed, the volume of business transacted during the year, the number and race of employees, rent paid for shop or other structure occupied, the net profit realized from the business, and the race of patrons, are shown for each establishment in General Table 22. The personal data collected are presented in other tables at the end of this report.

DATA RELATING TO JAPANESE BUSINESS.

Barber shops.—The number of barber shops conducted by Japanese has rapidly increased. There are now 44 as against 18 in 1904. These, with two exceptions, where the Japanese proprietor employs white barbers,[a] are all small shops, the majority with two chairs, the proprietor being assisted by his wife or one employee. The 8 investigated are typical of the greater number. Most of the shops are fairly clean, are simply furnished, and give the service characteristic of other small shops located in similar localities. The amount of business transacted varies from $1,200 per annum to something more than twice that amount. The barbers employed are paid $30, $35, $40, or $45 per month, with board and lodging, in the majority of shops; but in others, following the custom of the establishments conducted by white proprietors, the employees receive 60 per cent of the earnings of their chairs, without board or lodging.

---

[a] One Japanese proprietor employs 12 white barbers.

The prices charged are uniform—hair cutting 15 cents, shaving 10 cents, and corresponding sums for the various other services. All of the shops are freely patronized by other races as well as by Japanese, the proportions of the various races depending largely upon the character of the population residing or working in the immediate vicinity of each shop. The percentage of patrons other than Japanese in the 8 shops investigated varied from 10 to 99, the average being between 51 and 52. These races other than Japanese include some negroes and Mexicans as well as white men, chiefly foreign born. The Japanese proprietors are making very good profits. The profits of the 8 from whom data were obtained varied between $600 and $1,080, and averaged $832.50 for the year 1908. The capital invested varied from $300 to $2,000 per shop.

The first-class uptown shops have not been affected by Japanese competition, but the proprietors of the smaller shops in both sections of the city where Japanese are prominent complain of the loss of patronage. A number of shops along East First street have been closed, not because of any reduction of charges but because of the moving away of their patrons and the incoming of Japanese, who patronize shops conducted by members of their own race. In fact, they are usually not desired at shops conducted by white men giving as good service as at the shops conducted by Japanese. The union shops in the better parts of the city charge 25 cents for hair cutting and 15 cents for shaving, and their barbers receive $14 per week or $14 per week and 60 per cent of the gross earnings in excess of $23.33 per week. In many shops the price for hair cutting is 20 cents and for shaving 10 cents. In the districts where the Japanese shops are located, however, the prices are in almost every instance 15 cents and 10 cents for these services, while the barbers receive 60 per cent of their gross earnings, usually without a guaranty of a stipulated amount or a minimum wage, or wages no higher than those paid to Japanese barbers. Nor has there been any appreciable change in recent years, either in prices or in wages paid to employees. In five of these shops located near Japanese establishments 10 barbers employed by two native and one Norwegian proprietor earned about $61 per month on the percentage basis, while one barber employed by a Polish proprietor was paid only $10 per week.

Baths.—A large percentage of the Japanese barber shops have baths in connection. Some bathing establishments, however, are run independently. Some of the Japanese establishments have as few as 5 or 6 tubs, others as many as 25. Of three places investigated, all had white as well as Japanese patrons, the latter race constituting slightly more than one-half of the total number. The price charged in an ordinary bath is the same as that which has been charged in these districts, viz, 15 cents, while that for a " salt " bath is commonly 5 cents more.

Laundries.—In 1904 two small laundries were conducted by Japanese. In 1909 there were seven, but three proprietors maintained second shops in which ironing alone was done, while another maintained two of these establishments. The washing in such cases is done in the poorest parts of the Japanese quarter, while the ironing is done in good shops in the better residence districts, so as to attract trade. With two exceptions these laundries are small, employing a few persons each. The two largest employ 20 and 23 laborers, respectively, so that the total number regularly employed in laundries is about 75. A comparatively few others are employed by the day when additional help is needed. These laundries have little in the way of equipment. In fact, they do " hand work " almost exclusively and send most of the household linen delivered to them to the white steam laundries to be done at " family flat work " rates.

Those investigated reported that from 60 to 99 per cent of their patrons were of races other than Japanese. With the increase in the number of Japanese laundries, two steam laundries conducted by whites reported that they had lost the small percentage of patrons of that race which they formerly had. These Japanese laundries compete to a certain extent with some half dozen small French hand laundries located in the same parts of the city and a large number of steam laundries conducted by the various white races. In May, 1909, the Laundrymen's Association, a loose organization of which practically all of the white laundry proprietors are members, fearful of the results of Japanese competition, adopted a resolution providing that no member of the association should accept any work from Japanese laundrymen. There is also a " gentlemen's agreement " between the laundrymen and the laundry machinery supply houses to the effect that the latter shall not furnish equipment of any kind to the Japanese. The laundrymen fear the results of Japanese competition if their laundries are equipped with modern machinery.

From what has been stated it is evident that the competition between Japanese and other laundrymen is practically limited to those articles which are laundered as " hand work." A comparison of Japanese rates with those of the French and other laundrymen shows that while they are about the same on about one-half of the articles contained in " gentlemen's and ladies' lists," there is considerable variation, the Japanese rates in such instances almost without exception being the lowest. Their rates on articles which are preferably done as hand work are noticeably lower than those of their competitors.

The larger steam laundries have an 8½-hour day, but as is usual in this trade, there is much overtime work on certain days of the week. The smaller hand laundries and those conducted by the Japanese have a longer workday, 10 hours being reported as the normal, which is frequently exceeded. Four Japanese proprietors of laundries at the time of the investigation employed 33 persons. Two of these were German-Russian women, employed temporarily at $1.50 per day, or 15 cents per hour. The remaining 31 washermen or ironers were all Japanese men. Two of these were paid $45 and $40 per month, respectively, and received board and lodging in addition to their wages. The wages paid per month to the 31 men were as follows: Forty-five dollars to 1, $40 to 1, $35 to 4, $32 to 1, $30 to 7, $25 to 9, $20 to 5, and under $15 to 3. The average monthly wage paid to those who received board and lodging was $27.30. The average wage bill, allowing for board and lodging, was approximately $35 per month. Five of the steam laundries investigated employed 460 women and men. Various races were found among them—1

Armenian, 14 English, 10 French, 19 German, 8 Irish, 6 Italian, 8 Scandinavian, 3 Scotch, 3 Welsh, 3 Austrian, 1 Canadian, 4 Mexican. 9 American negroes, and 371 native-born whites being reported. The wages paid, both to men and women, varied from $1 to $2 or over per day. The median wage, without board and lodging, for males and females was $1.50 per day, or about $39 per month.

Pool rooms.—Playing pool is the chief amusement of the Japanese, and the number of pool rooms has kept pace with the increase of the Japanese population. In 1904 there were 13; at the end of the year 1908, 35 of these establishments. Some of them have only one or two tables, and are run in connection with some other branch of business, while others have as many as 18 tables. They are all located in the two districts in which the Japanese are colonized. Almost all are patronized by other races which live in these districts as well as by Japanese, but in most cases the members of the last-mentioned race constitute the majority of the patrons. The character of the patronage of some of the establishments is indicated by the fact that the prices charged and other matters are posted on the walls in the Japanese, Spanish, and English languages. The charge is uniform, viz, $2\frac{1}{2}$ cents " per cue " in the Japanese and in other pool halls, but as a result of the changes in the character of the population and the fact that Japanese patronize almost exclusively the halls conducted by their countrymen the profits of the white proprietors have been seriously affected by the competition of the increasing number of Japanese establishments. However, some of the larger pool rooms conducted by white men are well patronized and yield fairly large profits.

Restaurants.—From the time of their first settlement in Los Angeles the Japanese have conducted restaurants serving American meals. The number of such establishments in 1897 was 14; in 1904, 21; in 1909, 25. These are all comparatively small and serve low-priced meals. A few are conducted by the proprietor and his wife without other assistance; the largest has 11 employees. The average number of persons employed by the proprietor (who is frequently first cook) is about five. Some of these restaurants serve meals for 10 cents, others for " 15 cents and up." The latter are patronized in about equal proportions by white men, chiefly laborers, and Japanese, the former by Mexicans, negroes and white laborers, most of whom are foreign born, and a very few Japanese. Of three restaurants charging 15 cents per meal, two reported that their Japanese and white patrons were about equal in number, $97\frac{1}{2}$ per cent of the patrons of the third were members of the various white races. Of two serving 10-cent meals, one reported that 60 per cent of its patrons were Mexicans, 30 per cent white persons, and 10 per cent Japanese; the other, 5 per cent Mexicans, 25 per cent negroes, and 70 per cent white persons. The restaurants serving 15-cent meals have washable cloths on the tables, clean silverware, and fair " service," and serve good meals considering the lowness of the price. The restaurants serving 10-cent meals are very much inferior to these in every respect. Most of the Japanese restaurants are located in the district first occupied by the members of that race, but the number located in the newer quarter occupied by them is increasing. The restaurant keepers of other races in the former of these districts complain of the competition of the Japanese establishments. In the other districts, however, their competition has scarcely been felt. The number of white people living in the older of the two districts has diminished in recent years as the number of Japanese has increased. This has seriously affected the "white restaurants" for the Japanese, partly because they are clannish and partly because they are not, as a rule, welcomed elsewhere, almost invariably patronize restaurants conducted by their own countrymen. Moreover, it is the opinion of the agent of the Commission that the Japanese serve better meals than their competitors serve at the same price.

The agent of the Commission obtained data relative to the employees of several Japanese restaurants and of five conducted by white men—one Dalmatian and four natives—as well as regarding the wages paid by all, in the same localities, the restaurants of the two groups being of the same general type, except that those of the latter group were on the whole larger and did a larger business in the course of the year. The Japanese proprietors employed members of their own race only, though a few of those not included in the investigation employ white waitresses. The Dalmatian employed his own countrymen exclusively. Three of the other four white proprietors employed Japanese as dishwashers and "general help," while two of these three employed Japanese cooks. Only white waiters and waitresses were employed. On the whole, the white proprietors paid higher wages than the Japanese, though comparison is rendered difficult by the fact that while those employed by the former receive board only in addition to wages, those employed by the latter are usually provided with lodging as well.

The Japanese male waiters employed in the Japanese restaurants investigated were all paid $35 per month. The waiters employed in the white restaurants were paid from $10 to $16, the waitresses from $6 to $10 per week, the average for the two classes being $10.62 per week or about $45 per month. The dishwashers and "general help" employed in the Japanese restaurants were all paid $30 per month. The white men and Japanese employed in the other group of restaurants were paid from $6 to $9 per week, the average being $8.41 or about $36 per month. The wages paid to cooks in Japanese establishments varied from $30 to $70, and for the 9 averaged $48.33 per month, while the wages paid to the cooks in the somewhat larger competing establishments varied from $13 to $25 and averaged $17.45 per week or about $75 per month. Because lodging was not provided, the Japanese dishwashers employed in three white restaurants received $8 or $8.50 per week as against the $30 per month earned in Japanese restaurants.

The number of restaurants serving Japanese meals and patronized by Japanese only is much larger than that of restaurants serving American meals and patronized by the members of the various races. Of these, 12 were reported in 1904, 58 in December, 1908. Most of these were opened in 1906 and 1907, when the number of boarding and lodging houses with which some of them are connected greatly increased. Nearly all of these establishments are small, the employees of the 58 being reported as 182 in number, or an average of something more than 3 each. Japanese men are employed as cooks and "kitchen help," while Japanese women are almost exclusively employed as waitresses. The 15 waitresses from whom data were obtained received $25 per month with board and lodging. In most of these establishments the service is à la carte, but where table d'hôte meals are served the price is 15 cents.

Previous to May, 1909, about 30 of the restaurants serving Japanese meals were also selling intoxicating drinks, but were without licenses to conduct a business of that kind. During the latter part of the month mentioned these were closed by the police. In August following, 13 of them paid the city liquor license of $900 and were permitted to conduct their business as before.

Cobbler shops.—The number of Japanese cobbler shops has increased rapidly in recent years. In 1904 there were only 2; at the time of the investigation in 1909 there were 17, two of which also carried stocks of shoes. These are all small shops, and the old method of handwork is employed. The gross earnings of three typical shops for 1908 varied from $1,200 to $2,500, the net earnings from $720 to $900. Though the percentage of Japanese patrons is large, all of the three shops have many patrons of other races. Because of the increase in the number of small Japanese shops and of the racial changes in the locality, the cobblers of other races located in the older Japanese colony have lost much of their business. Those located in the newer district in which the Japanese are now settling have been affected to a less extent. These small cobblers have at the same time suffered from the competition of larger shops equipped with machinery, doing better work and turning it out more expeditiously.

The Japanese cobblers are all members of the shoemakers' union, controlling the shops conducted by the members of that race throughout California. The prices are fixed by this organization, but those actually charged by the cobblers of Los Angeles are, as a rule, somewhat less than those fixed by the union.[a] In some of the shops conducted by white men in the same localities prices of some kinds of work were the same as, of other kinds higher than, those fixed by the Japanese union. In the other shops practically all the prices were materially higher. In shops owned by white men the price for halfsoling men's shoes, hand sewed, was $1 or $1.25, in Japanese shops, $0.90. Corresponding differences were found to obtain in the prices charged for other kinds of repair work. Evidently there has been much underbidding by the Japanese cobblers.

Tailoring and cleaning establishments.—In 1904 there were only two Japanese merchant tailors; at the time of the investigation there were 14 tailoring and 2 dressmaking establishments. With the exception of 1, with 7 employees, 1 of whom is an Austrian, these are all small shops, with 1 or 2 employees at most. The total number of employees and proprietors is about 40. Most of the establishments are

---

[a] The prices fixed by the organization are as follows:

Men's shoes half-soled (hand sewed)	$1.00
Men's shoes half-soled (pegged)	.60
Women's shoes half-soled (hand sewed)	.80
Women's shoes half-soled (pegged)	.45
Heels placed on men's shoes	.30
Heels placed on women's shoes	.20
Patches, each	.10

The prices charged for the first four items are in practice 10 cents less.

engaged chiefly in cleaning, dyeing, and pressing suits. The standard price for pressing is 50 cents, for dyeing, cleaning, and pressing 75 cents per suit. These are the prices commonly charged at other small shops in these localities. Only a small percentage of the suits purchased by Japanese are made by these tailors, and their competition in the tailoring trade has been of little or no consequence. The percentages of white patrons of 4 shops investigated were from 20 to 50.

All of the employees of the 4 shops investigated, save 1, were Japanese. Two of the 10 Japanese were paid $50, another $60 per month. Of the other 7, one was paid $65, two $45, and the other four $40, $30, $25, and $20, respectively, with board and lodging. The wages of the Austrian employed in the largest shop was $15 per week.

Provision and grocery stores.—At the time of the investigation by the agents of the Commission there were 27 Japanese provision and grocery stores. In 1904 there were but 6. The expansion of this branch of business is given a somewhat undue importance by these figures, for the majority of the larger provision stores were opened previous to 1905, while most of the large number which have been subsequently established have comparatively little capital invested and a small annual volume of transactions. Nevertheless the growth of the Japanese provision and grocery trade was very rapid between 1904 and 1908. This is accounted for by the rapid increase in the number of agricultural laborers in the southern part of the State, the increasing number of Japanese farmers in Los Angeles County, the larger number of Japanese residing in Los Angeles, and the development of trade with other races. Previous to 1903 or 1904 the vast majority of the Japanese in the southern part of the State had been at work in large groups and chiefly on the railroads, and were provided with their supplies by a limited number of provision stores. More recently the number of men thus employed has diminished, while the number employed in small groups, chiefly as agricultural laborers, has rapidly increased. With this change and the rapid increase in the number of farmers in the vicinity of Los Angeles and a larger settled Japanese population in the city itself, it has been possible for more men to engage with profit in the provision trade. At the same time several small groceries have been opened to secure the trade of the members of the other races. During the year preceding the investigation, however, this branch of business, considered as a whole, did not prosper because many of the neighboring Japanese farmers were growing strawberries and the prices received for their crop were unremunerative. Indeed, because of the straitened circumstances of many of the farmers three or four Japanese provision and grocery stores had failed during the year preceding the investigation.

Agents of the Commission secured data from 9 of the 27 supply stores and groceries—one of the 9 carrying a stock of gentlemen's furnishing goods as well as groceries. These 9 were selected as typical of the larger number. It is noteworthy that of the 9 stores investigated, 2 had been established in 1903, 3 in 1906, 1 in 1907, and 3 in 1908. One employed a capital of $50,000, another $26,000, a third $7,500, a fourth $7,000. The amount of capital employed by the other 5 varied from $700 to $3,000. The amount of business transacted during the twelve months preceding the time of the investigation varied between $2,400 and $140,000, the total for the 9 establishments being $423,400. In some cases the figures were taken directly from the books, while in others, and chiefly in the case of the smaller establishments, they are only rough estimates. Four of the 9 establishments were so small that they were conducted by the proprietor and his wife or by the partners engaged in the business. The other 5 employed from 1 to 12 clerks. Of the 25 clerks and drivers employed, all but 1 were Japanese. The salaries of 2 managers were $125 and $90 per month, respectively. Of 21 other male Japanese employees, 3 were paid $50, 2 $45, 3 $40, 9 $35, and 4 $30 per month, while 1 female was paid $25 per month—all with board and lodging. The 1 native white employee was paid $60 per month.

One of the smallest groceries investigated carried a stock of American goods only. That much of the stock carried by the others is of non-Japanese origin is shown by the fact that from 20 to 80 per cent of the goods sold were reported to be of that character. Of sales reported aggregating $423,400 for the year, approximately 51.5 per cent were said to be of goods of non-Japanese origin. The largest single item among the sales was of rice, and that is purchased in Texas. The small grocery carrying a stock of "American" goods only has practically no Japanese customers. From 50 to approximately 100 per cent of the sales of the other stores were made to Japanese. According to the estimates made by the several proprietors, approximately 81.5 per cent of the business transacted was with the Japanese. These estimates are at best only approximately correct, but are believed to be sufficiently accurate to indicate in a general way the character of the supply and grocery business conducted by the members of this race. Though the number of white patrons of some of the Japanese stores is not small, such competition as has developed has been scarcely felt by the white grocers. At any rate no special complaint of Japanese competition was made by these men.

Fish and poultry and meat markets.—The Japanese also conduct three fish and poultry markets, which, together with the business of a fish peddler, were investigated by agents of the Commission. The markets are all located on East First street. With comparatively small capitals invested (aggregating $4,600), they do a large amount of business—their sales amounting to $6,000, $12,000, and $28,800 per year. The profits realized in all cases were comparatively large. The majority of the patrons of two of the markets were Japanese. Sixty per cent of those who patronized the largest markets, however, were members of other races. The fish peddler had Japanese patrons only. One meat market was found which was conducted by the proprietor with the assistance of one butcher and patronized by Japanese almost exclusively.

Art or curio stores.—Aside from the provision and grocery business, the curio or art stores, dealing in oriental wares chiefly, are the most important branch of retail trade engaged in by the Japanese of Los Angeles. Small shops were opened many years ago. In 1904 the number of stores, some of which carried large stocks of goods, was 7. In 1909 there were 15, 6 of which were investigated. Three of these 6 were very large establishments, with a combined capital of $120,000 and with 28 employees. The other 3 had a combined capital of $13,400 and had only 3 employees. White clerks, because of their superior knowledge of English, were employed in addition to Japanese in 3 of the stores. These were paid $65, $54, (2) $43, $35, and $30 per month without board or lodging. Three Japanese women were paid $43, $26, and $22 per month, respectively, without board or lodging. The remaining 22 Japanese employees were paid wages per month as follows: Three $75, seven $50, four $45, five $40, one $35, one $30, and one $25.

Some of these stores and shops are in the "shopping district." Except in the case of one store, the majority of the patrons were members of the white race. With unimportant exceptions, the classes of goods carried in stock are not sold by other dealers save the Chinese. The competition which exists is limited practically to the dealers of these two oriental races.

Other stores.—There are several retail shops of kinds other than those already mentioned. Among those investigated by the agents of the Commission were two "men's furnishing" stores, one with a capital of $5,000, the other with a capital of $2,500 invested; the first established in 1906, the other in 1907. Both of these are located in the center of the older "Japanese quarter," but each reports that 40 per cent of its patronage was by persons other than Japanese. One carries a small stock of Japanese goods. The sales for the year amounted to $21,000. There is also one shoe store, which was established in 1907. It carries a stock of goods worth only about $1,500, and 80 per cent of its patrons are Japanese. Of the 5 book and stationery stores, 2 were investigated. One of these reported that about 90 per cent, the other about 60 per cent, of its goods in stock were of Japanese origin, while 90 and 80 per cent of their patrons, respectively, were members of the Japanese race. Their combined capital was $6,000; their aggregate sales for the year amounted to $15,000. Three drug stores are reported, two of which were established in 1905, the other the following year. All three are located in the older "Japanese quarter" and each has a capital of $4,000 or a little more invested. Thirty per cent of the stock of two, and 50 per cent of that of the other, were reported to be Japanese patent medicines. From 50 to 60 per cent of their patrons are members of the Japanese race. Among the other patrons about one-fifth are negroes.

Of 5 watch and jewelry shops, 2—1 of which was established in 1902, the other in 1903—were investigated. One of these had a capital of $7,000 invested and employs two clerks, while the other is engaged in watch repairing almost exclusively. Fifty per cent of the patrons of the larger and 60 per cent of those of the smaller shop were reported as Japanese. One general merchandise store was reported. It had a small stock of American and Japanese goods worth perhaps $4,000. Sixty per cent of its patrons are Japanese. One liquor store, with a slightly larger capital, dealing in both American and Japanese intoxicating drinks and patronized by both white persons and Japanese (70 per cent of the latter class), was reported. Finally, one bicycle shop engaged in the sale of new bicycles, as well as in the repair of old ones, and patronized in about equal proportions by Japanese and white persons was investigated.

Cigar, confectionery, and ice-cream stands.—There are perhaps about 20 cigar, confectionery, and ice cream stands other than those conducted in connection with pool rooms and other establishments

already mentioned. These have all been started in very recent years.
Of 9, for which data were obtained, the oldest was started in 1905.
Most of them deal in vegetables, canned goods, candies, ice cream,
soda water, cigarettes, and cigars. Only 2 of the 9 reported a capital
in excess of $700. All but 1 is conducted without hired assistance
and all but 2 reported profits varying from $300 to $960 for the year.
These small shops are located in the most frequented part of the
Japanese colony. Most of them are patronized chiefly by Japanese,
but a few report that the majority of their customers are of the
various other races residing in the locality.

Boarding and lodging houses.—The conducting of boarding and
lodging houses for their countrymen engages the attention of a larger
number of Japanese business men than any other branch of business
enterprise, for the vast majority of those residing in the city are without families, and unless provided with board and lodging by their
employers, seek these establishments conducted by their countrymen.
Moreover, the agricultural class when not employed come here in
large numbers. In 1908 there were 104 such establishments, but at
the time of the investigation the number had decreased to 90. In 1904
only 18 were reported, but doubtless the list was incomplete and included only the more conspicuous among a much larger number.
Whatever the number at that time may have been it is certain that
with the influx of agricultural laborers to southern California and
the larger number of Japanese permanently located in Los Angeles,
it increased rapidly. More recently, however, as the number of Japanese laborers has diminished and as the Japanese population of the
city has become smaller, a comparatively large number of the less
profitable establishments have been closed and the profits of some of
the others are much smaller than they formerly were. The boarding
and lodging houses have very few patrons other than Japanese. Only
2 of some 30 known to the agents had any white patrons, and in those
instances they constituted for one 20 per cent and the other only about
1 per cent of the total number.

The 90 boarding and lodging houses are of diverse types, but in a
general way may be placed in three groups, according to the character of the patrons and the character of the accommodations provided. A large number provide meals and lodgings at low prices for
transient agricultural laborers and have a comparatively small number of regular boarders and lodgers employed in the city. An equally
large, if not greater, number provide meals and lodgings of the same
kind for house cleaners, restaurant employees, and others similarly
employed in the city, and have a small percentage of transients.
Finally, a smaller number provide better lodgings and, in some cases,
meals for the more well-to-do classes—business men, reporters, interpreters, etc. Six boarding and lodging houses were investigated.
The details reported by the agents show how a large percentage of the
Japanese in Los Angeles live and the cost of their board and lodging.
One of the boarding and lodging houses investigated was conducted
in an old two-story frame structure. There were 1 female and 18
male boarders and lodgers. Three of the latter did house cleaning,
2 were elevator "boys," 5 were restaurant employees, and 1 was a
ranch hand. Practically all of the males were regular boarders and
lodgers, who paid $9 per month for board and from $3.50 to $7 per

month for lodging. Transients pay 35 cents per day for meals and from 15 to 35 cents per night for lodging. With two exceptions the rooms were not crowded and were well ventilated and lighted. The rooms were furnished with iron beds and fairly clean bedding (including counterpanes) and cheap chairs and tables. The floors of the hallways and some of the rooms were carpeted. The care of the apartments, but not the toilets, was fairly good.

A boarding house of another type was conducted in a large dwelling house, which was in fair repair. The 34 boarders and lodgers included 7 men and their wives, 3 married men with wives abroad, and 17 single men. Of the men 18 were farm laborers, 2 were house cleaners, 2 were porters in saloons, and 2 were cooks. Of the women 4 were employed as waitresses. The price of meals was 10 cents each, of rooms per month from $5 to $10, of lodging per night 25 cents. The rooms were all clean, comfortably furnished, and well ventilated and lighted. Iron spring beds were used, the bedding (including counterpanes, etc.) was clean, and the apartments well cared for. Most of the rooms were carpeted. The proprietor has alliances with " bosses " of agricultural laborers, whereby he supplies them with men, but does not conduct a regular employment agency.

A boarding house of a slightly different type and conducted in an old frame dwelling had 29 boarders and lodgers. These 29 included 4 married couples, 5 married men whose wives were abroad, 14 single men, and 2 children. Ten of these men were ranch hands, 5 were restaurant employees, 2 were house cleaners, 1 a janitor, 1 a porter, 1 an elevator " boy," 1 an expressman, 1 an actor, 1 a " boss," and one a " day worker." Regular boarders paid $10 per month, transients 40 cents per day for their meals; regular lodgers paid from $3 to $10 per month, while transients paid 20 to 35 cents per night for their lodgings. Many of the rooms, which were not large, contained two double beds. For the greater part iron beds were used, the bedding (including, as elsewhere, counterpanes, pillowcases, etc.) was not clean, the furniture was of the cheapest kind, the floors were bare; the plumbing was poor and malodorous, the care of the apartments poor. The proprietor did not conduct an employment agency, but supplied laborers to ranch " bosses," " who, if it pleases them, send me money in acknowledgment of the services rendered." [a]

Another large establishment investigated was a three-story modern brick structure, the first floor of which was used for business purposes, the other two as lodgings. In every respect it was a very good rooming house, the rooms well furnished and well cared for. The price of lodgings was from $8 to about twice that sum per month. The lodgers were of the professional and business classes of Japanese. The other boarding and lodging houses, except in minor details, were duplications of these. As a group they compare favorably with those conducted by other foreign races, and are distinctly better than those conducted by some races represented by comparatively large numbers of single men and men whose wives are abroad, and most of whom are unskilled laborers or engaged in conducting petty shops.

Employment agencies.—Conducting employment agencies has been one of the most important branches of business enterprise engaged in

---

[a] Free translation of proprietor's statement to agent.

by the Japanese. It has usually been carried on in connection with the supply business or in connection with those boarding and lodging houses the patrons of which are largely transient laborers. Large agencies supplying railroad laborers have maintained branch offices here. Since the substitution of Mexicans as section hands on the southern route of the Southern Pacific and on the Santa Fe west of Albuquerque, however, this branch of the business has not been of great importance. Only one branch office of any great importance is now maintained in Los Angeles by an agency engaged in supplying Japanese laborers for railroad work.

Many of the lodging houses have until recently conducted agencies for supplying domestic and farm and other laborers, but the imposition in 1909 of a state tax of $50 on all employment bureaus in cities of the size of Los Angeles in addition to the city license tax of $48 per year, has caused most of these establishments to discontinue that part of their business. Many of the lodging houses, however, still supply farm laborers to ranch " bosses." These " bosses," who have their groups of laborers in different localities, correspond with lodging-house keepers or visit Los Angeles to secure more laborers when needed. Since Japanese laborers have become scarce the " bosses " usually pay the lodging-house proprietors for the men secured at their places. In several instances the payment was found to be 50 cents for each man secured.

Aside from the house-cleaning groups, which in a sense are employment agencies supplying men for domestic work by the hour or day, only 7 Japanese employment agencies were found by the agents of the Commission. The majority of the latter are general agencies engaged for the greater part in supplying domestics and general laborers. Some of them are patronized by both Japanese and white persons. The Commission collected from persons for whom employment is secured is usually 7 per cent of the first month's wages of domestics and general laborers, if paid in advance, or 10 per cent if paid later. The fee for agricultural laborers is usually $1.50 or $2.

Petty manufacture.—The Japanese have engaged in manufacture to a small extent. Establishments engaged in the manufacture of bamboo furniture, tofu (bean curd), soda water, and artificial flowers are reported, the entire number of establishments being about a half dozen. These are all small places, the work ordinarily being done by the proprietors. Most of the goods produced are sold to the members of the Japanese race.

Other business.—Several other kinds of business, practically all designed to serve the needs of their countrymen, are engaged in by the Japanese of Los Angeles. Among them are two banks engaged in commercial banking. These also serve as savings institutions and as agencies for forwarding money to Japan. There are also 11 expressmen. They do little business except for their countrymen. Their charges do not differ from those of negro and white expressmen, and they earn from $40 to $75 per month. There are 7 " job carpenters," one of whom employs two helpers at $35 and $30 per month, respectively, with board and lodging. These mechanics do cabinet work and " odd jobs "—chiefly in altering the interiors of buildings occupied by Japanese for business or residence purposes and in installing store fixtures. They are employed to only a small ex-

tent by the members of other races. Much of the work is done by
"contract," but the standard rate of wages—which is not necessarily
adhered to—is $3 per day of ten hours. Of small photograph gal-
leries there are now six. Only one studio has any considerable number of white patrons. With this exception, from 90 to 100 per cent
of their patrons are Japanese. Their gross earnings are comparatively small, and the annual profits of two investigated were reported
as being $360 and $600, respectively. There is also one "rubbish
man," who is said to have deprived a negro of the work of hauling
away débris and waste of various kinds for the members of the older
Japanese colony.

In addition to the various kinds of business thus far enumerated,
there are several small printing establishments. Two (and beginning
with the first of the year 1910, three) daily newspapers are published.
Five so-called magazines are published also, but most of them are
small leaflets and reports published by Japanese societies. There are
also two small job printing offices, which engage for the greater part
in printing "matter" in the Japanese language.

Japanese professional men.—Finally, in order to account for the
Japanese not working for wages, reference should be made to the
professional men. These at the close of the year 1908 included several interpreters, four physicians and surgeons, two dentists, and
three midwives. All of these, save the interpreters, serve their own
countrymen almost exclusively and do not compete for the patronage
of other races.

SUMMARY STATEMENT OF THE ESSENTIAL FACTS RELATING TO JAPANESE
BUSINESS.

From the details presented above, it is evident that the Japanese of Los Angeles have engaged in many branches of business
enterprise and that their business establishments are much more
numerous than in 1904. Practically all of these people, save the
domestic servants, live in the two colonies to which reference has
been made, and in many cases are not welcomed in desirable places
conducted by other races. This is true of hotels and lodging houses,
restaurants, barber shops, poolrooms, and similar places. In other
cases, because of convenience, language difficulties, personal taste, and
race sympathy, the vast majority of the Japanese patronize establishments conducted by their own countrymen, in so far as fairly
satisfactory service is available. As deduced from these several facts,
it is clear that the Japanese patronize almost exclusively the business
establishments of their own race, with the possible exception of those
selling American clothing. They usually patronize dentists, physicians, and photographers of their own race as well.

It is evident, also, from the details presented that in most lines of
business the Japanese establishments find many patrons among the
other races. The patrons of the curio and art stores are found among
all the races frequenting the shopping districts. In most other cases,
however, the non-Japanese patrons are practically all of the white
people, Mexicans, and negroes who live in or near the two districts
in which the Japanese have settled in large numbers. Much, if not
most, of the business of the cobblers, restaurants serving American

meals, laundries, barbers, groceries, fish markets, clothes-cleaning and pressing shops, pool rooms, watch-repairing shops, drug stores, and cigar and confectionery stands is done with the members of the various non-Asiatic races of the class mentioned. The competition of the Japanese establishments has not been of any special importance, however, except in the case of the cobbler shops, restaurants, pool rooms, barber shops, and laundries. Only the proprietors of the laundries have as yet offered any organized resistance to the inroads of the Japanese upon their business, the reason being that they alone are organized and in position to offer such resistance. One characteristic of most of the Japanese business establishments is the insignificant amount of capital employed and the small volume of business transacted. In fact, the proportion of small establishments is considerably greater than the number indicated in the investigation. Except for a few of the art stores and provision and grocery stores it may be properly called petty business. In this, however, if a few exceptions are allowed for, the Japanese business does not present any particular contrast to that of the other races—largely foreign—carried on in the same or similar districts of the city. The total capital employed by the 92 establishments investigated was $361,710. The indebtedness reported outstanding against this amounted to $63,460. Of this, $59,560 was on account of stock in trade, $2,000 on account of fixtures, and $1,900 on account of personal loans from friends.

The total number of employees reported by the 92 establishments was 177. Of these, 11 were white persons, 166 were Japanese. Of the latter, 116 were provided with board and lodging by the employer, 31 received board only, 5 lodging only, and 14 neither board nor lodging in addition to their wages. Most of the employees are single men or married men whose wives are abroad, so that an arrangement whereby they receive board and lodging is a convenience for most of them. In 65 cases the proprietors lived in the rear or over the rooms in which business was conducted. With very few exceptions the employees receive lodging and food from their employers. The lodgings of the men were inspected by the agent in 37 cases. The conditions found varied greatly. In 26 cases the rooms were well ventilated and comfortably furnished, the bedding clean, and all details at least fairly satisfactory. In the other 11 cases the lodgings were deficient in one or more respects, the rooms usually being in disorder and the bedding dirty. In 4 of these cases the rooms were, in the opinion of the agent, also inadequate for the needs of the number of persons occupying them.

PERSONAL DATA RELATIVE TO JAPANESE BUSINESS MEN.

Personal data were obtained from 100 Japanese men engaged in the business enterprises which have already been dealt with in this report. As shown by General Table 33 (which includes 3 male minors who were members of the families of these men), 33 had been in the continental United States ten years or over; 67, or two-thirds of the entire number, less than ten years; 2 had been in this country two years, 5 three years, 12 four years, 48 five to nine years, 27 from ten to fourteen years, 5 from fifteen to nineteen years. and only 1 for twenty years or over. Of 98 from whom data were obtained bearing upon the point, 8 had been laborers on the plantations in the Hawaiian Islands before coming to the continental United States. Thirty-eight of the 98 had been engaged in business on their own accounts just previous to their immigration. One of the others had been a laborer in an industrial establishment, 12 had been working for wages in other capacities, chiefly in cities, 19 had been associated with their fathers in farming or in business, while 18 had no occupation. From this it is evident that the majority of these men had come from the cities and that a large percentage had been engaged in some kind of business on their own account, while a comparatively small percentage had been members of the city wage-earning classes (General Table 24).

Most of those who had been engaged in business, however, were engaged in petty trade, came to the United States when comparatively young men, and brought little or no capital with them. Thirty of the 100 were 30 years of age or over, 70 under 30 years of age upon their arrival in this country. Ten were under 18, and 7 were 18 or 19 years of age—these comprising the majority of those who had not been occupied unless working with their fathers, and most of whom came to this country immediately upon leaving school. Of the others, 25 were between 20 and 25, 28 between 25 and 30, 13 between 30 and 35, 13 between 35 and 40, 1 between 40 and 45, and 3 45 or over, at the time of their arrival in this country. (General Table 31.) The amount of money in their possession upon arrival was reported by 98. Three partners coming together had $10,000, 4 sums between $500 and $1,000, and 9 others between $200 and $500 each. Sixty-six of the 98, or about two-thirds of the entire number, had less than $100, and of these, 37 had less than $50 upon their arrival in this country. It is evident that comparatively few came with sufficient capital to engage in business at the outset. Twelve came to pursue their studies, but practically all of the others came to this country on the ground that it presented the best opportunities for making money and expected to begin as wage-earners. Of 98, 16 engaged in business in this country, while the remaining 82 were first gainfully occupied as ·wage-earners. Eleven found their first occupation as railroad laborers, 30 as domestics, 20 as farm hands—a total of 61, who became wage-earners in employments well organized and controlled by Japanese " bosses." Of the remainder, 3 found employment in restaurants, 5 in stores, 10 in various other occupations, while the first occupation of 3 was not ascertained. (General Table 24.)

Most of those who did not engage in business immediately upon their arrival were enabled soon to do so, in several instances the formation of partnerships making it possible to establish themselves with less personal capital than is required for the kind of business they conduct. Information as to the number of years they worked for wages in this country before they engaged in business on their own account was secured from 89. Sixteen of these engaged in business at once: 8 worked for wages for less than one year; 30 for one year, but less than two; 17 for two years, but less than three; 7 for three, but less than four; 4 for four years, but less than five; 2 for five years, but less than six; 1 for seven, 1 for eight, 2 for nine, and 1 for eleven years before engaging in business for themselves. It is evident that most of them soon departed from the wage-earning class. They were enabled to do so because of the small amount of capital required in such business as they are engaged in and the opportunities presented for making profit in Los Angeles. Moreover, they found strong inducement in the fact that most of them had not been wage-earners at home, and that a large number were married men who found it impossible to lead a normal family life while working as wage-earners elsewhere than in the city. Indeed, those who have wished to have their families with them in this country have found it possible to make suitable provision for them only by becoming farmers or business men and thus severing their connection with the wage-earning class.

A comparison of the business now engaged in with the occupation before leaving their native land reveals the fact that the majority are conducting business in which they had had no experience abroad. Of 8 grocers and supply men, 1 had been a grocer abroad, 2 had been clerks, 1 a farmer, and 1 a sailor, while the other 3 had been otherwise occupied. Of the proprietors of haberdasheries, 1 had been a grain dealer, the other a farmer; the proprietor of the shoe store had been a fisherman; of 9 restaurant proprietors, 1 had engaged in the same kind of business abroad, 4 had been farmers or farmers' sons, 2 had been clerks, 1 a sailor, and 1 a metal worker. These are typical of the majority of the branches of business engaged in. There are exceptional cases, however, these being found among the proprietors of the larger art and curio stores, druggists, tailors, shoemakers, and barbers, most of whom had been engaged in the same or a closely related business in Japan. How well the Japanese business men from whom data were secured have succeeded is indicated by the net value of the property now owned by them as well as by the position they occupy as shown in the preceding section of this report. One of 98 reporting has property the net value of which is estimated to be in excess of $25,000; 4, $10,000 but less than $25,000; 8, $5,000 but less than $10,000; 16, $2,500 but less than $5,000; 25, $1,500 but less than $2,500; 16, $1,000 but less than $1,500; and 22, $500 but less than $1,000. The remaining six have less than $500 worth of property after indebtedness is deducted. Grouping in a different way, the wealth of 13 is estimated at $5,000 or more, of 57 at $1,000 but less than $5,000, of 28 at less than $1,000.

As would be expected, all of those who are worth more than $5,000 have been here five years or longer and most of them have been here from ten to twenty years or over. The details relating to length of residence and wealth are shown in General Table 25. The gross value of all property owned by the 98 was $337,070, the indebtedness of 35, $40,810, the net amount owned by all, $296,260, the average for each, $3,023.06. (General Table 28.)

The success of these business men is indicated also by the profits they report as realized in business and by their personal gains for the year preceding the investigation. The profits of each establishment are shown in General Table 22, the personal incomes of 97 in so far as derived from the main business in which they are engaged, in General Table 42. These are only estimates and at best only approximately accurate, but it is believed that they indicate in a general way the position that these men occupy. The incomes of the 97 men in so far as derived from the principal business or businesses in which they engaged, aggregated $111,995 or $1,154.59 per man. Four had incomes of between $300 and $400, 2 between $400 and $500, 26 between $500 and $750, 27 between $750 and $1,000, 22 between $1,000 and $1,500, 6 between $1,500 and $2,000, 3 between $2,000 and $2,500, while 7 had annual incomes of $2,500 or over. The incomes of the restaurant keepers varied between $400 and $2,600 and averaged $1,267.27. Those of the lodging-house keepers varied between $600 as a minimum and $2,250 as a maximum and averaged $1,151.67. The minimum for the shop and store keepers was $300, the maximum $6,000. Of the 39, only 6 had incomes as great as $1,500. The incomes of the 6 were $2,400, $2,880, $3,000, $4,000, $4,200, and $6,000, respectively. The incomes of 8 proprietors of small barber shops varied between $600 and $1,080 and averaged $832.50 for the year. Of 2 tailors, 1 made $1,080, the other $1,200. Of 3 shoemakers, 1 made $900, the other 2 $720 each. The 2 employment agents reported incomes of $720 and $840, respectively. The 6 proprietors of laundries reported incomes of $600 each in two cases, $1,920 each in two other cases, and $875 and $1,200 in the other two.

The incomes of the proprietors of pool rooms varied between $360 as a minimum and $1,200 as a maximum, and averaged $840 for the 6. The incomes of 11 of the 14, placed in a miscellaneous group, were less than $1,000 each. Fifteen of the 97 had subsidiary sources of income. Two received dividends on stocks aggregating $7,000. The remaining 13 had comparatively small incomes from other business or labor or from the renting of property, the total amount being $5,962. The total incomes of the 97, therefore, aggregated $124,957, an average of $1,288.14 each. Including incomes from all sources, the net incomes of the 97 were as follows:

Amount of income: Number.
$300 and under $400_____   4
$400 and under $500_____   2
$500 and under $750_____ 26
$750 and under $1,000_____ 27
$1,000 and under $1,500_____ 22
$1,500 and under $2,000_____   6
$2,000 and under $2,500_____   3
$2,500 or over_____   7

    Total _____ 97

For reasons already stated, the proportion of small incomes would be considerably larger were a complete census of all Japanese establishments made.

The surplus or deficit of 95 men, after meeting their personal expenses as reported to the agents, are shown in General Table 26. One had a deficit of $250 for the year, while 10 had neither surplus nor deficit. The remaining 84 had a surplus varying from $100 to $4,000 and averaging $621.61. The surplus of 19 was between $100 and $250; of 26, between $250 and $500; of 25, between $500 and $1,000; of 10, between $1,000 and $2,500; of 4, between $2,500 and $4,000 (General Table 27). The amount of money sent abroad ($5,035) was about one-tenth of the aggregate gains ($52,215) of these 84 men. Of the 98 men reporting, 32 sent sums of money abroad during the year. The disposition of the remainder of the profits, save for $1,200, the disposition of which was not ascertained, was as follows: Six thousand five hundred dollars was used by 11 to pay debts earlier incurred, $500 was invested in land, $28,150 was invested in the business or in other ways, while the remainder was placed in the bank. According to the report, the larger part of the profits were invested in this country, and chiefly in extending the business conducted.

DATA RELATING TO WAGE-EARNERS.

Corresponding personal data were obtained for only 40 Japanese wage-earners—with few exceptions men employed in the Japanese establishments investigated. Some of the data gathered may be presented at this point to bring out the similarities and contrasts between the business men and their employees.

Like the majority of the business men, the greater number of these wage-earners came from the cities of Japan. Two came to this continent from the Hawaiian Islands, where they had been engaged in agricultural work. Of the other 38, 5 had been in business for themselves, 4 had been employed in stores, 1 in an industrial establishment, while 5 had been wage-earners in other occupations, presumably in the cities. Of the other 24, 11 had worked for their fathers, while 12 had had no occupation before coming to the United States (General Table 24). At the time of arrival in this country all but 7 were under 30 years of age and 25, five-eighths of the entire number, were under 25. On the whole their ages were somewhat less than those of the business men (General Table 31). A much greater contrast, however, is found in the amount of money brought, for only 1 had more than $100 and 21 of the 40 had less than $50 on arrival (General Table 23). Being without capital, only 1 engaged in business when he arrived, 4 of the other 39 became railroad laborers, 21 domestics, 9 farm laborers—all well-organized trades—while the other 5 found employment in stores, restaurants, and other places in the city (General Table 24). Most of them have been in this country for five years and 7 of them for ten years or over, so that they have had sufficient time to find their way into city occupations, which are more agreeable and more remunerative than railroad and farm work. Indeed, from the incomplete data available it would appear that those who were first engaged in railroad and farm work left it after one or two years to seek employment in the city. A few have engaged in business; but, meeting with reverses, have fallen back into the wage-earning class.

The wages of the employees in the establishments investigated have been noted. The annual earnings of the 40 are shown in General Table 43. The earnings of 24 who received board and lodging in addition to wages varied from $270 for nine months' work to less than $800 for twelve months' work. All but 3 were employed for twelve months during the year; these three were employed for nine, ten, and eleven months, respectively. The median earnings was $420, the average $440. The annual earnings of 16 who did not receive board varied from $330 for eleven months' to $1,500 for twelve months' employment. Only two were not employed continuously, and these were without work only one month. The median was $720, the average earnings $719.38 (General Table 43). Of 38 reporting. 8 had neither surplus nor deficit for the year, while the remaining 30 realized a surplus varying from $50 to $1,750. The average amount of surplus was $326.66, the median $250. That two had gains amounting to $1,200 and $1,750, respectively, is explained by the fact that they held managerial positions and owned corporate stocks which paid them dividends (General Table 26). Fourteen sent a portion of their earnings abroad during the year, the total amount being $2,270, or more than 23 per cent of the surplus reported by the 30 reporting a surplus for the year. That the wage-earners sent a larger part of their gains abroad than did the business men is accounted for by the fact that fewer of them have their families with them in this country and that they have less opportunity for profitable investment here than do those conducting business. Of the much larger sum kept in the United States, $1,500 was invested in stocks, $200 used to pay a debt earlier incurred in business, and the remainder deposited in the bank. By retaining much of their gains in this country several of these wage-earners have been able to accumulate several hundred dollars' worth of property. Of 40, 8 have no property other than their personal effects, 14 have property worth less than $500, 10 worth from $500 to $1,000, 5 worth from $1,000 to $1,500, and 3 have still more (General Table 25).

SOCIOLOGICAL DATA.

As already stated, the Japanese population of Los Angeles was reported in December, 1908, as numbering 4,457. Of these, 3,925 were adult males, 427 adult females, 81 American-born children, and 24 foreign-born children. Complete data relating to various matters were obtained from 220 of these—140 men, 48 women, 7 foreign-born children between 6 and 13 years of age, and 25 Japanese-Americans under 6 years of age. (General Tables 29 and 32.) Practically all of the females over 16 years of age were married women, most of whom have come to the United States within recent years to join their husbands or to be married upon their arrival. Moreover, most of them are the wives of men engaged in business or in the professions. Of 100 business men from whom data were obtained 58 are married and 43 of the wives are now in this country. Twenty-one of them, including 1 who came from Canada and several who came from the Hawaiian Islands, accompanied their husbands to this country when they first immigrated, 5 joined their husbands later, 9 came to this country to be married here, while the remaining 11 married when their prospective husbands visited Japan, and all but 2 came to this country with them upon their return. Of 40 wage-earners, 10 are married. One of these was married during a visit to his native country, the other 9 previous to their immigration to the United States. Two of these men, who came from the Hawaiian Islands, were accompanied by their wives, and 1 was later joined by his wife. At present, therefore, 4 of the wives of the 10 wage-earners are in this country, 6 abroad. (General Tables 30 and 31.) In recent years a tendency is evident, especially among the men who engage successfully in business, to bring their wives to this country. This accounts for the fact that whereas in 1904 only 5 married women as against 493 adult males were reported, in 1908 427 adult females and 3,925 adult males were reported.

This change in the composition of the Japanese population of Los Angeles is indicative of the fact that many expect to remain indefinitely if not permanently in the United States. Of the 100 Japanese males engaged in business investigated, 73 stated that they expect to remain permanently in this country, 2 to return to Japan, while 25 were in doubt as to what they would eventually do. The wage-earners, who, on the whole, have had a shorter residence than the business men in this country, have been less successful and are not so well off, present a contrast to the business men in this regard. Of 40 from whom data were obtained, 9 stated that they expected to reside permanently in this country, 14 to return to their native land, while 17 were in doubt as to what they would do.·

Something has been said concerning the conditions under which the Japanese live. Most of the domestics and some of the laborers employed by white men are provided with lodging where they are employed. Though a few of the others live elsewhere, the majority reside in the two Japanese colonies. As already stated, most of the business men live in the rear or over the rooms housing the business conducted, and the majority of their employees live with them. The greater number of the remainder live in lodging and boarding houses. A few families live in small cottages on streets which were formerly occupied mainly by the families of white laborers of various races.

Data were collected from the households investigated relative to the cost of food and drink consumed. Excluding those groups whose heads were proprietors of restaurants or who were engaged in some other business where the articles were not purchased in the usual way, 71 groups, including 131 individuals, remained. Twelve of these, constituting 4 households, reported the cost as $5 per month; 12, constituting 6 households, as $7 but less than $8; 19, constituting 9 households, as $8 but less than $9; 6, constituting 3 households, as $9 but less than $10; 28, constituting 12 households, as $10 but less than $12; 14, constituting 8 households, as $12 but less than $14; and 40, constituting 29 households, as $14 or over per month. Of these 29 last-mentioned households, 1 of 5 persons reported a cost of $25 per person, 1 of 2 persons reported a cost of $30, while 2 single men reported the cost as $35 and $50 per month, respectively. The cost per month of lodging and board at the boarding and lodging houses has already been commented upon. The noteworthy fact made evident by these estimates—for they are only estimates—is the wide range of costs reported.

The percentage of illiteracy among the Japanese from whom data were obtained is small. Of 141 males, 10 years of age or over, all but 4, and of 48 females, all but 3, could read and write some language. (General Table 37.) Moreover, most of the males have a good command of the English language. Of 143, 6 years of age or over, 140 can speak, and of 141, 10 years of age or over, 95 can read and write, our language. Of 52 females 6 years of age or over, on the other hand, only 33 can speak English, and of 48, 10 years of age or over, only 8 can read and write. (General Tables 34 and 40.) The contrast between the sexes in this regard is partly explained by the difference in length of residence in this country. Thirty-four of 52 females had immigrated within five years, while of 143 males all but 34 had been in this country five years or more. (General Table 33.)

It is explained in part, also, by the fact that some of the men have been members of the " student class " and have learned English in schools in this country, while few or none of the Japanese women have had these advantages.   Finally, it is explained in part, also, by the greater contact the Japanese men have had with English-speaking people.   Few of the Japanese-American children have reached school age, and there are comparatively few Japanese children between 6 and 15 years of age in Los Angeles.   Indeed, most of the Japanese children born abroad have been left there until they have received their schooling.   Of 63 children of 33 fathers, 31 were in Japan, and 32, of whom approximately 25 were born in Hawaii or in the continental United States, were in this country. Eighteen of the 31 were with their mothers in Japan, 13 with other relatives, while they were being educated.   In spite of the fact that one-fourth of the families investigated where the marriage had taken place at least three years previous, were without children, and that most of those born abroad have been left there to be educated, 128 pupils of Japanese nativity were in attendance at the Los Angeles public schools in February, 1908.   The majority of these were over 15 years of age, a large percentage of them being young men of the " student class."

The various missions and religious organizations conduct schools for the instruction of Japanese classes.   The Buddhist Mission conducts a school for teaching children the Japanese language and history and has from 20 to 30 pupils each year.   There are seven schools for teaching English to adults.   These schools have from 20 to 50 pupils each.   Besides these classes conducted by missions, there are several instructors, both Americans and Japanese, who are giving private lessons in English.   This is one indication of the strong desire shown by adult Japanese to gain a knowledge of our language. Closely connected with the use of English is the matter of newspapers taken by the Japanese groups.   These also reflect the interests and indicate the standard of culture of the Japanese people.   Of 80 households reporting data, 4 were without newspapers or periodicals of any kind, while the other 76 had from one to nine each. Only 24 of these had any newspaper printed in English, 17 having one, and 7 two each.   Several of the households had newspapers and periodicals printed in their native language and published in San Francisco or Japan, as well as some or all of those published by Japanese in Los Angeles.

Few Japanese frequent the churches attended by the members of the other races living in Los Angeles.   They have seven missions and religious organizations of their own.   The Methodist Mission was established in 1896.   It has a membership of about 100, most of whom are young men of the " student class."   This mission now owns the building occupied by it.   It has a lodging department which can accommodate 25 persons.   The mission is provided with a dining room, a library, and an employment bureau.   As already indicated, a school to teach English is run in connection with it.

The Presbyterian Mission organized in 1902 is doing a similar work, and now has a membership of 114.   There are also three other smaller missions conducted by the various Christian organizations. More important than any of these, however, is the Buddhist Mission, which was organized in 1904 and which now has a membership of about 500. In general, its lines of work are the same as those of the Methodist Mission, as indicated above. Of the 110 men from whom data were obtained, 17 were members of the Buddhist Mission, 4 of the Congregational Mission, 2 of the Presbyterian Mission, and 1 of the Methodist Mission, a total of 24.

The Japanese also have various other organizations, but do not have membership in American societies. Most important among these organizations is the Japanese Association, which was organized in 1893 and has members in the rural sections of Los Angeles as well as in the city. Its membership now numbers about 500, of whom are 64 of the 100 business men and 2 of the 40 wage-earners investigated. Its objects are the same as those of similar organizations in other localities. There are 12 "prefectural societies." These supplement the work of the Japanese Association in various ways. Their primary function, however, is to render personal aid to members who may fall ill, meet with accident, or become incapacitated for work. Monthly dues, varying from 50 cents to $1, are collected to defray the expenses involved in maintaining their objects, and additional contributions are solicited in case of an emergency. In this way the Japanese who are unfortunate are cared for and not permitted to become public charges, and these organizations also create centers for Japanese social life.

Besides two Japanese student clubs and a ladies' temperance society there is a Japanese business men's association. According to the constitution of this association its "objects are to protect the mutual interests of the Japanese business men of Los Angeles, to uphold a high moral standard, and to promote an intimate association among its members." Sixty-six, or approximately two-thirds, of the business men from whom data were obtained had membership in it. Though the degree of assimilation found among the Japanese is greater than that found among the Mexicans, the Molekane-Russians, and a few of the less numerous races who have immigrated in recent years and settled in Los Angeles, it is evident from what has been stated above that the process of assimilation has not proceeded far, save in the learning of English and in the adoption of American clothes and some American business methods. The Japanese colonize and, except as domestics, do not live with white people. They are, as a rule, not given personal service in American shops. Save for an occasional business man who has membership in a general business organization, they do not have membership in American societies. On the contrary, they have their own organizations of various kinds, including religious institutions. Though various Christian organizations are represented among them, the majority adhere to the Buddhist faith. Though some of them subscribe for newspapers printed in English and reflecting American ideals and ideas, the majority, because of inability to read English, or because of their interests and sympathies, limit their reading to newspapers and periodicals published here or abroad in the Japanese language and reflecting the Japanese ideals and point of view. The associations between the Japanese and white races are limited, and, with few exceptions, not upon the basis of equality.

CHAPTER IV

JAPANESE IN CITY TRADES AND EMPLOYMENTS IN SACRAMENTO.

[For General Tables, see pp. 372–382.]

INTRODUCTION.

Because of its location in the Sacramento Valley the city of Sacramento has for twenty years been an important distributing point for Japanese laborers. Electric and steam railroads run to Oroville, Marysville, Newcastle, Woodland, and Vacaville to the east, north, and northwest of Sacramento, and down the valley to Stockton, Fresno, and other places. Boats on the Sacramento River carry laborers to various places as far down as Antioch and to the islands of the San Joaquin. The larger part of the land in all the communities about the localities mentioned and along the American River is devoted to producing deciduous and citrus fruits, berries, grapes, vegetables, sugar beets, and hops. The production of all of these involves much hand labor, and for ten years or more the Japanese engaged in work of this kind have been more numerous throughout this large district than all other races combined. Many of the laborers during periods of interruption in work spend their time in Sacramento. To supply their own needs while in the city and to supply provisions and Japanese goods to those working not far away many Japanese have engaged in business in Sacramento. At the same time others have engaged in businesses designed to secure the patronage of other races, while still others have found employment in the houses of and in establishments conducted by white persons.

The Japanese population of Sacramento is estimated to have been 12 in 1883 and 100 in 1893. According to the census it was 337 in 1900.[a] In June, 1909, it was estimated at 1,000. About 700 of these Japanese were connected with business enterprises and professions or were unoccupied members of the families of persons thus gainfully employed. Some 300 were employed as porters in saloons, clubs, and other places conducted by white persons, as domestics, or as general " help " in the city. The 1,000 just mentioned is the estimated number of the Japanese " settled " or regularly residing there. The " floating population " varies in number. The minimum number might be placed at 200 and the maximum at 2,500, the latter being the figure during the last two weeks of August, when the Japanese gather in Sacramento on their way to the hop fields near by.

When the transient Japanese laborers came to Sacramento in considerable number toward the end of the decade 1880–1890 they found no welcome in white boarding houses, and the accommodations available in the lodging houses conducted by Chinese were not regarded as suitable. Consequently there was great need for Japanese boarding

---

[a] U. S. Census, 1900, " Population," pt. 1, p. 802..

and lodging houses. A lodging house and two hotels were opened in 1891. Several others were soon established, four or more being opened in 1895 and 1896. The first provision store to supply Japanese with Japanese goods was opened in 1893. Another was started in 1894, and the number increased until it had reached 12 in 1909. The first restaurant serving American and Japanese meals was opened in 1893, and the first Japanese barber shop began business in the same year. The first bathhouse had been established two years earlier.

As the number of transient Japanese became larger the number engaged in these branches of business increased and many new branches were engaged in. Some of the establishments have been designed to serve the wants of persons other than Japanese. The number and kinds of business conducted by the members of this race in Sacramento are shown by the following table based upon an enumeration made in June, 1909, by Japanese and white agents employed by the commission.

TABLE 4.—*Business conducted by Japanese in Sacramento, Cal., June, 1909.*

Kind of business.	Number of establishments.	Kind of business.	Number of establishments.
(a) STORES AND SHOPS.		(b) PERSONAL AND DOMESTIC SERVICE—continued.	
Fish and vegetable markets	3	House cleaning	4
Groceries and general stores	12		
Gents' furnishing stores	9	(c) AMUSEMENTS.	
Shoe store	1		
Tailor shops	4	Moving-picture show	1
Confectioners' shops	4	Pool rooms	a 15
Jewelry and watch repairing	4		
Curio	1	(d) OTHER.	
Books and stationery	2		
Cigar stand	1	Banks	1
Drug stores	2	Bicycle shop	1
Dry goods	1	Employment and real-estate agencies	4
		Express	6
(b) PERSONAL AND DOMESTIC SERVICE.		Photograph galleries	3
		Printing shops	2
Boarding and lodging houses	37	Shoe-repairing shops	2
Restaurants (Japanese meals)	28	Tofu manufacturers	3
Restaurants (American meals)	8	Miscellaneous	12
Barber shops	a 26		
Baths	a 7	Total	b 207
Laundries	6		

a Some of the barber shops, baths, and pool rooms are conducted in the same establishment.
b Not including 1 artist, 9 carpenters, 5 interpreters, 5 physicians, and 2 dentists

The agents of the Commission investigated the general situation and collected details relating to the business carried on in 55 of these establishments conducted by Japanese and 23 conducted by other races in the same districts and in those branches of business enterprise where the competition between the Japanese and others was said to be of consequence. Detailed data were obtained from the following Japanese establishments: Seven boarding and lodging houses, 7 restaurants, 4 barber shops, 2 pool rooms, 2 tailor shops, 2 photograph galleries, 5 grocery stores, 4 labor and real-estate agencies, 2 men's furnishing stores, 1 dry goods, 1 drug, 1 shoe, 1 general store, 1 jewelry, and 5 confectionery and tobacco stores, 2 laundries, and from 8 other establishments indicated by tables printed in the appendix. Similar data were obtained from the following establishments conducted by members of other races: Four restaurants, 6 barber shops, 3 grocery stores, 2 groceries and saloons, 2 tailor shops, 1 men's furnishing store, and 5 laundries. The data relating to the date of establishing each place, the amount of capital employed, the amount of the capital borrowed, the value of annual transactions, the number of employees, the rent per year paid, the net profit realized, and the races of patrons are presented in tabular form in the appendix. Personal data were secured from the Japanese conducting the 55 establishments and other members of their households. The data are presented in a later part of this report, while the tables are printed in the appendix. With few exceptions—these being some of the shoe-repair shops, barber shops, laundries, and furnishing stores—the Japanese places of business are in the " Japanese quarter." This occupies both sides of L and M streets, between Second and Fourth, and the intersecting streets. Within a space of some 5 or 6 blocks most of the Japanese live and carry on the greater part of the business in which they engage. It is evident that they are closely colonized.

DATA RELATING TO JAPANESE BUSINESS.

Barber shops.—The Japanese barber shops number 26. With few exceptions they are small, having one or two chairs and are conducted by the proprietor, and possibly his wife or an apprentice, and infrequently a barber working for wages. Formerly all of the Japanese shops were located in the " Japanese quarter," but in recent years there has been competition for the patronage of persons other than the Japanese, and several shops have been established in another section of the city. Of those located outside the " Japanese quarter," there are now 10. These are in the oldest part of the business section and compete with shops conducted by Americans, Greeks, Italians, and Negroes. Fifty to 80 per cent of the patrons of the Japanese shops located there are members of the white race, Greeks and Italians being prominent among them.

Until recently the Japanese barbers charged 20 cents for hair cutting and 10 cents for shaving, but in July, 1909, the union scale was changed to 25 cents for hair cutting. All of the Japanese barbers belong to this Japanese organization. Most of the Greek, Italian, Negro, and some of the American shops charge the same prices as those recently established by the Japanese union. Some shops, conducted almost entirely by Americans, which are not far away, charge 15 cents for shaving. Though it is evident that there is little difference in the charges for the services rendered, the white barbers of this locality complain bitterly of Japanese competition—not underbidding through low prices, but an increase in the number of shops due to the incoming of the Japanese. One American proprietor whose barbers are employed on a commission basis (usually the barbers receive 60 per cent of the receipts, with a minimum wage of $14 per week guaranteed and a maximum fixed at $22) states that his four barbers earn on the average $5 less per week than before the Japanese shops were established. The shop in question was well equipped, well lighted, and clean, but 15 cents was charged for shaving.

It is interesting to note in this connection, however, that most of the shops conducted by white men have been established in recent years and while the Japanese shops were in process of becoming more numerous. Moreover, the majority of them are being conducted with profit. In the " Japanese quarter," which is not extensively frequented by other races, the Japanese shops in no case draw more than 30 per cent of their customers from among the members of the white races. The profits of the four Japanese shops, from whose proprietors detailed information was obtained, were $540, $600, $700, and $720. Only one of these had more than one " chair," and in that case the only employee was an apprentice working for his board and lodging. (See General Table 44.)[a]

Baths.—The seven baths are conducted in conrection with barber shops and pool rooms. They are patronized by Japanese only, for they are of the foreign type, i. e., with large tubs in which several people bathe before the water is changed.

Laundries.—Of the six Japanese laundries, four are " hand " and two are small " steam " laundries. The hand laundries have few while the largest of the steam laundries has but 9 employees. The smaller establishments are patronized by Japanese almost exclusively, while the larger are patronized chiefly by white persons. Eighty per cent of the patrons of the largest laundry are whites, 20 per cent Japanese. Though there are 20 Chinese " hand laundries " in addition to those conducted by the Japanese in the city, there has been little complaint of oriental competition. That the business of both Chinese and Japanese laundries is comparatively small is shown by the fact that five white steam laundries investigated had 227 employees. Moreover, the Japanese laundries with white patrons have practically the same list of prices as the steam laundries conducted by Americans and Italians investigated by the agent of the Commission. A comparison of the " lists " obtained shows as many instances in which the prices charged by the Japanese exceed those charged by the other laundries as the reverse. There is little or no underbidding by the Japanese in the laundry business.

Restaurants.—Of the 36 restaurants, 28 are located in the Japanese quarter, serve Japanese meals, and are patronized almost exclusively by members of that race. Seven of these 28 are licensed to sell intoxicating drinks. Most of the restaurants serving American meals are located in the Japanese district and have Japanese and white laborers as their patrons. Of the few located elsewhere, two have white patrons almost exclusively, these being largely of the laboring classes. The price of meals is 10 or 15 cents. The establishments are of the same general character as those conducted by Greeks, Italians, and Slavs in the same localities, and there is no material difference in the prices of meals served. The Chinese restaurateurs are more serious competitors than the Japanese. They conduct four large restaurants in the poorer quarters of the city, charge comparatively low prices, and have many patrons belonging to all races.

---

a See discussion of organizations, pp. 259 and 260.

The wages paid to cooks, waiters, waitresses, and dishwashers in the Japanese restaurants were found to be somewhat less than those paid in an American, a German, a Danish, and a Slovenian restaurant of the same general type and located in the same sections. Of five Japanese cooks, one was paid $50, one $45, two $40, and one $25 per month. Of four cooks employed in the white restaurants, one was paid $80, two $60, and one $40, while a second cook was paid $25 per month. The Japanese waiters were paid $30, eleven waitresses $25, two $20, and one $18 per month. Of the waiters in the other restaurants, four received $40 and one $32 per month. The dishwashers and kitchen help in the Japanese restaurants investigated were paid $20 per month; in the other restaurants $8 per week or $25 per month. All received board, and the Japanese, except in one case, received lodging in addition to wages. From a comparison of the data presented in the appendix it would appear that the rate of profit on the business transacted is larger in the Japanese restaurants than in the others and that the former are making larger net annual profits.

Hotels and lodging houses.—The keeping of hotels and lodging houses was the first branch of business engaged in by the Japanese in Sacramento, and these are now the most numerous of all the establishments conducted by members of that race in the city. They are located in the Japanese colony and have only Japanese lodgers and boarders. Some of the houses occupied are cottages, while others are two or three story buildings. Almost without exception the buildings are painted and in good repair and the premises are well kept. With very few exceptions the rooms are well furnished, having good beds and clean bedding, including pillow slips, counterpanes, etc., carpets or matting, and other furnishings of good quality. Both the exteriors and interiors of these places are superior in appearance to those conducted by orientals and most other foreign races in other cities investigated. The price of lodging is from 10 cents to 50 cents per night and from $5 to $15 per month. Some of these houses provide meals as well as lodging, the price per meal being 10 or 15 cents, but most frequently the latter sum. The lodging houses, considering the fact that most of the patrons are transient laborers, are orderly and well conducted. A boarding and lodging house keepers' association was established in 1901. Until 1907 all of the proprietors had membership in it. It was reorganized in that year and now has only 17 members of 37 who were eligible. The written agreement among the proprietors effected through this association provides, among other things, that all accounts must be collected in cash; that the association shall deal severely with all irresponsible patrons, and shall publish the names of patrons who have been guilty of dishonesty or misconduct; that each proprietor shall see that there is no disturbance after 11 p. m., and that patrons have returned to the house by that time. To prevent undue competition the association has also regulated prices.

Tailor shops.—The six Japanese tailor shops are all small, and most of them do little more than clean, dye, and press clothes. The price charged for pressing men's suits is 75 cents, which is the customary rate in the part of the city in which these shops are located.

The majority of their patrons are Japanese, though 50 per cent of the patrons of one of the shops are white. A large percentage of the Japanese purchase tailor-made suits. Until comparatively recent years these were made at white shops. Doubtless the majority are still made by white tailors, but some of this trade has been lost to the rival Japanese shops. Only one tailor (near two Japanese shops) was found, however, who had had so large a percentage of Japanese among his patrons that the partial withdrawal of that patronage had caused him serious loss. Where he had previously made four or five suits of clothes per week for men of that race, he now makes but one or two per month.

Men's furnishing stores.—Within the past few years the Japanese have engaged also in the men's furnishing business. At present there are nine establishments. These all carry small stocks of goods, chiefly of "American," i. e., non-Japanese, origin. The capital employed is in no case in excess of $5,000 and the annual transactions of the largest of the nine amount to only $8,000. With one exception, they are located in the Japanese quarter and have only a small percentage of white patrons. Seventy per cent of the patrons of the one store located outside of the Japanese quarter are white persons; their purchases aggregate between $5,500 and $6,000 per year. On the whole, however, the trade of the white persons at these stores is not of great importance. On the other hand, the partial withdrawal of Japanese trade from stores conducted by white persons has seriously affected the business of a few located within two or three blocks of the Japanese colony. The Japanese usually purchase American articles of dress which are of good quality, and before they engaged in this line of business their purchases at some of the American stores were an important factor in the business transacted. With the establishment of stores by their countrymen, however, the larger part of their patronage has been transferred to them. The proprietor of an American shop states that this has reduced the amount of his business by one-half. Others have been less seriously affected.

Grocery stores.—The most important branch of retail trade engaged in by the Japanese in Sacramento is the sale of groceries and supplies. The first store of this kind was established as early as 1893. The number has gradually increased, until it is now 12. These are all located in the Japanese quarter. Some of them are very small, while two are large, as compared with groceries conducted by other races. The smallest has a stock of goods valued at $1,000, and its annual transactions amount to $1,700. The largest, conducted by a corporation, has a stock valued at $60,000, and its annual transactions aggregate $120,000. Five of the 12 stores were investigated. All carried stocks of American as well as of Japanese goods, the percentage of the latter varying from 50 to 70. All have both white and Japanese customers. Many of the latter are farmers and laborers about Newcastle, Florin, the several towns along the Sacramento River, and elsewhere. This trade is an important part of the whole, for the " bosses " buy supplies in large quantities for the men who work under their control. Among the city customers, however, are many white people who buy at the Japanese stores because they sell some of their goods at lower prices than do their white competitors.

The situation is very well indicated for the five stores from which detailed data were secured by the following table:

TABLE 5.—*Data for five grocery stores conducted by Japanese in Sacramento, Cal., June, 1909.*

Value o annual transactions.	Per cent of—					
	Japanese customers.	White customers.	Japanese goods in stock.	"American" goods in stock.	Purchases by Japanese.	Purchases by white persons.
$1,700	40.0	60.0	50.0	50.0	60.0	40.0
$5,000	70.0	30.0	70.0	30.0	70.0	30.0
$4,000	50.0	50.0	50.0	50.0	80.0	20.0
$120,000	30.0	70.0	70.0	30.0	70.0	30.0
$10,000	70.0	30.0	70.0	30 0	85.0	15.0

An agent of the Commission secured data also from 5 grocery stores conducted by white men, 1 in and the other 4 within a block of the "Japanese quarter." Two of these were conducted by native Americans, 1 by a German, 1 by a French-Swiss, and 1 by a Greek. All were comparatively small stores, the stock of the Greek being valued at $300 or $400, the largest stock of the other 4 at $6,500. Their annual transactions varied from $1,500 to $20,000. Japanese were reported as purchasing at only 1 of these—the 1 in the midst of the Japanese colony—and in that case infrequently. All of the proprietors complain of Japanese competition. The stores conducted by that race, it is conceded by purchasers as by all others, sell at lower prices, but how much the average difference in prices is it is impossible to estimate, because of the difference in brands of goods and of the numerousness of the articles carried in stock. The chief disadvantage under which the white grocers were found to labor was, however, that their business is almost entirely local in character, and with the influx of the Japanese most of the white people have moved elsewhere. Two of these grocers had been engaged in business many years and since becoming established in their present locations the character of the population had almost completely changed.

The Japanese stores investigated employed 10 persons, while those conducted by members of other races had 15 persons engaged as clerks and drivers, the latter also serving as clerks when not delivering goods to the houses of purchasers. In comparing wages, the fact that all of the Japanese employees receive board and lodging in addition to wages, while the others do not, must be taken into consideration. Of the 10 male Japanese employees, 2 were paid $40 per month, 2 $35, while the remaining 6 earned between $30 and $25. Of the 13 males employed by the proprietors of the "white stores," none received less than $50. The 2 women employed were paid $52 and $40 per month, respectively.

Other stores.—The Japanese, as is indicated by Table 4, page 250, have a variety of other stores and shops, including 1 dry goods, 2 drug, 4 jewelry and watch repairing, 1 curio, 2 books and stationery, and 1 shoe store, 3 fish markets (1 dealing in vegetables also), 1 cigar and 4 confection " stands." All of those investigated had been established since 1904 and most of them in 1907 or 1908. They are all small shops, are located in the "Japanese quarter," and are patronized chiefly by members of the Japanese colony. The establishments for which data are presented in the tables in the appendix are typical of the larger numbers—a fish market with a capital of $1,400 and two-thirds of its patrons Japanese; a confectionery shop, capital $1,300, 80 per cent of its patrons Japanese; a cigar stand, capital $300, 60 per cent of its patrons Japanese; a dry goods store, capital $4,000, 80 per cent of its patrons Japanese; a shoe store, capital $1,500, 70 per cent of its patrons Japanese; a drug store, capital $500, 100 per cent of its patrons Japanese; and a watch and jewelry store, capital $2,400, 50 per cent of its patrons Japanese. Besides the shoe store, in which repairing is also done, there are two cobblers' shops. These are located outside of the "Japanese quarter," charge lower prices than the cobblers of other races, and have a large patronage, drawn almost entirely from white persons.

Employment and real estate agencies.—The employment agencies are connected with stores or, more frequently, with a real estate brokerage business. The employment agents provide Japanese laborers for all kinds of work. The commissions ordinarily collected from those who obtain employment through them are 10 per cent of the first month's wages of domestics, 5 per cent of the first month's wages of railroad laborers, and 50 cents each for farm hands.

The real estate agents serve as intermediaries between Japanese tenants and white real estate agents. The Japanese establishments frequently change location and new ones have been rapidly opened, so that there is much demand for the services of these men. The commission charged is 5 per cent of the consideration involved in the transaction.

Places of amusement.—The places of amusement conducted by Japanese are 1 moving-picture show and 15 pool rooms. The moving-picture show is of the usual American type, but frequently serves as a Japanese theater. A white woman is employed in the box office and about half of the patrons are white persons, chiefly those living in the poorer part of the city surrounding the Japanese colony. The pool rooms are patronized almost entirely by Japanese, though a few have white patrons, chiefly Italians and Greeks. No complaint of Japanese competition was found except that made by the proprietor of a Greek pool room located near several Japanese establishments. He had been compelled to reduce his to the more popular prices charged by his neighbors in order to retain his patronage.

Photograph galleries.—Of the 3 photograph galleries, 2 were investigated. Each of the proprietors had 1 assistant, and the annual transactions amounted to $3,000 in each case. Seventy per cent of the patrons of one and 25 per cent of those of the other were white persons.

Other branches of business.—The Japanese bank has only 6 or 7 white depositors, and these are Greeks. It finances Japanese enterprises and serves as a savings institution and as agent in sending money abroad. It was organized in 1906 and has a capital in excess of $65,000.

One newspaper is published and 2 job printing shops are conducted by Japanese. Their patronage, save some advertising matter, is almost entirely by the members of that race.

The 1 small bicycle shop is run in connection with a Japanese restaurant. Fifty per cent of its patrons are white.

The only other branches of business engaged in by the Japanese are the express business and carpentry and repair work. The first Japanese to engage in the former business began in 1901. There are now 6 Japanese express wagons. Five of the 6 expressmen belong to a union, which fixes the prices for hauling baggage. A schedule has been drawn up in which the prices vary with the character of the baggage and the distance it is hauled. The union also provides for the equal sharing among its members of baggage at the railway station and at the wharf.

There were 15 Japanese carpenters in Sacramento at the time of the investigation. Six of these resided there and were members of the Japanese Carpenters' Union, while 9 were transients, who were employed in Sacramento at that time. This Japanese Carpenters' Union was organized in October, 1908. Like the carpenters' union among the white men, it provides for an eight-hour day and prohibits work on Sundays and holidays. Wages are fixed at $3.50 or $4 per day, according to the efficiency of the individual members, but these standard rates are not closely observed. Most of the carpenters are independent workmen, who are employed almost exclusively in altering interiors of buildings rented by Japanese and in placing " fixtures " in business houses. Three, however, are employed by a Japanese " contractor and job carpenter," who reports that 40 per cent of his work is done for white people, 60 per cent for Japanese. The wages of these 3 employees for an eight-hour day are $2.70, $2.50, and $2.25, respectively.

Summary.—From the details presented it is evident that with the growth of the Japanese population the members of that race have engaged in many lines of business; that with the exception of 2 cobblers' shops, 1 " men's furnishing " store, 10 barber shops, and a few restaurants serving American meals, these establishments are located in the " Japanese quarter," and that many of them supply the needs of the Japanese population. It is found, however, that some of these establishments, and especially those located outside of the " Japanese quarter," have a large percentage of white persons among their patrons. The larger laundries, the restaurants serving American meals, the 2 cobbler shops, 10 barber shops, and 1 " men's furnishing " store have been established primarily to secure "American " patronage, while a large percentage of the establishments located in the Japanese quarter have many white persons among their customers. This is especially true of the grocery stores, some of which have large stocks of goods and do a substantial amount of business.

The instances of underbidding other dealers and tradesmen are not numerous, though several cases have been cited. But more important in its effects than the attracting of white patronage in some branches of trade has been the withdrawal of Japanese patronage from white shops when attractive shops conducted by their countrymen have been established, as they have been in several branches of business within the past five or six years. The withdrawal of Japanese patronage has seriously affected the profits of some white tradesmen. But more important in its effects has been the shifting of population with the influx of the Japanese and the expansion of their colony. It is evident that the Japanese are well provided for in most lines of business by tradesmen of their own race, and because of clannishness, inability to speak good English, convenience, and other reasons, trade very largely at Japanese stores. For the same reasons and because they are not welcome in barber shops, restaurants, and places of amusement of a good type conducted by white persons, they patronize Japanese barber shops, restaurants, and pool rooms. Under these circumstances the white men whose business establishments were located in or near the present " Japanese quarter " have lost a large share of their former patrons, as they have moved elsewhere with the influx of Japanese.

It is evident from what has been stated and from an examination of the data presented in the tables in the appendix that most of the stores, shops, and other business conducted by the Japanese are small. With the exception of two grocery and supply stores and a few restaurants the capital invested, the volume of transactions, and the number of employees are small. With the exceptions noted these places are in these respects like the establishments conducted by the various races in the poorer quarters of any typical American city. As a rule, however, the Japanese places are cleaner and more attractive than those conducted by the members of other races in the same localities. The tables presented in the appendix show also that much of the capital employed in business is borrowed. Taking 33 establishments where the capital employed was $1,000 or more, a part was found to be borrowed in 18 instances.

· *Labor employed.*—In the majority of cases the business of the Japanese is conducted by the individual proprietor, or the one or more proprietors, but with the assistance of wives in some cases. Persons were employed for wages in 25 of the 55 establishments at the time of the investigation, the total number of such employees being 72. With a single exception these were Japanese. As a general rule the system of " living in " prevailed, the proprietor providing board and lodging in addition to paying wages. Of the 71 Japanese employed, 54 were provided with board and lodging in addition to wages, 5 (restaurant employees) were boarded but not provided with lodging, 1 (a photographer's assistant) was provided with lodging only, while 11 were provided with neither board nor lodging. Seven of this last-mentioned group were employees of the bank and the contracting carpenter. The proprietor and his employees usually live in the rear or over the room used for business purposes. The agents of the Commission visited 19 of the apartments in which employees were provided with lodging. Eleven of them were well lighted, well furnished, well kept, and not crowded. In two other cases the same conditions regarding equipment prevailed, but the room was inadequate for the number living there. In the other six cases the lighting was bad, the ventilation poor, or the care of the apartment not good. On the whole, the lodging conditions found were fairly good considering that they represent the poorer section of a city.

Organization.—Japanese business men are highly organized. There are now seven local organizations, while the shoemakers belong to a general organization controlling Japanese cobblers in the various localities of California. The local organizations are the Boarding and Lodging House Keepers' Association, the Expressmen's Union, the Japansee Barbers' Union, two Japanese Restaurant Keepers' Associations, the Watchmakers Union, and the Carpenters' Union. All but the first two of these have been organized in recent years. The objects and the regulations of the Lodging House Keepers' Association, the Expressmen's Union, the Barbers' Union, and the Carpenters' Union have already been noted.

The members of the Barbers' Union pay 50 cents per month as dues. The organization is very strong and its work has many sides. It fixes the time for opening and closing shops and a scale of union prices. Violation of the regulations is punished by fine. Under the union's regulations the shops are closed on Sunday, as they are required to be by an ordinance of the city, are to be open from 7 a. m. to 12 noon on holidays and from 7 a. m. to 8 p. m. on regular week days. The union controls the matter of apprenticeship. During the first four months of his engagement the apprentice receives no wages and must provide his own board and lodging. During the next four months he is provided with board and lodging and may be paid not to exceed $10 per month. In the event that the apprentice leaves his master and starts an independent shop before the expiration of the term of his apprenticeship he must pay $40 to his former master. If a member of the union is obliged to return to Japan because of ill health, his fare is paid from the treasury of the organization. If any member is compelled to move his shop, the expense is paid by the union. If any member is sick for more than one month, each member of the union contributes $1 per month toward his support. If any member dies from sickness or accident, the organization sends his family a sum equivalent to the fare from San Francisco to Japan. In order that all shall be on the same basis the constitution of the union provides that a new member shall pay into the treasury a sum equal to the amount per capita then on hand.

The Japanese Restaurant Keepers' Union was organized in April, 1908, and reorganized in February, 1909. It now has 19 members. The dues are $1 per month. An effort is being made to induce each new establishment to join the organization, and when it does it must contribute a sum equal to the per capita amount then in the treasury. The organization fixes prices, forbids the sale of intoxicating drinks, and the serving of any save those provided by the patrons. Violation of a rule is punished by a fine of $10· Any member who retires from business is entitled to the redemption of his share in the union's fund.

There is a second Japanese restaurant keepers' union, having for its membership those restaurants which serve intoxicating liquors. It was organized July 1, 1908. It has seven members, which includes all who are eligible. The organization fixes the price of drinks of various kinds. It requires its members to take out the necessary license and to do a legal business, and if anyone fails to do this he is to be reported to the city authorities. The union compels its members to do business on a strictly cash basis. The dues are 50 cents per month. The union is to assist any member when assistance is needed.

This may extend to loans from the organization's treasury. Failure to obey any regulation or the commission of any act contrary to the interests of the union is punished by dishonorable expulsion from the union.

The Watchmakers' Union has an agreement written in English. It is as follows:

NOVEMBER, 1906.

(1) We, Japanese jewelers and watchmakers, who are carrying on our business in the city of Sacramento, State of California, hereby form a union in order to promote our welfare and credit in the eyes of our customers.

(2) We call this union the "Japanese Jewelers' and Watchmakers' Union of Sacramento."

(❸) We construct the regulations of the union by and with the mutual agreement of us all.

(4) We all swear that we will faithfully uphold and obey the regulations. In order to confirm our pledges, everyone of us deposit $50 in the lawful money of the United States of America.

(5) We agree and swear that if any of us either disobey or violate the regulations his $50 will be confiscated to the coffers of the union, and he will not complain of the loss, but will deposit another $50 in the same kind of money as above mentioned in order to retain membership in the union.

(6) The price of every sort of article sold at our shops will be fixed by us all according to the manufacturers' price, and everyone of us members of the union must sell the article for the fixed price. He must neither sell it higher nor lower than the fixed price.

(7) The charge for repairing watches and other articles will also be fixed by us all, and every member must charge for repairing the uniform rate, neither higher nor lower than the rate we have fixed.

(8) We all, being members of the Japanese Jewelers' and Watchmakers' Union of Sacramento, swear to conform to the regulations of the union, and in witness thereof we have hereunto set our hand and seal on this day of November, 1906.

This is signed by six members.

The Japanese and real estate values.—It has frequently been stated that the presence of Japanese in Sacramento has materially lowered the value of real estate in the section of the city occupied by them. It was found that because of the strong feeling against the Japanese, white people would not continue to occupy houses in blocks in which Japanese lived and pay the rentals they had been accustomed to pay. In fact most of the white people have moved from that section of the city as the Japanese have spread from street to street and from block to block. The movement has, however, been hastened by the fact that the Japanese have caused a rise of rents and market values of real estate in the blocks occupied by them. The assessed value of real estate in these blocks has steadily increased during the past five years. The Japanese usually conduct a business and live in the same structure and are willing to pay high rents for the property. One instance was noted where an apartment had been rented to a white family for $25 per month, but was then tenanted by Japanese who paid $60 per month for it. Another instance was noted where a man owned two cottages. He had lived in one and rented the other for $12 per month. The Japanese colony encroached upon the block in which his cottages were located, and he moved elsewhere, but each of the cottages was then rented to Japanese for $30 per month. In a third case an Italian barber had conducted a barber shop and lived with his family in a small apartment in a street outside of the Japanese quarter. He paid $15 per month rent. A Japanese barber desired to lease the premises, with the result that the rent was raised to $25 per month, but the Italian remained. Only a short time elapsed, however, until the rent was increased to $38 per month. The Italian could not pay this sum and vacated the property, which was then occupied by the Japanese at the rental just mentioned. These instances are rather extreme, but they are indicative of the facts as ascertained by the agents of the Commission, viz, that where there was a demand for property by Japanese, its rental and its market values were materially increased, but that property near the Japanese colony became less desirable and had less value until it was desired by Japanese tenants or purchasers.

PERSONAL DATA RELATING TO JAPANESE ENGAGED IN BUSINESS.

Personal data were obtained for 73 men conducting the 55 establishments investigated, also for 5 dependent males. Two-thirds of them had been in the United States less than ten years, one-third of them ten years or over. In greater detail, 19 had been in this country less than five years, 33 from five to nine years, 18 from ten to fourteen years, 7 from fifteen to nineteen years, and only 1 for twenty years or over. (General Table 25.) Of 75 reporting data, 12 had come from the Hawaiian Islands, where they had been employed as laborers on the sugar plantations, and 2 from Canada. Of the 61 who migrated to the United States directly from Japan, 24 had been engaged in business on their own accounts, 3 had been clerks in stores, 6 had been wage-earners in other city occupations, 2 had been farming on their own account, 13 had been working on farms for their fathers, 1 had been in other occupation, while 12 were young men with no occupation before migrating to the United States. (General Table 46.) It is evident that the majority of these men immigrated from the cities and that at least one-third of them had engaged in business in their native land on their own accounts. Yet, in spite of the large number who had been employed in Hawaii or had engaged in business in their native land before immigrating to the continental United States, all but 18 of the 75 were under 30 years of age at time of arrival. Ten were under 20, 33 between 20 and 25, and 14 between 25 and 30 years of age. (General Table 33.) With few exceptions, they came to this country to make money and brought little or no capital with them. Of 74 reporting the amount of money in their possession upon landing, only 1 had more than $1,000, 1 other more than $500, and 8 others more than $200. Thirty-three had $100 or more, 41, including 16 who had less than $50, less than that amount. (General Table 45.)

Of 74 whose first occupations in this country were ascertained, 2 engaged in business and 4 became farmers upon their own account immediately upon their arrival, while 68 became wage-earners. Twenty-seven of these became farm hands, 12 railroad laborers, 22 domestics, 3 assistants in stores, 1 a " helper " in a restaurant, and the remaining 3 wage-earners in other occupations. Thus it is seen that the vast majority became wage-earners in those occupations which were well organized and controlled by Japanese labor agents, and that the majority (39) found their first occupations in noncity employments. (General Table 46.) Most of them soon acquired sufficient English and accumulated enough capital to engage in business on their own account. In many cases they were aided by entering partnerships and by securing loans from personal friends and credit in various forms. Taking 57 from whom sufficient data were obtained relative to the length of time they had lived in this country before engaging in business on their own account, 6 began at once, 16 more after working for wages less than one year, 9 others after working for wages less than two years, 8 others after working for wages less than three years, 8 others after working for wages less than four years, and the remaining 10 after working for wages from four to ten years.

A comparison of occupations abroad and present business in the United States throws some light upon the matter in hand. Of 57 business men, 19 are found to be engaged in the same business as abroad or in a related business, 30 in entirely unrelated business, while 8 had had no occupation previous to coming to this country. Among 17 storekeepers, all but 4 are engaged in the same or in a business related to that engaged in abroad. Two tailors and 1 carpenter were engaged in the same trades abroad. So, too, was 1 of 4 labor agents. Practically all of the others are engaged in entirely unrelated business or had had no occupation before coming to this country. For example, of 7 restaurant keepers, 5 had been engaged in farm work, 1 had been an actor, and 1 a blacksmith abroad. A shoemaker had been a grocer, a watchmaker a farmer, a photographer a lumber dealer, a laundry proprietor a farmer. It is evident that the minority of the business men have soon engaged in business of the same type as that in which they had been trained abroad, while the majority availed themselves of the opportunities presented to engage in business in which they had had no previous experience.

The primary motive for immigrating to the United States has been to make money. How well these men have succeeded is shown by the property they have acquired. As already stated, many had only small sums of money upon their arrival. Three of 74 now have a net indebtedness outstanding against them. Of the other 71, 5 have property, after indebtedness is allowed for, worth between $100 and $250; 13, between $250 and $500; 13, between $500 and $1,000; 14, between $1,000 and $1,500; 12, between $1,500 and $2,500; 7, between $2,500 and $5,000; 4, between $5,000 and $10,000; 2, between $10,000 and $25,000; and 1, more than $25,000. Of the 25 who have been in the United States for ten years or over, 2 are in debt; 4 have between $250 and $500; 2, between $500 and $1,000; 4, between $1,000 and $1,500; 7, between $1,500 and $2,500; 2, between $2,500 and $5,000; 1, between $5,000 and $10,000; 2, between $10,000 and $25,000; and 1, more than $25,000. Of 49 who have been in this country less than ten years, 1 is in debt; 5 have between $100 and $250; 9, between $250 and $500; 11, between $500 and $1,000; 10, between $1,000 and $1,500; 5, between $1,500 and $2,500; 5, between $2,500 and $5,000; and 3, between $5,000 and $10,000. (General Table 47.) On the whole, these men have been successful, some of them very successful, in making money. Of course others, though not a large number, have been unsuccessful and have fallen back into the wage-earning class.

The gross value of property controlled by these 74 Japanese was $210,360; the indebtedness, $55,939; the net amount, $154,421; or an average of $2,086.77 per man. Thirty-eight, or slightly more than one-half of the total number, were in debt in sums varying from $50 to $9,000. (General Table 50.)

The profits realized in the 55 establishments investigated are shown in General Table 44. These have little significance, however, aside from the amount of capital invested and the amount of labor done by the proprietor or proprietors and others who do not receive wages. The annual incomes of the 63 men in business for the entire twelve months just preceding the time of the investigation, from the main or sole line of business engaged in, are shown in General Table 64. The average net income from this source was $1,124.13 for the twelve months. The extremes were $180 and $4,700. Of the 63, 7, or one-ninth, had net incomes of less than $500, 20, or almost one-third, between $500 and $750, 6 between $750 and $1,000, 16 between $1,000 and $1,500, 8 between $1,500 and $2,000, 4 between $2,000 and $2,500, and 2, $4,700 each. Of course the incomes derived from different branches of business differ greatly. The incomes of 5 proprietors of barber shops varied between $180 as a minimum and $720 as a maximum and averaged $492. Those of the proprietors of three small tailor shops varied between $700 and $1,000 and averaged $800. The minimum income of 8 boarding-house keepers was $600, the maximum $1,704, the average $937.50. The income of 7 restaurant proprietors varied between $240 and $1,800 and averaged $1,060. The corresponding figures for 16 storekeepers were $300, $4,700, and $1,553.75, respectively. The two laundry proprietors had net incomes from their laundry business of $1,200 each. The incomes of 5 real estate and labor agents varied between $700 and $1,200 and averaged $1,020. Though some of these incomes are comparatively small, as a whole they are in strong contrast to the incomes which might be made by the Japanese as wage-earners in any occupations open to them in this country. As already stated, the net incomes shown in General Table 64 are those from the main or sole business conducted. Some of these men, however, have other lines of business, while others have other sources of income. Four were also engaged in subsidiary lines of business from which they earned $1,780, 2 received dividends on stocks amounting to $80, and 11 received $5,401 from real estate leased for business purposes but in part subleased to others. Moreover, the wives of 4 of these men had outside interests or employments from which they earned $1,258.

The surplus and deficit of 69 of these men for the year 1908, after living and incidental expenses incurred by them and their families in this country were met, are shown in General Table 48. Nine had neither surplus nor deficit for the year, 7 incurred a deficit, while 53 had a surplus. The amount of deficit varied from $20 to $500, aggregated $1,645, and averaged $236.29 per man. The surplus of 53 reporting the amounts varied from $50 to $3,000, aggregated $35,706, and averaged $673.70 per man. Of 60 reporting the amount of surplus or deficit for the year 43 had a surplus of $250 or more, 26 of these of $500 or more, 11 of $1,000 or more, and 2 of more than $2,500. (General Table 49.)

Twenty-nine of 77 business men sent money abroad during the year 1908. The total amount sent was $9,346, or an average of $322.28 for each man sending money to Japan. Of the total amount sent $1,580 was for safe-keeping or investment, the remainder for use by their families or relatives. As against this $9,346 sent abroad $27,120 was retained in the United States. Of this total $1,150 was invested by 3 men in farm land, $350 in city real estate, $1,735 was used to pay debts earlier incurred, $7,260 added by 11 to the capital employed in the business conducted, $11,380 was deposited in the bank, and $5,245 otherwise invested, loaned to friends, or in hand.

PERSONAL DATA RELATING TO EMPLOYEES OF JAPANESE BUSINESS MEN.

Data relating to the same points as covered by the investigation of business men were secured from only 25 of their employees. Though the number is too small for statistical purposes, some of the data are indicative of the differences and similarities between them and their employers.

As regards length of time in the United States, the employees have come more recently, as indicated by the fact that only 3 of them had been in the United States as long as ten years and none of them as long as fifteen years. (General Table 55.) They came from the same classes. Only 4 were 30 years of age or over, and only 7 others were 25 years of age or over at the time they arrived in the continental United States. Four came from Hawaii. Of the others, 3 had engaged in business on their own account, 6 had been working for their fathers on the farm, 3 had been wage-earners in city trades, 1 had been store help, while 7 had had no occupation in Japan. (General Table 46.) Only 3 had as much as $150 upon their arrival in the United States (General Table 45) and all became wage-earners in this country. Like the majority of the men engaged in business, the majority of them engaged in occupations controlled by Japanese labor agents. Eight were first employed as farm hands, 7 as domestics, and 4 as railroad laborers, while the remaining 6 found employment in other occupations. (General Table 46.)

The rates of wages in different occupations have been noted earlier in this report. The number of months employed and the earnings in 1908, without reference to the various occupations in which the men were engaged, are shown in General Table 65. All but one man had been employed at least ten months, and 18 had been employed twelve months during the year. The yearly earnings of 13, with board and lodging, varied from $250 to $1,800. The earnings of 12, without board, but usually with lodging, from $270 to $1,200. The median earnings for the two groups were $350 and $400, respectively. Of 23 reporting, 4 had neither surplus nor deficit for the year, while 19 had a surplus varying from $50 to $550. The average amount was $245.53, the median $250. (General Tables 48 and 49.) Both incomes and surplus are very much less than those reported for men engaged in business on their own accounts. In this fact is found one reason why many have been eager to engage in business for themselves. A larger percentage of the employees sent money abroad during the year, but in smaller sums, the total amount sent by 14 being $1,845, or an average of $131.78 each, as against $322.28 sent by proprietors.

Of this amount sent, $70 was deposited in banks, $200 invested in land, while the remainder was for the use of parents and other relatives. As against this, $3,260 was retained in the United States, $630 being loaned, $500 used for paying debts earlier incurred in business ventures, and the remainder—$2,130—deposited in the bank or in hand. A larger percentage of the gains were sent abroad by the employees than by their employers.

As would be expected, because of difference in economic status, incomes, and disposition of their gains, the employees have much less property than the business men as a class. The average amount of property of the business men, indebtedness deducted, was $2,086.77. Of the 25 employees, 4 had no property, 10 less than $250, 9 had $250 but less than $500, while 2 had $500 and $800, respectively. The average amount was $232. (General Tables 47 and 50.)

SOCIOLOGICAL DATA.

Personal data relating to 173 Japanese and Japanese-Americans and general data relating to Japanese social, educational, and religious institutions in Scramento were obtained.

Of the 173 persons, 25 were male wage-earners, 148 were business men and the members of their families in the United States. Of this latter number, 37 were children under 16 years of age. There were 36 females 16 years of age or over, 34 of whom were the wives of business men, one a widow, and one a single woman. There were 100 males 16 years of age or over, 75 of whom were members of the business class, 25 of the wage-earning class. Of the former, 42 were married, one widowed, and 32 single; of the latter, 4 were married and 21 single. Thirty-four of the wives of the business men lived with their husbands, two lived elsewhere in the United States, and six abroad. The four wives of wage-earners had all remained in their native land. (General Tables 51, 52, 53, and 54.) Of the 42 business men, 13 have married in the United States, 6 have returned to Japan and married there, while 21 [a] were married in Japan before migrating to the United States. Ten of the last-mentioned number brought their wives with them when they immigrated to this country, while the other wives residing in this country have joined their husbands more recently after they had become established in business and could make suitable provision for them. (General Table 53.)

As is indicated by the presence of six-sevenths of the wives of the Japanese business men, many of them expect to remain long, if not permanently, in the United States. Of the 75 from whom data were secured, 31 stated that they expect to reside here permanently, 30 that they expect sooner or later to return to their native land, while the remaining 14 are in doubt as to what they will eventually do. A much smaller percentage of the wage-earners—most of whom are younger, have been in this country for a shorter time and are unmarried—on the other hand, have decided to become permanent residents of the United States. Of the 25, 6 expect to do so, 15 to return to Japan, while 4 are in doubt. These answers of course are not

---

[a] Place of marriage of two whose wives are now in the United States was not ascertained.

to be accepted as having any degree of finality, but as merely indicating the probability of a large number permanently settling in this country.

Few of the Japanese families occupy houses or cottages used only as residences. The vast majority of the business men, their families and employees live in the structures used for business purposes. A much smaller number live at lodging houses. The character of the tenements occupied in connection with the business conducted and of the lodging houses has been discussed earlier in this report. Their method of living is in striking contrast to that of the natives and well-assimilated immigrants with families, but not unlike that of the Chinese, Greeks, and other foreign-born races who engage in trade or are single men and have not as yet been assimilated.

The cost of food and drink was ascertained for 52 Japanese groups, containing 92 members. Proprietors of restaurants, lodging houses, or other business in which the cost of food and drink either could not be easily segregated or estimated with a fair degree of accuracy, together with the members of their households, have been eliminated from the computation. The cost per person was estimated as less than $6 per month by 9, $6 but less than $7 by 11, $7 but less than $8 by 14, $8 but less than $9 by 9, $9 but less than $10 by 9, $10 but less than $12 by 17, $12 but less than $14 by 3, and $14 or over by 20. The average cost for the men, women, and children 2 years of age or over was $8.32 each.

All but 3 of the 76 business men, 31 of the 36 women who were members of their households, and all of the 25 wage-earners were literate. Thus 129, or 93 per cent, of the 137 Japanese immigrants from whom data were obtained were literate. (General Table 59.)

Seventy-five of 76 males (over 14 years of age) engaged in business can speak English. So can 23 of 25 persons employed by them from whom information was obtained. In many cases this knowledge of English has been gained by attending classes or mission night schools in this country. Several, however, have belonged to the "student class" and have acquired a knowledge of our language by attending other institutions of learning. Less than one-half of the women and foreign-born girls, on the other hand, can speak English. Of 24 who have been in this country less than five years, 11 speak English; of 12 who have been here from five to nine years, 6; of 2 who have been here ten years or over, neither speak English. This difference between the sexes is explained partly by the difference in the length of time they have resided in this country, but chiefly by the fact that the females have seldom been members of classes for the study of English and have not come into contact with persons of other races to the same extent as the members of the male sex. (General Tables 58 and 62.)

As would be expected, a very much smaller percentage of the Japanese read and write than speak English. Yet of 76 business men, 42 can both read and write the language. So can 14 of the 25 employees from whom data were secured. Thus of 101 Japanese men, 98 can speak and 56 can read and write English. The women again stand in contrast, for while 15 of 36 can speak only 3, or 1 in 12, can read and write the English language. (General Table 62.)

The families of Japanese investigated had few children of school age. (General Table 63.) Fifteen of the 47 [a] married men had no offspring. This large percentage of families without children is accounted for partly by the fact that a few of the marriages took place only a year or two ago, but chiefly by the fact that most of the Japanese in this country have not been leading a normal family life. Many of the husbands and wives have been separated for years, and a large percentage of the latter have been gainfully employed. The remaining 32 families had 70 offspring all told. Of these, 37 were in the United States, and of these all but 5 were native-born. Sixteen were in Japan with their mothers, 2 were married and abroad, while 13 had been left by their parents with relatives in Japan to be educated. Few of the Japanese bring their children with them to this country; the majority of their offspring born abroad are left with their grandparents or other relatives to receive their schooling before they leave their native land. The foreign-born and the native-born of school age and many of the older girls in this country, however, attend the public schools. The Japanese accept the educational opportunities offered and the children are regular in their attendance.

All of the public schools of Sacramento are freely open to Japanese children of school age. At the time of the agent's investigation, 64 Japanese all told were attending the different educational institutions of the city. Forty-six of these (34 males and 12 females, ranging from 7 to 13 years of age) were attending the Lincoln Primary School. Eight more were attending the Chinese department of the same school. These 8 were all males ranging from 16 to 22 years of age. Six males from 12 to 22 years of age were at the Harkness Grammar School, while 1 male of 17 was attending the Sacramento Grammar School. Two males aged 18 and 20, respectively, were attending the Sacramento High School. Finally, 1 male, 4 years of age, was attending the kindergarten at the Lincoln school mentioned above.

That nearly all of these students attend the Lincoln Primary School is explained by the fact that it is located very close to the " Japanese quarter," and that the Japanese maintain a supplementary school close to the Lincoln School—a school to which these Japanese pupils repair for further instruction at the close of the regular school day at 3 p. m. That only 2 Japanese are attending the Sacramento High School is due largely to the fact that those who attend high school usually go to some place near a university, and chiefly San Francisco. The Lincoln School maintains a Chinese department in which are found those students who attend school more or less irregularly or who are too old for the regular primary grades and those who do not have a sufficient knowledge of English to attend the regular grammar grades and the high school.

The Japanese supplementary school, referred to above, is conducted by the Buddhist Mission. It is supported by the mission board and the Buddhist churches in Japan. However, it is not intended to give religious instruction. These children are taught Japanese history and geography and to read and write the language of their parents.

Some of the children at the supplementary school are boarders, while others come from their homes in Sacramento. All of the

---

[a] Including 1 man whose wife had died.

children go to the public school during the regular hours and then the supplementary school from 3 to 5 p. m. Those who do not board pay 50 cents per month tuition, while the 27 who do board at the school pay this tuition fee and $7.50 per month for their maintenance. In connection with this school it is interesting to note that of the 27 boarding pupils, 16 were born in Hawaii and 11 in Japan. Moreover, the interest of the Japanese in the education of their children, especially in their native language and history, is indicated by the fact that 9 of these boarders are children of farmers leasing about Florin, Acampo, Isleton, Courtland, Wheatland, and Oak Park; one is the son of a Stockton grocer and another the son of a Marysville restaurant keeper. The remaining 16 are the children of scattered farm hands employed in various localities.

Something should be said, too, concerning the classes conducted for teaching English to adult males. There are four of these. They are conducted by the Buddhist Mission, the Episcopal Mission, the Methodist Mission, and the Independent Mission. These classes are for the teaching of English to adult males exclusively, and most of these men belong to the laboring classes. Some of the teachers are Americans, while some are Japanese. It was found necessary for them to work together in order to get good results. English is taught to these adults by instructing them in reading, grammar, composition, and conversation. Each of these evening schools has from 20 to 30 pupils during the winter sessions. At the time of the investigation the work had closed in all of the schools save that conducted by the Buddhist Mission.

Closely related to the matters just discussed is that of newspapers and periodicals taken by the Japanese. These are also indicative of the standard of living and culture and of the interests of the members of this race. Of 56 households from which data were obtained all but one subscribed for one or more publications. Six subscribed for 1 publication only, 7 for 2, 9 for 3, 17 for 4, 6 for 5, 5 for 6, 3 for 7, 1 for 9, and 1 for 10. Eighteen, or slightly less than one-third of the entire number, subscribed for publications in English, while all but one (exclusive of the one with no publication) had one or more publications in their native language. A large number of subscribers are found for the Japanese paper locally published and the four published in San Francisco, a small number for the local papers printed in English and magazines published in Japan, and a few for such weeklies as Collier's.

The Japanese investigated were found to have membership in a great variety of organizations—most of them exclusively Japanese in membership. Their trade organizations have already been discussed. They have four missions—the Buddhist, Methodist, the Christian, and the Independent. Thirty-five of 101 males were members of some one of these. Of the 35 all but 5 were Buddhists. Forty-nine of the 101 are members of the Japanese Association of America—most of them of the Sacramento branch. Twenty-six are members of prefectural societies. Eight of these were represented, which shows that these immigrants had come from many different provinces of Japan. Through the Japanese Association and the various prefectural societies the Japanese further the general interests of their

JAPANESE IN CITY EMPLOYMENTS AND BUSINESS IN WASHINGTON, WITH SPECIAL REFERENCE TO SEATTLE.

[For General Tables, see pp. 382 to 395.]

JAPANESE IN CITIES OTHER THAN SEATTLE.

To supply the needs of their countrymen, Japanese tradesmen, using the term in a broad sense, are found in all of the cities and towns in or near which Japanese find employment. In many of these places some Japanese conduct business for "white trade" as well, while others engage in domestic and personal service. First in point of development and importance are those in Seattle. Because of that fact an intensive study of the work and business of the Japanese was made in that city. Before presenting the results of the study, however, something should be said of these matters in cities of less importance.

Tacoma was formerly the headquarters for many railroad laborers and sawmill hands. The Japanese consulate was also located there from 1895 to 1899, when it was removed to Seattle. These facts caused Tacoma to be an important place from which Japanese goods were supplied to Japanese laborers who used imported goods almost exclusively. In that city many of the Japanese laborers were provided with shelter, food, and amusements while not at work on the railroads or elsewhere. Finally, the offices of a few professional men supplying the needs of Japanese were located there. It was not until recent years, however, that any special attention was given to the American trade. Nor has Japanese business of this kind, save that of the restaurants serving American meals, laundries, tailor shops, and barber shops, assumed much importance. The number of establishments conducted by Japanese in 1905 and 1909 are shown in the table below (Table 6). It has been impossible to get accurate figures for any earlier year.

TABLE 6.—*Number of establishments in Tacoma, Wash., conducted by Japanese in 1905–1909.*

Kinds of business.	Number.		Kinds of business.	Number.	
	1905.	1909.		1905.	1909.
Industrial companies	1	3	Laundries	3	6
Tailor shops	2	3	Bath houses	2	5
Photographers	None.	1	Barber shops	2	9
Expressmen	None.	3	Billiard halls	1	4
Japanese curio stores	3	5	Fruit, tobacco, and cigar stands	None.	3
Hotels and rooming houses	3	8	Employment offices	None.	1
Restaurants:					
Serving American meals	4	5			
Serving Japanese meals	2	7			

The 6 laundries do a general business for both the Japanese and white races and employ about 75 men. The 3 tailor shops, cleaning and repairing suits for the most part, employ 15. The 5 restaurants serving American meals employ 40 persons and are well patronized. The 9 barber shops have 20 chairs all told. The 5 curio stores have 20 employees. The other establishments are small and give employment to about 30 people.

The employment office supplies domestic servants chiefly, while one of the industrial companies has the contract for supplying laborers to the Milwaukee, St. Paul and Puget Sound Railway. Another is interested principally in arranging for the leasing of agricultural land to Japanese.

Some 150 Japanese are working in families and hotels as cooks and domestic servants. They constitute a very small percentage of the persons so employed.

There are two Japanese missions and the usual Japanese association. The purpose of the latter is to protect and promote the interests of the Japanese race. The association has about 80 members, most of whom are business men and farmers. Two Japanese physicians are practicing among their countrymen.

Spokane is the center of the labor market for most of that part of the State lying east of the Cascades. As would be expected under the circumstances, many employment agents, boarding houses, restaurants, and barber shops have been established to meet the needs of a large floating population of common laborers. The Italian shops seem to be in the majority, but there are many conducted by Greeks, Austrians, and Japanese. Those conducted by Japanese are as follows:

Restaurants serving American meals	11
Restaurants serving Japanese meals	4
Grocery stores, selling American goods chiefly	5
Barber shops, patronized largely by white persons	5
Hand laundries, patronized largely by white persons	3
Steam laundry, employing 12 men	1
Tailors, doing cleaning and pressing	2
Dry goods merchants, doing general business	3
Bazaars and curio shops, selling Japanese goods to white persons almost exclusively	2
Pool rooms, patronized by Japanese chiefly	2
Hotels and lodging houses for Japanese	7

With the exception of the curio and dry-goods shops, these establishments are located in a district of some 12 blocks given over to immigrant laborers of various races.

The small grocery stores, cheap restaurants, small barber shops, and little tailor shops compare favorably with those conducted by the immigrant white men, with whose shops they are interspersed. Their business is with the same class of people, most of them immigrant laborers. The prices charged are the same as those charged by their competitors in that section of the city.

A number of Japanese in Spokane are employed in domestic service and as porters and other help about the hotels, restaurants, saloons, and clubs. They have recently entered these lines of employment and are now only a small percentage of the total number of persons so engaged.

In Bellingham there are, besides 3 hotels for Japanese, a restaurant, 3 tailor shops, 3 laundries, 2 barber shops, and 2 stores which compete for "American trade." It is stated that the competition of the Japanese in and near " Old Town " (the poorer quarter) is strongly felt by white restaurant keepers, barbers, and cleaning and dyeing establishments. This is particularly true of the cleaning and dyeing trades, in which, by cutting prices, the Japanese have secured most of the trade. Many Japanese are employed as domestics and as porters and bell boys in hotels.

Of the smaller cities in the interior of the State, Wenatchee and North Yakima are the only ones in which any considerable number of Japanese are engaged in business or domestic and personal service. In the latter city there are, in addition to a hotel, a restaurant and a billiard parlor for Japanese patrons, a laundry and 3 restaurants for white people, but the competition of the restaurants alone has been seriously felt. About 30 Japanese are engaged in personal and domestic service. The situation is much the same at Wenatchee, where there are 2 Japanese restaurants serving American meals and 1 Japanese laundry.

THE JAPANESE IN SEATTLE—HISTORICAL.

In 1884 there were 4 or 5 Japanese in Seattle, all employed in restaurants or hotels. During the following year one opened a restaurant for American patronage. In 1886 another opened a lodging house, which was patronized mainly by white laborers. A year later 25 Japanese came from California, one of them opening a second restaurant. In 1888 more came from San Francisco, and the number of restaurants, all patronized by white laborers, increased to 4. A bathhouse, a laundry, and a small general store for the sale of Japanese wares were opened during the same year. At that time the Japanese population aggregated about 100.

By 1894 the number of Japanese had increased to about 400 and the number of places of business to 10. There were 6 restaurants serving American meals; 2 general stores selling Japanese goods to Japanese chiefly; 1 bamboo-furniture store; and 1 barber shop, bath, and laundry, the 3 combined under one management.

Shortly after this the Japanese population of the State increased rapidly as a result of the establishment of direct steamship connection between the Orient and Seattle, the discovery of gold in Alaska, and the employment of Japanese by the railroad companies. The increase in the number of Japanese in Seattle was equally rapid. The number reported by the census of 1900 was 2,990. During the same time the number of business places conducted by that race increased to about 50. Many of them—especially the employment offices, the lodging houses, some of the restaurants, and barber shops—were established to answer the needs of the large Japanese colony in the city. The number of places devoted to each kind of business conducted is shown in the accompanying table (Table 7), which indicates the various kinds of business engaged in by Japanese in 1888, 1894, 1900, 1905, and in the spring of 1909.

TABLE 7.—*Growth of Japanese business in Seattle, 1888 to 1909.*

Business.	1888.	1894.	1900.	1905.	1909.
Newspapers and periodicals				3	12
Banks				1	3
Employment offices			3	5	17
Hotel and rooming houses			8	42	72
Crockery and curio stores			8	6	12
Grocery and provision stores	1	2		16	26
Watch and jewelry stores				4	7
Printing establishments				4	7
Tailor and dye shops			4	12	45
Shoe stores and shoe repairing shops				2	5
Restaurants, American meals	4	6	10	21	36
Restaurants, Japanese meals			3	22	51
Japanese cake stores				3	5
Liquor dealers				1	2
Fish dealers				2	5
Barber shops a		a 1	12	35	64
Baths a	1	a 1		16	26
Laundries a	1	a 1	1	20	37
Express			1	4	10
Book and drug stores					4
Billiard and pool halls a					25
Furniture stores		1			
Photographers				2	5
Miscellaneous				12	20
Total	7	12	50	233	496

a Barber shops, baths, laundries, and billiard and pool halls are frequently under one management. The number of places of business is therefore somewhat smaller than the totals given.

The increase of the Japanese population (and of the total) since 1900 has been very great, and the increase of business done by them still greater. From 2,990 Japanese returned for Seattle by the census for 1900, the number of that race residing in Seattle all or most of the year had increased to about 4,500 in 1908. The number of places of business conducted by Japanese increased from 50 in 1900 to 233 in 1905 and to 496 in the spring of 1909. The number of places already conducting the kinds of business which had been engaged in greatly increased, while many new kinds were established. All of this is shown by the table presented above.

With the increasing Japanese population, many have found employment as domestics, store " help," restaurant " help," bell boys, and in other callings.

JAPANESE EMPLOYED BY WHITE PERSONS.

Altogether, more than 2,400 Japanese are more or less regularly employed by white people. Some 1,600 more are employed in the various business enterprises conducted by Japanese. Of professional men, and men, women, and children without occupation, there are in normal times perhaps some 500.

Taking up the first-mentioned class for discussion, the 2,400 are distributed as follows:

(1) Domestics in private families, about 1,200.
(2) Cooks and waiters on board ships, some 300.
(3) Restaurant and hotel "help" and bell boys in hotels and clubs, some 400.
(4) Attendants in barrooms, some 200.
(5) Porters and miscellaneous employees in white stores, at least 300.

A few are employed in other capacities, but they are not of so much importance as those specified.[a] Any persons so engaged should be added to the number reported above to get the approximate number of Japanese employed in Seattle by white persons.

Because of the nature of domestic service, it is difficult to ascertain very accurately the total number of persons so employed, the wages the different races have been paid, and the effect of such competition as may have existed between them. The Japanese have been employed as domestics for several years, at first at somewhat lower wages than are now paid. The work is shared by these Japanese men (few Japanese women being so employed) and white women, a large percentage of whom are Scandinavian immigrants or of Scandinavian extraction. The Japanese constitute a minority of the persons so employed,[b] and the wages they command are about the same as are paid to others of equal efficiency. The average wage of Japanese cooks is $35, of other domestics $27 or $28 per month, with board and lodging. Some 300 of the total of 1,200 Japanese in domestic service are " school boys "—young men who work a few hours per day for board and lodging and a little money (frequently $1.50 per week) while attending school.

About 300 hundred Japanese men who make their headquarters in Seattle are employed as cooks and waiters on ships on Puget Sound. The wages of stewards are from $70 to $90, of cooks from $50 to $75, of waiters from $25 to $50, and board.

According to the secretary of the Cooks and Waiters' Union of Seattle, the great majority of the kitchen employees in restaurants and hotels are now Japanese. The displacement has been fairly general, though by no means complete. From data collected from such of these employees as live in lodging houses it was found that their wages are usually $10, less frequently $11, $12, or $13 per week (of seven days), with board included. It is asserted that there is no longer any regular scale for white employees engaged in this line of work, but from the data collected the wages of this class are about the same as or a little higher than those paid to Japanese. The change of races is explained by the fact that reliable white persons have found it easy to secure more remunerative and agreeable employment, while the Japanese, being more regular in their work, more willing to work long hours, and more easily secured when needed, have been preferred by the employers to the less desirable class of white persons available.

Japanese have not been employed as cooks or waiters in the hotels and white restaurants. The one trade requires skill, the other a good knowledge of English, while both are well organized. The combined influence of these factors has sufficiently protected the white employees.

---

[a] Among these are some 10 Japanese women employed in an establishment devoted to the manufacture of cloth gloves.

[b] The Census for 1900, Occupations, pp. 732–733, reported 1,217 female servants and waitresses in Seattle. With the growth of population the number has increased several fold. Of the 1,217 reported, 408 were native-born of native parents, 290 were native-born of foreign-born parents, and 466 were foreign-born whites, chiefly Germans and Scandinavians.

Many of the hotels, however, employ Japanese bell boys. Perhaps Japanese working in this capacity are almost as numerous as the other classes taken collectively. Such employment is of comparatively recent date. In some instance negroes, in others—and more frequently—white boys, have been displaced. The displacement appears to have been due to difficulties met with in securing a reliable class of young men for such work, rather than to a desire to economize in wages. The Japanese are paid from $15 to $25 per month, and from "tips" they frequently receive as much as $30 more.

The Japanese have come to predominate also as "helpers" in barrooms, clubs, and other places where liquors are sold, and for reasons much the same as those which have led to their employment in domestic service. They serve as porters, cleaners, and waiters, and are paid $10, $12, or $14 per week—wages which are too small to attract reliable men of other races.

Japanese porters are very generally found in the larger stores in the better shopping district. At least 300 are now so employed. In most places they have been given employment in recent years, when with the growth of the city it has been difficult to secure responsible men to serve in such capacities at the wages which have been paid. It was both difficult to get and to keep good white employees for such work. The Japanese, on the other hand, were made available through the employment agencies and were less prone to change employers. Their wages vary from $9 to $14 and average between $11 and $12 per week.

These are the most important occupations in establishments conducted by white proprietors in which Japanese are engaged as wage-earners. Combining employers and employees, there are some 1,600 more engaged in business conducted by Japanese—some 150 in hotels and rooming houses, 110 in tailor shops, 143 in barber shops,.210 in restaurants serving American meals, 250 in restaurants serving Japanese meals, 200 in laundries, 80 in grocery and provision stores, 150 in Japanese curio and general stores, and some 310 in various other kinds of business. The classes so employed may be discussed in connection with the business they conduct.

THE JAPANESE DISTRICT IN SEATTLE.

Until about 1900 the Japanese colony in Seattle centered at King street and Second avenue, the older business portion of the city. More recently, as the colony has grown and its business expanded, the center has moved eastward, where rent is lower; at present it is at Seventh avenue and Main street. Few establishments are located west of Third avenue or east of Thirteenth avenue, while few are located north of Yesler way or south of Dearborn street. The boundaries thus indicated inclose about 50 blocks. Nearly 20 of these, however, are now unoccupied, because of the prosecution of extensive improvements involving the cutting down of the hills, while in the remaining 30 about two-thirds of the houses are occupied by white people, largely European immigrants of the newer type. There are no solidly built blocks, such are found in a "Chinatown," occupied by Japanese. But the boundaries set by the streets mentioned are somewhat arbitrary. Beyond them, however, there are few Japanese restaurants, lodging houses, tailor shops, and residences. In this district most of the Japanese immigrants live and have their places of business.

From the European immigrants living in the territory just indicated most of the white patrons of Japanese establishments are drawn. The more important exceptions are those who patronize laundries, these living in all parts of the city; those who patronize the restaurants near stores and industrial establishments, to which men come from different parts of the city to perform their labor; and those in search of " bargains " in clothing, curios, and other things.

Most of the streets of the district in which the Japanese live are either unpaved or poorly paved, and most of the sidewalks are of wood and in a bad state of repair. Most of the buildings are one, two, or three story frame structures in poor condition. Here the Japanese and a large proportion of the recent European immigrants, those from north Europe excepted, live—many of them in the rear of or over the offices or small stores they or others conduct.

Of the business indicated in Table 7, page 274, much is conducted for Japanese almost or quite exclusively. This is true of the publication of newspapers, the banking establishments, the employment agencies, the bookstores, and the restaurants serving Japanese meals. The same is true of some of the general stores, drug stores, groceries, liquor dealers, job-printing establishments, photograph galleries, and billiard parlors and pool rooms. To these the expressmen and lodging houses may be added, for most of their patrons are Japanese. On the other hand, the tailors, curio dealers, watchmakers, dyers, shoe repairers, fish markets, restaurants serving American meals, barber shops, and laundries have as their patrons a very large percentage of white people. The competition of the Japanese in several of these lines has been sufficient to give their white competitors serious concern.

LAUNDRIES.

Though the Japanese started a laundry in Seattle in 1888, only one was reported as being conducted by them in 1900. More recently many have been established. In 1905 there were 20; in 1909, 37. Six of these, representing the different types, and 4 white laundries were investigated in detail by an agent of the commission. The data relating to the amount of capital employed, the value of annual transactions, rent, and the race of patrons are presented in General Table 66, page 383.

Most of the white laundries in Seattle are large. They employ a great deal of capital and many laborers and have large gross earnings from the business transacted. Most of the Japanese laundries, on the other hand, are small. Of the 20 in existence in 1905, 13 were connected with Japanese bathhouses and washed few clothes other than those left by persons (chiefly Japanese) who take baths. Of the 37 now in existence, 21 are of the same kind, and the vast majority of their patrons are Japanese. Of the 16 laundries not connected with bathhouses, one employs more than 40 persons, two others about 30 each, and a fourth 15. The remaining 12 are for the most part " hand laundries," employing on the average 8 persons each. It is with these 16 laundries, some large, others small, that the white laundries compete. Only one of the white laundries investigated had Japanese and Chinese patrons, and these were few. Of the Japanese hand laundries investigated, 2 reported 90 per cent each, another 80 per cent of their patrons as being white people, the others Japanese and (in one case) Chinese. The percentages of the white patrons of the 3 Japanese steam laundries investigated were 65, 70, and 90, respectively.

Two of the Japanese laundries employ white collectors. In this way they doubtless secure some white patrons who do not know that the laundries are conducted by Asiatics. However, most of the patronage secured by the Japanese laundries is accounted for on economic grounds. Their prices are generally lower than those charged by their white competitors.

The vast majority of the Japanese proprietors are members of a union which they have organized. While the standard price charged by white laundries for laundering plain shirts is 12½ cents; washing undershirts and drawers, 12 cents each; handkerchiefs, 3 cents; and socks, 5 cents per pair; the Japanese union prices are 10, 7½, 2, and 3 cents, respectively. The one nonunion laundry investigated made some further reductions. Furthermore, the majority of the Japanese laundry slips employed carry the note, " Goods buttoned and mended free of charge." But on items other than those specified the prices charged are the same. Both white and Japanese laundries have the standard prices of 5 cents for cuffs per pair, 3 cents each for collars, and 10 cents for nightgowns.

They usually also have the same rates printed on laundry slips for various kinds of household linen. These rates have little significance, however, for most such work is done for hotels, restaurants, saloons, and barber shops, and, whether by white laundries or Japanese, is done at prices agreed upon between the parties concerned. It is in such work—" soft washing "—that the Japanese have been most successful in gaining business at the expense of their white competitors. One laundry firm states that of " 50 hotels and lodging houses on our books a few years ago we now have only 10; Japanese have the rest." The various Japanese proprietors state that they give from 10 to 30 per cent discount on " soft wash in bulk," discounts sufficient to more than offset those given by their rivals.

Besides the two white men employed as collectors, working on commission, five white women were found working in a Japanese laundry as ironers. This employment of white ironers is exceptional, however. The other employees were all Japanese, and chiefly men. The races employed by three of the four American laundries investigated are shown in the first of the two tables following. These give the rate of earnings of those employed in the establishments conducted by the two races.

TABLE 8.—*Number of employees in three American laundries in Seattle earning each specified amount per day, by sex and general nativity and race.*

MALE.

General nativity and race.	Number earning each specified amount per day without board or lodging.								Total.
	Under $1.10.	$1.10 and under $1.25.	$1.25 and under $1.40.	$1.40 and under $1.55.	$1.55 and under $1.70.	$1.70 and under $1.85.	$1.85 and under $2.	$2 or over.	
Native-born of native father, White	2			2				24	28
Foreign-born:									
Armenian			1						1
English								3	3
Flemish								1	1
Hebrew								2	2
Norwegian								1	1
Scandinavian								9	9
Swedish								1	1
Total	2		1	2				41	46

FEMALE.

General nativity and race.	Number earning each specified amount per day without board or lodging.								Total.
	Under $1.10.	$1.10 and under $1.25.	$1.25 and under $1.40.	$1.40 and under $1.55.	$1.55 and under $1.70.	$1.70 and under $1.85.	$1.85 and under $2.	$2 or over.	
Native-born of native father, White	8	9	22	25	14	5	2	14	99
Foreign-born:									
Armenian		1							1
Australian					1				1
Bulgarian			1						1
Canadian			1	1	2			2	6
Danish			1						1
Finnish					1				1
Flemish			1					1	2
French						1			1
German			1		1				2
Iceland			1						1
Irish	1	1			2				4
Italian			2						2
Norwegian		1	2	2	2	1			8
Swedish			1	2	1				4
Total	9	12	33	30	24	7	2	17	134
All employees	11	12	34	32	24	7	2	58	180

TABLE 9.—*Number of Japanese employees [a] in Japanese laundries in Seattle earning each specified amount per day, by sex.*

Sex.	Number earning each specified amount per day with board and lodging.								Total.
	Under $1.10.	$1.10 and under $1.25.	$1.25 and under $1.40.	$1.40 and under $1.55.	$1.55 and under $1.70.	$1.70 and under $1.85.	$1.85 and under $2.	$2 or over.	
Male	6	17	8	16	2	2	1		52
Female	7								7
Total	13	17	8	16	2	2	1		59

[a] The two native white men employed earned $2 or over per day, while one woman earned $1.25, three $1.50, and one $2 per day. They did not receive board or lodging.

The first of these tables shows that of 180 employees reported 127 were native whites. The only large element among the foreign-born consisted of Scandinavians, and numbered all told 24 persons. No Japanese were employed in laundries conducted by white proprietors. One hundred and thirty-four of the 180 were women, while 46 were men.

The white laundry proprietors do not provide their employees with board and lodging. Of 46 men, 41 earned $2 or over per day, 2 between $1.40 and $1.55, 1 between $1.25 and $1.40, 2 less than $1.10. Of the 134 women, only 17 earned more than $2 and only 26 more than $1.70 per day (54 from $1.40 to $1.70 per day). Fifty-four, or two-fifths of the total number, earned less than $1.40. In some laundries the employees worked fifty-five, in others sixty hours per week. The earnings given are, therefore, for approximately a nine or a ten hour day.

The Japanese laundry workers all received board and lodging in addition to wages. The system of "living in" obtains, the employees usually, but not always, living in the building housing the business. Of the Japanese males only three earned $1.70 or over per day, twenty-one $1.40 or over. The Japanese laundries run regularly sixty-six or sixty-nine hours per week. In other words, if overtime is excepted, they have an eleven or an eleven and one-half hour day.

The board and lodging provided the Japanese hands should be reckoned at a little less than 30 cents per day. A wage of $1.40 paid by the Japanese proprietor corresponds closely, therefore, to a wage of $1.70 paid by the white competitor. Reckoning thus, it is possible to compare the earnings of the two races. Comparing Japanese men and women and white men and women it is found that 64.4 per cent of the former and 62.8 per cent of the latter earned, in effect, less than $1.70 per day. Japanese men and women earning less than $1.40 do about the same work as the white women employed in white laundries. Their wages (per day) are not very different, but the wages per hour of the white women are considerably higher. It should be added, also, that the wages per day of Japanese in the higher occupations are less than those paid white men doing the same kind of work. The differences in wages per hour are still greater. It follows, therefore, that unless there is a considerable difference in the efficiency of the two races, the labor cost in the Japanese laundries is less than in the laundries conducted by their competitors.

According to the data given in General Table 66, both white and Japanese proprietors are making good profits. The rates of profit on the capital invested in three white laundries conducted by Americans were in 1908, 13.3, 12, and 30 per cent, those of the larger Japanese laundries, where the manual labor of the proprietor was not important, 20 and 16.8 per cent.

It is stated that an effort has been made by the "Anti-Jap Laundry League" of San Francisco to organize a similar institution in Seattle to prevent the further increase of Japanese laundries and to check the growth of their business, but no organization has as yet been effected. There is, however, a general feeling among laundry proprietors in favor of effecting such an organization if the number of Japanese laundries continues to increase.

TAILOR SHOPS.

The first tailor shop conducted by Japanese was started in 1894 or 1895. In 1900 there were 4; in 1905, 12; in 1909, 45. Most of them are small. Only 5 employ more than 5 tailors, and few have an invested capital of more than $1,000. Of the 45 about one-half do cleaning and pressing chiefly.

Seven of these 45 Japanese establishments and 5 conducted by white men in the same district were investigated in detail. Of the latter, one was conducted by a Scandinavian, three by Russian Hebrews, and one by a native American.

All of the establishments investigated did some tailoring, but most of them did repairing, cleaning, and pressing as their main business. One of the Japanese tailors also carried a stock of ready-made clothing.

The Japanese establishments had as their patrons a rather large percentage of white persons. The percentages of their patrons who were Japanese was 70 in the case of one small and one large shop, 60 in another case, 50 in another, 30 in the case of the largest shop, and 10 in two smaller shops. The competing white establishments were patronized by white persons only.

The net profits made by all but one of the establishments are shown in General Table 66. Those of the Japanese vary between $600 as a minimum and $1,440 as a maximum, and those of their competitors between $800 and $1,800. All were making fair profits considering the kind of business conducted. The table referred to above gives, in addition to the earnings reported, the capital invested in the business, the gross value of transactions, the rent paid per year, and various other items of importance in investigating a business. From these figures it would be possible to ascertain the relation between rent paid and the amount of business transacted and other facts about the concern. However, it is the opinion of the agent that so many of the figures are inaccurate that it is not safe to draw any definite conclusions from comparisons in which they are involved.

The 7 Japanese shops reported 23 persons working for wages. All of these save 2 were Japanese. The 5 white establishments reported 14 employees, each employing, as a rule, a majority of the same race as the head. Ten of the Japanese were employed by the month. Of 5 who received board and lodging in addition to wages, 3 were paid $20, a fourth $30, and the fifth $50 per month. Of 4 who received lodging only, 1 was paid $40 per month, the other 3, $50. Two who received neither board nor lodging were paid $35 per month. Some of them who did work other than repairing and pressing were paid by the piece and reported earnings as high as $75 per month. Practically all of the employees in the white shops were paid by the piece. None received board and lodging from the employer. Three reported piece earnings of $52, one of $61, one of $73, three of $78, and five of $87 per month. The one not employed on a piece basis was paid $75 per month. It is apparent that, reckoning the board and lodging provided for the Japanese at $10 per month, their earnings are smaller than those of the men employed in the white establishments. Yet, because of differences in the work done and in efficiency, no conclusions can be drawn with reference to the labor cost as an item of expense in the business. Unfortunately so few Japanese establishments employ tailors on a piece basis that a comparison of that kind could not be made.

As a result of the investigation made by an agent of the commission it was found that "high-class" and even "second-class" tailors are not affected by Japanese competition, but the third-rate shops, especially those which do cleaning and pressing, are quite seriously affected. The Japanese make suits for less money than white men, and their workmanship is often as good. The charge for pressing suits has been reduced from $1 to 50 cents on account of low Japanese prices, and for pressing trousers to 15 cents. Even at these rates the white establishments have lost a good deal of their trade to Japanese.

In connection with the class of business affected by Japanese competition it should be added that they have not been long engaged in American tailoring or working with cloths used in this country.

BARBER SHOPS.

The competition of Japanese barbers has been even more serious than in the branches of business just discussed.

The first of these barber shops was established in 1893. In 1900 there were 12; in 1905, 35; in 1909, 64. Most of them are carried on in connection with baths or pool rooms or laundries. Usually the capital employed is not in excess of $800. Frequently the barbers are only the proprietor and his wife, and of 64 shops only 4 have more than three or four "chairs." The total number of barbers is 143. The rent paid seldom exceeds $90 per month, and in one instance it is only $15. The fixtures are not expensive.

These small barber shops are competing with less numerous similar shops conducted by various races and with several larger ones, these usually being conducted by Americans. Of ten Japanese shops investigated, one reported that 70 per cent of their patrons were Japanese; two, 50 per cent; one, 40 per cent; one, 20 per cent; three, 10 per cent; and two not reporting. White persons (largely laborers) constitute perhaps two-thirds of their patrons. Their competition has been seriously felt—more so than in any other trade—for they have caused a reduction of prices as well as shared the trade with the white shops. As a result of the competition some of the white barbers on First Avenue South have been forced out of business.

The prices charged by Japanese barbers varied somewhat before 1902. They then organized a union and provided for uniform prices—15 cents for hair cutting and 10 cents for shaving. Two years later they were compelled to suspend business for a time because of the refusal of the state examiner to renew their licenses, on the ground that the shops were insanitary—as most of them, in fact, were. In 1907 they reorganized and fixed prices as follows: Hair cutting, 25 cents; shaving, 10 cents; neck shaving, 5 cents additional. These prices generally obtain at present, but in some cases white patrons are charged "15 cents straight" for a shave.

The large number of Japanese shops charging low prices forced the white barbers to lower the union scale. Until the competition of the Japanese was seriously felt, this scale was 35 cents for hair cutting and 15 cents for shaving, the standard prices on the Pacific coast. To meet the Japanese competition the prices were changed to 25 cents for hair cutting. The rate for shaving remained the same, but most of the " downtown shops," in order to meet the Japanese competition, reduced the charge to 10 cents, thereby making themselves ineligible for membership in the union. The prices thus reduced, there is now practically no difference between those charged in shops conducted by Japanese and in those conducted by white men. The latter complain that the wages of white barbers and profits realized are too low. The figures given for capital invested, rent, and profit tend to bear out this statement. (See General Table 66.)

In competing with the Japanese shops the white proprietors are handicapped by paying higher wages. The Japanese proprietors pay their barbers $45 or $50 per month without board and lodging, or from $15 to $35 with board and lodging. The board and lodging may be reckoned at from $10 to $12 per month. In the large American shops, on the other hand, the barbers receive a commission, with a minimum wage guaranteed. Nineteen barbers employed in the shops investigated reported their average earnings as about $16 per week, while 24 reported their average earnings as $18 per week.

Some of the larger American shops employ Japanese as porters, paying them from $9.50 to $12 per week. In one shop with 16 chairs two negro porters were paid $12 per week each and two Japanese $9.50.

The Japanese bathhouses are usually connected with barber shops. The character of the baths provided is such, however, that the percentages of white patrons are much smaller than those of the barber shops, as indicated above. Their competition is of little importance.

A word may be added, also, concerning the billiard parlors and pool rooms which, though in a few cases conducted independently of or in conjunction with other kinds of business, are usually connected with barber shops. The number of these places has rapidly increased in recent years. They were not reported separately except for 1909, the number then being 25. Some of these, and especially those not connected with barber shops, are patronized exclusively by Japanese. Others have many white patrons, mostly immigrant laborers. These are in the minority, however, and no complaint has been heard of the Japanese invasion of this branch of business enterprise.

RESTAURANTS SERVING AMERICAN MEALS.

The restaurant business was the first engaged in by Japanese in Seattle. There were 4 such restaurants in 1888, 6 in 1894, 10 in 1900, 21 in 1905, and 36 in 1909. Many of them are small, having a capital of from $1,000 to $4,000 invested and with seating capacities for from 35 to 60 or 70 persons. Some of those serving American meals are located near the poorer shopping district, others near industrial establishments.

Some of these Japanese restaurants serving American meals derive a small percentage of their patronage from Japanese who prefer American food, while others have no Japanese patrons. Some of them serve meals for 10 and others for 15 cents. Their competition is with third and fourth class white restaurants of the " quick-lunch " variety.

Within the districts in which the Japanese restaurants are located their competition has been seriously felt, and a few white restaurants have closed because of the smallness of profit. The same is true of a few Japanese establishments not economically or intelligently managed.

Formerly the minimum price charged for a meal by Japanese restaurants was 10 cents. In 1907, however, a union was organized and the price advanced to 15 cents. Though this action was taken because of the higher prices paid for supplies, some of the proprietors did not become members of the Japanese Restaurant Keepers' Union and still continue to sell meals at the former price. But whatever the price, it has been somewhat lower than those charged by their white competitors, who serve meals of the same class and with similar "service." Furthermore, the rooms, furnishings, "service," and meals have been better in the majority of cases. The perceptible difference has been sufficient to attract many white patrons in spite of the odium attaching among certain classes to patronizing Japanese restaurants.

At one time the feeling against the Japanese because of the effects of their competition upon the employment of "restaurant help" was so strong that a general boycott was organized against them by white laborers. This boycott was directed chiefly against the restaurants, but ceased after a few months without seriously injuring their business. More recently, as a result of agitation against the Japanese restaurants, many of the unions have resolved that their members shall not patronize them, and in some instances penalties are imposed when they do. Yet the effect is evidently not great, for many union as well as nonunion men are numbered among the patrons.

The only apparent advantage the Japanese have in competing with the white restaurant keepers is found in the low wages they pay their employees and the smaller profits with which they are satisfied.

As a result of an investigation of 9 of the 36 Japanese restaurants serving American meals, it was found that first cooks were paid from $35 to $70 per month with board and usually lodging. The greater number are paid only $35, $40, or $45. One received $50 and another $70 per month. Second cooks were paid from $32 to $42 per month and third cooks from $30 to $40. In six white restaurants of the same type—two of them conducted by Slovenians and one by Greeks—cooks were paid $16, $17, and $18 per week, and two head cooks $100 and $150 per month, respectively. All of these received board and some of them lodging in addition to wages. Japanese male waiters (Japanese women are not employed as waitresses in restaurants serving American meals) were paid from $25 to $40 per month with board and usually lodging, the prevailing rate being $30 per month, or $1 per day. A few white waitresses were employed, being paid $8, $8.50, and $9 per week with board. White waiters in the other restaurants were paid, with board and, in a few cases, lodging, as follows: Eight at $10 per week, 3 at $12 per week, 2 at $14 per week, and 2 at $15 per week. Others were employed for "part days" only and so are not included. The waitresses received the same rates as those employed by the Japanese. The general and kitchen help in Japanese restaurants were paid, with board and lodging, as follows: Five at $25, 1 $28, 1 $29, and 3 $30 per month. In white restaurants, on the other hand, these men were paid $8, $9, $10, and $11, and women $8 per

week. The wages of the Japanese are thus shown to have been somewhat lower than those of white men employed in white restaurants.
In their smaller cost of labor per man the Japanese proprietors had
a distinct advantage over their competitors.

RESTAURANTS SERVING JAPANESE MEALS.

In restaurants serving Japanese meals Japanese foods are cooked
and served in the Japanese way; the patrons are all Japanese. The
price of meals is " 10 cents and up."

The number of these restaurants has increased rapidly as the Japanese population has grown, for most of these people are unmarried
men or men whose wives are in Japan, and unless provided with
board by the employer usually eat at restaurants. Comparatively
few buy American meals. The number of restaurants of this type
increased from 3 in 1900 to 22 in 1905 and to 51 in 1909.

These restaurants are a center of Japanese social life. Six of them
sell intoxicating drinks as well as meals. They take the place of the
American saloon and of a certain type of club.

Of the 51 restaurants serving Japanese meals 6 were investigated
by an agent of the Commission. The data relating to capital invested,
business transacted, etc., will be found in General Table 66.

Most of the restaurants are small, employing 5 persons each on
the average. Some of them have open dining rooms, boxes, and party
rooms; others no open dining room at all. The seating capacities
vary from 20 to 65. However, all of these establishments cater to
lodging houses and hotels, from 20 to 40 per cent of the meals being
sent out to these places.

The rents paid are usually small, as the buildings or rooms used
are not large and as nearly all are poorly built and in bad repair.
Some of the dining rooms presented a neat appearance; others did not.
In this they are not unlike small restaurants patronized chiefly by
other races whose members desire food and service of the kind to
which they were accustomed before migrating to the United States.

The work in the Japanese restaurants serving Japanese meals, except the attendance, is done by the proprietor, the members of his
family, and male employees. The wages paid the latter as cooks and
helpers are about the same as are paid by the proprietors of Japanese restaurants serving American meals. In the restaurants investigated only waitresses were employed in the dining room. The wage
was uniformly $25 per month with board. The receipts from " tips "
in some cases were estimated at $10 per month in addition to wages.
The earning of waitresses, therefore, may be estimated roughly at $1
per day with board.

JAPANESE STORES.

The Japanese conduct a great variety of shops, some of them patronized almost exclusively by white persons, others almost exclusively
by Japanese, and still others by the two races in proportions more
nearly equal.

The first of these in point of origin and importance are the grocery
and provision stores. One establishment of this kind was opened as
early as 1888, but none so described was in existence in 1900. In
1905, however, there were 16; in 1909, 26. They are all located in the

district in which the Japanese immigrants live, and the effects of their competition are limited to the competing stores in that part of the city.

In this part of Seattle there are many small stores conducted by Italians, Greeks, and Servians, and some by natives and north European immigrants. The few large stores are conducted by the latter classes only. The Japanese stores are all small, the capital of nine from which complete data were collected by an agent of the commission aggregating only $19,200, or a little more than $2,000 each. Their annual transactions aggregated $96,800, an average of a little less than $11,000. The rents paid by eight of the nine proprietors aggregated $3,964, or an average of about $495.50 per year.

The small shops (such as those for which data are given in General Table 66) conducted by Italians, Greeks, and Austrians are patronized very largely by persons of the same race as the proprietor. Few of the south European immigrants of this district trade elsewhere than with their countrymen. Nor do these grocers receive much patronage from the other races. A Greek shopkeeper reported that 10 per cent of his patrons were Japanese, while two Italians reported 2 per cent of this race among their patrons. However, the business done by them with Americans, north Europeans, and Japanese is not of great importance. And, on the other hand, the business done by the Americans, north Europeans, and Japanese with these classes is not of much greater importance. The vast majority of the Japanese and a considerable proportion of the natives and north European immigrants trade with the Japanese grocers. The native and north European grocers find most of their patrons among their own classes—practically none among the Japanese. In other words, the Japanese supply the wants of their own countrymen and share other trade with native and north European and, to a less extent, with south European storekeepers.

The Japanese grocers carry many Japanese goods to meet the needs of their countrymen, who use more foreign than American provisions. One reported that of his sales only 5 per cent were American goods, another 10, another 30, another 40. Half or more of the sales made by the others were American goods. The percentages reported by them were 50 in three cases, 75 in one, and 90 in the other. Of sales aggregating $96,800, roughly $45,000, or something less than half, were of American or of other non-Asiatic origin.

The percentages of Japanese and American customers were not the same as the percentage of American and non-American goods sold, for the Japanese buy a considerable quantity of non-Asiatic goods, and white people dealing with Japanese buy some foodstuffs imported from Asia. One grocer reported that 90 per cent of his customers were Japanese, another 70, another 60, two others 50, another 30, another 25, and another 10, while one did not report. The others were white persons. If the size of the stores is taken into consideration, it would seem that something less than three-fifths of the patronage was by others than Japanese. This patronage by white persons is explained partly by the fact that the stores may be the nearest, partly by the fact that the Japanese sell some goods, such as rice, at lower prices than their competitors.

The increasing number of Japanese provision stores, with their large percentages of white patrons, has rather seriously affected the business of white grocers not dependent upon their own countrymen for most of their trade. It has affected the south European immigrant less seriously than others.

The rents of 8 of the Japanese establishments were 4.5 per cent of the receipts reported, while in the case of 5 stores conducted by Italians, Greeks, and Servians it was 5.6 per cent, and in the case of 2 conducted by natives, 4.7 per cent. These latter were the large stores conducted by Americans, however.

In the matter of wages paid to clerks, on the other hand, the Japanese were found to have a distinct advantage over their white competitors. The Americans and north European clerks employed in the latter were paid from $65 to $100 per month, the average being about $70. Of 15 clerks, all Japanese, employed by 7 of the 9 Japanese stores (the other 2 had none, being conducted by partners), 7 were paid $25 per month, while the wages of the remainder were from $30 to $50 per month. In addition to the wages paid, the Japanese clerks were given board and lodging by the employer—usually in the building in which the business was conducted. These should be estimated at $10 or $12 per month extra.

There is very little difference between the Japanese stores and those conducted by the south European immigrants, save in the kind of goods carried in stock. Few other than the countrymen of the proprietors are employed, and if board and lodging for their employees are taken into consideration the wages paid are about the same. Taking three Italian stores, one clerk was paid $25 per month, two $50, two $60, and one $65—the others did not report wages—none receiving board and lodging.

There are also a few Japanese stores dealing in general merchandise. The largest of these is a supply store conducted by a large employment agent, and supplying the laborers working on railroads with Japanese and American goods. Most of the things purchased by laborers employed by the two largest railway companies are supplied by this company. The few other stores are very small, have little capital, and little white patronage. Though one of the larger reports 70 per cent of its patrons as white, most of them are engaged chiefly in selling American and Japanese goods in about equal proportions to Japanese.

In the third place, there are crockery and curio stores. Of these there were 8 in 1900, 6 in 1905, and 12 in 1909. These carry large stocks of Japanese goods only—art works, curios, etc. They are located in the shopping districts and are patronized exclusively or almost exclusively by white persons. Their competition is with white · stores having oriental departments and with Chinese shops. Judged by their effects upon white establishments, they have little importance. The wages paid to clerks vary from $35 to $60 per month, $45 and $50 being the most general figures. In most cases board and lodging are not furnished in addition to wages. Of 13 employees in 2 stores, 3 were white persons, these being employed on account of their superior knowledge of English.

It is only recently that book and drug stores have been conducted by Japanese independent entirely of other goods. There are at present four of these establishments. The books are Japanese publications, and there is no competition with other booksellers. Most of the drugs and toilet articles are also of Japanese manufacture.

All of the patrons of the one bookstore investigated were Japanese; of the drug stores, 90 per cent of one and 60 per cent of the other. With one exception the capital invested was very small. The competition with white establishments is scarcely felt.

Seven jewelry stores and watch-repairing establishments are conducted by Japanese. Two of the larger of these had a capital of $5,000 and $3,500 and did a business of $24,000 and $6,000 per year, respectively. The others are smaller. Of the larger of the two, only 30 per cent, and of the smaller 80 per cent, of the patrons were white persons.

Recently the Japanese have opened a number of small fish markets. They sell both fresh and canned fish, a part of the latter being imported for Japanese consumption. Of two of the five markets now in existence, one reported 90 per cent, the other 40 per cent, of its patrons as white persons.

HOTELS AND LODGING HOUSES.

Conducting hotels and lodging houses, chiefly for their countrymen, is one of the oldest enterprises engaged in by the Japanese in Seattle. The number of these establishments has rapidly increased with the number of Japanese in the city, for most of them are single men and, if not provided with lodging by their employers, must find shelter elsewhere. Furthermore, race lines are generally drawn against them and they are not welcomed in places where white persons take lodging. In 1900 there were 8 of these places; in 1905, 42; in the spring of 1909, 72. A few of them are hotels providing both board and lodging, while nearly 40 of them are like private rooming houses with comparatively few rooms. Of the others a few have as many as 50 rooms.

Most of the buildings used for this purpose are poorly constructed and some of them are old and in poor condition. The vast majority are cheaply but neatly furnished and are kept in an orderly condition. In most of these each room contains a double iron bed and is occupied by one or two persons. Counterpanes and similar linen are in general use. The typical room has furnishings costing about $75.

The rates charged for lodging vary considerably, but the vast majority of the rooms of the kind described rent for from 25 to 75 cents per night, from $2.50 to $6 per week, and from $5 to $20 per month. Most of the Japanese pay from $5 to $10 per month for their lodgings in these places; while many of them pay more, for many of the well-to-do live here.

In two or three of these hotels and lodging houses white laborers only are found. Perhaps in half of the others white men find lodging, frequently as many as 10, 15, or 20 per cent of the total number being white. The three hotels mentioned above as having white lodgers only are cheap places, where men get lodging for the night. One of them is in the basement of a large brick building. The room is undivided and has 150 cots which let for 15 cents per night. Another is in a building formerly used as a skating rink and is of the same character as the one just described. Such places are not patronized by Japanese. It is chiefly in conducting them that the Japanese are competing with other races. The lodging furnished does not materially differ from that supplied by others.

EMPLOYMENT AGENCIES.

Until within recent years some of the lodging houses served in a general way as employment agencies, but at present that business is usually carried on entirely independently. However, in a few cases lodging houses are conducted by employment agents whose chief business is to provide laborers for some given line of business. The most important instance of this kind is one where a contractor furnishing the vast majority of the Japanese laborers employed in Puget Sound and many of those employed in Alaskan canneries conducts two lodging houses. This is exceptional.

The first employment agency was started in 1896. As late as 1905 there were only 5, but more recently many have been established. In the spring of 1909 there were 17. Most of these supply work for Japanese only, but a few have Koreans and Filipinos as patrons. Domestics, bar and restaurant employees, farm, sawmill, cannery, and railroad hands—in short all kinds of laborers—are supplied to employers who have need for them.

The commission collected and rules under which the employment agents operate are in a general way controlled by an agreement entered into in 1906. The object of the agreement was to put an end to the competition which had brought loss to many of the agents. It was then agreed that domestics receiving both board and lodging should be charged 7 per cent of one month's wages, those receiving board alone 6 per cent, and those receiving neither board nor lodging 5 per cent. The commission on earnings where persons were employed temporarily by the hour was 10 per cent. The fee for "hands" of various kinds was fixed at $1.50. It was agreed that two-thirds of the fee collected should be returned if the laborer at the expiration of three days was not in employment. It was further agreed that in case an employer refused to pay the wages agreed upon, or in any way illtreated his employee, the matter should be reported to all parties to the agreement, who should then refuse to provide the offending party with labor.

The union thus formed has largely lost its importance, save that the terms of the agreement are very generally regarded by all employment agents, whether parties to it or not. The prevailing commission for domestics is 6 per cent of a month's wages—$1.75 to $2. The commission for all kinds of labor in the city is about the same. Farm laborers and sawmill hands are usually charged $1 or $1.50, but more frequently the latter amount. Cannery hands usually pay no commission; one large contractor has the privilege of supplying goods to the laborers under his control, and from this he makes from $10 to $15 per man for the season. Railroad laborers pay no commission, but the two contractors furnishing laborers to the Northern Pacific, Great Northern, and Milwaukee, St. Paul and Puget Sound railways pay from $2 to $3 for each man supplied to them. In turn they collect $1 and (with certain exceptions in one case) 5 per cent of the wages of these men as long as they are employed.

Most of the employment agents bind themselves to return a part or all of the commission to those who are not satisfied with the work to which they are assigned or who are not accepted by the employer to whom they are sent. There seems to be little or no exploitation of laborers by the Japanese employment agents; the exploitation which exists is practiced by the contractors for railroad and cannery work.[a]

Fifteen of these agencies deal in real estate. Many new Japanese enterprises are being established, and those in existence frequently change location or ownership, thus making the real estate business one of considerable importance. The commission charged is 5 per cent of the values involved in the transactions effected.

NEWSPAPERS AND PERIODICALS.

Beginning with 1899 many new newspapers and periodicals have been started in Seattle to meet the needs of the Japanese in Washington, Montana, and British Columbia. Most of these have failed for some reason. There remain 1 weekly and 3 daily newspapers and 11 magazines, 9 of which are organs of societies and do not have a general circulation.

Of the three daily newspapers, one dates from 1901 and two from 1905. The two larger papers each have about 2,000 subscribers, the other a smaller number. The two larger printing establishments have 37 employees, who are paid from $25 to $60 per month, with board and lodging. The weekly newspaper has a circulation of about 500, the two magazines with a general circulation of 500 and 200, respectively.

At these newspaper offices and a few others job printing is done. Most of the work is for Japanese and printed in the Japanese language. One of these offices, however, reported that 35 per cent of its work was done for white people. These printing plants are small and do a business of from $2,000 to $7,000 a year.

The Japanese colony also has professional men of the Japanese race. There are at present seven physicians and four dentists. Their practice is entirely among their fellow countrymen.

OTHER KINDS OF BUSINESS.

The other branches of Japanese business, because of the limited numbers of the establishments or the nature of the business conducted, are of little importance save in showing the extent to which the Japanese are supplying their own wants.

There are a few Japanese cake stores which sell pastries, ice cream, and fruits; two liquor dealers, supplying liquors to Japanese restaurants; one second-hand clothing store, with a large percentage of white patrons; and a few shoe-repairing shops, some of them carrying small stocks of shoes. The prices for repairing are about 25 per cent less than the standard prices charged by other cobblers, but the number of Japanese shops is as yet too small to afford serious competition. There are five small photograph galleries; of the two reported, 70 and 90 per cent of their patrons are Japanese. Of expressmen there are 10, but only 1 of these has sufficient business to warrant the keeping of an office, and he alone has any employees. Of three of these, one reports that 70 per cent of his patrons are Japanese, another 80 per cent, the third 100 per cent. There are also 16 carpenters, but they do little work except to make repairs and alter the interior of buildings occupied by their countrymen.

---

[a] See "Immigrant laborers employed by the steam railways of the Pacific Coast and Rocky Mountain States."

The Japanese have organized three banks, two in 1905 and one in 1907. Two of them have a total paid-up capital and surplus of $82,354 and deposits in excess of $150,000. The other is a private bank, not yet well started. These banks are used largely for financing the larger business enterprises and for the collection of Japanese savings. Four per cent interest is paid on deposits in the savings departments. The banks are also the agency through which Japanese remittances are forwarded to Japan. One of these reports that it forwards about $50,000 per month, saved by " day laborers " in Seattle and by laborers elsewhere sent out by contractors from that place.

SUMMARY.

From the preceding discussion it is seen that the Japanese have become conspicuous in several branches of employment, but chiefly in the field of domestic and personal service. They have found their way into these departments of work at a time when it was difficult to get and to keep reliable white employees at the wages which had obtained. It is seen, also, that the Japanese have engaged in many branches of business on their own account, two-fifths of the Japanese in Seattle being employed in establishments conducted by their countrymen. Few wants of their race can not be and, with the exception of clothing, are not supplied in this way. The laborers find employment through Japanese employment agencies; they are provided with board and lodging by the employer or are given lodging in Japanese lodging houses; they eat in Japanese restaurants; they purchase at Japanese stores, and they generally patronize Japanese laundries, barber shops, baths, and places of amusement; they have their own banks, photographers, newspapers, expressmen, and professional men. In several branches of business they have a considerable amount of white trade. This is true of the laundries, tailor shops, barber shops, restaurants serving American meals, grocery and other stores, and to a less extent of other branches of business. In some instances the trade has been shared by them; in two branches of business—barber and tailor shops—they have caused a reduction of prices. The white laundries, the third-rate tailors, the barbers, the third and fourth class restaurants, and the grocery stores have been affected by the Japanese competition. Japanese prices have generally been, and usually are, somewhat lower than those charged by their competitors for what is accepted as an equivalent service. Their chief advantages lie in the lowness of the wages paid to employees and, to a less extent, in a willingness to accept lower profits. They employ their own countrymen almost exclusively.

But in all this they differ only in extent and degree from some of the recent immigrants from Europe. Though less self-sufficient and less given to starting competing businesses, the Italians, Greeks, and Austrians are more or less clannish, conduct their own shops, lodging houses, and hotels, employ persons largely of their own races, and pay them frequently less than current wages.

The close approach to self-sufficiency found in the case of the Japanese is explained by the rapid influx of the members of that race during a comparatively short time, the shortness of their residence in the United States, the expectation of the majority of them to return shortly to their native country, their infrequent command of the English language, the race feeling and prejudice against them—all these combining to induce or force them to be clannish and to provide for their own wants. The competition for the trade of others is explained partly by their willingness to take risks, their ambition, and their excellent competitive ability. It is also explained partly by the fact that they desire to work for themselves, and to occupy the economic position they did in their native land. Further light will be thrown on some of these points by an examination of the character of the Japanese business men and their employees.

JAPANESE BUSINESS MEN OF SEATTLE.

Agents of the Commission secured personal information from 108 of the Japanese conducting the 86 business establishments investigated. Of the entire number, only 28, or slightly more than one-fourth, had been in the United States ten years or more, and none had been here as long as twenty. Twenty-eight had been in this country even less than five years. (General Table 77.)[a]

The majority of these business men came from the towns and cities of Japan. Three of the 108 had come to the continental United States from Hawaii, where two had been employed as plantation laborers, the third as a grocer's clerk. Their occupations in their native land are unknown. Of the remaining 105, 37, or more than one-third, had been engaged in business on their own account, 8 had been employed for wages in stores, 13 had been employed for wages in other occupations in cities, while only 5 are reported as having been engaged in farming on their own account. Of the remaining 42, 20 had been assisting their fathers on the farm, while 22 had not been gainfully occupied before emigrating to the United States. Thus it is seen that only 25 of 105 had belonged to the agricultural class in Japan. (General Table 68.)

The majority of the business men investigated had emigrated to the United States when comparatively young men and before they accumulated much, if any, money to serve as capital. Moreover, a large percentage of the older men who had been engaged in business had not been very successful and came to begin anew. A smaller number, however, came in the prime of life, and brought considerable capital with them in order to engage in business at once. Of 109 males reporting data, 8 were under 18 years of age; 15, 18 and under 20; 37, 20 and under 25; 30, 25 and under 30; 12, 30 and under 35; while only 7 were 35 years of age or over when coming to the United States. Approximately one-fifth were under 20, six-elevenths under 25, and nine-elevenths under 30 years of age upon their arrival in this country. (General Table 75.) Of 106 reporting the amount of money brought upon coming, 6 had more than $1,000 each; of these, 1 had $10,000, 2, $2,500 each, an equal number $1,500 each, and the remaining 1, $1,200. Twenty-one more had $100 or over. Of these, 5 had $100 but less than $150; 2, $150 but less than $200; 8, $200 but less than $300; and 6, $300 but less than $400. Seventy-nine, or 74.5 per cent of the entire number, had less than $100, and of these,

---

[a] This table includes two foreign-born male members of the families of these business men.

42 had less than $50 upon their arrival in this country. (General Table 67.)

In spite of the fact that only 20 of the entire number had more than $200 upon their arrival in this country, 22, by forming partnerships or otherwise, engaged in business to begin with. The remaining 86 became wage-earners, most of them in city trades and in Seattle, where the majority had landed upon coming. Thirty became domestics, a part of them no doubt as "school boys" working a part of the day for board and lodging and a small sum of money per week; 8 were employed in restaurants, 7 in stores, and 1 in a tailor shop. Twenty were first employed as railroad laborers, 7 as farm laborers, and 1 as a cannery hand. The remaining 12 found employment in other occupations. (General Table 68.) Thus about four-fifths of the entire number became wage-earners. It was not long, however, before the larger number of them took advantage of opportunities to engage in business requiring little capital and thus to rise from the wage-earning class.

The following table shows the occupations abroad of the 86 individual proprietors of, or head partners in, the establishments investigated, by kind of business conducted in the United States:

TABLE 10.—*Kind of business conducted by Japanese in Seattle at the present time, by occupation abroad.*

Kind of business conducted by Japanese at present.	Number reporting complete data.	Number who were abroad—			
		Without occupation.	In same business as in the United States.	On farm.	In miscellaneous occupations.
Barber	10	....	3	4	a 3
Billiard hall keeper	1	....	....	1	....
Bookstore keeper	1	1	....	....	....
Cake maker	1	....	1	....	....
Curio dealer	2	....	2	....	....
Druggist	2	....	2	....	....
Dyer	1	....	1	....	....
Employment agent	6	3	1	1	b 1
Expressman	3	1	....	1	c 1
Fish market keeper	2	1	....	....	d 1
General store keeper	4	1	3	....	....
Grocer	10	....	2	5	e 3
Laundry proprietor	7	1	....	2	f 4
Lodging house keeper	8	2	....	2	g 4
Photographer	2	....	1	....	h 1
Printer	2	....	2	....	....
Restaurant keeper	13	3	....	4	i 6
Second-hand clothes dealer	1	....	....	....	j 1
Shoe repairing	1	1	....	....	....
Tailor	7	1	5	....	k 1
Watchmaker	2	....	2	....	....
Total	86	15	25	20	26

a One cook; 1 clerk; 1 druggist.
b School-teacher.
c Dairy manager.
d Clerk.
e One fisherman; 1 draftsman; 1 matting maker.
f One lumber dealer; 1 fisherman; 1 cake maker; 1 restaurant proprietor.
g Four storekeepers.
h Printer.
i One cook; 1 clerk; 1 salesman; 1 policeman; 1 clothes dealer; 1 fish broker.
j Salesman.
k Liquor dealer.

It will be noted that of the 86, 25, including the larger number of those who had been business men at home, are engaged in the same business here as abroad, while 15 had not been gainfully occupied before immigrating to this country. Of the remaining 46, 20 had been on farms, while 26 had been engaged in branches of business different from those in which they are now engaged or employed for wages in various city occupations. The majority of the tailors, general-store keepers, curio dealers, watchmakers, druggists, printers, and one or two less important groups had established themselves in the same branch of business as engaged in abroad, while the majority of the others engaged in branches of business different from those in which they had been engaged as business men or as wage-earners.

Though a few of the Japanese came to the United States as members of the "student class," the vast majority came because of the better opportunity presented here than at home for making money. How well they have succeeded is shown by the net value of the property now owned by them and their financial gains.

The 108 have property with an aggregate estimated value of $475,900, or an average of $4,406.48 each. Forty-one of the 108 were in debt, however, the total amount of the indebtedness being $77,150. The net value of the property was, therefore, $398,750, an average of $3,692.13 for each man. (General Table 72.) Some of these have much while others have little property. Seven had property, less indebtedness, valued at $100, but less than $250; 4 at $250, but less than $500; 28 at $500, but less than $1,000; 19 at $1,000, but less than $1,500; 21 at $1,500, but less than $2,500; 18 at $2,500, but less than $5,000; 7 at $5,000, but less than $10,000; 3 at $10,000, but less than $25,000; and 1 at $170,000. Though 39, or more than 36 per cent of the 108, had less than $1,000, and 58 others less than $5,000, thus leaving only 11, or about 1 in 10, who have property worth $5,000 or more, when the comparatively short residences in this country are taken into consideration, the property owned is found to be comparatively large. The amount of property owned by years in the United States is shown in General Table 69. As would be expected, there is a rough correspondence between the number of years in the United States and the value of property owned. This is not an accurate test of the degree of success with which the Japanese have engaged in business, however, for it does not include representatives of the unknown number who have failed in business and again become members of the wage-earning class. For this reason the income derived from business conducted and the surplus realized or deficit sustained during the year 1908 is, in some respects, a better index of the degree of success they are meeting with.

The net incomes for the year 1908 from business engaged in were ascertained. The income of one was $240; of 2, $400 but less than $500; of 40, $500 but less than $750; of 28, $750 but less than $1,000; of 10, $1,000 but less than $1,500; of 6, from $1,500 to $2,000. The incomes of the remaining 8 were $3,000 in 2 cases and $2,400, $3,240, $3,600, $4,800, $5,400, and $24,000 for the other 6, respectively. The incomes of the restaurant proprietors varied between $480 as the minimum and $5,400 as a maximum, and averaged $1,388 for 20 investigated. They were less than $750 in one-half of the cases, however, and less than $1,000 in 14 of 20. The incomes of the lodging-house keepers varied between $840 as a minimum and $1,200 as a maximum and averaged $1,020. The stores conducted by Japanese differ greatly in size and so does the amount of the net income from the business conducted. The incomes of 4 were $600 each, of one at the other extreme, $24,000. Inasmuch as 18 of the 23 had net incomes from their business less than $1,000 and 2 others less than $1,500, the average of $2,011.30 for the group of 23 has no significance. The incomes of 11 barbers varied between $500 as a minimum and $960 as a maximum and averaged $727.64. The corresponding figures for the incomes of the 8 tailors were $600, $1,800, and $1,038.75. The incomes of 5 real-estate and labor agents investigated varied between $480 as a minimum and $3,000 as a maximum, the average being $1,776. Finally, the net incomes of the proprietors of 6 laundries from their business varied between $600 and $3,000 for the year. (General Table 86.)

The incomes discussed above are the net amount realized from the principal business or businesses conducted. Seventeen of the 95 had incomes from subsidiary business enterprises, the rental of property, or from investments. Including these, the incomes of the 95 from all sources for the year 1908 are shown in the following statement. The average was $1,372.63, the median income $840.

Amount of income.	Number of persons.
Less than $300	1
$300 and under $400	
$400 and under $500	1
$500 and under $750	38
$750 and under $1,000	25
$1,000 and under $1,500	15
$1,500 and under $2,000	7
$2,000 and under $2,500	1
$2,500 or over	7
Total	95

Seventy-five of the 108 business men reported the amount of surplus left, or deficit incurred, after their living and other current expenses were paid. Two of these had small deficits for the year, aggregating $920, 8 reported that they had neither surplus nor deficit, while the other 65 reported gains varying from $50 to $25,000. Between these extremes the surpluses reported by 12 were $100, but less than $250; of 28, $250 but less than $500; of 17, $500 but less than $1,000; of 3, $1,000 but less than $2,500; of 4, $2,500 or over. The average surplus reported by the 65 was $966.77, but as this was greatly affected by the large gains of a few, the median sum was only $400. (General Tables 70 and 71.) The greater part of the gains were left in this country, but about two-fifths of those investigated sent money abroad for the use of wives, children, parents, and other relations, or for investment. Only about 45 per cent of the money sent abroad was for the use of relations. Of 107 reporting data, 42 sent money abroad during the year, the total amount sent by the 42 being $18,835. The disposition of $47,240—the larger part of the amount retained in this country—was as follows: Invested in extending the business conducted, $32,610; used for the payment of debts, $4,900; placed in bank, $5,680; loaned or otherwise disposed of, $4,050.

JAPANESE WAGE-EARNERS IN SEATTLE.

Corresponding data were secured from 89 members of the laboring class, most of whom were employed in the Japanese business establishments investigated. Two of them had come to the continental United States from the Hawaiian Islands, where 1 had been employed as a plantation laborer and the other had been a small shopkeeper. Of the remaining 87, 11 had been engaged in business in their native land, 9 had been employed for wages in stores, 9 had been wage-earners in other occupations in cities, 7 had been farmers, 14 had been on farms with their fathers, while 37 had not been gainfully occupied before emigrating to the United States. Thus, like the business men from whom data were collected, the majority of these men in their native land had been members of the city wage-earning and business classes. The chief differences between them and the business men as a group are that they came at a somewhat younger age, fewer of them had upon their arrival sufficient money to engage in business for themselves, and more of them had been in the United States for a short period of time. Of the 89, 26 were under 20; 36, 20 but under 25; 13, 25 but under 30; 8, 30 but under 35; and 6, 35 but under 45 years of age, at time of arrival in the continental United States. (General Table 75.) Two of the 89 had upon their arrival more than $500 each, and 5 others had between $100 and $300, but the remaining 82 had less than $100, and 18 of them less than $50. With insufficient capital to engage in business on their own account, they all became wage-earners. The majority of them first found employment in city occupations and chiefly in Seattle. Seventeen secured their first employment in stores, 15 in restaurants, 20 as domestics, some of them "schoolboys," 5 as tailors, 1 as a barber, and 8 others in other occupations. As opposed to these, 5 became farm hands, 14 railroad laborers, and 1 a sawmill laborer. (General Table 68.) Of the 89 wage-earners, only 12 at the time of the investigation had been in the United States for ten years or longer, while 61 had been here for less than five years. (General Table 69.)

The number of months employed and the earnings for the year 1908 were ascertained for 88 of the 89 wage-earners. Seventy of the 88 received board and lodging in addition to wages, while 18 did not. Of the former group 2 were employed for eight of the twelve months and earned, as an average, $180 in addition to board and lodging. The remaining 68 were employed throughout the year, and their average earnings were $446.54. Five of these, employed in unimportant occupations, earned less than $250 per year; 21, $300 but less than $400; 23, $400 but less than $500; 4, $500 but less than $600; 11, $600 but less than $700; 2, $700 but less than $800; and 2, $800 or over. Of the 18 who did not receive board in addition to wages, 1 was employed for only six and another for eight months during the year, and earned $360 and $400 per year, respectively. The remaining 16 were employed throughout the year and earned, on the average, $656. (General Table 87.)

Data were secured from 61 of the 89 wage-earners as to the surplus over their expenditures, or deficit, for the year 1908. One, employed for only six months, incurred a deficit of $250, while another reported that he " came out even " at the end of the year.

The other 59 reported surpluses ranging from $30 to $1,000 and averaging $218.14. The median sum was $200. (General Tables 70 and 71.)

Thirty-five of those from whom data were obtained, sent a part or all of the surplus for the year abroad, the total amount sent being $7,395. Of this, $400 was for the purpose of bringing a wife and child to the United States, $1,450 for safe-keeping, and $5,545 for the use of wife, children, parents, or other relations, or to be disposed of by them. As against this, 41 retained $9,360 in this country, practically all of it in the absence of opportunities for investment, being placed in the bank, for safe-keeping. In the amount of surplus, the amount of money sent abroad, and the amount of money retained in the United States and its disposition, the wage-earning group stand in strong contrast to the business men as a group.

A large percentage of these wage-earners as a result of saving, have accumulated from several hundred to a few thousand dollars worth of property. Of the 89, 3 had property, indebtedness deducted, with an estimated value of $1,500 or more; 5, $1,000 but less than $1,500; 19, of $500 but less than $1,000. As against these 27, there were 62, 27 of whom had property valued at $250 but less than $500; 26, $100 but less than $250; five $50 but less than $100, while four had no savings and no property other than their personal effects. (General Table 69.)

SOCIOLOGICAL DATA.

Detailed information was obtained from the members of their households as well as from the 108 business men and the 89 male wage-earners. All told there were 199 male and 63 female foreign-born Japanese and 20 male and 21 female Japanese-Americans—a total of 262 foreign and 41 native born. Of the 41 native-born, 36 were under 6 years of age, 4 native-born and 2 foreign-born Japanese were between 6 and 13, and 1 native-born and 1 foreign-born were between 14 and 15. (General Tables 73 and 85.) With three exceptions the female foreign-born were married. (General Table 74.) Of the 109 males of the business class, 62 were married, 2 were widowed, and 45 were single. Of 89 male wage-earners, 28 were married, 2 widowed, and 59 single. (General Table 74.) Thirty-three of the former group were married previous to their immigration to the United States, 11 while upon visits abroad, and 18 in the United States, in the latter case usually upon the arrival of the women in this country. Of the 33 men who were married previous to their immigration, 7 were accompanied by their wives when they came to this country, while 15 have been joined by them more recently. Only 14 of the 62 wives of business men are now abroad. Of 89 wage-earning males, 22 were married previous to their immigration to this country, 4 have been married while on visits to Japan, while 2 have been married in this country. Six of the 22 who were married previous to their immigration were accompanied by their wives upon coming to this country, while 3 have been joined by them more recently. At the time of the investigation, then, 28 of the wage-earning males were married and 13 of their wives were abroad. (General Table 75.)

From these details it is evident that the great majority of those who were married previous to their immigration to this country were not accompanied by their wives, but a large proportion of them have been joined by them subsequently, while a large number have been married in this country or in Japan and now have their wives with them. It is evident, also, that there has been a large influx of women to join their husbands or to be married in the United States. This recent immigration of women accounts for the fact that of the 63 foreign-born females all but 4 have been in this country less than ten years, and all but 12 of the remaining 59 have been here less than five years. (General Table 77.)

In spite of the fact that many Japanese families have been reunited or established in Seattle, comparatively few of the Japanese men have definitely decided to remain permanently in this country. Of 109 men of the business group, 18 stated that they expected to remain permanently in this country, 44 that they expected to return to Japan, while 47 were in doubt as to what they would eventually do. The corresponding figures for the wage-earners were 3, 66, and 20.

It has been shown that most of the Japanese employed by white persons are engaged in domestic and personal service. The vast majority of them receive board and lodging in addition to wages. Few, other than those working in stores, must provide their own meals, and less than half must provide themselves with lodging. A similar situation obtains among Japanese employed by persons of their own race. Laundry employees all receive board and lodging, restaurant employees receive board and as a rule lodging, while the vast majority of clerks in stores, barbers, tailors, and others live with their employers. Those who are not provided with their food and lodging in this way usually live in the lodging houses, and those so doing generally eat at the restaurants. It is impossible to reckon the cost of rooms occupied by such persons with any degree of accuracy, but it is less than $5 per month. Nor was it possible to get much data with regard to the cost of meals. Of nine men employed by tailors and not boarded by their employer, three estimated the cost of food at $7 per month, two at $10, one at $12, and three at $15. The cost reported by clerks in stores was almost invariably about $13 and of barbers $15 per month. These figures must be used only to show the probable cost.

Some of the missions also furnish board and lodging for people of these classes and especially for women. The prices of rooms vary, but the price charged for "table board" by the month is usually about $9.

Of 40 business men, other than proprietors of hotels and lodging houses, and expressmen without offices, who had their families with them, 24 lived in the rear or over the shop, store, office, restaurant, or laundry conducted by them, while 16 did not. Of 34 single men or married men with families in Japan, 15 lived in the building housing the business, while 19 did not.

Taking 69 of these men for whom complete data were obtained, they, their families, and employees or other lodgers numbered all told 227. The 69 apartments occupied by them had a total of 180 rooms. The number of persons per room was, therefore, 1.26—approximately the figure for congested districts in some of the eastern cities. Thirty-four of the 227 were children under 15 years of age—a smaller proportion than usually obtains in the congested districts mentioned. This fact would be more than offset, however, by those cases where meals are regularly taken at restaurants and no cooking done in the apartments occupied.

In a few cases the rooms were crowded. As rather extreme examples of these cases, there were 4 men, 2 women, and 1 child occupying 2 rooms; 1 man, 4 women, and 3 children occupying 2 rooms; and 2 groups of men, one of 4 and one of 6, each group occupying 1 room. Nine families of husband and wife, with no children except infants, were living in 1 room each, while the other 2 out of 11 such families had apartments of 3 rooms.

Of 69 families, 9 had a room other than kitchen or bedroom used as a living room or parlor. The other 60 used shop, store, bedroom, or kitchen for this purpose. Almost without exception, the kitchen was used as both kitchen and dining room.

Something has already been said concerning the character of the buildings in the district in which the Japanese live. The agent of the commission described one apartment of 69 occupied by Japanese families as being in "good" condition, 30 "fair," 30 "bad," and 8 "very bad." The care of the apartments, i. e., the housekeeping, was described as "fair" in 28 cases, "bad" in 36, and "very bad" in 5. Most of the instances of bad housekeeping were where no women were living in the group.

In many instances it was difficult to ascertain the actual rental value of the apartment occupied because it was rented with other rooms used for business purposes. But apportioning the rent in such cases, the total amount per month paid for the 69 apartments was $1,067.50. This is an average of $15.46 per apartment, and a little less than $6 per room. The rent per occupant was $4.70; per adult, practically all of whom were gainfully employed, about $5.50.

Data were secured by the agents of the Commission relative to the cost of food and drink for the several households consisting of the proprietors of the business places investigated, their families, if in this country, and such of their employees as boarded with them. The data for 75 groups, excluding those the heads of which were restaurant keepers, boarding house keepers, or others where the food supplies were not purchased and consumed in the usual way, are presented. Four groups, with 15 members, reported the cost of food and drink as $6, but less than $7, per month per person; 4, with 22 members, as $7, but less than $8; 4, with 12 members, as $8, but less than $9; 1, with 2 members, $9, but less than $10; 20, with 68 members, as $10, but less than $12; 15, with 39 members, as $12, but less than $14; while 27 groups (and individuals) with 51 members reported the cost per month as $14 or over.

No effort was made to secure statistics relating to the cost of clothing and to miscellaneous expenses of the Japanese. It may be said, however, that their expenditures for clothing and amusements compare favorably with those of any other race similarly circumstanced with reference to employment and income.

All but one of the 262 Japanese and the one Japanese-American 10 years of age or over were literate (General Table 81), and the great majority could speak English. In fact, all but 2 of 199 males and 35 of 63 females 6 years of age or over had a speaking knowledge of English. (General Table 78.) Moreover, 180 of the males and 24 of the females could read and write that language as well. (General Table 84.) Some had studied English abroad, while many had attended classes for the study of our language in this country.

In Seattle at present there are six night schools conducted by the several missions and churches for teaching English (and in some instances religious doctrines) to adult Japanese. The fee is usually $1 or $2 per month. This is chiefly for incidental expenses, for most of the teachers donate their services. At the time of the investigation by the Commission there were only 64 students in the six night schools, but in the winter the enrollment may reach 200. The number is not so large as formerly, when all classes of Japanese not barred by the general immigration law were admitted without restriction.

The adults in the night schools are for the greater part domestics and store, restaurant, and bar employees. Besides these there are about 200 Japanese children in the public primary and grammar schools of the city, 42 in the high schools, and about 15 adults attending the University of Washington. Some of the children attend a school conducted under the auspices of the Japanese Association as well as the public schools, the children attending the former when the public schools are not in session. This "supplementary school" is maintained to teach Japanese children to read and write the Japanese language and something of the history and geography of Japan. At the time of the investigation there were 38 children enrolled, and the teaching staff consisted of three graduates of Japanese normal training schools.

Closely related to the matter of literacy and the use of English is that of newspapers and periodicals subscribed for by the Japanese households investigated. These also indicate the standard of living and culture of the Japanese, and show the sources from which their opinions of current events are largely drawn. Of 78 reporting data bearing upon this point, 2 subscribed for no newspapers at all, 6 for 1, 7 for 2, and the remaining 63 for from 3 to 10 each. Seventy-three of the 76 subscribed for newspapers and periodicals printed in their native language, and many of them published in Japan, while 3 subscribed for newspapers printed in English only. Besides these 3, 42, making three-fifths of the entire number, subscribed for from 1 to 6 newspapers and periodicals published in the English language. Of the 78 households reporting data, then, 33 did not subscribe for any newspaper printed in the English language.

There are six Japanese missions and churches in Seattle.[a]

Approximately half of the Japanese have no church affiliations; the vast majority of the others are nominal[b] or active adherents of the Buddhist faith. All of these organizations conduct night schools, and all but two (the Congregational and Episcopal) have other "institutional" work, such as maintaining dormitories for both men and

---

[a] The denomination, the date of organization, and approximate present membership are as follows: Baptist, 1890. 87 members; Buddhist, 1903, 2,000 members; Methodist, 1904. 70 members; Presbyterian, 1906, 60 members; Congregational, 1907, 50 members; Episcopal, 1907, 25 members.
[b] It is stated that only about 1,000 of the 2,000 members of the Buddhist mission pay dues regularly.

women. Upward of 100 Japanese had lodging in mission dormitories in the spring of 1909; in winter the number is larger.

A word should be said concerning the organizations among the Japanese of Seattle and their relations with people of other races.

Reference has been made to the laundrymen's alliance, the barbers' union, the Japanese restaurant-keepers' association, and the lodging-house keepers' association or union. These are all trade organizations for the regulation of prices and other matters of common interest. There are similar organizations also among the tradesmen and the shoemakers. Few lines of business conducted by Japanese are without an organization to protect and to promote the interests of those engaged in them.

Besides the business organizations, there are numerous others of a more general character. Most important among these are the Japanese Association and 24 prefectural societies. These care for the general interests of all Japanese residents and those coming from given provinces in Japan, respectively. The prefectural societies are, perhaps, more thoroughly organized in Seattle than in any other place. Of 199 men from whom data were secured, 117 had membership in them. Through the various organizations the Japanese care for those who are ill or meet with misfortune; they do not become public charges. In these societies and in places of amusement conducted by Japanese, their social life is found. Except in billiard and pool rooms and similar places frequented by some white men, there is little association between the adult Japanese and adult white persons, save that incidental to business and labor. The associations are closer among those in school, however, and a few Japanese business men find a place in the social life of the city. But here, as elsewhere, and for the same reasons of racial, language, and institutional differences and brief and more or less temporary residence, the Japanese are farther removed from normal American life than any European immigrant race.

Chapter VI

JAPANESE IN CITY EMPLOYMENTS AND BUSINESS IN PORTLAND.

The first Japanese came to Portland, Oreg., during the first half of the decade 1880–1889.[a] Following these some 40 or 50 cooks came from California. Some of the latter became domestic servants in private families. Direct immigration began near the end of the year 1887 when steamship service was established between Kobe and Portland. In that year 200 immigrants were sent to Oregon by an emigration company conducting its business at Kobe. Two years later a member of this company visited Portland. He soon returned to Japan, however, and sent over some 40 laborers to work as section hands on a railroad with one of its terminals at Portland. Three years later this same agent returned to Portland and entered into contract with another railroad company to furnish it 200 laborers.

Inasmuch as men were not at this time being sent out from San Francisco, Seattle, and Tacoma to work on the railroads, Portland became an important center for the distribution of Japanese laborers and the influx was rapid, many of the men being sent beyond the boundaries of the State. In 1885 the total number of Japanese in Oregon was estimated at 40 or 50, in 1889 at 300. By 1897 the number had increased to about 1,000, by 1900 to 2,500, by 1907 to 3,000.[b] In 1909 the estimated number was 3,872.[c] This figure includes those who make their homes in Portland during the winter, but during the summer go to Alaska or Washington to work in the salmon canneries. Some 500 are sent out by corporations from Portland and Astoria to Alaska, while a large number work in the canneries on the Washington side of the Columbia River. In all probability the Japanese population of the State during the summer months is about 3,000.

Since 1887 the majority of Japanese in Oregon have engaged in railroad work. At the maximum the number so engaged is estimated at 1,800. Many of these leave that employment during the summer months, however, to engage in cannery and farm work. Some 200 men all told go to Alaska each year, while from 75 to 100 find employment in Oregon salmon canneries. Roughly speaking, there are some 400 farm hands in the vicinity of Portland, 300 about Hood River, 30 at The Dalles, 125 at La Grande during the sugar-beet season, and from 150 to 200 about Salem during the hop train-

---

[a] The date is not more definitely established.

[b] According to the United States census the number of Japanese in Oregon in 1890 was 25, in 1900 (Population, Pt. I, p. 487), 2,501. According to the State census of 1905 (secretary of state report, 1906–7, pp. 105–106), the total number was 1,459, but the census of Chinese and Japanese was not complete.

[c] These figures are taken from Y. Kudo and T. Abe, The Japanese in Oregon. The figures for 1909 are based upon an investigation made under the direction of the consul (at Portland) in April, 1909.

ing and picking seasons. Some 200 men are employed in lumber and shingle mills. Most of the others are in the cities and towns of the State. The Japanese population of Portland varies between 900 in summer and 1,500 in winter. From 5 to 20 are found in each of several smaller cities—Salem, Baker City, Hood River, The Dalles, Eugene, and Astoria.

Most of the laborers engaged in railway, cannery, lumber mill, and farm work are distributed by contractors with offices in Portland, and are supplied with a large part of the necessaries of life from that place. Largely because of Portland's importance as a distributing point and supply center for Japanese laborers, many members of that race have engaged in business and in the professions in that city. Moreover, like the Chinese, they have shown a tendency to compete for the patronage of other races. At the same time a comparatively small number have engaged in domestic and personal service. The number so employed, however, has never been large because of the higher wages paid in railroad and other branches of employment.

The first business conducted in Portland by a Japanese was that of a restaurant serving American meals. This was established as early as 1888, when there were few Japanese in the State. With this as a beginning, the number of places of business has expanded as the Japanese population has increased and as the members of this race have gained a knowledge of American methods and wants. The kinds of business conducted by Japanese in 1891, 1900, and 1909 are shown in the following table:

TABLE 11.—*Data for Japanese in business in Portland, Oreg., in 1891, 1900, and 1909.*

Kind of business.	Number of establishments in—			Number of persons employed in 1909.
	1891.	1900.	1909.	
Restaurants serving American meals	4	14	14	94
Restaurants serving Japanese meals		4	11	48
Hotels and lodging houses	2	3	12	35
Laundries			2	8
Barber shops		2	10	31
Bath houses			a 13	37
Pool rooms			b 4	7
Art stores			4	6
Watch and jewelry store			1	5
Fish dealer			1	2
Japanese sauce dealer			1	2
Japanese cake store			1	4
Tofu maker			1	4
Other stores (chiefly general merchandise)		3	8	64
Shoemaker			1	2
Tailors			2	4
Mechanic			1	1
Carpenter shops			2	3
Garbage collector			1	4
Expressmen			2	4
Contractors	1	2	2	
Commercial agencies			2	6
Newspaper office			1	13
Total	c 7	c 28	d 97	e 384

a Three of these are connected with laundries.
b All connected with fruit and cigar stands or with bath houses and barber shops.
c Perhaps not complete.
d Slightly exaggerated because of duplication noted above.
e Not including office men of "contractors."

Though the figures for 1891 and 1900 may not be complete because of inadequate records, while those for 1909 are slightly exaggerated because of duplication, due to two or more businesses being at times conducted in one establishment, this table indicates that there has been a great increase in the number of different kinds of business engaged in and the number of establishments conducted by Japanese. In so far as can be ascertained, there were in 1891 only 4 restaurants serving American meals, 2 hotels and lodging houses making provision for the transient Japanese, and 1 contractor supplying laborers to two railroad companies. By 1900 the number of these establishments and contractors had increased, while restaurants serving Japanese meals, barber shops, and stores had been started. A much more rapid expansion took place later, especially just before the Portland exposition, for this attracted many Japanese to the city to engage in petty business. In fact, the number of establishments has not increased materially since that time.

The character of the business engaged in by Japanese is very well shown by the table just presented. Most of the stores, shops, and laundries are very small, represent but little capital investment, do little business, and yield only small profits. The chief exception is found in one store conducted by the largest of the contractors. Moreover, most of the business is incidental to supplying the needs of the Japanese. In fact, the barber shops, restaurants serving American meals, and the art stores alone have more than a small percentage of white patrons. Fifty per cent or more of the patrons of the barber shops are white men, principally laborers. White men constituted 50 per cent of the patrons of one, 70 per cent of those of another, and 96 per cent of those of a third shop from which complete data were obtained. The barbers are organized as the Japanese Barbers Union, which has established uniform prices—25 cents for hair cutting and 10 cents for shaving. These are the prices charged by the majority of the smaller shops conducted by white men. The barbers employed usually receive 60 per cent of the receipts and earn from $30 to $50 per month. The patrons of the Japanese restaurants serving American meals are almost all white laborers. One establishment doing a business of $9,600 per year, reported that 95 per cent of its patrons were white men, 5 per cent Japanese. Two others doing a business of $14,400 and $15,000 per year, respectively, had white patrons only. The proprietors of 12 of the 14 restaurants of this kind are members of the Japanese Restaurant Keepers Association, organized in 1896, to regulate prices and to protect the interests of its members. All of these establishments are of the " 10 cents and up " variety, and do the same class of business as is done by five Chinese and a many fold larger number of " white " restaurants. The wages of waiters and cooks vary from $30 to $40 and average about $33 per month, with board and lodging. The art stores selling brass ware and other " novelties " depend almost entirely upon white persons for their patronage. These establishments are all very small, however, and their competition is not felt by the dealers of other races.

As indicated in the table given, the various branches of business give employment to something more than 384 persons. Only Japanese are employed. In addition to these there are several professional men—2 interpreters, 3 dentists, and 5 physicians—the last two groups practicing among Japanese exclusively. The other Japanese gainfully employed, the official class and clergymen excepted, are employed for wages by white persons.

It is estimated that about 350 Japanese men are employed as domestics in private families. The more experienced command from $40 to $50 per month as cooks. These wages are much higher than those earned twenty years ago. The usual wage was then $14 or $15 per month. At no time has the number of Japanese domestics been sufficiently large seriously to affect the employment of other races. It is estimated that about 120 Japanese men are employed about hotels, bars, clubs, and in stores conducted by white proprietors. As porters they usually earn $12 per week or $50 per month and board. As bell boys, another capacity in which they are employed about hotels, they earn about $30 per month and board. In this latter capacity they are now employed to the exclusion of other races in most of the high-priced hotels of the city. The few employed in stores conducted by white men serve as porters and general workers. One newspaper is published by the Japanese in Portland. It is an eight-page daily with a circulation of about 800. The Japanese maintain two churches. The Methodist Mission was established in 1893 and has about 70 members. The Buddhist Mission was established ten years later. It has about 570 members, 270 of whom live in Portland and its vicinity, the others in more distant country places. The Japanese Association of Oregon was organized in February, 1909. It unifies the various kinds of organizations among the Japanese and serves to protect and promote the interests of that race as do the associations organized in other States.

Chapter VII

JAPANESE IN CITY EMPLOYMENTS AND BUSINESS IN DENVER.

The first Japanese settled in Colorado a little more than ten years ago. When they first came to the State they were engaged very largely in maintenance-of-way work on the railroads and in business in Denver. The latter city became a supply center. In 1900, however, they found employment in the coal mines, and somewhat later in an iron and steel plant at Pueblo. Shortly after that time they engaged in handwork in the sugar-beet fields, and subsequently became tenant farmers in large numbers. In 1909 the Japanese population of the State was estimated at 6,000. Of these, some 400 or more were engaged in coal mining, 128 in iron and steel manufacture, and 4,500 in agricultural and construction and railroad work, the agricultural laborers swelling the ranks of those otherwise employed during the seasons when little work is done in the beet fields. Denver is the supply center and the place of residence for the majority of the Japanese in the State when they are not employed.

According to an investigation conducted by the Japanese Association of Colorado, July 15, 1909, the number of Japanese in Denver was 526. Of these, 489 were adult males, 24 married women, and 13 children. This census contained few of the laborers who reside there when not at work. If these and miscellaneous persons not included in the above are added, the minimum number is estimated at about 725. During certain months of the year the number is much larger. About the middle of August, for example, many agricultural laborers come to the city to remain until the beet harvest begins toward the end of September. The Japanese population at that time is about 1,500. Again, at the close of the beet harvest in December a still larger number come to the city until they find other employment for the winter months or until agricultural work begins again in the spring. At that time the number is in excess of 1,500. With the growth of the Japanese population, Japanese have engaged in business in Denver primarily to provide for the wants of the remainder of that race residing there and to furnish supplies to those gainfully occupied in different parts of the State. Few have engaged in business in the smaller cities and towns. In 1909 five establishments were reported for Pueblo and two each for Colorado Springs and Eaton and one each for Greeley and Fort Collins, but the entire number outside of Denver does not greatly exceed a dozen. In Denver in 1903 there were two restaurants, one bamboo furniture manufacturer, and one boarding house. More recently, with the great influx of agricultural laborers to the beet fields, which began in 1903, the number of establishments conducted by Japanese has greatly increased. The number in July, 1909, as ascertained by an agent of the Commission, is shown in the table following. It shows also the number of persons gainfully occupied in the several establishments engaged in each kind of business specified.

307

TABLE 12.—*Japanese engaged in business in Denver, Colo., June, 1909.*

Kind of business.	Number of establish-ments.	Number of persons oc-cupied in same.	Kind of business.	Number of establish-ments.	Number of persons oc-cupied in same.
Banks *a*	1	2	Japanese confectionery *a*	2	2
Bamboo furniture shop *a*	1	1	Japanese drug store *a*	1	2
Barber shops	4	4	Jewelry shop	1	1
Bath houses (in barber shops)	3	0	Labor contractors *a*	7	8
			Laundries	3	9
Boarding and lodging houses *a*	7	20	Lodging houses	3	4
Curio shops	1	2	Massage parlor *a*	1	1
Dairy	2	3	Photograph gallery *a*	1	1
Dry goods stores (2 carry-ing provisions also)	4	18	Pool rooms	3	6
			Restaurants (Japanese meals)	10	33
Employment office *a*	1	2	Tailor shops	2	2
Express	2	2	Tea garden	1	3
Fish markets *a*	1	2	Tofu manufacturer *a*	1	1
Grocery stores	2	2			
Ice cream parlors	2	2	Total *b*	67	133

a Patronized by Japanese only.
b Not including 5 newspaper men with branch offices, 4 house-cleaning agencies with 130 men, 2 physicians, 2 dentists, a hospital, a "bamboo worker," a carpenter, a job painter, and 2 prostitutes.

The total presented, viz, 67 establishments, comprising 133 persons gainfully occupied, does not include 5 newspaper men, with branch offices; 4 house-cleaning agencies, with 130 men; 2 physicians, 2 dentists, several craftsmen, and a few others gainfully occupied in the Japanese colony or in connection with Japanese institutions.

The Japanese are more conspicuous in the general field of domestic service than in any other branch of employment in Denver. There are 4 house-cleaning agencies, controlling some 130 men, who do house-cleaning and domestic work by the day. There is also a group of Koreans, as large as any of these 4, likewise employed. Some 100 Japanese men are regularly employed as domestics in private families, but they are only a small percentage of the total number so employed. There were also, in 1908 and 1909, 22 students attending the public schools of the city and the University of Denver. This accounts for the vast majority of those residing in the city throughout the year other than those engaged as professional and business men and their few dependents.

An agent of the Commission made a general investigation of the business conducted in Denver by the Japanese. The number of the establishments was too few to warrant a general statistical analysis. The general results may be briefly presented. Most of the Japanese live and, with few exceptions, conduct their business in two or three blocks of the older part of the business district of the city. There, as elsewhere, the vast majority of the proprietors, their families, and employees live in the rear or over the rooms in which business is conducted.

The seven boarding and lodging houses are patronized exclusively by Japanese, chiefly farm and railroad laborers. These provide board as well as lodging. Besides these seven, there are three lodging houses which provide lodgings only and are patronized to some extent by white persons of the lower class. These 10 boarding and lodging houses are organized into a boarding-house association, the primary object of which is to prevent any unnecessary competition.

At the time of the investigation each member was contributing $5 per month to a fund for the purpose of establishing a cooperative supply house. There are 10 restaurants, all of which serve Japanese meals and " noodles " only. They have a few white and negro patrons, but the Japanese patrons are far more numerous than the others. These proprietors are organized into the Japanese Restaurant Keepers' Association, which regulates prices so that they may be uniform, and controls the location of restaurants, so that undue competition shall not develop. There are no Japanese restaurants serving American meals, and there is no competition between those serving Japanese meals and the restaurants conducted by the members of other races. When the Japanese first came to Denver, about ten years ago, however, several opened restaurants to serve American meals. It is said that the prices charged were lower than those which obtained at other cheap restaurants in the city, so that the competition of the seven or more Japanese establishments was keenly felt, especially by other establishments located near by. The white cooks and waiters were at that time strongly organized, and, acting in cooperation with the white restaurant keepers, they succeeded in cutting off very largely the supplies which had been furnished the Japanese restaurants by white dealers. This was done by means of a threatened boycott of offending dealers. Moreover, the Japanese were prevented from establishing a supply house of their own, and though the case was contested in the courts the Japanese restaurant keepers were soon forced to suspend business.

As indicated in the foregoing table, there were four dry goods stores. These are in fact supply stores. Two of them carry goods of every kind, save perishable articles, needed by railroad and farm laborers, and most of their trade is with out of town laborers of the kind mentioned, employed through and working under the control of the proprietors of these supply houses as labor contractors. In addition to this supply business they have some city customers, both Japanese and white, the latter being the more numerous. One of the larger of the supply houses does a business of approximately $100,000 per year, 70 per cent of which is with farmers and laborers in various parts of Colorado. The value of goods imported from Japan during the year was $55,000, or more than one-half of the value of the annual transactions.

Besides these dealers who serve as labor contractors, there are several other Japanese contractors in Denver, making a total of seven. These men are engaged in providing laborers for work in the mines, as section hands on the railroads, and for construction of dams, reservoirs, and other reclamation work. The relations between the contractors and men are practically the same as in Seattle, where conditions have already been noted. Besides these labor contractors there is one employment office patronized exclusively by Japanese and chiefly by domestics and casual laborers employed in Denver. The other branches of business engaged in by Japanese are of less importance. There are four barber shops with one chair each. Three also have baths. The prices are the same as those charged in other shops of the same type, viz, 20 or 25 cents for hair cutting and 15 cents for shaving. While all of the shops are patronized by other races, the Japanese are the most numerous of all.

There are three laundries. Two are conducted by the members of one family without the assistance of outside employees, while only 1 Japanese man and from 3 to 4 white women are employed in the other. The latter, alone, has patrons other than Japanese, the majority of its customers being white persons. The prices charged are higher than those which are maintained by some white laundries but lower than those of some others. The competition is negligible. The Japanese conduct two dairies supplying milk in Denver. One has 33, the other 15 milch cows. Both Japanese and white persons are found among their patrons, the latter being in the majority. Both Japanese are members of the Dairymens' Association, and there is no underselling of other dealers. The three pool parlors are frequented by members of other races as well as by Japanese. Taking the three together, the percentages of the various races represented among the patrons are about as follows: White persons, 10; negroes, 20; Japanese, 70. The other business conducted by the Japanese is of little importance. Moreover, as is indicated in the foregoing table, most of the establishments have Japanese patrons only.

From the table to which reference has just been made and from this brief review of different branches of business conducted by Japanese, it is evident (1) that while the number of Japanese business establishments in Denver has rapidly increased since 1903, they are not comparatively numerous; (2) that with the exception of the supply stores and some of the lodging houses, they are small; (3) that the more important branches of business, viz, the labor agencies, supply business, the boarding and lodging houses, and the restaurants, as well as the majority of the small establishments, have been started primarily to provide for Japanese laborers while in Denver as transients and while at work in other places; (4) that the only branch of business in which there has been serious competition between Japanese and white establishments is the restaurant trade, and that the Japanese thus engaged were compelled to suspend business because of the organized opposition of their competitors and their employees; (5) that while a comparatively large number of the small shops and some of the larger stores have non-Japanese patrons, such establishments occupy such an unimportant place in the trade of Denver that their existence is of no particular consequence to business men of other races.

The most important organizations among the Japanese other than the purely business organizations among the restaurant keepers and the boarding and lodging house keepers, to which reference has been made, are the Japanese Association of Colorado, the Business Men's Association, and two " prefectural " societies, with memberships of 639, 25, 25, and 66, respectively. The Japanese Association of Colorado was organized a few years ago when the opposition to immigrants of that race was organized and directed through the local Japanese and Korean Exclusion League, and was designed to protect the interests of the members of the race in Colorado. Since the opposition has become less pronounced, the association has served the same purposes as similar organizations in other localities. The Japanese Business Men's Association is chiefly of historical interest. It was organized in 1907 as a result of a factional fight within the

Japanese Association of Colorado over the requirements made by contractors of a deposit of $10 by each of their Japanese laborers when beginning work.   This requirement resulted in hardship and exploitation, and the association resolved that the practice was unjust and should be discontinued.   Thereupon some of the members withdrew from the association and organized a rival institution under the name of the Japanese Business Men's Association.   More recently the requirement of a $10 deposit has been abolished.

A small hospital and the Methodist Mission are the other Japanese institutions which should be noted in Denver.   Other religious denominations had not at the time of the investigation organized missions among the Japanese.

Chapter VIII

JAPANESE IN CITY TRADES AND BUSINESS IN SALT LAKE CITY AND OGDEN.

INTRODUCTION.

The first Japanese came to the State of Utah a little less than ten years ago, when a contractor brought in 200 of them to engage in railroad work. With this as a beginning, the members of this race have increased in number, engaged in more numerous occupations, become conspicuous as tenant farmers in certain agricultural localities, and engaged in business on a small scale in Salt Lake City, Ogden, and a few of the smaller towns. Most of the Japanese are common laborers, and many of them move rapidly from place to place and from one industry to another. The number in a given locality or engaged in any given industry varies greatly during the year. Consequently it is impossible to do more than give an approximate estimate of the total number in the State.

The following data were obtained in June and July, 1909, and are presented as showing the approximate number of Japanese [a] in the State and the occupations in which they were engaged at that time:

```
In the State:
    Railroad laborers—
        Section hands_____  813
        Shop laborers_____  107
                                                                      ——— 920
        Coal miners_____  126
        Smelter laborers_____  143
        Cement factory hands_____   20
        Construction laborers_____   48
        Sugar beet hands_____ [b]800
        Farmers and other agricultural laborers_____ [b]225
In Salt Lake City: [c]
        Business and professional men and assistants_____  150
        Domestics _____   90
        House cleaners_____    2
        Cooks _____   35
        Store help_____   15
        Students _____   24
        Without occupation _____   80
                                                                      ——— [c]396
In Ogden_____ [b][d]125
In towns_____ [b]20
Women and children_____  125
                                                                      ———
        Total_____[b]2,948
```

[a] Not including about 200 Koreans employed on railroads, in beet fields, and leasing land.

[b] Estimated.

[c] Exclusive of 93 included in above entries.

[d] Exclusive of laborers and helpers in railroad shops and roundhouse at Ogden, included under railroad laborers above.

The total number of Japanese in Utah is thus estimated to have been approximately 3,000. Something more than 1,000 of them were men engaged at the time in agricultural occupations. Though most of these men purchase the bulk of their supplies at "American" stores, practically all purchase some if not many supplies at Salt Lake City or Ogden, and chiefly at the latter place. Some 920 men were employed under 10 contractors as maintenance of way men or as shop and roundhouse laborers by the railroads. In addition to these, 1,340 were similarly employed in Nevada, Idaho, and Wyoming, thus making a total of 2,260 laborers under the control of 10 Japanese contractors with offices at Salt Lake City and Ogden. These men purchase by far the greater part of their supplies from Japanese supply stores, the majority of which are conducted by these labor contractors. The same is equally true of most of the 126 Japanese coal miners and the 143 smelter hands who are under the control of some of the same contractors. In addition to these 126 coal miners employed in Utah, several hundred are similarly employed in Wyoming through a contractor at Salt Lake City and purchase many of their supplies from him. Primarily to secure employment and to supply the wants of these men while at work and to provide for their needs when unemployed in the cities, a comparatively large number of business establishments have been opened by Japanese in Salt Lake City and Ogden, while a few have been opened in the small towns of the agricultural districts in which many Japanese laborers are employed. Still other establishments have been started to secure the patronage of other races. These various Japanese establishments provide gainful employment for perhaps 150 Japanese in Salt Lake City, for perhaps 125 in Ogden, and probably for as many as 20 in the small towns of the northern part of the State. Finally, in recent years a comparatively small number of Japanese have found employment as domestics in the homes of and as "help" in establishments conducted by white men.

JAPANESE IN CITY TRADES AND EMPLOYMENTS IN SALT LAKE CITY.

The "settled" Japanese population of Salt Lake City is estimated at about 441. Of women there were about 20; of children about 12. Of the men, 93 were, in July, 1909, employed in street construction and railroad work. Of the other 316, about 150 were connected with Japanese business establishments or engaged in the professions, about 127 engaged in domestic and personal service and related employments, 15 were employed in cleaning and similar work in "American" stores, while some 24 were students in public schools of the city and the University of Utah. In addition to these Japanese residents, there are a variable number of transient laborers. At the time of the investigation there were about 80 of these, but during the winter months this number increases to several hundred. The number of domestics employed regularly by the month in "American" families numbers about 75; the number of "school boys" who work a few hours per day for board and lodging and a small sum of money, about 15. The total number is so small as compared with the total number of persons engaged in domestic service that no appreciable effect has been wrought upon the wages and other conditions of employment of other persons similarly occupied. Only two men, in partnership, have engaged in house cleaning and similar work by the hour or day. Some 35 Japanese have found employment in white restaurants as cooks and " kitchen help." The number is too small to have had any appreciable effect upon the employment of other races in similar capacities. The same is true of the 15 employed as janitors, porters, and "general help" in stores conducted by white men. The kinds of business and the number of establishments of each kind conducted by Japanese in Salt Lake City in July, 1909, are shown in the following table:

TABLE 13.—*Japanese in business in Salt Lake City, Utah, July, 1909.*

Kind of business.	Number of establish- ments.	Kind of business.	Number of establish- ments.
Bamboo furniture manufacture	1	Newspaper	1
Barber shops	3	Photograph gallery	1
Bathhouses	2	Provision stores	4
Billiard and pool rooms	3	Restaurants serving American meals	5
Boarding houses	9	Restaurants serving Japanese meals	3
Contractors	7	Tailor shops	3
Curio shops	3		
Laundry	1	Total	a 46

a Not including 1 physician, 1 house-cleaning establishment conducted by 2 men in partnership, and 1 carpenter.

The total number of establishments was 46. Of these, 7 were employment agencies (most of which sell supplies also), while 4 were provision or supply stores, both closely connected with the employment of laborers in the mines and smelters and on the railways. The 7 contractors, from their Salt Lake City offices, in July, 1909, controlled 1,223 laborers, besides several hundred employed in the coal mines of western Wyoming. In the majority of cases the contractors collect an interpreter's fee of $1 per month and 5 per cent of the earnings of each laborer, the wages being paid by the employer through the contractor. A further source of profit is found in the supplies furnished the laborers working under the control of the several contractors or agents.

Besides the supply stores conducted by the contractors and not engaged in local retail trade, there are four provision stores conducted by Japanese. These are located in the Japanese quarter, which centers in a small street one block west of Main street (the center of the business district), between First and Second streets south. These stores are patronized almost exclusively by Japanese. Most of the 9 boarding and lodging houses and the 3 restaurants serving Japanese meals are also located in this district. Of these establishments, only one—a boarding and lodging house—is patronized by others than Japanese, and in this case the Japanese patrons constitute more than 90 per cent of the entire number. The prices charged for boarding and lodging range from 55 to 75 cents per day for transients. The charge for lodging alone is from 15 to 35 cents per night; that for single meals, 15 cents.

The restaurants serving American meals, the small laundry, the barber shops and baths, the curio shops, tailor shops, and billiard and pool rooms, unlike the business establishments already noted, have comparatively large numbers of white patrons. Until shortly previous to the investigation there had been seven Japanese restaurants serving American meals, but two of them had failed and had been closed. The five remaining were scattered through the business district and were found to be patronized chiefly by white men, the vast majority of whom were of the laboring class. They serve cheap but substantial meals at low prices—two at 20 cents, two at 15 cents, and one at 10 cents. These establishments in point of furnishings, service, food, and prices do not differ materially from a very much larger number of small "cheap" restaurants conducted by white men of various races. No opposition has as yet been aroused against the Japanese restaurants; their competition has not had any serious effect upon their competitors. The hand laundry employs only four men. The three barber shops are also small, two of them having only two chairs each, the other four. One of the barbers employed is a white man. The Japanese and white patrons of the smaller shops are about equal in number, but the latter class predominate among the patrons of the larger shop. The charge for hair cutting is uniformly 25 cents, for shaving 10 cents. These prices are the same as those which obtain in small shops of the same type conducted by men of other races, many of whom are foreign-born. However, in the majority of the shops conducted by white men the prices are 35 cents for hair cutting and 15 cents for shaving. The baths conducted by Japanese are run in connection with two of their barber shops.

The curio shops are small, and, as elsewhere, are patronized largely by white people. The three tailor shops are small, each being conducted by one man. Though each is an agent for Chicago merchant-tailoring houses, most of the business done consists of cleaning, repairing, and pressing suits. The price charged for cleaning and pressing is $1 per suit, the same as at other shops engaged in that business. Of three billiard and pool rooms conducted by Japanese two are small and are patronized by the members of that race almost exclusively, while a larger one with eight tables is patronized almost entirely by white men. The last-mentioned establishment sells soft drinks and cigars also, and does a large amount of business. The other branches of business engaged in by the Japanese are of little consequence. They have been indicated in the foregoing table.

The more essential matters relating to Japanese business in Salt Lake City may be stated in summary form as follows: (1) The more important establishments are directly connected with the supplying of laborers to capitalistic enterprises and providing these laborers with the necessaries of life; (2) the Japanese may supply most of their needs, save for clothing of superior quality, at establishments conducted by members of their own race; (3) their barber shops and baths, some of the pool rooms, the curio shops, tailor shops, and restaurants serving American meals are patronized largely by white persons, but these establishments are few and small, and maintain the same level of prices as are found in similar establishments conducted by other races, so that the competition between them and their competitors has been of little consequence.

JAPANESE IN BUSINESS IN OGDEN.

Ogden is a supply point for railway and for agricultural laborers engaged in truck gardening and sugar-beet growing. The 4 labor contractors in July, 1909, controlled 1,322 men employed by a number of railway companies. These laborers and the vast majority of those employed in the beet fields and the numerous farmers are provided with much of their food and some of their clothes by the Japanese provision and supply stores. During the seasons when many Japanese laborers are unemployed a large number live at the boarding and lodging houses conducted at Ogden. To supply their needs, and in some cases to secure white patrons, a comparatively large number of establishments have in recent years been started by Japanese. One important difference between the situation found in Salt Lake City and that which obtains in Ogden lies in the fact that to some extent Japanese are engaged in domestic service and related occupations in the former, while practically all of the approximately 175 Japanese residing throughout the year in Ogden are connected with business establishments conducted by the members of that race or work in the railroad shops. Another difference is found in the fact that less of the business conducted is for the American trade. The kinds of business engaged in by the Japanese in Ogden and the number of establishments conducted, in July, 1909, are shown in the following table:

TABLE 14.—*Japanese in business in Ogden, Utah, July, 1909.*

Kind of business.	Number of establishments.	Kind of business.	Number of establishments.
Bank (branch)	1	Provision stores	2
Barber shops	4	Laundry	1
Baths	a 2	Restaurant serving American meals	1
Contractors	4	Restaurants serving Japanese meals	8
Express	2	Tailor shop	1
Hotels and lodging houses	10		
Photograph gallery	1	Total d	c 43
Pool rooms	b 6		

a Connected with barber shops.
b Three of the 6 connected with barber shops.
c See notes "a" and "b."
d Not including 3 branch newspaper agencies dealing in Japanese newspapers and conducted in connection with other business.

The total number of Japanese establishments (including some duplication which can not be entirely eliminated in this case) was 43. Those of importance, with few exceptions, are directly connected with Japanese labor. What was said concerning the business of the labor contractors at Salt Lake City applies equally well to contractors with offices at Ogden. The two large provision stores, both of which are closely connected with, though conducted separately from, the contracting business, carry chiefly Japanese goods in stock and are patronized almost exclusively by Japanese. They ship large consignments of goods to groups of Japanese section hands and beet-field laborers. The 10 boarding and lodging houses are patronized exclusively by Japanese and practically all of these are of the transient class who come to Ogden " between jobs." The proprietors of these establishments have organized an association to limit the competition among them. The price of lodging is 20 cents for the night, without board, and 15 cents if meals are purchased also. The cost of meals is 15 cents each. The two expressmen are engaged principally in hauling the baggage of Japanese as they come to and depart from the city.

The number of establishments having any considerable percentage of their patrons among the white race are the one laundry, the one restaurant serving American meals, the four barber shops and the pool rooms. The laundry gives employment to four Japanese and five white women. About 50 per cent of the patrons are white. The prices charged, and especially those charged for laundering women's articles, are somewhat lower than those charged by the white steam laundries. Yet the prices are higher than those charged for work done for Japanese, for it is customary to make material reductions on articles laundered for the members of that race. Though the Chinese have several restaurants patronized almost exclusively, if not entirely, by white persons, the Japanese have not engaged in the serving of American meals to any considerable extent. At the time of the investigation there was only one small restaurant serving American meals. The price per meal was 15 cents.

From the point of view of American patronage the barber shops and the baths and pool rooms connected with them are by far the most important of all the establishments conducted by the Japanese. There are four small barber shops, each with two chairs. These are located in the most frequented parts of the city and 70 per cent of their patrons are white men. The price charged for hair cutting is 25 cents, for shaving 10 cents. These prices are the same as those charged at three nonunion white shops giving equally good service, and higher than at two others of a poorer quality at which the charges for hair cutting and shaving are 15 and 10 cents, respectively. The majority of the white shops are unionized, however, and the union price for hair cutting is 35 cents, and for shaving 15 cents. It is evident that the Japanese, together with about an equal number of white shops, are appealing to the " cheaper trade." The charge for a bath at the Japanese shops is 15 cents. The same rate obtains at some white establishments, though at a much larger number the charge is either 20 or 25 cents. There is no difference in the prices " per cue " at Japanese pool rooms, three of which are connected with barber shops and patronized largely by white persons, and those which prevail elsewhere.

The other business establishments are few in number, are small, and are patronized chiefly by the Japanese. The bank is a branch institution designed to serve as an agency for collecting and forwarding the savings of the Japanese laborers. The tailor is agent for a Chicago merchant-tailoring house, but is engaged chiefly in cleaning and pressing clothes. His shop is located in the Japanese quarter and is patronized chiefly by the Japanese who live in the boarding and lodging houses near by. The small photograph gallery is patronized chiefly by Japanese laborers. From the details presented it is evident (1) that most of the Japanese business establishments are small; (2) that white persons are relatively numerous among the patrons of a few establishments only; and (3) that the limited competition between the Japanese and white business men has as yet been of no particular consequence.

A very few Japanese are engaged in business in some of the smaller towns. Garland and Logan, in each of which there is a small Japanese restaurant largely patronized by white people, are typical of these. The entire number of Japanese business establishments in Utah, outside of Salt Lake City and Ogden, probably does not exceed six.

CHAPTER IX.

JAPANESE IN BUSINESS IN IDAHO.

The number of Japanese in Idaho varies greatly with the seasons, chiefly because of the importance of the beet fields as a source of employment. The number of persons engaged in some of the non-agricultural occupations also varies from season to season for the same reason. According to the best estimates the number of domestic servants varies between 40 and 70, of railroad laborers between 200 and several hundred. The number of Japanese engaged in the handwork of the beet fields reaches between 600 and 700 as a maximum. The number of Japanese farmers and employees perhaps numbers 50. The number engaged in reclamation work varies greatly from time to time. The number connected with business enterprises is about 80. In all probability the total number in the State at the minimum in winter is something less than 1,000, the maximum in summer not much less than 1,400.

The Japanese are employed in many parts of the State as laborers on the railroads, in the beet fields, and in the construction of irrigation ditches. Wherever they have been employed for a year or so a small number have engaged in business. While investigating the beet-sugar industry and railway labor, the agents of the Commission collected the data relative to Japanese engaged in business presented in the following table:

TABLE 15.—*Japanese engaged in business in Idaho in 1909.*

Location.	Provision and supply stores.	Boarding and lodging houses.	Restaurants serving Japanese meals.	Restaurants serving American meals.	Barber shops.	Pool rooms.	Tailor shops.	Curio stores.	Total.
American Falls				1					1
Boise		1		3					4
Gooding				1					1
Idaho Falls		1							1
Mindoka				1					1
Nampa	1	1				1	1		4
Preston				1					1
Pocatello	2	1	1	1	1	a 1		1	8
Shoshone				1		1			2
Twin Falls				2					2
Wendell				1					1
Total b	b 3	4	1	12	1	3	1	1	b 26

a With barber shop.

b Not including 1 railroad contractor and a few subcontractors under a general agency in several sugar beet growing districts, together with the supply business they conduct.

The preceding table is not complete. In all probability a few Japanese are engaged in business in other towns in the southern part of the State. The total number of establishments not reported, however, is small. Moreover, the table does not include a contractor for railroad labor at Pocatello and a few subcontractors working under a general agency and controlling many of the laborers in the beet fields and the supply business conducted by them. In spite of this incompleteness, however, the table shows (1) the comparatively slight extent to which the Japanese have engaged in business, and (2) that restaurants serving American meals are by far the most numerous of the enterprises conducted.

That the Japanese have not engaged more extensively in business in Idaho is due to the fact that there is no important center in the State from which Japanese laborers are supplied, and the comparatively short time they have engaged in any employment save railway work where they are provided with supplies by the contractors through whom they are employed. That a number of small restaurants serving American meals have been opened in small towns is an interesting fact. Both the Chinese and Japanese conduct restaurants patronized chiefly by white people of various classes who show no antipathy to the Orientals. Unlike the white residents of the Pacific Coast States, those of Idaho give no evidence of any hostile feeling toward either the Chinese or the Japanese.

PART III.—THE EAST INDIANS ON THE PACIFIC COAST.

Chapter I.

INTRODUCTORY.

Agents of the Commission made an investigation of East Indian immigrants in California, Oregon, and Washington. Data were secured for 36 groups including 159 members and from 395 other men found at work on farms and elsewhere. Information was obtained from the members of the 36 groups with reference to their occupations, wages, cost of living, housing, and related matters. Information was secured with reference to still other matters from 79 of the members of 24 of these groups. Corresponding data relative to most points of interest were obtained from the 395 from whom individual schedules were obtained. The number of these latter schedules is not so large or so well distributed by industries as desired because those employed as section hands on the railroad and in lumber mills could not be reached by the agents in person, and it was found impossible to secure the data otherwise because of the inability of the majority of these immigrants to read and write English, and because of the disinclination of the foremen under whom they worked to devote the time necessary to secure the desired information and to record it. Personal data were secured, however, from 474 East Indians. These are 15 per cent or more of the total number in the United States at the time the investigation was conducted. Inasmuch as practically all of these immigrants are engaged in common labor and are of the same class, the data secured are believed to show the essential facts with a fair degree of accuracy.

323

Chapter II

SETTLEMENT AND PROGRESS OF EAST INDIANS IN PACIFIC COAST STATES.

The East Indians in the Pacific coast States include Sikhs, Mohammedans, and Afghans (who are also of the Mohammedan faith). They are all known as " Hindus," though, strictly speaking, they are not all of the Hindu caste.

There are at present about 5,000 East Indians of the working class in the United States.

The census of 1900 does not specify by race the number of East Indians in the United States at that time, but it gives a total (exclusive of Hawaii and Alaska) of 2,050 persons born in India, and it is probable that the greater part of these were East Indians. The following table, compiled from the annual reports of the Commissioner-General of Immigration for the years 1900–1910, shows the number of East Indian immigrants admitted during the past eleven years.

TABLE 1.—*Number of East Indians admitted and departed during the years 1900 to 1910.*

Year ending June 30—	Admitted.			Departed.[a]			Increase.
	Immigrant aliens.	Nonimmigrant aliens.	Total.	Emigrant aliens.	Nonemigrant aliens.	Total.	
1900	9						
1901	20						
1902	84						
1903	83						
1904	258						
1905	145						
1906	271						
1907	1,072						
1908	1,710			124			1,586
1909	337	113	450	48	55	103	347
1910	1,782	85	1,867	b 74	b 78	b 152	

[a] Previous to 1908 no record of departures was kept. The distinction between immigrant and nonimmigrant aliens was first made in 1909, and the basis of the classification is thus explained: " In making the classification the following rule is observed: Arriving aliens whose permanent domicile has been outside of the United States who intend to reside permanently in the United States are classed as immigrant aliens; departing aliens whose permanent residence has been in the United States who intend to reside permanently abroad are classed as emigrant aliens; all alien residents of the United States making a temporary trip abroad, and all aliens residing abroad and making a temporary trip to the United States are classed as nonimmigrant aliens on the inward journey and nonemigrant on the outward " (p. 9, Report Commissioner-General of Immigration, 1909).
[b] For July, 1909, to March, 1910, inclusive.

This table shows that the immigration of East Indians in more than small numbers has been very recent, and it also shows how rapidly the number admitted has been increasing. In 1900, 9 were admitted to the United States, in 1904, 258, and in 1908, 1,710. The great decline in the number entering this country in 1909 was due to the fact that the Canadian government put in force a more stringent policy (hereafter explained) which barred East Indians from British Columbia, from whence they had been coming to the United States, and that the United States Bureau of Immigration was more rigid in its requirements than it had been before or is now. The provision of the immigration law excluding " persons likely to become a public charge " was strictly applied against East Indians and discouraged their coming in that year. In 1908 the number debarred from entering the United States was one-fourth as large as the number admitted; in 1909 the number debarred was three-fourths as large as the number of immigrant and nonimmigrant East Indians admitted, while in 1910 less than one-fourth as many were debarred as were admitted.

The reports for the years 1908, 1909, and for nine months of 1910 give the number leaving the United States as shown in the above table. Previous to 1909 the reports do not distinguish between immigrant and nonimmigrant aliens admitted. The number of East Indians debarred from entering and also the number deported are given in the following table:

TABLE 2.—*Number of East Indians debarred during the years 1900 to 1910, by cause.*

Year ending June 30—	Tuberculosis.	Trachoma.	Loathsome or contagious diseases.	Surgeon's certificate of defect mentally or physically which may affect ability to earn living.	Likely to become a public charge.	Contract laborers.	Idiots.	Under sec. 11, act of 1903.	Criminals.	Polygamists.	Total.	Deported.
1900											0	0
1901					1						1	0
1902											0	0
1903											0	1
1904			3		4						7	2
1905					12	1					13	2
1906			6		10	5	2	1			24	2
1907			102		286	29					417	1
1908	1	192		107	118	20					438	9
1909		94	2	54	146	17			2	16	331	1
1910		161	7	18	200	7				18	411	4

This table indicates the causes for rejecting applicants for admission and the number under each class by years. There are three main causes (1) trachoma and other loathsome or contagious diseases; (2) surgeon's certificate of mental or physical defect which may affect the ability to earn a living; and (3) danger of becoming a public charge. A number were debarred as contract laborers. Of the total number debarred during the 10 years, 1901–1910, nearly one-half were rejected owing to their being "likely to become a public charge." A little less than one-third were rejected as having trachoma or other loathsome or contagious diseases.

In this connection the following table, which shows the amount of money brought to the United States by 79 East Indians from whom schedules were secured, is given:

TABLE 3.—*Money brought to the United States by East Indians.*

Number reporting complete data.	Number bringing each specified amount.								
	None.	Under $25.	$25 and under $50.	$50 and under $100.	$100 and under $150.	$150 and under $200.	$200 and under $300.	$300 and under $400.	$400 and under $500.
73....	3	3	15	36	9	2	2	2	1

The next table shows the number of East Indian immigrants bringing $50 and over and the number bringing less than $50, as given in the reports of the Commissioner-General of Immigration.

TABLE 4.—*Money brought to the United States by East Indians during the years 1905 to 1909.*

Year.	Number bringing each specified amount.		Total amount of money shown.
	$50 or over.	Less than $50.	
1905	70	55	$13,575
1906	111	75	17,016
1907	255	745	39,278
1908	367	1,129	72,650
1909	189	123	24,834
Total	992	2,127	167,353

Table 5, also compiled from the reports of the Commissioner-General of Immigration, shows other salient facts in regard to the East Indian immigrants.

TABLE 5.—*General data for East Indian immigrants.*

Year.	Number of immigrants.	Sex.		Last permanent residence.		Occupation abroad.		
		Male.	Female.	India.	British North America.	Farmer.	Farm laborer.	Laborer.
1901	20	18	2	20	0	0	0	1
1902	84	82	2	84	0	0	0	14
1903	83	70	13	83	0	6	0	4
1904	258	241	17	224	0	0	4	7
1905	145	137	8	70	17	0	2	35
1906	271	252	19	155	6	19	0	42
1907	1,072	1,056	16	833	89	23	91	816
1908	1,710	1,702	8	999	593	58	123	1,380
1909	337	327	10	138	129	26	43	128
1910	1,782	1,768	14	1,615	23	22	371	1,222

TABLE 5.—*General data for East Indian immigrants*—Continued.

Year.	Intended destination.					Number who have been in the United States before.	Illiterates.
	New York.	California.	Oregon.	Washington.	Other States.		
1901	2	6	0	0	12	3	5
1902	42	8	0	3	31	6	4
1903	54	20	1	0	8	15	18
1904	82	19	1	8	148	30	76
1905	31	11	2	43	58	29	17
1906	67	25	24	57	98	25	77
1907	35	491	31	475	40	27	487
1908	63	736	70	713	128	58	985
1909	61	78	17	67	114	58	98
1910	43	1,343	61	48	a 60	....	936

a Not including 227 going to Hawaii.

The table shows the small number of females of this race who have come to the United States, and their number has not been increasing in proportion to the increase in number of immigrants, for members of the laboring class now coming in large numbers do not bring their wives.

This table indicates the number giving India or British North America as their last permanent residence. These have been the two main sources of the East Indian immigration. As shown under the head of " intended destination " previous to 1905 nearly all of the East Indians were bound for Eastern States. Of these New York received the majority. The immigration of East Indians to the three Pacific Coast States, Washington, Oregon, and California, practically began in 1905, when it will be noted they gave British North America as their " last permanent residence." For the years 1905 to 1909 inclusive, British Columbia was the principal source of East Indian immigration to the Pacific Coast States. Most of those giving India as their last permanent residence came via British Columbia. Since 1905 the Pacific Coast States have received nearly all of the rapidly increasing immigration of this race.

It will be noted in the table that since 1905 the proportion giving the three occupations " farmer," " farm laborer," and " laborer " has increased until in 1908 out of 1,710 immigrants 1,380 were laborers, 123 farm laborers, and 58 farmers.

Of the total of 5,317 admitted during the years 1905 to 1910, inclusive, 778 had been employed in agricultural work, while 3,623 had been " laborers " abroad. Of 473 East Indians in the United States from whom agents of the Commission secured personal data, 402 had been engaged in agriculture, 10 in business and in the trades, and 16 in the other occupations as wage-earners, while 16 had been soldiers and 6 had had no occupation before leaving their native land. That the Commissioner-General of Immigration reports more as laborers while the agents' schedules show more farm workers is due to the fact that in coming from Canada the East Indians gave their occupation as laborers, referring to their work in Canada. The East Indian immigrants came from the Punjab, a farming section of India. Previous to 1905 the majority of the few East Indians coming to the United States were professional men, merchants, and travelers. The great influx since 1905 has been of the " coolie " class. It will also be seen that the proportion of illiterates has greatly increased.

The first East Indians settling in the Pacific Coast States in noticeable numbers came from British Columbia, so that their migration to Canada will be considered. The number entering Canada is as follows: 1905, 45; 1906, 387; 9 months to March 31, 1907, 2,124; 1908, 2,623; 1909, 6. Total, 5,185.

In speaking of the causes of the East Indian immigration to Canada, the Hon. W. L. Mackenzie King, royal commissioner, says as follows:

The influx of recent years has not been spontaneous, but owes its existence in the main to (1) the activity of certain steamship companies and agents desirous of selling transportation and profiting by the commission; (2) the distribution throughout some of the rural districts of India of literature concerning Canada and the opportunities of fortune making in the province of British Columbia; and (3) the representations of a few individuals in the province of British Columbia, among the number a Brahmin named Davichand and certain of his relatives, who induced a number of the natives of India to come to Canada under actual or verbal agreements to work for hire, the purpose being that of assisting one or two industrial concerns to obtain a class of unskilled labor at a price below the current rate and at the same time of exploiting their fellow-subjects to their own advantage. Some of the natives may have emigrated to Canada of their own accord or because of the advice or desire of some relatives who had come to this country, but had the influence here mentioned not been exerted it is certain that their numbers would not have been appreciable.[a]

Later, in another report,[b] Mr. King says:

That Canada should desire to restrict immigration from the Orient is regarded as natural; that Canada should remain a white man's country is believed to be not only desirable for economic and social reasons, but highly necessary on political and national grounds. * * *

It is clearly recognized in regard to emigration from India to Canada that the native of India is not a person suited to this country; that, accustomed, as many of them are, to conditions of a tropical climate and possessing manners and customs so unlike those of our own people, their inability to readily adapt themselves to surroundings entirely different could not do other than entail an amount of privation and suffering which render a discontinuance of such immigration most desirable in the interest of the Indians themselves. It was recognized, too, that the competition of this class of labor, though not likely to prove effective, if left to itself, might, none the less, were the numbers to become considerable (as conceivably could happen were self-interest on the part of individuals to be allowed to override considerations of humanity and national well-being and the importation of this class of labor under contract permitted), occasion considerable unrest among the workingmen whose standard of comfort is of a higher order, and who, as citizens with family and civic obligations, have expenditures to meet and a status to maintain which the coolie immigrant is in a position wholly to ignore.[b]

The East Indian immigrants were not welcome in British Columbia, and the opposition to them led to insurmountable barriers being erected against them, which accounts for the decline in their numbers in 1909 when only 6 were admitted. The most formidable of these barriers is the application to East Indian immigrants of section 38 of the Canadian immigration act which provides that any immigrants who have come to Canada otherwise than by continuous journey from the country of which they are natives or citizens, and

---

[a] Report of the royal commissioner appointed to inquire into the methods by which oriental laborers have been induced to come to Canada. Ottawa, 1908. p. 76.

[b] Report by W. L. Mackenzie King, deputy minister of labor on mission to England to confer with the British authorities on the subject of immigration to Canada from the Orient and immigration from India in particular.

upon through tickets purchased in that country, may be excluded. This provision has been peculiarly efficient because there is no means by which a continuous journey from India to Canada can be accomplished. Another deterrent was an order in council dated June 3, 1908, by which the amount of money required in the case of East Indians was increased from $25 to $200.

The East Indians in Canada are engaged in sawmill and shingle mill work, in the construction and maintenance of way of railroads, and during the fishing season in the salmon canneries on the Frazer River. They are usually common laborers, but in the lumber mills of British Columbia they are engaged in more skilled positions than they ever have been in the United States. In Canada they are the cheapest grade of labor. In the lumber mills of British Columbia they receive from 80 cents to $1.25 per day without board, while Japanese get $1 to $1.75, and white men for the same work $1.75 and over per day.[a] The wages paid East Indians in British Columbia are less than those paid them in the mill work in the United States, and that caused many of them to come to the State of Washington.

The action taken in Canada in 1908, which prevented the further immigration of East Indians to British Columbia, reduced the number leaving British Columbia for the Pacific Coast States, and the number entering this country was also kept low by the more stringent policy of the immigration bureau in that year.

In the year 1910 the number of East Indian immigrants has again become large (1,782 entering from July 1, 1909, to June 30, 1910, inclusive), but this is mainly a direct immigration from India to our western ports, for very few are now coming from British Columbia. During the first nine months of the calendar year 1910, 1,401 were admitted, while 623 were denied admission at the Port of San Francisco.[b]

The East Indian coolie immigrants coming from British Columbia were first employed in Washington, but later they began gradually to go farther south into Oregon and later to California, until now the great majority of them are in the last-mentioned State. Their migration from one section to another and the industries in which they have been engaged are shown in the chapter next presented.

---

[a] Tariff Hearings, Committee on Ways and Means, Sixtieth Congress, 1908-9, Vol. III, p. 3171, et seq.

[b] Because of the criticism of the administration of the immigration law in the case of the East Indians, the following statement is given, showing the number of East Indians admitted at San Francisco and the number rejected, with the cause assigned, during nine months of 1910:

	January.	February.	March.	April.	May.	June	July.	August.	September.	Total.
Total admissions	95	377	47	169	231	183	65	189	45	1,401
Total rejections	7	4	28	68	23	105	67	138	183	623
Cause of rejection:										
Liable to become a public charge	1	1	14	42	10	90	45	124	162	489
Trachoma	6	3	14	26	13	15	20	13	11	121
Surgeon's certificate of defect which may affect alien's ability to earn a living								1	7	8
Assisted alien							1			1
Loathsome contagious disease (syphilis)							1		1	2
Polygamists									2	2

CHAPTER III

EMPLOYMENT OF EAST INDIANS IN COAST STATES.

IN LUMBER MILLS AND ROPE FACTORY.

When the East Indians came to the State of Washington they found their first employment in the lumber industry. In 1906 they were employed in considerable numbers in the mills between Tacoma and Bellingham. Reports of higher wages received in the United States soon brought a large number from British Columbia.

The East Indians met with little difficulty in entering the lumber industry because there was a scarcity of men to do the rougher and heavier work. It appears they were not used to undermine the existing wage scale or to replace striking lumbermen. In spite of their general willingness to work for less, East Indians have often been paid the same as white men, lest the latter should object on the ground that the wage scale had been undermined. Of 53 men employed in 6 mills visited, 1 received $1.50 per day; 3, $1.55; 16, $1.60; 17, $1.65; 6, $1.70; 2, $1.75; 2, $1.80; 3, $1.85; 3, $2. The average was $1.67, which is somewhat more than the Japanese, but less than white men, are paid. That the East Indians have not been worth this wage has been one cause of their decreasing number in this industry. At the time of this investigation they were found in 6 mills. Their general disappearance, however, has been due primarily to the hostile attitude of the white workmen. This prejudice against them is due partly to race feeling and partly to a dislike of the East Indian dress, religion, and manner of living, and, further, it may be attributed to the fact that they were cheap laborers in British Columbia and had been employed by a railroad company as strike breakers in Tacoma. At Bellingham, where most of the East Indians were employed, there was rioting against them, and they left the community fearing bodily injury. This experience has caused them to be generally discriminated against by employers. It is now difficult for them to find employment in the lumber mills of Washington.

A few East Indians have been employed in the lumber mills of Oregon and California, but not many are now so employed.

The members of this race have been employed only as common laborers, usually in the lumber yards. There is a difference of opinion among those who have employed East Indians at labor of this kind. One employer, whose East Indians had been soldiers in the British army, found them strong and industrious, but unadaptable and unprogressive, and hence capable only of doing the rougher kinds of work. As common laborers he found them less desirable than the Swedes and Norwegians, but more desirable than the class of Americans employed. Another employer found difficulty in giving the orders because of their limited knowledge of English. A third ranks them after Americans, Scandinavians, and Germans in desirability. A fourth regards them as the least desirable of the many races he has employed because they are so slow to comprehend instructions given. Two others agree with the latter opinion, while another found them too weak physically to do the heavy work required.

In Oregon 20 or more East Indians are working in a rope factory. They have been operating machines for a year. This is one of the few instances where they have found " inside " employment. In this cordage plant 1 receives $60 per month, another $50 per month, 1 $1.85 per day, and 17 $1.75 per day.

The following table gives the average yearly earnings of 63 men employed in the lumber mills and rope factory investigated:

TABLE 6.—*Yearly earnings (approximate) of East Indians 18 years of age or over, by number of months employed.*

Number of months employed.	Number working for wages and reporting amount.	Average earnings.	Number earning—									
			Under $100.	$100 and under $150.	$150 and under $200.	$200 and under $250.	$250 and under $300.	$300 and under $400.	$400 and under $500.	$500 and under $600.	$600 and under $700.	$700 and under $800.
2	1	$86.00	1									
4	2	156.00			2							
6	7	261.29				3	3	1				
7	3	309.33						3				
8	6	348.00						6				
9	2	392.00						1	1			
10	4	415.50							4			
12	38	532.76							4	32	1	1
Total	63		1		2	3	3	11	9	32	1	1

Of the 63 reported, 38 worked twelve months and earned $532.76 as an average. For the whole number the average number of months worked during the year was 10. Nine of the 63 earned less than $300 during the year. On the other hand, 34, or almost five-ninths of the entire number, earned $500 or more during the twelve months. These yearly earnings must be accepted as perhaps the largest made by East Indian laborers in the West, for the rates of wages were among the highest paid to laborers of that race and the amount of lost time during the year the least.

IN RAILROAD WORK.

As the East Indians in British Columbia very soon went into railroad work, so, also, in the United States they early entered that field of employment as common laborers. In 1907 they were employed at Tacoma to replace some striking Italians. A small number are still working on railroads in Washington. The East Indians who went south to Oregon and California also found employment with the railroads. At various times large numbers of them have been employed in construction work on the Ocean Shore, Western Pacific, and Southern Pacific in California, but at the time of this investigation few were found in construction work. It is reported that many of the East Indians arriving directly from India during the fiscal year

1910 have been employed by a railroad company in California in constructing a new line. Because of inefficiency, due primarily to physical weakness and lack of endurance, caused by poor and inadequate food, the East Indians have not long been employed in any piece of construction work.

In 1909, in the maintenance of way of railroads in the Western Division of the United States, 73 East Indians were reported out of a total of 34,919 employed in that department. Comparatively few of them are employed as section hands, for they are generally regarded as absolute failures, largely because of insufficient strength and endurance.

IN AGRICULTURAL WORK IN CALIFORNIA.

The majority of the East Indians have migrated from Washington and Oregon to California because of the warmer climate and because the opportunities for finding employment as farm laborers are greater in the last-mentioned State. The first of these immigrants coming from the north located near Marysville and Chico in 1907. They found employment temporarily in the industries of the community and with the railroads, but during the summer of 1908 they were principally engaged in agricultural work.

During the summer of 1908 about 500 of them made their appearance in the Newcastle fruit district, east of Sacramento, where they were more favorably received than they had been elsewhere. The orchardists, being short of help and being thoroughly tired of the Japanese because of their monopoly control of the labor supply, were glad to hire them. The fruit crop was large and the presence of the East Indians greatly relieved the labor situation. Their employment was in picking fruit and hoeing the weeds from the orchards. In 1909 this race was still present in the district, but not in such large numbers, as most of them had gone to other districts in the autumn of the preceding year and many did not return the following summer. Some, however, found employment here throughout the year 1908–9 in cutting wood, clearing land, etc.

At first the East Indians worked in this district for any rate of wages offered, and averaged about 50 cents per day less than the Japanese and white men in 1908, but they have been demanding higher wages until in 1909 they were usually paid only 25 cents a day less than Japanese. Of 40 East Indians on day-wage basis from whom personal data were obtained in 1909, five received $1.25; 16, $1.50; and 1, $1.60 per day, without board. Japanese were paid from $1.50 to $1.85 per day, without board. White men received $1.25 to $1.50 per day with board, or $1.50 to $2 without board. The difference of 25 cents per day in wages is probably no greater than the difference in the amount of work accomplished by the East Indians and the other races. It should be added, however, that a large percentage of the employers in this district who have employed both Japanese and East Indians were found to prefer the latter.

During the summer of 1908 some 300 East Indians were induced by a large shipper and grower of fruit to go into the Vaca Valley to work in the orchards. They served as a check on the Japanese, who were the most numerous race of laborers. The East Indians received at fruit picking 25 cents per day less than white men and Japanese.

Of 103 East Indians on the ranches visited in 1908, 86 were paid $1.25, and 17, $1.50 per day. The usual wage paid to white men and Japanese was $1.50 per day. The East Indians were regarded as dear at the lowest wages paid them.

Many East Indians secured work in the beet fields near Hamilton this same summer. They were employed in thinning, hoeing, and topping beets. In the Hamilton district where it was hard to get laborers in 1909, 425, or three-fourths of the total number of hand-workers, were East Indians.

Late in the fall of 1908, 400 or 500 East Indians went farther south into the fruit sections of the San Joaquin Valley. Most of these were employed about Fresno as grape pickers. In picking grapes, which is paid on a piece basis, the East Indians have not been found very satisfactory. They are slow and require much supervision, as they can not be made to understand the work. On account of their slowness their earnings were far below those of the Japanese. In this district, also, they succeeded in getting work only because help was scarce during the busy season and many ranchers wished to show the Japanese they were not entirely dependent upon them.

From the Fresno district many of the East Indians went back north to work on the railroads, while a number went farther south to the Tulare County citrus-fruit district and found work picking oranges.

It was in the fall of 1908, also, that the East Indians began to move down into the lower Sacramento River Valley. There were several hundred of them working in the delta lands of the lower Sacramento and San Joaquin rivers during the spring and summer of 1909. They were engaged in hoeing and other hand work in connection with the growing of beans, asparagus, and other vegetables. The East Indians were first paid less than the Japanese and Chinese in this work, receiving $1.10 and $1.25 per day as against $1.50 for the other two races. In 1909 all wages were higher. Of 139 East Indians on ranches visited in 1909, 47 per cent were paid $1.50, 32 per cent $1.55, and 19 per cent $1.60 per day, while 55 per cent of the 667 Japanese received $1.65 and 37 per cent received $1.75 per day. It is practically universal for employers to discriminate against East Indians in wages. They are generally considered the least desirable race of immigrants.

One grower of fruit and asparagus who paid white men $30 a month with board (which is regarded as equal to $1.65 per day without board), and Japanese $1.70, paid East Indians $1.10 per day without board, but discharged them when they wanted $1.50, as he says they were not worth $1.10 per day. Another grower of asparagus and vegetables preferred East Indians to Japanese, though he states that the East Indians are the least desirable race to have in the community, and they require a great deal of supervision. Another grower, disappointed with the other races he has hired, prefers the East Indians after one year's experience with them. A fourth rancher who hired East Indians to hoe beans found them so slow that he put a pace setter to work with them, but he had to discharge them, and they threatened violence to the pace setter unless he would slow down to their pace.

In the spring of 1909 the East Indians were also found in southern California for the first time. At Highgrove a group of East Indian

Mohammedans were picking oranges. They had wandered through the surrounding districts without success in finding anyone to employ them. It is stated that they were then growing desperate and practically demanded work of various employers. At Highgrove they had been employed only a few days previous to the agent's visit. They were paid $1.50 per day, while Japanese working for the same company received $1.75 and white men $2 per day. To avoid the prejudice of the people of the community against East Indians the employer was calling them " Turks," and the agent of the commission first heard of these East Indians as " Turks " through the Japanese, who were jealous of their new competitors. They were provided with lodging 2 or 3 miles from town in a deserted house, away from all neighbors. Their condition was pitiable. They claimed that they were hungry, and having been unable to find work, had nothing to eat.

In Orange County a gang of about a dozen East Indians had recently come from the northern beet fields and were employed in thinning beets. Labor was scarce, so they easily found work, and proved satisfactory.

Near Oxnard a gang of 25 East Indians was employed in hoeing beets in the spring of 1909. The sugar company operating there had expected a shortage of Japanese labor that season and had hired these East Indians to work in a new community where beets had not previously been grown. These three groups were the only East Indians in southern California in the spring of 1909.

The following table shows the earnings per day of 371 East Indians engaged in agricultural work and from whom personal schedules were obtained:

TABLE 7.—*Number of male East Indian employees 18 years of age or over earning each specified amount per day.*

Number reporting complete data.	Number earning each specified amount per day.					
	$1 and under $1.25.	$1.25 and under $1.50.	$1.50 and under $1.75.	$1.75 and under $2.	$2 and under $2.50.	$2.50 and under $3.
371..	45	104	149	43	28	2

Some of these earnings are reported on a piece basis. Indeed, this is true of all of those in excess of $1.75 per day, which is the maximum paid to any East Indians working on a time basis. It will be noted that 149 of the 371 earned less than $1.50 per day, and that an equal number earned $1.50 but less than $1.75 per day. Comparisons have been made between the earnings of the members of this and other races in the preceding paragraphs.

The wage data given were collected during the months when there was the greatest demand for labor in the several agricultural districts visited. They are materially higher than the rates paid at other times. Data for the yearly earnings and the number of months of the twelve employed were not secured for East Indian agricultural laborers. They are engaged in seasonal occupations, and, though they migrate from community to community, lose much time during the spring, summer, and autumn months, while in the winter they find little to do.

A few of the East Indians in California have found work in a pottery, and still another group were employed as common laborers in a stone quarry. In San Francisco personal data were secured from 17 East Indians who were engaged in the manufacture of tamales and the sale of them on the streets. They were Mohammedans and were not of those who had immigrated from British Columbia, but had been in the country four or five years and were of a higher type. These men were living in four groups and working in as many partnerships. They earned more than $30 per month per man. In some of the northern cities, also, some East Indians have owned peanut carts, but they have not been successful in business as peddlers.

From this review of the employment of East Indians in the Pacific Coast States it is evident that they are rarely employed at inside work. It is evident also that they are not employed in as large numbers as formerly in the lumber mills and that they have found little place in railroad work. In mining and smelting, the other industries of the Western States requiring many unskilled laborers, they have never been employed. The majority of those who came to this country from British Columbia have migrated south to California, while recently most of the direct immigration has been to that State. As a result, most of the East Indians in the West are now in that State, where the vast majority are engaged in seasonal handwork in various branches of agriculture. In only one or two instances have they been found working with a team. They migrate from ranch to ranch and from locality to locality, doing the most unskilled work, and, with few exceptions, at a lower rate of wages per day than the Japanese or any other race employed. They are usually regarded as dear at the price, and have been employed chiefly to supplement the Japanese, who have diminished in number.

In looking for work the East Indians go about in "gangs" of from 3 to 50 members, under a leader or "boss." The leader is one who can speak English, and acts as interpreter and carries on all dealings with an employer. These "gangs" are not as closely organized as the Japanese and Chinese "gangs," for the East Indian appears to be more individualistic, and the "gang" system is largely due to the fact that the majority of them can not understand English, and so can not find work for themselves. Unlike the Japanese "bosses," the East Indian leaders do not get a commission out of the wages of their men, but they themselves work and expect slightly higher pay from the employer for acting as interpreters. Very often the large gangs send their leaders out alone to look for work, and often into remote districts, and the members follow when work is found. The leaders usually offer to supply an employer with as

CHAPTER IV

AGE AND CONJUGAL CONDITION.

Personal data were secured from 474 East Indians. These reported their ages at time of coming to the United States as follows: Twenty-three were under 18, 26 were between 18 and 20, 142 between 20 and 25, 120 between 25 and 30, 84 between 30 and 35, 45 between 35 and 40, 16 between 40 and 45, and 16 were 45 years of age or over. Thus it is seen that about three-fourths of the entire number were between 20 and 35 years of age. The reports of the Commissioner-General of Immigration give the ages of 3,535 at the time of entry as follows:

TABLE 8.—*Number of East Indians admitted to the United States during the period 1905–1909, by age groups.*

Year.	Number within each specified age group.		
	Under 14.	14 to 44.	45 or over.
1905	3	122	20
1906	15	245	11
1907	4	1,055	13
1908	3	1,676	31
1909	4	312	21
Total	29	3,410	96

Over 96 per cent of those reported were between 14 and 44 years of age at the time of arrival in this country.

The conjugal condition and location of wife of the East Indians from whom the agent of the Commission secured data are shown in the following table:

TABLE 9.—*Conjugal condition of male East Indians, and location of wife, by age groups.*

Age.	Single.	Married.	Widowed.	Wife abroad.
16 to 19	17	2	1	2
20 to 29	130	89	5	89
30 to 44	79	104	17	104
45 or over	2	20	8	20
Total	228	215	31	215

More than two-fifths of them are married, but all of their wives are abroad. Having no families in this country the East Indian men live in groups of from 2 to 50 members.

CHAPTER V.

STANDARD OF LIVING.

AGRICULTURAL WORKERS.

The following table shows the size of a few groups of agricultural workers, and also their housing conditions and cost of food and clothes, and average earnings per month per man.

TABLE 10.—*General data for agricultural laborers.*

Number in group.	Number of rooms occupied.	Number of rooms for sleeping purposes.	Wages per week per individual.	Cost of food per month per individual	Cost of clothing per month per individual.	Saving per month per individual.
6	1	1	$7.50	$7.00	$2.00	$20.00
7	1	1	7.50	7.00	2.00	18.00
13	1	a 1	7.50	7.00	3.00	20.00
5	1	1	8.25	7.50	3.50	24.00
8	b 1	1	7.50	7.50	2.00	20.00
13	4	3	7.50	10.00	2.50	18.50
5	1	1	7.00	10.00	3.00	15.00
45	2	1	9.50	c 14.00	....	25.00

a Quite small.   b Tent.   c For food and clothing.

In the agricultural districts usually all the men in the group sleep in one room, as shown by the table above, and the cooking is done outside of the house. The quarters furnished them are generally dilapidated houses, woodsheds, or barns. The agricultural laborers have no furniture, and in many cases they sleep in their blankets on the bare floor. The space in the room not occupied by their bedding is usually taken up by boxes and supplies. Each man has his own blankets which, as a rule, are dirty and ragged and have been originally purchased second hand. The boxes serve as chairs, but the East Indians usually sit on the ground or floor. They often have a rough board table outside at which they stand to eat, or squat on the ground near by. Very few cooking utensils are used. Food is cooked over a fire built in a hole in the ground covered by an iron grating. Some of the groups eat from tin plates, but most of the farm laborers seen by the agent at meal time used no dishes. They put their vegetables on their flat " pancake " shaped bread, which is then rolled up and eaten from the hand.

The groups described above are of a more permanent character. The migratory groups of seasonal farm laborers are usually not as well provided for but live out of doors without shelter, both eating and sleeping on the ground under the trees. The groups included in the table are of the best established members of the East Indian laboring class and the earnings given are too large to represent those of all East Indians.

The table shows the average cost of clothing per individual to be about $2.50 per month. An East Indian's clothing usually consists of a shirt, a coat, a pair of overalls, a turban, coarse shoes, and, occasionally, socks. These articles are worn continuously and East Indians have seldom been seen to wash their clothing. Their unclean habits have constituted one of the great objections to them. The native article of dress, the turban, which is also allowed to become very dirty, has created prejudice. Some of the East Indians in California have cut their long hair because of the heat, but even these men continue to wear their native headdress.

The cost of food per month reported by these farm laborers is also given in the foregoing table. These figures must, however, be accepted as showing the outlay of the more well to do of the laborers. As a class they spend, on the average, less than $7.50 per month for food. Unleavened bread, made of whole wheat flour, and baked on the iron tops of the stoves already described in large, round, flat cakes, is the most important article of food. They also eat vegetables, chiefly dried split peas, rice, potatoes, and " greens." Milk is also an important item when it is available. Eggs, tea, and coffee are often used. Meat is eaten, but only occasionally. The Sikhs eat fish and most kinds of meat, but they tabu beef, as the cow is with them a sacred animal. The Mohammedans, on the other hand, eat all kinds of meat except pork. The fact that East Indians will not eat meat cut by the white butchers tends to keep their consumption of meat low. They confine themselves to chickens, lambs, and other small animals which they can afford to buy as a group and kill for themselves.

The caste system, which is still adhered to (though probably not as strictly as in India, for different castes are found sleeping under the same roof), tends to break up a mixed " gang " into separate groups. A " gang " of 45 engaged in thinning sugar beets was divided into six eating groups, partly because of the presence of different castes whose food had to be prepared by their own members only. The requirements as to the preparation of food are strictly adhered to. The members of one faith or caste can not prepare certain articles for those of another; the food must be prepared by members of the same caste as those who are to eat it.

The East Indians drink a great deal of beer and whisky, but each man buys his own liquor, so that this expense is not usually included in the cost of food. Their habit of heavy drinking has tended to limit their capacity to save in this country.

MILL WORKERS.

The table following shows the grouping, housing, and other facts relating to the lumber-mill laborers in Washington and Oregon from whom personal schedules were obtained.

TABLE 11.—*General data for mill hands in Washington and Oregon.*

Number in group.	Number of rooms occupied.	Number of rooms for sleeping purposes	Rent paid per month.	Amount paid for food per individual per month.
6	1	1	Free.	$10.00
10	2	1	Free.	10.00
4	2	2	$8.00	7.50
5	1	1	10.00	10.00
1	2	1	5.00	14.00
2	1	1	6.00	10.00
2	2	1	7.00	10.00
2	2	2	8.00	12.00
2	1	1	6.00	10.00
1	2	1	3.00	12.00
2	2	1	6.00	10.00
3	2	2	8.00	10.00
1	1	1	3.00	12.00
2	2	1	5.00	12.50
4	2	1	10.00	11.00
3	2	1	10.00	11.00
1	2	1	3.00	12.00
4	2	2	Free.	15.00
2	1	1	Free.	12.50
2	2	1	Free.	12.50

It will be seen from this table that the groups of lumber-mill hands are comparatively small, that they usually occupy two rooms, and, as a rule, the members of the group all sleep in one room. The East Indians engaged in millwork must usually provide their own quarters, and being in the city, their rent is an important item of expense, as is shown in the table. They usually rent small "shacks" or rooms in basements in parts of the city or town in which rents are cheap, and consequently their quarters are very poor. The mill hands get regular work and higher pay than the agricultural laborers in California, and their outlay for food appears to be proportionately higher. Their dress is also slightly better. Their food is practically of the same varieties, but they enjoy more delicacies. Much the same is true of the East Indians employed in a rope factory in Portland, Oreg., at $1.75 per day to $60 per month, shown by the following table:

TABLE 12.—*General data for cordage-factory hands in Portland, Oreg.*

Number in group.	Number of rooms occupied.	Number of rooms for sleeping purposes.	Rent paid per month.	Amount paid for food per month per individual.
7	4	3	Owned.	$20.00
5	2	1	$8.50	14.00
4	1	1	6.00	15.00
4	2	1	8.00	11.00

Of 79 of these East Indians in Washington and Oregon from whom schedules were secured, 4 reported the cost of food and drink as between $7 and $8 per month; 39 between $10 and $12; 15 between $12 and $14; and 21, $14 or over; or an average of $12.

TAMALE MEN.

The standard of living of 4 groups of partners engaged in the tamale business in San Francisco is shown by the following table:

TABLE 13.—*General data for tamale men of San Francisco, Cal.*

Number in group.	Number of rooms occupied.	Number of rooms for sleeping purposes.	Rent paid per month.	Wages per month per individual.	Food, rent, fuel, etc., per month per individual.	Clothing per month per individual.	Saving per month per individual.
4..............	2	1	$12.50	$32 00	$18.00-$21.00	$5.00	$7.50
5..............	2	1	20.00	35.00	22.00- 24.00	4.00	7.00
4..............	3	2	16.00	35.00	24.00	6.00	5.00
4..............	3	2	15.00	31.00	20.00- 22.00	7.00	3.00

These men usually rent basement rooms and have a kitchen and living room apart from their sleeping rooms. They have been in the United States several years and evidently did not come from British Columbia. They are in better circumstances than their countrymen more recently arrived. Like the others, however, they take no care of their quarters and allow them to become very dirty. They possess some furniture of a cheap quality—usually beds, tables, chairs, and stoves and occasionally other articles. Every group has a gas stove on which they manufacture their tamales in their quarters. The tamales are sold on the streets by the partners, and the profits, after deducting the expense of manufacture, are divided equally. Their work brings them in contact with Americans and they can all speak English.

On account of their business they wear good clothing and try to keep up a good appearance. They are all Mohammedans and consequently wear their hair short without turbans. As a result of these changes in their appearance they are not generally known to be East Indians. Their standard of living is higher than that of the great body of East Indians in the United States. Their food is of practically the same kind as that of the other East Indians and is prepared in the same way, but they apparently have more luxuries.

The peculiarities of the East Indian customs, religious beliefs, and the caste system all hinder their assimilation. The absolute refusal of East Indians to eat food prepared by others than those of their own caste and faith and the possible results of this requirement are well illustrated by the following incident in Placer County, Cal. An East Indian was convicted of beating and robbing some of his countrymen on a ranch located in that county. At the time of the agent's visit he was in the county jail pending an appeal. The prisoner for 12 days had refused to eat the food offered, and said he would starve before he would touch any food prepared by one not of his caste. Finally a small stove was put into the jail and he was there allowed to prepare his own meals. When the East Indians first came to Fresno County they occupied private yards and took articles against the wishes of the owners. Many of them were imprisoned, but they refused to eat the food given them and were freed in order to prevent them from starving.

the farm laborer being seasonal, however, their savings at this rate would only be possible for a few months in the year. The tamale men in San Francisco, as shown by preceding table, saved between $3 and $7.50 per month per individual, or an average of $5.70. Their lower rate of saving is accounted for by their higher standard of living and also by the fact that business was poor after the panic of 1907.

Chapter VI

SOCIOLOGICAL DATA.

Of these 79 East Indians in Washington and Oregon, 31 sent money abroad, in all $4,320, or an average of $139.35 each during the year 1908. Deducting this amount from the total amount reported as surplus by 36 mentioned above leaves $1,130 in the United States or a surplus of $31.40 for each of the 36. Of the 79, 62 reported that they owned no property whatever, and of the remainder, 10 owned less than $100. The work in the sawmills is quite regular throughout the year, but the above data show the insecurity of these men when thrown out of work.

The position of the East Indians engaged in agricultural work is still more precarious, as the work is generally seasonal and they have greater difficulty in finding such work. While the East Indians from whom personal data were secured showed an average saving per individual of $21 per month, it must be noted that as a rule this rate only applies for a part of the year. They, as a class, are out of work a considerable part of the year, partly because of the seasonal character of the work and partly because of the general aversion to employing them. It must also be noted that almost all of the savings are immediately sent to India, leaving them nothing to live on in case of unemployment. In the winter of 1907–8 the East Indians in northern California were desperate and in great distress. They were assisted by money sent to them by the British consul-general. During that winter the East Indians suffered a great deal, but by spring the local prejudice had so far subsided that some of the ranchers in the surrounding country employed them. In spite of their poverty these East Indians, for the eight months ending July, 1908, had sent money to India. During that period (through the Marysville post-office) over $34,000 had thus been sent.

The poverty and peculiar character and position of the East Indians is likely to make them a public charge at any time. That many of their groups have not already been thrown upon the public during the winter months is due largely to the fact that few of them speak English, so that consequently they live apart from white persons, to whom their condition does not become known. As yet the only apparent effect of their destitution has been to make them desperate and persistent in demanding employment.

The object of the East Indians in coming to the United States has been to accumulate enough money to enable them to return to their native land and live well. Two thousand dollars is the goal of many. Of 31 mill hands who sent money to India, 18 sent to wives, 9 to parents, 3 to brothers, and 1 for "investment." This money sent to relatives is probably partly for their support, but

principally it forms the fund which they set out to accumulate when
they came to the United States. On coming to the United States
they practically all intended to return to India within a few years.
According to the personal data secured from 79 in Washington and
Oregon, 36 expressed an intention to return to India, 6 intended
to remain permanently in the United States, while 37 were in doubt
as to what they would eventually do. Like the immigrants of many
other races who have changed their intentions after living in the
United States, it appears likely that the East Indians in large numbers will decide to remain in this country, especially since they are
now meeting with greater success in finding work. This seems the
more likely since a few of the East Indians have already taken out
their first papers. Many courts have refused to naturalize East
Indians, but there are others which admit them to citizenship. The
Bureau of Naturalization has instructed federal attorneys to
"oppose the granting of naturalization to Hindus or East Indians," but in so far as known no case directly involving the right
of East Indians to become naturalized citizens of this country has
been decided by the courts. Recently the United States circuit court
of appeals in the southern district of New York (180 Fed. Rep.,
695) rendered a decision holding that a Parsee—a native of India—
was eligible for citizenship, but the court made a clear distinction
between the Parsees and the Hindus.

Something has already been said concerning the literacy of the
East Indian immigrants. The following table shows the number of
those for whom personal data were obtained who are able to read and
write their native language and to speak and to read and write
English.

TABLE 14.—*Ability of foreign-born male East Indians 10 years of age or over
to read and write their native language and to speak, read, and write English,
by industry.*

Industries.	Number reporting complete data.	Number who read and write native language.	Number who speak English.	Number who read English.	Number who read and write English.
Agriculture	381	171	130	30	26
Lumber and other industries	91	45	65	10	10
Total	472	216	195	40	36

From this table it will be seen that only 45.7 per cent of the East
Indians investigated by the agent of the Commission can read and
write their native language. The reports of the Commissioner-
General of Immigration for the years 1905–1909 (see Table 5, pp.
327 and 328) show 1,664 out of 3,535 as unable to read and write. In
other words, 47.1 per cent were illiterate. That the Commissioner-
General's report should show a small percentage of illiterates is due
to the fact that the nonimmigrant aliens included in those reports are
usually literate.

Of 473 from whom data were obtained, 33 had been in the United
States less than one year, 117 had been here one year, 218 had been
here two years, 94 three years, 7 four years, 2 from five to nine years,

garded as the least desirable race of immigrants thus far admitted to the United States. In point of desirability they are placed far below the Japanese, Chinese, and other oriental races found in the Western States. The white workingmen regard them as a menace just as the previous unrestricted immigration of Japanese and Chinese was. They accept low wages and threaten to undermine the position of white men in such occupations as they are capable of entering. Experience so far has shown them that at the same wages they can not compete with white men, for they are generally the least efficient race employed, but they accept employment at low wages, and if they were admitted in large numbers might seriously affect the wages of the members of other races in those industries in which men of low efficiency can be employed. At present, as has been indicated, many employers discriminate against them even to the point of not employing them at any wage, yet they find a certain amount of favor among the employing classes (1) because they work for low wages at a time when the wages of the other orientals are rapidly rising because of the restriction placed upon their immigration to the United States, (2) because they migrate from place to place and are available for seasonable work, and (3) because they board themselves and are provided with any necessary lodging at little expense.

GENERAL TABLES.

JAPANESE IN SAN FRANCISCO: TABLES 1-21.
JAPANESE IN LOS ANGELES: TABLES 22-43.
JAPANESE IN SACRAMENTO: TABLES 44-65.
JAPANESE IN SEATTLE: TABLES 66-87.

351

GENERAL TABLES.

SAN FRANCISCO.

TABLE 1.—*Money brought to the United States by Japanese.*

	Number reporting complete data.	Number bringing each specified amount.										
		None.	Under $25.	$25 and under $50.	$50 and under $100.	$100 and under $150.	$150 and under $200.	$200 and under $300.	$300 and under $400.	$400 and under $500.	$500 and under $1,000.	$1,000 or over.
In business for self.........	112	.....	1	43	32	16	7	5	3	.....	2	3
Wage-earners...............	230	1	2	124	66	21	6	5	4	1	......	.....

TABLE 2.—*First occupation of Japanese in the United States, by occupation abroad.*

IN BUSINESS FOR SELF.

Occupation abroad.	Number.	In business for self.	Farmers.	Farm hands.	Railroad laborers.	Sawmill laborers.	Cannery hands.	Laborers in industrial establishments.	Store help.	Restaurant help.	House cleaners.	In domestic service.	Tailors and dyers.	Wage-earners in city.	In other occupations.	Occupation unknown.
In business for self.....	a 31	12	....	2	....	....	....	....	1	1	2	....	11	....	2	....	....
At home...............	22	1	1	....	....	....	....	....	....	1	....	19	....	....	....	....
Farming for father.....	b 29	3	....	8	1	....	1	....	....	....	4	8	....	4	....	....
Store help.............	c 8	4	....	....	....	....	....	....	2	....	....	2	....	....	....	....
Wage-earner in city....	de 21	5	....	3	....	....	....	....	1	1	....	10	1	....	....	....
In other occupation....	c 2	......	....	1	....	....	....	....	....	....	....	....	....	1	....	....
Total..............	113	25	1	14	1	....	1	1	4	4	4	50	1	7	....	....

WAGE-EARNERS.

In business for self.....	c 36	1	....	11	2	....	....	1	2	2	1	10	2	3	....	1
At home...............	d 70	1	....	9	1	1	2	1	3	1	1	44	....	6	....	....
Farming for father.....	fg 70	....	....	24	8	....	2	1	1	2	7	23	....	1	....	1
Farm hand.............	c 2	....	....	.....	....	....	....	1	....	....	....	1	....	....	....	....
Store help.............	d 16	....	....	5	....	....	....	....	3	1	....	4	....	1	1	1
Laborer in industrial establishment........	3	....	....	1	1	....	....	....	....	1	....	....	....	....	....	....
Wage-earner in city....	h 23	....	....	6	....	....	....	1	....	....	....	6	3	4	....	3
In other occupations...	ce 8	....	....	2	....	....	....	....	....	1	....	4	....	1	....	....
Occupation unknown..	1	....	....	.....	....	....	1	....	....	....	....	....	....	....	....	....
Total..............	229	2	....	58	12	1	5	5	9	7	10	92	5	16	1	6

a Including 4 who came to United States from Hawaii.
b Including 6 who came to United States from Hawaii.
c Including 1 who came to United States from Hawaii.
d Including 2 who came to United States from Hawaii.
e Including 1 who came to United States from Canada.
f Including 12 who came to United States from Hawaii.
g Including 1 who came to United States from Mexico.
h Including 3 who came to United States from Hawaii.

TABLE 3.—*Net value of all property now owned by Japanese, by length of residence in the United States.*

IN BUSINESS FOR SELF.

Length of residence in the United States.	Number reporting complete data.	None.	Under $50.	$50 and under $100.	$100 and under $250.	$250 and under $500.	$500 and under $1,000.	$1,000 and under $1,500.	$1,500 and under $2,500.	$2,500 and under $5,000.	$5,000 and under $10,000.	$10,000 and under $25,000.	$25,000 or over.
Under 1 year													
1 year	1				1								
2 years	6				1	1	1	3					
3 years	3						2		1				
4 years	13					3	7	3					
5 to 9 years	44	1			2	3	10	12	7	6	2	1	
10 to 14 years	34					2	9	8	8	5	1	1	
15 to 19 years	4						2			2			
20 years or over	8						2	1		1	1		3
Total	113	1			4	9	33	27	16	14	4	2	3

WAGE-EARNERS.

Length of residence in the United States.	Number reporting complete data.	None.	Under $50.	$50 and under $100.	$100 and under $250.	$250 and under $500.	$500 and under $1,000.	$1,000 and under $1,500.	$1,500 and under $2,500.	$2,500 and under $5,000.	$5,000 and under $10,000.	$10,000 and under $25,000.	$25,000 or over.
Under 1 year	1	1											
1 year	13			5	6	2							
2 years	39	5	2	6	19	4	3						
3 years	36	3	2	6	14	9	1	1					
4 years	19	3			10	1	1	2	2				
5 to 9 years	82	18		5	29	16	10	3		1			
10 to 14 years	26	4	2		9	3	4		2	2			
15 to 19 years	9	3			1	2	2		1				
20 years or over	6				3	1	2						
Total	231	37	6	22	91	38	23	6	5	3			

TABLE 4.—*Average surplus or deficit of past year, reported by Japanese.*

IN BUSINESS FOR SELF.

	Number.	Average.		Number.	Average.
Reporting:			Average surplus based on total number		$595.44
Surplus	102	$726.86			
Deficit	4	1,862.50			
Neither surplus nor deficit	6				
Total	112				

WAGE-EARNERS.

	Number.	Average.		Number.	Average.
Reporting:			Average surplus based on total number		$199.78
Surplus	198	$239.57			
Deficit	8	210.53			
Neither surplus nor deficit	23				
Total	229				

TABLE 5.—*Surplus or deficit of past year reported by Japanese, by classified amounts.*

IN BUSINESS FOR SELF.

Amount.	Number reporting.		Amount.	Number reporting.	
	Surplus.	Deficit.		Surplus.	Deficit.
$100 and under $250............	12	....	$2,500 or over..................	3	2
$250 and under $500............	40	1			
$500 aud under $1,000.........	30	1	Total....................	102	4
$1,000 and under $2,500........	17	....			

WAGE-EARNERS.

Under $100....................	24	2	$1,000 and under $2,500.......	1	....
$100 and under $250...........	83	3			
$250 and under $500...........	76	3	Total....................	198	8
$500 and under $1,000.........	14	....			

TABLE 6.—*Gross value of property, encumbrances, and net value of property now owned by male Japanese.*

	Number reporting complete data.	Gross value of property.		Encumbrances on property.			Net value of property.	
		Aggregate amount.	Average amount.	Number having encumbrances.	Aggregate amount.	Average amount.	Aggregate amount.	Average amount.
In business for self..	113	$352,520.00	$3,119.65	47	$63,830.00	$1,358.09	$290,690.00	$2,594.44
Wage-earners......	194	66,444.00	342.49	1	200.00	200.00	66,444.00	342.49

TABLE 7.—*Number of Japanese for whom detailed information was secured, by sex and general nativity.*

IN BUSINESS FOR SELF.

General nativity.	Male.	Female.	Total.
Native-born...	13	20	33
Foreign-born..	122	50	172
Total...	135	70	205

WAGE-EARNERS.

General nativity.	Male.	Female.	Total.
Native-born...	....	....	....
Foreign-born..	231	7	238
Total...	231	7	238

TABLE 8.—*Conjugal condition of Japanese, by sex and age groups.*

IN BUSINESS FOR SELF.

Sex.	Number within each specified age group.																			
	16 to 19.				20 to 29.				30 to 44.				45 or over.				Total.			
	Single.	Married.	Widowed.	Total.	Single.	Married.	Widowed.	Total.	Single.	Married.	Widowed.	Total.	Single.	Married.	Widowed.	Total.	Single.	Married.	Widowed.	Total.
Male	....	....	....	....	24	9	....	33	22	49	2	73	1	8	1	10	47	66	3	116
Female	....	....	....	....	....	28	....	28	....	19	....	19	....	1	....	1	....	48	....	48
Total	....	....	....	....	24	37	....	61	22	68	2	92	1	9	1	11	47	114	3	164

WAGE-EARNERS.

Sex.	Number within each specified age group.																			
	16 to 19.				20 to 29.				30 to 44.				45 or over.				Total.			
	Single.	Married.	Widowed.	Total.	Single.	Married.	Widowed.	Total.	Single.	Married.	Widowed.	Total.	Single.	Married.	Widowed.	Total.	Single.	Married.	Widowed.	Total.
Male	9	....	....	9	114	5	....	119	52	34	2	88	7	7	1	15	182	46	3	231
Female	....	....	....	....	....	3	....	3	....	2	2	4	....	....	....	....	....	5	2	7
Total	9	....	....	9	114	8	....	122	52	36	4	92	7	7	1	15	182	51	5	238

TABLE 9.—*Conjugal condition of foreign-born male Japanese 16 years of age or over, by age at time of coming to the United States.*

IN BUSINESS FOR SELF.

Age at time of coming to the United States.	Total number of arrivals.	Single or widowed at time of coming to United States.			Married at time of coming to United States.			
		Number.	Married during visit abroad.	Married in United States.	Number.	Wife abroad.	Accompanied by wife.	Wife joining later.
Under 18 years	14	14	a 3	1	....	....	....	....
18 and under 20 years	7	6	1	2	1	1	....	....
20 and under 25 years	36	31	a 4	7	5	2	1	2
25 and under 30 years	34	20	b 2	7	14	4	4	6
30 and under 35 years	14	5	....	a 2	9	a 2	5	2
35 and under 40 years	7	1	....	....	6	3	2	1
40 and under 45 years	3	2	....	....	1	....	1	....
45 years or over	1	....	....	....	1	1	....	....
Total	116	79	c 10	a 19	37	a 13	13	11

WAGE-EARNERS.

Age at time of coming to the United States.	Total number of arrivals.	Single or widowed at time of coming to United States.			Married at time of coming to United States.			
		Number.	Married during visit abroad.	Married in United States.	Number.	Wife abroad.	Accompanied by wife.	Wife joining later.
Under 18 years	29	29	....	a 1	....	....	....	....
18 and under 20 years	32	31	....	....	1	1	....	....
20 and under 25 years	77	71	1	1	6	5	1	....
25 and under 30 years	47	40	....	....	7	4	a 3	....
30 and under 35 years	21	10	....	....	11	8	3	....
35 and under 40 years	17	4	....	....	13	12	1	....
40 and under 45 years	6	1	....	....	5	5	....	....
45 years or over	2	2	....	....	....	....	....	....
Total	231	188	1	a 2	43	35	a 8	....

a Including 1 whose wife is visiting in Japan.
b Including 1 married abroad, wife remaining in Japan.
c Including 3 whose wives are in Japan.

TABLE 10.—*Number of Japanese within each age group, by sex.*

[This table includes persons in business for self as well as wage-earners.]

Sex.	Number within each specified age group.							
	Under 6.	6 to 13.	14 and 15.	16 to 19.	20 to 29.	30 to 44.	45 or over.	Total.
Male	11	7	1	9	152	161	25	366
Female	17	5			31	23	1	77
Total	28	12	1	9	183	184	26	443

TABLE 11.—*Number of foreign-born Japanese in the United States each specified number of years, by sex.*

IN BUSINESS FOR SELF.

[By years in the United States is meant years since first arrival in the United States. No deduction is made for time spent abroad.]

Sex.	Number reporting complete data.	Number in United States each specified number of years.								
		Under 1.	1.	2.	3.	4.	5 to 9.	10 to 14.	15 to 19.	20 or over.
Male	122	1	1	7	3	16	48	34	4	8
Female	50		6	5	5	10	22		2	
Total	172	1	7	12	8	26	70	34	6	8

WAGE-EARNERS.

Sex.	Number reporting complete data.	Under 1.	1.	2.	3.	4.	5 to 9.	10 to 14.	15 to 19.	20 or over.
Male	231	1	13	39	36	19	82	26	9	6
Female	7			2	2	1	2			
Total	238	1	13	41	38	20	84	26	9	6

TABLE 12.—*Ability to speak English of Japanese 6 years of age or over, by sex and general nativity.*

IN BUSINESS FOR SELF.

General nativity.	Number reporting complete data.	Male.		Female.		Total.	
		Number.	Number who speak English.	Number.	Number who speak English.	Number.	Number who speak English.
Native-born	5	2	2	3	3	5	5
Foreign-born	172	122	116	50	27	172	143
Total	177	124	118	53	30	177	148

WAGE-EARNERS.

General nativity.	Number reporting complete data.	Male.		Female.		Total.	
Foreign-born	238	231	200	7	5	238	205

TABLE **13.**—*Ability to speak English of foreign-born Japanese 6 years of age or over, by sex and years in the United States.*

IN BUSINESS FOR SELF.

[By years in the United States is meant years since first arrival in the United States. No deduction is made for time spent abroad.]

Sex.	Number reporting complete data.	Number who speak English.	Years in United States.					
			Under 5.		5 to 9.		10 or over.	
			Number.	Number who speak English.	Number.	Number who speak English.	Number.	Number who speak English.
Male	122	116	28	24	48	47	46	45
Female	50	27	26	12	22	13	2	2
Total	172	143	54	36	70	60	48	47

WAGE-EARNERS.

Sex.	Number reporting complete data.	Number who speak English.	Under 5.		5 to 9.		10 or over.	
Male	231	200	108	85	82	75	41	40
Female	7	5	5	3	2	2		
Total	238	205	113	88	84	77	41	40

TABLE **14.**—*Ability to speak English of foreign-born Japanese 6 years of age or over, by sex and by age at time of coming to the United States.*

IN BUSINESS FOR SELF.

Sex.	Number reporting complete data.	Number who speak English.	Age at time of coming to United States.			
			Under 14.		14 or over.	
			Number.	Number who speak English.	Number.	Number who speak English.
Male	122	116	7	7	115	109
Female	50	27	2	2	48	25
Total	172	143	9	9	163	134

WAGE-EARNERS.

Sex.	Number reporting complete data.	Number who speak English.	Under 14.		14 or over.	
Male	231	200	3	3	228	197
Female	7	5			7	5
Total	238	205	3	3	235	202

TABLE 15.—*Literacy of Japanese 10 years of age or over, by sex and general nativity.*

IN BUSINESS FOR SELF.

General nativity.	Number reporting complete data.	Male.			Female.			Total.		
		Number.	Number who read.	Number who read and write.	Number.	Number who read.	Number who read and write.	Number.	Number who read.	Number who read and write.
Native-born...........	1	1	1	1	....	....	....	1	1	1
Foreign-born...........	167	118	118	118	49	43	43	167	161	161
Total...........	168	119	119	119	49	43	43	168	162	162

WAGE-EARNERS.

Foreign-born...........	238	231	231	231	7	7	7	238	238	238

TABLE 16.—*Literacy of foreign-born Japanese 10 years of age or over, by sex and years in the United States.*

IN BUSINESS FOR SELF.

[By years in the United States is meant years since first arrival in the United States.]

Sex.	Number reporting complete data.	Years in United States.								
		Under 5.			5 to 9.			10 or over.		
		Number.	Number who read.	Number who read and write.	Number.	Number who read.	Number who read and write.	Number.	Number who read.	Number who read and write.
Male.................	118	25	25	25	47	47	47	46	46	46
Female..............	49	26	23	23	21	19	19	2	1	1
Total..........	167	51	48	48	68	66	66	48	47	47

WAGE-EARNERS.

Male.................	231	108	108	108	82	82	82	41	41	41
Female..............	7	5	5	5	2	2	2	....	....	....
Total..........	238	113	113	113	84	84	84	41	41	41

TABLE 17.—*Literacy of foreign-born Japanese 10 years of age or over, by sex and by age at time of coming to the United States.*

IN BUSINESS FOR SELF.

Sex.	Number reporting complete data.	Age at time of coming to United States.					
		Under 14.			14 or over.		
		Number.	Number who read.	Number who read and write.	Number.	Number who read.	Number who read and write.
Male.................	118	3	3	3	115	115	115
Female................	49	1	1	1	48	42	42
Total..............	167	4	4	4	163	157	157

WAGE-EARNERS.

Male.................	231	3	3	3	228	228	228
Female................	7	....	....	....	7	7	7
Total..............	238	3	3	3	235	235	235

TABLE **18.**—*Ability of foreign-born Japanese 10 years of age or over to speak, read, and write English, by sex.*

IN BUSINESS FOR SELF.

Sex.	Number reporting complete data.	Unable to speak, read, or write English.	Able to speak English, but not to read and write it.	Able to speak and read, but not write English.	Able to speak, read, and write English.
Male	118	6	37	....	75
Female	49	23	18	1	7
Total	167	29	55	1	82

WAGE-EARNERS.

Male	230	30	77	2	121
Female	7	2	3	1	1
Total	237	32	80	3	122

TABLE **19.**—*General occupation of Japanese under 16 years of age, by sex, age groups, and general nativity.*

IN BUSINESS FOR SELF.

Sex and general nativity.	Number within each specified age group.															
	Under 6.				6 to 13.				14 and 15.				Total.			
	At home.	At school.	At work.	Total.	At home.	At school.	At work.	Total.	At home.	At school.	At work.	Total.	At home.	At school.	At work.	Total.
Native-born:																
Male	11	....	....	11	....	1	....	1	....	1	....	1	11	2	....	13
Female	16	1	....	17	1	2	....	3	....	....	....	....	17	3	....	20
Total	27	1	....	28	1	3	....	4	....	1	....	1	28	5	....	33
Foreign-born:																
Male	....	....	....	....	2	4	....	6	....	....	....	....	2	4	....	6
Female	....	....	....	....	1	1	....	2	....	....	....	....	1	1	....	2
Total	....	....	....	....	3	5	....	8	....	....	....	....	3	5	....	8
Grand total	27	1	....	28	4	8	....	12	....	1	....	1	31	10	....	41

TABLE **20.**—*Total yearly income of male Japanese engaged in business for self, and income from principal business.*

Kind of business.	Number reporting complete data.	Number having each specified amount of yearly income.									Income from principal business.	
		Under $300.	$300 and under $400.	$400 and under $500.	$500 and under $750.	$750 and under $1,000.	$1,000 and under $1,500.	$1,500 and under $2,000.	$2,000 and under $2,500.	$2,500 or over.	Total income.	Average income.
Barber shop	3	....	....	....	2	1	....	....	....	....	$2,400.00	$800.00
Laundry	14	....	....	6	4	....	1	2	....	1	15,880.00	1,134.29
Lodging house	22	....	1	1	5	6	1	....	....	3	32,810.00	1,491.36
Pool room	3	....	....	....	2	1	....	....	....	....	2,280.00	760.00
Real estate and labor agencies	2	....	....	....	....	1	1	....	....	....	1,980.00	990.00
Restaurant proprietor	6	....	....	1	3	1	....	....	....	1	12,750.00	2,125.00
Shoemaker	18	....	....	2	6	9	....	....	1	....	14,660.00	814.44
Storekeeper	25	....	....	....	7	....	5	6	3	2	35,120.00	1,404.80
Tailor	6	....	....	....	....	1	2	3	....	....	8,940.00	1,490.00
Miscellaneous	11	....	1	....	3	3	2	....	2	....	11,740.00	1,067.27
Total	110	....	2	10	32	27	14	12	6	7	138,560.00	1,259.64

TABLE 21.— *Yearly earnings (approximate) of male Japanese 18 years of age or over, by number of months employed.*

WITH BOARD.

Number of months employed.	Number working for wages and reporting amount.	Average earnings.	Number earning—														
			Under $100.	$100 and under $150.	$150 and under $200.	$200 and under $250.	$250 and under $300.	$300 and under $400.	$400 and under $500.	$500 and under $600.	$600 and under $700.	$700 and under $800.	$800 and under $1,000.	$1,000 and under $1,250.	$1,250 and under $1,500.	$1,500 and under $2,000.	$2,000 or over.
4 months	3	$200.00		1		1	1										
5 months	2	187.50			1	1											
6 months	5	224.40		1	1	1	1										
8 months	1	360.00						1									
9 months	5	468.00						2	1	1	1						
10 months	2	365.00					1		1								
11 months	5	330.60		1		1		1	2								
12 months	83	444.54	2	1	2	4	2	29	23	2	7	4	6	1			
Total	106	415.82	2	4	4	8	5	34	27	3	8	4	6	1			

WITHOUT BOARD.

Number of months employed.	Number working for wages and reporting amount.	Average earnings.	Under $100.	$100 and under $150.	$150 and under $200.	$200 and under $250.	$250 and under $300.	$300 and under $400.	$400 and under $500.	$500 and under $600.	$600 and under $700.	$700 and under $800.	$800 and under $1,000.	$1,000 and under $1,250.	$1,250 and under $1,500.	$1,500 and under $2,000.	$2,000 or over.
6 months	2	$270.00			1			1									
8 months	1	2,000.00															1
9 months	8	303.75				1	3	3	1								
10 months	1	400.00							1								
11 months	1	385.00						1									
12 months	111	566.76			1	2		13	32	13	26	17	4	1		2	
Total	124	553.75			2	3	3	18	34	13	26	17	4	1		2	1

LOS ANGELES.

TABLE 22.—*General data on business conducted by Japanese and members of other races.*

ART AND CURIO STORES.

Race of proprietor and number of establishment.	Date established.	Amount of capital— Employed.	Amount of capital— Borrowed.	Rent per year.	Value of annual transactions.	Net profit.	Number of employees of— Same race.	Number of employees of— Other races.	Per cent white patrons.
Japanese:									
No. 1	1902	$90,000	$10,000	$16,200	$120,000	(a)	18	4	90.0
No. 2	1902	20,000	0	40,000	40,000	(a)	3	1	90.0
No. 3	1902	10,000	0	2,400	20,000	(a)	2	0	99.0
No. 4	1903	5,000	1,500	960	6,000	$1,000	1	0	99.0
No. 5	1904	3,000	300	324	4,000	700	0	0	30.0
No. 6	1908	5,400	400	4,200	12,000	850	1	1	99.0

BARBER SHOPS.

Race of proprietor and number of establishment.	Date established.	Amount of capital— Employed.	Amount of capital— Borrowed.	Rent per year.	Value of annual transactions.	Net profit.	Number of employees of— Same race.	Number of employees of— Other races.	Per cent white patrons.
Japanese:									
No. 1	1901	$700	0	$300	$2,600	$960	1	0	50.0
No. 2	1905	1,500	0	240	2,000	720	1	0	99.0
No. 3	1905	300	0	300	2,400	840	1	0	50.0
No. 4	1908	300	0	300	1,440	780	b 0	0	60.0
No. 5	1908	300	0	240	1,200	840	b 0	0	40.0
No. 6c	1905	2,000	0	720	2,500	1,080	1	0	50.0
No. 7c	1908	500	0	300	2,500	840	1	0	50.0
No. 8c	1908	1,400	$200	300	2,000	600	1	0	10.0
American:									
No. 9	1901	1,500	0	960	6,000	(a)	3	3	100.0
No. 10	1901	200	(a)	240	1,200	(a)	0	0	100.0
No. 11	1903	600	(a)	312	2,400	(a)	0	1	100.0
Norwegian:									
No. 12	1909	600	0	720	3,500	900	1	3	100.0
Polish:									
No. 13	1907	300	(a)	108	1,000	500	0	1	100.0

a Not reported.　b Wife of proprietor works also.　c Bathrooms connected with this establishment.

TABLE 22.—*General data on business conducted by Japanese and members of other races*—Continued.

BILLIARD AND POOL ROOMS.

Race of proprietor and number of establishment.	Date established.	Amount of capital—		Rent per year.	Value of annual transactions.	Net profit.	Number of employees of—		Per cent white patrons.
		Employed.	Borrowed.				Same race.	Other races.	
Japanese:									
No. 1	1903	$2,000	0	$720	$3,000	$1,200	0	0	20.0
No. 2	1907	2,000	$300	480	1.800	960	1	0	40.0
No. 3	1907	1,000	0	720	3,000	1,200	0	0	50.0
No. 4	1908	2,500	0	960	1,800	360	1	0	10.0
No. 5	1908	1,000	0	600	1,800	840	0	0	90.0
No. 6	1908	800	200	(a)	552	(a)	b 0	0	.0
American:									
No. 7	1908	2,000	(a)	480	2,400	900	1	0	100.0
German:									
No. 8	1907	900	(a)	720	4,000	(a)	4	0	100.0
No. 9	1905	3,200	(a)	2,400	8,400	1,800	2	0	100.0
No. 10	1907	1,000	0	240	3,000	(a)	0	0	100.0

BOARDING AND LODGING HOUSES.

Race of proprietor and number of establishment.	Date established.	Employed.	Borrowed.	Rent per year.	Value of annual transactions.	Net profit.	Same race.	Other races.	Per cent white patrons.
Japanese:									
No. 1	1904	$4,000	0	$520	$2,500	$700	1	0	0.0
No. 2	(a)	4,000	0	1,800	5,500	2,250	0	0	1.0
No. 3	1902	2,000	0	780	3,000	600	1	0	.0
No. 4	1906	2,000	$500	1,200	3,600	1,800	2	0	.0
No. 5	1908	650	0	900	2,000	720	0	0	.0
No. 6	1906	1,700	0	360	1,900	840	b 0	0	20.0

COBBLER SHOPS.

Race of proprietor and number of establishment.	Date established.	Employed.	Borrowed.	Rent per year.	Value of annual transactions.	Net profit.	Same race.	Other races.	Per cent white patrons.
Japanese:									
No. 1	1903	$700	0	$180	$1,440	$720	0	0	50.0
No. 2	1906	150	0	144	1,200	720	0	0	30.0
No. 3	1908	300	0	216	2,500	900	0	0	50.0
German:									
No. 4	1886	100	0	300	800	(c)	0	0	(a)
No. 5	1889	100	0	300	1,000	700	0	0	100.0
No. 6	1894	100	0	120	1,250	(a)	0	0	(a)
Italian, North:									
No. 7	1906	50	0	(c)	600	(c)	0	0	100.0

DRUGS AND BOOKS.

Race of proprietor and number of establishment.	Date established.	Employed.	Borrowed.	Rent per year.	Value of annual transactions.	Net profit.	Same race.	Other races.	Per cent white patrons.
Japanese:									
No. 1	d 1905	$4,000	0	$600	$12,000	$900	0	0	50.0
No. 2	d 1906	4,000	0	600	12,000	900	e 0	0	50.0
No. 3	d 1905	4,360	$360	660	6,800	1,440	1	1	40.0
No. 4	1903	4,000	500	720	12,000	4,200	1	0	10.0
No. 5	1904	2,000	1,000	240	3,000	1,200	0	0	20.0

FRUIT, CONFECTIONS, AND TOBACCO.

Race of proprietor and number of establishment.	Date established.	Employed.	Borrowed.	Rent per year.	Value of annual transactions.	Net profit.	Same race.	Other races.	Per cent white patrons.
Japanese:									
No. 1	1905	$500	0	$300	$3,600	$960	0	0	30.0
No. 2	1907	500	0	144	2,000	540	0	0	70.0
No. 3	1908	700	0	144	1,000	300	0	0	90.0
No. 4	1908	700	0	960	2,700	300	0	0	30.0
No. 5	1906	2,000	0	540	5,800	2,400	0	0	10.0
No. 6	1907	500	0	84	1,300	360	0	0	80.0
No. 7	1906	700	0	120	1,800	540	1	0	30.0
No. 8	1906	600	0	108	2,500	720	0	0	80.0
No. 9	1906	2,700	$700	144	2,000	1,000	f 0	0	5.0

a Not reported.
b Wife of proprietor works also.
c Very small.

d Drug stores.
e Three partners.
f Two partners.

TABLE 22.—*General data on business conducted by Japanese and members of other races*—Continued.

GROCERIES.

Race of proprietor and number of establishment.	Date established.	Amount of capital—		Rent per year.	Value of annual transactions.	Net profit.	Number of employees of—		Per cent white patrons.
		Employed.	Borrowed.				Same race.	Other races.	
Japanese:									
No. 1	1903	$26,000	$20,000	$1,200	$96,000	$2,600	4	0	20.0
No. 2	1903	7,000	1,000	720	50,000	6,000	2	0	20.0
No. 3	1906	50,000	15,000	2,160	87,000	900	6	0	.0
No. 4	1906	2,000	0	540	18,000	1,200	a 0	0	50.0
No. 5	1906	3,000	500	540	15,000	1,440	0	0	40.0
No. 6	1908	1,500	200	480	6,000	780	0	0	20.0
No. 7	1908	700	200	360	2,400	720	a 0	0	10.0
No. 8	1908	1,000	0	480	9,000	960	b 0	1	99.5
No. 9	1907	7,500	1,700	3,600	140,000	(c)	12	0	20.0

LAUNDRIES.

Race of proprietor and number of establishment.	Date established.	Amount of capital—		Rent per year.	Value of annual transactions.	Net profit.	Number of employees of—		Per cent white patrons.
		Employed.	Borrowed.				Same race.	Other races.	
Japanese:									
No. 1	1904	$3,000	$500	$300	$6,500	$1,200	b 8	0	90.0
No. 2	1907	1,400	0	420	9,000	1,200	7	0	60.0
No. 3	1908	1,500	0	384	3,000	(c)	3	0	80.0
No. 4	1908	1,000	0	900	8,000	(c)	6	2	80.0
No. 5	1908	700	0	420	2,000	(c)	2	0	80.0
No. 6	1906	2,000	0	1,140	10,000	(c)	10	0	75.0
No. 7	1909	800	0	540	2,400	(c)	1	0	99.0
American:									
No. 8	1900	100,000	0	6,000	120,000	(c)	140	0	100.0
No. 9	1903	30,000	0	1,560	75,000	(c)	(c)	0	100.0
No. 10	1903	40,000	0	2,400	124,000	18,600	100	0	100.0
No. 11	1904	50,000	0	(d)	123,000	18,450	120	0	(c)
English:									
No. 12	1893	60,000	0	(c)	125,000	(c)	100	0	100.0

MEAT AND FISH MARKETS.

Race of proprietor and number of establishment.	Date established.	Amount of capital—		Rent per year.	Value of annual transactions.	Net profit.	Number of employees of—		Per cent white patrons.
		Employed.	Borrowed.				Same race.	Other races.	
Japanese:									
No. 1	1906	$1,000	0	$540	$12,000	$3,000	2	0	20.0
No. 2	1908	600	0	720	6,000	1,200	1	0	10.0
No. 3	1902	3,000	0	900	28,880	2,400	b 3	0	60.0
No. 4	e 1908	200	0	(c)	1,500	600	0	0	.0
No. 5	f 1908	450	0	240	5,000	600	1	0	1.0

RESTAURANTS.

Race of proprietor and number of establishment.	Date established.	Amount of capital—		Rent per year.	Value of annual transactions.	Net profit.	Number of employees of—		Per cent white patrons.
		Employed.	Borrowed.				Same race.	Other races.	
Japanese:									
No. 1	1899	$2,000	0	$1,200	$18,000	$1,800	a 6	0	90.0
No. 2	1904	5,000	$1,500	960	10,000	2,000	11	0	.0
No. 3	1905	1,000	0	420	3,600	900	g 0	0	50.0
No. 4	1906	4,000	0	1,500	12,000	2,700	9	0	.0
No. 5	1906	400	0	240	3,000	840	a 0	0	.0
No. 6	1907	2,500	0	1,080	18,000	600	4	0	100.0
No. 7	1907	600	0	276	2,000	400	a 1	0	75.0
No. 8	1907	700	0	900	18,000	1,800	3	0	97.5
No. 9	1908	1,500	0	900	12,000	600	4	0	50.0
American:									
No. 10	1905	2,500	0	2,520	60,000	(c)	22	0	100.0
No. 11	1907	1,500	0	900	27,375	(c)	3	5	100.0
No. 12	1909	1,100	0	1,020	23,400	(c)	5	3	100.0
No. 13	1909	1,200	0	900	9,600	(c)	3	1	100.0
Dalmatian:									
No. 14	1902	3,000	0	1,620	18,000	(h)	9	0	100.0

a Wife of proprietor works also.
b Two partners.
c Not reported.
d Proprietor owns building.
e Fish peddler.
f Meat market.
g Wife and daughter of proprietor work also.
h Small.

TABLE 22.—*General data on business conducted by Japanese and members of other races*—Continued.

TAILORING AND CLEANING.

Race of proprietor and number of establishment.	Date established.	Amount of capital—		Rent per year.	Value of annual transactions.	Net profit.	Number of employees of—		Per cent white patrons.
		Employed.	Borrowed.				Same race.	Other races.	
Japanese:									
No. 1	1900	$2,000	$200	$720	$18,000	$1,200	6	1	20.0
No. 2	1906	1,000	0	360	8,800	840	1	0	20.0
No. 3	1906	700	0	336	4,800	600	2	0	20.0
No. 4	1907	500	0	240	1,800	1,080	0	0	50.0

MISCELLANEOUS.

Japanese (artificial flower maker):									
No. 1	1906	$500	0	$216	$3,000	$1,500	3	0	50.0
Japanese (bicycle shop and repairs):									
No. 1	1903	4,500	$1,000	780	6,000	1,200	1	0	50.0
Japanese (carpenters):									
No. 1	1905	500	0	96	800	600	0	0	10.0
No. 2	1906	250	(a)	192	2,000	840	2	0	10.0
Japanese (employment agencies):									
No. 1	1907	80	0	144	1,400	840	0	0	(a)
No. 2	1907	70	(a)	240	1,300	720	0	0	(a)
Japanese (general merchandise):									
No. 1	1905	4,000	1,500	480	30,000	2,500	0	0	40.0
Japanese (men's furnishings):									
No. 1	1906	5,000	2,000	720	7,000	960	2	0	40.0
No. 2	1907	2,500	0	720	14,000	1,200	b0	0	40.0
Japanese (liquor store):									
No. 1	1908	4,500	400	600	21,600	2,800	1	0	30.0
Japanese (photographers):									
No. 1	1907	1,000	0	300	1,500	360	0	0	.0
No. 2	1908	600	0	300	1,600	600	0	0	10.0
Japanese (shoe store):									
No. 1	1907	1,500	700	420	6,000	1,440	0	0	20.0
Japanese (watchmaker and jeweler):									
No. 1	1902	7,000	500	540	10,000	4,500	2	0	50.0
No. 2	1903	1,000	600	420	4,500	1,440	0	0	40.0

a Not reported.   b Two partners.

TABLE 23.—*Money brought to the United States by Japanese.*

	Number reporting complete data.	Number bringing each specified amount.									
		None.	Under $25.	$25 and under $50.	$50 and under $100.	$100 and under $150.	$150 and under $200.	$200 and under $300.	$300 and under $400.	$400 and under $500.	$500 and under $1,000.	$1,000 or over.
In business for self	98	1	......	36	29	8	8	5	3	1	4	3
Wage-earners	40	......	......	21	18	......	......	1	......	......	......	......

TABLE 24.—*First occupation of Japanese in the United States, by occupation abroad.*

IN BUSINESS FOR SELF.

Occupation abroad	Number	Number who were—															
		In business for self.	Farmers.	Farm hands.	Railroad laborers.	Sawmill laborers.	Cannery hands.	Laborers in industrial establishments.	Store help.	Restaurant help.	House cleaners.	In domestic service.	Tailors and dyers.	Barbers.	Wage-earners in city.	In other occupations.	Occupation unknown.
In business for self	a38	12		7	4				3	1		6			3		2
Farmer	b7	1		4						1		1					
At home	18	1			1				1	1		14					
Farming for father	a19			8	4							4			3		
Store help	1											1					
Laborer in industrial establishment	c1			1													
Wage-earner in city	12	2			1				1	1		4		1	1		1
In other occupations	2				1		1										
Total	98	16		20	11		1		5	3	1	30		1	7		3

WAGE-EARNERS.

Occupation abroad	Number	In business for self.	Farmers.	Farm hands.	Railroad laborers.	Sawmill laborers.	Cannery hands.	Laborers in industrial establishments.	Store help.	Restaurant help.	House cleaners.	In domestic service.	Tailors and dyers.	Barbers.	Wage-earners in city.	In other occupations.	Occupation unknown.
In business for self	2	1			1												
Farmer	c4			3	1												
At home	12			1								11					
Farming for father	c12			4	2					1		3			2		
Store help	4									1		3					
Laborer in industrial establishment	1									1							
Wage-earner in city	4											4					
In other occupations	1			1													
Total	40	1		9	4					1	2		21				2	

a Including 2 who came to United States from Hawaii.
b Including 3 who came to United States from Hawaii.
c Including 1 who came to United States from Hawaii.

TABLE 25.—*Net value of all property now owned by Japanese, by length of residence in the United States.*

IN BUSINESS FOR SELF.

Length of residence in the United States.	Number reporting complete data.	Number owning property valued at each specified amount.											
		None.	Under $50.	$50 and under $100.	$100 and under $250.	$250 and under $500.	$500 and under $1,000.	$1,000 and under $1,500.	$1,500 and under $2,500.	$2,500 and under $5,000.	$5,000 and under $10,000.	$10,000 and under $25,000.	$25,000 or over.
Under 2 years													
2 years	2						1	1					
3 years	5			1			2		1	1			
4 years	12				1		3	3	3	2			
5 to 9 years	48					2	9	8	13	10	3	3	
10 to 14 years	25				1	1	6	4	5	3	4		1
15 to 19 years	5						1		3		1		
20 years or over	1											1	
Total	98			1	1	4	22	16	25	16	8	4	1

WAGE-EARNERS.

Length of residence in the United States.	Number reporting complete data.	None.	Under $50.	$50 and under $100.	$100 and under $250.	$250 and under $500.	$500 and under $1,000.	$1,000 and under $1,500.	$1,500 and under $2,500.	$2,500 and under $5,000.	$5,000 and under $10,000.	$10,000 and under $25,000.	$25,000 or over.
Under 2 years													
2 years	2			1			1						
3 years	5				1	2	2						
4 years	7	1			1	2	3						
5 to 9 years	19	2			2	3	5	5	1	1			
10 to 14 years	4	3				1							
15 to 19 years	3	2										1	
20 years or over													
Total	40	8		1	4		10	5	1	1		1	

TABLE 26.—*Average surplus or deficit of past year reported by Japanese.*

IN BUSINESS FOR SELF.

	Number.	Average.		Number.	Average.
Reporting:			Average surplus, based on total number................	....	$547.00
Surplus...................	84	$621.61			
Deficit....................	1	250.00			
Neither surplus nor deficit....	10	....			
Total...................	95	....			

WAGE-EARNERS.

	Number.	Average.		Number.	Average.
Reporting:			Average surplus, based on total number................	....	$213.04
Surplus...................	30	$326.66			
Deficit....................	.....	.....			
Neither surplus nor deficit....	8	....			
Total...................	38	....			

TABLE 27.—*Surplus or deficit of past year reported by Japanese, by classified amounts.*

IN BUSINESS FOR SELF.

Amount.	Number reporting.		Amount.	Number reporting.	
	Surplus.	Deficit.		Surplus.	Deficit.
$100 and under $250...........	19	....	$2,500 or over................	4	....
$250 and under $500...........	26	1			
$500 and under $1,000.........	25	....	Total....................	84	1
$1 000 and under $2,500.......	10	....			

WAGE-EARNERS.

Amount.	Surplus.	Deficit.	Amount.	Surplus.	Deficit.
Under $100..................	1	....	$1,000 and under $2,500.......	2	....
$100 and under $250...........	14	....			
$250 and under $500...........	12	....	Total....:..............	30	....
$500 and under $1,000.........	1	....			

TABLE 28.—*Gross value of property, encumbrances, and net value of property now owned by male Japanese.*

	Number reporting complete data.	Gross value of property.		Encumbrances on property.			Net value of property.	
		Aggregate amount.	Average amount.	Number having encumbrances.	Aggregate amount.	Average amount.	Aggregate amount.	Average amount.
In business for self.	98	$337,070.00	$3,439.49	35	$40,810.00	$1,166.00	$296,260.00	$3,023.06
Wage-earners.......	40	31,415.00	785.37	....	....	....	31,415.00	785.37

TABLE 29.—*Number of Japanese for whom detailed information was secured, by sex and general nativity.*

IN BUSINESS FOR SELF.

General nativity.	Male.	Female.	Total.
Native-born..................................	10	14	24
Foreign-born.................................	103	48	151
Total......................................	113	62	175

General nativity.	Male.	Female.	Total.
Native-born..	....	1	1
Foreign-born..	40	4	44
Total...:..	40	5	45

TABLE 30.—*Conjugal condition of Japanese, by sex and age groups.*

IN BUSINESS FOR SELF.

Sex.	16 to 19.				20 to 29.				30 to 44.				45 or over.				Total.			
	Single.	Married.	Widowed.	Total.	Single.	Married.	Widowed.	Total.	Single.	Married.	Widowed.	Total.	Single.	Married.	Widowed.	Total.	Single.	Married.	Widowed.	Total.
Male...........	....	....	....	....	23	4	....	27	16	45	1	62	....	9	2	11	39	58	3	100
Female.........	1	2	....	3	....	24	....	24	....	17	....	17	....	....	....	....	....	1	43	....	44
Total.....	1	2	....	3	23	28	....	51	16	62	1	79	....	9	2	11	40	101	3	144

WAGE-EARNERS.

Sex.	16 to 19.				20 to 29.				30 to 44.				45 or over.				Total.			
Male...........	....	....	....	....	17	1	....	18	13	8	....	21	....	1	....	1	30	10	....	40
Female.........	....	....	....	....	....	3	....	3	....	1	....	1	....	....	....	....	....	4	....	4
Total.....	....	....	....	....	17	4	....	21	13	9	....	22	....	1	....	1	30	14	....	44

TABLE 31.—*Conjugal condition of foreign-born male Japanese 16 years of age or over, by age at time of coming to the United States.*

IN BUSINESS FOR SELF.

Age at time of coming to the United States.	Total number of arrivals.	Single or widowed at time of coming to United States.			Married at time of coming to United States.			
		Number.	Married during visit abroad.	Married in United States.	Number.	Wife abroad.	Accompanied by wife.	Wife joining later.
Under 18 years......................	10	10	1	3	....	....	....	....
18 and under 20 years...............	7	7	....	....	....	....	....	....
20 and under 25 years...............	25	22	3	3	3	....	2	1
25 and under 30 years...............	28	16	a 5	b 2	12	3	6	3
30 and under 35 years...............	13	2	2	....	11	2	8	1
35 and under 40 years...............	13	4	....	1	9	5	4	....
40 and under 45 years...............	1	....	....	....	1	1	....	....
45 years or over....................	3	1	....	....	2	1	1	....
Total......................	100	62	a 11	b 9	38	12	21	5

WAGE-EARNERS.

Age at time of coming to the United States.	Total number of arrivals.	Single or widowed at time of coming to United States.			Married at time of coming to United States.			
Under 18 years......................	6	6	....	....	....	....	....	....
18 and under 20 years...............	3	3	....	....	....	....	....	....
20 and under 25 years...............	16	15	1	....	1	....	1	....
25 and under 30 years...............	8	6	....	....	2	1	....	1
30 and under 35 years...............	4	1	....	....	3	2	1	....
35 and under 40 years...............	3	....	....	....	3	3	....	....
40 years or over....................	....	....	....	....	....	....	....	....
Total......................	40	31	1	....	9	6	2	1

a Including 2 married abroad whose wives remained in Japan.
b Including 1 whose wife is visiting in Japan.

TABLE **32.**—*Number of Japanese within each age group, by sex.*

[This table includes persons in business for self as well as wage-earners.]

Sex.	Number within each specified age group.							
	Under 6.	6 to 13.	14 and 15.	16 to 19.	20 to 29.	30 to 44.	45 or over.	Total.
Male	10	3	....	....	45	83	12	153
Female	15	4	....	3	27	18	....	67
Total	25	7	....	3	72	101	12	220

TABLE **33.**—*Number of foreign-born Japanese in the United States each specified number of years, by sex.*

IN BUSINESS FOR SELF.

[By years in the United States is meant years since first arrival in the United States. No deduction is made for time spent abroad.]

Sex.	Number reporting complete data.	Number in United States each specified number of years.								
		Under 1.	1.	2.	3.	4.	5 to 9.	10 to 14.	15 to 19.	20 or over.
Male	103	......	......	2	5	13	50	27	5	1
Female	48	1	8	1	10	11	15	2	......	......
Total	151	1	8	3	15	24	65	29	5	1

WAGE-EARNERS.

Sex.	Number reporting complete data.	Under 1.	1.	2.	3.	4.	5 to 9.	10 to 14.	15 to 19.	20 or over.
Male	40	......	......	2	5	7	19	4	3	......
Female	4	......	......	......	1	2	1	......	......	......
Total	44	......	......	2	6	9	20	4	3	......

TABLE **34.**—*Ability to speak English of Japanese 6 years of age or over, by sex and general nativity.*

IN BUSINESS FOR SELF.

General nativity.	Number reporting complete data.	Male.		Female.		Total.	
		Number.	Number who speak English.	Number.	Number who speak English.	Number.	Number who speak English.
Foreign-born	151	103	101	48	31	151	132

WAGE-EARNERS.

General nativity.	Number reporting complete data.	Number.	Number who speak English.	Number.	Number who speak English.	Number.	Number who speak English.
Foreign-born	44	40	39	4	2	44	41

TABLE **35.**—*Ability to speak English of foreign-born Japanese 6 years of age or over, by sex and years in the United States.*

IN BUSINESS FOR SELF.

[By years in the United States is meant years since first arrival in the United States. No deduction is made for time spent abroad.]

Sex.	Number reporting complete data.	Number who speak English.	Years in United States.					
			Under 5.		5 to 9.		10 or over.	
			Num-ber.	Number who speak English.	Num-ber.	Number who speak English.	Num-ber.	Number who speak English.
Male...................	103	101	20	20	50	48	33	33
Female.................	48	31	31	18	15	11	2	2
Total................	151	132	• 51	38	65	59	35	35

WAGE-EARNERS.

Male...................	40	39	14	14	19	18	7	7
Female.................	4	2	3	2	1	....	....	....
Total................	44	41	17	16	20	18	7	7

TABLE **36.**—*Ability to speak English of foreign-born Japanese 6 years of age or over, by sex and by age at time of coming to the United States.*

IN BUSINESS FOR SELF.

Sex.	Number reporting complete data.	Number who speak English.	Age at time of coming to United States.			
			Under 14.		14 or over.	
			Number.	Number who speak English.	Number.	Number who speak English.
Male......	103	101	3	3	100	98
Female....	48	31	6	6	42	25
Total.....	151	132	9	9	142	123

WAGE-EARNERS.

Male......	40	39	....	....	40	39
Female....	4	2	....	....	4	2
Total.....	44	41	....	....	44	41

TABLE **37.**—*Literacy of Japanese 10 years of age or over, by sex and general nativity.*

IN BUSINESS FOR SELF.

General nativity.	Number reporting complete data.	Male.			Female.			Total.		
		Num-ber.	Num-ber who read.	Num-ber who read and write.	Num-ber.	Num-ber who read.	Num-ber who read and write.	Num-ber.	Num-ber who read.	Num-ber who read and write.
Foreign-born..........	145	101	98	98	44	41	41	145	139	139

WAGE-EARNERS.

Foreign-born..........	44	40	39	39	4	4	4	44	43	43

TABLE **38.**—*Literacy of foreign-born Japanese 10 years of age or over, by sex and by years in the United States.*

IN BUSINESS FOR SELF.

[By years in the United States is meant since first arrival in the United States.]

Sex.	Number reporting complete data.	Years in United States.								
		Under 5.			5 to 9.			10 or over.		
		Number.	Number who read.	Number who read and write.	Number.	Number who read.	Number who read and write.	Number.	Number who read.	Number who read and write.
Male	101	19	19	19	49	47	47	33	32	32
Female	44	28	27	27	14	12	12	2	2	2
Total	145	47	46	46	63	59	59	35	34	34

WAGE-EARNERS.

Sex	Number reporting complete data.	Number.	Number who read.	Number who read and write.	Number.	Number who read.	Number who read and write.	Number.	Number who read.	Number who read and write.
Male	40	14	13	13	19	19	19	7	7	7
Female	4	3	3	3	1	1	1	......	......	......
Total	44	17	16	16	20	20	20	7	7	7

TABLE **39.**—*Literacy of foreign-born Japanese 10 years of age or over, by sex and by age at time of coming to the United States.*

IN BUSINESS FOR SELF.

Sex.	Number reporting complete data.	Age at time of coming to United States.					
		Under 14.			14 or over.		
		Number.	Number who read.	Number who read and write.	Number.	Number who read.	Number who read and write.
Male	101	1	1	1	100	97	97
Female	44	2	2	2	42	39	39
Total	145	3	3	3	142	136	136

WAGE-EARNERS.

Sex	Number reporting complete data.	Number.	Number who read.	Number who read and write.	Number.	Number who read.	Number who read and write.
Male	40	......	......	......	40	39	39
Female	4	......	......	......	4	4	4
Total	44	......	......	......	44	43	43

TABLE **40.**—*Ability of foreign-born Japanese 10 years of age or over to speak, read, and write English, by sex.*

IN BUSINESS FOR SELF.

Sex.	Number reporting complete data.	Unable to speak, read, or write English.	Able to speak English, but not to read and write it.	Able to speak and read, but not write English.	Able to speak, read, and write English.
Male	101	2	28	......	71
Female	44	17	19	......	8
Total	145	19	47	......	79

WAGE-EARNERS.

Sex	Number reporting complete data.	Unable to speak, read, or write English.	Able to speak English, but not to read and write it.	Able to speak and read, but not write English.	Able to speak, read, and write English.
Male	40	1	15	......	24
Female	4	2	2	......	......
Total	44	3	17	......	24

TABLE 41.—*General occupation of Japanese under 16 years of age, by sex, age groups, and general nativity.*

IN BUSINESS FOR SELF.

Sex and general nativity.	Under 6.				6 to 13.				14 and 15.				Total.			
	At home.	At school.	At work.	Total.	At home.	At school.	At work.	Total.	At home.	At school.	At work.	Total.	At home.	At school.	At work.	Total.
Native-born:																
Male..............................	10	....	....	10	....	....	....	....	....	....	....	....	10	....	....	10
Female............................	14	....	....	14	....	....	....	....	....	....	....	....	14	....	....	14
Total........................	24	....	....	24	....	....	....	....	....	....	....	....	24	....	....	24
Foreign-born:																
Male..............................	....			....	..	3	....	3	....			....	..	3	....	3
Female............................	....			....	2	2	....	4	....			....	2	2	....	4
Total........................	....			....	2	5	....	7	....			....	2	5	....	7
Grand total..................	24	....	....	24	2	5	....	7	....			....	26	5	....	31

WAGE-EARNERS.

Sex and general nativity.	At home.	At school.	At work.	Total.	At home.	At school.	At work.	Total.	At home.	At school.	At work.	Total.	At home.	At school.	At work.	Total.
Native-born:																
Male.............................	..			..												
Female...........................	1	....	....	1	....	....	....	....	....			....	1	....	....	1
Total.......................	1	....	....	1	....	....	....	....	....			....	1	....	....	1
Foreign-born:																
Male.............................	....	..		....												
Female...........................																
Total.......................	....			....												
Grand total.................	1	....	....	1	....	....	....	....	....			....	1	....	....	1

TABLE 42.—*Total yearly income of male Japanese engaged in business for self, and income from principal business.*

Kind of business.	Number reporting complete data.	Number having each specified amount of yearly income.									Income from principal business.	
		Under $300.	$300 and under $400.	$400 and under $500.	$500 and under $750.	$750 and under $1,000.	$1,000 and under $1,500.	$1,500 and under $2,000.	$2,000 and under $2,500.	$2,500 or over.	Total income.	Average income.
Barber shop.........................	8	....	....	....	2	5	1	....	....	....	$6,660.00	$832.50
Laundry.............................	6	....	....	....	2	1	1	2	....	....	7,115.00	1,185.83
Lodging house......................	6	....	....	....	3	1	....	1	1	....	6,910.00	1,151.67
Pool room..........................	6	....	1	1	2	2	....	....	....	....	5,040.00	840.00
Real estate and labor agencies....	2	....	....	....	2	....	....	....	....	....	1,560.00	780.00
Restaurant proprietors............	11	....	....	1	2	2	2	2	1	1	13,940.00	1,267.27
Shoemakers........................	3	....	....	....	2	1	....	....	....	....	2,340.00	780.00
Storekeepers	39	....	2	....	8	10	13	....	1	5	53,390.00	1,368.97
Tailors............................	2	....	....	....	....	....	2	....	....	....	2,280.00	1,140.00
Miscellaneous......................	14	....	1	....	7	3	1	1	....	1	12,760.00	911.43
Total......................	97	....	4	2	26	27	22	6	3	7	111,995.00	1,154.59

TABLE **43.**— *Yearly earnings (approximate) of male Japanese 18 years of age or over, by number of months employed.*

WITH BOARD.

Number of months employed.	Number working for wages and reporting amount.	Average earnings.	Number earning—										
			$250 and under $300.	$300 and under $400.	$400 and under $500.	$500 and under $600.	$600 and under $700.	$700 and under $800.	$800 and under $1,000.	$1,000 and under $1,250.	$1,250 and under $1,500.	$1,500 and under $2,000.
9 months................	1	$270.00	1	....	....	....	....	....	....	....	....	....
10 months................	1	300.00	....	1	....	....	....	....	....	....	....	....
11 months................	1	330.00	....	1	....	....	....	....	....	....	....	....
12 months................	21	460.00	....	4	12	3	1	1	....	....	....	....
Total...............	24	440.00	1	6	12	3	1	1	....	....	....	....

WITHOUT BOARD.

Number of months employed.	Number working for wages and reporting amount.	Average earnings.	Number earning—										
			$250 and under $300.	$300 and under $400.	$400 and under $500.	$500 and under $600.	$600 and under $700.	$700 and under $800.	$800 and under $1,000.	$1,000 and under $1,250.	$1,250 and under $1,500.	$1,500 and under $2,000.
11 months................	2	$495.00	....	1	....	....	....	1	....	....	....	....
12 months................	14	751.43	....	....	....	3	2	5	3	....	....	1
Total...............	16	719.38	....	1	....	3	3	5	3	....	....	1

SACRAMENTO.

TABLE **44.**—*General data on business conducted by Japanese and members of other races.*

BARBER SHOPS.

Race of proprietor and number of establishment.	Date established.	Amount of capital.		Rent per year.	Value of annual transactions.	Net profits.	Number of employees of—		Per cent white patrons.
		Employed.	Borrowed.				Same race.	Other races.	
Japanese:									
No. 1..............	1901	$200	0	$180	$1,000	$700	a 0	0	10.0
No. 2..............	1905	150	0	180	1,000	720	0	0	30.0
No. 3..............	1908	449	$99	120	800	600	0	0	.0
No. 4..............	1895	1,000	0	420	1,200	540	1	0	70.0
American:									
No. 5..............	1905	1,500	0	720	7,000	(b)	c 2	1	100.0
No. 6..............	1909	2,000	0	618	6,000	500	2	2	100.0
Greek:									
No. 7..............	1909	250	0	360	375	(b)	1	0	d 100.0
Italian (North):									
No. 8..............	1909	250	0	300	1,680	(b)	1	1	100.0
Negro:									
No. 9..............	1909	5	5	72	(b)	261	0	0	e .0
Portuguese:									
No. 10..............	1908	1,000	0	360	3,100	2,080	1	0	f 100.0

BILLIARD HALLS.

Race of proprietor and number of establishment.	Date established.	Amount of capital.		Rent per year.	Value of annual transactions.	Net profits.	Number of employees of—		Per cent white patrons.
		Employed.	Borrowed.				Same race.	Other races.	
Japanese:									
No. 1..............	1907	$1,500	0	$276	$2,500	$1,200	0	0	25.0
No. 2..............	1909	750	0	360	1,000	148	0	0	50.0

a One partner, brother.　　　c Two partners.　　　e All negro.
b Not reported.　　　d Mainly Greek.　　　f Approximately.

TABLE 44.—*General data on business conducted by Japanese and members of other races*—Continued.

BOARDING AND LODGING HOUSES.

Race of proprietor and number of establishment.	Date established.	Amount of capital.		Rent per year.	Value of annual transactions.	Net profits.	Number of employees of—		Per cent white patrons.
		Employed.	Borrowed.				Same race.	Other races.	
Japanese:									
No. 1............	1899	$200	0	$480	$1,800	$600	0	0	0.0
No. 2............	1901	2,000	0	1,080	3,500	1,200	0	0	.0
No. 3............	1902	3,000	0	780	5,680	1,700	2	0	.0
No. 4............	1903	1,700	0	480	3,000	900	0	0	.0
No. 5............	1907	1,700	0	900	5,300	2,196	a 0	0	.0
No. 6............	1908	1,450	$500	780	2,500	950	b 0	0	.0
No. 7............	1908	300	0	(c)	2,000	(c)	0	0	.0

CONFECTIONERY AND TOBACCO STORES.

Japanese:									
No. 1............	1907	$300	0	$42	$1,800	$600	1	0	40.0
No. 2............	1907	1,300	0	120	2,000	1,200	1	0	20.0
No. 3............	1909	2,750	$750	84	2,000	150	0	0	5.0
No. 4............	1901	500	0	60	1,200	600	0	0	.0
No. 5............	1901	1,200	0	180	800	600	0	0	.0

GROCERY STORES.

Japanese:									
No. 1............	1894	$60,000	$18,000	$1,236	$120,000	$4,700	8	0	70.0
No. 2............	1905	2,000	300	300	4,000	840	0	0	50.0
No. 3............	1906	3,000	1,500	600	5,000	2,400	1	0	30.0
No. 4............	1908	1,000	300	300	1,700	600	0	0	60.0
No. 5............	1906	3,300	300	720	10,000	1,800	1	0	30.0
American:									
No. 6............	1904	2,500	0	360	3,000	700	2	0	100.0
No. 7............	1879	5,000	0	1,025	20,000	(c)	7	0	100.0
German:									
No. 8............	1869	3,500	0	(d)	6,000	(c)	0	4	100.0
Greek:									
No. 9............	1908	300–400	0	540	5,000	(c)	b 0	0	e 100.0
Swiss (French):									
No. 10............	1896	6,500	0	(d)	1,500	(c)	1	1	100.0

LABOR AND REAL ESTATE AGENCIES.

Japanese: f									
No. 1............	1908	$500	0	$180	$1,500	$1,200	0	0	0.0
No. 2............	1906	200	0	180	2,000	1,000	0	0	40.0
No. 3............	1905	100	0	72	1,300	1,000	0	0	.0
No. 4 f............	1907	300	0	216	2,500	1,000	0	0	20.0

LAUNDRIES.

Japanese:									
No. 1............	1902	$2,000	0	$300	$7,000	$1,200	9	0	80.0
No. 2............	1907	630	0	48	2,000	1,200	1	0	.0
American:									
No. 3............	1887	30,000	0	(c)	86,000	(c)	17	16	100.0
No. 4............	1904	55,000	0	1,800	145,000	(c)	(g)	(g)	100.0
No. 5............	1906	25,000	0	1,860	95,000	(c)	16	17	100.0
No. 6............	1907	(c)	0	300	6,000	(c)	21	3	100.0
Italian, North:									
No. 7............	1902	90,000	0	(d)	100,000	(c)	28	33	(c)

a Three partners.
b Two partners.
c Not reported.
d Proprietor owns building.
e Mostly Greek.
f Also acts as interpreter and as broker in vegetables and fruits.
g 76 employees, including all races.

TABLE 44.—*General data on business conducted by Japanese and members of other races*—Continued.

MEN'S FURNISHINGS.

Race of proprietor and number of establishment.	Date established.	Amount of capital.		Rent per year.	Value of annual transactions.	Net profits.	Number of employees of—		Per cent white patrons
		Employed.	Borrowed.				Same race.	Other races.	
Japanese:									
No. 1	1907	$5,000	$1,500	$600	$8,000	$700	0	0	90.0
No. 2	1909	4,900	900	720	(a)	(b)	c 2	0	30.0
American:									
No. 3	1893	10,000	0	1,080	32,000	2,500	0	2	100.0

PHOTOGRAPHERS.

Japanese:									
No. 1	1901	$1,500	0	$180	$3,000	$1,800	1	0	70.0
No. 2	1904	1,880	$380	480	3,000	1,200	1	0	25.0

RESTAURANTS.

Japanese:									
No. 1	1900	$600	0	$480	$9,600	$1,920	d 2	0	e 100.0
No. 2	1904	2,500	0	360	10,000	2,400	c 5	0	.0
No. 3	1907	1,400	$200	500	9,000	1,800	6	0	.0
No. 4	1907	400	0	150	2,000	360	0	0	e.0
No. 5	1908	500	0	120	2,000	1,016	f 0	0	50.0
No. 6	1908	1,500	0	360	9,000	700	6	0	30.0
No. 7	1909	1,800	0	108	2,500	240	2	0	e.0
American:									
No. 8	1884	2,500	0	900	13,500	(b)	5	1	e 100.0
Danish:									
No. 9	1908	800	0	(g)	12,000	1,200	1	1	e 100.0
German:									
No. 10	1907	800	0	720	9,600	1,200–1,500	d 0	1	100.0
Slovenian:									
No. 11	1907	2,000	700	624	20,000	1,200	4	2	100.0

TAILOR SHOPS.

Japanese:									
No. 1	1902	$1,000	0	$480	$5,000	$1,400	f 2	0	10.0
No. 2	1902	300	0	180	2,000	1,000	0	0	50.0
German-Hebrew:									
No. 3	1884	15,000	0	1,380	28,000	2,500	0	10	100.0
Italian, North:									
No. 4	1907	3,000	0	660	8,000	h None.	4	3	100.0

MISCELLANEOUS.

Japanese:									
No. 1 (bank)	1906	$66,650	$16,650	$360	$1,072,745	(g) $720	4	0	7.0
No. 2 (bathhouse)	1904	450	0	90	900		0	0	.0
No. 3 (bicycle repairing and noodle restaurant)	1907	1,200	200	180	1,800	500	0	0	50.0
No. 4 (carpenter)	1905	200	0	180	1,800	1,560	3	0	40.0
No. 5 (drug store)	1908	500	0	180	2,000	720	0	0	.0
No. 6 (dry goods)	1908	4,000	2,000	216	5,400	1,100	0	0	20.0
No. 7 (fish and vegetable market)	1908	1,400	400	180	10,000	1,000	1	0	33.33
No. 8 (general business agency)	1908	800	0	300	36,000	2,100	1	0	.0
No. 9 (general store)	1904	31,000	17,300	1,632	70,000	2,000	6	0	23.0

a In business only three months.
b Not reported.
c Four partners.
d Wife works also.

e Approximately.
f Two partners.
g Proprietor owns building.
h Lost $1,600 during year.

TABLE 44.—*General data on business conducted by Japanese and members of other races*—Continued.

MISCELLANEOUS—Continued.

Race of proprietor and number of establishment.	Date established.	Amount of capital.		Rent per year.	Value of annual transactions.	Net profits.	Number of employees of—		Per cent white patrons.
		Employed.	Borrowed.				Same race.	Other races.	
Japanese—Continued.									
No. 10 (moving pictures)	1907	$3,500	0	$960	$5,500	$1,320	4	1	50.0
No. 11 (shoe store and repairing)	1908	1,500	$500	240	5,000	1,800	1	0	30.0
No. 12 (shoe repairing)	1907	400	150	(a)	1,200	420	b 1	0	99.0
No. 13 (watchmaker and repairer)	1907	2,400	400	162	3,000	800	0	0	50.0

a Proprietor owns building.　　　　　　　　b One apprentice.

TABLE 45.—*Money brought to the United States by Japanese.*

	Number reporting complete data.	Number bringing each specified amount.										
		None.	Under $.	$5 and under $.	$9 and under $.	$100 and under $150.	$150 and under $200.	$200 and under $300.	$300 and under $400.	$400 and under $500.	$500 and under $1,000.	$1,000 or over.
In business for self	74	3	2	11	25	19	4	4	2	2	1	1
Wage-earners	25		2	1	13	6	1		1	1		

TABLE 46.—*First occupation of Japanese in the United States, by occupation abroad.*

IN BUSINESS FOR SELF.

Occupation abroad.	Number.	Number who were—								
		In business for self.	Farmers.	Farm hands.	Railroad laborers.	Store help.	Restaurant help.	In domestic service.	Wage-earners in city.	Occupation unknown.
In business for self	a 28	2		10	4	2	1	8	1	
Farmer	b 3			3						
At home	12			1	2	1		7		1
Farming for father	a 17		4	6	3			4		
Farm hand	b 1				1					
Store help	3			1	1			1		
Laborer in industrial establishment	c 1			1						
Wage-earner in city	b 7			3	1			2	1	
In other occupations	b c 3			2					1	
Total	75	2	4	27	12	3	1	22	3	1

WAGE-EARNERS.

In business for self	3			1				2		
Farmer	1			1						
At home	7				3	1		2	1	
Farming for father	d 9			2	1		2	3	1	
Store help	1			1						
Wage-earner in city	b 4			3					1	
Total	25			8	4	1	2	7	3	

a Including 4 who came to United States via Hawaii.
b Including 1 who came to United States via Hawaii.
c Including 1 who came to United States from Canada.
d Including 3 who came to United States via Hawaii.

TABLE 47.—*Net value of all property now owned by Japanese, by length of residence in the United States.*

IN BUSINESS FOR SELF.

Length of residence in the United States.	Number reporting complete data.	Number owning property valued at each specified amount.											
		None.a	Under $50.	$50 and under $100.	$100 and under $250.	$250 and under $500.	$500 and under $1,000.	$1,000 and under $1,500.	$1,500 and under $2,500.	$2,500 and under $5,000.	$5,000 and under $10,000.	$10,000 and under $25,000.	$25,000 or over.
Under 2 years													
2 years	4	1			2			1					
3 years	4						2		1	1			
4 years	8				1	2	3		1		1		
5 to 9 years	33				2	7	6	9	4	3	2		
10 to 14 years	17	1				3	2	3	6	2			
15 to 19 years	7	1				1		1		1	1	1	1
20 years or over	1											1	
Total	74	3			5	13	13	14	12	7	4	2	1

WAGE-EARNERS.

Length of residence in the United States.	Number reporting complete data.	None.a	Under $50.	$50 and under $100.	$100 and under $250.	$250 and under $500.	$500 and under $1,000.	$1,000 and under $1,500.	$1,500 and under $2,500.	$2,500 and under $5,000.	$5,000 and under $10,000.	$10,000 and under $25,000.	$25,000 or over.
Under 2 years													
2 years	3			1	1	1							
3 years	3				3								
4 years	2					1	1						
5 to 9 years	14	4			3	6	1						
10 to 14 years	3				2	1							
Total	25	4		1	9	9	2						

a Gross value of property minus indebtedness is nothing or less than nothing.

TABLE 48.—*Average surplus or deficit of past year, reported by Japanese.*

IN BUSINESS FOR SELF.

	Number.	Average.		Number.	Average.
Reporting:			Average surplus based on total number		$493.51
Surplus	53	$673.70			
Deficit	7	236.29			
Neither surplus nor deficit	9				
Total	69				

WAGE-EARNERS.

	Number.	Average.		Number.	Average.
Reporting:			Average surplus based on total number		$202.82
Surplus	19	$245.53			
Deficit					
Neither surplus nor deficit	4				
Total	23				

TABLE 49.—*Surplus or deficit of past year reported by Japanese, by classified amounts.*

IN BUSINESS FOR SELF.

Amount.	Number reporting.		Amount.	Number reporting.	
	Surplus.	Deficit.		Surplus.	Deficit.
Under $100	2	1	$1,000 and under $2,500	9	
$100 and under $250	8	3	$2,500 or over	2	
$250 and under $500	17	2			
$500 and under $1,000	13	1	Total	53	7

TABLE 49.—*Surplus or deficit of past year reported by Japanese, by classified amounts*—Continued.

WAGE-EARNERS.

Amount.	Number reporting.		Amount.	Number reporting.	
	Surplus.	Deficit.		Surplus.	Deficit.
Under $100...................	4	....	$500 and under $1,000.........	2	....
$100 and under $250..........	3	....			
$250 and under $500..........	10	....	Total....................	19	....

TABLE 50.—*Gross value of property, encumbrances, and net value of property now owned by male Japanese.*

	Number reporting complete data.	Gross value of property.		Encumbrances on property.			Net value of property.	
		Aggregate amount.	Average amount.	Number having encumbrances.	Aggregate amount.	Average amount.	Aggregate amount.	Average amount.
In business for self..	74	$210,360.00	$2,842.70	38	$55,939.00	$1,472.08	$154,421.00	$2,086.77
Wage-earners......	25	6,050.00	242.00	3	250.00	83.33	5,800.00	232.00

TABLE 51.—*Number of Japanese for whom detailed information was secured, by sex and general nativity.*

IN BUSINESS FOR SELF.

General nativity.	Male.	Female.	Total.
Native-born..	16	16	32
Foreign-born.......................................	78	38	116
Total..	94	54	148

WAGE-EARNERS.

Foreign-born.......................................	25	....	25

TABLE 52.—*Conjugal condition of Japanese, by sex and age groups.*

IN BUSINESS FOR SELF.

Sex.	Number within each specified age group.																			
	16 to 19.				20 to 29.				30 to 44.				45 or over.				Total.			
	Single.	Married.	Widowed.	Total.	Single.	Married.	Widowed.	Total.	Single.	Married.	Widowed.	Total.	Single.	Married.	Widowed.	Total.	Single.	Married.	Widowed.	Total.
Male..........	....	....	....	....	15	7	1	23	17	32	....	49	....	3	....	3	32	42	1	75
Female........	1	2	....	3	....	18	1	19	....	14	....	14	....	....	....	....	1	34	1	36
Total.....	1	2	....	3	15	25	2	42	17	46	....	63	....	3	....	3	33	76	2	111

WAGE-EARNERS.

Male..........	2	....	....	2	12	....	....	12	7	4	....	11	....	....	....	....	21	4	....	25

TABLE **53.**—*Conjugal condition of foreign-born male Japanese 16 years of age or over, by age at time of coming to the United States.*

IN BUSINESS FOR SELF.

Age at time of coming to the United States.	Total number of arrivals.	Single or widowed at time of coming to United States.			Married at time of coming to United States.			
		Number.	Married during visit abroad.	Married in United States.	Number.	Wife abroad.	Accompanied by wife.	Wife joining later.
Under 18 years....................	5	5	....	1	....	....	....	....
18 and under 20 years.............	5	5	....	1	....	....	....	....
20 and under 25 years.............	a 31	28	3	6	3	1	1	1
25 and under 30 years.............	14	8	1	2	6	2	3	1
30 and under 35 years.............	11	5	2	3	6	....	4	2
35 and under 40 years.............	5	1	....	....	4	1	2	1
40 and under 45 years.............	1	....	....	....	1	1	....	....
45 years or over..................	1	....	....	....	1	1	....	....
Total......................	a 73	52	6	13	21	6	10	5

WAGE-EARNERS.

Under 18 years....................	3	3	....	....	....	....	....	....
18 and under 20 years.............	5	5	....	....	....	....	....	....
20 and under 25 years.............	6	6	....	....	....	....	....	....
25 and under 30 years.............	7	6	....	....	1	1	....	....
30 and under 35 years.............	2	1	....	....	1	1	....	....
35 and under 40 years.............	2	....	....	....	2	2	....	....
40 years or over..................	....	....	....	....	....	....	....	....
Total......................	25	21	....	....	4	4	....	....

a Not including 2 not reporting complete data.

TABLE **54.**—*Number of Japanese in each specified age group, by sex.*

[This table includes persons in business for self as well as wage-earners.]

Sex.	Number in each specified age group.							
	Under 6.	6 to 13.	14 and 15.	16 to 19.	20 to 29.	30 to 44.	45 or over.	Total.
Male..................................	17	1	1	2	36	58	4	119
Female................................	15	3	....	3	19	14	....	54
Total........................	32	4	1	5	55	72	4	173

TABLE **55.**—*Number of foreign-born Japanese in the United States each specified number of years, by sex.*

IN BUSINESS FOR SELF.

[By years in the United States is meant years since first arrival in the United States. No deduction is made for time spent abroad.]

Sex.	Number reporting complete data.	Number in United States each specified number of years.								
		Under 1.	1.	2.	3.	4.	5 to 9.	10 to 14.	15 to 19.	20 or over.
Male..................................	78	....	1	4	6	8	33	18	7	1
Female................................	38	1	7	10	3	3	12	2	....	....
Total........................	116	1	8	14	9	11	45	20	7	1

WAGE-EARNERS.

Male..................................	25	....	....	3	3	2	14	3	....	....

TABLE 56.—*Ability to speak English of Japanese 6 years of age or over, by sex and general nativity.*

IN BUSINESS FOR SELF.

General nativity.	Number reporting complete data.	Male.		Female.		Total.	
		Number.	Number who speak English.	Number.	Number who speak English.	Number.	Number who speak English.
Native-born....................	1	....	....	1	1	1	1
Foreign-born..................	115	77	76	38	17	115	93
Total......................	116	77	76	39	18	116	94

WAGE-EARNERS.

Foreign-born..................	25	25	23	....	....	25	23

TABLE 57.—*Ability to speak English of foreign-born Japanese 6 years of age or over, by sex and years in the United States.*

[By years in the United States is meant years since first arrival in the United States.]

IN BUSINESS FOR SELF.

Sex.	Number reporting complete data.	Number who speak English.	Years in United States.					
			Under 5.		5 to 9.		10 or over.	
			Number.	Number who speak English.	Number.	Number who speak English.	Number.	Number who speak English.
Male.........................	77	76	18	18	33	32	26	26
Female.......................	38	17	24	11	12	6	2	....
Total.......	115	93	42	29	45	38	28	26

WAGE-EARNERS.

Male.....................	25	23	8	8	14	12	3	3

TABLE 58.—*Ability to speak English of foreign-born Japanese 6 years of age or over, by sex and by age at time of coming to the United States.*

IN BUSINESS FOR SELF.

Sex.	Number reporting complete data.	Number who speak English.	Age at time of coming to United States.			
			Under 14.		14 or over.	
			Number.	Number who speak English.	Number.	Number who speak English.
Male.........................	77	76	1	1	76	75
Female.......................	38	17	2	2	36	15
Total......................	115	93	3	3	112	90

WAGE-EARNERS.

Male.........................	25	23	....	....	25	23

TABLE **59.**—*Literacy of Japanese 10 years of age or over, by sex and general nativity.*

IN BUSINESS FOR SELF.

General nativity.	Number reporting complete data.	Male.			Female.			Total.		
		Number.	Number who read.	Number who read and write.	Number.	Number who read.	Number who read and write.	Number.	Number who read.	Number who read and write.
Foreign-born...........	112	76	73	73	36	31	31	112	104	104

WAGE-EARNERS.

Foreign-born...........	25	25	25	25	....	....	....	25	25	25

TABLE **60.**—*Literacy of foreign-born Japanese 10 years of age or over, by sex and years in the United States.*

IN BUSINESS FOR SELF.

[By years in the United States is meant years since first arrival in the United States.]

Sex.	Number reporting complete data.	Years in United States.								
		Under 5.			5 to 9.			10 or over.		
		Number.	Number who read.	Number who read and write.	Number.	Number who read.	Number who read and write.	Number.	Number who read.	Number who read and write.
Male...................	76	17	16	16	33	32	32	26	25	25
Female.................	36	22	20	20	12	10	10	2	1	1
Total.............	112	39	36	36	45	42	42	28	26	26

WAGE-EARNERS.

Male...................	25	8	8	8	14	14	14	3	3	3

TABLE **61.**—*Literacy of foreign-born Japanese 10 years of age or over, by sex and by age at time of coming to the United States.*

IN BUSINESS FOR SELF.

Sex.	Number reporting complete data.	Age at time of coming to United States.					
		Under 14.			14 or over.		
		Number.	Number who read.	Number who read and write.	Number.	Number who read.	Number who read and write.
Male.................................	76	1	1	1	75	72	72
Female...............................	36	....	....	....	36	31	31
Total.....................	112	1	1	1	111	103	103

WAGE-EARNERS.

Male.................................	25	....	....	....	25	25	25

TABLE **62.**—*Ability of foreign-born Japanese 10 years of age or over to speak, read, and write English, by sex.*

IN BUSINESS FOR SELF.

Sex.	Number reporting complete data.	Unable to speak, read, or write English.	Able to speak English, but not to read or write it.	Able to speak and read, but not to write English.	Able to speak, read, and write English.
Male	76	1	33	....	42
Female	36	21	12	....	3
Total	112	22	45	....	45

WAGE-EARNERS.

Male	25	2	9	....	14

TABLE **63.**—*General occupation of Japanese under 16 years of age, by sex, age groups, and general nativity.*

IN BUSINESS FOR SELF.

Sex and general nativity.	Number within each specified age group.															
	Under 6.				6 to 13.				14 and 15.				Total.			
	At home.	At school.	At work.	Total.	At home.	At school.	At work.	Total.	At home.	At school.	At work.	Total.	At home.	At school.	At work.	Total.
Native-born:																
Male	16	....	....	16	....	....	....	....	....	....	....	....	16	....	....	16
Female	15	....	....	15	....	1	....	1	....	....	....	....	15	1	....	16
Total	31	....	....	31	....	1	....	1	....	....	....	....	31	1	....	32
Foreign-born:																
Male	....	1	....	1	....	1	....	1	....	1	....	1	....	3	....	3
Female	....	....	....	....	....	2	....	2	....	....	....	....	....	2	....	2
Total	....	1	....	1	....	3	....	3	....	1	....	1	....	5	....	5
Grand total	31	1	....	32	....	4	....	4	....	1	....	1	31	6	....	37

TABLE **64.**—*Total yearly income of male Japanese engaged in business for self, and income from principal business.*

Kind of business.	Number reporting complete data.	Number having each specified amount of yearly income.									Income from principal business.	
		Under $300.	$300 and under $400.	$400 and under $500.	$500 and under $750.	$750 and under $1,000.	$1,000 and under $1,500.	$1,500 and under $2,000.	$2,000 and under $2,500.	$2,500 or over.	Total income.	Average income.
Barber shop	5	1	....	1	3	....	2	....	....	....	$2,460.00	$492.00
Laundry	2	....	....	....	....	....	2	....	....	....	2,400.00	1,200.00
Lodging house	8	....	....	....	4	2	1	1	....	....	7,500.00	937.50
Pool room	1	....	....	....	....	....	1	....	....	....	1,200.00	1,200.00
Real estate and labor agencies	5	....	....	....	1	....	4	....	....	....	5,100.00	1,020.00
Restaurant	7	1	1	....	1	....	2	2	....	....	7,420.00	1,060.00
Shoemaker	2	....	....	1	....	....	....	1	....	....	2,220.00	1,110.00
Storekeeper	16	....	1	....	5	2	2	1	3	2	24,860.00	1,553.75
Tailor	3	....	....	....	2	....	1	....	....	....	2,400.00	800.00
Miscellaneous	14	1	....	....	4	2	3	3	1	....	15,260.00	1,090.00
Total	63	3	2	2	20	6	16	8	4	2	70,820.00	1,124.13

TABLE **65.**— *Yearly earnings (approximate) of male Japanese 18 years of age or over, by number of months employed.*

WITH BOARD.

Number of months employed.	Number working for wages and reporting amount.	Average earnings.	Number earning—										
			$200 and under $250.	$250 and under $300.	$300 and under $400.	$400 and under $500.	$500 and under $600.	$600 and under $700.	$700 and under $800.	$800 and under $1,000.	$1,000 and under $1,250.	$1,250 and under $1,500.	$1,500 and under $2,000.
10 months	2	$287.50	1	....	1	....	....	....	....	....	....	....	....
11 months	1	220.00	1	....	....	....	....	....	....	....	....	....	....
12 months	10	501.00	2	....	4	3	....	....	....	....	....	....	1
Total	13	446.54	4	....	5	3	....	....	....	....	....	....	1

WITHOUT BOARD.

Number of months employed.	Number working for wages and reporting amount.	Average earnings.	$200 and under $250.	$250 and under $300.	$300 and under $400.	$400 and under $500.	$500 and under $600.	$600 and under $700.	$700 and under $800.	$800 and under $1,000.	$1,000 and under $1,250.	$1,250 and under $1,500.	$1,500 and under $2,000.
8 months	1	$400.00	....	....	....	1	....	....	....	....	....	....	....
10 months	2	735.00	....	1	....	....	....	....	....	....	1	....	....
11 months	1	385.00	....	....	1	....	....	....	....	....	....	....	....
12 months	8	412.50	....	....	3	3	1	1	....	....	....	....	....
Total	12	462.92	....	1	4	4	1	1	....	....	1	....	....

SEATTLE.

TABLE **66.**—*General data on business conducted by Japanese and members of other races.*

BARBER SHOPS.

Race of proprietor and number of establishment.	Date established.	Amount of capital.		Rent per year.	Value of annual transactions.	Net profit.	Number of employees of—		Per cent white patrons.	Per cent of American goods sold.
		Employed.	Borrowed.				Same race.	Other races.		
Japanese:										
No. 1 a	1900	$800	0	$780	$3,120	$960	1	0	30.0	0.0
No. 2 a	1900	3,000	0	600	11,220	504	(b)	(b)	(b)	.0
No. 3 a	1903	2,000	0	1,080	6,660	720	3	0	90.0	.0
No. 4 c	1905	2,000	0	1,680	5,400	900	d 5	0	50.0	.0
No. 5 c	1907	2,900	0	900	3,220	960	d 1	0	(b)	.0
No. 6 e	1908	800	0	384	1,620	480	0	0	50.0	.0
No. 7	1908	250	$200	180	960	640	d 0	0	80.0	.0
No. 8	1908	700	350	600	6,000	720	2	0	60.0	.0
No. 9	1909	550	400	360	1,080	500	d 0	0	90.0	.0
No. 10	(b)	800	(b)	720	(b)	720	2	0	90.0	.0
American:										
No. 11	1889	2,000	0	2,400	20,000	2,000	10	2	100.0	.0
No. 12 a	1899	21,000	0	3,780	50,000	6,000 to 8,000	25	4	100.0	.0
No. 13	1900	2,000	0	1,200	5,500	900	4	2	100.0	.0
No. 14	1906	1,000	0	1,500	7,500	(b)	4	0	100.0	.0
Norwegian-American:										
15 a	1900	25,000	0	1,800	18,000	(b)	8	2	100.0	.0

a Bathrooms connected with this establishment.
b Not reported.
c Baths and laundry connected with this establishment.
d Wife of proprietor works also.
e Pool room connected with this establishment.

GROCERIES.

Race of proprietor and number of establishment.	Date established.	Amount of capital.		Rent per year.	Value of annual transactions.	Net profit.	Number of employees of—		Per cent white patrons.	Per cent of American goods sold.
		Employed.	Borrowed.				Same race.	Other races.		
Japanese:										
No. 1	1898	$2,400	$300	$720	$7,200	$600	1	0	70.0	5.0
No. 2	1904	2,500	300	(a)	8,000	1,200	2	0	a.0	50.0
No. 3	1904	2,000	1,000	760	12,000	1,200	4	0	10.0	50.0
No. 4	1907	1,500	600	120	6,000	600	b 0	0	50.0	50.0
No. 5	1907	1,000	300	480	4,800	600	1	0	30.0	30.0
No. 6	1907	1,500	900	240	14,400	960	3	0	50.0	90.0
No. 7	1907	3,500	500	600	12,000	600	0	0	90.0	10.0
No. 8	1908	1,800	700	324	18,000	480	1	0	75.0	75.0
No. 9	1908	3,000	0	720	14,400	900	3	0	40.0	40.0
American:										
No. 10	1901	16,000	0	3,000	80,000	(a)	4	3	99.0	100.0
No. 11	1902	8,000	0	3,600	60,000	10,000	5	0	100.0	100.0
Greek:										
No. 12	1907	2,000	0	840	5,500	1,100	0	1	90.0	100.0
Italian, North:										
No. 13	1900	12,000	2,300	1,680	48,000	c 900	3	0	98.0	100.0
No. 14	1902	2,000	500	1,200	12,000	(a)	d 1	0	98.0	100.0
Italian, South:										
No. 15	1907	2,000	1,000	480	12,000	1,800	4	0	100.0	100.0
Servian:										
No. 16	1906	1,500	0	720	9,600	1,600	0	1	100.0	100.0

LAUNDRIES.

Race of proprietor and number of establishment.	Date established.	Amount of capital.		Rent per year.	Value of annual transactions.	Net profit.	Number of employees of—		Per cent white patrons.	Per cent of American goods sold.
		Employed.	Borrowed.				Same race.	Other races.		
Japanese:										
No. 1	1899	$3,000	$1,000	$780	$9,600	$600	e 4	0	65.0	0.0
No. 2	1902	15,000	4,000	1,440	42,000	3,000	32	5	90.0	.0
No. 3	1905	10,000	0	900	26,400	1,680	25	0	70.0	.0
No. 4	1907	350	0	360	1,440	600	0	0	80.0	.0
No. 5	1908	500	300	240	1,920	615	b 1	0	90.0	.0
No. 6 f	1908	1,500	0	240	2,700	960	b 0	0	80.0	.0
American:										
No. 7	1887	150,000	0	18,000	182,000	(a)	33	31	(g)	.0
No. 8	1890	80,000	0	6,000	130,000	(a)	20	13	100.0	.0
No. 9	(a)	50,000	0	2,220	100,000	(a)	(a)	(a)	100.0	.0
Swedish:										
No. 10	1905	18,000	(a)	3,000	70,000	(a)	(a)	(a)	(a)	.0

RESTAURANTS.

Race of proprietor and number of establishment.	Date established.	Amount of capital.		Rent per year.	Value of annual transactions.	Net profit.	Number of employees of—		Per cent white patrons.	Per cent of American goods sold.
		Employed.	Borrowed.				Same race.	Other races.		
Japanese:										
No. 1	1901	$4,000	0	$2,160	$26,100	$1,440	8	0	0.0	0.0
No. 2	1901	2,500	0	2,400	42,000	5,400	12	0	g0.0	.0
No. 3	1905	2,500	$200	720	18,000	600	5	0	h.0	.0
No. 4	1905	5,000	0	1,800	15,000	1,200	7	0	h.0	.0
No. 5	1906	1,000	0	900	4,800	960	b 1	0	75.0	.0
No. 6	1906	1,000	0	840	7,200	1,400	e 4	0	h.0	.0
No. 7	1907	3,000	0	1,920	36,000	4,800	8	0	99.0	.0
No. 8	1907	1,500	0	480	7,200	960	5	0	h.0	.0
No. 9	1907	3,500	0	1,800	18,000	1,920	j 6	2	100.0	.0
No. 10	1908	1,500	0	720	18,000	540	6	0	90.0	.0
No. 11	1908	1,000	0	900	7,200	960	b j 4	0	h.0	.
No. 12	1908	1,500	500	1,200	13,000	600	b 6	0	100.0	.0
No. 13	1908	1,200	400	756	18,000	600	5	0	90.0	.0
No. 14	1908	2,500	400	1,980	14,400	1,270	2	1	100.0	.0
No. 15	1908	800	200	180	8,400	570	1	0	h.0	.0

a Not reported.
b Wife of proprietor works also.
c Profit for each proprietor; number of proprietors not given.
d Daughter of proprietor works also.
e Wife and son of proprietor work also.
f Bathrooms connnected with this establishment.
g Almost 100.
h Sells Japanese meals only.
i Two daughters of proprietor work also.
j Two partners.

TABLE 66.—*General data on business conducted by Japanese and members of other races*—Continued.

RESTAURANTS—Continued.

Race of proprietor and number of establishment.	Date established.	Amount of capital.		Rent per year.	Value of annual transactions.	Net profit.	Number of employees of—		Per cent white patrons.	Per cent of American goods sold.
		Employed.	Borrowed.				Same race.	Other races.		
American:										
No. 16.......	1900	$2,500	0	$500	$30,000	(a)	14	0	100.0	0.0
No. 17.......	1908	1,000	$200	720	9,000	$800	3	0	100.0	.0
No. 18.......	1909	1,400	(a)	1,500	18,000		8	0	100.0	.0
Greek:										
No. 19.......	1906	3,000	0	1,500	32,000		6	4	100.0	.0
Norwegian:										
No. 20.......	1907	900	0	780	(a)	1,000	0	5	100.0	.0
Slovenian:										
No. 21.......	1906	1,200	0	960	9,000	(a)	5	0	100.0	.0

TAILOR SHOPS.

Japanese:										
No. 1........	1903	$5,000	$2,000	$1,440	$20,400	$1,200	b 5	2	70.0	0.0
No. 2........	1903	800	0	300	9,000	1,440	4	0	50.0	.0
No. 3........	1904	700	0	360	7,200	960	2	0	90.0	.0
No. 4........	1906	400	0	180	4,800	840	b 1	0	30.0	.0
No. 5........	1907	2,500	0	360	8,400	900	7	0	30.0	.0
No. 6........	1907	500	0	120	1,500	840	0	0	40.0	.0
No. 7........	1908	500	(a)	240	2,400	600	2	0	90.0	.0
American:										
No. 8.......	1900	2,000	200	1,200	8,000	1,500	4	1	100.0	.0
Hebrew (Russian):										
No. 9........	1891	300	0	660	3,600	1,000	0	1	100.0	.0
No. 10.......	1907	200	0	900	3.000	800	1	0	100.0	.0
No. 11.......	1908	300	0	300	840	(a)	0	0	100.0	.0
Scandinavian:										
No..12........	1891	300	0	600	7,500	1,800	5	2	100.0	.0

MISCELLANEOUS.

Japanese (billiard hall):										
No. 1.......	1908	$2,400	$900	$1,200	$4,200	$960	1	0	0.0	0.0
Japanese (bookstore):										
No. 1.......	1907	1,200	50	390	6,500	720	0	0	.0	30.0
Japanese (cake store):										
No 1.......	1906	800	0	336	4,800	840	b 0	0	.0	80.0
Japanese (cake and ice cream store):										
No. 1.......	1908	1,200	600	720	4,200	720	1	0	20.0	50.0
Japanese (curio dealers):										
No. 1.......	1904	35,000	20,000	4,800	70,000	3,600	5	1	100.0	.0
No. 2.......	1907	50,000	0	1,200	110,000	(a)	5	2	100.0	.0
Japanese (drug stores):										
No. 1.......	1903	5,000	0	600	8,400	960	2	0	10.0	30.0
No. 2.......	1907	700	0	192	3,600	720	b 0	0	40.0	30.0
Japanese (dyeing):										
No. 1.......	1908	600	0	300	4,800	750	1	1	100.0	.0

a Not reported.　　　　　　　b Wife of proprietor works also.

TABLE 66.—*General data on business conducted by Japanese and members of other races*—Continued.

MISCELLANEOUS—Continued.

Race of proprietor and number of establishment.	Date established.	Amount of capital.		Rent per year.	Value of annual transactions.	Net profit.	Number of employees of—		Per cent white patrons.	Per cent of American goods sold.
		Employed.	Borrowed.				Same race.	Other races.		
Japanese (employment agencies):										
No. 1........	1907	$300	0	$240	$2,160	$1,200	0	0	0.0	0.0
No. 2........	1907	500	0	288	3,000	1,800	1	0	.0	.0
No. 3........	1908	300	0	192	1,800	960	0	0	.0	.0
No. 4........	1908	600	0	300	4,200	2,400	1	0	.0	.0
No. 5........	1908	150	0	180	1,200	540	0	0	.0	.0
Japanese (express companies):										
No. 1	1902	1,000	0	(a)	1,800	840	0	0	.0	.0
No. 2	1904	5,000	0	360	9,600	1,800	b 5	0	20.0	0
No. 3	1908	850	0	(c)	3,600	1,440	d 0	0	30.0	.0
Japanese (fish market):										
No. 1	1908	1,700	$1,500	600	18,000	600	4	0	90.0	.0
Japanese (fish market and meat store):										
No. 1	1904	2,500	200	588	54,000	1,920	d 6	0	40.0	.0
Japanese (general merchandise):										
No. 1	1894	200,000	50,000	1,980	300,000	24,000	17	0	e .0	20.0
No. 2	1902	10,000	3,000	720	12,000	840	2	0	70.0	50.0
No· 3	1907	2,000	500	600	9,600	960	4	0	.0	50.0
Japanese (hotel and contracting business):										
No. 1	1899	800	0	600	13,000	3,000	4	0	.0	.0
Japanese (job printing):										
No. 1	1907	3,600	300	720	7,200	1,800	2	0	35.0	.0
No. 2	1907	1,800	450	144	2,100	720	0	0	.0	.0
Japanese (lodging houses):										
No. 1	1905	2,800	0	1,800	5,280	d 1,800	f 0	0	1.0	.0
No. 2	1905	5,000	0	1,800	1,800	1,440	1	0	50.0	.0
No. 3	1906	3,500	0	2,400	6,000	1,200	1	0	100.0	.0
No. 4	1906	3,000	0	2,820	6,000	1,680	2	0	5.0	.0
No. 5	1907	2,000	300	780	2,760	960	0	0	20.0	.0
No. 6	1908	2,500	0	2,880	6,000	840	2	0	80.0	.0
No. 7	1908	3.700	2,300	1,320	4,560	1,676	f 0	0	.0	.0
No. 8	1909	600	400	900	1,800	504	0	0	.0	.0
Japanese (photographers):										
No. 1	1907	500	0	432	1,000	240	0	0	10.0	.0
No. 2	1908	2,000	0	432	3,600	1,200	d 2	0	30.0	.0
Japanese (second-hand clothing store):										
No. 1	1907	800	0	420	4,800	1,200	0	0	70.0	100.
Japanese (shoe repairing):										
No. 1	1908	600	0	180	2,400	720	1	0	70.0	.0
Japanese (watches and clocks):										
No. 1	1903	3,500	0	450	6,000	900	1	0	80.0	100.0
No. 2	1906	5,000	1,000	1,020	24,000	720	3	0	30.0	100.0

a No rent; 60 per cent of work done for 1 company.
b 3 partners.
c No fixed headquarters.
d 2 partners.
e Except in December, when 50 per cent of trade is American.
f Wife of proprietor works also.

TABLE 67.—*Money brought to the United States by Japanese.*

	Number reporting complete data.	Number bringing each specified amount.										
		None.	Under $25.	$25 and under $50.	$50 and under $100.	$100 and under $150.	$150 and under $200.	$200 and under $300.	$300 and under $400.	$400 and under $500.	$500 and under $1,000.	$1,000 or over.
In business for self	106		1	41	37	5	2	8	6			6
Wage-earners	89	1		17	64	2	1	2			2	

TABLE 68.—*First occupation of Japanese in the United States, by occupation abroad.*

IN BUSINESS FOR SELF.

Occupation abroad.	Number.	Number who were—												
		In business for self.	Farm hand.	Railroad laborer.	Sawmill laborer.	Cannery hand.	Laborers in industrial establishment.	Store help.	Restaurant help.	In domestic service.	Tailor and dyer.	Barber.	Wage-earner in city.	Occupation unknown.
In business for self	37	12	2	9	1			1	1	7			4	
Farmer	5		1	1	2				1					
At home	22	3		3		1		3	1	9			2	
Farming for father	20		2	5	2				4	7				
Farm hand	a2	1			1									
Store help	b9	2	1					2	1	3				
Laborer in industrial establishment	5	4							1					
Wage-earner in city	8		1	2					1	3	1			
Total	108	22	7	20	6	1		7	8	30	1		6	

WAGE-EARNERS.

Occupation abroad.	Number.	In business for self.	Farm hand.	Railroad laborer.	Sawmill laborer.	Cannery hand.	Laborers in industrial establishment.	Store help.	Restaurant help.	In domestic service.	Tailor and dyer.	Barber.	Wage-earner in city.	Occupation unknown.
In business for self	b12		1	2				2	2	2	1		1	1
Farmer	7			3						3		1		
At home	37			2	1		2	9	8	11	2		1	1
Farming for father	14			5				2	4	2			1	
Farm hand	b1													1
Store help	9			1				4	1	1			2	
Laborer in industrial establishment	3										2		1	
Wage-earner in city	6		4	1						1				
Total	89		5	14	1		2	17	15	20	5	1	6	3

a Including 2 who came to United States from Hawaii.
b Including 1 who came to United States from Hawaii.

TABLE 69.—*Net value of all property now owned by Japanese, by length of residence in the United States.*

IN BUSINESS FOR SELF.

Length of residence in the United States.	Number reporting complete data.	None.	Under $50.	$50 and under $100.	$100 and under $250.	$250 and under $500.	$500 and under $1,000.	$1,000 and under $1,500.	$1,500 and under $2,500.	$2,500 and under $5,000.	$5,000 and under $10,000.	$10,000 and under $25,000.	$25,000 or over.
Under 1 year													
1 year	2				1					1			
2 years	10				2	2	4		1	1			
3 years	11				1	1	5	1	2	1			
4 years	3						1		2				
5 to 9 years	54				2	1	11	14	12	9	4	1	
10 to 14 years	18				1		5	3	1	6	1	1	
15 to 19 years	10						2	1	3		2	1	1
20 years or over													
Total	108				7	4	28	19	21	18	7	3	1

WAGE-EARNERS.

Length of residence in the United States.	Number reporting complete data.	None.	Under $50.	$50 and under $100.	$100 and under $250.	$250 and under $500.	$500 and under $1,000.	$1,000 and under $1,500.	$1,500 and under $2,500.	$2,500 and under $5,000.	$5,000 and under $10,000.	$10,000 and under $25,000.	$25,000 or over.
Under 1 year	1						1						
1 year	15	2		1	7	4		1					
2 years	24	1		1	7	10	4	1					
3 years	15	1			3	5	5		1				
4 years	6				2	2	2						
5 to 9 years	16			3	4	4	1	3	1				
10 to 14 years	10				2	1	6		1				
15 to 19 years	2				1	1							
20 years or over													
Total	89	4		5	26	27	19	5	3				

TABLE 70.—*Average surplus or deficit of past year reported by Japanese.*

IN BUSINESS FOR SELF.

	Number.	Average.		Number.	Average.
Reporting:			Average surplus based on total number		$825.60
Surplus	65	$966.77			
Deficit	2	460.00			
Neither surplus nor deficit	8				
Total	75				

WAGE-EARNERS.

	Number.	Average.		Number.	Average.
Reporting:			Average surplus based on total number		$206.88
Surplus	59	$218.14			
Deficit	1	250.00			
Neither surplus nor deficit	1				
Total	61				

TABLE **71.**—*Surplus or deficit of past year reported by Japanese, by classified amounts.*

IN BUSINESS FOR SELF.

Amount.	Number reporting—		Amount.	Number reporting—	
	Surplus.	Deficit.		Surplus.	Deficit.
Under $100	1	....	$1,000 and under $2,500	3	....
$100 and under $250	12	1	$2,500 or over	4	....
$250 and under $500	28	....			
$500 and under $1,000	17	1	Total	65	2

WAGE-EARNERS.

Under $100	3	....	$500 and under $1,000	3	....
$100 and under $250	36	....	Total	59	1
$250 and under $500	17	1			

TABLE **72.**—*Gross value of property, encumbrances, and net value of property now owned by male Japanese.*

	Number reporting complete data.	Gross value of property.		Encumbrances on property.			Net value of property.	
		Aggregate amount.	Average amount.	Number having encumbrances.	Aggregate amount.	Average amount.	Aggregate amount.	Average amount.
In business for self	108	$475,900 00	$4,406.48	41	$77,150.00	$1,881.70	$398,750.00	$3,692.13
Wage-earners	85	35,375.00	416.18	....	....	....	35,375.00	416.18

TABLE **73.**—*Number of Japanese for whom detailed information was secured, by sex and general nativity.*

IN BUSINESS FOR SELF.

General nativity.	Male.	Female.	Total.
Native-born	17	19	36
Foreign-born	110	51	161
Total	127	70	197

WAGE-EARNERS.

	Male.	Female.	Total.
Native-born	3	2	5
Foreign-born	89	12	101
Total	92	14	106

Sex.	Number within each specified age group.																			
	16 to 19.				20 to 29.				30 to 44.				45 or over.				Total.			
	Single.	Married.	Widowed.	Total.	Single.	Married.	Widowed.	Total.	Single.	Married.	Widowed.	Total.	Single.	Married.	Widowed.	Total.	Single.	Married.	Widowed.	Total.
Male	1	....	....	1	27	12	....	39	17	47	2	66	....	3	....	3	45	62	2	109
Female	2	2	....	4	1	28	....	29	....	15	....	15	....	1	....	1	3	46	....	49
Total	3	2	....	5	28	40	....	68	17	62	2	81	....	4	....	4	48	108	2	158

WAGE-EARNERS.

Sex.	Single.	Married.	Widowed.	Total.	Single.	Married.	Widowed.	Total.	Single.	Married.	Widowed.	Total.	Single.	Married.	Widowed.	Total.	Single.	Married.	Widowed.	Total.
Male	9	...	....	9	41	5	2	48	9	23	....	32	....	....	....	....	59	28	2	89
Female	....	3	....	3	....	4	....	4	....	5	....	5	....	....	....	....	....	12	....	12
Total	9	3	....	12	41	9	2	52	9	28	....	37	....	....	....	....	59	40	2	101

TABLE 75.—*Conjugal condition of foreign-born male Japanese 16 years of age or over, by age at time of coming to the United States.*

IN BUSINESS FOR SELF.

Age at time of coming to the United States.	Total number of arrivals.	Single or widowed at time of coming to United States.			Married at time of coming to United States.			
		Number.	Married during visit abroad.	Married in United States.	Number.	Wife abroad.	Accompanied by wife.	Wife joining later.
Under 18 years	8	8	....	2	....	....	....	....
18 years and under 20 years	15	14	1	2	1	1	....	....
20 years and under 25 years	37	29	a 6	8	8	2	b 2	4
25 years and under 30 years	30	22	4	5	8	2	1	5
30 years and under 35 years	12	2	....	1	10	6	b 3	1
35 years and under 40 years	4	1	....	....	3	....	....	3
40 years and under 45 years	2	....	....	....	2	....	1	1
45 years and over	1	....	....	....	1	....	....	1
Total	109	76	a 11	18	53	11	c 7	15

WAGE-EARNERS.

Age at time of coming to the United States.	Total number of arrivals.	Number.	Married during visit abroad.	Married in United States.	Number.	Wife abroad.	Accompanied by wife.	Wife joining later.
Under 18 years	10	10	1	1	....	....	....	....
18 years and under 20 years	16	15	....	....	1	1	....	....
20 years and under 25 years	36	33	2	1	3	2	1	....
25 years and under 30 years	13	8	1	....	5	4	1	....
30 years and under 35 years	8	1	....	....	7	3	2	2
35 years and under 40 years	3	....	....	....	3	2	....	1
40 years and under 45 years	3	....	....	....	3	1	2	....
Total	89	67	4	2	22	13	6	3

a Including 1 whose wife remained in Japan.
b Including 1 whose wife returned to Japan.
c Including 2 whose wives returned to Japan.

TABLE **76.**—*Number of Japanese within each age group, by sex.*

[This table includes persons in business for self as well as wage-earners.]

Sex.	Number within each specified age group.							
	Under 6.	6 to 13.	14 and 15.	16 to 19.	20 to 29.	30 to 44	45 or over.	Total.
Male.	17	4	....	10	87	98	3	219
Female.	19	2	2	7	33	20	1	84
Total.	36	6	2	17	120	118	4	303

TABLE **77.**—*Number of foreign-born Japanese in the United States each specified number of years, by sex.*

IN BUSINESS FOR SELF.

[By years in the United States is meant years since first arrival in the United States. No deduction is made for time spent abroad]

Sex.	Number reporting complete data.	Number in United States each specified number of years.								
		Under 1.	1.	2.	3.	4.	5 to 9.	10 to 14.	15 to 19.	20 or over.
Male.	110	1	2	10	12	3	54	18	10	......
Female.	51	4	9	10	8	5	11	3	1	......
Total.	161	5	11	20	20	8	65	21	11	......

WAGE-EARNERS.

Sex.	Number reporting complete data.	Under 1.	1.	2.	3.	4.	5 to 9.	10 to 14.	15 to 19.	20 or over.
Male.	89	1	15	24	15	6	16	10	2	......
Female.	12	1	4	5	1	......	1	......	......	......
Total.	101	2	19	29	16	6	17	10	2	......

TABLE **78.**—*Ability to speak English of Japanese 6 years of age or over, by sex and general nativity.*

IN BUSINESS FOR SELF.

General nativity.	Number reporting complete data.	Male.		Female.		Total.	
		Number.	Number who speak English.	Number.	Number who speak English.	Number.	Number who speak English.
Native-born.	5	3	3	2	2	5	5
Foreign-born.	161	110	109	51	29	161	138
Total.	166	113	112	53	31	166	143

WAGE-EARNERS.

General nativity.	Number reporting complete data.	Male.		Female.		Total.	
Foreign-born.	101	89	88	12	6	101	94

Male	89	88	61	60	16	16	12	12
Female	12	6	11	5	1	1		
Total	101	94	72	65	17	17	12	12

TABLE 80.—*Ability to speak English of foreign-born Japanese 6 years of age or over, by sex and by age at time of coming to the United States.*

IN BUSINESS FOR SELF.

Sex.	Number reporting complete data.	Number who speak English.	Age at time of coming to United States.			
			Under 14.		14 or over.	
			Number.	Number who speak English.	Number.	Number who speak English.
Male	110	109	1		109	100
Female	51	29	2	2	49	27
Total	161	138	3	2	158	136

WAGE-EARNERS.

Sex.	Number reporting complete data.	Number who speak English.	Under 14. Number.	Under 14. Number who speak English.	14 or over. Number.	14 or over. Number who speak English.
Male	89	88	1	1	88	87
Female	12	6			12	6
Total	101	94	1	1	100	93

TABLE **81.**—*Literacy of Japanese 10 years of age or over, by sex and general nativity.*

IN BUSINESS FOR SELF.

General nativity.	Number reporting complete data.	Male.			Female.			Total.		
		Number.	Number who read.	Number who read and write.	Number.	Number who read.	Number who read and write.	Number.	Number who read.	Number who read and write.
Native-born............	1	....	....	....	1	1	1	1	1	1
Foreign-born...........	161	110	110	110	51	50	50	161	160	160
Total............	162	110	110	110	52	51	51	162	161	161

WAGE-EARNERS.

General nativity.	Number reporting complete data.	Male.			Female.			Total.		
Foreign-born...........	101	89	89	89	12	12	12	101	101	101

TABLE **82.**—*Literacy of foreign-born Japanese 10 years of age or over, by sex and years in the United States.*

IN BUSINESS FOR SELF.

[By years in the United States is meant years since first arrival in the United States.]

Sex.	Number reporting complete data.	Years in United States.								
		Under 5.			5 to 9.			10 or over.		
		Number.	Number who read.	Number who read and write.	Number.	Number who read.	Number who read and write.	Number.	Number who read.	Number who read and write.
Male..................	110	28	28	28	54	54	54	28	28	28
Female...............	51	36	35	35	11	11	11	4	4	4
Total............	161	64	63	63	65	65	65	32	32	32

WAGE-EARNERS.

Sex.	Number reporting complete data.	Under 5.			5 to 9.			10 or over.		
Male..	89	61	61	61	16	16	16	12	12	12
Female...............	12	11	11	11	1	1	1	....	....	....
Total............	101	72	72	72	17	17	17	12	12	12

Male	89	1	1	1	88	88	88
Female	12	....	....	....	12	12	12
Total	101	1	1	1	100	100	100

TABLE 84.—*Ability of foreign-born Japanese 10 years of age or over to speak, read, and write English, by sex.*

IN BUSINESS FOR SELF.

Sex.	Number reporting complete data.	Unable to speak, read, or write English.	Able to speak English, but not to read and write it.	Able to speak and read, but not write English.	Able to speak, read, and write English.
Male	110	1	8	....	101
Female	51	22	8	....	21
Total	161	23	16	....	122

WAGE-EARNERS.

Sex.	Number reporting complete data.	Unable to speak, read, or write English.	Able to speak English, but not to read and write it.	Able to speak and read, but not write English.	Able to speak, read, and write English.
Male	89	1	9	....	79
Female	12	6	3	....	3
Total	101	7	12	....	82

TABLE 85.—*General occupation of Japanese under 16 years of age, by sex, age groups, and general nativity.*

IN BUSINESS FOR SELF.

Sex and general nativity.	Number within each specified age group.															
	Under 6.				6 to 13.				14 and 15.				Total.			
	At home.	At school.	At work.	Total.	At home.	At school.	At work.	Total.	At home.	At school.	At work.	Total.	At home.	At school.	At work.	Total.
Native-born:																
Male	13	1	....	14	....	3	....	3	....	....	....	....	13	4	....	17
Female	15	2	....	17	....	1	....	1	....	1	....	1	15	4	....	19
Total	28	3	....	31	....	4	....	4	....	1	....	1	28	8	....	36
Foreign-born:																
Male	....	....	....	....	....	1	....	1	....	....	....	....	....	1	....	1
Female	....	....	....	....	....	1	....	1	....	1	....	1	....	2	....	2
Total	....	....	....	....	....	2	....	2	....	1	....	1	....	3	....	3
Grand total	28	3	....	31	....	6	....	6	....	2	....	2	28	11	....	39

WAGE-EARNERS.

Sex and general nativity.	Under 6.				6 to 13.				14 and 15.				Total.			
	At home.	At school.	At work.	Total.	At home.	At school.	At work.	Total.	At home.	At school.	At work.	Total.	At home.	At school.	At work.	Total.
Native-born:																
Male	3	....	....	3	....	....	....	....	....	....	....	....	3	....	....	3
Female	2	....	....	2	....	....	....	....	....	....	....	....	2	....	....	2
Total	5	....	....	5	....	....	....	....	....	....	....	....	5	....	....	5

TABLE 86.—*Total yearly income of male Japanese engaged in business for self, and income from principal business.*

Kind of business.	Number reporting complete data.	Number having each specified amount of yearly income.									Income from principal business.	
		Under $300.	$300 and under $400.	$400 and under $500.	$500 and under $750.	$750 and under $1,000.	$1,000 and under $1,500.	$1,500 and under $2,000.	$2,000 and under $2,500.	$2,500 or over.	Total income.	Average income.
Barber shop	11	....	....	....	7	4	....	....	....	....	$8,004.00	$727.64
Laundry	6	....	....	....	3	1	....	1	....	1	7,560.00	1,260.00
Lodging house	6	....	....	....	....	4	2	....	....	....	6,120.00	1,020.00
Real estate and labor agencies	5	....	....	1	....	....	1	1	1	1	8,880.00	1,776.00
Restaurant proprietors	20	....	....	1	9	4	1	2	....	3	27,760.00	1,388.00
Shoemakers	1	....	....	....	1	....	....	....	....	....	720.00	720.00
Storekeepers	23	....	....	....	8	10	2	1	....	2	46,260.00	2,011.30
Tailors	8	....	....	....	2	3	2	1	....	....	8,310.00	1,038.75
Miscellaneous	15	1	....	....	10	2	2	....	....	....	10,800.00	720.00
Total	95	1	....	2	40	28	10	6	1	7	124,414.00	1,309.62

.....	70	438. 93	....	2	1	4	....	21	23	4	11	2	2	....	....	....	....

WITHOUT BOARD.

.....	1	$360. 00	....	....	....	....	....	1	....	....	....	....	....	....	....	....	....
.....	1	400. 00	....	....	....	....	....		1	....	....	....	....	....	....	....	....
.....	16	656. 00	....	....	....	....	....		3	2	5	2	4	....	....	....	....
.....	18	625. 33	....	....	....	....	....	1	4	2	5	2	4	....	....	....	....

LIST OF TEXT TABLES.

PART I.—THE JAPANESE IMMIGRANTS IN THE UNITED STATES.

CHAPTER I.—Introductory:

Page.

Table 1.—Total number of foreign-born Japanese for whom information was secured, by sex and by industry.................................... 3, 4

CHAPTER II.—Japanese population of the United States:

Table 2.—Number of Japanese (exclusive of those coming from the Hawaiian Islands) admitted to the Continental United States, fiscal years 1893 to 1910... 5

Table 3.—Departures of orientals from Hawaii to the mainland............ 6

Table 4.—Age of foreign-born Japanese males at time of coming to the United States, by industry: Numbers................................. 7

Table 5.—Age of foreign-born Japanese males at time of coming to the United States, by industry: Percentages............................. 7, 8

Table 6.—Occupation of Japanese aliens arrived at ports of United States and Canada, as reported by Commissioner-General of Immigration...... 8

Table 7.—Wages of males in specified occupations in Japan.............. 10, 11

Table 8.—Japanese arrivals in continental United States, fiscal year 1909. 17

Table 9.—Occupations of Japanese admitted to the continental United States, fiscal year 1909 18

Table 10.—Number of Japanese debarred or deported from the United States, 1893 to 1910, by cause....................................... 20

Table 11.—Japanese population (estimated) of the continental United States in 1909.. 21

Table 12.—Conjugal condition of foreign-born Japanese wage-earners, by sex, age groups, and industry: Numbers.............................. 23

Table 13.—Conjugal condition of foreign-born Japanese wage-earners, by sex, age groups, and industry: Percentages.......................... 24

Table 14.—Conjugal condition of foreign-born Japanese in business for self, by sex, age groups, and industry: Numbers........................... 25

Table 15.—Conjugal condition of foreign-born Japanese in business for self, by sex, age groups, and industry: Percentages..................... 26

Table 16.—Location of wives of foreign-born Japanese, by industry....... 26

Table 17.—Per cent of foreign-born Japanese husbands who report wife in the United States and per cent who report wife abroad, by industry.... 27

Table 18.—Conjugal condition at time of coming to the United States of foreign-born Japanese males now 16 years of age or over, and subsequent changes in conjugal condition and location of wife, by occupation and industry: Numbers... 27

Table 19.—Conjugal condition at time of coming to the United States of foreign-born Japanese males now 16 years of age or over, and subsequent changes in conjugal condition and location of wife, by occupation and industry: Percentages.. 28

Table 20.—Time of arrival of wives of foreign-born Japanese males who were married before coming to the United States, by occupation and industry... 29

Table 21.—Intention of Japanese males 18 years of age or over to stay permanently in United States, by occupation and industry................ 29

Table 22.—Number of foreign-born Japanese in the United States each specified number of years, by sex and industry..................... 30, 31

Table 23.—Per cent of foreign-born Japanese in the United States each specified number of years, by sex and industry..................... 31, 32

CHAPTER III.—Japanese wage-earners in industry: Page.
   Table 24.—First occupation of Japanese in the United States, by present
     occupation and industry..   34
   Table 25.—Occupation of foreign-born Japanese males before coming to the
     United States, by present industry....................................   35
   Table 26.—Per cent of foreign-born Japanese males in each specified occu-
     pation before coming to the United States, by present industry......... 35, 36
   Table 27.—Yearly earnings (approximate) of Japanese coal miners 18 years
     of age or over...   55
CHAPTER IV.—Japanese in agriculture:
   Table 28.—Day wages of Japanese in farm work in California............   65
   Table 29.—Comparison between the average wages of the Japanese on a
     time basis and the averages of other races............................   65
   Table 30.—Approximate earnings during the past year of Japanese farm
     laborers 18 years of age or over......................................   74
   Table 31.—Approximate earnings during the past year of Japanese farm
     laborers.. 74, 75
   Table 32.—Land farmed by Japanese in 1909, by form of tenure and esti-
     mated number of holdings...   76
   Table 33.—Kinds of farming in which the Japanese are engaged   77
CHAPTER V.—Japanese in city employments and business:
   Table 34.—Number of Japanese establishments engaged in each specified
     kind of business in selected localities in 1909.......................   100
   Table 35.—First occupation in the United States of foreign-born Japanese,
     by occupation abroad... 104, 105
   Table 36.—Number of persons having each specified income during the
     past year and average income, by branch of business engaged in.......   106
   Table 37.—Net value of all property now owned by Japanese 18 years of age
     or over.. 108, 109
   Table 38.—Capital employed in Japanese establishments investigated, by
     branch of business   110
   Table 39.—Volume of transactions during the past year, by branch of busi-
     ness...   111
   Table 40.—Amount of profits realized during the past year, by branch of
     business...   112
   Table 41.—Number of male Japanese employees with each specified
     amount of earnings per month, with board and lodging, by branch of
     business...   132
   Table 42.—Number of male Japanese employees with each specified amount
     of earnings per month, with board, by branch of business.............   132
   Table 43.—Number of male Japanese employees with each specified amount
     of earnings per month, with lodging, by branch of business...........   133
   Table 44.—Number of male Japanese employees with each specified amount
     of earnings per month, without board or lodging, by branch of business..   133
   Table 45.—Yearly earnings (approximate) of male Japanese 18 years of age
     or over, by months worked...   134
CHAPTER VI.—Other economic considerations:
   Table 46.—Cost of food and drink per month per person of Japanese 2 years
     of age or over, by occupation and industry...........................   135
   Table 47.—Average surplus or deficit income for past year of Japanese
     males, by occupation and industry...................................   139
   Table 48.—Surplus or deficit for past year reported by Japanese, by classi-
     fied amount and by occupation and industry.........................   139
   Table 49.—Money sent abroad by Japanese males during past year, by
     occupation and industry...   140
   Table 50.—Net value of all property owned by Japanese 18 years of age or
     over, by occupation and industry....................................   142
   Table 51.—Money brought by Japanese males upon coming to the United
     States, by occupation and industry..................................   143
CHAPTER VII.—Social and political considerations:
   Table 52.—Ability to speak English of foreign-born Japanese, by sex, years
     in the United States, and industry.................................. 145, 146
   Table 53.—Per cent of foreign-born Japanese who speak English, by sex,
     years in the United States, and industry............................ 146, 147
   Table 54.—Number of foreign-born Japanese wage-earners who read their
     native language and number who read and write their native language,
     by sex and industry...   150

CHAPTER VII.—Social and political considerations—Continued.   Page.
  Table 55.—Per cent of foreign-born Japanese wage-earners who read their
    native language and per cent who read and write their native language,
    by sex and industry.. 150
  Table 56.—Number of foreign-born Japanese who read English and number
    who read and write English, by sex and industry.................... 153, 154
  Table 57.—Per cent of foreign-born Japanese who read English and per cent
    who read and write English, by sex and industry..................... 154
  Table 58.—Number of foreign-born Japanese who read and number who
    read and write, by sex and industry................................. 156
  Table 59.—Per cent of foreign-born Japanese who read and per cent who
    read and write, by sex and industry................................. 157
  Table 60.—Newspapers taken by Japanese households.................... 159

PART II.—THE JAPANESE IN CITY EMPLOYMENTS AND BUSINESS IN THE PRINCIPAL CITIES OF THE PACIFIC COAST AND ROCKY MOUNTAIN STATES.

                                                                                  Page.
CHAPTER II.—Japanese in city employments and business in San Francisco:
  Table 1.—Business conducted by Japanese in San Francisco, as reported
    by the Japanese-American Yearbook................................ 188
  Table 2.—Number of employees working in steam laundries earning each
    specified amount per month, by sex................................ 192
CHAPTER III.—Japanese in city employments and business in Los Angeles, Cal.:
  Table 3.—Business conducted by Japanese in Los Angeles, Cal., December,
    1904, and June, 1909... 225
CHAPTER IV.—Japanese in city trades and employments in Sacramento:
  Table 4.—Business conducted by Japanese in Sacramento, Cal., June, 1909. 250
  Table 5.—Data for five grocery stores conducted by Japanese in Sacra-
    mento, Cal., June, 1909.. 255
CHAPTER V.—Japanese in city employments and business in Washington, with
  special reference to Seattle:
  Table 6.—Number of establishments in Tacoma, Wash., conducted by
    Japanese in 1905–1909.. 271
  Table 7.—Growth of Japanese business in Seattle, 1888 to 1909.......... 274
  Table 8.—Number of employees in three American laundries in Seattle
    earning each specified amount per day, by sex and general nativity and
    race... 279
  Table 9.—Number of Japanese employees in Japanese laundries in Seattle
    earning each specified amount per day, by sex...................... 279
  Table 10.—Kind of business conducted by Japanese in Seattle at the
    present time, by occupation abroad................................ 293
CHAPTER VI.—Japanese in city employments and business in Portland:
  Table 11.—Data for Japanese in business in Portland, Oreg., in 1891, 1900,
    and 1909.. 304
CHAPTER VII.—Japanese in city employments and business in Denver:
  Table 12.—Japanese engaged in business in Denver, Colo., June, 1909.... 308
CHAPTER VIII.—Japanese in city trades and business in Salt Lake City and
  Ogden:
  Table 13.—Japanese in business in Salt Lake City, Utah, July, 1909...... 315
  Table 14.—Japanese in business in Ogden, Utah, July, 1909.............. 317
CHAPTER IX.—Japanese in business in Idaho:
  Table 15.—Japanese engaged in business in Idaho in 1909............... 319

PART III.—THE EAST INDIANS ON THE PACIFIC COAST.

CHAPTER II:
  Table 1.—Number of East Indians admitted and departed during the years
    1900 to 1910.. 325
  Table 2.—Number of East Indians debarred during the years 1900 to 1910,
    by cause.. 326
  Table 3.—Money brought to the United States by East Indians.......... 327
  Table 4.—Money brought to the United States by East Indians during the
    years 1905 to 1909.. 327
  Table 5.—General data for East Indian immigrants.................... 327, 328

CHAPTER III.—Employment of East Indians in Coast States: Page.
    Table 6.—Yearly earnings (approximate) of East Indians 18 years of age or
        over, by number of months employed.................................   332
    Table 7.—Number of male East Indian employees 18 years of age or over
        earning each specified amount per day.............................   335
CHAPTER IV.—Age and conjugal condition:
    Table 8.—Number of East Indians admitted to the United States during
        the period 1905–1909, by age groups...................................   339
    Table 9.—Conjugal condition of male East Indians, and location of wife, by
        age groups...   339
CHAPTER V.—Standard of living:
    Table 10.—General data for agricultural laborers.........................   341
    Table 11.—General data for mill hands in Washington and Oregon........   343
    Table 12.—General data for cordage-factory hands in Portland, Oreg......   343
    Table 13.—General data for tamale men of San Francisco, Cal............   344
CHAPTER VI.—Sociological data:
    Table 14.—Ability of foreign-born male East Indians 10 years of age or
        over to read and write their native language and to speak, read, and
        write English, by industry...   348

LIST OF GENERAL TABLES.

JAPANESE IN SAN FRANCISCO.

Page.

Table 1.—Money brought to the United States by Japanese.................. 353
Table 2.—First occupation of Japanese in the United States, by occupation abroad... 353
Table 3.—Net value of all property now owned by Japanese, by length of residence in the United States... 354
Table 4.—Average surplus or deficit of past year, reported by Japanese........ 354
Table 5.—Surplus or deficit of past year reported by Japanese, by classified amounts... 355
Table 6.—Gross value of property, encumbrances, and net value of property now owned by male Japanese.. 355
Table 7.—Number of Japanese for whom detailed information was secured, by sex and general nativity.. 355
Table 8.—Conjugal condition of Japanese, by sex and age groups............. 356
Table 9.—Conjugal condition of foreign-born male Japanese 16 years of age or over, by age at time of coming to the United States......................... 356
Table 10.—Number of Japanese within each age group, by sex................ 357
Table 11.—Number of foreign-born Japanese in the United States each specified number of years, by sex.. 357
Table 12.—Ability to speak English of Japanese 6 years of age or over, by sex and general nativity.. 357
Table 13.—Ability to speak English of foreign-born Japanese 6 years of age or over, by sex and years in the United States.................................... 358
Table 14.—Ability to speak English of foreign-born Japanese 6 years of age or over, by sex and by age at time of coming to the United States............ 358
Table 15.—Literacy of Japanese 10 years of age or over, by sex and general nativity.. 359
Table 16.—Literacy of foreign-born Japanese 10 years of age or over, by sex and years in the United States.. 359
Table 17.—Literacy of foreign-born Japanese 10 years of age or over, by sex and by age at time of coming to the United States............................ 359
Table 18.—Ability of foreign-born Japanese 10 years of age or over, to speak, read, and write English, by sex... 360
Table 19.—General occupation of Japanese under 16 years of age, by sex, age groups, and general nativity.. 360
Table 20.—Total yearly income of male Japanese engaged in business for self, and income from principal business... 360
Table 21.—Yearly earnings (approximate) of male Japanese 18 years of age or over, by number of months employed.. 361

JAPANESE IN LOS ANGELES.

Table 22.—General data on business conducted by Japanese and members of other races... 361–364
Table 23.—Money brought to the United States by Japanese.................. 364
Table 24.—First occupation of Japanese in the United States, by occupation abroad.. 365
Table 25.—Net value of all property now owned by Japanese, by length of residence in the United States... 365
Table 26.—Average surplus or deficit of past year reported by Japanese....... 366
Table 27.—Surplus or deficit of past year reported by Japanese, by classified amounts.. 366
Table 28.—Gross value of property, encumbrances, and net value of property now owned by male Japanese.. 366
Table 29.—Number of Japanese for whom detailed information was secured, by sex and general nativity... 366, 367
Table 30.—Conjugal condition of Japanese by sex and age groups............. 367
Table 31.—Conjugal condition of foreign-born male Japanese 16 years of age or over, by age at time of coming to the United States......................... 367

401

Page.
Table 32.—Number of Japanese within each age group, by sex 368
Table 33.—Number of foreign-born Japanese in the United States each speci-
fied number of years, by sex 368
Table 34.—Ability to speak English of Japanese 6 years of age or over, by sex
and general nativity 368
Table 35.—Ability to speak English of foreign-born Japanese 6 years of age
or over, by sex and years in the United States 369
Table 36.—Ability to speak English of foreign-born Japanese 6 years of age or
over, by sex and by age at time of coming to the United States............. 369
Table 37.—Literacy of Japanese 10 years of age or over, by sex and general
nativity.. 369
Table 38.—Literacy of foreign-born Japanese 10 years of age or over, by sex
and by years in the United States.. 370
Table 39.—Literacy of foreign-born Japanese 10 years of age or over, by sex
and by age at time of coming to the United States 370
Table 40.—Ability of foreign-born Japanese 10 years of age or over to speak,
read, and write English, by sex.. 370
Table 41.—General occupation of Japanese under 16 years of age, by sex, age
groups, and general nativity... 371
Table 42.—Total yearly income of male Japanese engaged in business for self,
and income from principal business.. 371
Table 43.—Yearly earnings (approximate) of male Japanese 18 years of age or
over, by number of months employed....................................... 372

JAPANESE IN SACRAMENTO.

Table 44.—General data on business conducted by Japanese and members of
other races.. 372–375
Table 45.—Money brought to the United States by Japanese.................. 375
Table 46.—First occupation of Japanese in the United States, by occupation
abroad... 375
Table 47.—Net value of all property now owned by Japanese, by length of
residence in the United States... 376
Table 48.—Average surplus or deficit of past year, reported by Japanese....... 376
Table 49.—Surplus or deficit of past year reported by Japanese, by classified
amounts... 376, 377
Table 50.—Gross value of property, encumbrances, and net value of property
now owned by male Japanese.. 377
Table 51.—Number of Japanese for whom detailed information was secured, by
sex and general nativity... 377
Table 52.—Conjugal condition of Japanese, by sex and age groups............. 377
Table 53.—Conjugal condition of foreign-born male Japanese 16 years of age
or over, by age at time of coming to the United States..................... 378
Table 54.—Number of Japanese in each specified age group, by sex........... 378
Table 55.—Number of foreign-born Japanese in the United States each speci-
fied number of years, by sex... 378
Table 56.—Ability to speak English of Japanese 6 years of age or over, by sex
and general nativity... 379
Table 57.—Ability to speak English of foreign-born Japanese 6 years of age or
over, by sex and years in the United States................................ 379
Table 58.—Ability to speak English of foreign-born Japanese 6 years of age or
over, by sex and by age at time of coming to the United States............. 379
Table 59.—Literacy of Japanese 10 years of age or over, by sex and general
nativity.. 380
Table 60.—Literacy of foreign-born Japanese 10 years of age or over, by sex
and years in the United States... 380
Table 61.—Literacy of foreign-born Japanese 10 years of age or over, by sex
and by age at time of coming to the United States......................... 380
Table 62.—Ability of foreign-born Japanese 10 years of age or over to speak,
read, and write English, by sex.. 381
Table 63.—General occupation of Japanese under 16 years of age, by sex, age
groups, and general nativity... 381
Table 64.—Total yearly income of male Japanese engaged in business for self,
and income from principal business.. 381
Table 65.—Yearly earnings (approximate) of male Japanese 18 years of age or
over, by number of months employed....................................... 382

JAPANESE IN SEATTLE.

Page.

Table 66.—General data on business conducted by Japanese and members of other races... 382–385

Table 67.—Money brought to the United States by Japanese............... 386

Table 68.—First occupation of Japanese in the United States, by occupation abroad 386

Table 69.—Net value of all property now owned by Japanese, by length of residence in the United States...................................... 387

Table 70.—Average surplus or deficit of past year reported by Japanese....... 387

Table 71.—Surplus or deficit of past year reported by Japanese, by classified amounts... 388

Table 72.—Gross value of property, encumbrances, and net value of property now owned by male Japanese.. 388

Table 73.—Number of Japanese for whom detailed information was secured, by sex and general nativity.. 388

Table 74.—Conjugal condition of Japanese, by sex and age groups............. 389

Table 75.—Conjugal condition of foreign-born male Japanese 16 years of age or over, by age at time of coming to the United States...................... 389

Table 76.—Number of Japanese within each age group, by sex............... 390

Table 77.—Number of foreign-born Japanese in the United States each specified number of years, by sex.. 390

Table 78.—Ability to speak English of Japanese 6 years of age or over, by sex and general nativity... 390

Table 79.—Ability to speak English of foreign-born Japanese 6 years of age or over, by sex and years in the United States................................ 391

Table 80.—Ability to speak English of foreign-born Japanese 6 years of age or over, by sex and by age at time of coming to the United States............ 391

Table 81.—Literacy of Japanese 10 years of age or over, by sex and general nativity... 392

Table 82.—Literacy of foreign-born Japanese 10 years of age or over, by sex and years in the United States.. 392

Table 83.—Literacy of foreign-born Japanese 10 years of age or over, by sex and by age at time of coming to the United States............................ 393

Table 84.—Ability of foreign-born Japanese 10 years of age or over to speak, read, and write English, by sex.. 393

Table 85.—General occupation of Japanese under 16 years of age, by sex, age groups, and general nativity.. 394

Table 86.—Total yearly income of male Japanese engaged in business for self, and income from principal business...................................... 394

Table 87.—Yearly earnings (approximate) of male Japanese 18 years of age or over, by number of months employed.................................... 395